Timeline (BC/AD): 1000 900 800 700 600 500 400 300 200 100 BC/AD 100 200 300 400 500

Musical instruments: harps, lyres

Ptolemy

Musical instruments: kissar, harps, lyres, dulcimers, asor

Sargon II

Nebuchadnezzar II

Dur-Sharrukin reliefs **Epic of Gilgamesh**

4: GREECE

First Olympic games
Homer

Herodotus
Thucydides

Darius
Xerxes
Pericles
Pythagoras

Socrates
Plato
Aristotle

Alexander the Great

Dipylon vase
Kouroi

Parthenon
Tragic plays: Aeschylus, Sophocles, Euripides
Makron
Myron

Black- and red-figure vases

Epidaurus theatre
Halicarnassus
Temple of Athena Nike
Polyclitus
Kritios boy
Praxiteles

Dying Gaul
Winged Victory of Samothrace
Laocoön group

Temple of Olympian Zeus

5: ROME

Etruscans

Gauls invade Rome

Romans conquer western Greece

Punic Wars
Hannibal

Julius Caesar
Augustus

Nero

Seneca

Temple of Jerusalem destroyed
Eruption of Vesuvius

Constantinople founded

Fall of Rome

Etruscan warrior

Plautus
Terence

Portrait busts
Boscoreale

Forum of Augustus

Virgil
Horace
Ara Pacis
Petronius

Colosseum
Basilica Ulpia
Herculaneum wall paintings

Pantheon

THE CREATIVE IMPULSE

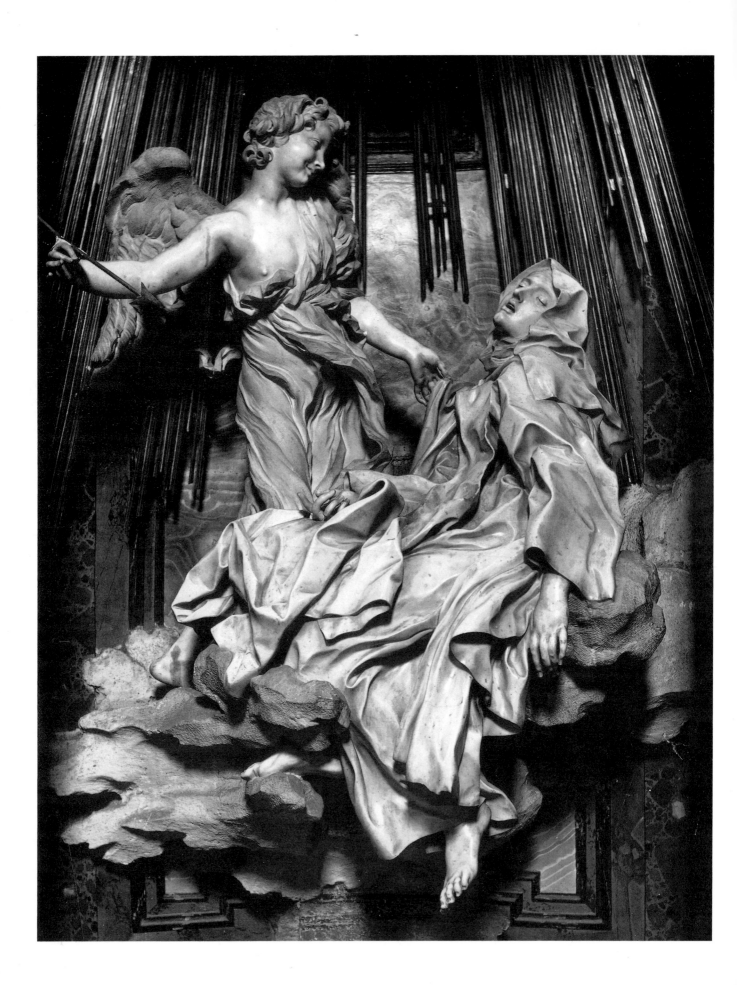

The Creative Impulse

An Introduction to the Arts

DENNIS J. SPORRE

Prentice-Hall, Inc. Englewood Cliffs, New Jersey

This book was designed and produced by
John Calmann and King Ltd, London
Designer: Richard Foenander

Typeset by Tradespools Ltd, England
Printed in Singapore by Toppan Ltd

Cover illustration:
Titian, *Bacchus and Ariadne*, 1523 (detail).
Oil on canvas, 69 × 75ins (175 × 191cm).
National Gallery, London.

Back cover:
Van Gogh, *The Starry Night*, 1889. Oil on
canvas, 29 × 36¼ins (73.7 × 92.1cm).
Museum of Modern Art, New York (Lillie
P. Bliss Bequest).

Frontispiece:
Bernini, *Ecstasy of St Teresa*, 1645–52.
Marble, height c. 11ft 6ins (350cm).
Cornaro Chapel, S Maria della Vittoria,
Rome.

Acknowledgements

The authors, the publishers and John Calmann &
King Ltd wish to thank the museum, galleries,
collectors and other owners who have kindly allowed
their works to be reproduced in this book. In general,
museums have supplied their own photographs;
other sources are listed below:

AEG Aktiengesellschaft, Frankfurt: 13.54 Actors'
Theatre of Louisville/David S. Talbott: 13.43, 44
Archivi Alinari, Florence: 6.24 9.27 10.31 Ancient Art &
Architecture Collection, London: 10.43, 44 Wayne
Andrews, Chicago: 11.29 13.52 The Architectural
Association, London: 13.56; Roger Schluntz: 13.62;
F.R. Yerbury: 13.51 The Architectural Press, London/
Unilever Ltd.: 13.57 BBC Hulton Picture Library,
London: 10.23 11.30 John Bethell, St. Albans: 12.44
Bildarchiv Preussischer Kulturbesitz, Berlin: 11.31
Bilderberg/Wolfgang Volz, Hamburg: 13.38
Bridgeman Art Library, London: 9.13, 14 11.6, 14 12.7,
13, 17, 21 13.1 CNMHS/SPADEM, Paris: 1.18, 21 7.25,
30 Cement & Concrete Association, Slough: 13.61
Centre National de Préhistoire, Perigueux: 1.8 Martin
Charles, Middlesex: 12.46 Cliché des Musées
Nationaux, Paris: 2.28 4.5 6.14, 15 7.31, 32 10.8, 17, 39,
40 11.13 Trudy Lee Cohen © 1986, Philadelphia:
12.30, 31 Courtauld Institute of Art, London: 10.24, 30
Deutsches Archäologisches Institut, Rome: 5.32 Jean
Dieuzaide, Toulouse: 7.21 John Donat, London: 13.55
Dumbarton Oaks (Byzantine Photograph Collection),
Trustees of Harvard University, Washington D.C.:
6.18, 19 Egypt Exploration Society, London: 3.33 Esto
Photographics Inc., Mamaroneck, New York: 13.58
Werner Forman Archive, London: 3.28 Alison Frantz,
Princeton, New Jersey: 4.34 6.20 Solomon R.
Guggenheim Museum, New York: 13.59 Sonia
Halliday Photographs, Weston Turville, U.K.: 4.1
Robert Harding Picture Library Ltd., London: 9.35
10.41, 42 Clive Hicks, London: 7.20, 22, 8.19, 21, 22, 23
Colorphoto Hans Hinz, Allschwil, Switzerland: 1.1, 17,
19, 20 Hirmer Fotoarchiv, Munich: 2.5, 7, 8, 29 3.3, 9,
11, 12, 14, 15, 16, 17, 18, 19, 20, 21, 22, 23, 47 4.16, 23,
28 6.7, 8, 13, 25, 28, 29 Michael Holford, London: 1.9
A.F. Kersting, London: 3.2, 4 4.31, 35 8.1, 26, 27, 28, 29,
30, 31, 32 9.30, 32 10.1, 28, 32, 36, 37 11.26, 12.43 G.E.
Kidder Smith, New York: 6.27 12.42 Lauros-Giraudon/
Bridgeman, London: 8.12, 14, 15, 20 Ralph
Liebermann, North Adams, MA: 13.50, 53, 60 The
Mansell Collection, London/Alinari: 4.14, 15, 21, 22
5.6, 17, 24, 25, 28 8.6 9.5, 9, 10, 11, 21, 24, 25, 29, 31
10.12, 13, 14, 15, 16, 20, 29 12.24 Bildarchiv Foto
Marburg, Marburg: 11.25, 34, 35 Jean Mazenod, L'Art
De L'Ancienne Rome, Editions Mazenod, Paris: 5.13
Lucia Moholy, Zürich: 13, 65, 66 The Henry Moore
Foundation, Hertfordshire, U.K.: 13.27, 28, 29 Ann
Münchow, Aachen: 7.34, 36 Musée D'Art et D'Histoire,
Auxerre: 7.26 Musei Capitolini, Rome (Barbara
Malter): 5.29 National Film Archive, London: 13,45, 46
Courtesy of the Oriental Institute, University of
Chicago: 2.11, 25, 26 Österreichische Akademie der
Wissenschaften – Mosaikenkommission, Vienna: 6.9
Scala, Florence: 2.1 5.10 6.1, 21, 22, 23 7.1 8.7 9.1, 15,
19, 20, 34, 41 10.7, 21, 33, 34, 35 Edwin Smith, Saffron
Walden: 11.32, 33 Wayne E. Upchurch, Wilmington:
12.36 Vatican Museums: 9.33 University of Virginia
Library: 11.27 Weidenfeld & Nicolson, London: 11.28
    The following illustrations are © DACS 1986:
12.28 13.6, 7, 8, 9, 10, 12, 14, 15, 17, 21, 22, 34
© ADAGP 1986: 13.13, 25, 26, 33, 39
© ADAGP, Paris & COSMOPRESS, Geneve 1986:
13.36

CONTENTS

PREFACE

The purpose of this book is to present an overview of the visual arts, music, theatre, dance, film, and architecture in western civilization by focusing on selected developments in the context of the philosophy, literature, religion, aesthetic theory, and political events surrounding them. It is an introduction to the humanities. The reader of this text should gain a basic familiarity with major styles in western arts history, some understanding of the ideological, chronological, and technical implications of those styles, and also a feeling for the historical development of individual arts disciplines. In addition, this work attempts to provide the humanities instructor with a helpful textbook for courses which touch upon the arts in an inter- or multi-disciplinary manner. To achieve these ends I have been necessarily selective and practical. This text should not be considered an attempt to develop a profound or detailed history. It is comprehensive only in the sense that it spans time from pre-history to the present day and does so by treating all the arts as consistently as possible.

Use of this text will encourage use of other source materials. The instructor should develop emphases or foci of his or her own choosing by adding, in lecture or other form, detailed development of particular areas to the very general overview provided here. What I hope I have done is provide a convenient, one-volume outline with enough flexibility to allow adaptation to a variety of purposes. In many cases I have provided suggestions for, rather than details of, examination. I suggest that when this book is used for the classroom, instructors carefully advise students which names it is necessary to memorize. My listing of artists who share the styles of those examined in the text is intended to be helpful, not burdensome.

Material is organized vertically and horizontally. One may isolate any subdivision, such as the general history or sculpture sections, and study the overview of that one area from ancient to modern times. Or one may read entire chapters or portions of chapters so as to gain a basic understanding and comparison of events and elements within a particular era. On the multisided debate concerning how a teacher should approach the arts, of course, this text takes a definite point of view. My focus, format, and choice of materials are based on the belief that one must be able to describe before one attempts to theorize. The issue is not a matter of right or wrong. Nearly all approaches have some merit. The issue, which is up to the individual instructor, is how and when a particular approach is applicable. This is one approach.

In discussing artworks I have for the most part kept to description and compositional analysis. By so doing I hope to assist the reader in polishing his or her skills of technical observation. By avoiding meaning and relationships I have left room for the classroom instructor to move discussion in whatever direction is deemed appropriate to the course. At the end of each chapter there is a section entitled "Synthesis". Here I have narrowed my vision to one specific location whose arts (or in two cases, art) provide us with a microcosm of the period or part of the period. Here we may gain a fuller understanding of interrelationships than the broad treatment in the remainder of the chapter allows.

At the end of each chapter I have also made suggestions for discussion and thought. By so doing I have tried to leave the text itself free from associations which may not suit a particular course or circumstance. The text contains the facts only. The challenges to thought and the interrelationships to be drawn from the facts are up to the reader and/or the instructor.

A significant problem in developing any inter- or multidisciplinary arts text is balancing thematic, chronological, and practical considerations. A strictly chronological approach works fairly well for histories of single or closely related disciplines because major movements tend to be compressed. When all the arts are included, however, we find a progression of shifting, sliding, overlapping, and recurring fits and starts which have not conformed to convenient chronological patterns. A strictly thematic approach, on the other hand, tends to leave the reader in limbo. Chronological guideposts simply cannot be ignored. So I have tried to maintain a broad and traditional chronological framework within which certain liberties can be taken to benefit thematic considerations.

The proper length for a book attempting to accomplish these ends is difficult to determine. How many pages can a student read in a semester, and how much detail can he or she be expected to learn? How much detail obscures the overview or curtails the flexibility of the individual instructor? How little detail makes the book detrimentally superficial? How many pages make the book impractical to print or impossible to buy? The answers to these questions are debatable and unquestionably demand certain compromises. No longer does a textbook writer have the luxury of including more information than is necessary for a given course. Nevertheless, a study of arts history must treat all the arts uniformly. I have severely curtailed two components normally included in arts histories. One is biographical material. That choice is arbitrary and practical and not an implication that biography is irrelevant. Biography can be very important in understanding meaning in works of art. However, my task, as I see it, is to suggest an outline with a few principles and illustrations on which the reader or the instructor is free to build in whatever direction or manner suits his or her fashion. The second area of abridgement lies in analysis of specific musical and theatrical works. Analyzing a specific musical work or play, as opposed to a painting, has limited value in a text such as this, because the student does not have the artwork immediately at hand and thus cannot link analysis to object. Musical notation and playscripts cannot be substitutes for musical or theatrical illustrations. Music is sound; plays are performances. Nothing less is adequate. In addition, either classroom or outside study can always be linked to a picture in a text; availability of a given symphony or play for classroom use or outside study may be problematic. So I hope those who use this text will view it as a skeleton from which the student can gain a basic conception of the entire form. Adding flesh to the form for clarification or substantiation becomes, again, a matter of individual choice.

Basic to this discussion is a belief that teachers of arts survey courses should assist students to view the arts as reflections of the human condition. A work of art is a view of the universe, a search for reality, revealed in a particular medium and shared with others. Men and women similar to ourselves have struggled to understand the universe, as we do; and often, though separated by centuries, their concerns and questions, as reflected in their artworks, were alike. In the same vein, artworks from separate eras may appear similar even though the historical context is different. Sometimes the medium of expression required technological advancement which delayed the revelation of a viewpoint more readily expressed in another medium. Sometimes disparate styles sprang from the same historical context. We need to be aware of similarities and differences in artworks and to try to understand why they occurred. We may even need to learn that we did not invent a certain style or form. Through such efforts we gain a more enriched relationship with our own existence.

Therefore, I trust that those who read this text will go beyond its facts and struggle with the potential meanings of the artworks included or suggested here. They should ask questions about what the artist may have been trying to accomplish; draw relationships from the social and intellectual contexts and concepts and the artworks; finally, seek to understand how they as individuals see these creative expressions in relation to their understanding of the universe.

To keep the text as flexible as possible I have not drawn detailed cause and effect relationships between the arts and history. Significant uncertainty exists in many quarters as to whether art is a reflection of the society in which it is produced or derives entirely from internal necessity, without recourse to any circumstances other than artistic ones. I believe both cases have occurred throughout history and do not consider it within my purpose here to try to argue which or where. I also find continual linkages of general events to six (or seven) arts disciplines problematically repetitious. Therefore, I begin each chapter with a brief historical summary to provide a cultural context for the arts of that period. Some relationships of style to political, philosophical, literary, and/or religious developments are obvious; others are not entirely clear or may be questionable. In all cases the reader or instructor is free to draw whatever connections or conclusions he or she deems appropriate. My purpose is merely to provide a relatively neutral overview.

One further observation is implicit. Artworks affect us in the present tense. Hard-edged abstraction cannot invalidate our personal response to realism. Whatever the current vogue, the art of the past can stimulate meaningful contemporary responses to life and to the ideas of other humans who tried or try to deal with life and death and the cosmos. Nonetheless, discussing dance, music, painting, sculpture, drama, film, and architecture falls far short of the marvelous satisfaction of experiencing them. Black and white and even color reproductions cannot stimulate the range of responses possible from the artwork itself. No reproduction can approximate the scale and mystery of a Gothic cathedral or capture the glittering translucence of a mosaic or a stained glass window. No text can transmit the power of the live drama or the strains of a symphony. One can only hope that the pages which follow will open a door or two and perhaps stimulate the reader to experience the intense satisfaction of observing actual works of art, of whatever era.

I have tried to keep descriptions and analyses of individual artworks as nontechnical as possible, but technical vocabulary cannot be avoided entirely. For that reason a Glossary is included. I have endeavored to define technical terms either in the text or in the Glossary. (Instructors using this book might wish to consider *Perceiving the Arts* [Prentice-Hall, 2nd ed., 1985] as a collateral text.) In addition, my approach sometimes varies from discipline to discipline and era to era. Although that variation creates some inconsistency, I have tried to let the nature of artistic activity dictate the treatment given. Sometimes a broad summary of a wide-ranging style suffices; at other times an ethnographic separation is necessary; at still other times a more individualized or subdisciplinary approach is required. Regardless of what the circumstances appear to dictate, I have tried to keep my focus, ultimately, on style, or at least I have tried to develop the examination in such a way that the reader can infer stylistic characteristics.

I have separated the visual arts into architecture, sculpture, and two-dimensional art. The first two are fairly obvious, but the third is less so. At all stages in the history of art, pictorial art has encompassed more than easel painting. Drawing, printmaking, manuscript illumination, vase and mural painting, photography, and mixed media have also played a role, and we will note those roles where appropriate. Traditional painting, however, has formed the backbone of the discipline and will be our primary focus.

Theatre as an art form or discipline must be seen as a live performance, which actuates a script with live actors in some kind of physical environment. So our description of theatre will try to illuminate production, with a ready acknowledgement that the script is the basis, the style of which often determines the production style. As we examine theatre, we will focus on the production of plays written in the same period in which they were produced; but occasionally revivals of earlier plays give strong indications of the idea or style of production in that period.

Dance presents a problem because although it has been an intimate part of creative expression since the dawn of history, it is also an ephemeral art and a social activity. Even though I have a fundamentally relativistic approach to the question "What is art?", for the purposes of this text I have tried to limit dance to what for want of a better term we may call theatre dance, that is, dance which involves a performer, a performance, and an audience. Such a limitation, still, is not entirely satisfactory since certain dances may, in some cases, be theatre dance, in other cases, social dancing, and in still other cases, both or neither. However, I hope the reader will understand that my choices are more or less practical, and that my purpose is to provide a general overview and not to argue for or against any particular theory.

Architecture and sculpture provide us with only a few minor problems either in definition or description. Both disciplines have the properties of immortality and, in general, give us a few excellent examples to draw upon, even from humankind's earliest days, Music, though also ephemeral, poses few problems, at least from the Middle Ages on. Finally, Chapter Thirteen presents a new subject —film. A twentieth-century discipline, film has developed its own aesthetics and form, and is fully a part, if only a recent one, of Western arts history. So I include it as such.

I am guilty, as are most textbook writers, of robbing the arts of much of their excitement and rich interrelationships by using neat, taxonomical divisions in each chapter so that one can see at a glance or focus conveniently on one art form or another. A history of the arts should read like a complex novel, because the history of the arts is a lively story—a story of humankind—full of life, breath, and passion. The ebb and flow of artistic history has created intricate crosscurrents of influence from society to individual to art; from other arts, to individuals, to society or societies, and so on in infinite variety. I would challenge those who use this book, again, to go beyond its covers to try to capture that excitement.

It should be clear that a work such as this does not spring fully from the general knowledge or primary source research of its author. Some of it does, because of my long-term and close affiliation with the various arts disciplines. Much is the result of notes accumulated here and there as well as research specifically directed at this project. However, in the interest of readability and in recognition of the generalized purpose of this text, copious footnoting has been avoided. I hope the method I have chosen for presentation and documentation of others' works meets the needs both of responsibility and practicality. The bibliography at the end of this work is a comprehensive list of cited works. I am indebted to many of these authors, to my colleagues around the country and specifically to John Myers, Sherrill Martin, and David Kechley.

D.J.S.

INTRODUCTION

This book is a story about us. It is a story about our perceptions of the world as we, humankind, have come to see it, both cognitively and intuitively, to respond to it, and to communicate our understandings of it to our fellow human beings. We have been doing this as part of our being human since the great Ice Age more than 35,000 years ago. We have not developed into our humanity since then. Our human characteristics of 'being human' have been with us from the earliest times. Certainly we have learned, in a cognitive way, more about our world and how it functions. We have changed our patterns of existence and interdependence. But we have not changed our humanness. As archeological and anthropological evidence has been synthesized over the last one hundred years, we have come to see that the fundamental characteristic of what makes us human, that is, our ability to intuit and to symbolize, has been with us from our beginnings. Our art tells us this in terms which are inescapable. So a story of humankind's artistic ventures is our story.

I have called this book the *Creative Impulse* because I hope that its content will suggest to the reader that creativity in the artistic sense is an intrinsic part of being human. Try as we may in these modern times to escape from the suggestions of our right cerebral hemisphere to the absolutes of the left brain, that is, the cognitive, we cannot escape the fact that we can and do know and communicate at an affective or intuitive level. The mistake of insisting only on cognitive knowing and development may already have robbed us of something of our capacity for being human.

The subtitle of this work is "An Introduction to the Arts". Courses of the same name or scope exist throughout the United States and comprise the market to which this text is directed. The Arts or the humanities as a series of disciplines deal with the issues addressed in the previous paragraphs, and require more examination if the approach of this work is to be clear to its readers. I therefore turn to a short essay by Warren S. Smith which also appears in my book *Perceiving the Arts* (Prentice-Hall, 2nd ed., 1985).

The Humanities and the Arts

In our passion for categorizing we have sometimes tried to gather the more humanizing elements of our civilization into a vague general area called the humanities. There is no sharp boundary separating these aspects of life from the sciences, technology, and the social sciences. Still, the curiosity to know the secrets of the natural universe, or to know how something works, or even how people behave en masse, is motivated by a perceptibly different spirit than the one that drives a human being to try to comprehend humankind. In the traditions of formal scholarship—that is to say, in the way universities divide these things—the humanities are thought of as philosophy, literature, the fine arts, and (sometimes) history. But these very often simply constitute a convenient administrative unit. Some of the current studies in these fields turn out to be largely quantitative with computerized data, while over in the microbiology department it may well be that a scientist is far less concerned about the phenomenon he is observing under the microscope than about its meaning for the human race. The humanities (if the term is to have a meaning beyond taxonomy) are marked by a point of view rather than by the names of certain disciplines. It is the point of view that wants to know what humanity is about, what kinds of creatures we are, and how we got to be this way. Are we civilized? What are our hopes and fears? What do we think about and dream about? What do we believe? How do we behave?

The answers to such questions are not likely to be as neat as those demanded by the scientist. The evidence is too scattered. It lies in the legends of storytellers and dramatists, in biographies and autobiographies, in the thoughts of the philosophers and the images of

11

the poets. It also lies in the millions of artworks that the human race has left strewn about the planet, from the caves of Lascaux and Altamira to the fleeting images of the latest film festival. The artworks are themselves expressions of the humanities, not—as they are so often presented—merely illustrations of literature or history.

Any definition of a work of art (like any definition of religion or of love) is destined to be inadequate for some people. For me, a work of art is some sight, sound, or movement (or combination)—some sensible manifestation—intended as human expression. This is obviously not a value-laden definition aimed at placing a work of art on a pedestal. It accepts as an artwork whatever is intended as an artwork, whether it is a childish effort or a renowned masterpiece. As an expression each artwork carries within itself some evidence of that seeking that characterizes the human condition. Its banality or profundity, its innocence or sophistication, its light-heartedness or solemnity are descriptive, not restrictive, qualities.

Within whatever range the artwork falls, and regardless of whether its creator intended it or not, the artwork has form: it occupies space or time, or both. A painting or print or photograph takes its shape on a two-dimensional surface. A piece of sculpture or architecture must occupy three-dimensional space. The sounds of music occupy no space at all but weave their shapes within the duration of time. The performing of a play or an opera or a dance requires both space and time, both visual and auditory elements. So do film, and, of course, television, though they reduce space to two dimensions, however much the illusion of depth remains.

But the concept of form extends beyond the mere shapes in space and time. Form is concerned not only with the overall structure that contains the work of art, but with the smaller patterns that compose its inner designs as well. It is therefore closely tied to the artist's choice of medium and materials—watercolors or oils, lithography or steel etching, strings or brass or electronic synthesizer, clay or bronze or stone, prose or verse, and so on. The artist's work is a continuous process of making choices, and the only guiding rules he or she has are

self-imposed. Traditionally the artist has sought both unity and variety. The most admired forms from the past are those in which the separate parts are clear, but not wholly predictable, so that one can say at the same time "Of course!" and "How surprising!"

There are styles and fads in art forms, but unlike advances in technology and the sciences, a new form in the arts never really replaces an old one. Obviously not all styles and forms can survive indefinitely, but a Picasso cannot do to a Rembrandt what an Einstein did to a Newton, nor can the serialism of Schoenberg banish the tonality of Mozart as the evolutionary evidence of Darwin banished the eighteenth-century world of William Paley. The arts, even more than literature, survive by direct impact, and continue to swell the ever-growing reservoir of human manifestations. Times and customs change, the passions that shaped the artist's work disappear, his cherished beliefs become fables, but all of these are preserved in the form of his work. "All the assertions get disproved sooner or later," Bernard Shaw observed, "and so we find the world full of a magnificent debris of artistic fossils, with the matter-of-fact credibility gone clean out of them, but the form still splendid." No doubt one can often read much history or biography in the arts, and no doubt, too, a knowledge of history or of an artist's life can often enhance a work of art, but the response to an artwork is always in the present tense.

Furthermore, a work of art is always a *gestalt*: its form and its content are inseparable. We may pay particular attention to the form today and consider the content more thoroughly tomorrow. But even as we determine to do so we are instantly aware that the two are one. The two concepts are interdependent and inseparable, even though we may attempt verbally to place them in separate paragraphs!

The content of an artwork may include certain subject matter. The sculpture may be a human form, the painting a landscape, the music the description of a storm, the dance a depiction of a fanciful story, the play or film a representation of a family crisis. But in none of these cases will the subject matter be mistaken for the real thing, and in some cases it may be the merest excuse, a framework for the sights, sounds, or movements that the artist has cre-

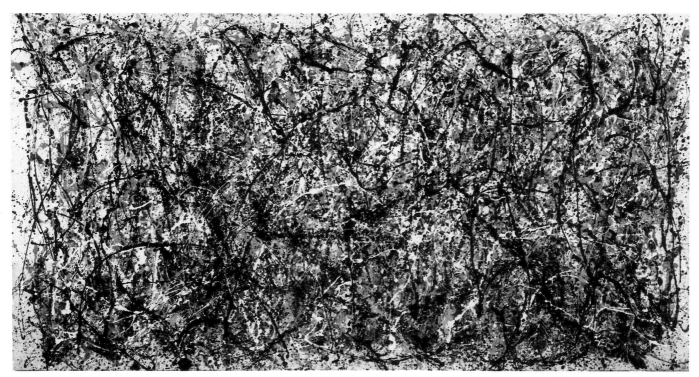

0.1 Jackson Pollock, *One* (*Number* 31, 1950). Oil and enamel paint on canvas, 8 ft 10 ins × 17 ft 5⅝ ins (2.695 × 5.31 m). Museum of Modern Art, New York (Sidney and Harriet Janis Collection Fund).

ated. Indeed, in many artworks there is no perceptible subject matter at all. Music, for example, quite frequently gets along very well without words, without a descriptive title, without being "about" anything. Very often dance does too. And in more recent years painting, sculpture, and even film have often departed from subject matter. Only the live theatre, it seems, must be tied—however tenuously—to some recognizable activity.

All of this brings us inescapably to the concept of abstraction. Every work of art, no matter how literal or representational, is an abstraction, in that it is a thing *apart*—removed from the indiscriminate and chaotic world beyond the picture frame, beyond the pedestal, the stage, the lighted screen, the privileged sound chamber in which the artwork resides. Some works are, of course, more abstract than others, but abstraction should not be regarded as an attribute only of so-called abstract art but of all art in varying degrees. There comes a point, however, when subject matter seems to disappear altogether and the other arts enter the realm that music and dance have always in some sense occupied—a realm in which recognizable subject matter is not necessarily ex-

pected, and therefore not missed. At this point it is proper to speak of an artwork as being non-objective, since there is no longer any evidence of its having been abstracted from a recognizable object or activity (Fig. **0.1**).

So we must conclude that the content of an artwork necessarily extends beyond mere subject matter. Obviously it must also be closely linked with the arrangement of lines, masses, colors, rhythms, timbres, dynamics—all the elements that, from another viewpoint, we regarded purely as form. But beyond this the content must at last be assumed to be what we get out of the work—or, perhaps more accurately, what the artist has put into it. It may offer us a profoundly emotional or a rigorously intellectual experience. All of the elements come together to affect us in some way. We cannot say exactly in what way because there are as many ways as there are artworks. It is not even possible to say that the same artwork will offer the same content to every respondent, for everyone brings to it a different set of experiences and a different level of sophistication. And although there may be no single correct way to respond to an artwork, it would seem worth some effort to discover its true content, to determine what the artist has put into the work that will now communicate with us as respondents.

This is a delicate and sensitive business, involving as it does the ability to sense an artist's *style*. This undefinable quality is a synthesis that carries the same connotation for an artwork that the term personality carries for an individual. One style, like one personality, may be easily distinguishable from another, though not easily explainable. An understanding of style comes not from any verbal explanation, but from practice in responding. It is safe to assume that practice is needed, for a complete aesthetic response requires a perception that can make fine distinctions. It also requires a willingness to accept the abstraction of the work in the manner in which the artist has composed it, together with whatever emotional overtones he or she has tried to communicate.

It is, I suppose, impossible to confront a work of art without developing some attitude towards it and placing some personal value on it. Your own response may vary from boredom to adoration to outrage. If your attitude on these matters is firmly fixed—if you have some clear idea of what music ought to sound like, what kind of action ought to constitute a drama, what a picture ought to look like—you will have little trouble in making value judgments. An artwork will be good art to the degree that it fits your preconceptions and bad art to the degree that it does not. These limits were more clearly set in former times when the church or the court or the academy was the accepted arbiter of taste. The advantage of having such guidelines was, however, short-lived, for many of the works we have come to admire the most were created by rebels from the establishments of their times. Nevertheless, for many people certain ideals of beauty and proportion that evolved in earlier centuries are still significant "taste-makers" today, and a study of aesthetics will still probably begin with Aristotle's conception of what is beautiful.

There runs through any discussion of the arts the question of how much we should be influenced by words that are spoken or written about them, and how much by the artwork itself. What part, in other words, should criticism play in our own responses to art? It is easy—and tempting—to say that our re-

sponses are to be purely our own, unencumbered by what some "expert" thinks. But it must be remembered that we live in a highly verbal society where *all* our responses tend to be verbalized. Even the respondent who is most outspokenly opposed to art criticism will try to share his own responses with others—and this in itself is an elementary form of art criticism. At its finest, art criticism does not merely set up value systems for what is and what is not acceptable. It also shows us ways to look and listen that may have escaped us, so that whether we agree with the critic's judgment or not, his or her words have given us an enriched perception of the work.

The value systems in our culture are so pluralistic, not only concerning the arts but concerning politics, religion, morals and manners, that it is not surprising that there are today no universally accepted arbiters of taste. The absence of such arbiters sets us free to accept or reject art experiences as we choose, but it also leaves us in the midst of a plethora of styles (also a plethora of conflicting commentary and criticism) with no guide but our own perception. Many people find this situation so frustrating that they literally beg for guidance. Guidance is, of course, available, but not in the old-fashioned sense of providing a clear-cut scale of aesthetic values. Some of the frustrations of living in today's world are unavoidable.

The arts are always a system of relationships, a careful, tenuous equilibrium between one thing and another—so much so that it has often occurred to me that almost any substantive question one can ask of a work of art must be answered initially with "That depends..." What should be its size? its complexity? its focal point? its relationship to nature? to society? to the artist? Multiply these questions to infinity, and ask them of any artwork, from an acknowledged masterpiece to a student work in progress. For an answer we must first discover the relationships, both within the work itself and outside itself. "It depends..."

Such a relativistic approach to the arts cannot result in giving every artwork a good or bad label, extolling one as a masterpiece and condemning another as a fraud. An enormous amount of nonsense is generated by such questions as "Is it really art?" or "Will it live?" A more proper question would always be, "What can we get out of it at this moment?" If the work engenders some response, there is little point in arguing whether it is art. Nor is it profitable to concern ourselves too much with the possible response of our grandchildren. History has provided us with no reliable pattern for the survival of art. Moreover, the number of variables involved in forming the taste of our posterity is nearly infinite. If we cannot know what kind of world they will be living in (if indeed the race survives) or what kind of pressures or passions will be driving them, surely we cannot pick their art for them. We cannot even be assured that the great masters, as we judge them, will continue to nourish them. It seems unlikely that Shakespeare, Rembrandt, or Beethoven might one day be passé, but we shall not be alive to defend them.

Actually, to "pick the survivor" is merely an academic game that no one can ever live long enough to win or lose. And it is not entirely healthy to think of art only in terms of the great masters who outlast the centuries. Art is legitimately a day-to-day activity, and it is natural that some of it should turn out to be ephemeral. The pace of living has accelerated so much that it becomes more and more essential to have some symbol of the passing tide held before us, if only for a moment. In a somewhat romantic vein Willa Cather asked, in the *Song of the Lark*, "What was any art but an effort to make a sheath, a mold, in which to imprison for a moment the shining, elusive element which is life itself—life hurrying past us and running away, too strong to stop, too sweet to lose?"

We should be wiser, I believe, to think of the arts more as we think of people. We learn, most of us, at a very early age that an adequate adjustment to the world cannot be made from social responses that simply divide the "good people" from the "bad people." We have learned to be skeptical even of such categories as "the people I like" and "the people I don't like." If we do maintain such divisions, we find individuals constantly moving from one group to the other. Eventually we find human differences too subtle for easy classification, and the web of our relationships becomes too complex for analysis. And we try to move toward more and more sensitive discrimination, so that there are those we can learn from, those we can work with, those good for an evening of light talk, those we can depend on for a little affection, and so on—with perhaps those very few with whom we can sustain a deepening relationship for an entire lifetime. When we have learned this same sensitivity and adjustment to works of art—when we have gone beyond the easy categories of the textbooks and have learned to regard our art relationships as part of our own growth—then we shall have achieved a dimension in living that is as deep and as irreplaceable as friendship.

Things cognitive and affective

Language and communication come in many forms. Most familiar to us is the language of the written and spoken word and the signs and symbols of science and mathematics. In addition there exists the language of sound, that is, music, and the language of gesture, which we could call dance, although gesture or body language often occurs in circumstances extrinsic to dance. Non-verbal modes of communication comprise significant and meaningful avenues for our understanding of the world around us. In coming to grips with the variety of means of communication we have available to us, we often separate these not only into verbal and non-verbal categories but also into cognitive and affective realms. The term cognitive connotes generally those things which are factual and objective; affective connotes feelings, intuition, and emotions. Each of these areas, that is, the cognitive and the affective, comprises separate ways of coming to understand or to know, as well as ways of communicating, and appears to be directly related to activities of either the left or right cerebral hemispheres. Roger Sperry, among others, has shown that

> The left and right hemispheres of the brain are each found to have their own specialized form of intellect. The left is highly verbal and mathematical, and performs with analytic, symbolic, and computer-like sequential logic. The right, by contrast, is spatial, mute, and performs with a synthetic, spatioperceptual and mechanical kind of information processing not yet simulatable in computers.[1]

What Sperry's work tells us is that there is a scientific basis for our assumptions that we can know and communicate through affective experiences, which do not conform to verbal, mathematical, or sequential cognitive systems.

Finally, let us consider one further, related concept. That is the concept of aesthetic knowledge—the total experience surrounding our involvement with a work of art and/or its creation. Aesthetic knowledge stems from a unique synthesis of affective and cognitive, of emotive and intellectual skills that deal with the relationships between colors, images, sounds, forms, and movements. As we move through the material ahead of us in this textbook, we need to keep in mind that the facts and descriptions presented here comprise only the beginnings of an experience with our cultural heritage. We really must go beyond these facts and try to discern meaning. In the classroom that task will require discussion and some help on the part of the instructor. For those reading this book for pleasure, it will entail some additional reading.

What is style?

Our discussion of arts history will focus to a large degree on style. So before we begin we need to understand some of the things the term style implies. A standard dictionary definition would indicate that style comprises those characteristics of an artwork that identify it with a period of history, a nation, a school of artists, and/or a particular artist. We might say that style is the individual personality of the artwork. That definition is fairly concise, but how does it affect us? How do we use it? When we look at a painting, for example, or listen to a piece of music, we respond to a complex combination of all the elements that make up the work—elements of form and of content. In the painting we see, among other things, colors, lines, and even perhaps the marks made by the brush as the paint was applied. In the musical piece we hear melodies, rhythms, harmonies, and so on. No two artists use these elements of their medium identically. Each artist has individual preferences and techniques. So when an expert compares several paintings by more than one artist, the expert can tell which paintings were painted by which artists. The expert extracts clues from the artwork itself: Are the colors bright, dull, or some combination? Are the lines hard or fuzzy, the contrasts soft or hard? Are the rhythms simple or complex? Those individual clues, those applications

of elements, help to indicate the artist's style, a style which may or may not be a reflection of society or philosophy, of biography or artistic considerations.

Groups of artists often work in close contact with each other. They may study with the same teacher, or they may share ideas of how their medium of expression can overcome technical limitations or more adequately convey the messages or concerns they all share. As a result, artworks of these artists may show characteristics of such similarity that the trained individual can isolate their works. The similarities which would allow for such identification would comprise the style of the group. Further expert examination could also isolate the works of individuals within the group. This same process of isolation and identification can be applied to artworks coming from certain nations, and even to rather large slices of history, as we shall see.

Finally, how does a style get its name? Why is some art called classical, some pop, some baroque, and some impressionist? Some styles were named hundreds of years after they occurred, with the definition accruing from extended, common usage or an historical viewpoint. The Athenian Greeks, whose works we know as classical, were centuries removed from the naming of the style they shared. Some labels were coined by artists themselves. Many stylistic labels are attributed to individual critics who, having experienced the emerging works of several artists and noting a common or different approach, invented a term (sometimes a derogatory one) to describe that approach. Because of the influence of the critic or the catchiness of the term, the name was adopted by others, and commonly used. Thus, a style was born.

We must be careful, however, when we use the labels by which we commonly refer to artworks. Occasionally such labels imply stylistic characteristics; occasionally they identify broad attitudes or tendencies which are not really stylistic. Often debate exists as to which is which. For example, romanticism has stylistic characteristics in some art disciplines, but the term connotes a broad philosophy toward life in general. Often a style label is really a composite of several styles whose characteristics may be dissimilar, but whose objectives are the same. Terminology is convenient but not always agreed upon in fine detail. Occasionally experts disagree as to whether certain artworks fall within the descriptive parameters of one style or another, even while agreeing on the definition of the style itself.

In addition, we can ask how the same label might identify stylistic characteristics of two or more unrelated art disciplines, such as painting and music. Is there an aural equivalent to visual characteristics, or vice versa? These are difficult questions, and potential answers can be troublesome as well as debatable. More often than not, similarity of objectives and date, as opposed to directly transferable technical characteristics, result in the same stylistic label being used for works in quite different disciplines. Nevertheless, some transference is possible, especially in a perceptual sense. For example, undulating line in painting is similar in its sense-stimuli to undulating melodic contours in music. However, the implications of such similarities have many hidden difficulties, and we must be careful in our usage, regardless of how attractive similarities in vocabulary may seem.

Styles do not start and stop on specific dates, nor do they recognize national boundaries. Some styles reflect deeply held convictions or creative insights; some styles are imitations of previous styles. Some styles are profound; others are superficial. Some styles are intensely individual. However, merely dissecting artistic or stylistic characteristics can be a dull experience. What makes the experience come alive is the actual experience of artworks themselves, describing to ourselves and to others such things about our reactions as can be described, and attempting to find the deepest level of meaning possible. Within every artwork there is the reflection of another human being attempting to express some view of the human condition. We can try to place that viewpoint in the context of the time or the specific biography that produced it and speculate upon why its style is as it is. We can attempt to compare those contexts with our own. We may never know the precise stimuli that caused a particular artistic reflection, but our attempts at understanding make our responses more informed and exciting, and our understanding of our own existence more profound.

CHAPTER ONE

PREHISTORY

In the Upper Paleolithic era some 50,000 years ago we learned, as *homo sapiens*, to grasp the notions of our selfhood and individuality—and thereby became human. We began to make symbols as part of our strategy for comprehending reality and for communicating what we found there. We learned to make art in order to express more fully what we believed was the unique essence of our common humanity. We thought. We became aware of death, and buried our dead with care and reverence. We realized that we had a complex relationship with the world into which we were born in mystery, in which we lived in mystery, and which we departed in mystery. We were fully human then. Our progress since that early time in technological and socio-economic sophistication has been immense—but we are no more human than we were at the first.

1.1 Black bull, detail, c.16,000–14,000 BC. Paint on limestone, total length of bull 13 ft (3.96 m). Lascaux, France.

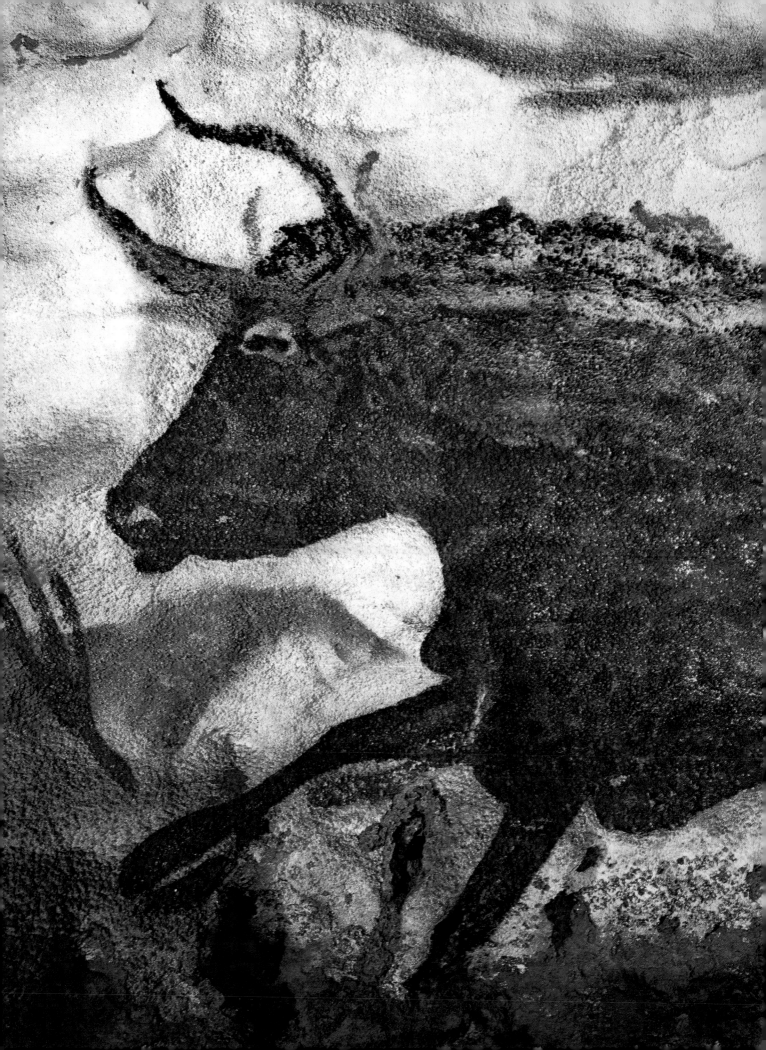

CONTEXTS AND CONCEPTS

If we have any tendency to think of our prehistoric predecessors as somehow less human than ourselves or as lacking intuitive or cognitive functioning, we have only to consider the profundity of their art to set our thinking straight. Because the period we are about to examine is prehistoric, that is, before recorded history, only the broadest of conjectures based on the slimmest of evidence leads us forward. Studies of prehistoric art and prehistoric societies leave us with a less than unified consensus on which to build. We may not be able accurately to grasp the whys or wherefores of the examples which present themselves for our study, but we cannot escape the power of the human spirit which they express.

When I first began to research Ice Age art, my task seemed rather straightforward, that is, to summarize those wonderful, and in some cases contemporary-appearing, artworks which have survived for tens of thousands of years. What makes this task different from the remainder of the book, however, is the fact that we are dealing with prehistory. The context and, therefore, the meaning of these works eludes us. Of course, we can examine these artworks in terms of line, form, color, and so on. But what of meaning? Eager to sort out the plethora of conclusions of various scholars from various finds in various places, I turned to the Museum of Natural History in New York City, whose 1978 exhibition of Ice Age art was one of the most stimulating I had ever seen. They, in turn, put me in touch with Alexander Marshack, to whose book, *The Roots of Civilization*, I have turned as my primary guide for what follows.

Social and natural environment

We begin our study of this very long period of humankind's creative activity with a brief look at the social and natural environment in which the artists lived and to one degree or another perceived and attempted to communicate through their artworks. To set the stage for our look at our ancestors' earliest creative expression we need to return to that time known as the Pleistocene Period, the beginning of which is dated variously between 500,000 and one million years ago. The Pleistocene Period saw great shifts of climate ranging from temperate to arctic; four glacial periods, separated by three interglacial periods, wrought tremendous changes on geographic and animal life. During the glacial periods in northern Europe (Fig. **1.3**) glaciers in the mountain ranges such as the Alps expanded to occupy huge areas. During the interglacial periods the same glaciers contracted. When the ice-sheets were at their maximum extent they averaged approximately 1,000 meters in thickness, which resulted in a drop in the levels of the oceans of nearly ninety meters. As Figure **1.3** illustrates, during the last glaciation, the sea level dropped so much that the British Isles and the Scandinavian peninsula were joined to the European continent. In the interglacial periods the phenomenon was reversed and the sea level rose to twenty or thirty meters above what it is today. Stretches of Pleistocene beaches containing shells from tropical seas can still be found high above the Mediterranean shores. Between 10,000 and 8,000 years ago the climate changed drastically. The Ice Age ended. The ice receded and the seas rose. Forests sprang up where only tundra had existed.

From the Pleistocene glacial and interglacial periods come some of our most fabled animals. The *Machairodus* or sabre-toothed tiger, the *Elephas meridionalis* or southern elephant, the hippopotamus, Merk's rhinoceros, and the *Elephas antiquus* or ancient elephant were succeeded by creatures more adapted to cold climates as glaciation occurred: the long-haired, thick-furred pachyderms called mammoths or *Elephas primigenius* and the woolly rhinoceros, *Rhinoceros tichorhinum*. Fossilized remains of mammoths have been found throughout Europe, and in Siberia complete carcasses have been retrieved from the frozen earth. However, these animals come alive to us not so much through their fossilized remains as through vibrant images in the caves of our prehistoric ancestors.

Compared to the timespan of recorded history the Pleistocene Period is enormously long. Even the relatively brief period which will concern humankind and Paleolithic art, from roughly 35,000 BC to 10,000 BC, is still overwhelming in comparison with recorded history, which starts with the ancient Mesopotamians and Egyptians some 5,000 years ago.

Early human symbols

Humankind's predecessors shaped stone weapons as early as one million years ago. The rough chipped tools of the pre-human period led to more fully developed hand axes of flint or similar stones shaped to create a cutting edge (Fig. **1.2**). These tools from the Middle Pleistocene era are about 250,000 years old. Some scholars speculate that it was about this time that early humankind developed the ability to create symbols, the requisites of language and of art. No other creature has this skill. For example, when an ape wishes to warn of danger, let us say a lion, it screams. However, the ape does not have the ability to communicate the symbol for "lion" when no lion is present. Such a transition involves a level of cognitive sophistication unique, and basic, to humanity. Such is one theory; there are others regarding how we made the transition to humanness.

Our early ancestors moved slowly to the acquisition of artistic capacity: stereoscopic vision, manual dexterity, communicative ability, conceptual thought, symbol-making, and aesthetic intuition all formed parts of such development. Two hundred thousand additional years of development from the hand axe of Figure **1.2** brought us to the last Ice Age and an ancestor of far greater complexity, self-awareness and clear artistic gifts. Marshack believes that "as far back as 30,000 BC the Ice Age hunter of western Europe was using a system of notation that was already evolved, complex, and sophisticated."[1] Scratched and engraved in bone and stone, examples of *Homo sapiens*' notation cross Europe from Spain to Russia and emerge from every period of the Upper Paleolithic.

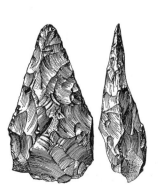

1.2 Hand-axe from Swanscombe, Essex, England, c. 25,000 B.C. Flint, 6⅜ ins (15.8 cm) high.

Neanderthal man may characterize for us the physical type which lived into the relatively warm period after 40,000 BC. *Homo neanderthalensis* was clearly more intelligent than his ancestors. He created tools by striking stone against stone. He was aware of death and created authentic burial places. Neanderthal man's posture was reasonably erect, although he stood on somewhat bowed legs, carrying his weight on the outward sides of his feet. His neck was short and squat. He possessed a low, slanted forehead with massive suborbital ridges. A broad jaw and receding chin completed the facial characteristics of this rather beast-like being. He was probably capable of speaking in a somewhat embryonic language. He did not, as far as we know, produce any art. *Homo sapiens*, completely evolved and distinguished by a defined chin and high, smooth forehead, appeared in Europe at the same time.

Early humans

Around 27,000 BC, south of the great ice-sheet across the middle part of Europe from Czechoslovakia to Poland and eastward to Siberia, herds of mammoths migrated across a barren tundra of rolling hills, rivers and streams. *Homo sapiens* hunted the mammoth, built huts, and even large houses (caves were rare in this part of Europe), of skin, bone, wood, clay and stone. These people buried their dead with ceremony and ornamentation, wore leather and skin clothes, some of which seem to have included a hood or parka, and decorated themselves with jewelry including rings, bracelets, necklaces and carved ivory headbands.

Homo sapiens comprised several sub-groups. The best known representative was Cro-Magnon, who stood at times six feet four inches tall and had a powerful build and a high forehead; not much different, in fact, from many Europeans of the twentieth century. Another variety of early *Homo sapiens*, the Combe Capelle man, had a smaller stature, more delicate bones, and a general appearance similar to contemporary Mediterranean people. These "modern men" made new types of tools and retained some tools of the Neanderthal. Most important, as Marshack points out, "he appears, apparently for the first time, with a skill in art, a skill for making images and symbols, that soon blossomed in every form: painting, sculpture, decoration, drawing, and engraving. He appeared also

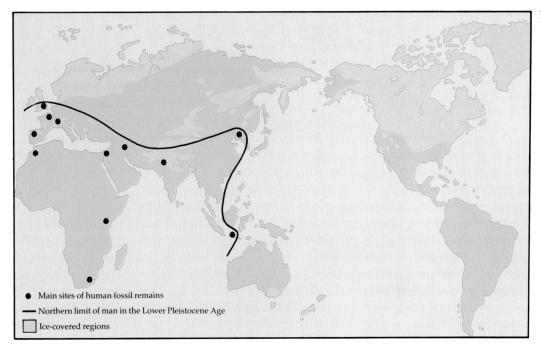

● Main sites of human fossil remains

— Northern limit of man in the Lower Pleistocene Age

☐ Ice-covered regions

with a skill in music, as excavated bone whistles and flutes from the early Upper Paleolithic indicate."[2]

The cranial capacity of *Homo sapiens* remains the same today as it was on his first appearance in Europe. There is a logic, then, in assuming that the basic functioning of the brain was the same then as it is now. Ice Age humankind may have lacked our world-view and technological achievement, but they were no less human than ourselves in feelings and the ability to perceive and respond. In capacity, ability, functioning and intelligence, Ice Age men and women were our peers.

During the entire Pleistocene Period our ancestors appear to have lived on game and wild fruits and vegetables; they made weapons and tools from stone, wood and bone. Agriculture and herding were unknown. This era is called the Old Stone Age or Paleolithic era (See Fig. **1.5**), and has been divided by some scholars into three periods: Lower, Middle, and Upper. Other scholars, however, compress it into merely Lower and Upper. Our study centers on the latest, or Upper, period, which begins around the middle of the final glaciation.

Primitive culture

We frequently and readily refer to Ice Age humankind as "primitive," but what does this term really imply? Traditionally, the historical study of humankind begins with recorded history and with what

some call high or mature cultures. Certainly, at least until very recently, prehistoric cultures have not appeared worthy of serious study if for no other reason than the lack of any apparent direct link with our own Western culture, which we perceive as beginning in Athens around 600 BC.

At issue is the word primitive itself. In an historical context the word loses all meaning, because it can include the societies of Paleolithic hunters as well as the Aborigines of contemporary Australia. Apparently, then, the word implies a qualitative distinction between levels of development even in coexisting societies. Some would argue that a distinction can be made which would separate, for example, the vigorous, changing, growing and dynamic primitive cultures of prehistory from what appear to be static, non-vital primitive cultures which are at odds with our modern world.

Paleolithic art may be the product of a technologically and economically primitive civilization, but it is not the product of the vision of a primitive human being. According to Marshack human culture existed at a modern level even in the Ice Age. It was complex in its use of art, symbol, rite, and story. "Art and symbol are products that visualize and objectify aspects of a culture, and no one image in human art is ever entirely explicable in terms of that representation and the limited meaning of that one image."[3] However, "the art, symbols and imitations ... do imply a structure, continuity and periodicity in the economic and cultural life of the Upper Paleolithic hunter."[4]

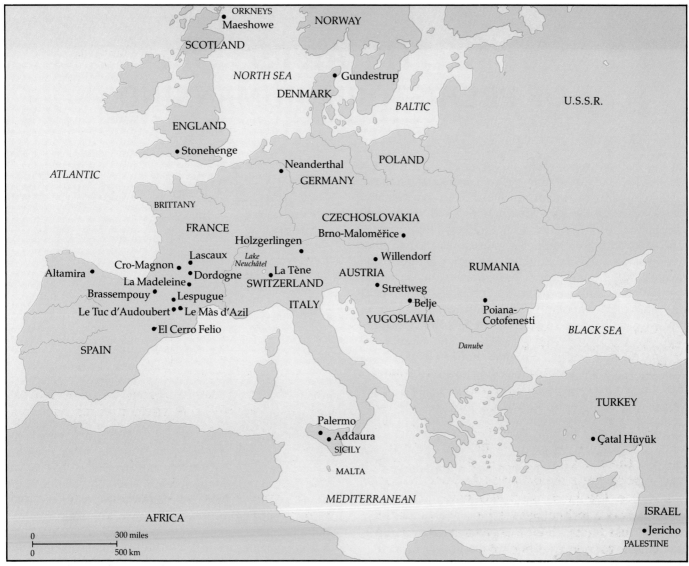

1.4 Prehistoric Europe.

1.5 Timeline of Prehistoric Eras.

BC				GENERAL EVENTS	LITERATURE & PHILOSOPHY	VISUAL ART	THEATRE & DANCE
1,000,000				Stone weapons			
600,000 540,000 480,000 380,000 240,000 180,000 120,000	Lower Paleolithic	Early Middle Pleistocene	1st Glacial 1st Inter-glacial 2nd Glacial 2nd Inter-glacial 3rd Glacial 3rd Inter-glacial	Flint axes	Human Symbols		
	Middle Paleolithic	Late Middle Pleistocene					
95,000							
40,000				Neanderthal			
30,000	Upper Paleolithic	Aurignacian	Last Glacial (Würm)	Tool making Homo Sapiens	Human Notation System	Lady from Willendorf (**1.11**) Man from Brno (**1.10**) Animals from Vogelherd (**1.14**)	
25,000		Solutrian				Woman from Dolní (**1.13**) Vulvae	Dancing Figures
20,000						Venus of Lespugue (**1.12**) Horse from Gargas (**1.7**) Bison from La Grèze (**1.8**) Cave of Lascaux	
15,000 12,000		Magdalenian				Cave of Altamira	
12,000	Mesolithic Neolithic			Domestication of the dog Pottery			
6,000				Mining and quarrying			

THE ARTS
OF PREHISTORIC HUMANKIND

In the material which follows, I am not going to trace a comprehensive picture nor explain in any great detail the archeological backgrounds which in a more specific study would accompany such descriptions. Rather, we will sample some of the fascinating products of our ancient ancestors and, if nothing else, gain an insight into their vision of the world around them. The nature of their vision may span the thousands of years between us, raise our awareness of our own vision, and cause us to marvel at the amazingly "modern" and sophisticated insights of these so-called primitives. I cannot help but recall my own reaction to Ice Age sculpture in the Museum of Natural History in New York. Had I not known that I was viewing sculpture and painting from over 20,000 years ago, I might have suspected that I was in a gallery in the Museum of Modern Art, a short distance downtown. The remarkable perception and execution of many of these prehistoric works has created profound and unanswerable questions for scholars about the psychological development of early humankind. Interpretations of these sophisticated representations are many. However, our present reaction to this prehistoric art can go far beyond historic or anthropological speculation, and bring us to a meaning of our own relationship to and understanding of the world in which we dwell.

TWO-DIMENSIONAL ART

Western European art probably began approximately 25,000 to 30,000 years before the Christian era, and at its earliest, consisted of simple lines scratched in damp clay. The people making these line scratchings lived in caves and seem, eventually, to have elaborated their simple line "drawings" into the outlines of animals. This development from what appears to be idle doodling into the sophisticated art to which we have referred, seems to have come in three phases. The first comprised black outline drawings of animals with a single colored filler. Next came the addition of a second color within the outline, so as to create a sense of light and shade, or modelling. As we shall see, these depictions often incorporated projecting portions of the cave walls to add a sense of three-dimensionality. In many cases it appears as though the artist picked an actual rock protrusion or configuration specifically for his animal drawing. The third step in the development of Ice Age art brought forth exciting multi-colored paintings which show an impressive naturalistic style. In this category are the well-

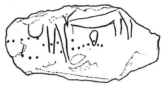

1.6 Animal's legs, vulva and dots, c.30,000–27,000 BC. Engraving on stone, 26½ ins (67.5 m) long. Musée des Eyzies, France.

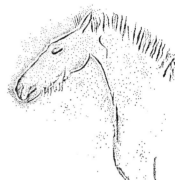

1.7 Horse's head, c.17,000–13,000 BC. Engraving on rock, about 8 ins (20 cm) high. Gargas, France.

known paintings of Altamira (Fig. **1.9**). Here the artists have captured detail, essence, mass, and a remarkable sense of power and movement in the subject matter, using only basic earth colors and charcoal.

Early in the twentieth century Henri Breuil traced the development of Paleolithic art over a period of 20,000 years. According to Breuil, art began with simple animal outlines and progressed to the multicolored animals just noted, changing stylistically from naturalistic depiction towards greater abstraction until, in the Mesolithic period (see Fig. **1.5**), an animal was represented by only a few characteristic strokes.

The first drawings of which we have knowledge date to the period from approximately 23,000 to 15,000 BC. The figures in these earliest drawings were scratched on stones and are found in deposits on cave floors among tools and weapons which scholars have used to date them. Figure **1.6** represents a rock found at La Ferrassie, France. Probably carved with a flint burin, such drawings show female sexual organs and animals. Figure **1.7** depicts a horse engraved on a cave wall at Gargas, France. The strong, curving outline captures the grace and strength of the horse; it is a smooth and sophisticated depiction which captures realistic proportions and details like the hair under the muzzle. Although employing economy of line, it nevertheless accurately captures the essentials of the subject. The drawings at Gargas raise some question as to their date; the caves were occupied by much later peoples. Nonetheless, they provide us with a remarkable illustration of the perceptions and style of our prehistoric ancestors.

The same may be said for a bison found on the wall of the cave of La Grèze in the Dordogne (Fig. **1.8**). Here we find a representational drawing so situated on the rock wall as to suggest the contours of the bison's rib cage and flanks. Further, to suggest plasticity of form, the artist has turned the face and horns of the bison to face outward, while the body and legs remain in profile. Only two legs appear.

Paleolithic artists seem to have shied away from the difficulties of suggesting three-dimensionality, keeping their subjects in profile (as, much later, the Egyptians were to do). Only an occasional turning of head or antlers tests the artist's skill at dimensional portrayal.

SCULPTURE

Humankind's first known sculpture predates drawings and occupies the period from approximately 30,000 to 15,000 BC. The head and body of a man carved from mammoth ivory were found in a burial site at Brno, Czechoslovakia (Fig. **1.10**). Although many body parts are missing, we can see that the head, in contrast to the body, shows a remarkable degree of verisimilitude. The hair is closely cropped, the brow is low and the eyes are deeply set.

Venus figures

Other burial sites yield a number of Venus figures. The possible meanings of these figures are numerous and elusive. The best known is the Lady from Willendorf (Fig. **1.11**), carbon-dated at approximately 30,000 to 25,000 BC. She was carved from limestone and originally colored red. She is remarkable in several aspects. Her obesity lends the figure a certain vitality; the bulging fat of breasts, sides, belly and thighs creates a subtle repetition of line and form which perpetually moves the eye of the viewer inward toward the reproductive organs. She may very well be an Earth Mother or goddess of fertility. She remains faceless and generalized, and yet her form strongly suggests an individual woman rather than an abstract type, however grossly exaggerated her torso appears to be at first viewing.

A remarkable similarity can be seen in two additional Venus figures from elsewhere in Europe. Figure **1.12** shows the restored Venus of Lespugue, carved in mammoth ivory. In this figure the sweeping, bulbous quality of the Lady from Willendorf is repeated. However, the symmetrical proportions give us, in this figure, a much less naturalistic portrayal. Whereas it is not difficult for us to imagine an actual woman of the obese proportions of

1.8 Bison, c.23,000–17,000 BC. Engraving on rock, 2 ft (60 cm) long. La Grèze, France.

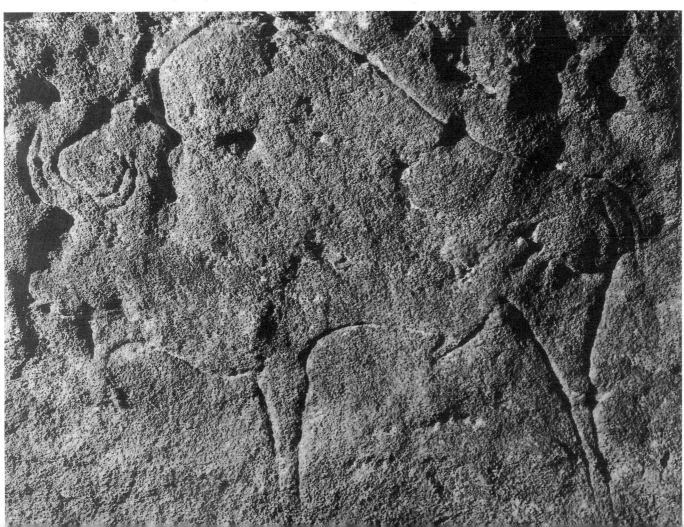

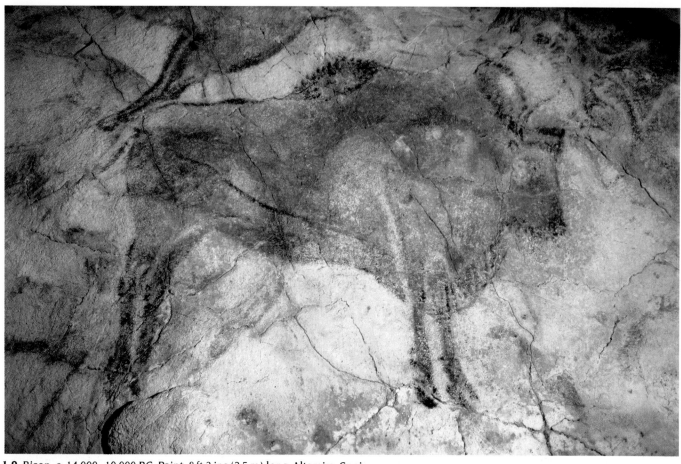

1.9 Bison, c. 14,000–10,000 BC. Paint, 8 ft 3 ins (2.5 m) long. Altamira, Spain.

1.10 Man from Brno, c.27,000–20,000 BC. Ivory, 8 ins (15 cm) high. Moravian Museum, Brno, Czechoslovakia.

1.11 Woman from Willendorf, Lower Austria, c.20,000–18,000 BC. Limestone, 4⅓ ins (11 cm) high. Naturhistorisches Museum, Vienna.

1.12 Woman from Lespugue, France, c.20,000–18,000 BC. Ivory, 6 ins (15 cm) high. Musée de l'Homme, Paris.

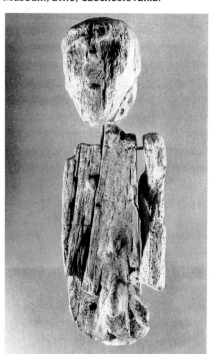

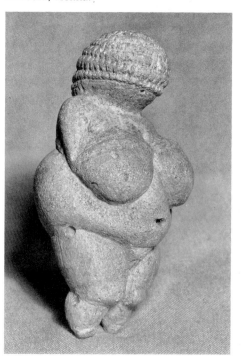

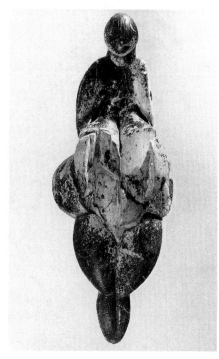

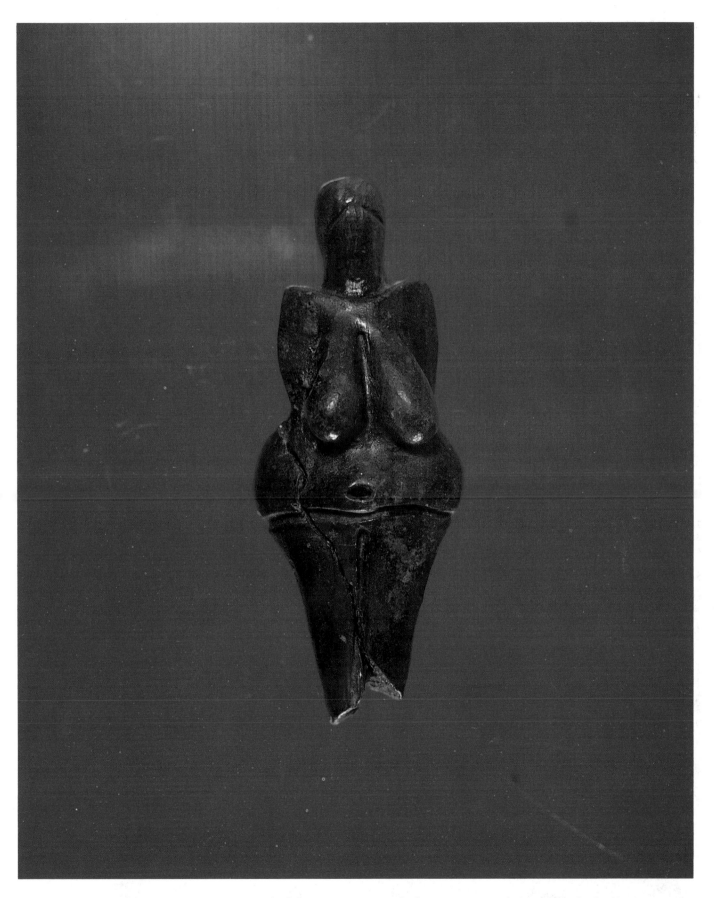

1.13 Woman from Dolní Věstonice, c.23,000 BC. Baked clay, 4½ ins (11.5 cm) high. Moravian Museum, Brno, Czechoslovakia.

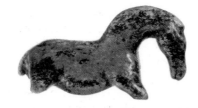

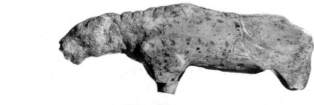

1.14 Animals from the Vogelherd cave, c.26,000 BC. Bone and ivory, lion 3⅔ ins (9.2 cm) long. Institut für Urgeschichte, Universität Tübingen, Germany.

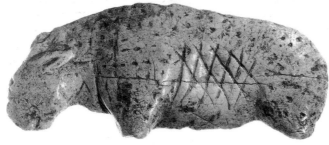

technique of high aesthetic sophistication. The compositional qualities of these three pieces exhibit rational control and closed qualities we might find, although in a more naturalistic style, in the High Renaissance.

Animal carvings

The same period produced animal carvings which illustrate, again, the naturalistic vision of their artists (Fig. 1.14). From these examples we sense the vision and skill of the Paleolithic artist. These works exhibit sensitivity to the grace, power, and spirit of the animal. Well modelled and proportioned, they are the product of a sensitive and perceptive human being.

Human figures in Paleolithic art

As we have seen, human images accompany animals in Upper Paleolithic art. Interestingly, none of the human images appears with weapon in hand. Usually the image depicts a naked man or one robed in animal skins; posture and attitude suggest a ritualistic or ceremonial relationship with the animals. Only later, after the Upper Paleolithic, when the ice had receded and a considerable change in culture had taken place, do humans appear in art along with weapons. Even then, it is not clear whether the paintings depict an actual hunt or a ceremonial one.

DANCE

We can, with some hesitancy, conclude that a number of Upper Paleolithic art objects portray dancing of some sort. Marshack presents a line rendition of both faces of a broken engraved bone disc or plaque (Fig. 1.15) which he describes as showing "human figures in dancelike stances before the paws of a standing bear".[5] One side shows a masked dancer and the other, a "dog-faced" dancer.

the Willendorf figure, the Lespugue figure is clearly a stylized abstraction of magnificent compositional unity. A faceless, neutral image casts an eyeless glance downward, reinforcing the sweep of uniformly curvilinear line which leads our eyes to focus on breasts, belly, and *mons veneris*, all of which have been placed in close proximity. The artist has given us an image of sexuality and fertility in a most dramatic manner.

A third and more geometric treatment of the same theme is shown in Figure 1.13. Although much less sensual than the two previous examples, the similarities are obvious. The obese spread of waist, thighs, and breasts tapers into highly stylized appendages for legs which indicate their unimportance in the meaning of this figure. Here, as with the Lespugue figure, a sophisticated compositional balance is achieved by carrying the linearity of the legs into the geometric configuration of the shoulders. A slight outward curvature of the arms reinforces the inward curvature of the legs and creates a central focal area in the breasts as the bulbous waistline gracefully picks up the reverse curves of the legs and joins the line of the arms. The curvature of the pendulous breasts creates a reinforcing rhythm with the waist in a unifying repetition of form. Finally, the head, with its almost helmet-like appearance, stares outward through mask-like slits whose oblique slant subtly but precisely leads our eyes downward to pick up the line of the shoulder and arm, thereby returning us to the breasts. The innate sexuality of the previous figures is lacking in this piece, but there can be little question that in all three works we are communicating with an artistic vision and

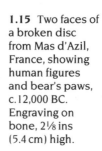

1.15 Two faces of a broken disc from Mas d'Azil, France, showing human figures and bear's paws, c.12,000 BC. Engraving on bone, 2⅛ ins (5.4 cm) high.

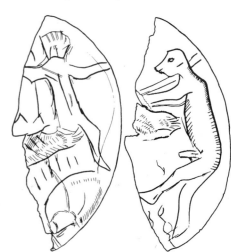

SYNTHESIS
The Cave of Lascaux

We cannot study humankind's earliest known art without considering what many believe to be the most significant and miraculous repository of works from the dawn of humanity, the Cave of Lascaux. It lies slightly over a mile from the little French town of Montignac, in the Valley of the Vézère River. Lascaux was discovered by a group of children who, investigating a tree uprooted by a storm, scrambled down a fissure into a world undisturbed for thousands of years.

Here, underground, we find ourselves in the undeniable presence of our early ancestors. The Lascaux paintings exist in great number. Hundreds of paintings add to those found elsewhere in France, Spain, and the remainder of Europe. The significance of the Lascaux paintings lies both in the quantity and the quality of an intact grouping of works. The diagram in Figure **1.16** helps to orient us to the wealth of paintings in the cave.

An overwhelming sense of the power and sweep of Lascaux emerges from the Main Hall or Hall of the Bulls (Fig. **1.17**). The thundering herd moves below a sky of rolling contours formed in the stone ceiling of the cave, sweeping our eyes forward as we travel into the cave itself. At the entrance of the Hall an eight-foot unicorn begins a monumental montage of bulls, horses, and deer, whose shapes intermingle one with another and whose colors radiate warmth and power. With heights ranging to twelve feet, these magnificent creatures overwhelm us and remind us that the artists were fully capable technicians who, with a genius seemingly equal to or exceeding our own, captured the essences beyond the photographic surface of their world. Although the paintings in the Main Hall were created over a long period of time and by a succession of artists, the cumulative effect of this thirty- by one hundred-foot domed gallery strikes us as that of a single work, carefully composed for maximum dramatic and communicative impact. We must remember, however, that our experience of the work illuminated by

1.16 Diagram of Lascaux cave, France.

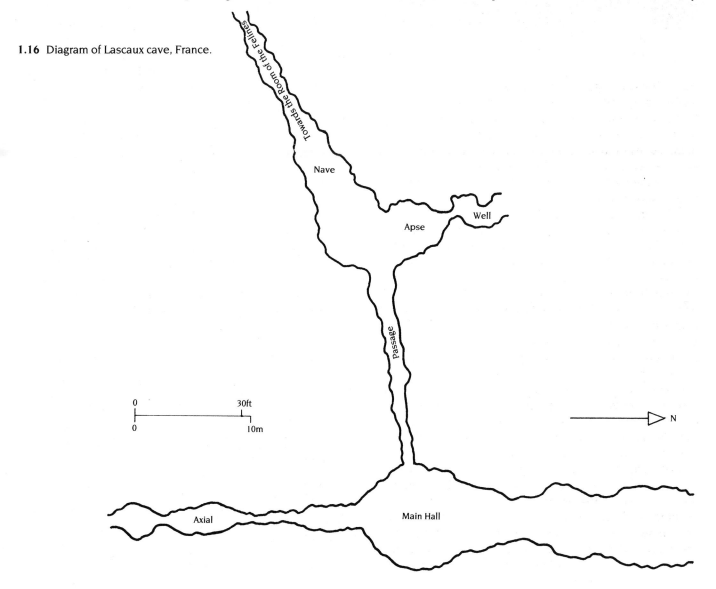

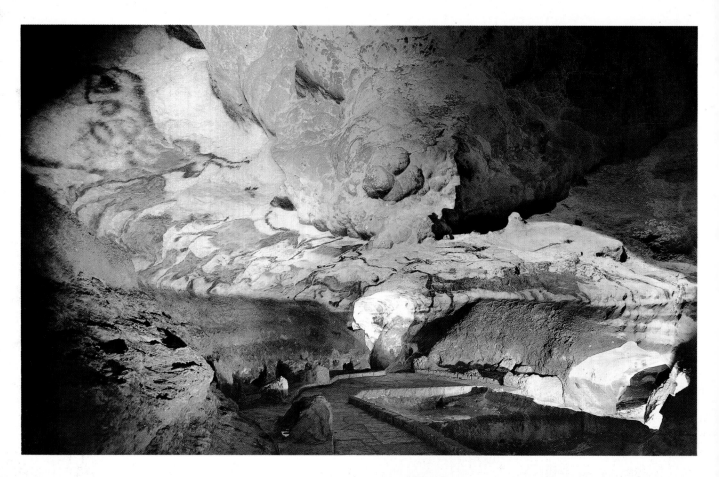

1.17 Main hall, or 'Hall of Bulls', Lascaux.

1.18 Head and back of deer, the 'Baying Stag', c.16,000–14,000 BC. Paint on limestone, 4 ft 11 ins (1.5 m) high. Lascaux.

1.19 Geometric figures at the feet of a cow, left square about 10 × 10 ins (25.4 cm). Lascaux.

1.20 Entrance to the axial gallery from the main hall, Lascaux.

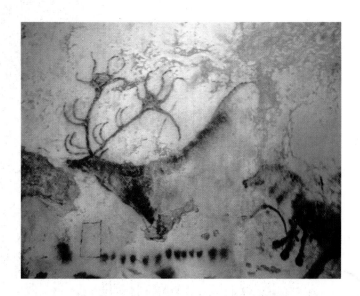

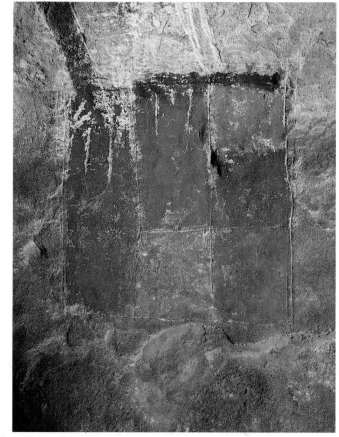

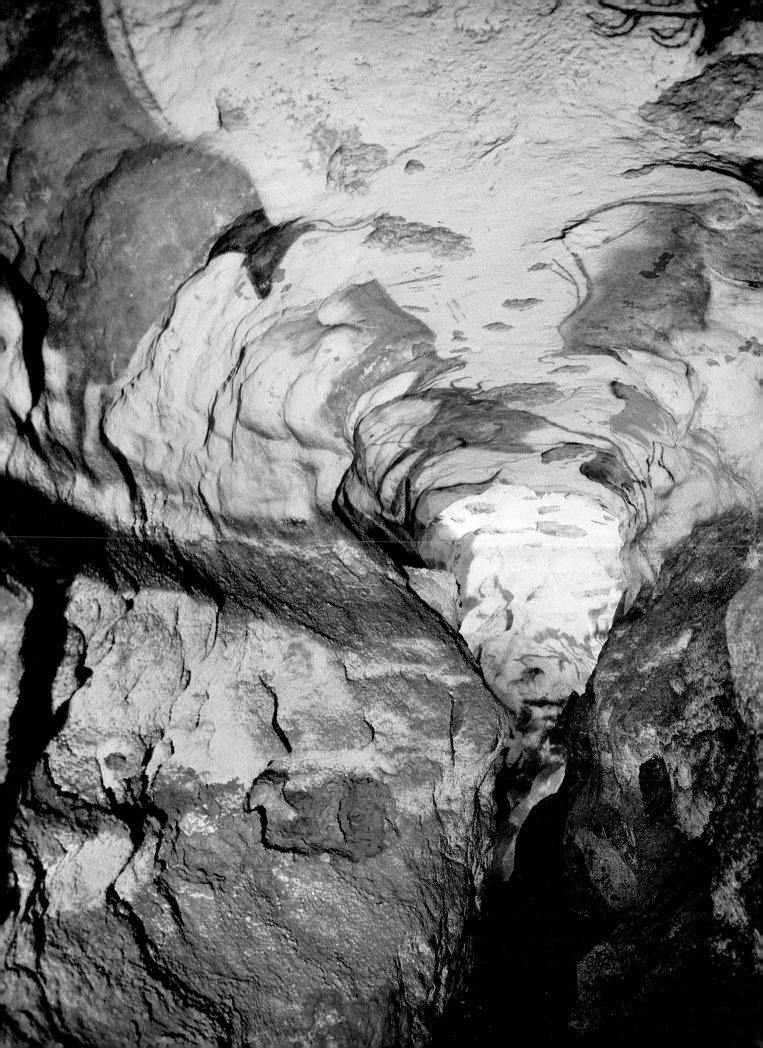

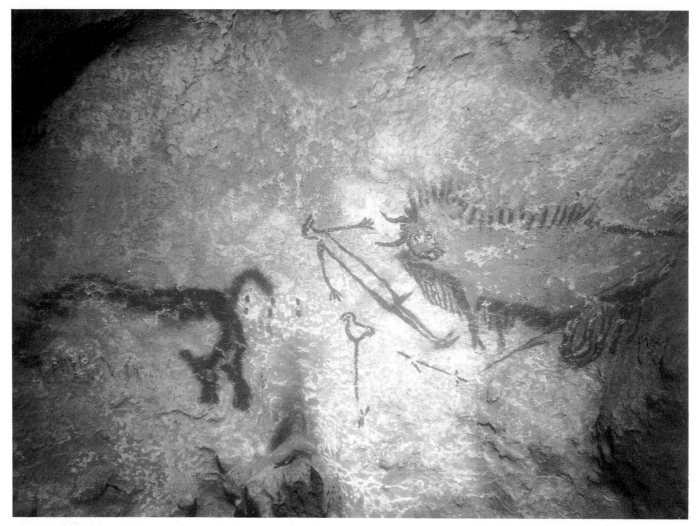

1.21 Rhinoceros, bird-headed 'dead' man, bird-topped rod, long spear and wounded bison, 6 ft 6 ins (1.98 m) long. 'The Well', Lascaux.

electric floodlighting may be very different from that of people who could only ever see small areas at a time, lit by flickering stone lamps of oil or animal fat.

From the Main Hall one can move straight ahead to a dead end Axial Gallery whose walls and ceiling swirl in colorful and profuse images, alive and vital. The effect is awesome and breathtaking (Fig. **1.20**). Rich in texture and color, the walls sparkle with horses, ibexes, cows and bulls, amidst which we find the head and back of a baying stag (Fig. **1.18**). Here the figures are much smaller than in the Main Hall, and are detailed with great delicacy. Like the Main Hall, the Axial Gallery seems to form a remarkably unified design whose parts, like a baroque design, stand on their own, distinct, and yet rationally assembled into an emotional complexity which overwhelms the viewer and draws us into an emotional experience.

From the Main Hall, a turn to the right leads through a small passageway to the Nave and the Apse. In the high-vaulted Nave, the paintings are spaced further apart and

depict, on one wall, a frieze of ibexes, a group of horses, a bison, a very large black cow which dominates the wall, a second group of horses, and a further two bison. On the opposite wall a frieze of deer heads appears to show a swimming herd.

Swelling out from the Nave is a chamber called the Apse. Every surface is decorated, often with paintings layered one over the other and reflecting immense activity over many years. Two additional spaces, the Well and the Hall of Felines, complete the ensemble of spaces that comprise the Lascaux Cave. Were we to descend into the Well, we would encounter a remarkable portrayal which dates back 15,000 to 20,000 years (Fig. **1.21**).

There is some disagreement concerning the actual dating of the Lascaux paintings. Abbé Breuil dates most of them from Arignacian-Perigordian, with some from the Magdalenian, whereas others have suggested Solutrean to Magdalenian III and IV (see Fig. **1.1**). Unimpressive by comparison with the colorful and dynamic work we previously encountered, this four by six and one half foot depiction shows a naked, bird-headed man with an erect phallus lying beside or falling in front of a bison whose entrails are spilling out and from whom a spear emerges. Under the man appears a bird on a stick. To the left stands a rhinoceros with six black dots in front of it. The composition includes other symbols apparently implicit with meaning.

Another enigma emerges from Lascaux, and that is a series of geometric figures or symbols which occur throughout the cave (Fig. **1.19**). Scholars have conjectured numerous interpretations for these figures, but the mystery remains; we do not and probably cannot know their meaning. Elsewhere in the cave appear what seem to be arrows or at least lines. Abbé Breuil attributed them to hunting magic and called them flying arrows.

On the other hand, Leroi-Gourhan has called them barbed signs, sexual and masculine, and his interpretation is based on the fact that in the caves these signs are often associated with pregnant animals or with feminine symbols. . . . Possibly [there is] a different meaning. If we consider . . . [the] horse to be female and pregnant or female and potentially pregnant—then the image might be considered a branch and, therefore, a sign of late spring and a time of calving or, if the form is intended to represent a bare, sparse branch, it may be a sign of autumn-winter. . . . Given the possibility of this sort of interpretation, a whole class of compositions or associations in the caves is given new potential meaning, with some hint as to the possible seasons of the rites or myths that may be involved.[6]

SUGGESTIONS FOR THOUGHT AND DISCUSSION

The artworks from humankind's earliest times reveal a human being who may have been fully developed in mental capabilities, and perhaps in communicative capabilities as well. If Marshack is correct in his analyses, our ealiest ancestors were not only artistic, but literate as well. Their vision was profound and their technical ability, masterful. They seem to have moved in visual art from the naturalistic style into the abstract.

■ What characteristics of Paleolithic art seem similar to other artworks you may have experienced?

■ Can you express your own reactions to the examples in this chapter?

■ How do you react to the suggestion that Paleolithic humans were equal in mental ability to us?

■ Is Ice Age art more or less sophisticated than other so-called primitive "art" you may have experienced, for example, African art?

■ What meanings can be transmitted through abstract as opposed to naturalistic images?

■ Some peoples believe that image and reality are the same. If such a belief existed in Paleolithic times, what practical or other results might Paleolithic humans have expected to occur from the representations we have seen in this chapter?

■ Do you think that Paleolithic humans might merely have painted the walls of their caves for the pleasure of decoration, in the same sense that we hang pictures on the walls of our homes?

■ What does the art of the Paleolithic period tell you about the humans who lived then?

■ Why might Paleolithic artists have chosen the deep, inaccessible parts of caves for some of their artworks?

CHAPTER TWO

MESOPOTAMIA

The mythological Tower of Babel rose to connect heaven and earth. In much the same way the arts of the Mesopotamians symbolized humankind's relationship to its kings and, through them, its gods. Bridging prehistory and history, the cities and empires of the Fertile Crescent, the "land between the rivers"—the Tigris and the Euphrates—were our prototype civilizations. Here, for the first time, agriculture, metal technology, literacy, the specialization of labor and a hierarchically organized urban community were combined. Kingdoms rose and fell as one power plundered its enemies, obliterated their cities, and was, in turn, itself plundered and obliterated, until, spilling out of the Crescent north into Asia Minor and south as far as Egypt, the vast empires of Mesopotamia reached outward in space and forward in time to clash with and influence our more immediate cultural forebears—the Greeks.

2.1 Head of an Akkadian ruler, from Nineveh, 2300–2200 BC. Bronze, 12 ins (30.5 cm) high. Iraq Museum, Baghdad.

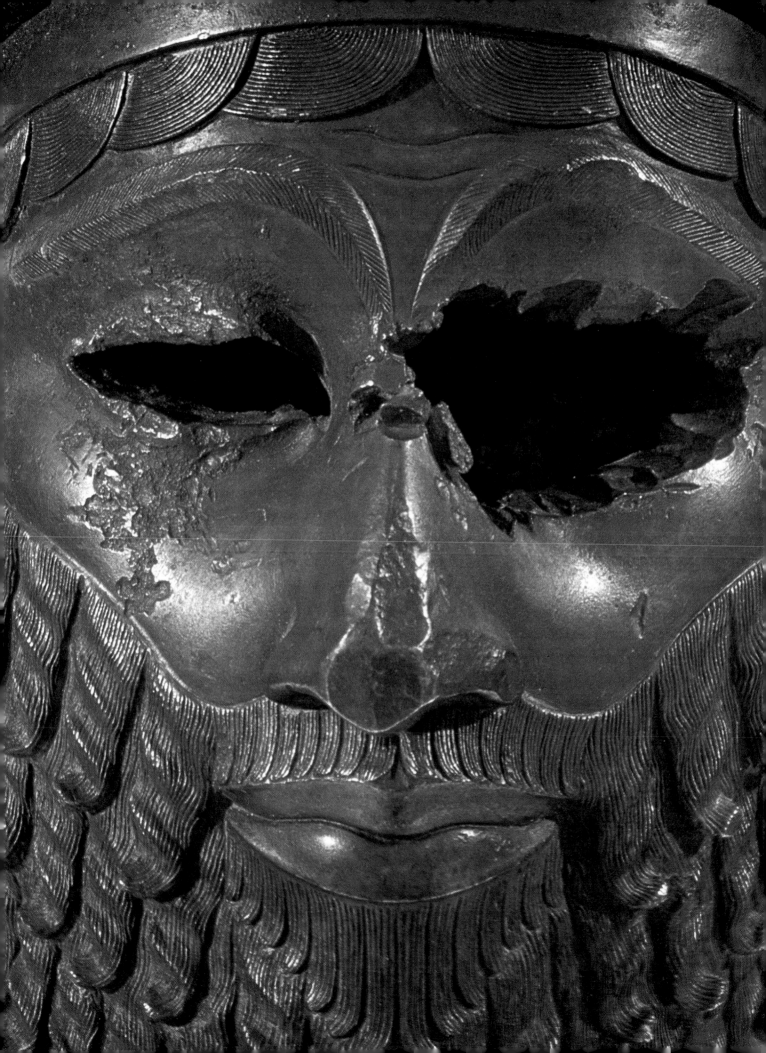

CONTEXTS AND CONCEPTS

From pre-history to history

Although this book is not a social history, it does to some degree treat cultural history in its social context. We must, therefore, be as careful with our general terminology as we are with our artistic terminology. The four terms noted above mark watersheds not so much in our development as human beings, as in the development of the social arrangements under which we live. There was, however, no single point at which humankind emerged into history from pre-history or became civilized after having been primitive. Nonetheless, we need some understanding of what these terms mean before we can move on to what historians call the ancient, historical, civilized world.

In the terms used by archeologists, the Paleolithic Age (Old Stone Age) was followed by the Mesolithic (Middle Stone Age); that in turn was followed by the Neolithic (New Stone Age) (see Fig. **1.2**). In the last of these our ancestors provided the beginnings from which a literate civilization could arise, although, if Marshack is correct, we may have to qualify the conditions of literacy we apply here.

The word history implies a conscious and intentional recall of the past which is a vital tradition communicated from one generation to another. This pursuit demands the existence of a continuous organization "which has reason to care for transmitting the historical traditions to future generations."[1]

Civilization, on the other hand, implies something more. First, humankind had first to produce an economic surplus above its daily needs. To reach such a stage, humankind needed to progress from hunting to gathering to agriculture. As our ancestors moved from the Neolithic Age, which began and ended in widely separated times across the ancient world, to the Age of Metals, they also, and at slightly different times, moved from hunting to agriculture. Societal complexity, which perhaps constitutes the basic quality of civilization, then began to emerge. We now find ourselves at some time around 6000 BC, when the first civilization appeared in a part of the Near East which we call Mesopotamia (see Figs. **2.3** and **2.4**).

A succession of cultures

In the southern part of Mesopotamia, in a strip of land some seven hundred miles long and one hundred and fifty miles wide between the Tigris and Euphrates rivers, we find a cluster of farming villages. The oldest of these appeared in Neolithic times in the extreme south of the Fertile Crescent, where drainage from the uplands and annual flooding deposited a rich topsoil in which crops flourished. As in Egypt, the livelihood of these peoples depended upon the rivers, since no significant rainfall occurred. Nonetheless, water was plentiful and wheat harvests appear to have been abundant. A surplus emerged. Even then, the challenge to humankind produced improved techniques such as diking and ditching to raise the marshy flood plain above river level. Irrigation and drainage, at first done individually, came to be jointly organized in collectively managed areas, with a resulting development of complex social and administrative structures. At some point these increasingly sophisticated organizational units must have faced conflicts of opportunity. The resolutions of such conflicts could be either conquest or cooperation. Undoubtedly both solutions were tried at one time or another, and the wiser choice appeared to be further conglomeration and organization. Larger units of government then emerged. Towns were established, mutual defenses were erected, and in one specific location these factors appeared to coalesce more effectively than in others. The result was Sumer—the first truly urban settlement, and the first that can be described as a civilization.

Sumer

Unlike their neighbors, the Sumerians appear to have been of Caucasian origin. Their way of life, however, was similar to that of the other peoples in the region. They lived in villages and organized themselves around several important religious centers, which grew rapidly. In time, these Sumerian religious centers grew into cities.

Religion and government shared a close relationship in Sumer. The Sumero-Akkadian religion permeated the social, political and economic, as well as spiritual and ethical life of society. From the Gilgamesh Epic we gain an insight into this religion around which Sumerian society was organized. The list of gods is a long one. By about 2250 BC the Sumerians had a well-developed and accepted pantheon of gods. Temples were erected throughout Sumer for the sacrifices necessary to ensure good harvests. It appears that each individual city had its own god, and these local gods were organized into a form of hierarchy. Like the Greeks, the Sumerians gave human form and attributes, as well as an individual role, to their gods. Ishtar was the goddess of love and procreation, for example. There was also a god of the air, one of the water, one of the plow, and so on. At the top of this pantheon were three male gods who demanded sacrifice and obedience; all was accomplished through elaborate and intricate rituals. Very simply, to those who obeyed the gods came the promise of prosperity and longevity. Ritual itself focused upon the marriage and rebirth cycle drama of creation as witnessed in the seasons.

Religion

Sumerian religion dwelt on life, and seems to have perceived the afterworld as a rather dismal place. Nonetheless, evidence suggests not only ritual suicide, but also the need for kings and queens to depart from this life with a full retinue of worldly goods and possessions.

In its political ramifications, Sumerian religion ascribed ownership of all lands to the gods. The king was a king-priest responsible to the gods alone. Below the king-priest there was an elaborate class of priests who enjoyed worldly power, privilege and comfort. To the priestly class fell responsibilities for education and the writing of texts. Writing undoubtedly represents the Sumerians' greatest contribution to the advancement of general civilization.

Writing

Sumerian writing began with the use of pictorial symbols—a qualitatively different means of message conveyance from the picture writing used by various primitive peoples. Advances came as the Sumerians (and later the Egyptians) started using pictures to indicate syllabic sounds which occurred in different words. Sumerian language consisted of monosyllables used in combinations, and so Sumerian writing came to consist of two types of signs, one for syllables and one for words. Writing materials consisted of unbaked clay tablets and a reed stylus, which, when pressed into the soft clay, produced a wedge-shaped mark. The wedges and combinations of wedges which made up Sumerian writing were called cuneiform writing, from the Latin *cuneus*, meaning wedge.

Written language does many things to a society, and also reveals many things about that society. While opening up new possibilities in the area of communication, it also has a stabilizing effect on society because it turns the past and its functions into a documentable chronicle. In Sumer records of irrigation patterns and practices, tax-collections, harvest and storage records were among the first things written down. Writing was also a tool of control and power. Those who had it could maintain a certain leverage over those who did not. In the earliest years the government and the priestly class of Sumer held a monopoly on literacy, and literacy served to strengthen government. Nonetheless, literacy also led to literature, and the oldest known story in the world comes to us from Sumer in the form of the Gilgamesh Epic, which dates from this era, although the most complete version dates only from the seventh century BC. A fascinating part of this epic of Gilgamesh, an actual person who ruled at Erech (or Uruk), is the description of the flood, which parallels the story of Noah's ark in the Bible. Other epics and even love songs have survived from the literature of ancient Sumer and, taken in total, these manifestations of society in written form, from tax records to love songs, with the addition of the art we shall examine, represent all that we know of humankind's earliest civilization.

Everyday life

Domestic life in Sumer provides us with an additional insight into the humans who made up this ancient civilization. Marriages were, apparently, monogamous, and depended upon the consent of the bride's parents. Once a marriage occurred, a new family unit was established, governed by a formal contract. Its head was a patriarchal husband who ruled his relatives and his slaves. Nonetheless, evidence suggests that Sumerian women held a higher position in family life and society as a whole than do many Middle Eastern women today. That role seems to reflect the importance of women's sexual power in Sumerian religion. Women also held important rights, including rights granted to female slaves who had children by free males. Divorce accorded fair treatment to women, although a wife's adultery was punishable by death.

The people of Sumer were curious about the world around them. They sought answers to basic questions about the nature of the universe. In some cases these questions were answered intuitively through reflections in art. In other cases the questions sought scientific answers. Insofar as the Sumerian was capable of discerning scientific knowledge, he also was capable of applying that knowledge as technology. Sumerian mathematics employed a system of counting based on sixty, and used that system to measure time and circles. The invention of number positioning, for example, 6 as a component of 6 or 60, gave Sumerian mathematics an unusual level of sophistication. Mathematical calculation formed the basis for architectural achievement, which in turn developed the technology of brick-making to high levels. Pottery was mass produced using the first known application of the potter's

wheel. The wheel itself appeared as a transportation device in Sumer as early as 3000 BC. By the third millennium BC Sumerian technology accomplished the casting of bronze and the invention of glass. Technology created a need for raw materials, which led to the growth of trade and commerce and took the ancient Sumerians to the far reaches of the Middle East.

Sumer comprised a dozen or so small cities and the territories around them, and the feudal nature of Sumerian society constantly pitted one city against its neighboring city, which often was within sight. Conflicts among these independent cities usually developed over water and pasture rights. However, Sumerians shared a common language, customs, religion, and an intolerance for non-Sumerians.

The Archaic period

History, however, provides a constantly changing

BC		GENERAL EVENTS	LITERATURE & PHILOSOPHY	VISUAL ART	THEATRE & DANCE	MUSIC	ARCHITECTURE
8,000	Neolithic	Mesopotamian farming villages Sumer		Ritual painted vases Stamp seals	Religious dances		
3,300				Head of a goddess (2.9) Sacred lambs			
3,000	Archaic Period	Invention of the wheel Dynasty I Bronze Casting Dynasty II		Tell Asmar statues (2.11) Cylinder seals			Ground level temples Sin Temple at Khafaje (2.20) Tell Asmar Temple (2.21)
2,500		Dynasty III		Royal Harp (2.14) He-goat from Ur (2.15)			
2,400	Akkadian Period	Sargon I Naram-Sin		Stele of Naram-Sin (2.12)			
2,300		Composite bow	Sumerian Pantheon well developed				
2,200	Neo-Sumerian Period		Early Gilgamesh epic				
2,100		Ur	Epics, love songs				Ziggurat at Ur (2.23)
2,000							
1,900	Babylonia		Babylonian literature Rage of the God Ezra Love Songs				
1,700		Hammurabi					
1,000	Assyrian Empire				Social and religious dances Fire festival	Musical instruments: kissar, harps, lyres, dulcimers, asor	
900							
800							
700		Sargon II		Alabaster relief & Winged bull (2.26) from Dur Sharrukin			Citadel at Dur Sharrukin
600	Neo-Babylonian	Nebuchadnezzar II	Gilgamesh epic Complete version				
500	Persian Empire	Darius I Xerxes I		Basalt Relief			
400							

2.2 Timeline of Mesopotamian culture.

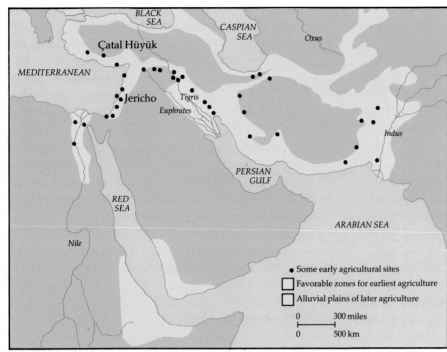

2.3 The Ancient Middle East.

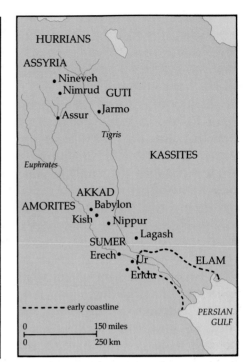

2.4 Mesopotamia.

scenario. We gain a clearer overview of the changes in Mesopotamian civilization if we consider certain periods in turn. The first of these is the period from 3300 to 2400 BC. Called the Archaic period, it saw numerous wars and conflicts between the cities. Military matters predominate as we sift through the evidence which survives.

We have noted that the Sumerian city-states each had a ruler or king-priest. The king was obliged to build temples; he also built roads. In addition, he was a warrior. Various illustrations depict kings leading troops into battle, conquering enemies, and receiving tribute from fallen foes. We find pictures of chariots and infantry. Chariots had solid wheels and were drawn by a breed of ass. Charioteers carried javelins. Infantry soldiers wore uniforms and wielded short spears, pikes and axes. Interestingly, with all the conflict among the city-states of Sumer, there does not appear to have been any attempt by the Sumerians to extend their territories to the North, where another civilization, the Akkadian, had grown up.

The proximity of these civilizations was a catalyst for change. The distance between them was tiny by our standards. In fact, the distance from the Sumerian city of Kish to the Akkadian city of Babylon was only ten miles, a distance well within the city limits of any number of modern urbanizations. But these were different times, and the fastest means of

transportation was not even the horse but, rather, the donkey. Nonetheless, contact occurred, and the Akkadians became interested in things Sumerian. In many of the border regions Akkadians lived and dressed like Sumerians. Sumerian culture permeated Akkadian civilization, and the Sumerian script was adopted. Curiously, though, as the Archaic period came to a close it was the Sumerizing of the Akkadians which brought the latter to a position where they could conquer their older neighbor to the South. A new era was about to begin.

The Akkadian period

Between 2400 and 2350 BC Sargon I of Akkad led his semitic people to victory over the Sumerians and thereby gained supremacy for Akkadian civilization. Sargon's empire stretched from the Mediterranean Sea to the Persian Gulf. Known for a thousand years as the King of Battle, he is known to us through inscriptions written in Sumerian and Akkadian. The reign of Sargon I is significant because he created a truly united empire with a centralized government. A division between secular and religious authority was maintained, but the king ruled by the authority of the gods. In the East Enlil, the supreme god of Sumer, granted his authority, and in the West, Sargon paid obeisance to the semitic god Dagon.

Sargon also ruled with the authority of the army, and the essence of Akkadian presence was that of force. Their military supremacy stemmed largely from two innovations. One was the composite bow, which is made from strips of wood and can shoot arrows faster and further than the non-composite bow. The other was a military maneuver which proved its effectiveness even in the time of the wars between Athens and Sparta. In Greek times it was called the Dorian phalanx; its strength came from discipline and professionalism. Thousands of soldiers ranked together in a tight formation with shields overlapping and spears projecting. This solid and impenetrable wall then moved steadily and forcefully forward, dispersing or crushing whatever stood in its path.

Sargon's grandson Naramsin called himself King of the Four Regions and seems to have been a fierce warrior. Depictions show him as standing taller than those around him, leading his loosely arranged soldiers to victory. Nonetheless, the Akkadian phase was a relatively brief one by ancient standards and within two hundred years a third phase, the neo-Sumerian, began as a mountain people called the Guti overthrew Sargon's great-grandson.

The neo-Sumerian period

Until approximately 2000 BC this period brought to ascendancy the city-state of Ur. The rulers of Ur called themselves the Kings of Sumer and Akkad. The art of the period indicates a new tendency to exalt the ruler of the land. The area from the Persian Gulf to the Zagros mountains was reunited. Government was centralized and the economy flourished. New temples appeared and architecture reflected in its scale the vigor and pride of the society and its rulers. Ziggurats, great terraced towers, inspirations for the biblical Tower of Babel, rose skyward. The neo-Sumerian period ended as more powerful neighbors, the Elamites, conquered Ur and turned an empire once more into a conglomeration of city-states of reasonably equal status. It was, however, the end of the Sumerian civilization.

Hammurabi

As Sumerian civilization had coalesced, corresponding developments took place among the tribes and peoples at the periphery of its sphere of influence. One of the cultures emerging at this time was that of an Arabian nomadic people called the Amorites, who had helped to overthrow Ur. As they rose to ascendancy they established their power in a series of kingdoms encompassing Assyria, that is, upper Mesopotamia, and stretching from Damascus to Babylon to the coast of Palestine. The region, which by this time had begun to feel the influence of the Egyptian civilization, remained in flux until the next great ruler emerged in the early 1700s BC.

That ruler was Hammurabi. His capital was Babylon, and Babylon became the hub of the world—at least for a while. The first Babylonian empire encompassed the lands from Sumer and the Persian Gulf to Assyria. It included the cities of Nineveh and Nimrud on the Tigris and Mari on the Euphrates, and extended up the Euphrates to present-day Aleppo (see Fig. **2.4**). An Empire of approximately seventy thousand square miles, it rested on an elaborate centralized administrative system, and maintained its order through a wide-ranging judicial code we have come to call the Code of Hammurabi. His laws consist of 282 articles which addressed the legal questions of the time.

Foremost in importance among the articles was the precept of "an eye for an eye". In the times prior to Hammurabi, damages for bodily injury were assessed on a monetary basis, for example, a lost eye would be assessed at sixty shekels. Under Hammurabi, the monetary system was retained for any injury inflicted by a free man on one of lower status. If, however, the parties were of equal status, exact retribution was called for: "An eye for an eye, a tooth for a tooth", and so forth. We do not know what retribution was exacted for injury inflicted by a man on one of higher state, but the penalty in such a case was undoubtedly very severe. Hammurabi's code was pragmatic and clearly based on a rigid class system in which only the rich were allowed to escape retributive mutilation by monetary payment. A sliding scale based on ability to pay determined compensation for medical expenses and legal fees.

The rights and place of women, likewise, were specifically spelt out. The purpose of a wife was to provide her husband with legitimate sons and heirs. The penalty for adultery (by a wife) was drowning for both wife and paramour. Men were allowed "secondary" or "temporary" wives as well as slave concubines. On the other hand, beyond the area of procreation women were largely independent. They could own property, run businesses, lend and borrow money. A widow could remarry, which made for a more efficient use of the population than was possible in cultures where the wife had to throw herself on her husband's funeral pyre.

In essence, the Code of Hammurabi dealt with wages, divorce, fees for medical services, family matters, commerce, land and property, which included slaves. Hammurabi, like the rulers who preceded him, took his authority from the gods, and his law came likewise. From the earliest of times the concept of law as a derivative of extraordinary and supernatural powers continued unchallenged.

The Assyrians

Hammurabi reigned for only forty-two years but he accounted well for himself in that time. Cuneiform writing saw further development and spread widely throughout the Near East. Astrology stimulated the observation of nature. The patron god of the Babylonians, Marduk, surpassed his rivals to assume headship of the pantheon. One hundred and twenty-five years after Hammurabi's death, his dynasty ended as yet another power from Asia Minor and northern Syria, the Hittites, plundered Babylon. The conquerors apparently maintained control until nearly 1100 BC, but no notable figures emerged. By the year 1000 BC a new power rose in Mesopotamia—the Assyrians. These were northern peoples from Ashur on the Tigris River. Their military power and skill enabled them to maintain supremacy over the region, including Syria, the Sinai peninsula, and as far as Lower Egypt, where they destroyed Memphis. For nearly four hundred years they appear to have engaged in almost continuous warfare, ruthlessly destroying their enemies and leveling their cities. Finally, they too felt the conqueror's sword and saw the utter destruction of all their cities.

The neo-Babylonian period

The phase of Mesopotamian culture is called the neo-Babylonian period. It lasted for less than one hundred years but produced some notable accomplishments and individuals. After the destruction of the Assyrian empire by the combined forces of two local peoples, the Scythians and the Medes, a new ruler rose in Babylon, which although politically impotent had retained a cultural centrality. Nebuchadnezzar II restored order and built a palace with a ziggurat which we know from biblical accounts as the Tower of Babel.

The Persians

The Persian Empire unified the Middle Eastern world from approximately 539 to 331 BC. Nomads by tradition, the Persians nonetheless kept a tight administrative hold on a vast empire that stretched from Mesopotamia to Syria, Asia Minor, Egypt, and India. Under Cyrus the Great, Darius I and Xerxes I, the Persian Empire occupied an area nearly twice as large as any previous empire in the region. Had not the Greeks of the Delian League turned them back at the battle of Marathon, the Persians would have marched into Europe as well. Carefully organized into provinces called Satrapies, the Empire functioned smoothly under kings who regularly moved the administrative capital, but whose great palace was located at Persepolis. The Persian religion centered on Ahuramazda, the god of light. Their places of worship were marked by outdoor bonfires, and so, unlike their predecessors, they are not noted for temples or ziggurats for worship.

Literature

The Sumerian scribes began recording literature at some point between the years 2700 and 2100 BC. Their texts ranged, as we have seen, from epics to love songs. Since reading and writing were rare skills, however, most stories remained in the oral tradition. By 1900 BC literature in Babylonia was more developed but, true to the spirit of the civilization, tended to be produced for some practical purpose. A poem about the rage of the god Era was used as a charm against pestilence. Lyrics for love songs exhibited a frankness which left nothing to the imagination, mostly because they belonged to fertility rites.

A great many literary texts have come to us on school tablets. Students copied classic texts in order to learn spelling and style. The Gilgamesh Epic appears to have been very popular at the Hittite court, recounting, as it does, the adventures of King Gilgamesh of Erech. In it we discover the quest for immortality and the effects of wanton pride.

Elsewhere in Mesopotamia scribes copied the myth of Adapa-Oannes, the wisest of men, who had ascended into the heavens and yet failed to attain immortality. The Sumerian tradition is strongly evident in Mesopotamian literature; almost all gods, heroes and men, especially of Akkadian classical literature, are Sumerian.

THE ARTS
OF MESOPOTAMIA

TWO- AND THREE-DIMENSIONAL ART

Early Sumerian art

The majority of surviving artworks from Mesopotamia prior to 3000 BC consists of painted pottery and stamp seals. The decoration of pottery served to satisfy the creative urge of providing the functional with an aesthetic appeal. Decoration was abstract. Stamp seals, whether round or rectangular, went beyond tool status and clearly came to be regarded as surfaces ideally suited to exercise the artist's creative ingenuity. Later, for reasons unknown to us, the cylindrical seal came into being. A carved wooden roller was applied to wet clay to produce a ribbon-like design of indefinite length. The creative possibilities for individuality in design in the cylinder seal, a stamp of sorts, were far greater than those of the stamp seal. Figure **2.4** shows both a cylinder seal and its impression. What must have fascinated the Sumerians is the intricate design capable of infinite repetition starting with and returning into itself.

Monsters seem to provide an alluring subject matter for the Sumerians, and many design characteristics occur in their groupings and composition. One reason for the popularity of monsters may be their emotional and unrealistic character, which enhances their decorative possibilities. In Figure **2.5** a snake-necked lion combines two aspects of fertility, the lioness and the intertwined snake. This fertility-based design and the cycle it pre-

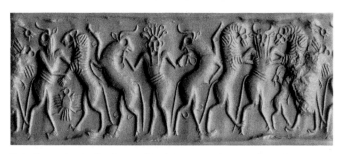

2.6 Sumerian cylinder seal impression, showing hero figure with bulls, surrounded by bull-men fighting lions, c.2500 BC. Aragonite seal, 1⅝ ins (4.3 cm) high. British Museum, London.

sents exemplifies the cyclical Sumerian religious philosophy, and it appears again and again in Sumerian art. Another, later, example of the cylinder seal explores the subject matter of raging beasts in the necessarily repetitive pattern imposed by this medium (Fig. **2.6**). Here intricate line patterns move through elaborate interlocking forms as bull and man wrestle for supremacy in symbolism and design. Scenes of sacrifice, hunting, and battle all appear in the examples of cylinder seal art which have survived. Throughout the early periods of Sumerian art there seems to be a conflict, or at least an alternation, between symbolism and naturalism in the depictions in cylinder art.

Low relief art of the early Sumerians provides further insights into Sumerian life. In works such as the relief-vase of Figures **2.7** and **2.8** we find a preoccupation with ritual and the gods. This alabaster vase, which stands

2.5 Mesopotamian cylinder seal and impression, showing snake-necked lions, c.3300 BC. Green jasper seal, 1¾ ins (4.5 cm) high. Louvre, Paris.

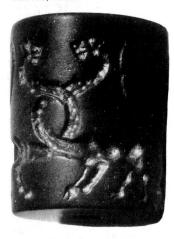 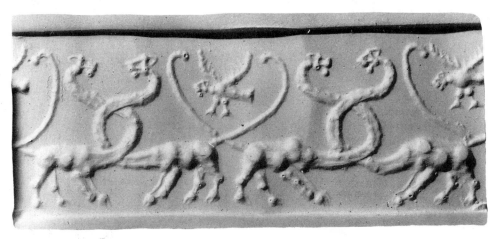

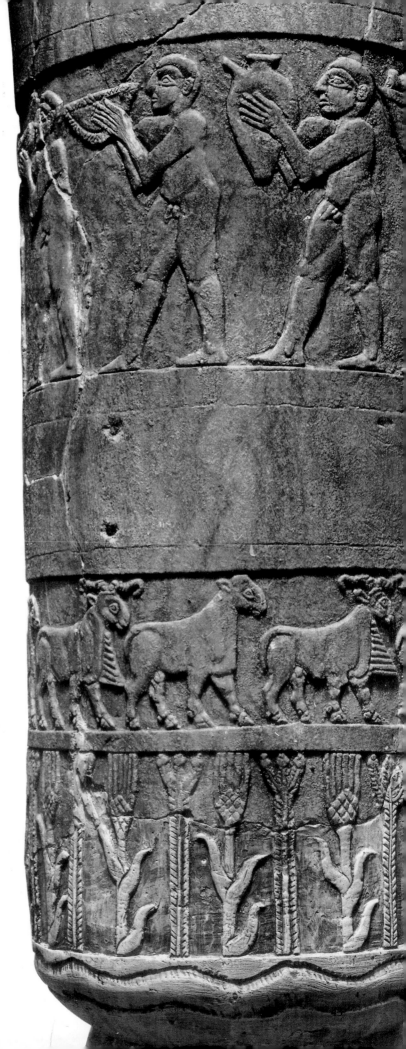

three feet tall, celebrates the cult of E-Anna, goddess of fertility and love. The vase is divided into four bands, commemorating the marriage of the goddess, which was re-enacted to ensure fertility. The bottom band has alternate stalks of barley and date palms; above it, rams and ewes. In the third band we see naked worshippers carrying baskets of fruit and other offerings. At the top the goddess herself stands before her shrine, two coiled bundles of reeds, to receive a worshipper or priest, also nude, whose tribute basket brims with fruit.

The composition exhibits an alternating flow of movement from left to right in the rams and ewes, and right to left in the worshippers. Conventions of figure portrayal are similar to but not as rigid as those in Egyptian art. Here bodies are depicted in profile, as are heads. However, the representation of the torso seems more naturalistic. On the other hand, anatomical proportions, especially in the torso, display varying degrees of adherence to reality. Yet the muscular little men seem

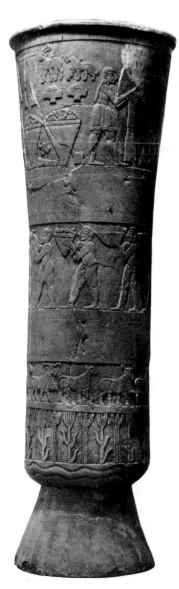

2.7 Vase with ritual scene in relief, from the Eanna precinct, Uruk (Warka), Iraq, c.3500–3100 BC. Alabaster, 36 ins (91.4 cm) high. Iraq Museum, Baghdad.

2.8 Detail of Uruk vase, showing tribute bearers, rams and ewes.

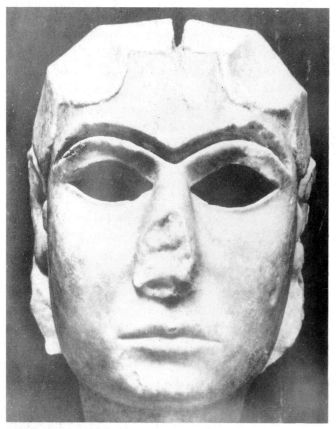

2.9 Head of a woman (female goddess) from Uruk, c.3500–3000 BC. Marble, 8 ins (20.3 cm) high. Iraq Museum, Baghdad.

shrine of the goddess from which lambs emerge on either side. The symmetry of the design exhibits a fair degree of life and vitality as it portrays animals in motion and countermotion. The rams and ewes move toward the shrine; the young lambs emerge from it. Strong diagonal line creates active dynamics in the picture.

The Archaic period

In the years from 3000 to 2340 BC persons and events become less anonymous. Here we find kings portrayed in devotional acts rather than as warlords. We also grasp a sense of the cylindrical mass of Sumerian sculpture, so different from the heavy, block-like style of the Egyptian. The famous statues from Tell Asmar and the Temple of Abu illustrate this for us (Fig. **2.11**). Undoubtedly the most striking features of these figures are the enormous, staring eyes. In contrast to Figure **2.9** the eyes remain intact, and their shell, lapis lazuli and black limestone composition rivets our attention. Representing the god Abu (the large figure), a goddess assumed to be his spouse, and a crowd of worshippers, the statues occupied places around the inner walls of an early temple. Each figure exhibits great dignity in a stylized depiction which is rather crudely executed. In addition to the staring eyes, we are drawn to the detached carving of the arms, whose line and demeanor suggest a votive character of a profoundly emotional nature. The entire use of line carries the eye of the viewer upward and inward to the heart of the statue. The composition is closed and self-contained, and reflects those same characteristics applied to prayer.

to show the strain of the weight of their burden far more realistically than the always upright, relaxed figures of Egyptian art. Finally, the faces are clearly not portrayals of individuals.

The mother goddess also emerges as the central focus in Figures **2.9** and **2.10**. The head of a goddess (Fig. **2.9**), carved from white marble, may originally have adorned a wooden statue. Lapis lazuli eyebrows, lapis lazuli and shell pupils, and gold sheeting over the hair undoubtedly completed the work in its original form. The modelling of the mouth is remarkably sensuous and gentle.

In Figure **2.10** a stone trough depicts the symbolic

If crudity marks the depiction of the human figure in the votive statues, grace and delicacy mark two other works from this period (Figs. **2.13** and **2.14**). These works illustrate the golden splendor of the Sumerian court. Inlaid in gold, the bearded bull symbolizes the royal personage of ancient Mesopotamia. Also laden with the symbolism of masculine fertility is the equally dazzling golden goat from the royal graves at Ur (Fig. **2.15**). Here we see what was basic to the Sumerians, and that is the divine revelation and incorporation of animal power,

2.10 Carved trough from Uruk, showing animals of the 'sacred herd' of the mother goddess, E-Anna, beside a reed-built byre, c.3500–3100 BC. Alabaster, 7.9 ins (20 cm) high. British Museum, London.

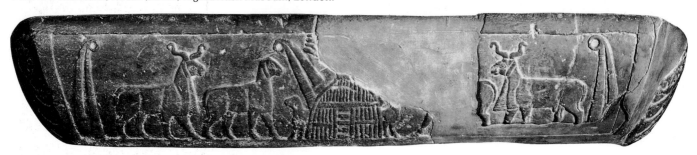

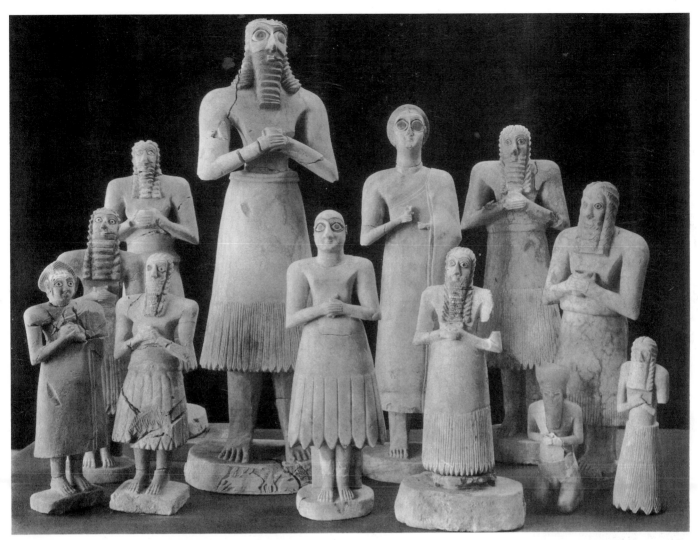

2.11 Statues of worshippers and deities from the Square Temple at Tell Asmar, Iraq, c.2750 BC. Gypsum, tallest figure 30 ins (76 cm) high. Iraq Museum, Baghdad, and The Oriental Institute, University of Chicago.

wisdom, and perfection. The goat clearly manifests on Earth the character of the god Tammuz. He is crisp and elegant in portrayal and undoubtedly superhuman.

The Akkadian period

Moving to the Akkadian period (2340 to 2180 BC) we find a uniquely dramatic and dynamic portrayal, high in emotion, and yet illustrative of the conventions of figure depiction we noted before. The Stele of King Naramsin (Fig. **2.12**) depicts an historical event and, unlike the earlier works we have seen, records a strictly human accomplishment. Composed in decorative fashion to fit the shape of the stone, the composition seems to rise and fall in rhythmic spasms as one figure moves our eye upward while another figure holds our eye down. The king in his horned helmet towers over his enemies and establishes the focal area of the work.

2.12 Victory stele of Naram-Sin from Susa, Iran, c.2300–2200 BC. Pink sandstone, 6 ft 6 ins (1.98 m) high. Louvre, Paris.

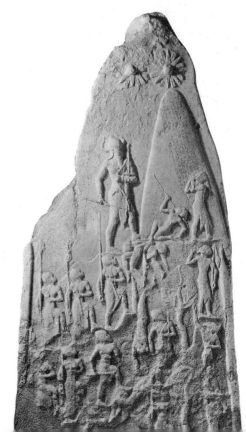

2.13 Soundbox panel of the royal harp from the tomb of Queen Puabi at Ur, Iraq, 2650–2550 BC. Shell inlay set in bitumen, 13 ins (33 cm) high. University Museum, University of Pennsylvania.

2.14 Royal harp from the tomb of Queen Puabi at Ur. Wood with gold, lapis lazuli and shell inlay. University Museum, University of Pennsylvania.

2.15 He-goat from Ur, c.2600 BC. Wood with gold and lapis lazuli overlay, 20 ins (50.8 cm) high. University Museum, University of Pennsylvania.

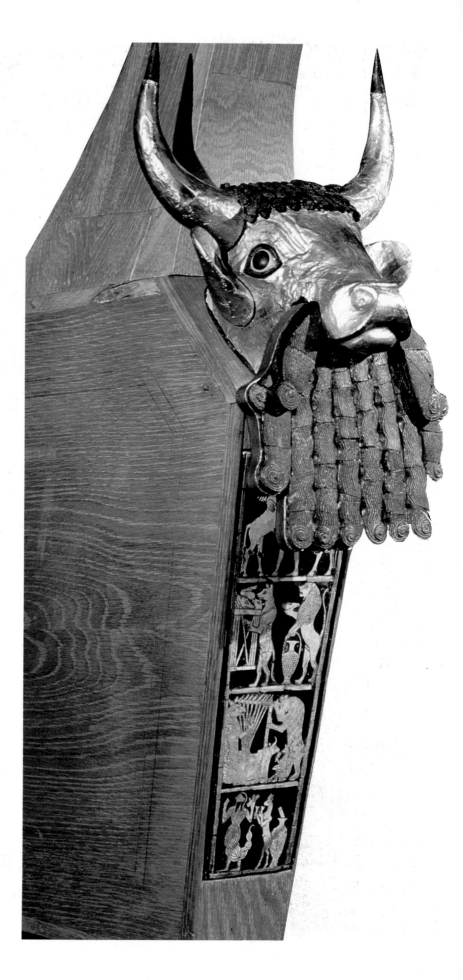

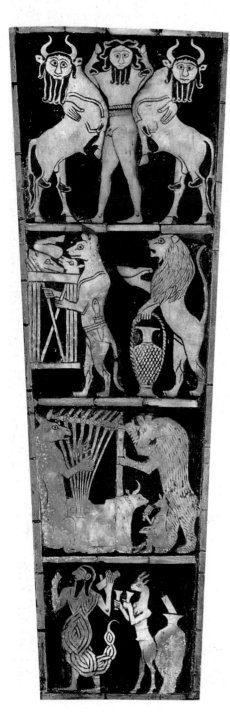

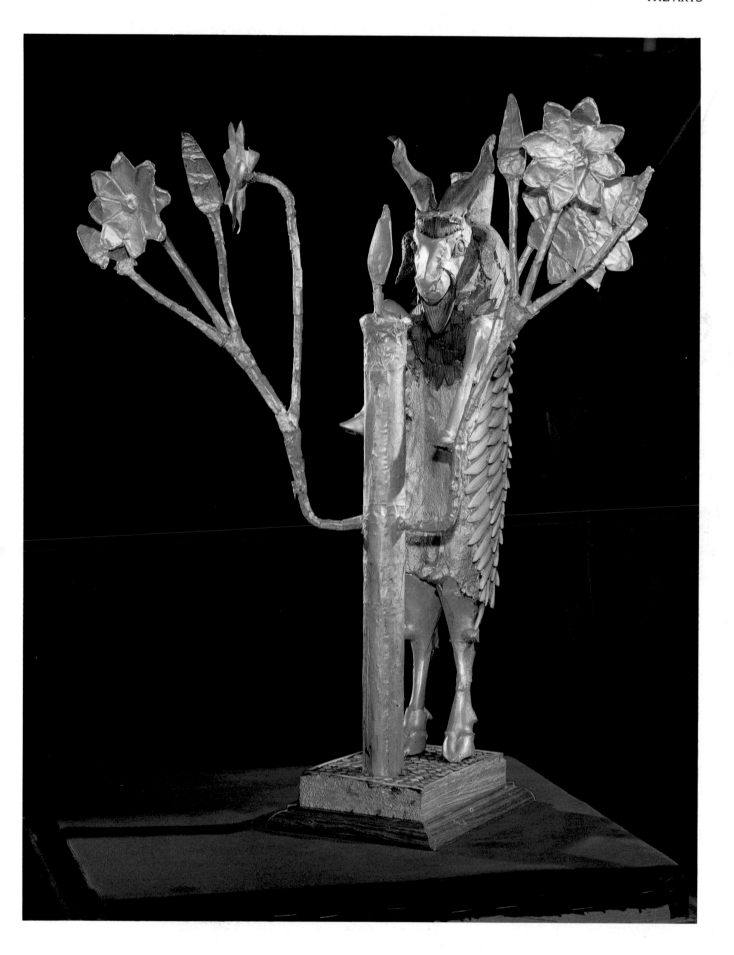

MUSIC

The early Sumerians utilized numerous musical instruments and held music as an essential and lively part of their culture. Lyres, pipes, harps and drums all featured prominently in Sumerian music, and these appear in the visual arts of the later Babylonian and, especially, Assyrian cultures. We have already seen one (reconstructed) example of an actual musical instrument in Figure 2.14.

Assyrian and Babylonian sculpture depicts musicians playing harps similar to the ancient kissor (Fig. 2.16). This instrument has a movable slant bar for the strings, which made it possible for the player to change the pitch of the strings by a simple pressure. Such illustrations as we have yield a fleeting glance of Mesopotamian music. The Assyrians possessed a variety of instruments, wind, string, and percussion. They apparently used stringed instru-

ments in a solo capacity, in ensembles, and as accompaniment for vocal music. Stringed instruments show evidence of finger boards and, therefore, indicate some degree of sophistication in musical development.

The harp was a basic instrument in Assyrian music, and Figure 2.17 illustrates the character of the instrument. The sounding board for the instrument is at the top. Hanging from the bottom of the instrument are various tassels and strings, which make the instrument seem larger than it actually is. The lyre as pictured in extant sculpture appears to have taken at least three different shapes (Fig. 2.18). There is also evidence of a dulcimer-type instrument and another stringed instrument, apparently played with a stick, called the asor (Fig. 2.19).

In the category of wind instruments, the Assyrians had both a double pipe and some variety of straight trumpet, whose illustration makes it appear to have been a military instrument. Finally, we find the usual variety of hand-held drums, bells, cymbals and tambourines.

As suggested earlier, Mesopotamian musical practice was very diverse. It seems to have been most popular as a form of secular entertainment, but religious ceremonies also employed music. In one bas-relief in the British Museum we find a king standing in front of an altar offering a libation for two lions he has just slain. Musicians with asors stand on the opposite side of the altar. Solo performances, instrumental ensembles of single and mixed instruments, and solo and choral vocal music with instrumental accompaniment are all documented.

We can only speculate on the character of Mesopotamian music with regard to its rhythms, scales, and textures, although we can imagine something of its timbre and dynamics from such scant evidence as we have. Clearly, stringed instruments were predominant. Percussion and rhythm instruments seem to have been less popular, and the blaring trumpet mostly military in application. So we may assume that Mesopotamian, like Egyptian, music seems to favor lyrical, soft, restrained qualities rather than loud or brash ones.

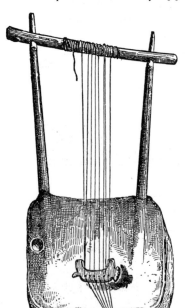

2.16 Kissor.

2.17 Assyrian harp.

2.18 Assyrian lyres.

2.19 Assyrian dulcimer and asor.

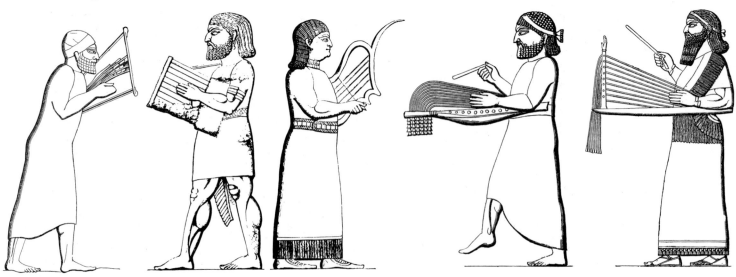

DANCE

Dance formed some part of ancient Mesopotamian culture, although the evidence for its character is scanty. In Sumer we find sacred dances of various forms. One form seems to have required a procession of singers, moving slowly to liturgies played on flutes. A second form employed dancers prostrating themselves before an altar. In Assyrian bas-relief sculpture depictions of dancers are fairly common, in both religious and secular contexts. The fire festival of the goddess of fertility, Ashtoreth, apparently witnessed drunken, orgiastic dancing involving self-mutilation with knives.

ARCHITECTURE

Evidence of Mesopotamian architecture dates back to well before the Sargonid unification. A group of temples from around 2700 BC have been called ground-level temples because, in contrast with later temple architecture, they were not built on a raised platform. The Sin Temple at Khafaje (Fig. **2.20**) exemplifies this early style. It follows a traditional plan of Sumerian temples. A long, rectangular sanctuary focuses on an altar at one end. An entrance and cross-axis occur at opposite ends of the sanctuary from the altar. Chambers were added on each side of the sanctuary.

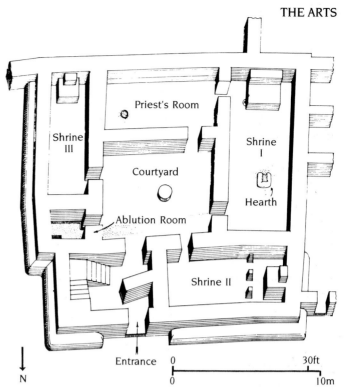

2.21 Projected plan of the Square Temple at Tell Asmar, c.2750–2650 BC.

2.22 Diagram of Sumerian method of brick laying, used c.2750–2250 BC.

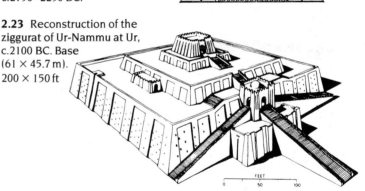

2.23 Reconstruction of the ziggurat of Ur-Nammu at Ur, c.2100 BC. Base (61 × 45.7 m). 200 × 150 ft

2.20 Projected plan of Sin Temple VIII at Khafaje, Iraq, c.2750–2650 BC.

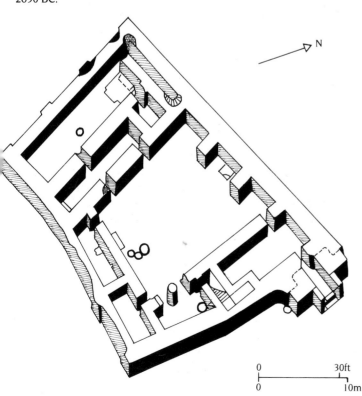

The Tell Asmar Temple (Fig. **2.21**), which yielded the group of statuettes we examined earlier, is from the same period. Its plan is similar to that of the dwelling houses of the time, and shows a priest's room (a), a shrine (b), a hearth (c), a second shrine (d), the entrance (e), an ablution room (f), and a third shrine (g), all grouped around a central courtyard (h).

Sumerian buildings were of mud sun-dried in brick-shaped molds. In early buildings courses were laid in a flat, horizontal arrangement. Later, bricks were made larger and plano-convex in shape, and placed on edge. Successive courses leaned in opposite directions and created a herring-bone pattern (Fig. **2.22**).

From the neo-Sumerian Period, dating to 2120 BC, we have the surviving structures of Ur, capital of an empire. Inside the city walls lies the colossal ziggurat built by Ur-Nammu and completed by his son Sulgi (Fig. **2.23**). It rises in three stages from a mud brick core. The lowest and largest stage measures approximately 190 by 138 feet and rises to a height of approximately forty-five feet.

We will examine the great palace of Sargon II in the next section of our text, but as we close our very brief discussion of Mesopotamian architecture we need to bear in mind that although construction of buildings in the ancient Near East was of brick, two factors militate against the survival of very much architecture. The first is the length of time we are dealing with—over five thousand years can separate us from some of these buildings. People need new buildings to replace old ones and, space being at a premium, old buildings were simply torn down or built over. Secondly, the incessant warfare of the area and the practice of destroying conquered cities gave buildings a short life-expectancy.

SYNTHESIS
Sargon II *at Dur Sharrukin*

Under Sargon II, who came to power in 722 BC, the high priests of the country regained many of the privileges they had lost under previous kings, and the Assyrian Empire reached the peak of its power. Early in his reign he founded the new city of Dur Sharrukin (on the site of the modern city of Khorsabad), about nine miles northeast of Nineveh. His vast royal citadel occupying an area of some quarter of a million square feet (Fig. 2.24) was built as an image not only of his empire, but of the cosmos itself. A reconstruction of the citadel shown in Figure 2.25 yields insights into the style of architecture and the priorities of Assyrian civilization at this time. It is quite clear that in Sargon's new city secular architecture takes precedence over temple architecture. The rulers of Assyria seem to have been far more preoccupied with building fortifications and pretentious palaces than with erecting religious shrines. Here we find a clear statement much in contrast with other Assyrian sites, which reflect the additive construction of successive rulers. Dur Sharrukin represents, like Akhenaton's Tell el Amarna (see pp.83–7), a city built, occcupied and abandoned within a

2.24 Plan of the citadel of King Sargon II's capital city, Dur Sharrukin, at Khorsabad, Iraq, c.721–705 BC.

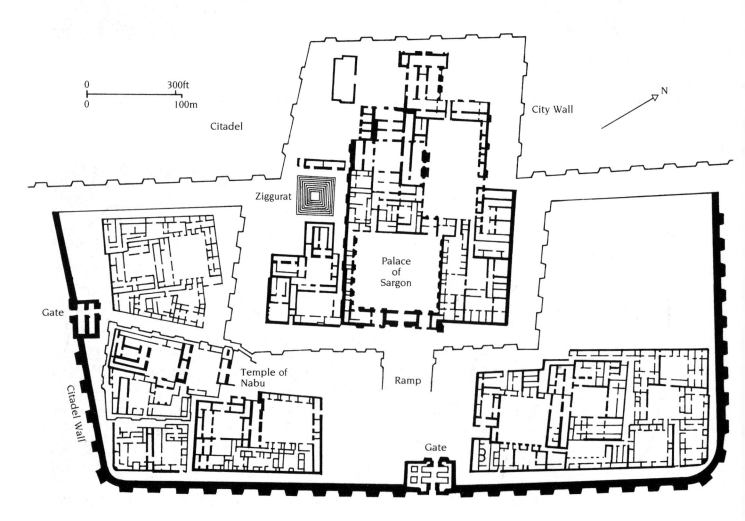

Citadel

Ziggurat

Palace of Sargon

Gate

Temple of Nabu

Ramp

Citadel Wall

Gate

City Wall

N

0   300ft
0   100m

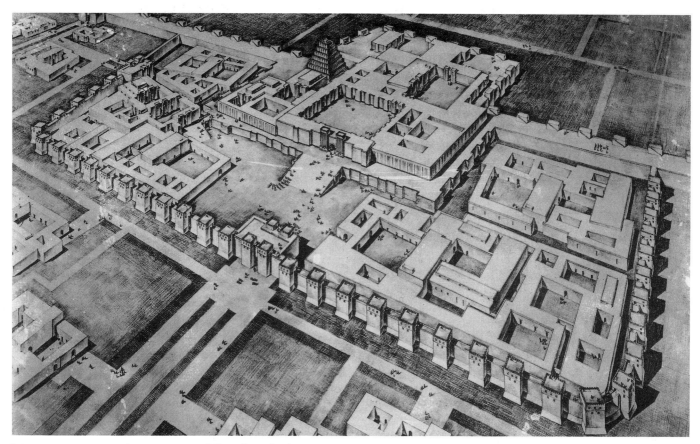

2.25 Reconstruction of Sargon II's citadel at Khorsabad.

2.26 Gate of Sargon II's citadel at Khorsabad (during excavation) with pair of winged and human-headed bulls. Limestone.

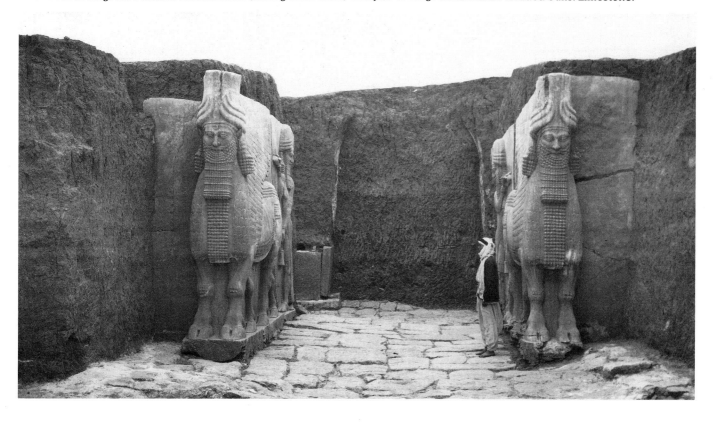

single generation. Its integrity remains intact and its message seems clear.

The citadel, representing the ordered world, rises like the hierarchy of Assyrian gods, from the lowest levels of the city through a transitional level, to the king's palace, which stands on its own elevated terrace. Two gates connect the walled citadel to the outside world. The first was undecorated; the second was adorned with and guarded by winged bulls and genii (Fig. **2.26**).

Remarkably, excavations at the site have shown building methods to be fairly inadequate. Buildings are arranged haphazardly and the terrace is asymmetrical. Near one gate a temple to the god Nabu sits at an awkward angle to the wall and adjacent buildings. Raised on its own terrace, the temple was connected to the palace by a bridge over the street. Within the inner walls, five minor palaces were crowded with obvious difficulty into the available space, revealing evidence of a lack of planning.

The main palace comprises an arrangement of ceremonial apartments around a central courtyard. Entrances to the throne room were guarded by winged bulls and other figures. The walls of the room itself stood approximately forty feet high and were decorated with floor-to-ceiling murals. Three small temples adjoined the palace and beside these rose a ziggurat with successive stages painted in different colors, connected by a spiral staircase. Construction was of mud brick, laid without mortar while still damp and pliable, and of dressed and undressed stone. Some roof structures utilized brick barrel vaulting, although the majority appear to have had flat ceilings with painted beams.

Corresponding to the vast scale and attitude of the buildings are the great guardian figures of which Figure **2.26** is representative. Undoubtedly symbolizing the supernatural powers of the king, these colossal hybrids are majestically powerful in stature and scale. Carved partly in relief and partly in the round, they are rationalized to be seen from front or side: the sculptor has provided the figure with a fifth leg, with the result that the viewer can always see four legs. Each of these monoliths was carved from a single block of stone upwards of fifteen feet square. Roughly shaped in the quarry, these blocks were transported to the site and the final carving was done in situ.

Subject matter in murals and relief sculpture consisted primarily of tributes to the victorious campaigns of the king. Predominant in many works is the onward press of chariots. Since warfare tended to be a seasonal activity, the intervening time was, apparently, spent in hunting; and so we find the royal personage engaged in the alternating slaughter of men and beasts, as well as some cult ceremonies. These scenes represent narratives, and while probably more symbolic than actual, the historicizing of these events appears to have yielded a greater naturalism in style than we have seen previously. Significantly, the concept of space in works from Sargon's palace takes on a pictorial quality quite different from the abstract space of Egyptian and other Mesopotamian art.

As we examine reliefs such as Figures **2.27** and **2.28** we recognize a composition of pictorial space more like that of the medieval period. Here is an artist's attempt to portray deep space, that is, to remove the image from the surface plane of the work and to suggest perspective. Of

2.27 Mural relief from the palace of Sargon II at Khorsabad. Basalt, 5 ft 10 ins (1.78 m) long. British Museum, London.

2.28 Mural relief from the palace of Sargon II at Khorsabad. Basalt, 4 ft 2 ins (1.27 m) high. Louvre, Paris.

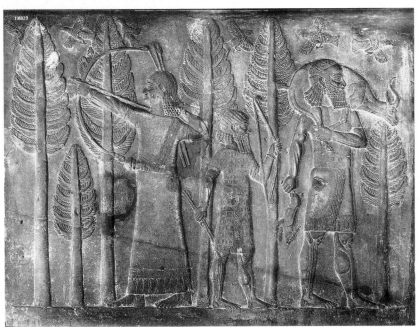

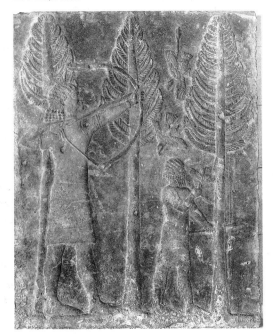

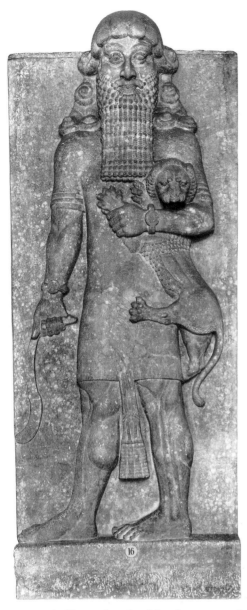

2.29 Relief from a facade of the throne room in the palace of Sargon II at Khorsabad. Alabaster, 15 ft 5 ins (4.7 m) high. Louvre, Paris.

SUGGESTIONS FOR THOUGHT AND DISCUSSION

Mesopotamian culture perhaps extends over too great a time, with too few surviving examples, to represent anything other than a geographically related sampling of several disparate peoples. Nonetheless, a certain characteristic style can be identified. As one people conquers another, cultures overlap and interact. Despite changes in the realism of figure depiction and spatial arrangement, the visual art of the area, whether Sumerian, Akkadian or Assyrian, remains recognizably Mesopotamian. Try to summarize the characteristics of the artworks we have examined to see if you can determine precisely what factors make such recognition possible.

■ How are the religious and political characteristics of Sumer and Akkad reflected in their artworks?

■ Trace the changes from stylized to realistic portrayal of the human form as they appear in the examples shown in this chapter.

■ If the eyes are the windows of the soul, what meaning can be attributed to the Tel Asmar sculptures?

■ Discuss the concept of divine right as we have seen it in Mesopotamian religion, politics, and art.

■ How was the king glorified in Mesopotamian art?

■ What implications for art and architecure derive from the nomadic character of Mesopotamian peoples?

■ What can we discern of the structure and power base of Mesopotamian societies from their arts?

■ Given the warlike character of Mesopotamian civilizations, to what would you attribute the apparent softness of their musical timbres?

■ Explain how Dur Sharrukin represents the late Assyrian concept of the structure of the universe.

course, the understanding of vanishing points and horizon lines, which was to revolutionize visual art in the Renaissance, is absent. Nonetheless, the attempt to portray distance through diminution stands out clearly in both works. A hurried roughness haunts the works, and the stylization of the figures counteracts spatial naturalism. On the other hand, these lively and charming depictions show some individuality among the figures; and, if attention to detail is any indication, the Assyrian love of animals and the animal spirit, as we have noted elsewhere in this chapter, remains pre-eminent. Yet, throughout, we cannot escape the presence of the king as protector and lord, as a final example illustrates. In Figure **2.29** Sargon himself subdues a lion, whose reduced size further points to the king's majesty and power. We should, in closing, take note of the convention of depiction whereby the body and head are now portrayed frontally while the feet remain in profile.

CHAPTER THREE

ANCIENT EGYPT

Protected by deserts and confined to a narrow river valley, ancient Egypt experienced a relatively isolated cultural history, virtually unbroken for thousands of years. It was a civilization uniquely dependent upon the regular annual flooding of a single river, and every year, as the Nile overflowed its banks to deposit a rich and fertile silt on the surrounding fields, it bore witness to the rhythmic permanence of a beneficent established order which would continue beyond the grave. Death—or, rather, everlasting life in the hereafter—was the focus of the arts of the Egyptians. Appearing mostly in the service of the cult of a god or to glorify the power and wealth of a pharaoh, art and architecture centered on the provision of an eternal dwelling-place for the dead—the recreation and celebration of life in images which would provide an everlasting substitute for the mortal body.

3.1 Stele of Chancellor Neferyu, "Sole Companion to the King", from Dendereh or Keneh, near Thebes, Egypt. First Intermediate Period or later (c.2280–2052 BC). Painted limestone, 45½ ins (115.6 cm) high. Metropolitan Museum of Art, New York.

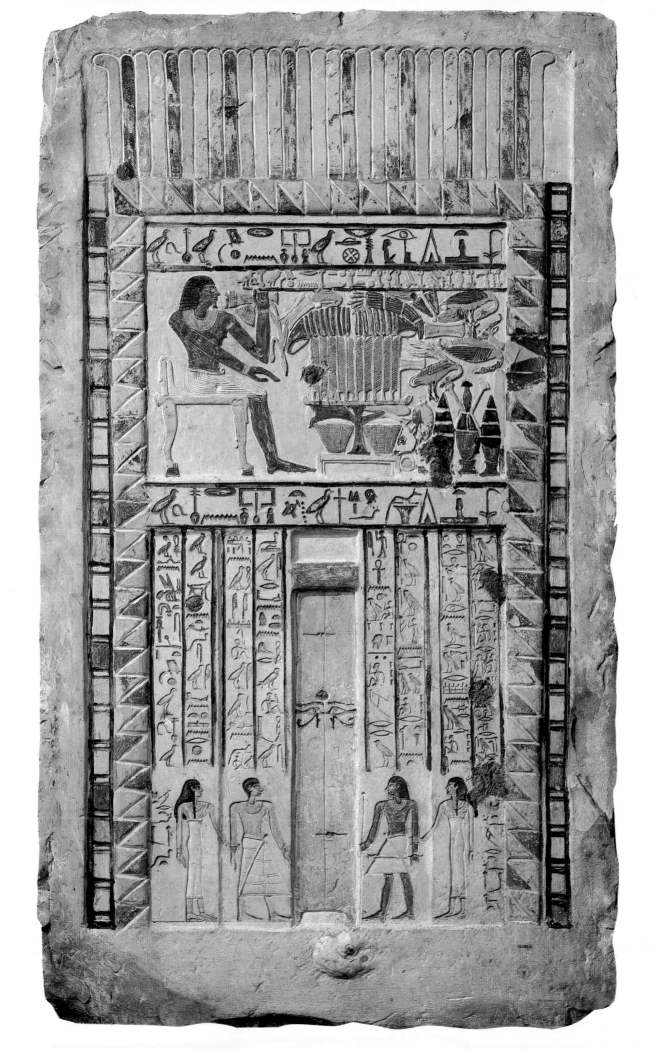

CONTEXTS AND CONCEPTS

Egyptian civilization spans thousands of years, encompassing the time before and after the start of history recorded in written form. Some scholars find in this civilization a kind of original source of human development, that is, one which sprang forth, without noticeable assistance from anywhere else, to influence all that succeeded it.

Egypt was a river-valley civilization, organized around and dependent upon the floods of the Nile River for sustenance. The flood waters are rich in silt, whose organic deposits renew the topsoil. After flooding the soil is so tillable that Egyptian farmers needed nothing more elaborate than a wooden hoe to work it. Two and three crops per year could be harvested almost without effort according to Greek authors, who spoke enviously of Egyptian agriculture. Nonetheless, effort was required to prevent the wind-blown sands of the desert encroaching and to keep the unpredictable Nile at maximum benefit. Dikes and canals were built, and as early as the dawn of written history the Egyptians had marked the height of the successive rises of the Nile.

Old Kingdom

Egypt's political organization centered around its all-powerful rulers, the pharaohs, and traditionally the chronology of Egyptian development follows the dynasties of its rulers; the Egyptians marked no other dating system than that of its pharaonic dynasties. The first significant achievement we can mark is the establishment of the Old Kingdom (c. 2778–2263 BC). With Memphis as its capital, the Old Kingdom had a planned economy and strict social order while maintaining a reliance on the agricultural system inherent in the annual Nile floods. During the reign of Snofru and other rulers of the Fourth Dynasty, about which we know little, emerged the pyramid, which has come to symbolize Egyptian accomplishment. According to one ancient source Snofru "arose as a beneficent king over all the earth". Snofru was a great builder and his mortuary temple contains a list of the strongholds and cities he founded. True to the characteristics which the ancient Egyptians assigned to beneficent rulers, Snofru built many temples and more than satisfied the appetites of the gods for offerings. This propensity for building was a reflection of the fact that no ruler wished to dwell in the palace of his father, preferring instead to build his own, as close as possible to his mausoleum.

During this early dynasty the horse and the cart were apparently unknown in Egypt, the ship being the only means of transportation. So it comes as no

3.2 Rhomboidal Pyramid, Dahsur, Egypt, Dynasty IV (2680–2565 BC).

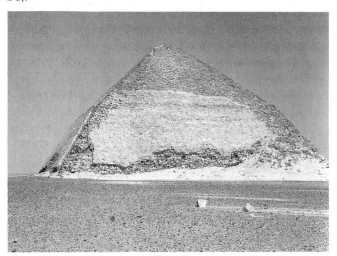

3.3 Step Pyramid of King Zoser, Saqqara, Egypt, Dynasty III (2780–2680 BC).

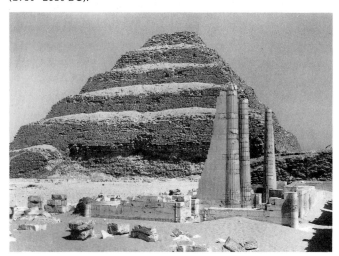

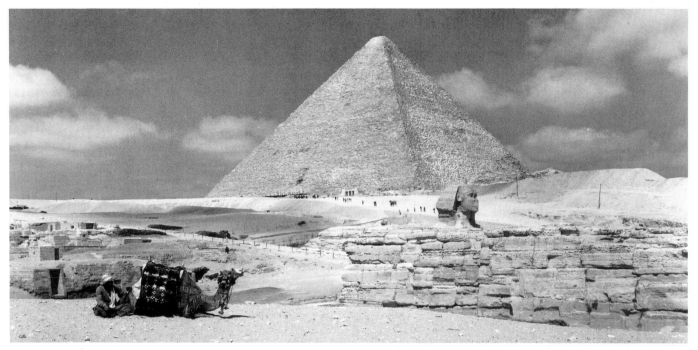

3.4 Great Pyramid of Cheops, Giza, Egypt, Dynasty IV (2680–2565 BC).

surprise that a pharaoh as capable as Snofru also excelled in shipbuilding. This provides us with an additional insight into the nature of Egyptian civilization because Snofru, as did his predecessors dating at least to Dynasty II, built his ships and barges of wood. Egypt has no forests and the source of wood was Byblos, north of Beirut, indicating early and healthy commerce and political relationships encompassing a large area around the eastern end of the Mediterranean.

But it is to pyramids that our attention and interest naturally turn. How did this ancient people, without access to machinery, bring large stones to the building site and put them into position on the pyramid? Many answers have been suggested to these questions, including the intervention of visitors from outer space; none, however, appears definitive. In any case, Snofru is credited with no less than three pyramids. His pyramids include the Rhomboidal Pyramid at Dahsur (Fig. **3.2**), and a step pyramid similar to that built by Imhotep at Saqqara for the Pharaoh Zoser (Fig. **3.3**).

Snofru's son Cheops (a Greek derivative of Chnum-Khufwey, Chnum being the principal god of the area) proved to be a demanding and authoritarian ruler. Reigning for twenty-three, fifty, or sixty years (sources vary), his presence forces itself on us even now in the form of the Great Pyramid (Fig. **3.4**). Like his father, Cheops took an interest in nations

beyond the fringes of his own kingdom. A bas-relief from Cheops' burial chamber indicates that visitors from afar, the Helu-Nebut, visited his court. The Helu-Nebut are presumed to be the ancient ancestors of the Hellenes.

These early dynasties witnessed rulers of well-defined personality and individuality. As time passed, the social organization, centered on an omnipotent god-king, changed through crisis after crisis and collapsed, finally, under weak and ineffectual rulers. We can see evidence of the changing social order in the tendency of royal burial chambers to diminish in size while those of wealthy courtiers and landowners grew larger.

Pepi II of Dynasty VI, pictured in Figure **3.8** as a child on his mother's lap, assumed the throne at the age of six, and lived for over a hundred years. We know from the king's own writings that by this time the Egyptian state was growing poor. Numerous temples were exempted from contributing to the administration's coffers. A further glimpse at Egyptian society in the reign of Pepi II comes through a story about the king's morals, which, apparently, were contrary to those of society. Apparently Pepi was fond of leaving the palace unescorted at night in order to rendezvous with one of his unmarried generals. The liaison was discovered, but the scandal was quashed before serious consequences arose. Pepi II nonetheless retains a place as the last

BC		GENERAL EVENTS	VISUAL ART	THEATRE & DANCE	ARCHITECTURE
3000	Archaic	Dynasties I & II			Temple at Khentiamentiu (**3.29**) Temple of Sethos I (**3.30**) Tomb 3038 at Saqqara (**3.33**) Abydos tomb of Merneith (**3.31**) Merneith tomb at Saqqara (**3.32**)

2778
2620
 	
2480
	Old Kingdom	Dynasty III
		Dynasty IV
		  Snofru
		  Cheops
		  Chephren
		  Mycerinus
		Dynasty V
			Tombs of Rahotep
			Prince Rahotep and his wife Nofret (**3.16**)
			Grazing geese (**3.11**)
			King Mycerinus between two goddesses (**3.17**)
			Presentation of cows and poultry (**3.18**)
				Stride dances	Zoser tomb at Saqqara (**3.35**)
					
					Pyramid of Cheops (**3.4**)
					Pyramid of Chephren
					The Sphinx (**3.38**)

2340	First Intermed.	Dynasty VI Dynasties VII & VIII Dynasties IX & X Dynasty XI	Sarcophagus of Queen Kawit (**3.21**)	Dwarf who Danced like a God Fertility dances	
2212	Middle Kingdom	Dynasty XII Ammenemes I (Amenemhet) Sesostris I Ammenemes II Sesostris II Ammenemes III	Maned Sphinx (**3.19**) Ka statue of King Hor (**3.20**)	Coronation festival play Osiris Passion Play	
	Second Intermed.	Dynasties XIII-XVII (Including the Hyksos)			

1575
1510
1490
1405
1367
1347
 	
1308
1290
 	
1182
1151
 	
1100
	New Kingdom	Dynasty XVIII
		  Thutmose II
		  Hatshepsut
		  Amenhotep III (Amenophis)
		  Amenhotep IV (Akhnaton)
		  Tutankhamun
		Dynasty XIX
		  Ramesses I
		  Ramesses II
		Dynasty XX
		  Ramesses III
		  Ramesses IV
		  Ramesses V-XII
			Theban rock tombs
			Tomb of Sennufer
			
			Gold mask of Tutankhamun (**3.22**)
			Tutankhamun as a sentry (**3.23**)
			
			Paintings from Nefertari's tomb
				Funeral dances	Temple at Luxor (**3.41**)
					Tell el Amarna (**3.42**)
					North Palace; Queen Nofretete

270		Ptolemy			

3.5 Timeline of Ancient Egyptian culture.

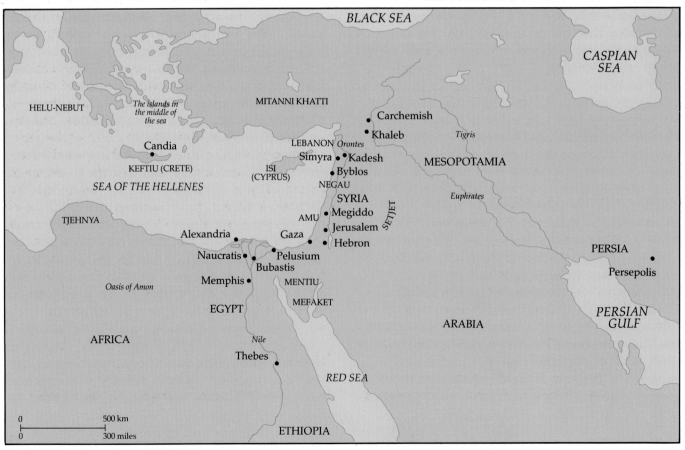

3.6 Ancient Egypt and the Middle East.

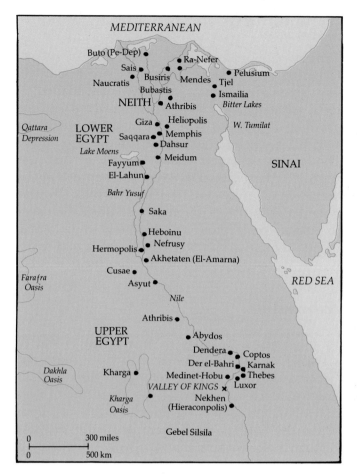

3.7 Ancient Egypt.

3.8 Seated statue of a Queen holding small figure of King Pepi II, Dynasty VI (2420–2258 BC). Alabaster, 15½ ins (39.2 cm) high. The Brooklyn Museum (Charles Edwin Wilbour Fund).

great ruler of the Old Kingdom. After Pepi II, Egyptian history fades somewhat from our view for a while. Centralized authority waned, landowners increased their power, and individual cities (*nomes*) gained in independence. It took until the pharaohs of Dynasty XI for Egypt to reemerge as a significant political entity.

Middle Kingdom

About the year 2130 BC the governor of Thebes successfully subdued his rivals and claimed a new dynasty (XI) which unified Egypt and, with Dynasties XII and XIII, maintained an organized, effective central government for the next four hundred years, a period known as the Middle Kingdom. This was an age of recovery, expansion, and material replenishment. Egypt conquered Nubia to the south, and expanded its trade to regions previously unreached. Theological changes also occurred, bringing more and more consolidation of diverse religious cults under the sun-god Ra.

Life, however, remained tenuous, even for a Pharaoh. Like many of his predecessors,

Amenemhet I, the founder of Dynasty XII, was assassinated in a palace conspiracy. He had assumed the throne twenty-nine years earlier in the same way by overthrowing the last ruler of Dynasty XI.

By the mid-nineteenth century BC the entirety of the Egyptian domain was administered directly from the palace of the Pharaoh. Its sphere of influence included the conquered Nubia, and extended to Southern Syria. By the end of the nineteenth century the Rulers of Byblos used hieroglyphs and Egyptian titles. A carefully designed system of fortresses guarded and controlled the southern approach to Egypt and the Isthmus of Suez. There was tight control of who could enter Egypt proper, even for commercial purposes, although it appears that access for the Bedouins of Palestine was fairly free, as evidenced by the biblical story of Abraham who, when famine was in his land, went down to sojourn in Egypt.

The scribes

In the Middle Kingdom the importance of scribes to

the economy increased, as did their numbers. The profession of scribe was open to anyone of talent, and those without title could send their children to the scribal school along with the children of the highborn. Early in the second millennium BC the profession had become a proud and important one, serving not only the Pharaoh but also overseeing workers in the fields. Scribes were essential and they were everywhere. All governmental functions needed to be recorded—the movement and activities of armies, the counting of crops, the monthly inspection of utensils in the temples, and even the registered wicks of old rags used for work in royal tombs. In a carefully organized hierarchy lower scribes labored diligently to become higher scribes, and even the most highly born youth was compelled to start at the bottom of the bureaucratic ladder. As early as the twenty-first century BC we find the aphorism, "the pen is mightier than the sword".

Second Intermediate period

Late in the eighteenth century BC the Hyksos succeeded in conquering lower Egypt. These invaders were described as "wretched Asiatics" and *hyksos* meant "rulers of foreign lands". At approximately the same time local princes gained control of the areas to the south of Elephantine. Two hundred years later the princes of Thebes rose in revolt against the Hyksos and their collaborators, drove them out, reconquered Nubia, united Egypt with Thebes as its capital, and heralded in the New Kingdom.

The two hundred year span of the Hyksos conquest was called the Second Intermediate Period. The success of their conquest was probably due to their military superiority over the Egyptians which relied upon the iron-fitted chariot and the composite bow. The importance of this brief incursion lay in the effects it wrought when the Hyksos were driven out and the New Kingdom was established. The outlook of the Egyptians was considerably broadened and from that time onward there existed an Egyptian foreign policy *per se*. In addition, the very weapons which had been used to defeat the Egyptians—the chariot and the composite bow—were now available to them, and enabled them first to turn on their adversaries, and in subsequent years to expand militarily.

New Kingdom

Dynasty XVIII produced an outpouring of activity including a renaissance in the arts, significant military accomplishments, and the consolidation of royal authority, centralized and powerful beyond anything of previous note. In a novel event around 1486 BC, a woman, Hatshepsut, came to the throne. Commerce expanded during her reign and was reinforced in successive reigns by further military and imperial expansion. Thutmose III took Egyptian boundaries to the Euphrates River. Royal marriages to Asiatic princesses are documented in monuments. Temple decoration grew lustrous, and sculpture in the round came into prominence.

Akhenaton

By the time of the reign of Amenhotep III and IV, *c.*1400–1340 BC, the Hittites well to the north had become a destabilizing force for the Egyptian Empire, which had relied on the friendship of Syria and Mitanni to protect Egyptian interests, and upon whom the Hittites were exerting greater pressure through their own ambitious motives. Amenhotep III brought Thebes to its peak as a capital city. Booty from captured lands continued to stimulate the economy, and the skills of captured craftsmen contributed to growth and development. Trouble lay in store for Amenhotep IV, who took the name Akhenaton or Ikhnaton, and set about to reform the religion of Egypt. He attempted to substitute the monotheistic cult of Aton for the ancient religions. His theology was based on the premise that he alone knew the god Aton and was his sole image on earth. Throughout Egypt the names of other gods were erased, and the outrage of the populace was only checked because the army remained loyal to the Pharaoh. Fifteen years after Akhenaton's death his name was damned. Akhenaton's accomplishments will be examined in greater detail later in this chapter.

Hittite pressure continued to build on the peripheries. From the fourteenth to the thirteenth century the outlook of the Egyptians shifted toward greater pessimism. Tomb paintings of the fourteenth century depict women in diaphanous dresses and unclad dancing girls, while in the thirteenth century great pain is taken to cover the bodies of females. Funerary subjects change from optimistic scenes of perpetual delight to prostrated praying.

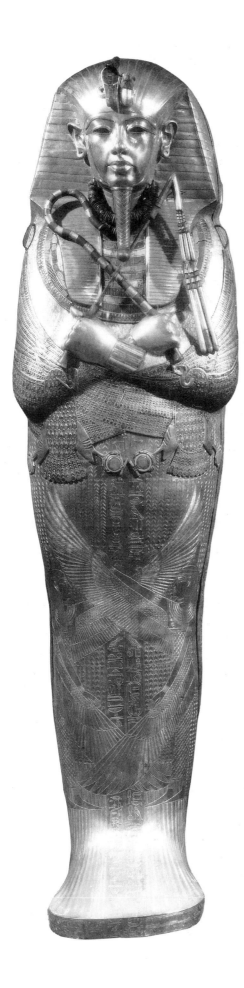

Tutankhamun

Akhenaton was succeeded by the Pharaoh perhaps best known to us, Tutankhamun (Fig. **3.9**). Amenhotep IV had changed his name to Akhenaton to erase the relationship with the cult god Amun-Ra. Tutankhamun changed his name from Tutankhaton for precisely the opposite reasons. The splendor of his burial may, in fact, be attributed to the gratitude of the people for this reversal of policy. Tutankhamun reigned only very briefly. After his death Egypt began a two hundred year slide toward the end of the New Kingdom. After 1150 BC strikes and economic troubles proliferated. The power of the Pharaoh gradually declined and internal disorganization increased. Ramesses III died as a result of a harem conspiracy, while the last king of Dynasty XX, Ramesses XI, was a virtual prisoner in his own palace. By the end of the New Kingdom in 1102 BC Egyptian civilization as a forceful, singular entity had deteriorated to a point where to all intents and purposes it was dead. Of course, Egypt continued to exist as a political entity, and the scholar Manetho, at the command of Ptolemy II in about 270 BC, continued the dynastic chronology to his day with the Later Period, Persian Period, and Ptolemaic Period, whose very names suggest the external dominance under which Egypt had fallen.

RELIGION

From the beginning of Egyptian civilization the king was always referred to as a god. At the time when Upper and Lower Egypt were united in Dynasty I, the king was considered to be the earthly manifestation of the god Horus, deity of the sky. The king was also considered to be the Son of Ra, and thus represented a direct link between the royal line and the creator sun god.

Egyptian religion is a complex combination of local and national gods and in a cumulative process new beliefs and gods were added over the thousands of years of Egyptian dynastic history. Two gods could be assimilated and yet remain separate entities. The same god may appear in various manifestations, for example, Horus, who may be the avenger of his father, Osiris, or the infant son of Isis,

3.9 Coffin of King Tutankhamun, c.1340 BC. Gold, 6 ft 1 in (185.5 cm) high. Egyptian Museum, Cairo.

or the shy god whose wings span the heavens and whose eyes are the sun and the moon.

Local deities appear in the shape of animals or are occasionally represented by a plant or inanimate object. Later they may become human but retain an animal head. The list of local deities and their variations and derivations appears endless and complex, but we need only briefly survey this diverse panoply and acknowledge its presence and importance in the general life and scheme of things Egyptian. Representations of many of these deities occur in the funerary art which comprises the bulk of extant Egyptian art, and to which we will turn our attention later in this chapter.

Religion played a central role in Egyptian societal and civil organization and life. Death was believed to be a doorway to an afterlife in which the departed could cultivate his or her Elysian Field with water apportioned to the individual by the gods. Life continued for the dead as long as the corpse, or some material image of it, subsisted. Careful burial in dry sand which preserved the corpse was therefore essential, as was careful mummification. The art of embalming had reached a proficient level as early as 3000 BC. Great pains were taken to ensure long life for the corpse, and mortuaria became the most important architectural features of the culture, properly reflecting their role as eternal home. From the tombs and burial places, rich in funereal imagery and narrative, we have gathered most of what we know of Egyptian history. Religious practice, however, did dictate that only good things be said of the departed, and we must be careful to temper immediate impressions of an Egypt populated by young, handsome, well-fed men and women, and ruled by beneficent Pharaohs who inspired productivity and optimism among even the lowest slaves.

The Pharaoh acted as a link between mortals and the eternal. Priests, or servants of the god, were delegates of the Pharaoh. The common people relied on their ruler for salvation, for access to the afterlife. The offerings which would secure existence in the afterlife were the Pharaoh's gift. They were the only key to the eternal. It was therefore in every Egyptian's interest to be sure that the Pharaoh's tomb could sustain and maintain him. Images and inscriptions in the tombs included the lowliest servants ensuring that they, too, would participate

forever in the Pharaoh's immortality. Magic charms to make certain the revivification of the deceased, which were once spoken by priests, came to be inscribed on the walls of the tomb so that if necessary the deceased could read them. These magic formulas were finally usurped by all manner of nobles, so that by the end of the twenty-first century BC, they were copied regularly and assisted just about anyone in sharing the unique privilege of the Pharaoh. The Pharaoh joined the gods in the nether world after death. As befitting a ruler whose entourage also existed in the afterlife, he became associated with Osiris, king of the dead.

The King's person and potency

The theory of kingship set forth in the Memphite Theology, which retained currency throughout the periods we have noted, commonly refers to the king as Horus. The king therefore shared the attributes of the god, Horus. Alternatively the king is often called simply, "the god". In Egypt, the Pharaoh was Horus, whose symbol was the falcon, although "we do not know whether the bird was thought in some way to be merely the god's manifestation; whether the god was embodied, temporarily or permanently, in a single bird or in the species as a whole."[1] The falcon may have been merely a sign "referring to a more intangible deity."[2] The image of Horus as the king's person is majestic and compelling—"His outstretched wings are the sky, his fierce eyes the sun and moon."[3]

The Ka

The Egyptians had a particular view of the human personality. Central to Egyptian understanding of human personality was the notion of the Ka. Ka is traditionally translated as spirit. It is a quality possessed by all men, but the king's Ka or vital force was greater than that of commoners and differed in essentials. The Ka of the common person was never pictured, whereas that of the king had its own symbol (see Fig. **3.19**). The Ka—the force of life— left the body in death, only to rejoin it in the afterlife.

THE ARTS
OF ANCIENT EGYPT

The most productive artistic periods in ancient Egypt were those when prosperity was high and the nation was at peace. There also appears to be a strong correlation between artistic vitality and the presence of strong rulers. To a certain degree religious forces also affected the focus and tenor of artistry. For example, when Mena, the first historic king, made Memphis his capital, art flourished and reached high levels of prominence because the major god of Memphis happened to be Ptah, the god of art and all handicrafts. The high priest of Ptah carried as one of his offices that of "Chief of the Stone Cutters and Artist to the King". As long as Memphis retained a central position in Egyptian life, until the fall of the Middle Kingdom, art maintained its importance. In Dynasty XXVI (see Fig. **3.2**) Memphis re-emerged as a political center, and art was once again cultivated and appreciated.

TWO-DIMENSIONAL ART

Egyptian painting took a subordinate position to sculpture, and may not, according to some sources, even have been regarded as an art form by the Egyptians. Painting for the most part was a decorative medium which provided a surface finish to a work of sculpture. Sculptures in relief and in the round were painted. Flat surfaces were also painted, although such painting appears to be a substitute for relief sculpture. In the Middle Kingdom painting largely replaced relief sculpture and the scenes presented vividly portrayed a genuine human interest and original insight. The same may be said of painting in the New Kingdom. Here we often find humor in portrayals of daily life and, again, a high level of technical craftsmanship. Nonetheless, the only time when painting was regarded as a true art was in the New Kingdom during the reign of Akhenaton. Painting appears to have died out as even a subsidiary art after the New Kingdom.

Materials and conventions

We know a little about the materials used by Egyptian painters thanks to analysis by the scholar Petrie of the tomb decorations of Rahotep and Nefermaat at Meydum, dating from the Old Kingdom. Rahotep's tomb walls showed careful preparation. The sun-dried mud brick was covered with an inch and a half thick layer of mud plaster mixed with chopped straw, which was in turn covered by a very thin layer of fine gesso. Paint was then applied with a

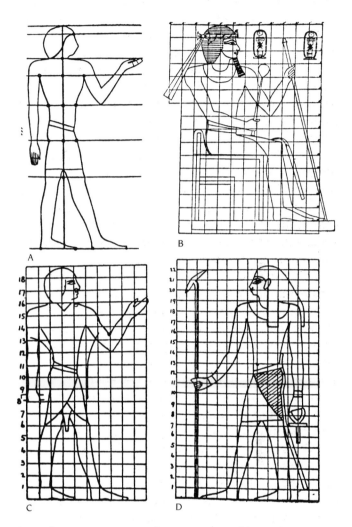

3.10 The Egyptian Canon of Proportion. A: Old Kingdom B: New Kingdom. C & D: Late Period.

brush. Petrie's analysis did not determine the actual painting medium, but the colors used were black, blue, brown (of several values), green, grey, orange, red, white, and yellow. White gypsum was used to lower the saturation or raise the value of any hue.

It is clear that the Egyptian artist followed a formularized approach to the human figure, although proportions varied from one period to another. To maintain proper proportion, the painting surface was first ruled into squares, each of which comprised one half unit. The standing male figure was produced accordingly (Fig. **3.10**). The different proportional variations are illustrated here by the Middle Kingdom canon.

Head (hair to shoulder)	1 unit
Shoulder to hem of kilt	5 units
Hem to ground	3 units
Ground to nipple	7 units
Ground to belt (front)	5 units
Ground to base of hip	4½ units
Ground to base of knee	2½ units
Across shoulders	2½ units
Across waist	1⅛ units
Across feet	3¾ units[4]

As we examine painting from the Old, Middle, and New Kingdoms, we will see some prevailing conventions and some changes. In the Old Kingdom verisimilitude and intricacy are combined with a flat, two-dimensional figure portrayal. In the Middle Kingdom color replaces technique and verisimilitude loses its importance; portrayal of fabric is clearly stylized. At this time focus also shifts to lesser nobles, and humor and liveliness inhabit the paintings. Two-dimensionality remains. New Kingdom painting continues the tradition of two-dimensional figure depiction, with some variations, and color remains vibrant and important.

Old Kingdom

Egyptian tomb painting often portrayed scenes of daily life. In Figure **3.11**, from the tomb of Nefermaat at Maidum, we find an appealing depiction of high verisimilitude much in the spirit and style of later genre paintings. While lively representation of animals appears common in Egyptian art, these geese are certainly not common in their execution. The artist has countered the rather dry composition, forced on the scene by its structure within a register, with a delicate subtlety in shading and by a remarkably wide palette including virtually the entire color spectrum and value scale. Despite the careful and intricate detailing of the scene, however, it is a picture composed on the surface plane, and shows its subjects in two-dimensional relief without any suggestion of perspective or chiaroscuro. Such treatment is characteristic of Egyptian two-dimensional art. In comparision with the works we examined from the Ice Age, we find here an attempt to show activity, but without the dynamic force which characterized the Paleolithic works. Here everything rests in a two-dimensional plane, capturing detail without essence, and form without depth.

Middle Kingdom

Painting gained greater prominence as an art form in the Middle Kingdom than it had had in the Old Kingdom. In a practical sense it allowed lesser nobles to decorate their tombs elaborately at lesser expense than using sculpture involved. Color in Middle Kingdom painting appears more important to the artist than drawing technique. Flat surface details and outlined figures comprise form, and highly coloristic details carry the works. Naturalistic detail such as that in the geese of Nefermaat was replaced by flat, but colorful, convention.

Theban rock tombs

The painted tombs of Thebes provide most of our knowledge of Egyptian painting of this period. Representations of gods are found for the first time in these tombs. Ceiling decorations are common and elaborate. The paintings portray the vivacity and humor of daily life. Theban tombs portray workmen and peasants differently from those of the Old Kingdom, particularly in the shape of the heads and in the garments worn.

The basic form of these tombs consists of a generally square-shaped forecourt leading into a transverse hall. From there we enter a long, narrow hall leading to the ritual chapel which contained seated statues of the deceased and his family. Beneath the chapel lay the burial chamber, access to which was via either a sloping corridor, steep stairs, or a vertical shaft. Walls of the transverse and long halls were often decorated with paintings depicting hunting or farming scenes thereby ensuring supplies of food for the dead in the hereafter. Figure **3.12** depicts a ceremonial purification from the pillared burial chamber of Sennufer, Superintendent of the Garden of the Temple of Amun under Amenophis II. As befits Sennufer's vocation, the burial chamber is decorated with vineyard scenes, with ceilings like vine bowers. The illustration, according to the custom of the period, shows the dead as they appeared when living. Sennufer is pictured with his wife, wearing the clothes and jewels of an earthly festival. The part of the ceremony shown is the purification of the dead, conducted by a priest attired in a leopard skin. Names and titles appear over the celebrants, and in front of Sennufer's face there is a text indicating the departed's wish to accompany the god Amun when he goes to the Feast of the Valley. Again, the conventional two-dimensionality and stylization of Egyptian painting present themselves. The palette is limited, and outlining completes the portrayal. Unlike the subtle details of the geese in Figure **3.11**, we find here an almost careless treatment of objects such as the bunches of grapes and vines. The bunches of grapes are portrayed by an oblong, flat wash of color overpainted with blue circles to represent individual grapes, in a manner consistent with depictions in other Theban tombs. Finally of interest in this painting is the apparent diaphanous quality of the garment over the legs, through which the flesh tones show as a pale red-brown, a convention which became more common as time elapsed.

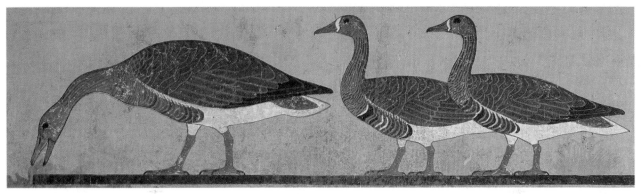

3.11 Grazing geese from the mastaba of Nefermaat at Maidum, early IV Dynasty (c. 2680–2600 BC). Painting on plaster, height of register 11.2 ins (28.5 cm), total length 68 ins (172.7 cm). Egyptian Museum, Cairo.

3.12 The ceremonial purification of Sennufer and his wife Meretjj, from the tomb of Sennufer at Thebes, Egypt. Dynasty XVIII (second phase: 1450–1372 BC).

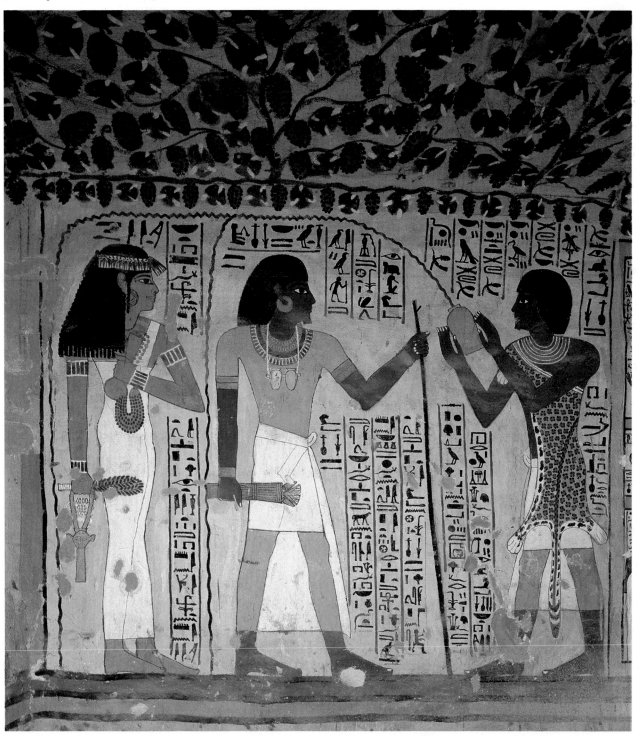

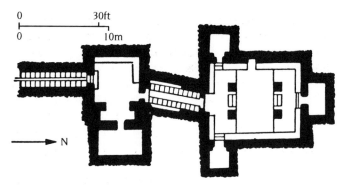

3.13 Ground Plan of Tomb of Queen Nefertari-mi-en-Mat in the Valley of the Queens in Western Thebes, Egypt. 1290–1224 BC.

New Kingdom

The Tomb of Nefertari

Queen Nefertari-mi-en-Mat, of Dynasty XIX (See Fig. **3.1**) was one of the four principal wives of King Ramesses II, and her tomb lies in the Valley of Queens in Western Thebes. Nefertari was Ramesses' favorite. Her tomb rests under the precipitous cliff walls at the end of the gloomy valley of Biban el Harin. Exemplifying a style of painting done in low relief, the paintings adorning the walls of Nefertari's tomb exhibit great elegance, charm, and vivacious color. The tomb is entered through a first room (1), shown in Figure **3.13**. Off this room and to the south lies the Main Room or offering chamber. Connected to these chambers is the major part of the tomb in which the Hall of Pillars or Sarcophogus Chamber provides the central focus. Off and surrounding the Hall of Pillars lie three side rooms (5–7).

The north-east wall of the First Room houses a vibrant painting showing, on the extreme left, the goddess Selkis with a scorpion on her head (Fig. **3.14**). On the extreme right appears the goddess Maat. On her head rests her hieroglyph, the feather. The rear wall of the recess depicts Queen Nefertari led by Isis toward the beetle-headed Khepri, a form assumed by the sun god which implies his everlasting resurrection. Over the door to the main room, on the extreme right of the illustration, we see the vulture goddess Nekhbet of El-Kab. Her claws hold the shen-sign, which symbolizes eternity and sovereignty. The goddess Isis wears on her crown the horns of a cow, surrounded by the sun-disc from which hangs a cobra. In her left hand she carries the divine sceptre. Queen Nefertari is dressed according to the fashion of the time, and over the vulture hood she wears the tall feathered crown of the Divine Consort. In the hieroglyphic text Isis says, "Come great king's wife Nefertari, beloved of Mut, justified, so that I may allot thee a place in the holy land [the hereafter], and the great king's wife and lady of the two lands, justified before Osiris, the Great god."

The painting itself is rich and warm, elegant, and highly stylized. A black base borders the composition,

provides it with a solid anchor, and raises the main body of the painting well above the floor of the chamber. A black band forms the upper terminal accent of the central, recessed panel. The black ceiling with its conventionalized ochre stars ties the sky to the ground and unifies the entire composition. A small black band decorated with stars runs just below the upper motif on the left panel. Strangely, a similar black band without the stars adorns the extreme right panel. The limited palette uses four hues, which never change in value throughout the work. Yet, the overall effect of this wall decoration is one of great variety. The composition maintains the conventionalized style established since Dynasty I, which treats the human form in flat profile.

The composition lies strictly on the surface. Naturalistic proportions are adhered to only minimally. Eyes, hands, head, and feet show no attempt at verisimilitude. Quite the contrary, the fingers become extenuated designs elongating the arms to balance the elegant and sweeping lines of legs and feet. The matching figures of Selkis and Maat, extreme left and right, exhibit arms of unequal length and proportion. Although the basic style remains consistent, we can observe a significant change in body proportions from those of the Middle Kingdom.

Figure **3.15** shows the north and part of the east walls of the Main Room of the tomb. The east wall depicts Queen Nefertari dedicating a rich offering. She holds a scepter in her hand. The offering is for Osiris-Khentamenty-Unnefer, "The King of the Living, the great God, the Lord of the Necropolis, the Lord until Eternity, the Lord of Infinity". Osiris sits on his throne holding his crook-scepter (crosier) and flail. Before him are the four sons of Horus—Hapi, Duamutef, Qebhsenuef, and Amsety. In return for Nefertari's offering, the god promises her immortality and good fortune in his kingdom. The north wall, on the left of the illustration, shows the queen standing in front of Thoth, the Lord of Hermopolis, the god of writing, wisdom, and judgement. Between Nefertari and Thoth rests a writing palette and an ink pot with a frog adorning its edge. The hieroglyphs indicate Nefertari's title and her words to the god, asking for the ink pot and the writing palette. She is "The great Royal Wife, the Lady of the Two Lands, Nefertari, beloved of Mut, true of voice".[5]

In this illustration we can see another Egyptian convention, in which the upper torso shows the shoulders, but not the breasts, in a full frontal depiction. The differing proportions of the arms may, perhaps, denote some accommodation of perspective, acknowledging the phenomenon that objects closest to us appear to be larger than objects further away. We also can see in this and the previous illustration indications of fabric texture; the diaphanous quality of Nefertari's outer gown reveals the silhouette of her tightly fitting inner garment and the flesh of higher value in the legs and upper arms. The pleated or gathered quality of the shoulder wrap is revealed in a fairly obvious, although not naturalistic, way as white stripes across the upper arms.

Until the nineteenth century AD and the invention of the camera, an artist's responsibilities have always included the recording of the details of society. Historians, social scientists, philosophers, and artists from later times gain many insights into civilizations from the depiction of clothing and ornamentation in the art of the period, regardless of the degree of verisimilitude employed. For example, the silhouette of the costume can reveal basic attitudes such as dynamism, passivity, gracefulness, discomfort, naturalness, exaggeration, simplicity or extravagance. Indications of morality and idealism can be revealed in which parts of the body are focused upon, and which parts are left unadorned, covered or uncovered.

In the paintings we have previously examined, we can see a change in the slope and configuration of the headgear. Likewise we can observe the addition of corselets with shoulder straps, armlets, bracelets, and anklets. These do not appear on gods until later times. The long, transparent gowns do not seem to have appeared until Dynasty XIX.

SCULPTURE

Old Kingdom

Sculpture was the major art form of the Egyptians. By the time of the Old Kingdom the sculptor had overcome many of the technical difficulties that plagued his predecessors of the pre-dynastic period. It may also be the case that religious tenets confounded the sculptor during those archaic times. Many primitive peoples throughout history have regarded the naturalistic portrayal of the human figure as inviting danger. Making a likeness of an individual may be thought to capture the soul. Concerning technical problems, pre-dynastic sculpture left detailing rough and simple. Convention rather than naturalism prevailed. It seems certain that sculptors relied on memory to portray the human form rather than working from live models. Since pre-dynastic sculpture is also pre-written history, we really cannot do more than speculate as to how much convention reflected technical mastery, or philosophy, or both. As we examine classic Greek sculpture, for example, we are certain that the idealized form of its sculpture was philosophical because the technical skill was obviously there. In pre-dynastic Egypt the reverse appears more logical.

Old Kingdom sculpture shows technical mastery and is well crafted. Life-size sculpture which captured the human form in exquisite natural detail, came to the fore. At the same time conventional portrayal of certain ideals of pharaonic demeanor also prevailed. The divine characteristics of the Pharaoh dictated a dignified and majestic portrayal. Although such rigidity of treatment lessened as time went on, the softening and human-centered qualities such softening connotes never completely divested the pharaonic statue of its divine repose.

The dual sculpture of Prince Rahotep and his wife Nofret (Fig. **3.16**) comes from the tomb of Prince Rahotep, one of Snofru's sons. The striking colors of the statues exemplify the Egyptian tendency to use painting to provide a decorative surface for sculpture, but the work is in no way commonplace. It is remarkable. The eyes of both figures are dull and light colored quartz. The eyelids are painted black. Both figures wear the costume of the time. In a somewhat conventionalized treatment, the skin tones of the woman are several shades lighter than those of the man. A woman's skin traditionally exhibited a creamy yellow hue, whereas a man's ranged from light to dark brown. In Dynasty IV the kings rose from peasant stock, an ancestry which is apparent in the sturdy, broad-shouldered, well muscled physique of the king. At the same time his facial characteristics, particularly the eyes and expression, exhibit alertness, wisdom, strength, and capacity. The portrayal of Nofret expresses similar individuality. Probably for the first time in Egyptian art we find in this work the full development of the naturalistic, three-dimensional female body. She is wearing the typical gown of the period cut to reveal well-formed and voluptuous breasts. Here, as is the case with all the details of the upper portion of both statues, the artist has been meticulous in his observations and depictions.

Egyptian admiration for the human body reveals itself clearly in both statues. Precise modelling and attention to detail are seen in the smallest item. In the statue of Nofret the gown at once covers and reveals the graceful contours of the body beneath. Comparison of facial features reveals in Nofret an individual of less distinct character than that of her husband. She has a sensual and pampered face. Her hair is obviously a wig shaped in the style of the day. Beneath the constricting head band we can see Nofret's own hair, of much finer character, parted in the middle and swept back beneath the wig. A precise and delicate treatment of the hand held open against the body reveals the artist's skill and perception and also reveals the care and attention Nofret has given to herself. The hand is, indeed, delicate and feminine. Small dimples decorate the fingers and the nails exhibit extraordinary care. The unpainted nails are correctly observed as being lighter than normal skin tone. In both statues the artist's attention and precision, so maturely and carefully expressed in the upper body, deteriorates almost to the point of juvenile crudity in the lower body, as is typical of sculpture of this era. The legs of both figures are lumpy, ill-defined, and coarse. The feet, with the exception of possessing five toes each, are nearly unrecognizable as parts of the human anatomy. The thrones on which the figures sit show even less attention to detail—they remain unpainted, rough blocks

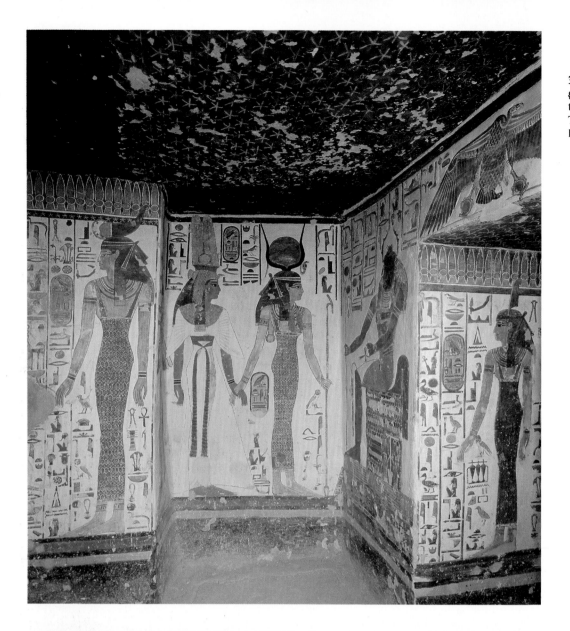

3.14 Queen Nefertari guided by Isis, from the tomb of Queen Nefertari at Thebes, Egypt. 1290–1224 BC.

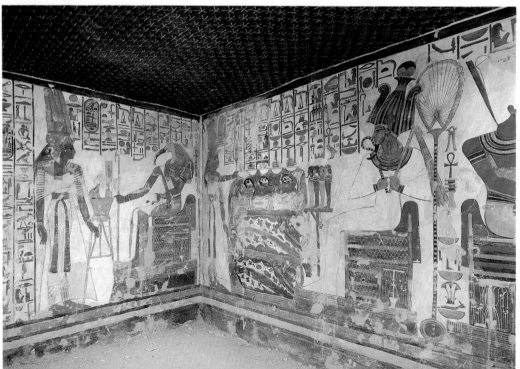

3.15 Queen Nefertari before the god Thoth (left) and the god Osiris (right), from the tomb of Queen Nefertari at Thebes, Egypt. 1290–1224 BC.

3.16 Prince Rahotep and his wife Nofret from Medum, c.2580 BC. Painted limestone, 47½ ins (120 cm) high. Egyptian Museum, Cairo.

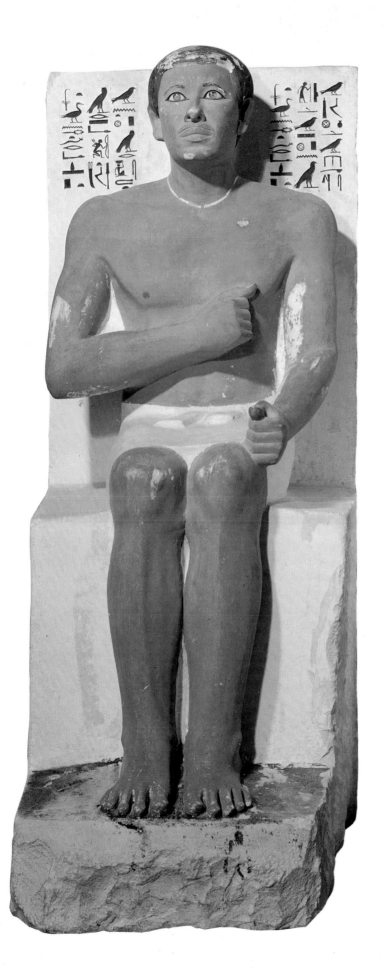
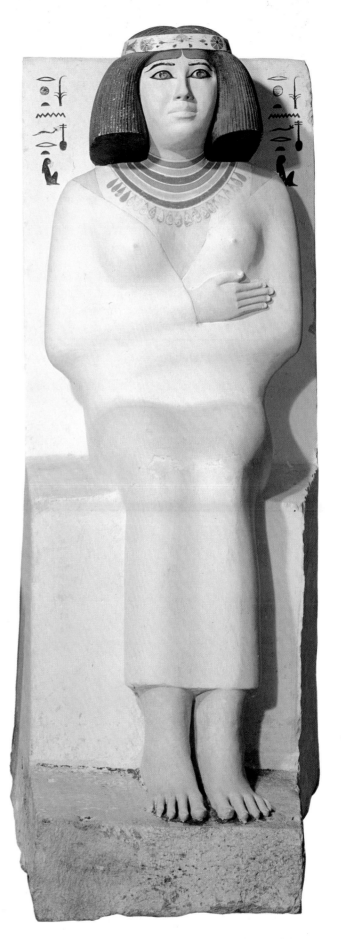

of limestone plainly hacked from their quarry and left unfinished.

Notwithstanding the curious lack of attention to detail in certain parts of Old Kingdom sculptures in the round, the fact remains that these and other works of the period are naturalistic and vital. Portrayals would soften over time, but as is the case with Rahotep and Nofret, we can see in Old Kingdom sculpture a powerful, solid formality and dignity which reflects the social and political centrality and stature of the Egyptian Pharaoh. No action is portrayed. In some cases a forward step can be seen in male figures (Fig. **3.17**) but the axis of the body pose remains rigid and stable. We can see clearly the effect of this convention if we compare this statue with that of the counterpoised stance of the form in Figure **4.16**. There the axis of the torso and hip twist naturally, throwing the weight onto one leg, and exhibiting movement and a dynamic quality not present in the Egyptian portrayal. Other conventions of the Old Kingdom style include the placement of the head in exact adherence to the median line of the body, with the eyes staring straight

3.17 King Mycerinus between Hathor and the local deity of Diospolis Parva, Dynasty IV (2680–2565 BC). Green slate, 38½ ins (97.8 cm) high. Egyptian Museum, Cairo.

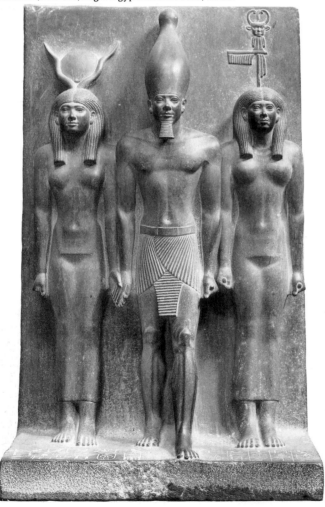

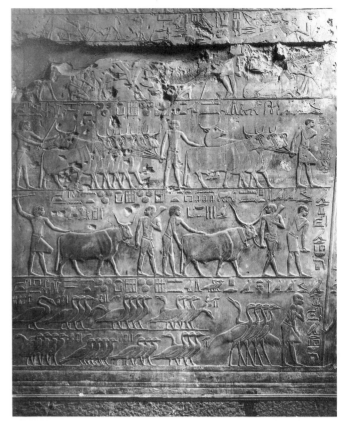

3.18 Presentation of cows and poultry, in the tomb of Ptahotep at Saqqara, Egypt. Dynasty V to early Dynasty VI (c.2565–2350 BC).

forward. Finally, the woman, when part of a dyad, embraces the man's shoulders or waist.

There are two distinctly different forms of Egyptian sculpture. We have just examined one form—sculpture in the round or statuary, that is, sculpture which has a full or nearly complete three-dimensionality. The second form is relief sculpture, or that which emerges from a background in a more two-dimensional manner. Artists of the Old Kingdom produced numerous relief sculptures, and more have been preserved from this period than from any other. Many of these works are of extraordinarily high quality. Figure **3.18** is from the tomb of the priest Ptahotep at Saqqara.

Typical of tombs from approximately Dynasty V onward, this is the multi-chambered tomb of a high functionary. As we examine the relief shown in this illustration several things may strike us. There is the dullness of the subject matter—cows and ducks. The artist, perhaps recognizing the nature of his subject, has accepted the challenge of turning the commonplace into the beautiful. The subject matter and its portrayal are constrained by the parameters of the individual registers or bands in which the depiction must be composed. The artist has skilfully turned both subject matter and form into an intricately composed work. Subtle variations and dynamic use of line turn each individual register into an active and interesting composition. Triangular development of form in which line swells and ebbs across the band can be seen clearly in the top two registers. The eye is led upward from the left border from the arms of the herdsman to his staff, sharply ascending to the horns of the cow which faces in the opposite direction from the others. The line of the composition then falls along the back of the single cow to rise again across the horns of the group of cows to focus on the central herdsman. Two juxtaposed triangles created by the single cow and the groups of cows here create a dynamic counterpoint carried on in the downward glance and line of skirt of the herdsman on the far right. Further interest is added by variations in detail in both registers. For example, although the cattle create a regularity of form and rhythm, they are not alike in detail. Notice how the downward curve of the foremost horn of the lead cow in the upper register carries the eye downward. Composition in all registers is carefully thought out, employing sophisticated devices and arrangements. The composition of ducks, geese, and cranes in the lower register exhibits an equally sophisticated design.

Constrained by the formal device of horizontal registers, the artist has done all in his power to tie the entire wall section into a single composition rather than several compositions piled on top of each other. Register lines actually break so as to allow the spatial integrity of one to flow into that of another. In other places forms and hieroglyphs touch register lines at places where the eye of the observer can be swept immediately up or down into an adjoining register. The conventions of figure portrayal are also apparent, but are modified by the artist's individual craftsmanship. Forms are delicately and meticulously carved. The muscle striations in the human legs, the precisely rendered feet, and the accurately depicted animal legs, heads, and eyes demonstrate considerable technique. One further detail stands out, and that is the apparent attempt at spatial development in the third dimension in raising the bull behind the grouping above the register base. This is a treatment quite at odds with prevailing convention and is not present, for example, in the lower registers where the legs of the fowl, which stand behind the forward group, are not depicted at all.

Middle Kingdom

In the Middle Kingdom artistic style moved toward simplicity of form. General form was emphasized at the

3.19 Maned sphinx of King Ammenemes III, Dynasty XII (1991–1786 BC). Black granite, 72 ins (183 cm) long. Egyptian Museum, Cairo.

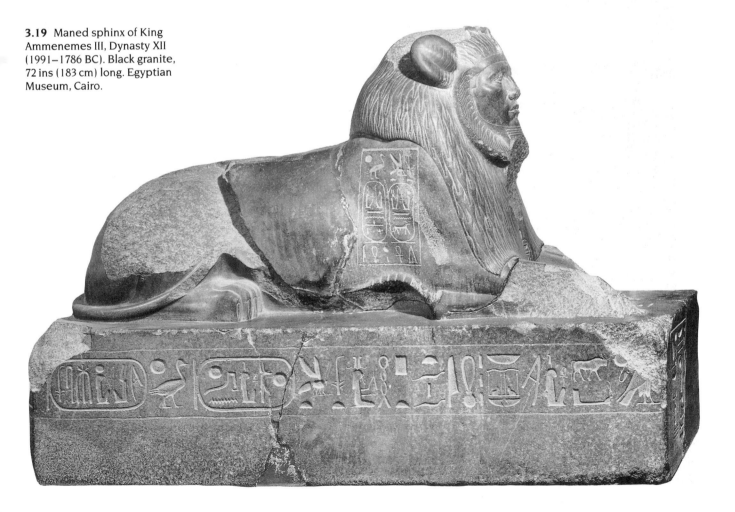

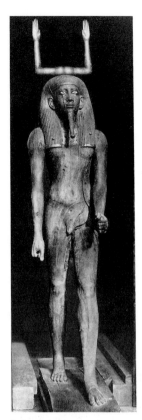

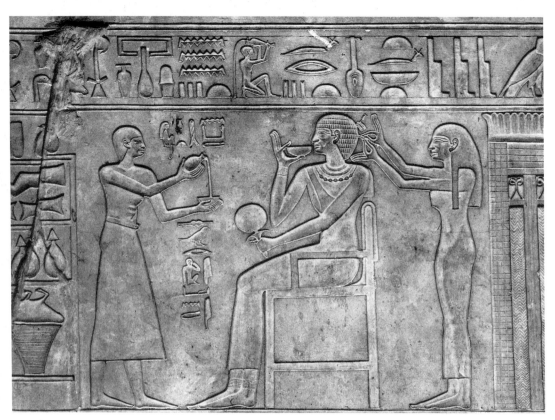

3.20 Ka statue of King Hor in its shrine, Dynasty XII (1991–1786 BC). Wood, 70 ins (177.7 cm) high. Egyptian Museum, Cairo.

3.21 Detail from the sarcophagus of Queen Kawit, Dynasty XI (2134–1991 BC). Limestone with traces of coloring. Egyptian Museum, Cairo.

expense of detail but not of clarity and accuracy. Lack of detail has been suggested by some scholars as indicative of the fact that sculpture in the Middle Kingdom was intended to be viewed in an architectural setting from a distance. Royal portraiture appears to have lost some of its power and dignity, and yet representations of royalty continued to express calmness and stability. A certain sadness seems to pervade royal visages, while the artist no longer attempts to capture expression. The vitality and vigor of Old Kingdom style has also been lost.

Turning to specific examples, we find in the maned sphinx of King Ammenemes III (Fig. **3.19**) a strong symbolism typical of the early part of the Middle Kingdom. This is one of four sphinxes of the same type found at the same site. Partially restored, it dates from the time of Ramesses II. The concentrated strength of this powerfully compact work is characteristic of the period it represents, that is the period following the expulsion of the Hyksos.

The Ka statue of King Hor (Fig. **3.20**) provides an example of late Middle Kingdom sculpture. The statue is of an otherwise unknown king, and was found in a tomb in the southern brick pyramid at Dashur. King Hor's statue shows softer modelling of form. Apparently it was originally clothed in an apron and girdle of another material. Nude statues other than those of small children were extremely rare in ancient Egypt. The style of the depic-

tion, particularly apparent in the shoulders, is less naturalistic than that of other dynasties. The lower body, legs, and ankles nonetheless reflect a higher degree of anatomical accuracy than the earlier dyad of Rahotep and Nofret. The overall tone of the statue is less solid and powerful than that of previous works, and shows a rather delicate and slender king, willowy in contrast to the powerful physiques of his predecessors. Hor stands with one foot forward to denote motion, but again is not in the *contrapposto* stance of Classical Greece. The feet are square rather than realistic and the sculptor has made the large and second toes on each foot of equal length. The eyes, as in earlier works, are inset in alabaster and a metal, which might be silver or bronze. The ears, in keeping with the style of Dynasty XII, are exaggerated. On the top of his head Hor wears the upraised hands and arms which represent the hieroglyphic Ka sign. The treatment of the hands and arms in the Ka sign is less naturalistic than in the figure of Hor himself. According to some scholars the hands once grasped great scepter staffs and were covered by a layer of painted stucco.

Figure **3.21**, from Dynasty XI, is a detail from a sarcophagus sculpture in relief found in the Deir el Bahari

3.22 Funerary mask of King Tutankhamun, c.1340 BC. Gold inlaid with enamel and semi-precious stones, 21¼ ins (54 cm) high. Egyptian Museum, Cairo.

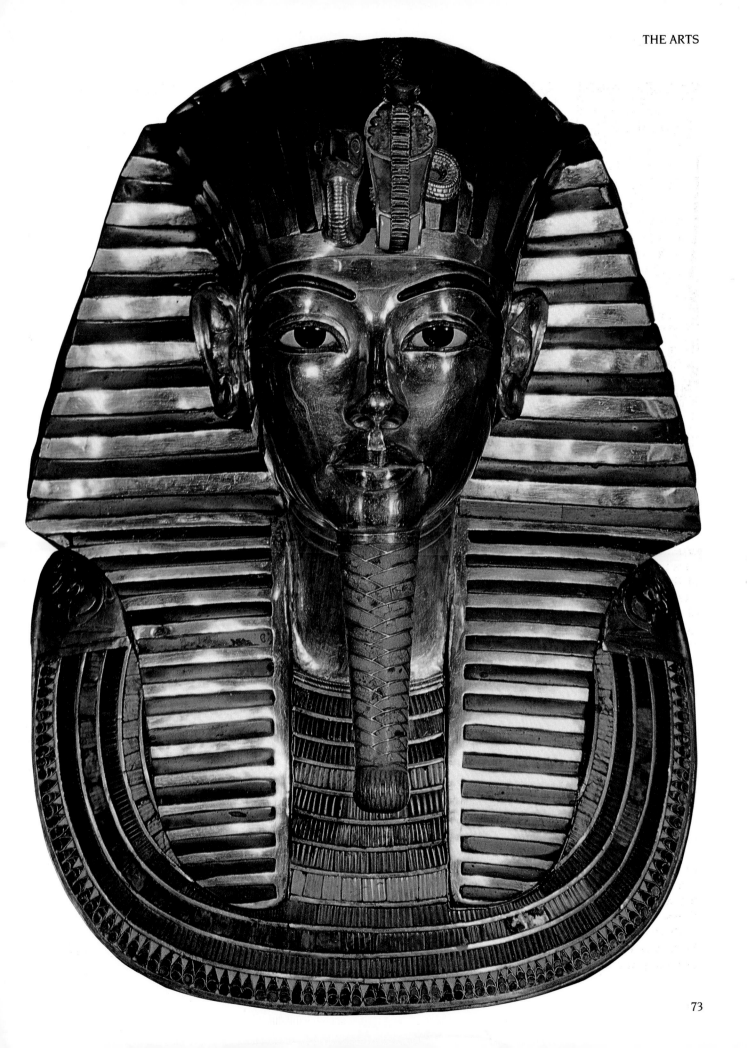

temple. The limestone material of this work also shows traces of once having been painted. We observe Queen Kawit seated on a chair with a drinking cup raised to her lips. A maidservant attends to ringlets in the queen's hair, and a manservant stands before the queen, pouring liquid into another cup. The style of this relief uses forms cut into the surface, called sunken relief as opposed to raised relief. Our attention is drawn to the rather fussy details such as the wigs and jewelry, while other parts of the sculpture remain plain and flat. The faces here are not pleasant and their treatment reflects an almost crude harshness. Bulbous nostrils and coarse treatment around the mouth, with little modelling of the cheeks and jaws, give the work an appearance of stylization much closer to parody than to realism. The eyes are highly stylized in both queen and maidservant, perhaps more suggestive of elaborate eye make-up than of the eye itself, but nonetheless conventionalized. The eye turns downward at the inward corner. The position of the hands and general tension of the work give us a sense of nervous energy. Clearly this style sets out to deny naturalism in favor of a very mannered presentation, in a somewhat similar way to works of the late sixteenth century AD in Europe.

Other anatomical details draw our attention. The manservant appears to be of middle age and a product of decadent living. Rather than the trim musculature we are used to seeing, his mid-section displays rolls of fat. The ears are far too large. In addition, the male figure has two right hands, the result of either carelessness or convention. On all the figures the big toes lie on the side of the foot nearest the viewer—a fairly common "mistake" in Egyptian relief sculpture. The overall mood of this work is not optimistic.

New Kingdom

One of the most popular artifacts to have survived from this period must be the exquisite sculpture from the tomb of Tutankhamun (Fig. **3.22**). The tomb of Tutankhamun was discovered in the Valley of Kings near Thebes. The sheer quantity of artifacts recovered is staggering, and makes us wonder just how much must have been lost over the centuries from looting of the burial chambers of the other pharaohs. The funerary mask is of solid beaten gold inlaid with semi-precious stones and colored glass. Designed to cover the face of the king's mummy, the mask is highly naturalistic in style, and apparently a true likeness of the young king. The mask wears the royal *nemes* head-dress with two lappets hanging down at the sides. A ribbon holds the king's queue at the back. The hood formed by the head-dress exhibits two symbolic creatures, the uraeus serpent and the vulture goddess Nekhbet of El-Kab, divinities who protected Lower and Upper Egypt.

The statue of King Tutankhamun posted like a sentry

to the entrance of the sepulchral chamber stands five feet nine inches tall, and must be nearly life-size (Fig. **3.23**). It is one of two identical Ka statues of Tutankhamun which stood facing each other guarding the door to his walled-up burial chamber. The statue is carved from wood and covered with a shining black resin. The eyes and eyebrows are made of gold. The head-dress, staff, armlets, wristlets, apron, sandals, and scepter are painted gold. Although the work is highly naturalistic, several conventions draw our attention. There is the forward placement of the left leg. Then there is the conventionalized treatment of the girdle and apron. Form here is treated not as cloth, but rather as a decorative part of the composition. The striations intended to depict pleats in the fabric do not reflect the way in which any fabric would fall, but suggest fabric within the decorative scheme of the sculpture, adding to the work a dynamic and elegant form, line, and silhouette. However, the overall treatment of detail is not particularly careful or precise. The

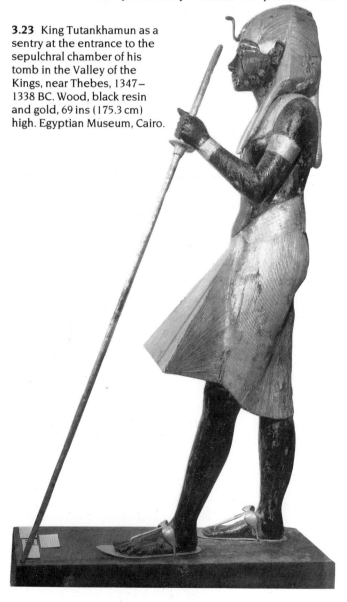

3.23 King Tutankhamun as a sentry at the entrance to the sepulchral chamber of his tomb in the Valley of the Kings, near Thebes, 1347–1338 BC. Wood, black resin and gold, 69 ins (175.3 cm) high. Egyptian Museum, Cairo.

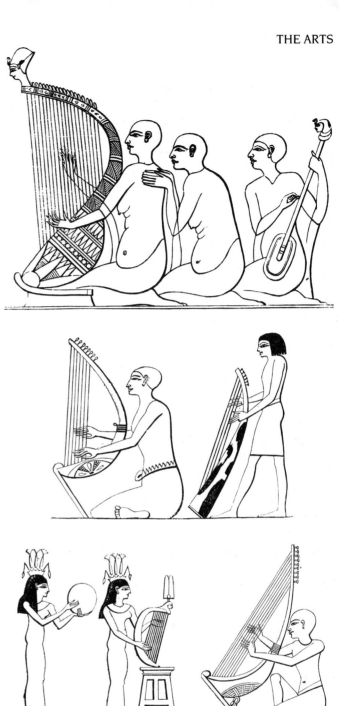

treatment of hands, head-dress, armlets, and wristlets exhibits only passing attention and perception. The face, likewise, is undefined and unrefined, in contrast with the careful treatment found on the death mask.

MUSIC

We noted earlier that the Egyptians had many contacts with other peoples of the Mediterranean world. Cross-cultural influence appears to have been strong in the area of music. Although we can point to, for example Egyptian fondness for Assyrian music and vice versa, we cannot know how these musical systems sounded. We do not have musical scores, and even if we did, we would not know how to play them. Scales, if any, harmonies, textures, pitches, intervals, dynamics, and so on, remain a mystery. We can nonetheless examine some of the instruments and perhaps, with some imaginative specu-lation, we can get some feeling for musical timbre, the basic quality of sound.

As more and more discoveries were made in the field of Egyptology, the modern world became better ac-quainted with Egyptian musical instruments. Sculptures and paintings depict them, and fragments and even fairly complete instruments have been found. Harps, lyres, and numerous other stringed instruments, pipes, flutes, sistra, cymbals, and bells were all in the storechest of the Egyptian musician. Probably the basic instrument in the Egyptian scheme was the harp. Harps varied tremen-dously in size, complexity, shape, and ornamentation. One variety had ten strings, while another had twenty. A third variety had seven strings, and yet another had only four. Some were very plain, and others were ornate and brightly colored. How much of this variety is actual and how much rests in the depictive license of the painter, we do not know. The frequent depiction of the harp in wall paintings and sculpture does assure us of its popularity. Wall paintings also indicate that the larger harps, some of which appear to stand nearly six feet tall, were played essentially as modern harps are. Figure **3.24** illustrates the diversity of harps available.

A second popular stringed instrument was the trigo-non. As its name suggests, the trigonon was a triangular stringed instrument, perhaps a hand-held variety of the harp or a more complex derivative of the lyre. This kind of instrument has been found throughout the ancient Middle East.

The lyre also came in a great variety of shapes and sizes, and was popular throughout the ancient world. It is famous for its references in the Bible, as are many other instruments found in Egypt. Some of the lyres found in the tombs of ancient Egypt still produce sound on their ancient strings.

Extrapolating from the shape of the stringed instru-ments and the number of strings and from the number of

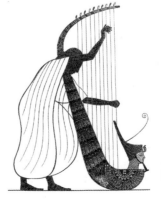
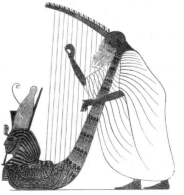

3.24 Egyptian harps.

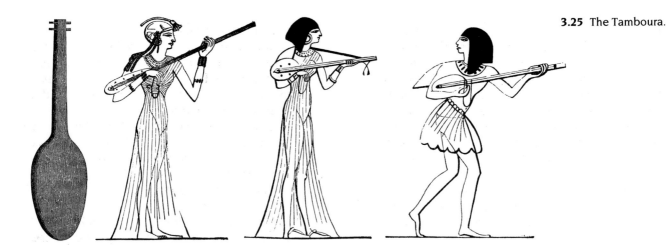

3.25 The Tamboura.

finger holes in flute-type instruments, it has been suggested that Egyptian music must have been based on pentatonic scales, tetrachords, and so on. Some scholars have also argued that Egyptian musical theory exerted a profound influence on Greek music.

The tamboura of ancient Egypt had two basic shapes—one oval and the other with sides slightly incurved like a modern violin or guitar. The overall design of this long, narrow, guitar-like instrument reminds us more of a simple, home-made stringed instrument than anything else (Fig. **3.25**). Various illustrations show from two to four tuning pegs and also indicate that the tamboura could be either with or without frets. The number of frets on some illustrations, if accurately portrayed, suggest that the tamboura could produce a large number of pitches on each string. Analysis of tamboura found with strings intact indicates that the ancient Egyptians had discovered the viability of cat gut as a musical aid. Additional stringed instruments of innumerable shapes and sizes defy classification, but certainly indicate that music, whatever its texture and tonal nature, held a firm and important place in Egyptian art.

Wind instruments were equally varied in shape, size, and ornamentation. Small pipes made of reed with three, four, five, and more finger holes have been found in great

3.26 The Double Pipe.

3.27 The Darabukkah of the modern Egyptians.

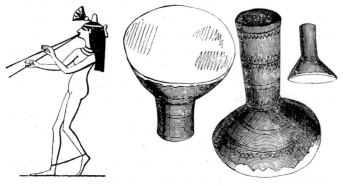

quantity. Some of these appear to have been played by blowing directly across the opening at the end, and others seem to have required a reed as in our clarinet or oboe. The long, double pipe illustrated in Figure **3.26** was made of wood or reed. As with the stringed instruments, scholars have tried to determine whether the number of finger holes relates to pentatonic or other scales, but none of the extant instruments is in good enough condition to produce tones accurate enough to constitute proof either way.

The trumpet also formed a part of the instrumental complement. Apparently of brass, the trumpet appears infrequently in paintings and sculpture, and its shape was unbent, in the later Roman fashion. If anything is to be concluded about the qualities of Egyptian music from the appearance of these various instruments in sculpture and painting, it is that Egyptians preferred the mellow and soft timbres of strings and woodwinds to the blare and volume of brass.

They also enjoyed rhythmic emphasis, as we can deduce from a variety of percussion instruments. Three kinds of drum appear. One is a small and longish hand drum. A second appears more like an American Indian tom tom, with cords stretching from drum head to drum head. A third type is still found in Egypt and is called a darabukkah (Fig. **3.27**). Tambourines, bells, cymbals, and other rhythm instruments are also depicted.

THEATRE

Aristotle, the Greek philosopher of the fourth century BC, wrote that human beings are instinctively imitative, that they enjoy imitating others and seeing imitations, because people like to know how it would feel to be another individual and why others act as they do. Such a statement might seem to be a logical argument for assuming that, whether we have traces of it or not, theatre must have been a part of every human civilization. This would, however, be a false assumption. Just as our definition of dance implies a performance/audience situation and not just dancing, the presence of dramatic devices or techniques alone does not constitute theatre, which is a formally organized performance. Theatre in its artistic sense must be divorced from the dramatic elements of ritual. Not every society has taken this step, so although Aristotle's observation may be correct, we cannot conclude that every society has theatre. It could be argued that the Egyptians had developed this separate activity by as early as 3000 BC. The Greek historian Herodotus makes ample reference to Egyptian dramatic activities, but it is not at all clear whether these references, noting religious festivals, are to what we have identified as theatre.

Theatre historians often refer to the famous *Abydos Passion Play*, also known as the *Osiris Passion Play*, whose text is unknown, but about which contemporary commentary by participants and spectators is recorded. According to Friedley and Reeves, many types of Egyptian drama existed, dating back to 3200 BC. Although none of the suggested evidence comprises what we would consider a playscript, some scholars have found in records such as the *Pyramid Texts* what they claim are stage directions for roles played by temple priests. This may have been the case, and records of endowments for such "performances" exist. However, it is equally logical for these "performances" to be labeled as religious incantations or formulas designed to ensure the safe passage of the departed to the afterlife. The same interpretation may be given to the other sources cited as theatrical activity, notably the *Coronation Festival Play* from Dynasty XII—ritual, undoubtedly, drama, unquestionably, theatre, probably not.

Less certain is our understanding of the *Abydos* or *Osiris Passion Play*. It appears to be mentioned in the *Pyramid Texts* as well as in inscriptions dating to Dynasty XII (just prior to 2500 BC). The text recounts the story of the death and dismemberment of Osiris.

According to Ikhernofret, who refurbished the play for Senworset III, he participated in the drama, which he described as follows. This outline of the play is all that has been written down and preserved:

(1) "I celebrated the 'Procession of the god Up-wawet' when he proceeded to champion his father [Osiris]." (This was probably a mock fight in front of the House of Osiris at Abydos in which the audience participated.)

(2) "I repulsed those who were hostile to the Neshmet barque, and I overthrew the enemies of Osiris." (This indicates a mock naval encounter on the Nile in which the audience joined.)

(3) "I celebrated the 'Great Procession', following the god in his footsteps." (In this scene probably Osiris was slain by Seth, an episode too sacred

for Ikhernofret to mention.)

(4) "I sailed the divine barque, while Thoth . . . the voyage." (Here the body of Osiris was recovered by his family led by Thoth, the god of speech, after a voyage in a boat, followed by the audience in their barques.)

(5) "I equipped the barque [called] 'Shining in Truth', of the Lord of Abydos, with a chapel; I put on his beautiful regalia when he went forth to the district of Pekar." (This suggests the embalment or possibly a description of Ikhernofret's production duties.)

(6) "I led the way of the god to his tomb in Pekar." (This scene was the funeral procession to the tomb of Osiris, the audience following as mourners. The actual setting was the tomb of King Djer of the 1st Dynasty, at some distance away.)

(7) "I championed Wennofer [Osiris] on 'That Day of Great Battle'; I overthrew all the enemies upon the shores of Nedyet." (In this scene Seth dug up the body of his brother, Osiris, and dismembered it. Half the audience supported Seth while the other half joined Horus and the family of Osiris who reassembled his limbs after the battle.)

(8) "I caused him to proceed into the barque [called] 'The Great'; it bore his beauty; I gladdened the heart of the eastern highlands; I [put] jubilation in the western highlands, when they saw the beauty of the Neshmet barque. It landed at Abydos and they brought [Osiris, First of the Westerner, Lord] or Abydos to his palace." (This was the great Resurrection scene, also too sacred to mention.)[6]

These plays, if plays they were, were performed in mortuary temples, which a few scholars believe were constructed specifically for the purpose of staging plays.

DANCE

There can be no question that music and dance contributed significantly to Egyptian culture. Dances of a highly formal character had developed, and the love of dance is clearly expressed in the testimonies which have survived in the tombs. In Dynasty VI of the Old Kingdom, Pepi II received news that in the land of Yam between the first and second cataracts of the Nile dwelt a dwarf who danced like a god. The sovereign's response was that it was absolutely essential that the dwarf be brought back to the court "alive, well, and happy".[7]

In the wall paintings of the tombs of Giza from Dynasty V there are significant examples of what Sachs

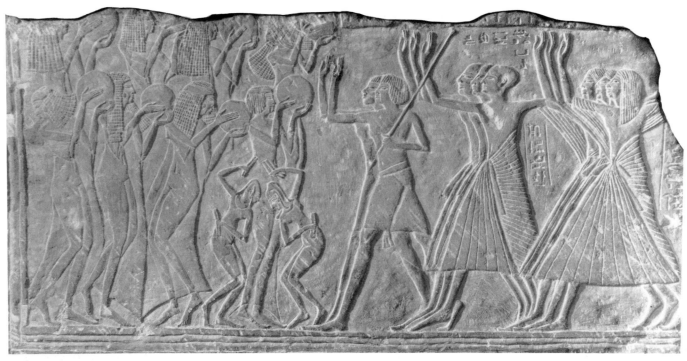

3.28 Funeral Dance, Dynasty XIX (1314–1197 BC). Limestone relief. Egyptian Museum, Cairo.

calls stride dances.[8] They occur in both the harvest dances and run dances of the king. Stride dances are typified by a forward thrust of motion, a characteristic based on motives. Several examples of stride dancing appear in funeral dances. Here the dancers seem to take exaggerated, long strides, throwing the leg forward so as to break the life-destroying power of death. From Dynasty VI come examples of dancers accompanying a coffin, throwing their legs in a wide spread above the heads of the dancers in front of them. Other forms of dance movements are depicted in the Theban tombs dating to 1300 BC. Here a dark-skinned woman, probably a slave, whirls in a circular motion. The example in Figure **3.28** shows yet another dance position, undoubtedly for a funeral dance of the New Kingdom. Fertility dances were also a prominent part of Egyptian ritual dance, and in examples which apparently show these dances we find women dancers covered in grape vines and swinging branches. In a wall painting from the Middle Kingdom a fertility dance is depicted in which three women mime what the hieroglyphs call the wind. One dancer is upright, the second bends under the outstretched arms of the first, and the third appears to be making a bridge.

ARCHITECTURE

Dynasties I and II

Architecture of a monumental character developed early in the pre-historic, pre-dynastic period in Egypt. Con-

siderable skill in the quarrying of large blocks of stone, mainly white limestone found in the eastern cliffs opposite Memphis, was acquired at this time. Evidence of this can be found in the burial chambers from the second half of Dynasty I. It has been suggested that less evidence exists for the "use of worked stone in the much larger brick tombs which were being constructed in the western edge of the valley at Saqqara from the time of Aha, the second king of Dynasy I".[9] Here burial chambers were cut out of the rock cliffs themselves.

An important shrine in the first two dynasties was the temple of Khentiamentiu (Fig. **3.29**), the jackal god. Khentiamentiu was later assimilated by Osiris, whose temple would remain at Abydos (Fig. **3.30**). Abydos became a sanctified location probably because of its use as a burial place for the kings of Dynasty I. We know little of the actual superstructures of Abydos, however, because time has destroyed them. Several reconstructions have been proposed, such as that shown in Figure **3.31**. It suggests a low brick structure filled with gravel and surrounded by a wall which enclosed an offering place housing two round-topped stelae bearing the name Horus. Another Dynasty I tomb for which part of the superstructure remains can be seen in Figure **3.33**. Credited to the time of Az-ib, sixth king of Dynasty I, the structure comprises three step sides and a flat fourth face. In the flat face an opening led to stairways to the upper and lower stories of the burial pit. Figure **3.32** illustrates an elaborate reconstruction of Merneith's tomb at Saqqara.

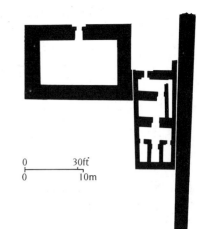

3.29 Plan of the Temple of Khentiamentiu, Dynasties I–II (3200–2780 BC).

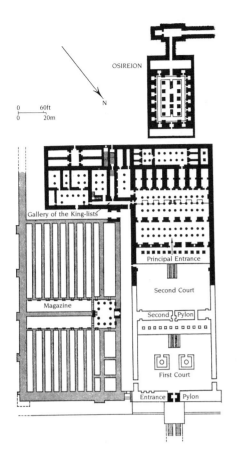

OSIREION

0 ____ 60ft
0 ____ 20m

N

Gallery of the King-lists

Magazine

Principal Entrance

Second Court

Second Pylon

First Court

Entrance   Pylon

3.30 Ground plan of the Temple of King Sethos I and the Osireion at Abydos (1304–1290 BC).

0 ____ 30ft
0 ____ 10m

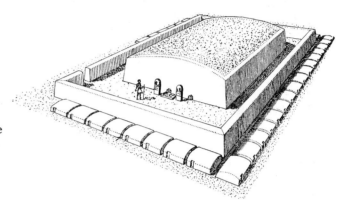

3.31 Reconstruction of the Abydos tomb of Merneith, Egypt, Dynasty I (3200–2980 BC).

3.32 Reconstruction of the Tomb attributed to Merneith, Saqqara, Egypt, Dynasty I (3200–2980 BC).

3.33 Superstructure of Tomb 3038, Saqqara, Egypt, Dynasty I (3200–2980 BC).

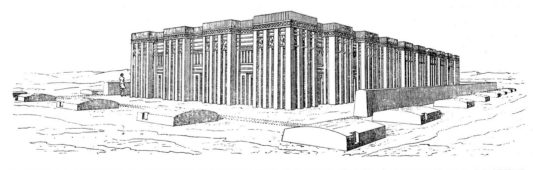

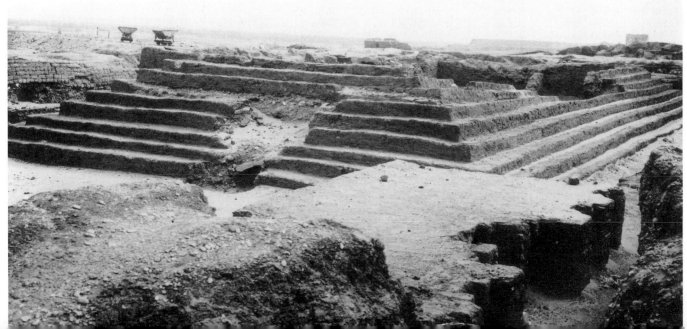

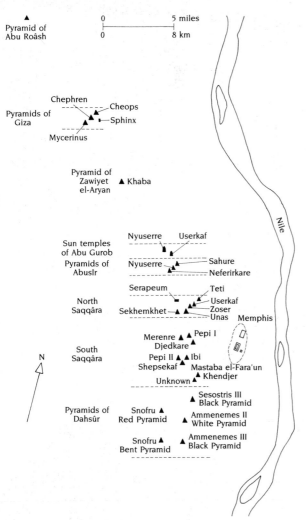

Pyramid of
Abu Roâsh

0 ___ 5 miles
0 ___ 8 km

Chephren
Pyramids of
Giza — Cheops
Sphinx
Mycerinus

Pyramid of
Zawiyet ▲ Khaba
el-Aryan

Sun temples
of Abu Gurob
Pyramids of
Abusîr

Nyuserre   Userkaf

Nyuserre — Sahure
Neferirkare

Serapeum   Teti
North   Userkaf
Saqqâra   Sekhemkhet — Zoser
Unas   Memphis

Merenre ▲ ▲ Pepi I
Djedkare ▲
South   Pepi II ▲ ▲ Ibi
Saqqâra   Shepsekaf ▲ Mastaba el-Fara'un
▲ Khendjer
Unknown ▲

Sesostris III
▲ Black Pyramid

Pyramids of
Dahsûr   Snofru ▲   Ammenemes II
Red Pyramid   ▲ White Pyramid

Snofru ▲   ▲ Ammenemes III
Bent Pyramid   Black Pyramid

N

Nile

Old and Middle Kingdoms

The proliferation of pyramids from Dynasties III to XII is illustrated in Figure **3.34**. The time period encompasses the Old and Middle Kingdoms, and the illustration shows the geographic relationship of these important burial places. Perhaps the most notable of the pyramids before the great building spree of Dynasty IV, which we noted in the introduction to this chapter, is that of King Zoser at Saqqara (Figs. **3.35** and **3.36**). As we can see, a number of smaller buildings surround the pyramid, all of which are enclosed in a walled enclave. These buildings include temples, chapels, and palaces, which were used by the king on various festival occasions. This complex appears to have been built using the predominant technique of mud brick construction, in which bundles of reeds were used for wall supports along with wooden logs, and wooden beams served as ceiling supports.

It was Dynasty IV, however, that gave us the most remarkable edifices of Egyptian civilization, whose images come to mind whenever we think of Egypt—the pyramid area of Giza (Fig. **3.38**). In addition to the three most obvious pyramids, the area comprises burial places for almost all of the important individuals of Dynasties IV and V. Each pyramid complex has four buildings. The largest pyramid, that of Cheops (Fig. **3.4**) measures approximately 750 feet square (440 cubits) and rises at an angle of approximately fifty-one degrees to a height of

3.34 The location of pyramids in the lower Nile Valley, Dynasties III to XII.

3.35 The Tomb Complex of King Zoser at Saqqara, Egypt, Dynasty III (2780–2680 BC).

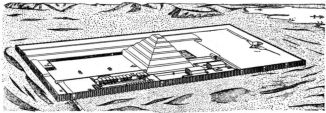

3.36 Plan of the area of the tomb of King Zoser at Saqqara, Egypt, Dynasty III (2780–2680 BC).

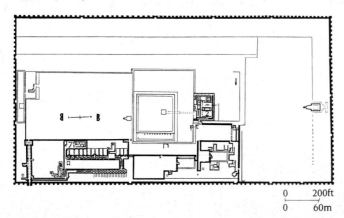

0 ___ 200ft
0 ___ 60m

3.37 Plan of the Giza pyramid complex.

3.38 (Opposite) The Sphinx, Giza, Egypt, c.2650 BC.

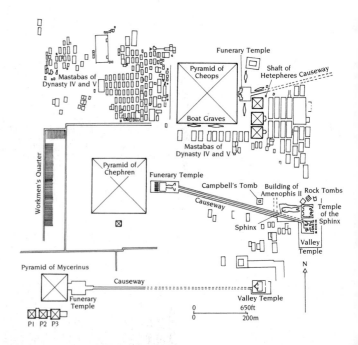

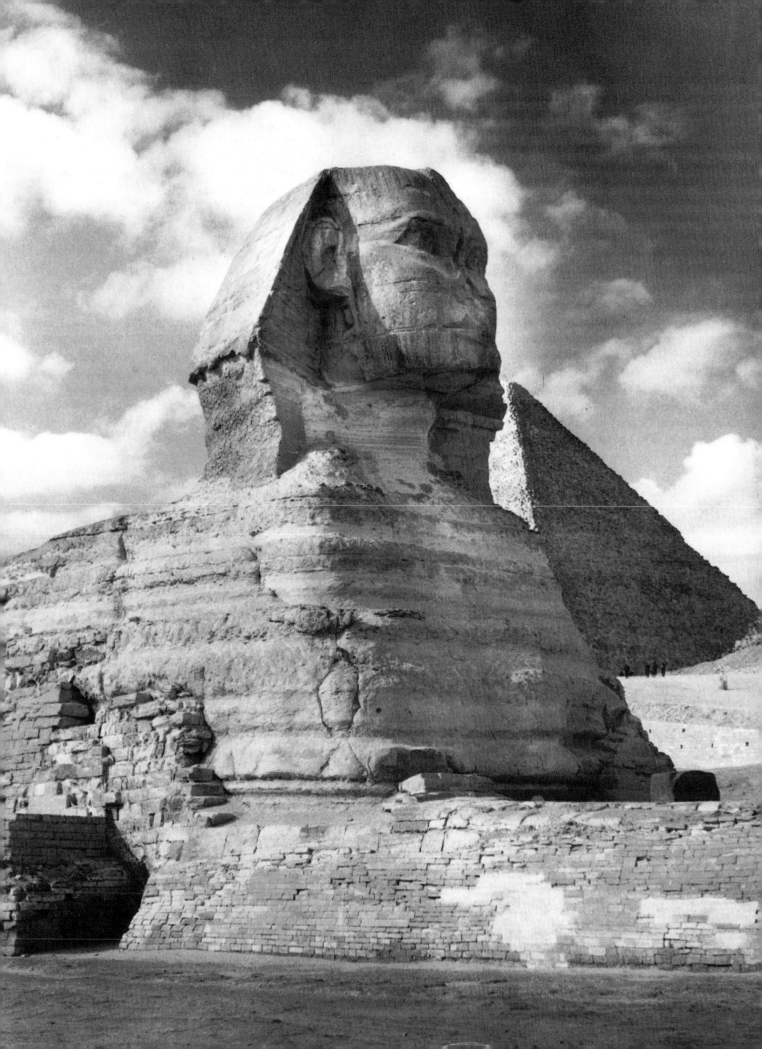

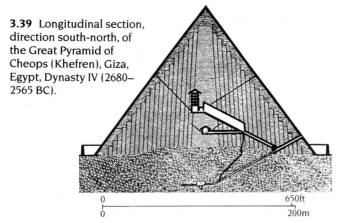

3.39 Longitudinal section, direction south-north, of the Great Pyramid of Cheops (Khefren), Giza, Egypt, Dynasty IV (2680–2565 BC).

481 feet. The burial chamber of the king lay hidden in the middle of the pyramid (Fig. **3.39**). Construction consisted of irregularly placed, rough-hewn stone blocks covered by a carefully dressed limestone facing approximately seventeen feet thick. The famous Sphinx (Fig. **3.37**) lies at the head of the causeway leading from the funerary temple adjoining the pyramid of Cheops' son Chephren, whose pyramid originally measured 707 feet square, and rose at an angle of fifty-two degrees to a height of 471 feet.

New Kingdom

Leaving the pyramids behind, we move to Dynasty XVIII and a building of great luxury and splendor—the Temple at Luxor (Fig. **3.41**). It approaches more nearly our conception of architecture as a useful place for mankind to spend the present rather than eternity. Built by Amenhotep III the temple is dedicated to Amun, Mut, and Chons. Known for his diplomacy, Amenhotep III was a great builder. His taste for splendid buildings drew sustenance from a number of architects, who appear to have been the best Egypt had produced since the time of

Sesostris. Notable among these was Athribis whose likeness at age eighty is preserved in a magnificent statue. We can tell from the statue that Athribis had retained his intellectual and physical abilities to that age, and that he hoped and expected to reach the age of one hundred ten, which the Egyptians considered to be the natural human life span.

Amenhotep III removed all traces of the Middle Kingdom at Luxor, erecting in their place the magnificent Temple. The pylon, obelisk, and first courtyard were added by Ramesses II. In the time of Dynasty XVIII we would have entered the temple through a vestibule comprising giant pillars with palmiform capitals (Fig. **3.40**). From the vestibule we would have progressed to a huge courtyard surrounded by bunched columns, followed by the hypostyle room, and the Holy of Holies. The temple served two purposes. First, it was the place of worship for the Theban Triad of Amun, Mut, and Chons. Second, during the great feast of the middle of the flood, the barques of Amun, Mut, and Chons were anchored there for several days. We cannot escape the loveliness of the columns. The balance between the open spaces and the mass of the columns creates a beautiful play of light and shade. We can get a feel for the proportions of the great Temple of Luxor when we realize that the seven pairs of central pillars in the Hall of Pillars stand nearly fifty-two feet tall. Surviving the centuries, the temple grew by the addition of a forecourt by Ramesses II. The inner sanctuary served as a sanctuary for Alexander the Great, and in the early Christian period it was used as a Christian church.

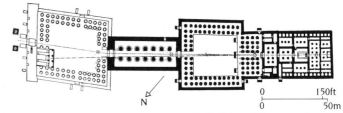

3.40 Plan of the temple at Luxor.

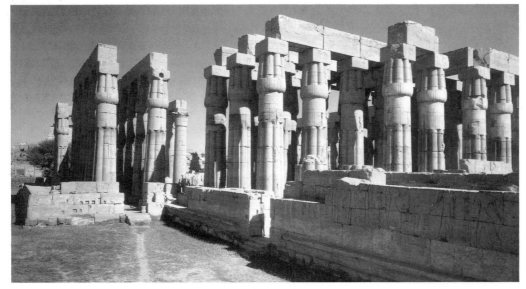

3.41 The temple at Luxor, Egypt, 1417–1397 BC.

SYNTHESIS
Akhenaton and monotheism: The Tell el Amarna period

As we examine the works of Egyptian art in this chapter it becomes clear that the reign of Akhenaton marked a break in the continuity of artistic style. The stiff poses disappear and a more natural form of representation replaces them. The Pharaoh, moreover, is depicted in intimate scenes of domestic life rather than in the formal ritual or military acts which were traditional and expected. The Pharaoh is no longer seen associating with the traditional gods of Egypt. Rather, he and his queen are depicted worshipping the disc of the sun, whose rays end in hands that either bless the royal pair or hold to their nostrils the *ankh*, the symbol of life.

What accounts for this revolution in the Egyptian tradition is not certain, but some evidence suggests that the priesthood of Heliopolis, the ancient seat of the sun cult, had sought to re-establish the primacy of their god.

Amenhotep IV, as Akhenaton was called before changing his name to reflect his god, was himself unusual. He possessed a "strange genius" for religious experience and its expression. Depictions of him also show that he apparently suffered from physical deformity. The realistic trends of the period and Akhenaton's desire for truth seem to have resulted in graphic representation of this abnormality. He is depicted as a man with a misshapen body, an elongated head and drooping jaw. Yet, the eyes are deep and penetrative. The effect is one of a brooding genius.

In a hymn of praise to Aton, thought to have been written by the king, Akhenaton exhibits a spirit of deep joy and devotion to the deity. In it we glimpse an Akhenaton of sensitive character, lyrical in his descriptions of the reactions of the earth and humankind to the rising and setting of the sun. Akhenaton's vision is universal—Aton is not merely a god of Egypt, but of all humankind, and Akhenaton is the sole mediator between the two.

In the fifth or sixth year of the reign of Akhenaton, the

3.42 Plan of the excavated areas of Tell El Amarna, Egypt.

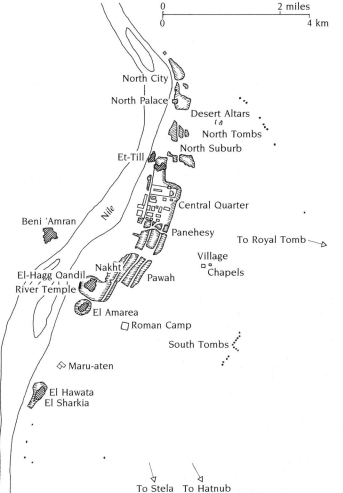

3.43 Plan of the North Palace, Amarna, Egypt, Dynasty XVIII (1570–1314 BC).

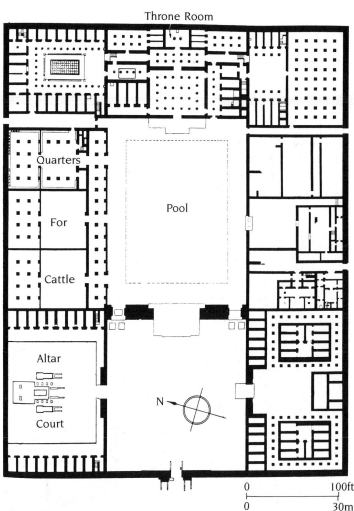

king moved his court to a sandy desert ground on the east side of the Nile to the newly constructed city of Tell el Amarna (Fig. **3.42**).

It was a new city for a new king intent on establishing a new order based on a new religion. Because Akhenaton's movement failed and the city was abandoned, we are left with an encapsulated artistic synthesis including the city itself. Tell el Amarna lay away from cultivated land, and once abandoned was never built over.

The town itself is dominated by the large estates of the wealthy, who chose the best sites and laid them out in the style of the Egyptian country house with large gardens and numerous out-buildings. The entire estate was enclosed within a wall. In between these large estates lay the smaller dwellings of the less wealthy. The new city was complete, it seems, with even a slum area which stood outside the northern suburb. Near this slum area was the grand North Palace (Fig. **3.43**).

Several characteristics can be identified in the architecture of Tell el Amarna. In many ways Amarna reflects the regular features of New Kingdom domestic architecture, but seems much less sumptuous in comparison. Its lines and style seem relatively simple. Structures are open, in contrast to the dark and secret character of the Temple of Luxor, for example. At Amarna numerous unroofed areas lead to the altar of the god, Aton, left open to provide access to the rays of his sun.

The originality of many of the structural details of Amarna architecture is also striking. The plant ornamentation of the columns served as a prototype for later Roman architecture (Fig. **3.44**). The palm column seems to have been especially favored, and the stone version

has a certain stoutness or heaviness which typifies Egyptian architecture. Also popular at Amarna were papyrus-bundle columns with capitals of clustered, open flowers, sometimes made of alabaster inlaid with blue paste. Even most original are the kiosk-like structures carved to display convolvulus vines. Everything was richly colored, including the palace walls which dazzled with colored glazed tiles and painted stone reliefs. The entire city must have shimmered in the sunlight of Akhenaton's single god, the god of the sun, Aton.

In the wall paintings and relief sculptures we find a significant difference in the conventions of body proportions compared with those of the other periods. In the Old, Middle, and early New Kingdom, head and body proportions seem to be close to a 1:8 ratio. As Murray points out, the total figure then becomes nine head lengths from top to bottom.[10] At Tell el Amarna the proportion is seven to eight head lengths. The head, therefore, becomes larger. Body proportions are also different at Amarna. Arms are thinner and hands are larger. Emphasis appears to fall on the abdominal and pelvic areas, in contrast to earlier periods wherein focus lay on the shoulders and upper torso.

Painting was confined to the walls and floors of palaces and, in contrast to other periods, did not appear in tombs. Plant and animal life were abundantly and colorfully portrayed in painting as in architecture. In Figure **3.45** we find a new approach to plants in decorative motifs and animals in rapid motion. Papyrus plants bend in the wind and a kingfisher swoops toward a pond. Delicate detailing complements a wide palette including the complete range from reds to blues. In contrast to the stark single value treatment of colors we noted earlier, value changes occur here within the same hue. So the color areas have texture and variety. The water ripples subtly and the papyrus reeds come alive with variegated mixtures of green and blue. Other wall paintings display a sense of three-dimensionality, and we see highlight and shadow in figure depiction. Plasticity in the painted human form is rudimentary and yet clearly original to the Amarna period.

As with painting, sculpture at Amarna represented a departure from tradition. It became more a form of secular art with less emphasis, apparently, on sculpture for tombs and temples. Perhaps as a result of the king's religious fervor, the Amarna sculptor seems to have sought to represent the uniqueness and individuality of humankind through the human face. In one sense Amarna sculpture is highly naturalistic, and yet, in another, departs from the merely natural into the realm of the spiritual. The bust of Queen Nofretete illustrates these characteristics (Fig. **3.46**). The statue of Akhenaton shown in Figure **3.47** depicts the king as the curious physical

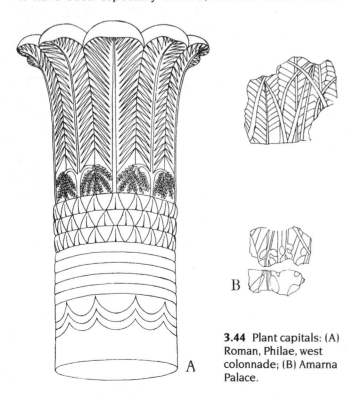

3.44 Plant capitals: (A) Roman, Philae, west colonnade; (B) Amarna Palace.

3.45 Kingfisher in papyrus marsh, c.1350–1334 BC. Wall painting, detail 25¼ ins (64 cm) × 19¼ ins (49 cm). The Oriental Institute, University of Chicago.

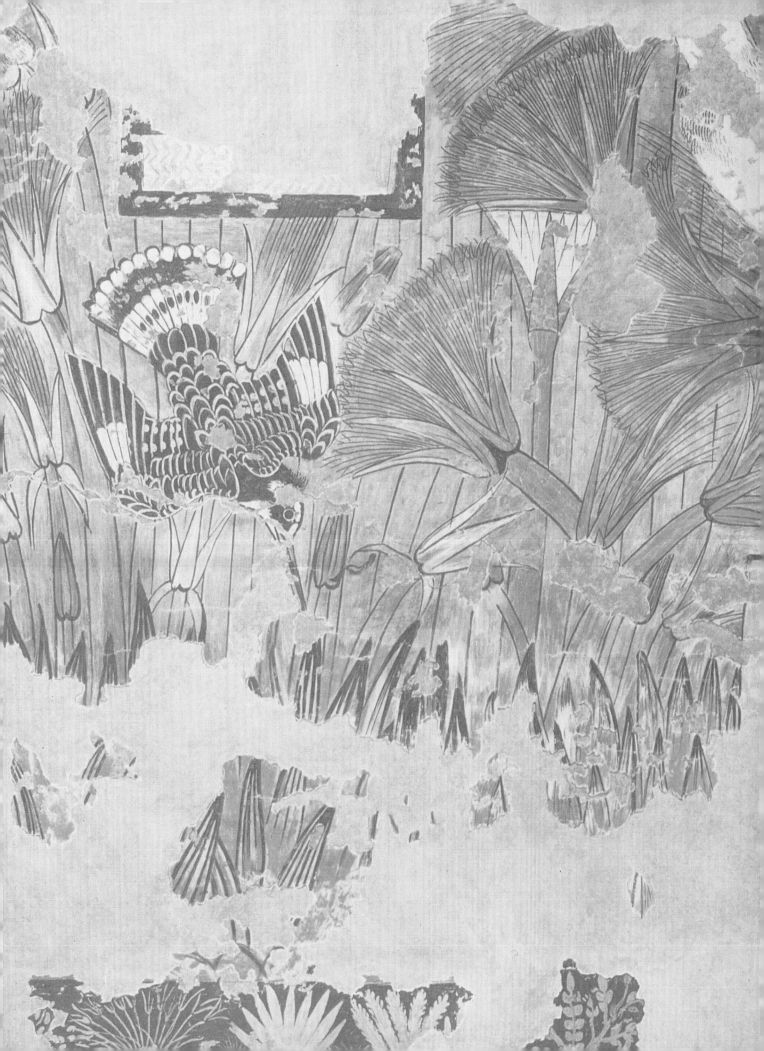

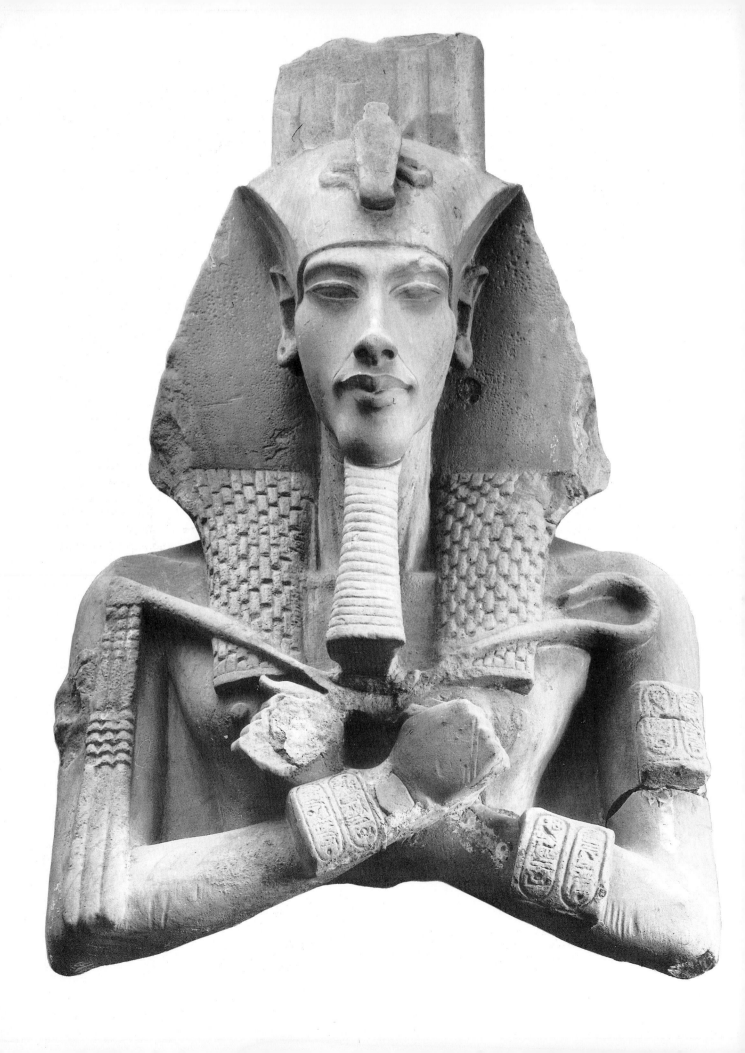

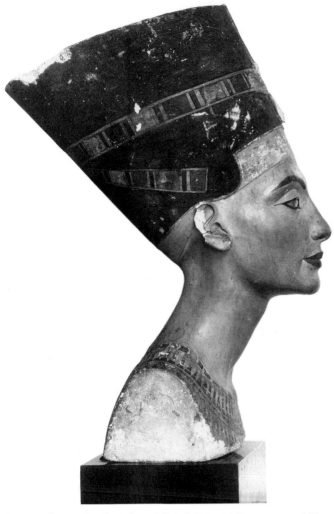

3.46 Nofretete (Nefertiti), c.1360 BC. Painted limestone, c.19 ins (48 cm) high. Egyptian Museum, Berlin.

entity we noted earlier, and yet the stylism of the approach seems clear, as is the change of focus from upper torso to abdomen.

Isolated from other periods by geographical and religious circumstance, the Tell el Amarna period brings us a complete and vivid encapsulation of artistic inter-relationships centered on a philosophical and religious concept. The religious reforms of Akhenaton were doomed to failure. What some scholars have labeled as an Egyptian experiment in monotheism has, nonetheless, left us with a clear portrait of an integrated scheme of life and culture.

3.47 King Amenophis IV, later Akhenaton, from a pillar statue in the temple of Aton near the temple of Amun at Karnak, 1364–1347 BC. Sandstone, 13 ft (396.5 cm) high. Egyptian Museum, Cairo.

SUGGESTIONS FOR THOUGHT AND DISCUSSION

Inasmuch as most extant examples of Egyptian records, including art and architecture, relate to funerary matters, we must assume that Egyptian civilization was hierarchical, with the Pharaoh at the top acting as the singular access to what appears to have been the focus of earthly life, that is, life after death. The remains of Tell el Amarna illustrate that not all art was temple or tomb art, but whether the art of Tell el Amarna was unique in the way that its artistic style and religion were is not certain. Nonetheless, as we found in Mesopotamian art, certain conventions and characteristics of Egyptian art held relatively constant over thousands of years, and give the label "Egyptian" meaning. Variations among the Pre-dynastic, Old, Middle, and New Kingdoms, and the Tell el Amarna period, also yield to stylistic identification. Once we accommodate and understand the conventions of Egyptian art and its variations, we can pull together religion, politics, and art into a fairly complete picture of this remarkable and long-lived civilization.

■ What relationships can be seen between pharaonic power and image and art and architecture in the various periods?

■ How does the concept of divine rule compare in Egypt with that of Mesopotamia?

■ What evidence suggests an early and strong Egyptian influence and presence in the eastern Mediterranean area?

■ How do the tomb paintings of various dynasties reflect the general social outlook of the times? How does the portrayal of domestic life and objects change over time?

■ How did conventions in painting and sculpture compare and how did they change from the Old to the Middle and New Kingdoms? Which conventions stayed the same?

■ How did the reign of Akhenaton affect artistic style and other cultural and religious developments?

■ Discuss the assumption that theatre and dramatic ritual are different concepts.

■ What conclusions about lifestyle can be drawn from the musical instruments of Egypt and the layout of Egyptian homes as seen in Tell el Amarna and the Tomb of Sennufer?

CHAPTER FOUR
THE GREEKS

Under the ruler Pericles, Classical Greek culture reached its miraculous zenith. To that civilization and its works Western culture has returned for nourishment for over two thousand years. In the brief span of time between approximately 600BC and 200BC Greek influence and civilization spread throughout the Mediterranean world until, under Alexander the Great, it stretched—for the space of a single lifetime—from Spain to the Indus. All this was achieved by a people whose culture, at its height, took as its measure the human intellect. In society as in the arts, rationality, clarity and beauty of form were the aim; although as the style we call Hellenistic developed in the fourth century BC, artists increasingly sought to imbue their works with the expression of feeling. Plato and Aristotle meanwhile explored complementary paths to an understanding of reality and the possibility of its representation.

4.1 The Parthenon, Athens, 447–438 BC.

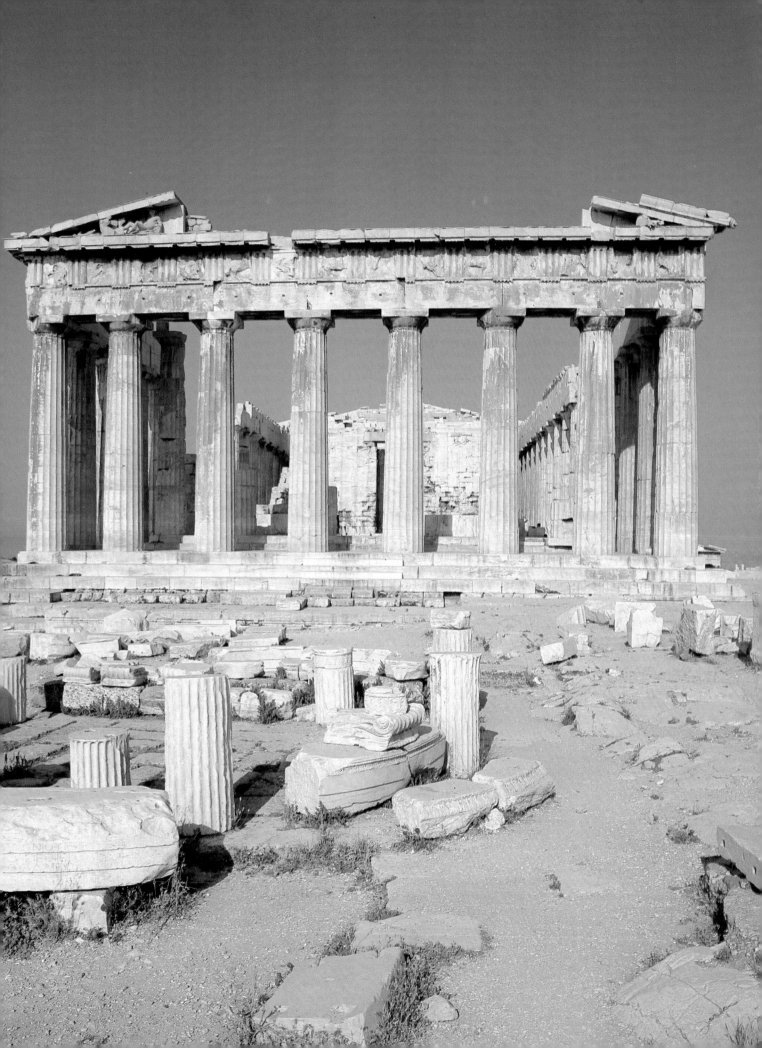

CONTEXTS AND CONCEPTS

Aegean civilizations

For the very beginnings of Western culture that we know today, we must look to the area of the Aegean Sea, a part of the Mediterranean stretching from the island of Crete to Asia Minor. Two civilizations draw our attention briefly as we move towards the cradle of Western culture, ancient Greece—the Minoan and Mycenaean civilizations. Around 3000 BC on the island of Crete small towns began expanding into large urban centers, and Minoan civilization emerged, so called after the legendary King Minos. The best known of the urban centers of Minoan civilization is Knossos. Others included Phaistos, Mallia, and Zakro. Not much is known about the Minoans, but we can tell from the ruins of their palaces and their wall paintings that they were rich and adventurous. They depended upon their naval power for defense, and their palaces were not fortified. Minoan palaces were elaborate complexes. The Palace of Minos at Knossos supposedly contained the mythical labyrinth of the Minotaur. Around the palace were located the private homes of the aristocracy and religious leaders. The wall paintings of the Minoans display a spontaneous quality and a deep love of nature. The color is brilliant and the scenes of nature are accurately observed.

Minoan influence on the later Mycenaean civilization is evident. The Mycenaeans were early Greek tribesmen who inhabited the south-eastern coastline of mainland Greece. The central city of Mycenae boasted a great palace complex. From approximately 1400 to 1200 BC Mycenaean traders travelled throughout the Mediterranean. By the fourteenth century BC they had become the rulers of Crete, supplanting the Minoans. Shortly after 1200 BC the Mycenaean civilization mysteriously collapsed, in spite of its great defenses and massively fortified palaces. Mycenaean culture as seen in its fortifications, some with walls fifteen feet thick and fifty feet high, was war-like, and yet their wall paintings were lively and much like those of the Minoans.

The Hellenes

According to early Greek historians, civilization flourished on the Greek islands and peninsula in the eighth century BC. They recorded the year 776 BC as the date of the first Olympic games and counted forward from that date as we now count forward from the birth of Christ. Primary among the factors which united the different peoples of this area—the Ionians, Dorians, and Aculians—was a common language. The language was old, but its written form had only recently developed. The earliest surviving Greek written characters are found on a jug dating to 725 BC. The characters appear to be an adaptation of Phoenician script, an example of one of the many outside influences, especially Asian, which helped to shape Greek culture, destined to become the cornerstone of all Western culture. Central to Greek civilization were the Athenians, citizens of the city-state of Athens, and part of the group of Greeks who called themselves Ionians.

Athenian culture grew from complex inter-relationships of politics, philosophy, religion, geography, and economics, and from previous civilizations in the Mediterranean world, including Egypt. The ancient Greeks pointed with pride to some of the external roots of their culture. Athens shared a common heritage and religion with many independent city-states in the region. The people of these city-states called themselves Hellenes, and the development of their civilization was partly influenced by two geographic factors. One was the mountainous terrain of the Peloponnesian peninsula and surrounding areas, which kept the city-states isolated from each other and which kept their confederations rather loosely organized. The other was the Aegean Sea, which provided an open highway for trade and commerce with the entire Mediterranean world. The seaport of Athens was particularly well positioned to benefit from these factors.

War and victory hurled Athens into its Golden Age and spawned a revitalized culture. Early in the fifth century BC the Persians under Xerxes I threatened conquest of the Greek peninsula. In 480 BC the Persians occupied Athens whose citizens had evacuated and destroyed it. The Greeks retaliated and within a year they had defeated the Persian fleet at Salamis and driven out the Persian armies. Claiming to be the saviors of Greece, the Athenians set about liberating the rest of Greece. Several city-states banded together with Athens to form the Delian League in 478 BC. The League took its name from Delos, the Ionian island shrine of Apollo, where it met and stored its money. Sanctuaries were always chosen for treasuries so that the god would always be on guard. The states made a contract and the signatories agreed to follow a common foreign policy and to contribute ships and/or money, as Athens deemed necessary. Athens contributed the most money and commanded the fleet. What followed was a systematic liberation of the Greek cities around the Aegean, and the conquest of some islands populated by non-Greeks. The Delian League became, in fact, a highly prosperous Athenian Empire.

The destruction of Athens, the victory over the Persians and the formation of the Delian League were three significant events in the transformation of the young democracy of Athens with her thriving commerce, unique religion, and inquisitive philosophies, into a culture of immense artistic achievement. The ruined city had to be rebuilt; a spirit of victory and heroics prevailed; the Delian treasury, moved to Athens by Pericles, was available to help finance the immense costs of artistic and reconstruction enterprises.

Athens had witnessed a succession of rulers and a fascinating form of democracy had gradually emerged. Historians estimate that when Pericles came to power in 461 BC the population of Athens was approximately 230,000 people. Approximately 40,000 were free male citizens; 40,000 were Athenian women; 50,000 were foreign born; and 100,000 were slaves. In Athenian democracy, however, only free male citizens were allowed to vote, and the Tyrant, or ruler, wielded considerable power. This power emanated principally from ownership of land. They owned estates which provided not only for their individual welfare, but also for the horses and arms necessary to make them leaders in warfare. Nonetheless, the central factor in Greek politics remained the concept and sanctity of the *polis* or city. More than an organized conglomeration of people, the polis was a community, a body of men aware of the interests of the community as opposed to individual interest. The word tyrant did not assume negative connotations until much later. In fact, the Greek tyrants seem to have been especially benevolent. They were not necessarily of the aristocracy, and their claim to leadership was based on their popularity among the citizens.

By the fifth century BC Athens was the richest of the Greek city-states. Greek laws had been reformed by the great lawmaker, Solon. After 508 BC constitutional changes created a complex of institutions which became the foundations of an almost pure form of democracy. All political decisions were made, in principle at least, by a majority vote of the ingeniously organized citizenry.

Conditions were right for a golden age of culture. By historical standards the Golden Age of Athens was very brief, indeed, less than three-quarters of a century. However, that fifth century BC was one of the most significant periods in Western civilization.

If war and victory ushered in the Golden Age of Athens, war and defeat brought that age to a close: it began to crumble with the onset of the Peloponnesian Wars between Athens and the rival city-state of Sparta, in the middle of the century. Although the Athenians showed military skill in the defeat of the Persians early in the fifth century BC, theirs was not a militaristic society. What they accomplished in the arts they lacked in judgement in pursuing military strategy. Through what appears from our vantage point to be a series of blunders, Pericles led Athens toward defeat in a war of attrition with their Spartan adversaries. As Athenian glory waned, an increasing attitude of realism or naturalism grew. The heroics of victory and idealism turned into the reality of defeat. This change in outlook or attitude marked a change in style in the arts as well.

However, although Sparta commanded political dominance, it did not assume a cultural leadership. Spartan society was a rigorous, militaristic, and uncultured one. In fact, the term spartan denotes conditions of austerity, self-discipline, political rigidity, and general fortitude—conditions basic to Sparta and its values. Therefore, Athenian impetus and influence in things aesthetic were not superseded by Sparta and continued to flourish despite their diminished role as a political power.

During the late fifth and early fourth centuries, a new and more powerful Athenian middle class arose. The stinging wounds of defeat, the rational Sophistic philosophy of the middle class, the sup-

BC		GENERAL EVENTS	LITERATURE & PHILOSOPHY	VISUAL ART	THEATRE & DANCE	MUSIC	ARCHITECTURE
1230	Geometric Period	Destruction of Troy					
800		First Olympic Games First surviving Greek writing	Homer Hesiod	Dipylon vase (4.6)			
700			Ionian Poets Herodotus Thucydides				
600	Archaic Period		Sappho of Lesbos Pythagoras	Kouros figure (4.13) Black and red figured vases Archaic style Nessos Painter Gorgon Painter Kleitias Lydos	Choric dance festivals Dithyrambs Tragic contests begin		
500	Classical Period	Persian occupation Delian league Pericles Golden Age of Athens	Sophistry Protagoras Socrates Plato	Classic Style Makron Douris Myron Polyclitus Achilles Painter Kritios (4.16) Parthenon Sculptures	Aeschylus Second Actor added by Aeschylus Theatre of Dionysos Sophocles Euripides Aristophanes		Parthenon (4.31) Halicarnassus Temple of Athena Nike (4.34)
400		Alexander the Great	Aristotle	Suessula Painter Praxiteles Lysippos	Theatre at Epidaurus		
300	Hellenistic Period		Theocritus Epigrams	Dying Gaul (4.22) Winged Victory of Samothrace (4.23)			
200			Apollonius Rhodius	Laocöon Group (4.24)			Temple of the Olympian Zeus (4.35)
100							

4.2 Timeline of Ancient Greek culture.

planting of Plato's absolute ideas by Aristotle's search for the essence of things in the nature of things themselves, dominated Athenian thought. Idealism and intellectualism gradually gave way to emotionalism.

Religion

The Greek mind was an earthy one, and Greek thought and religion centered on this life. An ancient Greek often directed his view toward the constellations, but his universe counted "Man as the measure of all things".

The basis of Greek religion was a large family of Olympian gods of superhuman qualities. Their mythical history had been traced by the poet Homer in the *Iliad*. Greek religion had no scriptures or holy books, even though the Greeks were highly literate; but the stories of the gods were well known through oral tradition and through books such as Hesiod's *Theogony*. The Olympian gods dwelt on the mythical (and also real) Mt. Olympus and were descended from Uranus, representing the heavens, and Gaia,

representing the earth. The struggles and genealogies of these deities were the subject of numerous and varied myths which, although central to Greek religion, were nevertheless confusing and to some degree confused. In addition to the central family of gods, the Greeks worshiped local deities who were thought to preside over certain human activities and to protect various geographical features such as streams and forests. Gods had individual human form and, sometimes, very human characteristics.

Zeus, king of the Greek gods, is portrayed as a well-intentioned but bumbling and self-indulgent amorist. Aphrodite, the goddess of love and fertility, wears her femininity and accompanying vanities and preferences like an ordinary mortal. Unlike the religions of Egypt and the East and Near East, Greek mythology and art usually represented the gods in human terms, sometimes better but sometimes worse. The differences in approach to, for example, the monsters of Assyria and Babylonia, constituted a radical departure from earlier religious thought. The implication was clear—humans could be god-like. The Greek supernatural provided for an intimacy between the gods and their human counterparts. Life on earth was very similar to that of the gods.

Humanism and intellectualism

The emphasis on human rationality and the intellect that characterized fifth-century Greek thought did not preclude a profound respect for the irrational and the mysterious. The Greeks recognized such agencies as oracles and omens. The shrines of the Oracle of Apollo at Delphi and at Didyma were the objects of pilgrimage and the source of respected, if not always lucid, advice. Numerous religious cults celebrated the cycle of the seasons and the implied fertility references with mysterious and secret rites. Greek dance and drama developed from these cults, and the supernatural and darker forces of human irrationality lie close to the heart of even the great classical tragedies.

Philosophy was an important discipline in Greek culture. A keen mind and a desire to answer life's critical questions were noble qualities. In the years prior to the zenith of Athenian civilization under Pericles, philosophers such as Thales, Anaximander, and Heracleitus had great influence. They wrestled with questions such as, "What is the basic element of which the universe is composed?" (Water); "How do specific things emerge from the basic elements?" (By "separating out."); "What guides the process of change?" (The universe is in a process of flow. Nothing *is*; everything is *becoming*.) The most important philosopher in Periclean Athens was Pythagoras. In his search for reality Pythagoras concluded that mathematical relationships were universal. His deduction and postulation of what we call the *Pythagorean theorem* illustrates his viewpoint: "The square of the hypotenuse of a right angled triangle equals the sum of the squares of the opposite two sides." Pythagoras saw this as a

4.3 Ancient Greece and the Eastern Mediterranean.

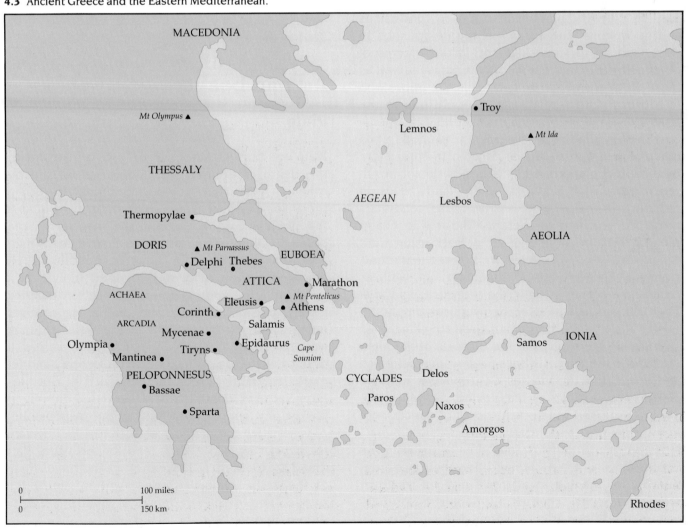

universal constant, a concept applicable to all circumstances. He differed from other philosophers in that his universe was constant, with a single reality existing apart from substance, whereas others imagined a universe based on a single physical element and constantly in a state of change. He also saw mathematics as fundamental to all life, including the arts.

Sophistry: The distrust of reason

"Man as the measure of all things"

The middle of the fifth century BC saw a skeptical reaction to previously constructive activity. The constructive cycle had ended and a period of criticism and turmoil was at hand. All established beliefs and standards, whether religious, moral, or scientific, came under fire. Reason, it was argued, had led only to diametrically opposed conclusions and deceptions. The agonies of the Peloponnesian Wars, and an awareness of the value systems of other cultures, which seemed to work just as well as those of Athens, gave rise to a realism in opposition to idealism, and a relativism in opposition to the absoluteness of the views previously held in Athens.

The formulation of skepticism emanated from a group of men whose star was rising in an Athens torn by disputation and ruled by a form of democracy in which persuasion and practicality made skills in debating an absolute necessity. These conditions produced teachers of rhetoric. Those who championed this new utilitarian art of persuasion were called sophists or wise ones. Well versed in rhetoric, grammar, diction, logical argument, as well as behind-the-scenes intrigue, the sophists taught well. They charged high fees for their services, an unethical act according to traditional Greek thinking.

Placing themselves at the disposal of the highest bidder, the Sophists became servants of the rich and enemies of the masses. Conservative Athenian elders were aghast at the manner in which the Sophists seemed to infect the youth of the city with irony, cynicism, and foreign "broad-mindedness". Most of the Sophists were non-Athenians. The Sophists were often indicted for their apparent purpose of winning at all costs and by whatever means, although whether all Sophists were unscrupulous is a matter of some debate. Certainly

Protagoras and Gorgias, the two great sophistic philosophers escaped such charges, although their approach to morality appears to deal more with external appearance than with belief. Virtue, morality and truth were relative to circumstance.

Protagoras, in his treatise *On the Gods* indicates that man "cannot feel sure that they [the gods] are, or that they are not, nor what they are like in figure, for there are many things that hinder sure knowledge, the obscurity of the subject and the shortness of human life." Such religious doubt is amplified into a denial of any absolute truths. "Man is the measure of all things, of things that are that they are, and of things that are not that they are not." That is, truth is absolutely relative and subjective. What appears true to any given man at any given moment is true, and vice versa. What appears as real is real so far as any one person is concerned, and vice versa. There is no means of measuring one man's truth against another's. Protagoras, apparently, was returning to Heraclitean teaching. Everything was in flux. However, it was Plato and Aristotle who laid the philosophical base of classical Greece, especially in the field of the arts.

Art and beauty

Plato

Plato was born in Athens in 427 BC, two years after the death of Pericles. His family was of the old Athenian aristocracy. He grew up during the years of the Peloponnesian Wars, which brought an end to the Athenian empire. Escaping the financial ruin that befell many Athenian aristocrats, Plato's family managed to give him the best of educations. He emerged a thoroughly well-rounded individual, a good athlete, and with experience of painting, poetry, music, literature, and drama. He received military training and fought in the wars. Although well suited and well connected for a career in politics, Plato turned instead to philosophy and fell more and more under the influence of Socrates. After Socrates' death Plato concentrated entirely on philosophy, and took on himself the responsibility of vindicating the memory of Socrates. Anti-Socratic feeling ran high in Athens, and for ten years Plato found it expedient to leave the city and travel. Many of the early "dialogues" were written during this period, and we learn much of Plato's aesthetic theory from the Socratic dialogues.

Plato founded philosophical aesthetics. Western thought has been profoundly influenced by the metaphysics of Plato's dialogues, in which the basic problems of the philosophy of art are laid out, explored, and resolved. Although not systematic and somewhat tentative, Plato's writings constitute a clear philosophy of art and beauty.

For Plato art derived primarily from the skill of knowing and making or *techne*. *Techne* was the ability of an artist to be in command of a medium, to know what the end result will be, and to know how to execute the artwork to achieve that result. The fundamental principles of *techne* were measurement and proportion. Standards of taste—the good and the beautiful—cannot be achieved unless the work is correct in proportion and measure. In *Statesman*, the young Socrates and a stranger discourse upon the nature of proportion and the mean, to which the stranger asserts,

> ...we shall some day require the notion of a mean with a view to the demonstration of absolute truth; meanwhile, the argument that the very existence of the arts must be held to depend on the possibility of measuring more or less, not only with one another, but also with a view to the attainment of the mean, seems to afford a grand support and satisfactory proof of the doctrine which we are maintaining; for if there are arts, there is a standard of measure, and if there is a standard of measure, there are arts; but if either is wanting, there is neither.

Plato's theory of beauty and art went on to focus on the concept of imitation. The artist imitates the Ideal which exists even beyond the universe, because the universe itself is only an imitation of Ideas or unchanging Forms. This point is crucial to all of Platonic thought. The nature of Platonic Ideas or Forms poses many dilemmas and questions for any student of Plato. To simplify a complex notion, Ideas or Forms are reality. Everything earthly is an imitation of reality. Ideas are not thoughts of either the individual mind or the divine mind—they exist independently of whether and what we think of them. Forms are the objects of thought. The arts are practiced as imitations of Ideas or Forms, but this becomes problematical for Plato because the individual artist may fail to know the ultimate reality, and may present instead merely an "appearance of perceivable nature". The arts, especially drama, which Plato mistrusted greatly, must therefore fall under the critical view of the statesman, who "envisages the human community according to the Ideas of

justice, the good, courage, temperance, and the beautiful".[1] What is proper as imitation depends upon the "moral ends of the polis".

Possession of *techne* and ability to imitate Ideas were dependent on a third quality—artistic inspiration. An artist cannot ascend to the highest levels of artistry without divine inspiration and assistance. Plato equates artistry with a form of madness which "relates men to the gods and to the beauty of the eternal realm they inhabit".[2]

Aristotle

Born in 384 BC Aristotle did not share by birth the golden opportunities of Plato. Aristotle's family was middle class, and his father was court physician to Amyntas of Macedon, grandfather of Alexander the Great. Left an orphan while still young, Aristotle gained a new home and an education through the generosity of a family friend. At eighteen he became a student at Plato's academy. Apparently his affectations and narcissism were the cause of some difficulties with the school's authorities. After Plato's death Aristotle left the Academy and married. Around 343 BC he obtained a very favorable position, that of tutor to Alexander the Great. Aristotle sought to teach Alexander to revere all things Greek and despise anything barbarian, that is, non-Hellene. When Alexander acceded to the throne in 336 BC, Aristotle returned to Athens to set up his own school, the Lyceum. Over the next twelve years came a prolific outpouring of writings as well as research in physics, astronomy, biology, physiology, anatomy, natural history, psychology, politics, ethics, logic, rhetoric, art, theology, and metaphysics. Aristotle's "is probably the only human intellect that has ever compassed at first hand and assimilated the whole body of existing knowledge on all subjects, and brought it within a single focus—and a focus, at that, which after more than two thousand years still stands as one of the supreme achievements of the mind of man."[3]

Aristotle's major work on the philosophy of the arts is the *Poetics*. It is not complete, however, and we need to refer to several other writings to complete our understanding. Aristotle's theory differs considerably from Plato's. Aristotle maintains that all the arts imitate nature, and that imitative character is rooted in human psychology. In the *Poetics* we see a philosophy of art focusing on one sort of *techne*. Art is different from nature and from acting. Art is "a capacity to make, concerned with contriving the coming-into-being of ends determined by reason."[4]

Aristotle may be summarized as follows. The end of artistic creating or making determines the appropriate means for its realization. In order to assess excellence of workmanship we must determine whether the artistic work has a perfection of form and a soundness of method, which will make the work a satisfactory whole. Excellence requires that the elements of composition display symmetry, harmony, and definiteness. Plato, in contrast to Artistotle, insists that artistic imitation, especially tragedy, fuels the passions and misleads the seeker of truth. Aristotle responds that the arts repair deficiencies in nature, with tragic drama particularly making a moral contribution, and therefore the arts are valuable and justifiable. In contrast to Plato, Aristotle further depreciates the centrality of beauty and erotic love. Aristotle rejects Plato's metaphysical idealism and treats beauty as a property of the artwork or object, thereby emphasizing the moral benefit of tragedy, whereas for Plato the proper end of art is the inspired search for the Beautiful. He does agree with Plato "that art is a kind of *techne*, that there is a measure and mean appropriate to the exercise of *techne*, and that the most important human arts, such as music, painting, sculpture, literature, are imitative of human souls, bodies and actions."[5]

The purpose of art, however, does not lie in edifying or teaching a moral lesson. The purpose of art is to give pleasure and in the measure by which it gives pleasure, it is to be judged good art. The pleasurable exciting of the emotions and passions purges, lightens, delights, and heals the soul. The highest art does make us think, but if we are to exercise our faculties at their best, it also needs to amuse and relax us. Aristotle further states that the arts are desirable because they provide the lower classes, who are incapable of appreciating the higher arts, with the entertainment and repose to which they are entitled. It is better that they enjoy some kind of art than to be cut off completely from aesthetic pleasure. So Aristotle's aesthetics provide for higher and lower arts, the difference lying in the degree of aesthetic value worked into the material by the artist.

Alexander

In the fourth century a new star was rising to the north, and by the middle of the century King Philip of Macedon had united Greece in an empire. It was to this throne that Alexander the Great came in 336 BC. Under the influence of the Alexandrian or Hellenistic Empire, which stretched from Egypt in the West to the Indus River in the East, civilization and the arts flourished. The influence of Hellenistic art continued for centuries beyond the fall of the Empire to the Romans and carried well into the Christian era.

Alexander's rule began with an expedition to Asia with an army only one fourth of which was Greek. Yet the brilliant twenty-two year old carried Greek (Athenian) culture throughout a wider and expanding world. After reaching Asia, Alexander cut the Gordian knot according to legend, and then defeated the Persian king, Darius III, at the battle of Issus. From there Alexander led his forces against Tyre, Syria, and finally and victoriously on to Egypt where he founded Alexandria, one of the most influential and important cities in the Hellenistic world. A second defeat of Darius and the subsequent sacking of Persepolis led to Alexander's installation as successor to the Persian throne. After pushing as far as the Indus river, Alexander's army refused to go further. Alexander returned to Babylon and died in 323 BC at the age of thirty-two, only ten years after leaving Macedonia.

The Hellenistic period

The success of Alexander's conquests depended to a great extent on his forceful personality, and on his death in 323 BC the Empire began to crumble. Regional fragmentation and struggles for power marked the post-Alexandrian, Mediterranean world. Nevertheless, the creation of so vast an empire fostered an internationalism in culture that persisted and strengthened under the Roman Empire. Commerce flourished and international communication carried Greek thought and artistic influence to all parts of the known world. Intercultural relationships blossomed. Buddhist sculpture in India, for example, showed signs of Greek influence, and the European pantheon of gods reflected a more emotional, Eastern approach. Athens remained an important nucleus for ideas and cultural accomplishments, however weak her commercial and military power may have become.

Alexander's generals divided the empire into kingdoms after his death. By the year 276 BC after a series of wars for supremacy, three prominent local families had established themselves as rulers of the entire Hellenistic world: the Antigonids ruled Macedon, the Ptolemies ruled Egypt, Palestine, Cyrenaica, and Cyprus, and the Seleucids ruled Asia, from Anatolia to Afghanistan. At the same time another power was taking shape and beginning to exert its influence on the Italian peninsula—Rome. Prosperity reigned throughout the Hellenistic world and the riches gleaned from rifling the Persian treasury provided the economic base for ships and farms alike. Standards of living rose appreciably. As often seems to be the case, economic security spawned a cultural revival. Outlooks and styles had changed. The happiness of the individual, viewed as psychological equilibrium, became the basis of a new philosophy. Philosophy came to be a training with this objective in mind. One should strive to live as well as possible, independently of luck and environment.

Cynics, Stoics, and Epicureans

Three schools of thought vied for philosophical supremacy. Led by Diogenes, the Cynics taught that humans are animals and that the good life lay simply in satisfying one's animal needs. Since needs can be troublesome, however, a wise man will have as few as possible and will then disregard any social conventions which stand in the way of his personal satisfaction. The Stoics, founded by Zeno, believed that humankind was an incarnation of reason, which produces and directs the world. The good life was defined as that which follows reason, wisdom and virtue. Awareness of one's own wisdom and virtue allows one, through asceticism, to disregard public opinion, misfortune, and even death. The Epicureans, followers of Epicurus, concluded that human beings consisted of a temporary arrangement of atoms, which dissolved at death. The good life was an untroubled life. Wisdom dictates that one avoid entanglements, maintain good health, tolerate pain, and accept death without fear. The indifference and intellectual arrogance of Hellenistic philosophy provoked a reaction in later times, from which rationalism began to emerge.

The center of Hellenistic culture was Alexandria. At this time it was the greatest city in the world, endowed with phenomenal wealth. Legally it was a Greek city "by" not "in" Egypt. Brilliant writers and new literary forms emerged. The Ptolemies lavished great patronage on science and scholarship. Royal funds paid for buildings, including an enormous library which became the focal point of the Hellenistic intellectual world.

Literature

The heroic ideal of the early years of the first millennium BC found its way into the books of the Old Testament, the Homeric poems, and probably numerous other writings, although these two are our only complete collections. The Homeric epic poems, the *Iliad* and the *Odyssey*, date to the eighth century BC. Both poems deal with minor events of the story of Troy, which was destroyed about 1230 BC. The poems became the basic texts for elementary and secondary education in ancient Greece, and have influenced Western literature ever since.

The growth of individualism in Greece produced a new literature, a personal lyric poetry. Ancient lyrics, anonymous, and often intended for use in rituals, had been concerned with common experiences. By the seventh century BC poets appeared along the Ionian coast who tell us their names and sing of themselves, their political contests, military adventures, travels, homesickness, drinking parties, poverty, loves and hates. The greatest of the love poets was Sappho of Lesbos (*c*.600 BC). Her poems celebrate love between women.

Prose was also important in Greek literature and was read for pleasure. The greatest prose works were the histories of which those of Herodotus and Thucydides survive. Herodotus writes of the eastern Mediterranean world from approximately 672 BC to the end of Xerxes' expedition in 479 BC. Thucydides treats the events of the Peloponnesian Wars. Herodotus maintains a masterful scope in his work, and Thucydides provides a remarkable conception of history as a concatenation of specific causes with specific results.

By the Hellenistic period the wealth lavished on Alexandria brought to its confines a cadre of brilliant writers. New literary forms flourished—the epigram, the pastoral of Theocritus, and the literary epic of Apollonius Rhodius. Very slowly, the literature of Greece also penetrated the Hellenistic world. Histories of Egypt and Babylon, Jewish law, and original literary works of the various regions were cast into Greek, and, conversely, Greek literature was translated into numerous other tongues.

THE ARTS
OF THE GREEKS

TWO-DIMENSIONAL ART

Humans throughout history have sought order in chaos, rational explanations, and intellectual challenge, while at the same time recognizing that emotions and intuitive feelings cannot be denied. The struggle between intellect and emotion is one of the most significant undercurrents in human existence. Although the two forces are not mutually exclusive, the history of Western arts often reflects the conflict between the two. The fifth-century Athenians recognized the struggle. Indeed, Greek mythology tells a story which demonstrates Periclean belief in the superiority of intellectual appeal over emotional. Marsyas, a mortal, discovered an aulos discarded by the goddess Athena. (An aulos is a musical instrument associated with the wild revelries of the cult of Dionysus.) (See Fig. **4.4**.) With Athena's aulos in hand Marsyas challenged the god Apollo to a musical contest. Apollo, patron of the rational arts of reflection, chose the lyre (a stringed instrument). According to mythology Apollo won the contest thereby proving the dominance of intellect over emotion.

4.4 Attributed to Eucharides Painter, amphora showing Apollo playing a lyre and Artemis holding an aulos before an altar, c.490 BC. 18½ ins (47 cm) high. The Metropolitan Museum of Art, New York (Rogers Fund, 1907).

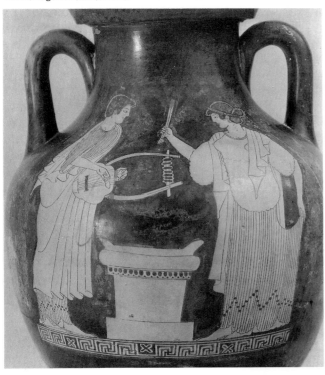

Appeal to the intellect was the cornerstone of classical style in all the arts. In painting, as well as in other disciplines, four characteristics reflected that appeal. First and foremost is an emphasis on form, on the formal organization of the whole into logical and structured parts. A second characteristic is idealization, an underlying purpose to portray things as better than they are as according to Aristotle in his *Poetics*, or to raise them above the level of the mundanely human. For example, the human figure is treated as a type rather than as an individual. A third characteristic is concession to convention. A fourth characteristic is simplicity. Simplicity does not mean lack of sophistication. Rather, it means freedom from unnecessary ornamentation and complexity.

These emphases were basic to Greek classicism, the predominant style of the era and the foundation of Western artistic tradition. The antitheses also existed, and as the Age of Pericles gave way to the Hellenistic period, the dominant characteristics of classicism were gradually modified to a less formal, more naturalistic, and more emotional style.

Such few examples of Greek classical painting as have survived can best be understood if we compare them with an example of an earlier style. Figure **4.6** shows a painted vase of the archaic style, just prior to the classical age. Compositional format, degree of realism, and use of convention help to make the point. Even though the figures are recognizably human, they are handled in a geometric manner and appear primitive. Less obvious, but quite critical, is the convention of portraying the torso frontally while the head and legs are in profile. By convention, turning the head alone to the rear would have denoted a figure in motion.

Sixth-century Attic pottery can be divided into two types—black-figure and red-figure. In black-figure vases the design appears in black against the light red clay background. Details are incised and white and dark red colors are added. White tends to be used for women's flesh and for old men's beards. Red is used for hair, horses' manes and for parts of garments. Red-figure, which appears around 530 BC, reverses the scheme and the figures appear in the natural red clay against a glazed black background. Contours and inner lines appear in glaze and often stand out in slight relief. In the earliest stages of red-figure, incision occurs occasionally for the contours of the hair, with touches of white and red. Other techniques also existed, including, in the fifth and fourth centuries BC, the use of palmettes and other motifs impressed in the clay and covered with black glaze.

Until the middle of the sixth century figure representation remained two-dimensional. Depiction was restricted to full profile or a full-frontal torso attached to legs in profile. The head, shown in profile, contained a full-frontal eye. Fabric was stiff and conventionalized. By 550 BC figure depiction shows attempts to portray the body in more of a three-quarter position. At the same time a new feeling for three-dimensional space occurs, and the eye is detailed in a more naturalistic manner. Fabric begins to assume the drape and folds of real cloth. By the end of the fifth century the convention we have seen in Egyptian and Mesopotamian art of putting all the figures along the base line on the front plane of the design gave way to suggestions of depth as some figures are occasionally placed higher than others. By the end of the fourth century attainment of depth and foreshortening were complete.

Fifth-century Athenian painting of the classical style reflected some of the earlier characteristics, including the principally geometric nature of the design. Such a compositional format indicated a concern for form and order in the organization of space and time. What separated the classical style in vase painting (our only extant evidence of Greek two-dimensional art of this period) from earlier styles was a new sense of idealized reality in figure depiction.

In addition to a change in attitude, such realism also reflected a technical advancement. Many of the problems of foreshortening, the perceivable diminution of size as the object recedes in space, had been solved, and, as a result, figures had a new sense of depth. Depth and reality were also heightened in some instances by attention to light and shadow. Some records imply that mural painters of this period were highly skilful in representation, but we have no surviving examples to study. The restrictions inherent in vase painting do not unfortunately allow us to assess the true level of skill and development of the two-dimensional art of this period. Vase painting does demonstrate, however, concern for formal design, that is, logical, evident, and perfectly balanced organization of space.

The vase painters

Although we speak of general stylistic tendencies in the pre-classical and classical periods, there was, in fact, a great deal of diversity among individual artists who painted vases. Some of these artists we know from their signatures. Scholars have assigned names to others based on the subject or the location of the artist's work. One of the earliest and best artists of black-figure is the Nessos Painter. He drew large-scale figures with strong features and serious expressions. His monsters and animals reflect the style and interest found in Mesopotamian art. The Gorgon Painter (Fig. 4.5), so called because of the Gorgons which decorate his work, and Kleitias, whose mythical figures reflect neatness, order, and vivaciousness, were also significant sixth-century painters. Lydos, another painter, is responsible for one of the largest surviving terracotta kraters (Fig. 4.7). In this work we see Hephaistos returning to Olympus, surrounded by a coterie of satyrs and maenads. Sixth-century conventions mark the depiction of the figures, whose lively postures reflect movement and instil in the work a varied rhythm and strong character.

Moving nearer to the classical period we find a striking comparision in a skyphos painted by Makron in the early fifth century (Fig. 4.8). Makron painted nearly all the vases signed by the potter Hieron, and in our illustration the subtle folds of fabric reflect delicacy and idealization of line and form. Here he tells the story of

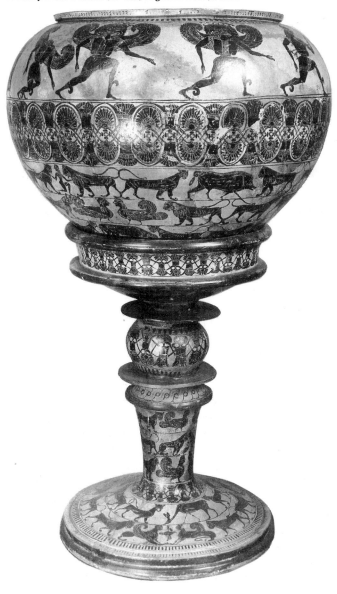

4.5 Attic Bowl showing Perseus and the Gorgons, early 6th century BC. 36½ ins (93 cm) high. Louvre, Paris.

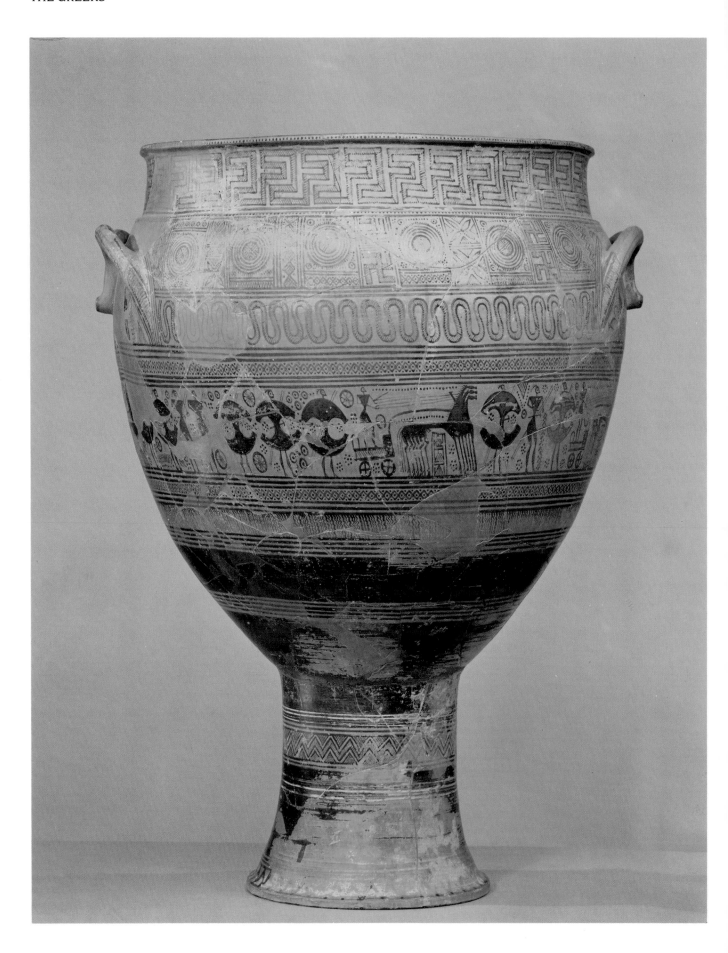

4.6 Dipylon Vase, Attic Geometric amphora, 8th century BC. 42⅝ ins (108.3 cm) high. The Metropolitan Museum of Art, New York (Rogers Fund, 1914).

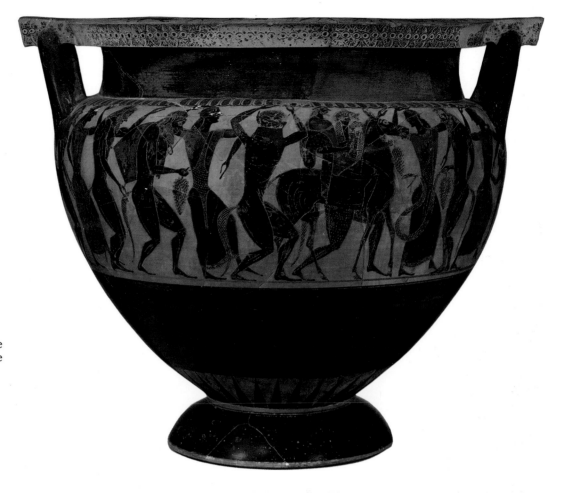

4.7 Attributed to the painter Lydos, black-figure column krater, showing the return of Hephaistos to Olympus escorted by Dionysus, Satyrs and Maenads, c.560–550 BC. 22 ins (55.9 cm) high. The Metropolitan Museum of Art, New York (Fletcher Fund, 1931).

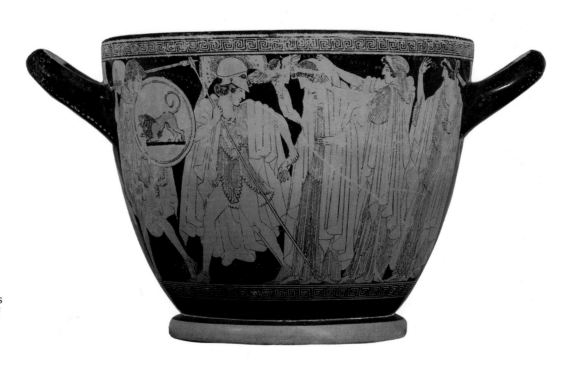

4.8 Skyphos by Hieron, painted by Makron, showing Paris abducting Helen, 500–480 BC. 8½ ins (21.5 cm) high. Museum of Fine Arts, Boston (Francis Bartlett Donation).

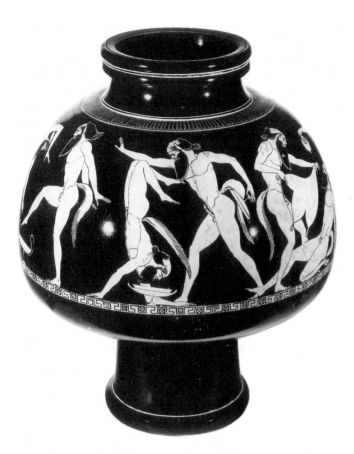

4.9 Douris, psykter showing dancing satyrs, c.500–480 BC. 11⅜ ins (28.7 cm) high. British Museum, London.

4.10 Achilles Painter, white ground lekythos from Gela(?), showing woman and her maid, 440 BC. 15 ins (38.4 cm) high. Museum of Fine Arts, Boston (Francis Bartlett Fund).

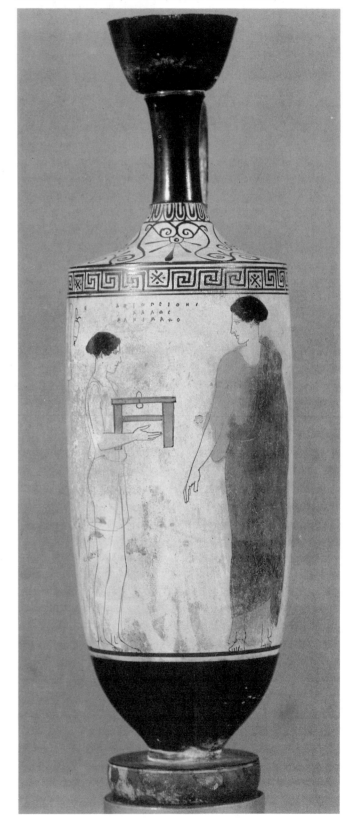

Menelaus and Helen with graceful rhythms and repetitions of form tempered by careful variation.

The work of the painter Douris spans the years 500 to 470 BC. Over thirty vases survive with his signature, and scholars have assigned to him more than two hundred others by matching the style. Figure **4.9** illustrates Douris' rhythmic animation.

The fifth century also saw many of the most talented artists turn to sculpture, mural painting, and architecture. The idealism and dignity of the classical style is nonetheless aptly portrayed by such artists as the Achilles Painter seen in Figure **4.10**. Here a quiet grandeur infuses the figures, whose elegance and stately presence reflect the intellectual approach of the classical period. The portrayal of feet in the frontal position is a significant development, a reflection of the skill and spatial mastery achieved by this time.

Characteristic of changes we find in other media and other art forms, vase painting around the year 400 BC had a highly ornate style. Thick lines, dark patterns on garments, and a generous use of white and yellow characterized compositions of crowded figures represented mainly in three-quarter views. Illustrative of this change in style is the *Combat Scene* from an amphora painted by the Suessula Painter (Fig. **4.11**). Here we see not only the characteristics just noted, but also a concern for spatial depth as the figures leave the base line of the frontal plane.

We generally relate style to treatment of form, rather

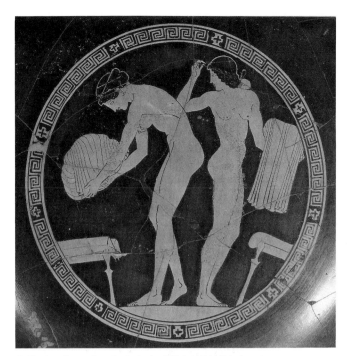

4.12 Attributed to Douris, red-figured kylix showing two women putting away their clothes, c. 470 BC. Diameter 12½ ins (31.7 cm). The Metropolitan Museum of Art, New York (Rogers Fund, 1923).

Later, in the Hellenistic era, mundane scenes, sometimes comic and vulgar, were common in wall painting. Remarkable in these scenes is the use of aerial and linear perspective to indicate deep, receding, three-dimensional space.

Unfortunately for us, the few extant examples of classical and Hellenistic two-dimensional art furnish us with only a glimpse of these two important styles, so closely linked, but reflective of such different attitudes.

SCULPTURE

We are more fortunate when our examination turns to sculpture. Stone and metal are more durable, and sculpture often exceeds all the arts in its ability to survive the centuries. However, great quantities of Greek sculpture do not exist, and more than likely some of the greatest examples have been lost forever. Much of what we surmise of Greek classical sculpture actually comes from inferior copies made at a later time. Existing sculpture can be divided into two categories: independent sculpture created for its own sake; and architectural, executed to serve as part of the decoration of a building.

Styles do not start on a given date and end on another, even when they are as local and compressed as those of the small city-state of Athens during the rule of Pericles. The Greek classical style, especially in sculpture, was a style continually in a state of change, and one artist's works will be different from another's even though, in general, they reflect the basic characteristics described earlier.

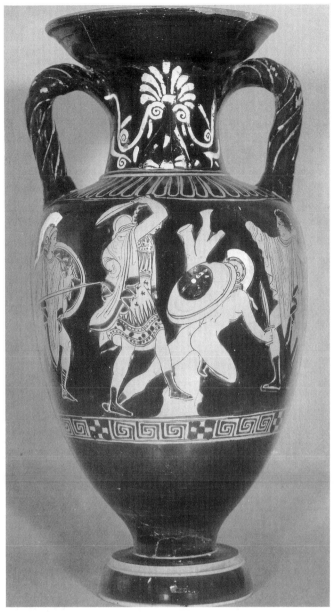

4.11 Attributed to the Suessula painter, amphora showing combat of Greeks and Amazons, 5th–6th century BC. 14 ins (35.5 cm) high. The Metropolitan Museum of Art, New York (Fletcher Fund, 1944).

than content or subject matter; but often form and content cannot be separated. When classicism was modified by a more individualized and naturalistic treatment of form, its subject matter broadened to include the mundane, as opposed, for example, to the heroic. In some vase painting we find an early transition. Figure **4.12** depicts *Women Putting Away Their Clothes*. The graceful curves and idealized form of the classical style are present, but the subject matter is clearly drawn from everyday life. The implications of this apparent departure are not entirely clear. Perhaps the utilitarian, as opposed to ceremonial, purpose of vases of this variety accounts for the early change.

Again, a contrast with the archaic style is useful. In Figure **4.13**, the *Kouros* or heroic youthful athlete (*c*. 600 BC), we find two significant characteristics. The first is a clear attempt to depict the human figure in fairly realistic form. The figure, however, is not a person. It is a stereotype, a symbol, and, in a sense, an idealization of heroism. Nevertheless the sculpture lacks refinement. It may be idealized, but it does not depict ideal or perfect human form, and this difference helps separate the archaic from the classical style. The second characteristic is an attempt to indicate movement or dynamics. Even though the sculpture is severely positioned and static, notice that the left foot is extended forward in an attempt to create a greater sense of motion than would be the case if both feet were in the same plane. However, the weight of the body remains equally divided between the two feet, as we saw in Egyptian sculpture.

The age of Greek classical style probably began with the sculptors Myron and Polyclitus in the middle of the fifth century BC. Myron's best-known work, *Discus Thrower*

(Fig. **4.14**), displays concern for restraint, subdued vitality, subtle control of movement coupled with balance, and a concern for flesh and idealized human form. Although our example of the *Discus Thrower* is a much later marble copy, Myron worked in bronzes and, because of the characteristics of that medium, was able to free his sculpture from many of the constraints of marble. A work of statuary, as opposed to relief sculpture, must stand on its own, and supporting the weight of a marble statue on the small area of one ankle poses significant structural problems. Metal, having greater tensile strength, provides a solution to many of these problems.

A second sculptor, Polyclitus, also contributed to the development of cast sculpture, and he is reported to have achieved in his *Lance Bearer* (Fig. **4.15**) the ideal proportions of the male athlete. It is important to note, again, in our pursuit of the elements of Greek classical style, that the *Lance Bearer* represents *the* male athlete, and not *a* male athlete. In this work the body's weight is thrown onto one leg in the *contrapposto* stance. The

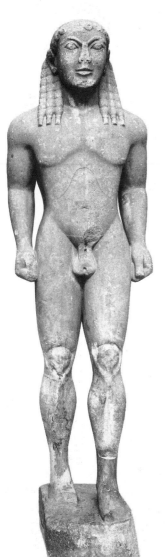

4.13 Polymedes of Argos, Kouros, c.580 BC. Stone, 6 ft 5½ ins (197 cm) high. Archeological Museum, Delphi, Greece.

4.14 Myron, *Discobolus* (*Discus Thrower*), c.450 BC. Roman marble copy after a bronze original, life-size. Museo Nazionale Romano, Rome.

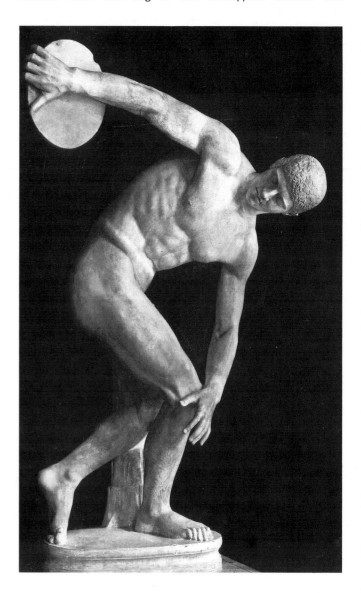

resulting sense of relaxation and controlled dynamics in the realistically treated human body and the subtle play of curves made possible by this simple but important change in posture are also characteristic of Greek classical style. The same reflection can be seen in Figure **4.16**, the *Kritios Boy*.

The east pediment of the Parthenon contains marvelous sculptural examples (Figs. **4.17** and **4.18**). What strikes us first is the compositional accommodation to the confines of the pediment. This group of *Three Goddesses* or the *Fates* is now a breathtaking separate display in the British Museum in London. Originally, however, it formed part of the architectural decoration high on the Parthenon. It depicts the mythological story of the birth of Athena from her father's head. Also from the east pediment is the figure of Theseus. Together they illustrate Greek idealization of their suprahuman deities. We can learn much about Greek style and technique from these superb but battered figures. To begin with, treatment of cloth is highly sophisticated. The drape and flow of fabric care-

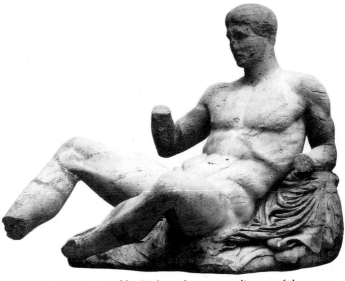

4.17 *Dionysus* (Herakles?), from the east pediment of the Parthenon, c.438–432 BC. Marble, over life-size. British Museum, London.

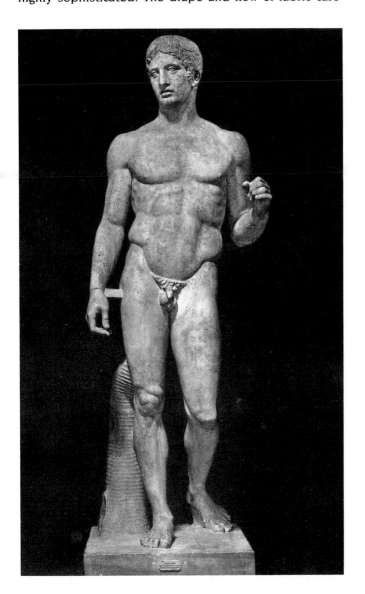

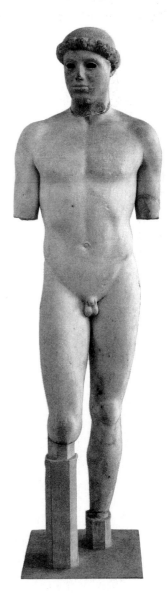

4.15 *Doryphorus* (*Lance Bearer*), Roman copy after an original of c.450–440 BC by Polyclitus. Marble, 6 ft 6 ins (198 cm) high. Museo Archeologico Nazionale, Naples, Italy.

4.16 *Kritios Boy*, c.480 BC. Marble, c.34 ins (86 cm) high. Acropolis Museum, Athens.

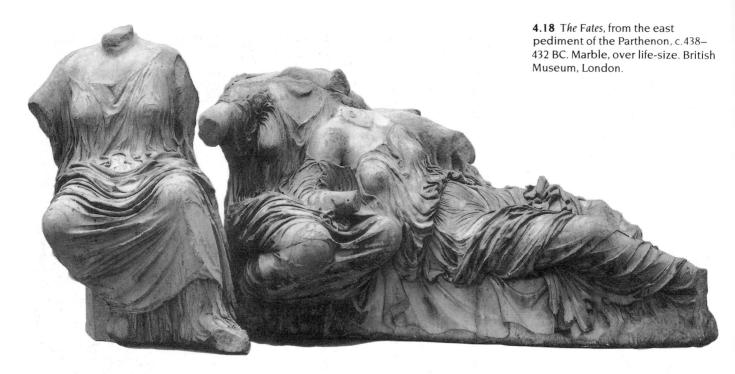

4.18 *The Fates*, from the east pediment of the Parthenon, c.438–432 BC. Marble, over life-size. British Museum, London.

fully reinforce the overall but reasonably simple line of the work, representing considerable technical achievement. However, this depiction is far from mere decoration—the cloth is used to reveal the perfected human female form beneath it in a way which once again demonstrates the classical purpose—not naturalism but the ideal. The purpose here is to raise these forms above the human or the specific to a symbolic level. Even in repose these figures show subtle and controlled grace and movement. The dynamic counterthrust of tensions and releases is obvious, but it always is restrained, never explosive or emotional.

The overall form and design of these figures, although constrained by the geometric parameters of the space of the pediment, show comfortable harmony in rhythmic flow of line as our eyes move from one part to the next. Control, again, is evident, with formal restraint an objective. Compare these figures with those of a later style in Figure **4.19**. The composition of the latter is more open, its movement violent and emotional, and subtle curvatures are replaced with a nearly geometric triangularity in a line that leads the eye in jerkily from one form to the next.

Sculpture of the fourth century BC illustrates clearly the change in attitudes reflected in post-classical styles. Praxiteles is famous for individualism and delicacy of themes such as the *Cnidian Aphrodite* (Fig. **4.20**). There is a looking inward in this work, which is different from the formal detachment of earlier sculpture such as *Theseus* (Fig. **4.17**). Female nudity also appears for the first time.

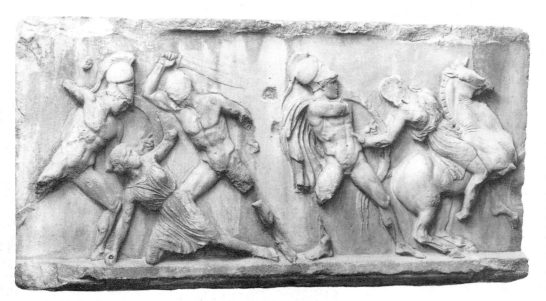

4.19 Scopas (?), Battle of Greeks and Amazons, from the east frieze of the Mausoleum, Halicarnassus, 359-351 BC. Marble, 35 ins (88.9 cm) high. British Museum, London.

4.20 *Opposite top left Cnidian Aphrodite*, probably Hellenistic copy of 4th century BC bronze original by Praxiteles. Marble. 60½ ins (153.7 cm) high. The Metropolitan Museum of Art, New York (Fletcher Fund, 1952).

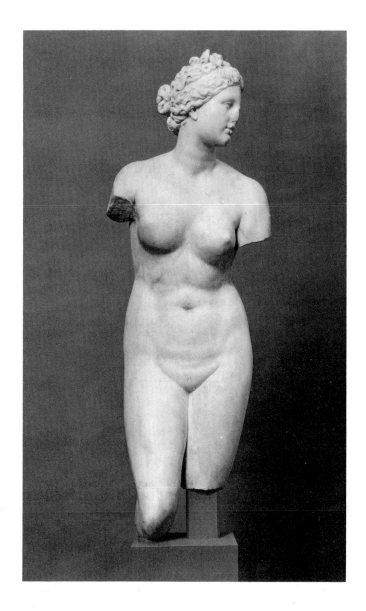

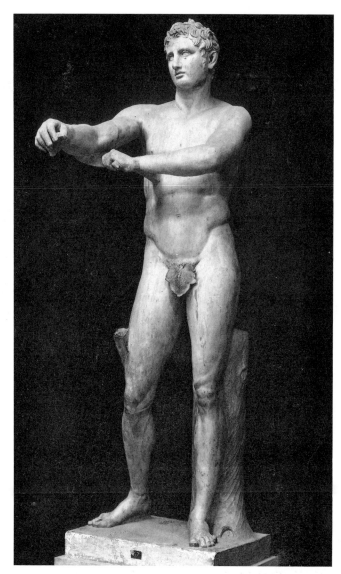

4.21 *Apoxyomenos (Scraper)*, Roman copy, probably after a bronze original of c.330 BC by Lysippos. Marble, 6 ft 9 ins (205.8 cm) high. Vatican Museums, Rome.

4.22 *The Dying Gaul*, Roman copy of a bronze original of c.230–220 BC. Marble, life-size. Museo Capitolino, Rome.

Originally, Aphrodite rested her weight on one foot. Her body sways to the left in the famous Praxitelean S-curve. Strain on the ankle of the sculpture was minimized by the arm's attachment to drapery and a vase.

The late fourth century found in the sculpture of Lysippos (a favorite of Alexander the Great) a dignified naturalness and a new concept of space. His *Apoxyomenos*, or *Scraper* (Fig. **4.21**), illustrates an attempt actually to put the figure into motion, in contrast to the posed figures at rest we have seen previously. The theme of the *Scraper* is mundane—an athlete scraping dirt and oil from his body. The proportions of the figure are even more naturalistic than those of Polyclitus; but the naturalism is still far from perfect. Style had moved dramatically from earliest classical reflections, but classical influence remained.

Hellenistic style in sculpture continued to dominate the Mediterranean world until the first century BC; and as time progressed, style changed to reflect an increasing interest in individual human differences. Rather than

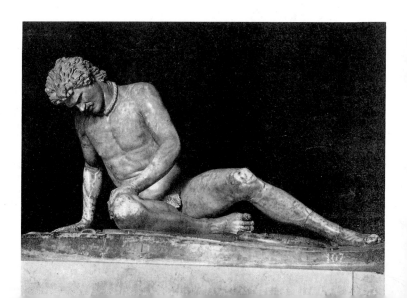

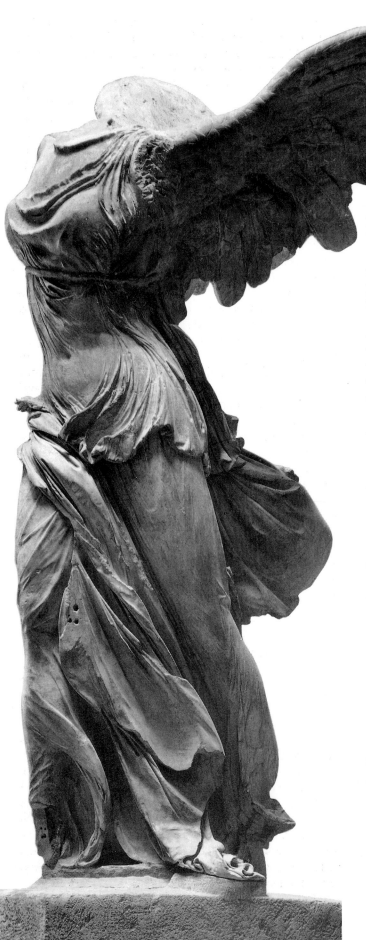

4.23 *Victory of Samothrace*, c.190 BC. Marble, 8 ft (244 cm) high. Louvre, Paris.

idealization, the Hellenistic sculptor often turned to pathos, banality, trivia, and flights of individual virtuosity in technical exploration. These characteristics appear in Figures **4.22**, **4.23**, and **4.24**. The *Dying Gaul* is a powerful expression of emotion and of pathos as it depicts a noble warrior on the verge of death. The *Winged Victory of Samothrace* displays a dramatic and dynamic technical virtuosity that has made it one of the most popular sculptures ever created. Finally, the *Laocoön Group* removes nearly all restraint from movement and emotion in an explosive moment, which might find a comfortable home in the baroque style.

4.24 Hagesandrus, Polydorus and Athenodorus, *Laocoon and his Two Sons*, 1st century AD. Marble, 8 ft (244 cm) high. Vatican Museums, Rome.

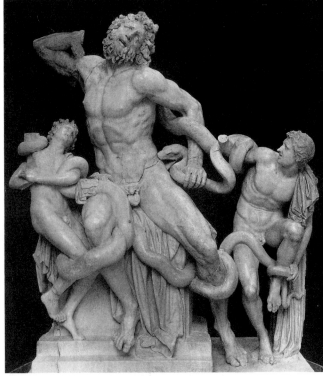

MUSIC

Very few examples of Greek music exist of any era—merely a handful of fragments and no clue as to how they were supposed to sound. However, thanks to surviving vase paintings and literature we can at least speculate on Greek classical philosophy or theory of music and about tone quality or timbre. The lyre and the aulos were the basic instruments of Greek music, and each had a significant role in pre-classical ritual. In the era of classicism both the lyre and the aulos were used as solo instruments and as accompaniment. The spirit of contest which was so popular among the Greeks apparently extended to instrumental and vocal music. As with all the arts, music was regarded as essential to life, and participation was widespread among the Athenian population. Perhaps the word dilettante, a lover of the arts, would describe the average citizen of Athens. Professionalism and professional artists, however, were held in low esteem, and Aristotle urged that skill in music stop short of the professional. Practice should develop talent only to the point that one could "delight in noble melodies and rhythms", as he says in *Poetics*. He also called for restraint from excessive complexity.

So during the classical age complexity apparently existed in some Greek music. We should not infer too much from such an observation. Complexity for the Greeks would no doubt still be simplicity by our musical standards. It appears reasonably clear, for instance, that all Greek music of this era was monophonic. Complexity might instead imply technical difficulty within the scope of the instruments used and perhaps melodic ornamentation, but not textual complication. Whether that is contrary to the classical spirit we do not know. A specific reaction against complexity occurred sometime after 325 BC, and it is from the Hellenistic era that our only remnants of Greek music come. Scholars can only guess how the fragments must have sounded and only extrapolate from them concerning the music of the Periclean era and the Greek classical style. A few characteristics of some types of music are apparent. As stated in Aristotle, the idealizing characteristic was implicit. Music should lead to noble thought. There is no question that some music in the Greek repertoire led to the opposite. Dionysiac rituals were emotional and frenetic, and music played an important role in these. We can assume that calls for restraint and pursuit of the ideal imply the presence of at least some music of an intellectual spirit.

If Plato's *Republic* can be taken as an accurate guide, then Greek music relied on convention. Most of the performances in Periclean Athens appear to have been improvised, which may seem a bit at odds with order and formality. However, improvisation should not be interpreted here as excessively spontaneous or unrehearsed. The Greeks had specified formulas or rules concerning acceptable musical forms or modes for nearly every occasion. So the musician, though free to seek the momentary inspiration of the Muses, the mythological sisters who presided over the arts, was constrained by the conventions applicable to the occasion.

The reliance on form which characterized classical style was reflected in music through relationships to mathematics in philosophy and religion. Greek classicism exemplified an orderly, formal, and mathematical approach to life, that is, reality. Pythagoras taught that an understanding of numbers was the key to an understanding of the entire spiritual and physical universe. Those views, expressed in music, as well as the other arts, led to a system of sounds and rhythms ordered by numbers. The intervals of the musical scale were determined by measuring vibrating strings. The results yielded relationships which even today are fundamental to Western musical practice: 2:1 = an octave; 3:2 = a fifth; 4:3 = a fourth. Since the characteristics of vibrating strings are the same today as they were then, this aspect of Greek music, at least, is comprehensible.

The Greek musical system was technical and highly organized, and those familiar with music history and theory will recognize the terms enharmonic, chromatic, and diatonic, as well as tetrachord and Mixolydian and Dorian modes, terms which continue to be used in our music today.

Some musical fragments from the Hellenistic period give us a view of life and love among mortals—subject matter beyond the bounds of classical idealization but consistent with Hellenistic naturalism. For example, *Skolian*, a drinking song composed as an epitaph in the second century BC, commented on the ephemeral nature of earthly pleasures.

Finally, the Hellenistic period (in about 265 BC) gave us a musical invention of great consequence, the organ. It was called *hydraulos*, water organ, and sound was produced by using water to force air upward through the pipes.

THEATRE

The theatre of Periclean Athens was a theatre of convention, and the term convention, as it applies here, takes on another dimension. Every era and every style have their conventions, those underlying, accepted expectations and/or rules which influence the artist subtly or otherwise. In some styles conventions are fundamental; in others the conventions are unconventional. Theatre of convention implies a style of production lacking in illusion or stage realism. So in contrast to sculpture and painting which pursued the noble and the ideal with fair dependence upon a verisimilar but idealized treatment of subject matter, the Greek classical theatre pursued the same ends through a slightly different means.

Theatre of convention is to a large extent freer to

explore the ideal than theatre of illusion, in which scenic details are realistically portrayed, because dependence upon stage mechanics does not hamper the playwright. An audience will accept a description in poetic dialogue, but by convention does not demand to see it. Imagination is the key to theatre of convention. The Greek dramatist found that with freedom from the restraints imposed by dependence on illusion or depiction, he was much better able to pursue the lofty moral themes fundamental to his perception of the universe. Although we have some extant plays from the era indicating what and how the playwright wrote, we are at a loss to know specifically how that work became theatre, that is, a production. Nevertheless, we can try to build a picture of production from descriptions in the plays themselves, other literary evidence, and from a few extant archeological examples.

Theatre productions in ancient Greece were part of three-yearly religious festivals, the City Dionysia, Rustic Dionysia, and Lenaea. The first of these was a festival of tragic plays and the last, of comic. The City Dionysia was held in the Theatre of Dionysus in Athens. The contests were begun in 534 BC, before the classical era. Our knowledge of Greek theatre is enhanced somewhat by the fact that although we do not have most of the plays, we do know the titles and the authors who won these contests from the earliest to the last. From the records (inscriptions in stone) we know that three playwrights figured prominently and repeatedly as winners in the contests of the era.[6] They were Aeschylus, Sophocles, and Euripides. Our entire collection of complete tragedies is from these three playwrights—seven from Aeschylus, seven from Sophocles, and eighteen from Euripides.

A playwright entering the contests for tragedy or comedy was required to submit his plays to a panel of presiding officers who selected three playwrights for actual production. The early plays of the classical style had only one actor plus a chorus, and at the time of play selection the playwright was assigned the chief actor plus a *choregus*, a patron who paid all the expenses for the production. The playwright was author, director, choreographer, and musical composer. He often played the leading role as well.

Aeschylus

At the same time as the *Kritios Boy* (Fig. **4.16**) was created, Aeschylus, the most famous poet of ancient Greece, began to write for the theatre. Clearly fitting the classic mold, he wrote magnificent tragedies of high poetic nature and lofty moral theme. In *Agamemnon*, the first play in the *Oresteia* trilogy, Aeschylus' chorus warns us that success and wealth are insufficient without goodness:

Justice shines in sooty dwellings

Loving the righteous way of life,
But passes by with averted eyes
The house whose lord has hands unclean.
Be it built throughout of gold.
Caring naught for the weight of praise
Heaped upon wealth by the vain, but turning
All alike to its proper end.[7]

Aeschylus probed questions that we still ask: How responsible are we for our own actions? How much are we controlled by the will of heaven? His characters were larger than life; they were types rather than individuals, in accordance with the idealism of the time. Yet his characters were also human, as evidenced by his portrayal of Clytemnestra in *Agamemnon*. Aeschylus' early plays consisted of one actor and a chorus of fifty, conforming to the convention of the time. He is credited with the addition of a second actor, and by the end of his long career a third, and a chorus reduced to twelve.

In Aeschylus' plays we find a strong appeal to the intellect. Aristophanes, the master of Greek comedy, has Aeschylus, a character in the *Frogs*, defend his writing as an inspiration to patriotism, to make men proud of their achievements. This is inspiration in an intellectual, not a rabble-rousing, sense. Aeschylus lived through the Persian invasion, witnessed the great Athenian victories, and fought at the battle of Marathon. His plays reflect this experience and spirit.

Sophocles

Overlapping with Aeschylus was Sophocles, who reached the peak of his personal career during the zenith of the Greek classical style with works like *Oedipus tyrannus*. Sophocles' plots and characterizations illustrate a trend toward increasing realism similar to that of classical sculpture. The movement toward realism was not a movement into theatre of illusion, and even Euripides' plays, the most realistic of the Greek tragedies, are not realistic in our sense of the word. However, Sophocles was a less formal poet than Aeschylus. His themes are more humane and his characters more subtle, although his exploration of the themes of human responsibility, dignity and fate is of the same intensity and seriousness as we see in Aeschylus. His plots show increasing complexity, but with the formal restraints of the classical spirit. Sophocles lived and wrote beyond the death of Pericles in 429 BC and so he experienced the shame of Athenian defeat. Even so, his later plays show nothing of the "action" noted in sculpture. Classical Greek theatre was mostly discussion and narration. Themes often dealt with bloodshed, but, though the play led up to violence, blood was never shed on stage.

Euripides

Euripides was younger than Sophocles, although both men died in 406 BC. They did, however, compete with each other. They do not share the same style. Euripides' plays carry realism to the furthest extent we see in Greek tragedy. His plays deal with individual emotions rather than great events, and his language, though still basically poetic, is higher in verisimilitude and much less formal than that of his predecessors. Euripides also experimented with, and ignored, many of the conventions of his theatre. He explored the mechanics of scenography and questioned in his plays the religion of his day. His tragedies are more tragicomedies than pure tragedies. Some critics have described many of his plays as melodramas. He was also less dependent on the chorus.[8]

Plays such as the *Bacchae* reflect the changing Athenian spirit and dissatisfaction with contemporary events, and show the same trend toward the mundane noted in sculpture and vase painting. Euripides was not particularly popular in his time, perhaps because of his less idealistic, less formal, and less conventional treatment of dramatic themes and characters. We might speculate whether his lack of popularity illustrated a question we can ask of any artwork that we find objectionable. Do our objections stem from the fact that the artwork tells us something about our world that we do not wish to hear or to acknowledge? Was Euripides' work too close to the reality of his age? His plays elicited much greater enthusiasm in later years and are unquestionably the most popular of the Greek tragedies today.

Aristotle's theory of Tragedy

We cannot pass from our discussion of classical and post-classical Greek theatre without noting Aristotle's analysis of Tragedy. His concepts are still basic to dramatic theory and criticism despite the fact that they have often been seriously misunderstood and misapplied over the last 2,400 years. One hundred years after the fact and drawing principally on Sophocles as a model, Aristotle laid out in the *Poetics* six parts for tragedy, in order of importance: first, plot, which includes exposition, discovery, reversal, point of attack, foreshadowing, complication, climax, crisis, and dénouement; second, character; third, thought; fourth, diction; fifth, music; and sixth, spectacle. Aristotle's analysis implies special meanings for each of these terms, in the same sense that special meanings exist for the analytical concepts of mass, line, shape, and color in visual art, or motif, phrase, binary, ternary, and sonata in music. Aristotle's analysis has evoked endless controversy about how such criteria ought to be applied to plays themselves.

Aristophanes

Tragedies and satyr plays (Euripides' *Cyclops* is the only example we have of that genre) were not the only works produced in the theatre of the classical era in Athens. The Athenians were extremely fond of comedy, although no examples survive from the Periclean period. Aristophanes (*c.* 450–*c.* 380 BC), of whose plays we have eleven, was the most gifted of the comic poets, and his comedies of the post-classical period, such as the *Acharnians*, are highly satirical, topical, sophisticated, and often obscene. Translated productions of his comedies are still staged, but the personal and political targets of his invective are unknown to us, and so these modern productions are mere shadows of what took the stage at the turn of the fourth century BC.

The characteristics of theatre of convention held sway over Aristophanic comedy. In fact, Aristophanes uses the conventions of his theatre to lay the groundwork for audience expectation. The obscenity present in Aristophanic comedy appears to serve two main functions.

> It is used both generally and in detail to articulate the main moral theme of his work, that natural behaviour produces more happiness than artificial systems of thought or action. This is particularly obvious in the peace plays, where bawdy sexuality is one of the principal symbols of the restoration of normality sought by the characters.... Its other (equally important) function is that it is funny in its own right—as a producer of laughter as any other of the human activities portrayed in the plays, and a primary means of communication between comedian and audience.[9]

New comedy

In the period from the middle of the fourth to the middle of the third century, comedy was the staple of the Hellenistic theatre. Only five incomplete plays by Menander survive, but the characteristics of his style are fairly clear. In this New Comedy in contrast with the Old Comedy of Aristophanes, the action is still bawdy, but the biting political invective is gone. The situations are pleasant and domestic, as opposed to the heroic nature of classical tragedy, and for the most part superficial and without satire. Religion no longer played a central role in the theatre, and the chorus had disappeared.

Costumes

If the plays of the Greek classical style treated lofty themes with language high in theatricality or poetic value, production style showed no less formality, idealism, and

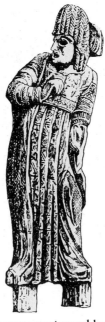

4.25 Greek statuette of a tragic actor, wearing a mask and a rich costume.

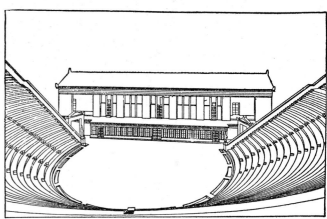

4.26 Reconstruction of the Hellenistic theatre at Ephesus, Turkey, c.280 BC, rebuilt c.150 BC.

convention. Larger-than-life characters were portrayed by actors in larger-than-life conventionalized costumes. Actors and chorus wore brightly colored robes whose colors signified specific information to the audience. The robes were padded to increase the actor's size, his height was increased by thick-soled boots called *kothurnoi* and large masks whose fixed, conventionalized expressions were readily identified by the sophisticated and knowledgeable audience. (Fig. **4.25**). His height was further increased by an *onkos*, a wiglike protrusion on top of the mask.

Scholars are divided about the exact layout of the classical Greek theatre building and the nature of its acting area and scenery. Since our purpose is an overview, we can summarize some of the architectural and archeological speculation, bearing in mind that it is only speculation. Nothing of substance remains of the classical Greek theatre building except its auditorium—the seating area—and parts of the *orchestra*—the original, circular acting and dancing area. The presence or absence of a stage and scenic background and at what date these were introduced are subjects of great debate.

Theatre design

The form of the Greek theatre owes much to the choral dances associated with the worship of Dionysus from which it originated. In 534 BC Thespis is reported to have introduced a single actor to these choric dances or dithyrambs. In 472, Aeschylus added a second actor, and in 458, Sophocles added a third. So throughout its history the Greek theatre comprised a large circular *orchestra* with an altar at its center, and a semicircular *theatron*—auditorium or viewing place—usually cut into or occupying the slope of a hill. Since the actors played more than one role, they needed somewhere to change costume, and so a *skene*—scene building or retiring place—was added. The gradual development of the *skene* into a

raised stage is somewhat obscure and problematical, but by later, Hellenistic times, it had become a rather elaborate, two-storied affair (Fig. **4.26**) with projecting wings at each end and a raised stage.

The earliest extant theatre is the theatre of Dionysus on the south slope of the Acropolis, dating from the fifth century BC, where the plays of Aeschylus, Sophocles, Euripides, and Aristophanes were staged. Its current form dates back to a period of reconstruction work around 338–326 BC. The theatre at Epidaurus (Figs. **4.27** and **4.28**) is the best preserved, and was built by Polykleitus the Younger about 350 BC. Its sheer size demonstrates the monumental character the theatre had assumed by that time. The orchestra measures eighty feet in diameter, with an altar to Dionysus in the center. The auditorium, comprising slightly more than a semicircle, is divided by an ambulatory about two-thirds of the way up, and by radiating stairways. All the seats were of stone, and around the first or lowest row were seats for the dignitaries of Athens. These seats had backs and arms, and

4.27 Plan of the theatre at Epidaurus.

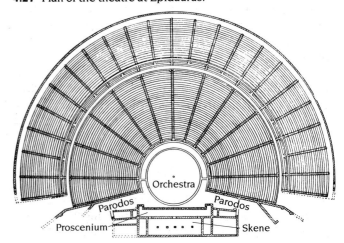

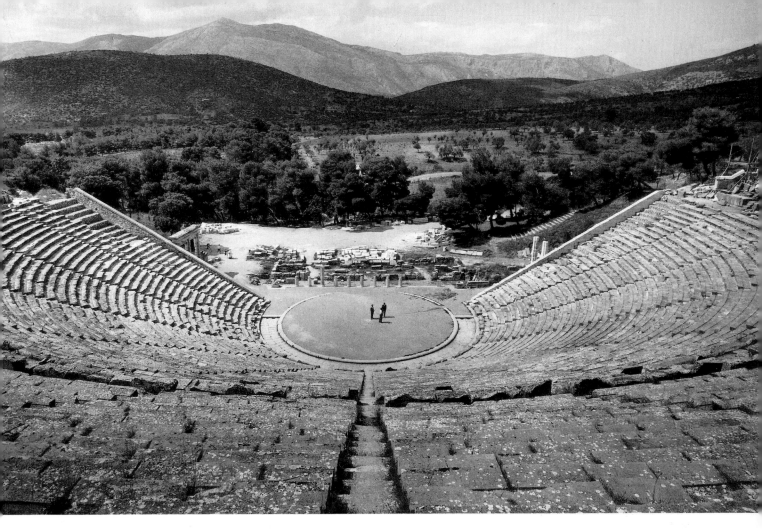

some were decorated with relief sculptures.

There was undoubtebly variation in the design of theatres in different locations, but, again, time has removed most examples from our grasp. The many theories of how Greek theatre productions worked, how scenery was or was not used, and whether or not and when a raised stage was present make fascinating reading, and the reader is encouraged to explore this area in detail elsewhere.

DANCE

The religious rituals of ancient Greece centered on dance. These great festivals brought choruses of dancers from each tribe together on special occasions for competition. Most scholars agree that the Greek theatre developed directly from these dances with their chorus of fifty. Dance, music, and drama were inseparably entwined, and each played a fundamental part in early and classical Greek philosophy, religion, and life. The term dance had a broader definition for the Greeks than it does for us and denoted almost any kind of rhythmic movement. Just as dance and music were inseparable, so were dance and poetry. A Greek could dance a poem, "interpreting with rhythmic movements of his hands, arms, body, face, and head the verses recited or sung by himself or another person."[10] Convention, apparently, was fundamental.

4.28 Polykleitus the Younger, theatre at Epidaurus, Greece, c.350 BC. Diameter 373 ft (114 m), orchestra 66 ft (20 m) across.

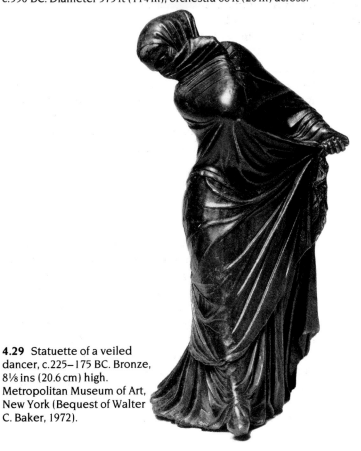

4.29 Statuette of a veiled dancer, c.225–175 BC. Bronze, 8⅛ ins (20.6 cm) high. Metropolitan Museum of Art, New York (Bequest of Walter C. Baker, 1972).

Dance in the Age of Pericles illustrates both classical and anti-classical styles. Certainly the dance of the Dionysiac cult revels, which may have decreased in popularity but certainly continued under Periclean rule, must have disregarded form, order, restraint, and idealization. Their appeal was to emotional frenzy, not the intellect. However, the philosophies of the era, the relationship of dance to music and drama, and the treatment of dance by Plato and Aristotle indicate that those aspects of dance which were associated with the theatre, at least, must have reflected classical characteristics.

Dance, though, is an evanescent art form. Today, even with labanotation—the system of writing down dance movements—we cannot know what a dance work looks like if we do not see the live, or at least filmed, event. So the treatises in literature, the musical fragments, and the archeological evidence from which so many have tried to reconstruct the dances of the Greeks give us no picture whatsoever. In fact, the very conventional nature of Greek art is our most formidable obstacle. It is clear that some vase paintings and sculpture depict dancers (Fig. **4.29**), but we do not know to what set of abstractions the conventions of these forms belong, and, therefore, we cannot reconstruct the acts in life that they symbolize.

ARCHITECTURE

Existing examples of Greek architecture, to which the arts of the Western world have returned over the past 2,300 years, offer a clear and consistent picture of basic classical style. Nothing brings that picture so clearly to mind as the term Greek temple. We all have an amazingly accurate concept of the structure and proportions of a Greek temple. H. W. Janson makes an interesting point in his *History of Art* when he suggests that the crystallization of the characteristics of a Greek temple is so complete that when we think of one Greek temple, we basically think of all Greek temples. Even so obvious a structure as a Gothic cathedral does not have this capacity, for we can only call to mind a specific Gothic church when we employ this recollection technique. Despite the explicit symbol of the Gothic arch, its employment is so diverse that no one work typifies the many.

The classical Greek temple, as seen in Figures **4.30**, **4.31**, and **4.32**, has a structure of horizontal blocks of stone laid across vertical columns. This is called post and lintel structure. It is not unique to Greece, but certainly the Greeks refined it to its highest aesthetic level. This type of structure creates some very basic problems. Stone is not high in tensile strength, the ability to withstand bending and twisting, although it is high in compressive strength, the ability to withstand crushing. Downward thrust works against tensile qualities in horizontal slabs (lintels) and works for compressive qualities

in vertical columns (posts). As a result, columns can be relatively delicate, whereas lintels must be massive. Only limited open space can be created using this structural system. Such a limitation was not of great concern to the Greeks because a Greek temple was to be seen and used from the outside. The Greek climate does not dictate that worshippers crowd inside a building. Exterior structure and aesthetics were of primary concern.

Greek temples were of three orders—Ionic, Doric, and Corinthian. The first two of these are classical, the third, though of classical derivation, is of the later, Hellenistic period. The contrasts between these types make an important, if subtle, stylistic point (Fig. **4.33**). Simplicity was an important characteristic of the Greek classical style, and the Ionic and Doric orders maintain clean and simple lines in their capitals. The Corinthian order has more ornate and complex capitals. When taken in the context of an entire building, this small detail does not appear to be of great consequence; but it is significant in understanding the rudiments underlying this style. Columns and capitals are convenient tags for identifying the order of a Greek temple. Differences are apparent in column bases and the configuration of the lintel, as well as in the columns and capitals.

The Parthenon typifies every aspect of Greek classical style in architecture. It is Doric in character and geometric in configuration. Balance is achieved through symmetry, and the clean, simple line and plan represent a perfect balance of forces holding the composition together in perfect unity here on earth. We can compare

4.30 The Nereid Monument, c. 400 BC. British Museum, London.

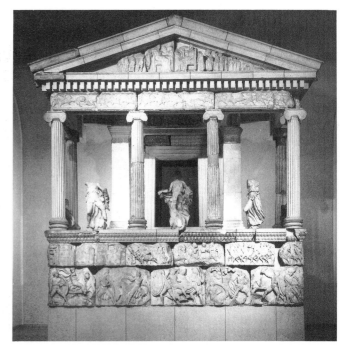

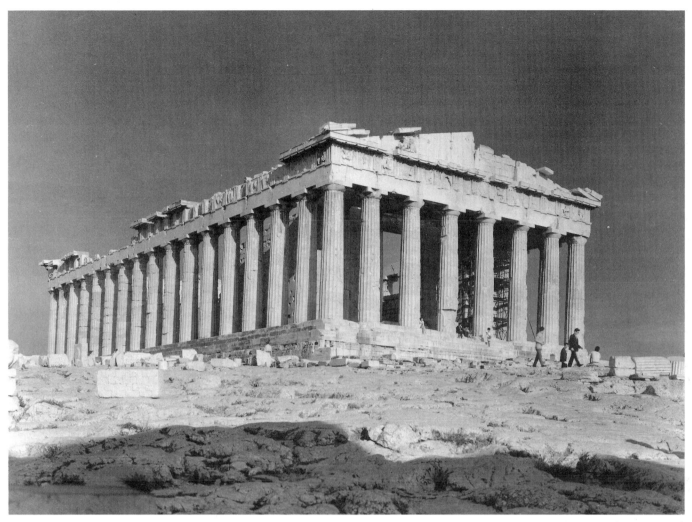

4.31 The Parthenon, Athens, from the north west, 447–438 BC.

4.32 Reconstructed model of the Parthenon. The Metropolitan Museum of Art, New York (Purchase 1890, Levi Hale Willard Bequest).

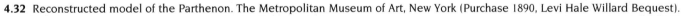

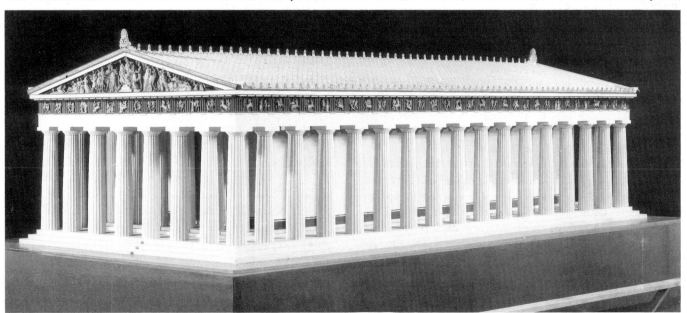

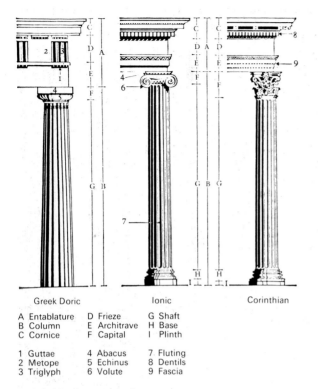

Greek Doric   Ionic   Corinthian

A Entablature   D Frieze   G Shaft
B Column   E Architrave H Base
C Cornice   F Capital   I Plinth

1 Guttae   4 Abacus   7 Fluting
2 Metope   5 Echinus 8 Dentils
3 Triglyph   6 Volute   9 Fascia

4.33 The Classical Orders.

the implications of this plan with those of a Gothic cathedral in which the upward striving line, in leading the eye to the apex of a spire and then off into space, becomes a symbol for an unknowable God. But for the Greeks, deities were just slightly more than mortal men, and in the Greek temple, deity and humankind met in an earthly rendezvous reflected clearly in the compositional factors just noted. The human-centered philosophy is also represented in the human scale of the temple.

The number of columns across the front and down the sides of the temple reflect specific conventions. The internal harmony of the design shows consonant harmony in the regular repetition of unvaried form. Each column is alike and spaced apparently equidistantly from its neighbor, except at the corners where the spacing is clearly lessened in subtle, but important, aesthetic adjustment. Such sophisticated variations create a sense of regular repetition and balanced grace and perfection, but they save the building from the boredom of overregulated and unvaried repetition. The proportions of the parts are delicate and graceful but not weak. There is never a hint of feebleness in a classical Greek temple, nor is there ever a hint of ponderousness. The balance of forces is classical, that is, perfect. Perfection is achieved by sophisticated understanding of perception and not through slavery to mechanics or pure mathematics. Each element is carefully adjusted. A slight outward curvature of horizontal elements compensates for the tendency of the eye to perceive a downward sagging if all elements are

actually parallel. Each column has about a seven-inch, gradual dilation to compensate for the tendency of vertical parallel lines to appear to curve inward. The columns also tilt inward at the top so as to appear perpendicular. The stylobate is raised toward the center so as not to appear to sag under the immense weight of the stone columns and roof. Even the white marble color, which in other circumstances might appear stark, was chosen to harmonize with and reflect the intense Athenian sunlight. There is some debate concerning the adjustments and refinements noted above. Vitruvius, the Roman architect, is the earliest known source to describe these adjustments as aesthetic. Some scholars now believe that practical concerns also played a role.

So here we have the perfect embodiment of classical characteristics: convention, order, balance, idealization, simplicity, grace, and restrained vitality; of this earth but mingled with the divine.

A final example of classical architecture takes us slightly beyond the classical period of the late fifth century. Although no inscriptional information or other evidence provides a certain date for the Temple of Athena Nike (Fig. 4.34), this Ionic temple probably dates to the last quarter of the fifth century BC. The pediments contained sculptures, but none of these have survived. What remain are sculptures from the balustrade and the friezes. The Battle of Marathon is the subject matter for the friezes on the South side of the temple, "the only known example in temple sculpture of a conflict from near-contemporary rather than legendary history"[11], although the battle had, even by 420 BC, apparently assumed a legendary status.

The two previous examples show the fundamental differences between Doric and Ionic orders, which go beyond mere identification of column capitals. The earlier of the two types, the Doric, has a massive appearance compared to the Ionic. The Ionic, with a round base, has a curved profile which raises the column above the baseline of the building. The flutings of the Ionic order, usually twenty-two per column, are deeper and separated by wider edges than are those of the Doric, giving it a more delicate appearance. The Ionic capital is surrounded by a crown of hanging leaves or a *kymation*. The architrave, or lintel, shows a three-part division, each section of which diminishes downward, creating a much lighter impression than the more massive architrave of the Doric.

The temple of the Olympian Zeus (Fig. 4.35) illustrates Hellenistic modification of classical style in architecture, similar to that in painting, sculpture, and theatre. Scale and complexity are considerably different from the Parthenon, and the philosophy of emotionalism is clearly evident. Order, balance, moderation, and consonant harmony are still present, but in these huge ruins we can see the change in proportions from the Parthenon in the slender and ornate Corinthian columns.

4.34 The Temple of Athena Nike, Acropolis, Athens, 427–424 BC.

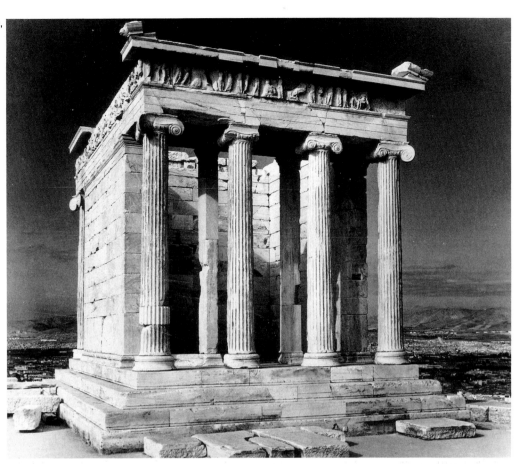

4.35 The Temple of Olympian Zeus, Athens, 174 BC–AD 130.

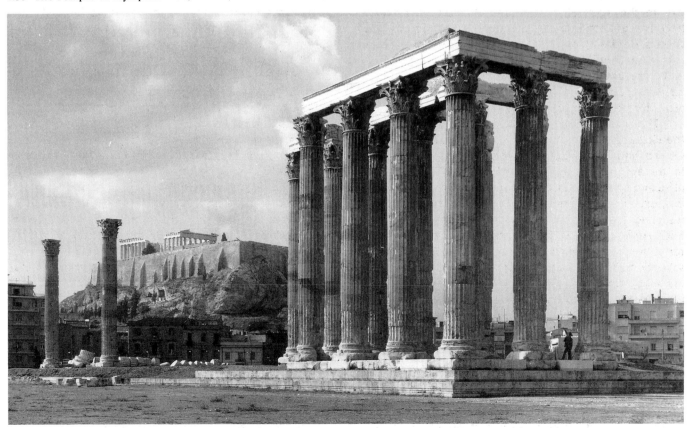

SYNTHESIS
From idealism to realism: Prometheus and Hecuba

In other chapters, the wide ranging character of the time period and geography lead us to synthesize by focusing on several disciplines from the same time and place, which may have evolved around a singular occurence or theme. In this case, however, the relatively compact and easily summarized characteristics of Athenian artistry have enabled us to perform this exercise of synthesis while examining the various artforms. A perhaps more revealing exercise when dealing with Greek culture is to isolate change, and particularly to see how much change occurred over a brief time in a single discipline, the theatre. We can take as our basis two plays which bracket the classical period in Athens—Aeschylus' *Prometheus Bound* and Euripides' *Hecuba*.

According to legend Prometheus frustrated the plans of Zeus by giving fire to a race of mortals whom Zeus sought to destroy. The legend embodies classical Greek idealism by attributing to human achievement the power to remedy shortcomings by reason and the capacity for infinite improvement. In punishment for his presumption, Prometheus is chained to a rock. In Prometheus' explanation of what he did for men, however, he suggests that humankind, through technology and reason, has dominion over nature.

Prometheus is extreme, even for Aeschylus, in its dependence on dialogue and character, and in its lack of action. The hero is motionless, chained to a rock, and nothing happens. There is only conversation with a parade of personages, by which the playwright reveals character and situation.

In this extract, the scene is set for an exchange between Force, Violence, and Hephaestus, the fire god. Violence does not speak, however, as there are only two actors. Force presents the situation:

> Far have we come to this far spot of earth,
> This narrow Scythian land, a desert all untrodden.
> God of the forge and fire, yours the task
> The Father laid upon you.
> To this high-piercing, head-long rock
> In adamantine chains that none can break
> Bind him—him here, who dared all things.
> Your flaming flower he stole to give to men,
> Fire, the master craftsman, through whose power
> All things are wrought, and for such error now
> He must repay the gods; be taught to yield
> To Zeus' lordship and to cease
> From his man-looking way.

Each character is revealed—Force, a villain and Hephaestus, a weak but kindly fool. After Force, Violence, and Hephaestus exit, Prometheus is discovered. He may have been revealed on a low wagon called an *ekkyklema*, which was rolled out from the central door of the *skene*. He speaks:

> O air of heaven and swift winged winds,
> O running river waters,
> O never numbered laughter or sea waves,
> Earth, mother of all, eye of the sun, all seeing,
> On you I call.
> Behold what I, a god, endure for gods.
> See in what tortures I must struggle
> Through countless years of time.
> This shame, these bonds, are put upon me
> By the new ruler of the gods.
> Sorrow enough in what is here and what is still to come.

And so the myth unfolds itself in high poetry as Prometheus discourses with the chorus, a group of kindly sea-nymphs, with Hermes, with Ocean, a humorous old busy-body, and with Io, an ephemeral creature. As the dialogue has run its course Prometheus summarizes:

> An end to words. Deeds now,
> The world is shaken.
> The deep and secret way of thunder
> Is rent apart.
> Fiery wreaths ⸱ lighting flash.
> Whirlwinds toss the swirling dust.
> The blasts of all the winds are battling in the air,
> And sky and sea are one.
> On me the tempest falls.
> It does not make me tremble
> O holy Mother Earth, O air and sun,
> Behold me. I am wronged.[12]

If *Prometheus* is an idealistic exploration of human achievement and power, written as the zenith of the Golden Age of Athens approached, *Hecuba*, by Euripides, is a bitter tragedy of the inter-relationships between those who rule and those who obey. It was written at a time when failure of leadership had sucked Athens downward through a long war of attrition with Sparta. Here again we deal with myth, in this case of the sack of Troy. Two separate events give the plot an episodic character. On the one hand is the slaughter of Polyxena by the Greeks, and on the other, the discovery of the body of Polydorus which causes Hecuba's revenge on Polymnestor. Hecuba rides over both of these actions. Each successive occurrence takes her one step further from grief to despair. She seeks Agamemnon's help in her revenge on Polymnestor for the murder of her son, and receives only pity and the summation, "What woman on this earth was ever cursed like this?" To which Hecuba replies in language less poetic and more realistic than that of Aeschylus:

There is none but goddess Suffering herself.

But let me tell you why I kneel
At your feet. And if my suffering seem just,
Then I must be content. But if otherwise,
Give me my revenge on that treacherous friend
Who flouted every god in heaven and in hell
To do this brutal murder.

At our table
He was our frequent guest; was counted first
Among our friends, respected and honoured by me,
Receiving every kindness that a man could meet—
And then, in cold deliberation killed
My son.

Murder may have its reasons, its motives,
But this—to refuse my son a grave, to throw him
To the sea, unburied! . . .

See me whole, observe
My wretchedness—

Once a queen, and now
A slave; blessed with children, happy once,
Now old, childless, utterly alone,
Homeless, lost, unhappiest of women
On this earth. . . .

Step by step she progresses toward her final atrocity. The focus of the play seems to lie on the way she is forced by her tormentors to yield, one at a time, her values, her self-respect, and "the faith which makes her human". What she suffers leads her to her ultimate dehumanization. Underlying the play is a stark condemnation of the logic of political necessity. When faced with power over which she has no control, she pleads honor, decency, the gods, and moral law, all of which fail. When her humanity is destroyed, she undertakes a savage brutality so base as to take her beyond the reach of judgement. Logic and sophistry are exposed by Euripides' furious pen. The chorus condemn the tragic waste of war and question the necessity of imperialism in their comments on the Archidamian War. Euripides finally attacks the gods themselves by implying that, even if they exist, their justice is so far removed from humans that it has no relevance.

Having slain all of Polymnestor's sons, whose abandoned corpses litter the stage, Hecuba and her women exit to their tent. The chorus files out with a final ode:

Files to the tents,
File to the harbor.
There we embark
On life as slaves.
Necessity is harsh.
Fate has no reprieve.[13]

SUGGESTIONS FOR THOUGHT AND DISCUSSION

The classical period in Greece, which reached its peak during the brief but lustrous "Age of Pericles", put the concept of humanism at the center of philosophy, aesthetics, and the arts. Man was the measure of all things. The gods displayed human characteristics and characters. Earthly life was of primary concern, and the *polis* was fundamental. In Greek temple architecture an earth-bound design of human scale further reinforced the humanism of philosophy and religion.

A second concept, that of intellectual rationalism, was part of Greek life and art. From *Prometheus* to the geometric designs of vase painting, order and form predominated. Appeal to the intellect and humanity's ability to address all issues successfully through reason comprise the canon underlying all things classically Greek. A third concept, idealism, further reinforced the classical Greek emphasis on humanity raised to its highest potential. From Plato to Aristotle to the sculptors, architects, and playwrights, we see this theme played out again and again.

As the Golden Age dissolved into the reality of Athenian defeat, however, we seen a change in tone, in attitude. Types become individuals, and idealism comes down to earth. The Cynics, Stoics, and Epicureans developed more pragmatic approaches to life and happiness. As the Hellenistic period arrived, simplicity in artistic form gave way to complexity. The aesthetics of the Doric Parthenon were replaced by the aesthetics of the Corinthian Temple of the Olympian Zeus. Appeal to the emotions took over from appeal to the intellect.

■ In what ways can you relate the philosophies of Plato to the classical style in painting, sculpture, and drama?
■ How do Aristotle and Plato differ in their aesthetic theories?
■ What is the relationship between the political history of Athens and the nature of its philosophical and aesthetic tone during the age of Pericles?
■ What relationships can be identified between the concepts of democracy and the *polis* and Aristotle's rejection of professionalism in the arts?
■ What practical circumstances made the "Golden Age" possible?
■ Trace the stylistic changes in vase painting and sculpture and compare these with changes in theatre art from the early classical to the post-classical and Hellenistic periods.

CHAPTER FIVE

THE ROMANS

The Romans were the conquerors of their world. By AD 70 they had destroyed the Temple of Jerusalem and colonized Britain, spreading their pragmatic and pluralistic version of Hellenistic Mediterranean civilization to peoples of the Iron Age in north and west Europe. Under Augustus, Roman culture turned again to Greek Classicism and in that spirit glorified their city, its Emperor and Empire. The Augustan period, falling at the opening of the Christian era, represents the plateau between the Roman Republic and Empire of the preceding one hundred and fifty years, and the gradual but accelerating slide into chaos and ultimate extinction which was to follow over the next three hundred years. Inventive and utilitarian, Roman culture left us roads, fortifications, viaducts, planned administration and a sophisticated yet robust legal system—in contrast to the temples and ideas of the Greeks. They provide us with the foundations for our society and its culture and represent the final and most historically important flowering of Classical civilization.

5.1 *Gemma Augustea* (detail), early first century AD. Onyx, 7½ × 9ins (19 × 23cm). Kunsthistorisches Museum, Vienna.

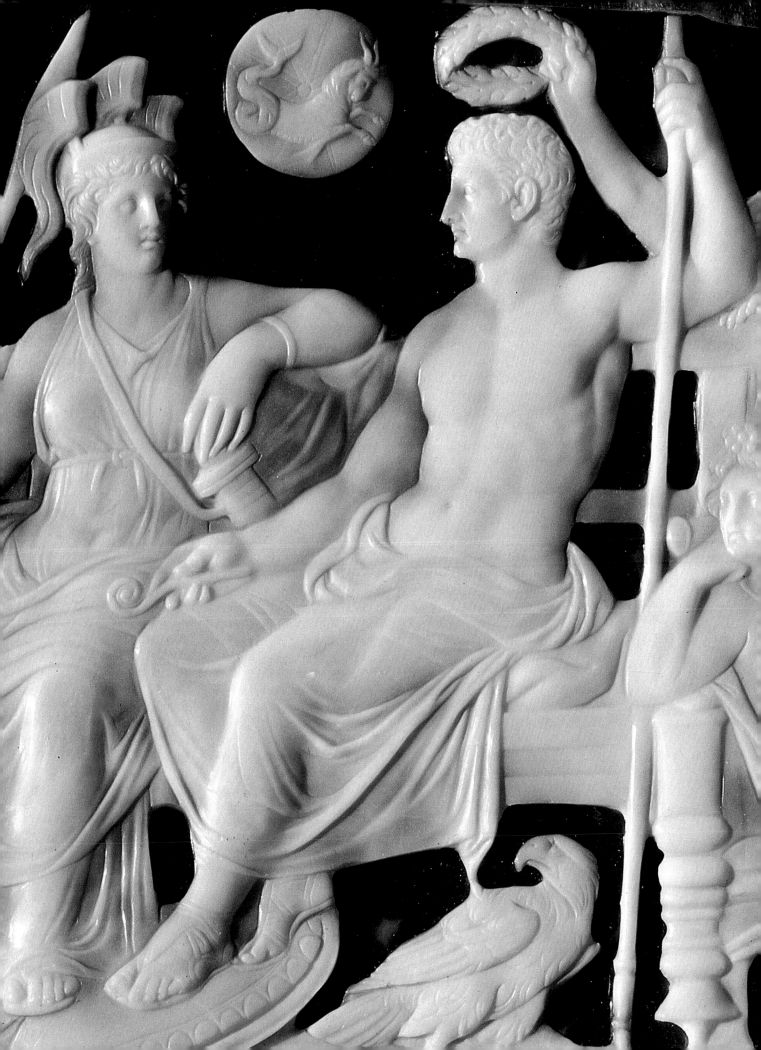

CONTEXTS AND CONCEPTS

The rise of Roman civilization parallels historically that of ancient Greece. By the sixth century BC Asian-Greek invaders, the Etruscans, dominated the Italian peninsula, bringing to that area a militaristic and practical society, an anthropomorphic conception of the deities, and arts of Greek influence roughly equivalent to the archaic style (Fig. **5.2**). During the centuries of the Greek classical and Hellenistic periods, Rome existed under a Republic characterized by class struggle and frequent attempts to assimilate other Italian peoples.

Roman legend held that Rome was founded by

5.2 Etruscan warrior supporting a wounded comrade, early 5th century BC. Bronze, height without base 5¼ins (13.4cm). The Metropolitan Museum of Art, New York (Rogers Fund, 1947)

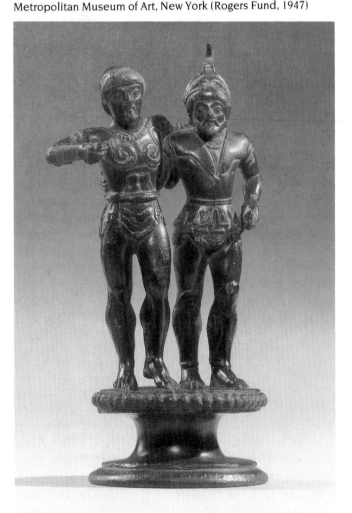

Romulus in 753 BC, and that he and his twin brother Remus had been suckled by a wolf, who became foster-mother to the orphaned boys. The legend of the founding of Rome provides further evidence of the Etruscan roots of Roman civilization, because one Etruscan religious cult revered wolves. Despite the rich archeological record left by the Etruscans, very little is known about them as a people. Several hypotheses exist as to where the Etruscans originated. One suggests that they came from Asia at the end of the Hittite Empire, reinforcing the concept of cross-cultural influence in the Mediterranean areas. They joined with other groups occupying the Italian peninsula perhaps as early as 1000 BC. It is clear that these early peoples had advanced cultures. Metallurgy developed as early as the tenth century BC. The Etruscans were also literate, and used an alphabet much like the Greek. Politically and economically they comprised a wealthy group of city-states governed by kings. One of these cities at the southern edge of Etruria, the Etruscan region, was Rome. Although small, Rome occupied an important location as a bridging-point across the river Tiber.

Towards the end of the sixth century BC the Romans instigated a revolt, involving other Latin cities, against Etruscan domination. In 509 BC, according to Roman tradition, the last Etruscan king was expelled from Rome, and the Romans set on a road that would lead them to all corners of the then-known world across nearly nine hundred years. Etruscan influence continued, however, and it was largely due to that influence and its links with Greece that the Romans inherited and carried forward the basic classical ideas and philosophies which still permeate our approach to life.

The Roman Republic

Once free of Etruscan domination, the Romans developed a Republican form of government which lasted until the first century BC, and provided important continuity for Roman institutions. The motto "S.P.Q.R."—*Senatus Populusque Romanus*, "The

Roman Senate and People"—reflected the philosophy of the early Roman political and social order and remained the watchword of Roman society until Imperial times. It meant that sovereignty rested in the people themselves, and not in any particular governmental form. Yet in many ways the Roman Republic functioned as a democracy. Decisions affecting society were made at a series of assemblies which all citizens attended to express their will. The Senate, on the other hand, conducted the business of government including the passage of legislation and the supervision of elected magistrates. Over the centuries the greatest issues affecting Roman society were played out as dramas created by tensions between people and Senate.

The Senate itself was an hereditary institution comprising an assembly of heads—*patres*—of old patrician families and later wealthy members of the citizenry—*plebs*. The three hundred members therefore represented old and new money, power, and social interest. It was a self-renewing oligarchy. The two most important officers who ruled the state were the *consuls*, elected by the representative assemblies for one-year terms, at the end of which they became members of the Senate. In Rome the rich ruled via the Senate. The general citizenry were little more than peasants. By the third century BC the division between aristocrat and peasant had widened appreciably—the former growing in riches and the latter sinking further and further into poverty. Yet the constitutional framework of the Republic held the small Roman social order together, warding off revolution, permitting change, and providing the body politic with reasonably well-trained leaders who knew how, above all else, to keep the Republic functioning and alive. It was, in fact, the internal stability of the Republic which made expansion possible, bringing about the next phase of Roman history.

Roman expansion was based on military conquest. Very little commerce and industry existed in Rome, unlike Athens, and the quality of life in Rome came to depend directly upon the wealth of conquered regions brought back to Rome as spoils of military victory. By the middle of the second century BC Rome had conquered Carthage in North Africa and Corinth in Asia Minor, and had thus assumed a position of political dominance in the Hellenistic world. The internationalization of culture, evident in Hellenic times, increased further under the Romans. Later, Rome would extend its control throughout Europe and eventually to the British Isles.

Imperialism and Empire

Because Roman expansion and conquest depended upon strong military power, the Roman army became a powerful institution. Every male citizen (citizenship was bestowed on conquered peoples as well) who held property also had an obligation to serve up to sixteen years in the army, if conscripted. The basic unit of the army was the legion, comprising 5,000 men. Apparently the only occasion during the early period on which the army did not successfully discharge its responsibilities occurred in 390 BC, when the Gauls succeeded in sacking Rome itself. By 272 BC the Romans had conquered western Greece and placed themselves in direct confrontation with the other major power of the period, Carthage. Over the next hundred years in the three stages of the Punic Wars, Rome and Carthage set upon each other in a battle for total control of the Mediterranean world. During the Second Punic War, which began in 218 BC, came the great march over the Alps to Italy by the Carthaginian general, Hannibal. The end of the Second Punic War in 202 BC left Rome in a position of advantage and at a watershed.

A choice presented itself, either to consolidate order and security in the West or to expand the Empire toward the East. The Romans chose to move eastward, and the outcome, though unforeseen at the time, left Rome as overlord of the entire Hellenistic world. What was foreseen was the possibility of new riches from the conquered territories. A second motive was the desire to rid the world of the Carthaginian threat, once and for all. The onset of the Third Punic War came in 149 BC, and ended three years later with the destruction of Carthage. The Roman Empire was at hand.

Control of such a vast empire for so long a time was the greatest monument to Roman genius. The Romans were supreme managers and administrators. They brought to their world a significant code of law and innumerable engineering projects such as aqueducts and roads, many of which are still in use. Concern was for the utilitarian and the practical, as befitted Rome's Etruscan heritage, and such concern can be seen in the focus of Roman architecture. Greek architecture had centered around religion and nearly always reflected mythical or religious conventions. Roman architecture solved practical problems. The temple symbolized Greek architecture, while the Triumphal Arch, the bath, and the amphitheatre (Fig. **5.6**) symbolized Roman.

BC/AD	GENERAL EVENTS	LITERATURE & PHILOSOPHY	VISUAL ART	THEATRE & DANCE	MUSIC	ARCHITECTURE
753 BC	Legendary founding of Rome by Romulus and Remus Development of Etruscan Civilization					
500	Roman Revolution		Etruscan Warrior (5.2)	Phlyakes farces		
400	Gauls invade Rome			Mime		
300	Roman conquest of Western Greeks First Punic War	Chryssipus-Stoicism		Development of Roman comedy Plautus		
200	Second Punic War Hannibal Marius	Middle Stoa Diogenes		Terence First stone theatres in Rome		The Pantheon (5.25)
100 BC	Julius Caesar elected Consul Julian Calendar Battle of Actium Augustus	Panaetius Posidonius Seneca Epictetus	Exedra of the Villa at Boscoreale Portrait of an Unknown Roman *Augustus* – 1st–3rd types	Pantomime invented: Pylades of Cilicia Bathyllus of Alexandria		Ara Pacis (5.33)
0	Nero Roman destruction of the Temple of Jerusalem Mt. Vesuvius erupts	Virgil Horace Martial Juvenal Homiletic Stoicism Satire Petronius Apuleius Lucian	Hercules and Telephos (5.10) Lady playing a kithara (5.11) Herculaneum wall paintings			Forum of Augustus (5.32) The Colosseum (5.23) Arch of Titus (5.28)
100 AD			Sarcophagi			
200		Plotinus				
300	Split between Rome and Byzantium		Head of Constantine (5.17)			

5.3 Timeline of Roman culture

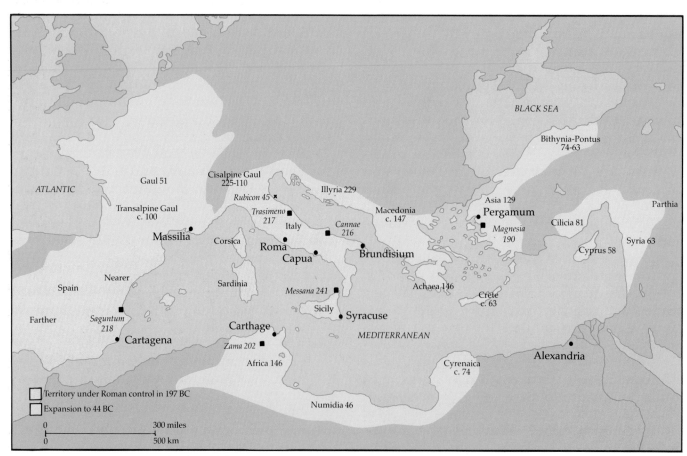

5.4 The Roman Empire under the Republic.

Rome assimilated much of its philosophy, science, and arts from the Greeks and the Hellenistic world. An example would be Stoicism. Reason or *logos* governed the Stoic's world, and the Great Intelligence was God. Specific guidelines for goodness and nobility gave order to life. The main tenets of Stoicism were acceptance of fate and duty, and the brotherhood of all men. The last belief had significant effect on the Western world because it gave Roman law, one of Rome's great contributions to Western culture, the ideal of providing justice for all men. Essentially, however, Stoicism was pessimistic. All things were believed to be controlled by the Great Logos, and man could do nothing but submit to this greater Will.

Julius Caesar

The continual state of war on the borders of the Empire and the practicalities of effective government placed ultimate power and authority in the hands of the Roman Senate, with a diminution of participation and franchise for the ordinary citizen. An emergent force in Roman political affairs, brought about because of the immense wealth to be gained in conquered lands, were the territorial governors and generals, who came from the patrician families. The institutions of the Republic gave way to the expediencies of the Empire. How to balance the needs imposed by running an empire with those required by the constitution taxed even the most scrupulous of politicians. The Empire was seething with turmoil and ripe for revolution. The conflict lay between rich and poor and both had a vote. Nevertheless there was a Hellenistic surge in culture at this time encouraged by ease of communication within the Empire.

The last century of the Republic and its Empire, that is, from approximately 112 to 27 BC, witnessed a parade of individuals stepping into the breach. The first of these was Marius. Then came a power struggle in the late first century from which the dictator Sulla emerged, followed by Pompey. In 59 BC Marius' nephew, Julius Caesar, was elected consul. During a five-year campaign against the Gauls, Caesar watched Roman politics carefully. "Gangsterism, corruption, and murder continued to disfigure public life and discredit the Senate." After great intrigue, Caesar crossed the Rubicon in 49 BC,

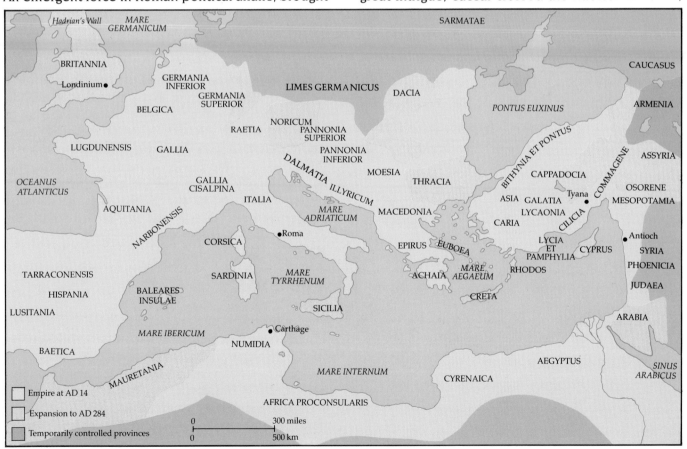

5.5 The Roman Empire AD 14–284.

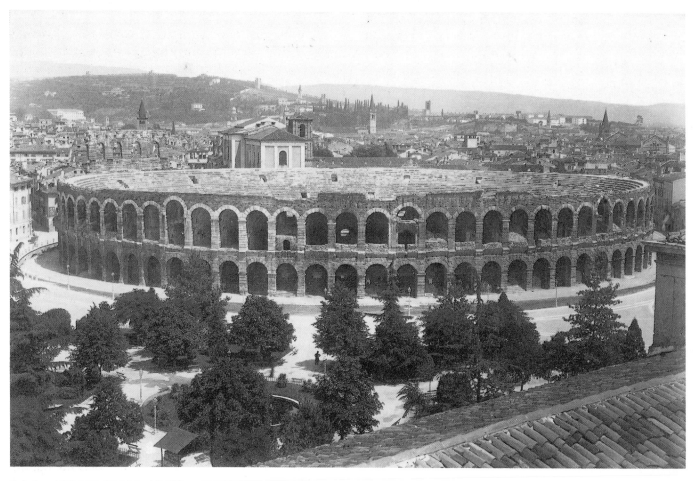

5.6 Amphitheatre, Verona, AD 290.

5.7 Map of Imperial Rome.

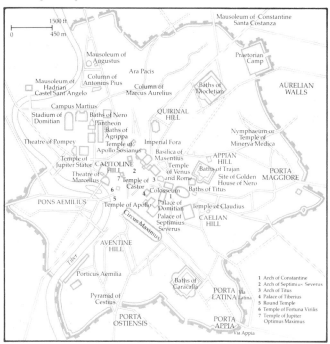

and by 44 BC he had returned to Rome in triumph to be voted dictator for life. His life was cut short only days later, however, on 15 March 44 BC at the hands of assassins in the Senate. Nonetheless, it is Caesar whom we credit with the reform of the calendar and the creation of the Julian calendar of 365 days, with an additional day every four years. The new calendar began 1 January 45 BC. Caesar's assassins were condemned and Caesar was proclaimed a god. The Republic, stagnant for years, was dead.

The Stoics

The philosophy of Stoicism followed a wandering course over the years, unlike other philosophies such as Epicureanism, which remained unchanged. Stoicism, as defined in Chapter 4, traced its roots back to Zeno and dealt primarily with a scheme of salvation and a way of life, that is, a definition of human happiness and a means of attaining it. By 280 BC, the Stoic philosophy had fallen under the charge of Chryssipus, who redefined it according to parameters which were to go unchanged for as long as Stoicism remained a vital philosophy. Called the Old Stoa, this period witnessed a modification of some of the more extreme tenets and a thrust which resulted in the Romans turning Stoicism into a religion. On its way to Rome, Stoicism passed through the hands of Diogenes in the second century BC, a period known as the Middle Stoa. Diogenes brought Stoicism to Rome, where he gave lectures and favorably impressed the Romans. The fate of Stoicism finally, however, depended upon the skills of Panaetius and Posidonius in the early first century BC. Under Panaetius and Posidonius Stoicism lost much of its cynicism, became more cultured and universal, and more attuned to the sprituality of the Roman world. Panaetius adopted Aristotle's definition of virtue as a golden mean and espoused the belief that physical goods might not only be a means to right living, but could also be pursued as an end in themselves. An emphasis on temperance, propriety in daily life, and the performance of daily duty made Stoicism even more attractive to the Roman way of thinking.

As a result of the work of Panaetius and Posidonius, Rome became the home of Stoic philosophy and Stoicism entered its Late Stoa. The worldliness and common sense of the Romans made it into a mellower, more urbane, and more tolerant set of beliefs, and freed it from intellectual and moral dogmatism.

Seneca

The changes forced on the Stoics by the Roman genius and the general nature of the times are illustrated by the life and writings of Seneca. "Austere and somewhat sanctimonious by nature, he was given to deploring human weakness and to bewailing the vanity and wickedness of the world, from which he professed himself to await impatiently release in a happier home beyond the grave."[1] He was not, however, averse to success in his own life. His business sense was shrewd, and he was tireless in his attempts to increase the considerable fortune he had inherited. While the Cynics and Epicureans deprecated wealth, Seneca staunchly defended the "righteousness of great wealth" in his philosophic sermons. Reflecting the changes in Stoicism during its final stages, he believed that reason was bankrupt. He substituted for it sentimental and moral needs as sufficient ground for religious convictions.

Marcus Aurelius and Epictetus

By the time of Augustus Caesar Stoicism had gained popularity among the masses as well as the upper classes. It accepted "popular theology as an allegorical and pictorial expression of Stoic truth." By the time of Nero, who sought to suppress all freedom of thought, Stoicism, which propounded free inquiry and discussion, had fallen on hard times. It was seen as a threat to the state, and many of its leaders were executed or exiled. In only a few years, however, Stoicism re-emerged as a central doctrine under the Stoic Emperor Marcus Aurelius who, along with the slave Epictetus gave final definition and popularity to the philosophy. The *Discourses* and the *Manual* of Epictetus and the *Meditations* of Marcus Aurelius show us a Stoicism, old-fashioned in many respects, leaning toward "cynic austerity" and concerned mainly with the moral and religious aspects of Stoicism. Physical and metaphysical concerns, as well as logic, were disregarded as a waste of time. Stoicism was a healer of souls, appealing to the moral sense rather than the intellect, and turning men to the "way that led to happiness and peace". Salvation lay in cultivating independence from external circumstance, enriching oneself by religious sentiment, and having faith in "an assurance that all is for the best". Central to the beliefs of both Marcus Aurelius and Epictetus was faith in the brotherhood of all men. "All men are the children of one Father." All men, regardless of race or status are brothers, and should be loved as such. Above all, the order of the world is rational. "All things and events are expressions of a divine Reason which finds them all equally necessary and equally perfect." Death is the end of the individual, merging each of us with "the elements from which we sprang", and reuniting "the reason within us with the *Logos* of which it is a part". Death is not to be feared or desired, but merely accepted. After Marcus Aurelius' death, Stoicism lost ground to the emerging Christianity.

Roman Law

Very likely the most significant conceptual development of Roman civilization was in jurisprudence—the law and specifically the technique of legal interpretation which enabled its practitioners to decide whether and with what effect a general law would apply in a given case. Such questions had always faced judges and juries wherever actions were judged and disputes settled in accordance with fixed laws. In Rome, however, their settlement became the province of a special group of private individuals called jurisconsults ... who were recognized experts on the meanings of the laws. Their opinions gradually acquired almost the force of law because a judge was limited in practice to choice between the opinions submitted to him by jurisconsults.[2]

Thus it was that a legacy of expert opinion and knowledge of the law was established. The prestige of learning separated itself from that of position. Legal knowledge and tradition became a base of knowledge requisite to the practice of the law.

The jurists applied philosophical methods—exact definition, classification, logical inference—to the topics of Roman law and thus transformed the isolated traditions of their predecessors into a legal system ... Their concern was to determine how the rules would apply in particular cases. By such determination in many exemplary cases they made the meaning of the law predictable and the same for all.[3]

5.8 Scale model of ancient Rome. Museo della Civilta Romana, Rome.

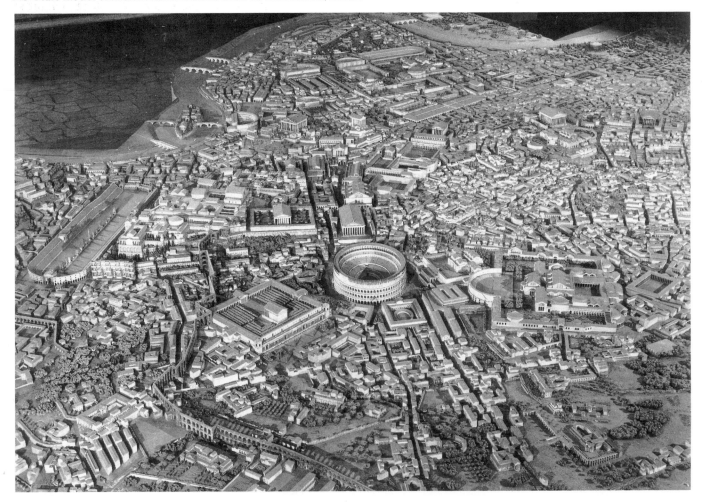

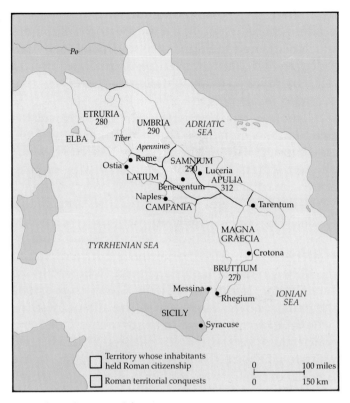

5.9 Italy at the time of the Roman Empire.

The final years

By the turn of the Christian age the Emperor Augustus (27 BC–AD 14) had launched Rome into a significant rebuilding period which emphasized arts and literature. This was the age of the poets Virgil and Horace, and Virgil's *Aeneid* is said by some critics to have brought instant mythology to the Romans. Virgil recognized the greatness of the Golden Age of Athens and the influence that Homer's earlier *Iliad* and *Odyssey* had had upon that era. The *Aeneid* created a mythical history of Rome complete with a founding hero, Aeneas. The Flavian–Antonine period of the late first and second centuries AD produced the architectural style we identify today as typically Roman, with its vaults and arches. In this era Roman expansion moved eastward, culminating in the siege and destruction of the Temple of Jerusalem in AD 70.

In AD 180 the army took command, and for all intents and purposes central authority in Rome collapsed. For the succeeding century and a half emperors came and went, largely at the whim of the army, until early in the fourth century when Constantine I assumed the throne. During his reign two vitally important events occurred. First, Christianity was recognized as the state religion in AD 337.

Second, a new Rome was founded in the East at Byzantium, which became Constantinople, and the Empire thenceforth had two capital cities. By the fifth century AD Rome had fallen to the Goths, and a new era in the history of Western art and civilization was beginning.

Plotinus: Beauty and Symbol

Plotinus (*c.* AD 205–*c.* AD 270) was an Egyptian-born philosopher and the greatest exponent of the neo-Platonist school. The neo-Platonist viewpoint will reappear much later in the works of Michelangelo, but here it is expressed in the midst of a Roman world sliding into decline.

> The beauty of art and nature is a manifestation of the unity of being ... individual beauty is, as it were, a symbol of cosmic harmony and a symbol of the higher reality to which all beautiful things are related and upon which all individual experiences of beauty depend.
>
> Artists' products are therefore valuable chiefly as symbols. It is with Plotinus that the symbolic nature of art receives its first comprehensive formulation. Not only is the beautiful object a symbol of cosmic harmony, but the cosmic order is best alluded to by metaphors themselves of a poetic nature ... An interesting use of art as an image of a metaphysical principle is Plotinus' reference to the dance in explaining the harmony of nature as a living whole (*Ennead* IV, 4.33). The Good radiates beauty from itself and is the source of beauty, while Beauty itself is second in the order of emanations. Thus the beauty of a man-made object (statue) is an imitation of Beauty and ultimately of the Good. And below the beauty of the created are the incomplete beauties of natural things which the arts are able to perfect. Hence, works of art stand midway between the somewhat obscured beauties of nature, which they ennoble and bring to fulfilment, and Beauty itself, which the mind can know through its ascent beyond the beautiful object. Art is a symbol in a double sense: of that lower reality which it perfects and that ultimate reality which it mirrors.[4]

Literature

At such time when literature became reasonably acceptable to the practical Romans, it was chiefly through the contributions of Greek slaves that it was nurtured. At first literary works were imitations of Greek works and written in Greek. Latin was initially seen as a peasant language with few words capable of expressing abstract notions. The credit for developing a Latin prose style and vocabulary for the expression of philosophical ideas probably belongs to Cicero.

During the reign of Augustus, the poets Horace and Virgil were commanded to write verses glorifying the emperor, the origins of Rome, the simple honesty of rural Roman life, patriotism, and the glory of dying for one's country. Livy set about retelling Roman history in sweeping style. Virgil's *Aeneid*, an epic account of the journey of Aeneas from the ruins of Troy to the shores of Italy, far surpassed any merely propagandistic brief. The influence of these three writers—Horace, Virgil, and Livy—on Western culture is difficult to overestimate; "they are so much a part of us that we take their values for granted and their epigrams for truisms."[5] As far as the Emperor Augustus was concerned, they fully expressed the Roman tradition and Roman language. Horace, Virgil, and Livy created a literature which distracted the upper classes from Greek "free thought" and which the Emperor could exploit to rally them to the ancient Roman order as represented in his person.

Throughout the literature of the Augustan period runs a moralizing stoicism. The most remarkable product of stoicism in poetry was satire, which allowed writers to combine morality with popular appeal. Martial and Juvenal utilized poetry to attack vice, and were thereby able to describe it in graphic detail. Petronius produced satirical picaresque novels of verse and prose, whose details were as readable as Martial's and Juvenal's but void of their morality. Finally, Apuleius and Lucan followed in the same literary tradition. Apuleius' *Golden Ass* is among the earliest novels ever written. The author creates a fictional biography describing how he was tried and condemned for the murder of three wineskins. He was brought back to life by a sorceress, and in the process of trying to follow her in the form of a bird, he was changed instead into an ass. The only cure for his affliction appeared to be the procurement of rose leaves, and in his search for these, he fell into some bizarre and fantastic adventures.

THE ARTS
OF THE ROMANS

TWO-DIMENSIONAL ART

Very little Roman painting has survived. Most of what there is comes from Pompeii, preserved by the cataclysmic eruption of Mt. Vesuvius. Frescoes—paintings on wet plaster which become a permanent part of the wall surface—appear to have comprised the bulk of two-dimensional art, much of which was an outright copy of classical and Hellenistic works. Greek artists and craftsmen were brought to Rome and it was they who produced most early Roman artworks. It is therefore not surprising that Roman paintings reflected classical and Hellenistic characteristics, although certain uniquely Roman qualities were added. It is difficult to state with any certainty that the illustrations which follow are typical, but they are typical of what survives of Roman artworks.

The work *Hercules and Telephos* (Fig. **5.10**) clearly displays the naturalism of figure depiction characteristic of the Hellenistic style, and we note with interest the mythical and heroic nature of the subject matter. In contrast, the painting *Lady Playing the Cithara* (Fig. **5.11**) combines naturalistic detail with everyday or genre subject matter. Each of these is a formally composed picture, with a self-imposed boundary.

Some Roman painting combines landscape representation with painted architectural detail on a flat wall surface to create a panoramic vista seen through an imaginary window. The detailed complexity of ornamentation of such landscapes, framed by fake architectural detail, has been suggested by some scholars to be remarkably similar to the rococo style of the eighteenth century.

Rooms painted in what is called the Second Style reflect the tastes of late Republican aristocratic society which took as its model the opulence and stylishness of the late Hellenistic princely courts still influential around the Mediterranean. Mystery cults, especially that of Dionysius, were fashionable, and appear in various manifestations in wall paintings, such as those from the villa near Boscoreale (Fig. **5.12**).

The rich iconographical repertory of Greek mythology became part and parcel of Roman wall decoration, and not alone with its forms but also with its wealth of significant content. This had to do also with the affinity of the wall painting to the scenery in Roman theatres.... Related concepts underly these two forms of art ... Vitruvius (*De Architectura* 6.5.2)

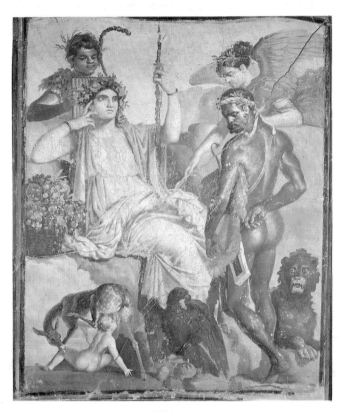

5.10 Hercules and his infant son Telephos, Roman copy of a Greek work of the 2nd century BC. Wall painting from Herculaneum, 5ft 7½ins (171cm) high. Museo Archeologico Nazionale, Naples.

tells us that at a certain point the wall painters took to imitating theatrical décors as used in tragedies, comedies, and satyr plays. Elsewhere (5.6.9), he specifies that these represent three standard types, whose decorations are entirely different. The tragic décor involves columns, pediments, statues, and all the other things fitting to a royal palace.... The comic décor, on the other hand, shows private dwellings with balconies and projecting bays broken up by windows just as in ordinary houses. Satyric décors, finally, are decked out with trees, grottoes, mountains and like rustic features found in country places, all treated in the manner of a landscape painting.[6]

There is debate among scholars as to the degree to which illusionistic wall painting relates to theatrical scenery and which to real architecture.

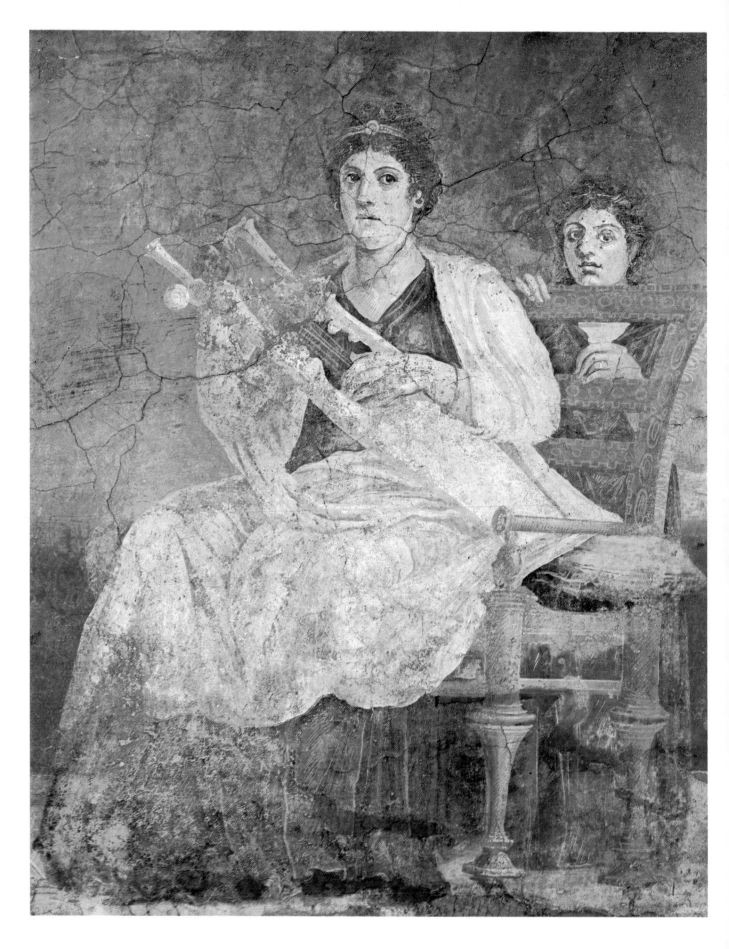

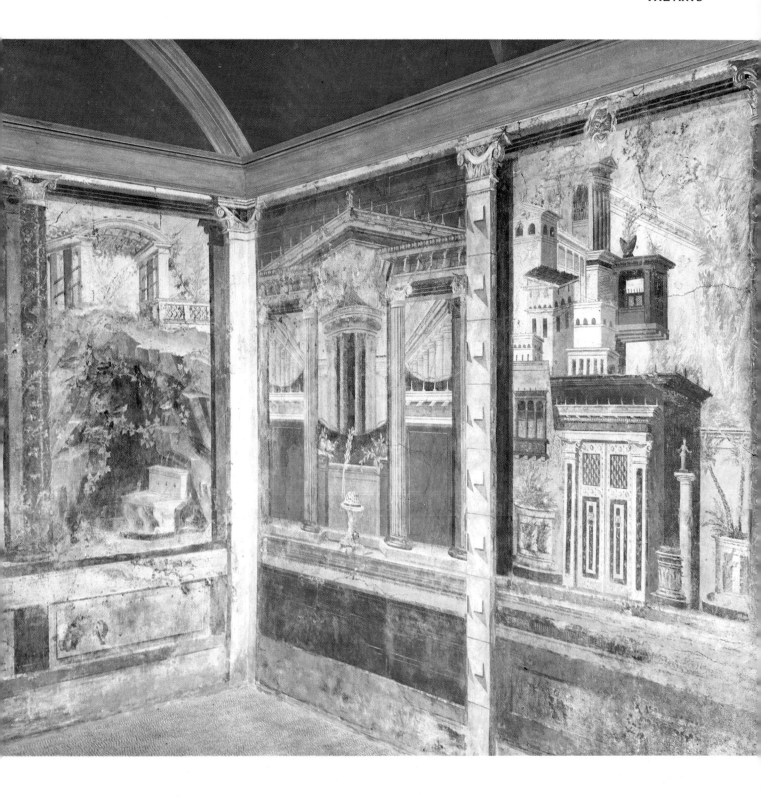

5.11 Lady playing the kithara, c. 50 BC. Wall painting, 6ft 1½ins (187 cm) square. The Metropolitan Museum of Art, New York (Rogers Fund, 1903).

5.12 Cubiculum from a villa at Boscoreale, showing painted decorations, c. 50 BC. Wall painting, average height 8ft (2.44m). The Metropolitan Museum of Art, New York (Rogers Fund, 1903).

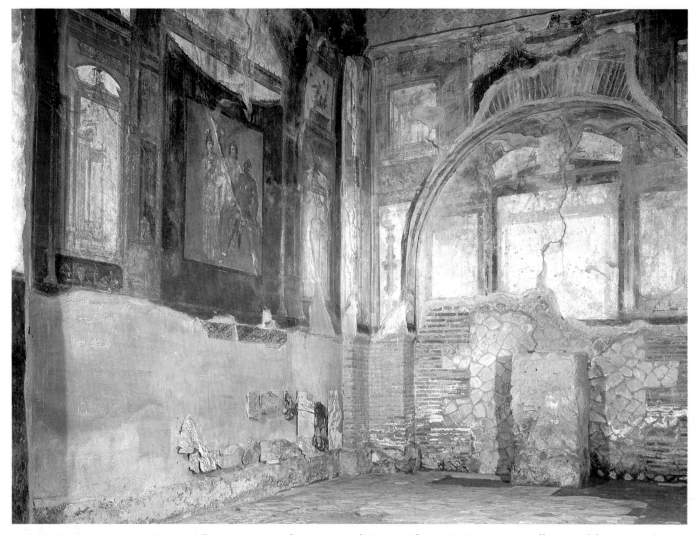

5.13 Wall decoration, c. AD 70–79. Wall painting, room dimensions 14ft 2ins × 13ft 4ins (4.32 × 4.06m). Collegium of the Augustales, Herculaneum.

A final example of wall painting from the Flavian period of the first century reinforces our image of highly forceful color usage and broad surfaces depicting architectural detail (Fig. **5.13**). In this shrine devoted to the cult of the emperor, the central panel depicts the introduction of Hercules into Olympus in the presence of Minerva and Juno.

SCULPTURE

We should beware of classifying all Roman art as an imitative and sterile reconstruction of Greek prototypes. Certainly some Roman statues fit that category. Figure **5.14** is a Roman copy of a Greek statue of Hermes dating back to before the Christian era. It represents not only mythological subject matter, but also Hellenic qualities of an earlier era.

Some Roman sculpture, however, displays vigorous creativity that is uniquely Roman and uniquely expressive of Roman circumstances. All the same, scholars are divided not only on what various works of Roman sculpture reveal, but also on what motivated them. The *Portrait of an Unknown Roman* (Fig. **5.15**) dates from a time when Hellenistic influence was becoming well established in Rome, as the fresco painting of the previous section illustrates. It is tempting to attribute the highly naturalistic representation of this work to the same artistic viewpoint which governed Hellenistic style, and conclude that it is a copy of Hellenistic work. Such a conclusion, however, neglects an important Etruscan–Roman religious practice, undoubtedly of stronger influence. Portraits were an integral part of household and ancestor worship, and the image of a departed ancestor was maintained in a wax death mask. Wax is not a substance ideally suited for immortality, and there is a possibility that the naturalism of portraiture of this bust stems from the fact that it was made from a death mask.

However, there may be more than mere portrait accuracy in this work, and some scholars point to an apparent selectivity of features and a reinforcement of an idea or ideal of ruggedness and character.

The straightforward naturalism of the Republican era changed during the Augustan period. Hellenistic influence had grown by the late first century BC. In certain quarters Greek classical influence dominated, but always with a Roman, that is, a more practical and individual character. By the time of the Empire, classical influence had returned sculpture to the idealized characteristics of Periclean Athens.

5.14 Hermes, Roman copy of a Greek work of c. 400 BC. Marble, 5ft 11ins (1.8m) high. The Metropolitan Museum of Art, New York (Gift of the Hearst Foundation, 1956).

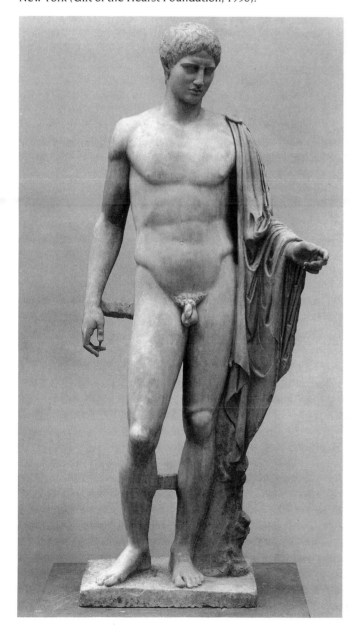

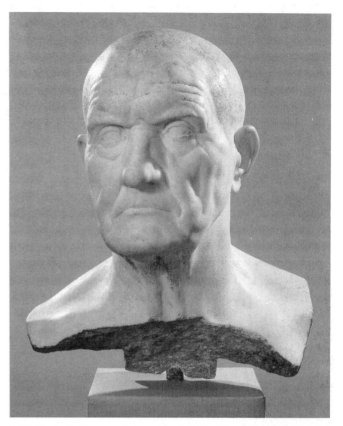

5.15 Bust of a Roman, 1st century BC. Marble, 14⅜ins (36.5cm) high. The Metropolitan Museum of Art, New York (Rogers Fund).

Augustus (Fig. **5.16**) boasted that when he took Rome over it was a city of sun-dried bricks, and that when he left it it had become a metropolis in marble. Greek classical form in sculpture was duplicated, recast, and translated into vital forms of the present. The Greek concept of the "perfect body" predominated. There was also a common practice of copying the idealized body of some well known Greek statue and adding to it a highly realistic portrait head of some contemporary Roman. Other figures were similarly Romanized. One statue portrayed a male figure draped in a toga, while another showed Augustus in armor. The aesthetics of sculptural depiction thus remained Greek with Roman clothing added. The pose, rhythm, and movement of the body originated in the past. The purpose of much sculpture at this time was the portrayal of the emperor. Emperors were raised to the status of gods, perhaps, as some have speculated, because a far-flung empire required assurances of stability and suprahuman characteristics in its leaders.

The reality that men are men and not gods was not long in returning to Roman consciousness, however, and third-century sculpture exhibited a stark and expressive reality. In the fourth century AD a new and powerful emperor had taken the throne, and his likeness (Fig.

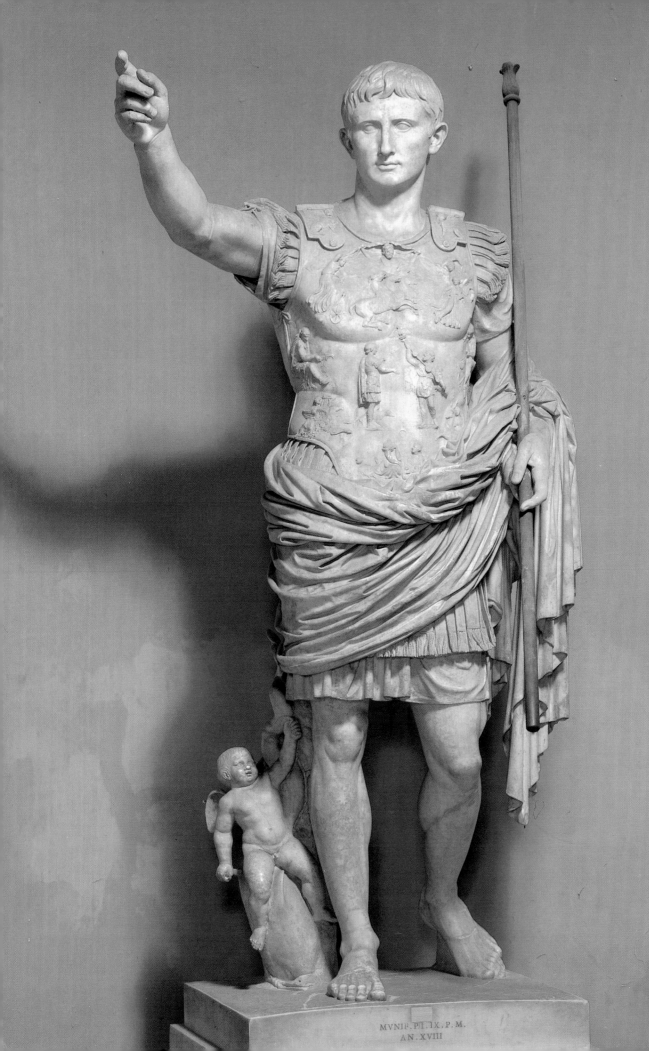

5.17), part of a gigantic sculpture (the head is over eight feet tall), shows an exaggerated, ill-proportioned intensity that we can compare with expressionist works of the early twentieth century. This work is not an actual likeness of Constantine. Instead, it is the artist's view of Constantine's perception of himself as emperor and of the office of emperor itself.

Finally, Roman funerary sculpture needs to be mentioned. We have touched already upon funerary art in the form of the death mask. The intricate relief sculpture which decorated Roman sarcophagi shows Roman artistry as it reflected private life. This type of sculpture emerged early in the second century AD when the practice of cremation fell out of favor. Marble sarcophagi were adorned with rich and varied relief decoration. There were three major centers of sarcophagus production—Rome, Athens, and Asia Minor. Sarcophagi were often exported in an uncompleted state and finished at the site by accompanying sculptors. Attic sarcophagi showed decoration on all four sides with scenes drawn from Greek mythology. They were typically carved in high relief in a somber tone. Asiatic sarcophagi exhibited figures carved almost in the round against a background of architectural detail. Roman sarcophagi were carved on three sides, with the fourth side designed to sit against a wall. The front side typically contained a mythological scene while the two ends showed low relief, decorative motifs (Fig. 5.18).

MUSIC

We know that music was very popular among the Romans. Extant reports describe festivals, competitions, and virtuoso performances. Large choruses and orchestras performed regularly, and the *hydraulus*, the water organ, was a popular attraction at the Colosseum. The *hydraulus*, apparently, was so loud that it could be heard a mile away, and the fact that it provided "background music" for the infamous feedings of the Christians to the lions banned it from Christian churches for centuries. Many Roman emperors were patrons of music, and Greek music teachers were popular and very well paid.

Aristotle deplored professionalism in the pursuit of music. Music for him was art for its own aesthetic qualities and a moral factor in character development; it was a

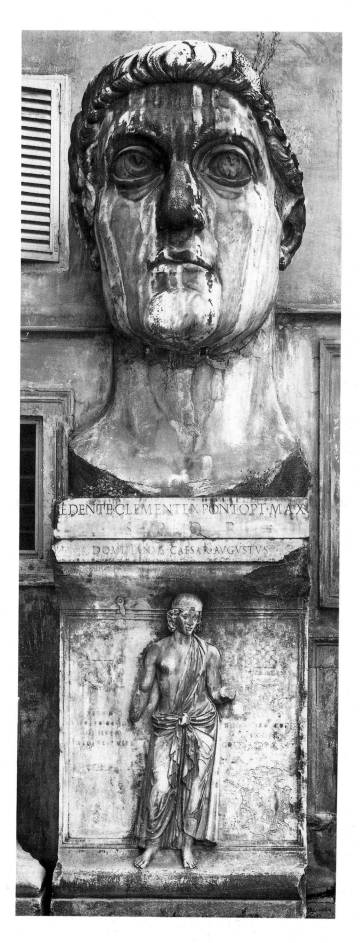

5.16 Augustus in armor, from the Villa of Livia, Prima Porta, c. 20 BC. Marble, 6ft 8ins (2.03m) high. Vatican Museums, Rome.

5.17 Head of Constantine the Great (part of an original colossal seated statue), AD 313. Marble, 8ft 6⅜ins (2.61m) high. Palazzo dei Conservatori, Rome.

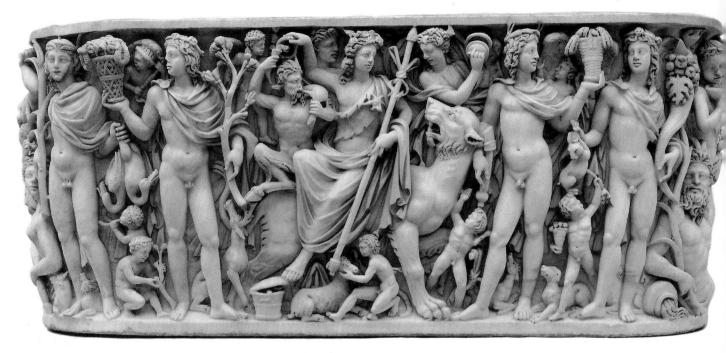

5.18 Roman sarcophagus, showing Dionysus, the Seasons and other figures, c. AD 220–30. Marble, 7ft 3¾ins (2.23m) long. The Metropolitan Museum of Art, New York (Purchase, 1955, Joseph Pulitzer Bequest).

measure of intelligence. Clearly the pragmatic Romans did not regard music in these terms. Professional dexterity and virtuosity were used as social tools, and such inane accomplishments as who could blow the loudest tone or hold a note the longest were heralded with great acclaim. Musical entertainment, very different from the Greek concept of art and inspiration, did fulfill an important social and political function for the Romans. As more and more people flocked to Rome from conquered territories, and the numbers of unemployed grew, the state provided entertainments to keep them occupied and under control. "Bread and Circuses" came to be regarded as the answer to the dissatisfactions of the poor and the oppressed, and music played an important role in keeping the lid on some of the trouble. Music became less and less an individual activity and more and more an exclusively professional enterprise.

It appears doubtful that the Romans contributed much to musical practice or theory. They took their music from the Greeks after Greece became a Roman province in 146 BC, absorbing both Greek instruments and theory. They did invent some new instruments, principally brass, such as the trumpet and horn for practical, military usage. As with Greek music, we may know of the presence of music in this society and a little of its theory, practice, and instrumentation, but we have no real conception of how Roman music may have sounded, melodically or rhythmically.

By the end of the fifth century AD all mention of secular music had virtually disappeared. Certainly secular music must have existed, but we have no record of it.

THEATRE

The Romans loved entertainment, and particularly drama. Roman drama, for the most part, occupied the opposite end of the intellectual spectrum from Greek classicism. Roman theatre was wild, unrestrained, lewd, and highly realistic. Accounts of stage events suggest that very little was left to the audience's imagination. We might find the Roman theatre buildings somewhat strange in their conventions, and we would need to learn the conventions of various masks, but for the most part we would have little difficulty understanding the events portrayed. Undoubtedly we would find the grotesquely padded costumes and farcical actions as hilarious as the Romans did.

Dramatic forms

Three important dramatic forms were prevalent at various times in Roman history: *phlyakes* farces, Roman comedy, and the mime. The earliest of these was the *phlyakes* farce, which some authorities trace to Grecian origin as early as the fifth century BC in Sicily. Whatever its sources, the *phlyakes* (from the word for gossips) had an earthy style. Its themes first parodied mythology and, later, burlesqued tragedy. Very little literary evidence exists about the *phlyakes*, but a considerable number of vase paintings testify to its existence and character. If such evidence can be taken at face value, the *phlyakes* were bawdy and lewd with actors suggestively padded and extravagantly masked. Apparently these farces used a raised stage consisting of a rough wooden platform containing a simple background and doors for entrances and exits by the actors. Curtains masked the area below the stage.

Roman comedy developed from third and second century BC influences of Hellenistic comedy, with its large theatres, high stages, and elaborate scene buildings as we noted in Chapter Four. The New Comedy of Menander was easily understood by the Romans and was assimilated quickly. From the importation to Rome of Greek New Comedy came the rise of two of Rome's most important playwrights, Plautus (c. 254–184 BC) and Terence (c. 185–159 BC). Twenty of Plautus' plays survive, and they provide a picture of a playwright who was principally a translator and adaptor. He copied Greek originals, changing the locations to Rome and inserting details of Roman domestic life. His characters were types, not individuals: the braggart soldier (miles gloriosus), the miser, the parasite, and the wily but mis-treated slave. These stock characters were extremely important in later developments like commedia dell'arte, influencing both Shakespeare and Molière. Plautus' plays depend upon slapstick humor and "sight gags" for their effect. They are full of farcical energy and appeal directly to the emotions, not the intellect. They are not particularly well-written, and as is the case with much theatre, these works play better than they read.

Terence was a more literary writer and was better educated than Plautus, and enjoyed the support of a wealthy patron. From his six extant plays we find a dramatist capable of drawing universal situations and characters. Like Plautus, he had a tremendous influence on the theatre of later ages. Perhaps because he did not make use of banality and buffoonery, he was not particularly popular with Roman audiences.

The third form of Roman theatre, the mime, was probably as old or older than the other two forms, but it did not achieve prominence in Rome until the time of the Empire. Mimes dealt with low life, and appealed to all classes of Romans. Some mimes were adventures, a style copied by some dramatists in Elizabethan England. Some mimes ridiculed Christianity, particularly the rite of baptism, and consequently were not well favored by the Christian community. Early Christian writers condemned the obscenities of the mimes, noting that adulteries actually took place on stage. That may be an exaggeration, however. The style of Roman theatre in general clearly was anti-classical. Idealization, formality, simplicity, and appeal to the intellect were not its characteristics.

Like music, the theatre fulfilled an important social function in keeping the minds of the masses off their grievances. Yet it also served as a forum in which the general public could address grievances to the bureaucracy. When an official of the state had betrayed his trust, when a wrong had been suffered, or when an impropriety of state had become flagrant, the satirical bite of the

Roman theatre was brought fully to bear, with grotesque masks, bright costumes, and penetrating directness.

Theatre design

The design of theatre buildings in Rome changed over the centuries. For years the rough, raised stage of the *phlyakes* sufficed, and it was not considered necessary to construct theatres from anything but wood until the second century BC. The attempt to build a permanent stone theatre brought to a head some of the conflicts within Roman philosophy, morality, and government. In 54 BC, one year after construction of the first stone theatre had begun, the Roman Senate decreed that no seats should be provided in any theatre, that no one should sit down at any theatre production in the city or within a mile of its gates on the grounds that theatre was injurious to public morals. Three years later the consul Pompey nevertheless built a permanent stone theatre (seating 40,000), copied, according to Plutarch, from the Hellenistic theatre at Mytilene. To circumvent the Senate, he placed a shrine to Venus at the highest point in the rear of the auditorium so that all the seats served as steps to the shrine. By the turn of the Christian era the orchestra of the early Greek theatre had been infringed upon by scene building and the theatre had become a single architectural unit. The Romans added two new features to their theatres. One was a curtain, which could be raised and lowered from a slot across the front of the stage. The second was a roof over the stage which served both to protect the *scaenae frons* and to improve acoustics.

The ground plan of the Marcellus Theatre (Fig. **5.19**) demonstrates how the vestiges of the Greek theatre building were developed into a unified, single building. Rather than being carved out of a natural amphitheatre or

5.19 Plan of the Theatre of Marcellus, Rome, 23–13 BC.

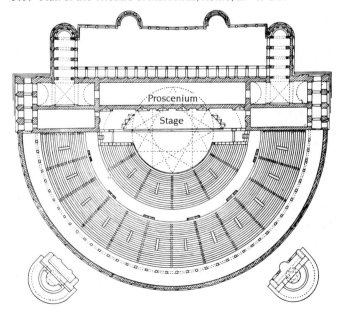

hillside as the Acropolis was, the Roman theatre stands as a building. The circular orchestra of the classical Greek theatre, which was first intruded upon by the stage of the Hellenistic theatre, now becomes barely a semi-circle. The action of the play occupies a raised stage and the entire acting area and its background become an elaborate *proscenium*, usually ornamented with columns and niches. An elaborate and imagistic *scaenae frons* rises behind the actors. The auditorium (*cavea*) is also reduced from its Greek proportions to a semi-circle. We see not only the details but also the single architectural unity of the Roman theatre in a recreation of the Theatre at Aspendos (Fig. **5.20**). The elaborate stage and *scaenae frons* of the Roman theatre seen in Figures **5.21** and **5.22** reflect the classical convention of three entrance door-ways in the back wall and the Hellenistic addition of two entrances at each end of the stage. What is most striking in these representations, apart from the elaborate detail of the *proscenium*, is the scale of the *proscenium* relative to the actor. As well as the addition of a roof over the stage, the *cavea* could apparently be covered with an awning, and as a result, the Roman theatre came very close to being an indoor theatre. The final detail of the front curtain made the Roman theatre very similar to a modern theatre.

The lot of the Roman actor, who had a very low social status, was probably a consequence of the changing and deteriorating condition of Roman theatre. The formation of professionally managed dramatic troupes whose actors were slaves became typical. Unlike the Greek actor, whose costume elevated his height and idealized his presence, the Roman actor wore contemporary dress. The

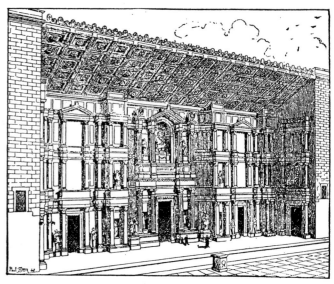

5.21 Reconstruction of the stage of the theatre at Orange.

large mask of the classical theatre with its *onkos* and grandeur was replaced with a smaller wig and less idealized mask. Costume at the time of Plautus and Terence in the second century BC did maintain much of the character of Hellenistic theatre production. Throughout the history of the Roman theatre, color symbolism in costume and mask remained a convention. Old men usually wore white; young men, purple; parasites, grey; and courtesans, yellow.

By the end of the Roman Empire, however, theatre had virtually disappeared as an art form. The playwright's art became one of reading, not of performing. The only

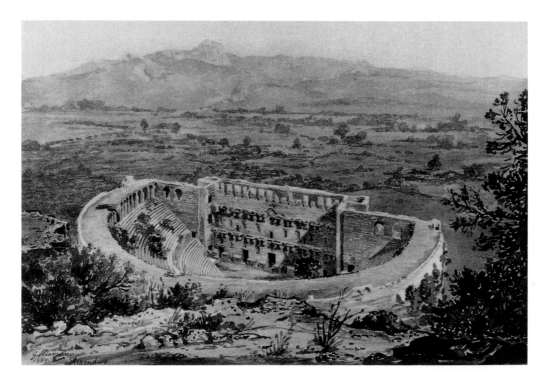

5.20 The theatre of Aspendos, 2nd century AD.

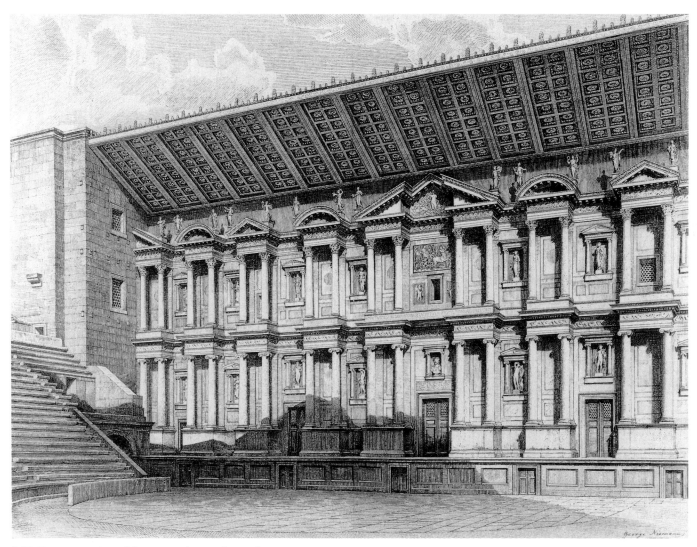

5.22 Reconstruction of the *scaenae frons* at Aspendos.

remaining theatrical entertainments were those of the mime and pantomime.

DANCE

One of Rome's significant legacies to the Middle Ages and the Renaissance was the unique dance form called pantomime. Although the words mime and pantomime are sometimes used interchangeably in our vocabulary, they were two completely different art forms. Around 22 BC Pylades of Cilicia and Buthyllus of Alexandria are said to have invented pantomime by combining dance elements, some of which dated to prehistoric Greece.

The purpose of the pantomime was serious and interpretative. Some pictorial evidence suggests that a single dancer portrayed many roles through costume change and the use of masks. He was accompanied by wind, brass, and string instruments as he leaped, twisted, and performed acrobatic feats or delicate interpretations. Themes occurring in pantomimes were often tragic, apparently taken from Greek and Roman tragedies and mythology. Many pantomimes were sexual in orientation, and some sources call them pornographic. It is clear that the pantomime fell into disfavor as its lewdness increased. It may be that lewdness, comically treated as in the mimes, has a tolerable and endearing quality, whereas the same subject treated seriously, as in the pantomime, becomes tedious, even to the pragmatic (and decadent?) Romans. The more notorious emperors, such as Nero and Caligula, apparently loved pantomime, as did certain segments of the populace. Eventually, however, pantomimists were forced to leave the major cities, wandering throughout the countryside as itinerant entertainers. Some opinion suggests that these itinerants helped to keep the Hellenistic and Roman spirit alive, and with it the concept of theatrical dance, through the Middle Ages and into the Renaissance.

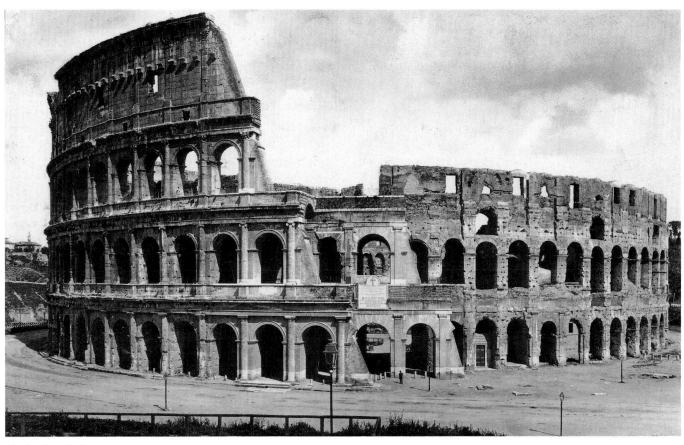

5.23 Colosseum, Rome, c. AD 70–82.

5.24 Colosseum, interior.

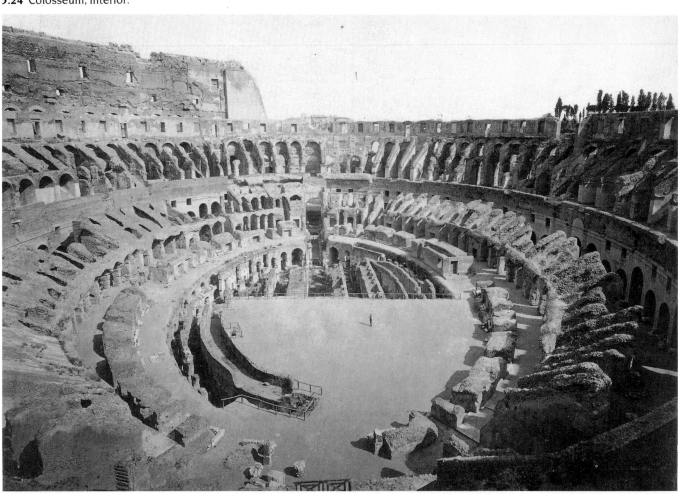

ARCHITECTURE

Given the practicality of the Roman viewpoint, we should not be surprised to find that it is in architecture that an immediately distinctive Roman style is most evident. The clear crystallization of form we found in the post and lintel structure of the classical Greek temple is also apparent in the Roman arch. However, here the whole is suggested, and to a certain degree summarized, by the part, whereas the Greek composition finds the part subordinate to the whole.

Very little remains of the architecture of the Republican period, but what there is suggests a strong Hellenistic influence with Corinthian orders and fairly graceful lines. There were notable differences, however. Hellenistic temples were on an impressive scale. Roman temples were even smaller than the classical Greek, principally because Roman worship was mostly a private rather than public matter. Roman temple architecture also employed engaged columns, that is, columns partly embedded in the wall. As a result, on three sides Roman temples lacked the open colonnade of the Greek.

In the Augustan age at the turn of the Christian era a refashioning of Roman architecture according to Greek style, as we saw in the case of sculpture, took place. This accounts to a large extent for the dearth of surviving buildings from previous eras. Temples were built on Greek plans, but the proportions were significantly different from those of the classical Greek.

The first through fourth centuries AD brought us what we typically identify as the Roman style, the most significant characteristic of which is the use of the arch as a structural system in arcades and tunnel and groin vaults. The Colosseum (Figs. **5.23** and **5.24**), the best known of Roman buildings and one of the most stylistically typical, could seat 50,000 spectators. Combining an arcaded exterior with vaulted corridors, it was a marvel of engineering. Its aesthetics are reminiscent of Greek classicism, but fully Roman in style. The circular sweep of each level is carefully countered by the vertical line of engaged columns flanking each arch. Doric, Ionic, and Corinthian columns mark each level and progress upward from heavy to lighter orders.

The Pantheon (Figs. **5.25** and **5.26**) fuses all that is Roman in engineering, practicality, and style into a domed temple of unprecedented scale dedicated, as its name suggests, to all the gods. Around the circular interior are niches carved out of the massive walls and occupied by statues of the gods. Corinthian columns mark the lower level, adding grace and lightness. Heavy horizontal moldings accentuate the feeling of open space made possible by the expansive dome, which is 140 feet

5.25 Pantheon, Rome, c. AD 118–128.

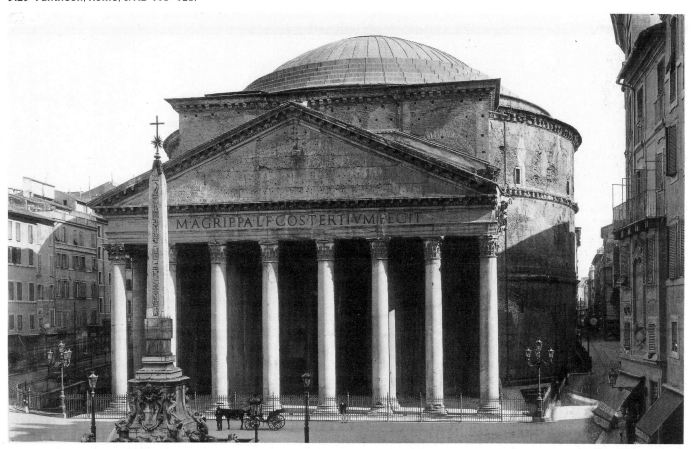

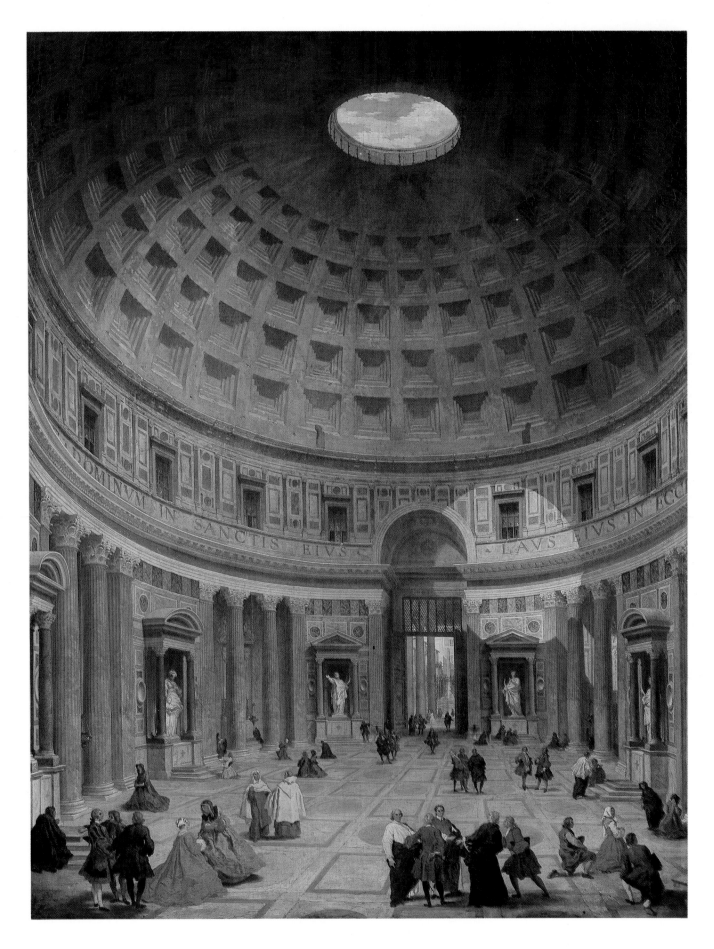

5.26 Giovanni Paolo Panini, *Interior of the Pantheon*, c. 1740. National Gallery of Art, Washington DC (Samuel H. Kress Collection).

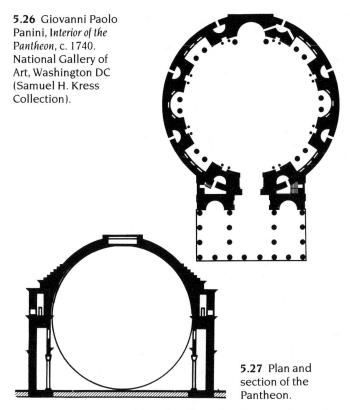

5.27 Plan and section of the Pantheon.

What then? Probably they perform a function similar to the buttresses of a Gothic cathedral ... The extra weight of the rings ... helps stabilize the lower portion of the dome: "Rather than functioning like a conventional dome, the Pantheon behaves like a circular array of arches, with the weight of the rings holding the end of each arch in place."[7]

Roman triumphal arches were impressive as architectural monuments, as demonstrated by the second Arch of Titus (Fig. **5.28**). The Roman classical style (the two pylons were completed by neo-classical architect Valadier in Napoleonic times) survives here in a memorial to Titus raised by his younger brother, Domitian. It memorializes the accomplishments which Titus shared with his father Vespasian in the conquest of Jerusalem. The sculptural reliefs on the arch show Titus alone as *Triumphator*. The reliefs represent allegories of political reverence rather than illustrations of an historical event. Accompanying Titus in these reliefs are figures such as the *Genius Senatus* and the *Genius Populi Romani*, embodiments of the spirit of the Senate and general populace rather than actual senators and citizens. What is important to recognize in this work is the contrast of external appearance, that is the richly and delicately ornamented façade, with the massive internal structure of the arch, a characteristic which will reappear in Renaissance architecture.

both in diameter and height (from the floor to the *oculus*, or eye, the round opening at the top of the dome). The circular walls supporting the dome are twenty feet thick and seventy feet high. Recessed square coffers on the underside of the dome give an added sense of lightness and reflect the framework into which concrete was poured. Originally the dome was gilded to suggest "the golden dome of heaven".

An informative recent analysis of the Pantheon discusses the force factors which hold up the one hundred and forty foot dome (Fig. **5.27**). Until now, architects have attributed its endurance to the sheer strength of Roman concrete. But the new study at Princeton University suggests that the real explanation may lie in the curious step-like rings at the base of the dome.

> The traditional view of these rings is that they act like a hoop, keeping the 14-story-high dome in compression and preventing it from collapsing under its weight. But Princeton engineer Robert Mark had his doubts. Even modern concrete, which is stronger than the Romans', has very little tensile strength, or ability to resist being torn apart....
>
> So ... he devised a computer model to simulate the stresses acting within the Pantheon. Only when the researchers assumed that the concrete had little or no tensile strength did the model accurately predict the pattern of cracks in the building. This suggested that the rings aren't acting as a hoop.

5.28 Arch of Titus, Forum Romanum, Rome, AD 81. Marble.

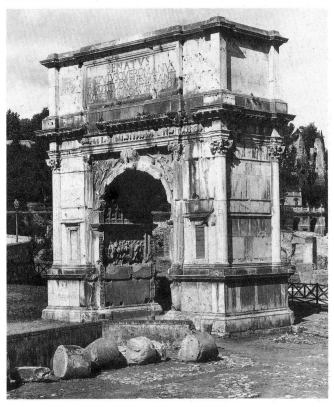

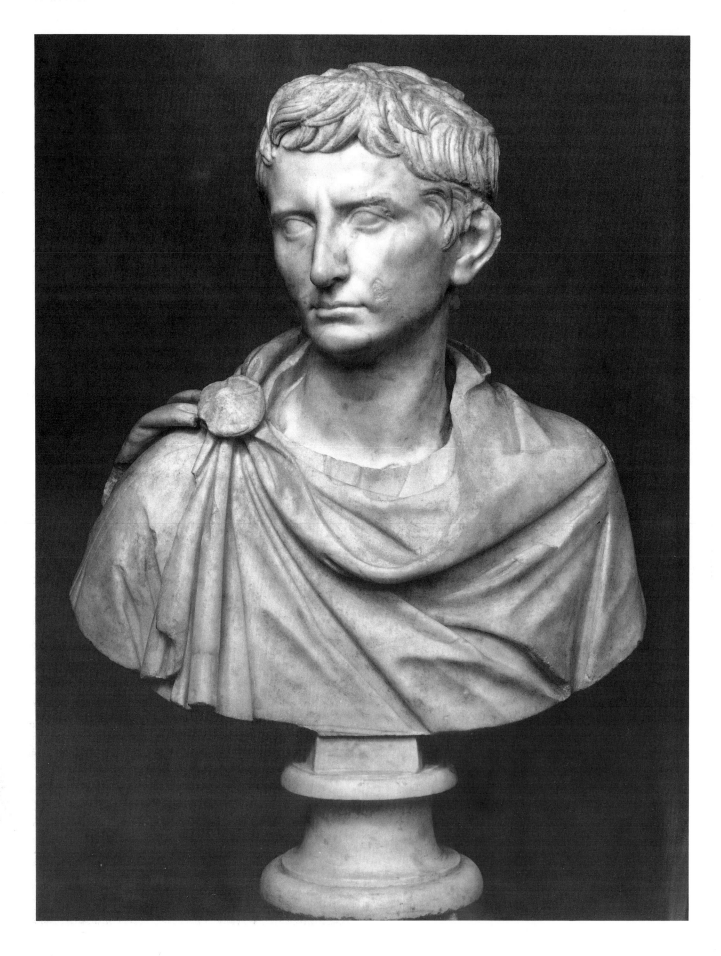

SYNTHESIS
Augustus: Classical Visions

The assassination of Julius Caesar made it clear that links with the past, to the Roman Republic, had run their course. If any Roman hoped that the assassination of the dictator would return things to Republican rule, he must surely have been disappointed. Artistic and political turbulence continued until Octavian defeated Marc Antony at the battle of Actium in 31 BC. The death of Marc Antony and the suicide of Cleopatra brought some relief to the chaos. "It was then, in the thirty-seventh poem in his first book of *Odes*, that Horace imitated the jubilation of Alcaeus over the death of the tyrant Myrsilos and cried: '*Nunc est bibendum nunc pede libero pulsanda tellus!*' ('Now is the time for drinking, now, with unshackled foot, for dancing!')." Octavian took absolute power, and was hailed as Caesar in Horace's Ode.

Attitudes had changed. Octavian, however, knew how to adorn reality with an outward form the public could accept—to replace democracy with autocracy, and make the public like it. As a result, the services of culture,

religion, literature, architecture, and the visual arts were called on to help in the creation of a new picture of the world. The result was a politically inspired aesthetic revolution. It all led to the legalizing of absolute power in 27 BC when Octavian formally divested himself of authority and was promptly reinvested with it as Augustus by the Senate and the will of the people. One of the ramifications of this new political order in art was the emergence of the neo-Attic style.

Sculptural works, with their new emphasis on portraying the Emperor, can be divided into three main types, differentiated primarily by hair style. Facial features remained relatively the same. An example of the Actium type (Fig. **5.29**) depicts Octavian with his hair in realistic disorder. The second type (Fig. **5.30**) shows more refined and nobler facial characteristics, but depicts the hair above the right eyebrow divided into two strands. In the third type (Fig. **5.31**) the forelock is removed and the hair is combed to the side.

The essence of Roman neo-Attic sculpture is nevertheless to be found in the statue of Augustus shown in Figure **5.16**. The portrait head of the Emperor sits on an idealized youthful body as depicted by Polyklitus in his

5.29 Octavian, copy of a type created in 31 BC. Marble, 14⅝ins (37.2cm) high. Museo Capitolino, Rome.

5.30 Augustus, copy of a type created in 27 BC. Bronze, 16⅞ins (42.9cm) high. British Museum, London.

5.31 Augustus, final type before 12 BC. Marble, 12ins (30.5cm) high. Museum of Fine Arts, Boston (Gift of Edward W. Forbes).

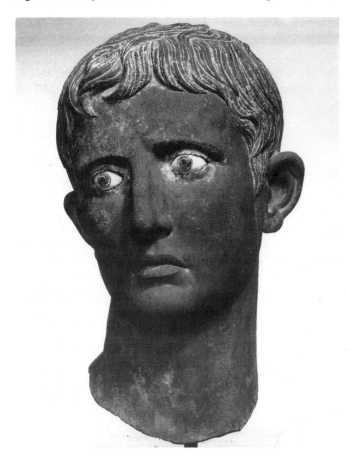

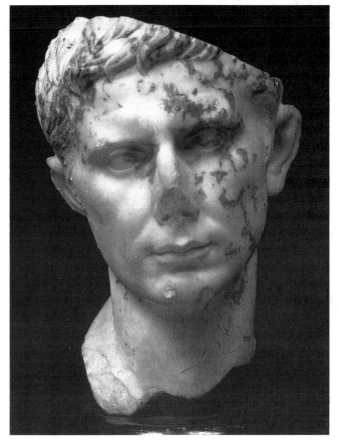

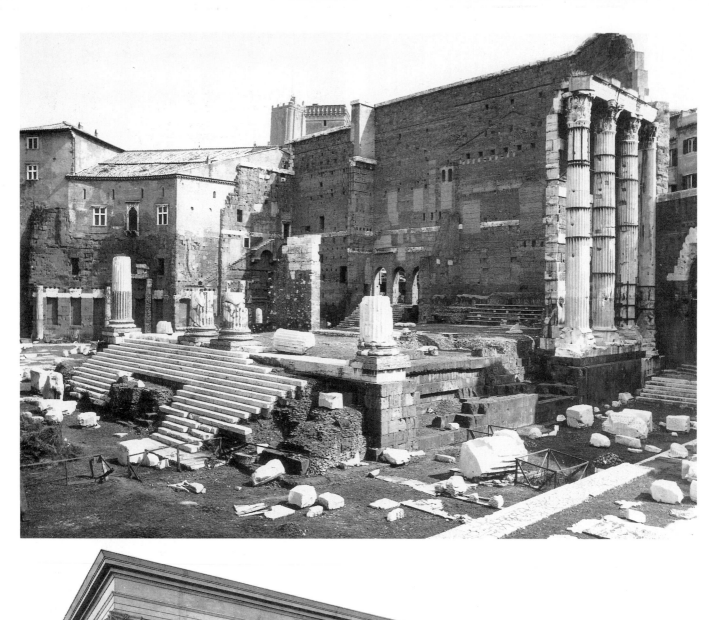

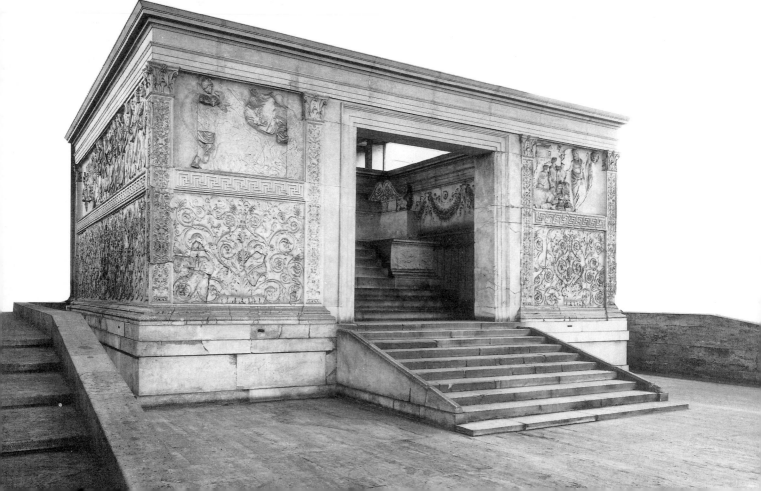

Lance Bearer (Fig. **4.15**). However, unlike in Polyklitus' work, Augustus here reaches outside the cube of compositional space, the final effect being quite different from that of its prototype.

The Forum of Augustus (Fig. **5.32**) represents monumental imperial art bedecked with grandeur. It represents greatness in both conception and dimension. Constructed from war booty, it is a dedication to the god Mars the Avenger, from a vow made by Octavian in his wars against the assassins of Julius Caesar. It reflects Augustan classicism and was based "on the conviction that, as far as depiction of the visible world was concerned, in all the aspects we subsume under the term figurative arts the Greeks had achieved everything permitted to man"[8], and in all this Augustus was to appear the greatest among *summi viri*, to stand out "among all the great men of Roman history".[9] Augustus' success finds testimony in the *Odes* of Ovid: "*Tua Caesar, aetas fruges et agris rettulit uberes*" ("Thy age, Caesar, restored rich harvests to our fields").

Finally, we turn to a jewel amidst the monuments of Augustan classicism, the Ara Pacis (Fig. **5.33**). In the frieze "royal dignity is conveyed by the noble but nonetheless perfectly natural poses and movements of the figures.... The Ara Pacis was no more than an early step in a gradual but inexorable progress toward a rigorously systematic point-for-point symbolism that was the goal to which all Roman art aspired."[10] Symbolism abounds in the decoration from the allegorical Peace of the garlands strung from ox skulls to the varieties of fruits, none of which ripen at the same time, woven into the garlands. In their entirety they symbolize the golden age of Augustus.

SUGGESTIONS FOR THOUGHT AND DISCUSSION

From Plotinus' first formulation of the symbolic nature of art we begin to find in Roman consciousness the seeds of aesthetic purpose which goes beyond the purely practical. Our overall impression of Roman culture as unoriginal and predominantly utilitarian, however, remains unaltered. Clearly the arts held a broad appeal for the Roman populace from the earliest days of the Republic to the late Empire years under Constantine, whether as a theatrical outlet for popular discontent or as a tool for the glorification of the emperor in the neo-Attic cult of Augustus. Roman arts served their constituency—engineering and technology were used to create marvelous architectural structures such as the Pantheon and the Colosseum, and music and drama became adjuncts to social welfare used to keep the vast army of the unemployed in check. At the same time, the utilitarian yielded somewhat to the aesthetic as sarcophagi took on delicate sculptural detail and the triumphal arch displayed masterly decoration. Indeed, the triumphal arch, as crude interior with superficial delicacy, aptly summarizes the culture of Rome.

■ In what ways did Roman arts adopt or change classical Greek and Hellenistic styles?
■ In what ways is the classical vision of Augustus similar to or different from the efforts of Akhenaton at Tell el Amarna?
■ In what ways does Stoicism still influence Western society?
■ What similarities or differences do Plotinus' concepts of beauty and symbol have with those of Aristotle and Plato? What is neo-Platonism?
■ What characteristics of Roman theatre make it closer to contemporary theatre than it was to its immediate predecessor, Greek theatre?
■ Do you agree or disagree with the comments made regarding the popularity of the Roman mime and the disfavor into which Roman pantomime fell?

5.32 Forum of Augustus, Rome, from the south, dedicated 2 BC.

5.33 *Ara Pacis* ("Altar of Peace"). Rome, 13–9 BC. Marble.

CHAPTER SIX

BYZANTIUM

Astride the main land route from Europe to Asia and its riches, Byzantium possessed tremendous potential as a major metropolis. In addition, Byzantium was a defensible deep water port which controlled the passage between the Mediterranean and the Black Sea; and blessed with fertile agricultural surroundings, the city formed the ideal "New Rome". For this was the objective of the Emperor Constantine when he dedicated his new capital in 330 and changed its name to Constantinople. The city prospered, and became the center of Christian Orthodoxy and mother to a unique and intense style in the visual arts in architecture. When Rome fell to the Goths in 476 it had long since handed the torch of its civilization to Constantinople. Here it was that the arts and learning of the Classical world were preserved and nurtured for future generations, while Western Europe underwent the turmoil and destruction of wave upon wave of barbarian invasion.

6.1 Empress Theodora and attendants, c. AD 547. Detail of wall mosaic. S Vitale, Ravenna.

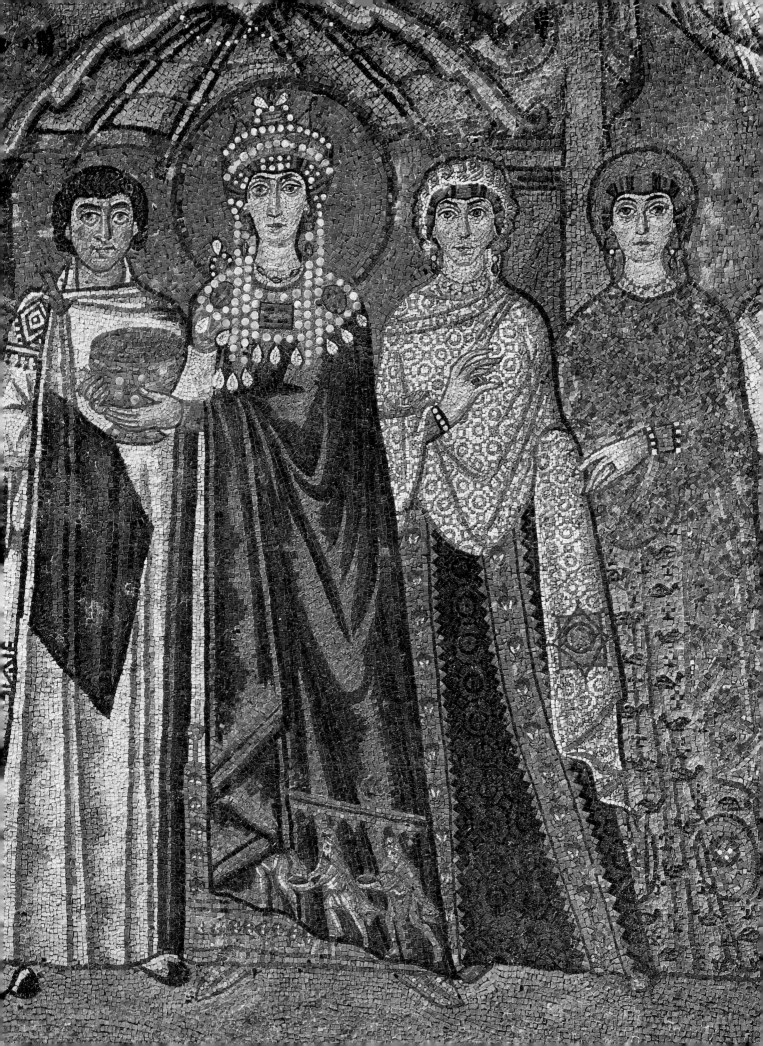

CONTEXTS AND CONCEPTS

Although Byzantium is geographically part of the Eastern world, its relationship with and influence on Western thought and art was highly significant. This chapter traces the history and culture of the capital of the Eastern Roman Empire from AD 330 until its conquest by the Turks in 1453. Parallel developments in the West are examined in Chapters 7 and 8.

The Byzantine Empire was founded on 11 May 330 when Constantine created the second capital of the Roman Empire, Byzantium, renaming it Constantinople. The geographical location of the city, bridging Europe and Asia, made it ideal. The cultural influences in the region were a mix of Hellenistic tradition and Christian thought. It was seen as a New Rome, promising new hope. While Eastern in many aspects of its society, Constantinople maintained Roman tradition beyond the fall of the Roman Empire in 476 until the end of the sixth century. From then on it followed its own course. Nominal separation from the Western Roman Empire became fact as early as 395 when Theodosius the Great died leaving a divided succession to his sons Arcadius and Honorius.

Two early crises contributed to the distinctive character of the Eastern half. The first came with the barbarian invasions of Europe in the fifth century— the Visigoths led by Alaric, the Huns by Attila and the Ostrogoths by Theodoric. Successful in the West, the barbarians carved up the Western Empire, and yet were unable to make anything but peripheral inroads into the Eastern Empire. So the New Rome assumed a new political focus. The second crisis was a religious crisis. In the fourth and fifth centuries the Eastern Empire was the seedbed of several "heresies" in the Christian Church which, in typically Greek spirit, revelled in "subtle theological metaphysics". These heresies conflicted with the official theology of the Latin Church and caused a schism between the Eastern and Roman episcopacy out of which the concept of a purely Eastern empire emerged. Its government was an absolute monarchy in the Eastern tradition. Its church was of Greek language and closely linked with the government which ruled it.

Justinian

The move toward total separation from the Western Empire lost momentum somewhat under the rule of the Emperor Justinian (527–565), who aspired to be Roman Emperor and sought to promote imperialism and Christianity. He was heir to the Caesars and proud of his heritage of Roman greatness, and his great ambition was to re-establish Roman unity. This ambition was partly achieved as he reconquered Africa, Italy, Corsica, Sardinia, the Balearic Islands, and part of Spain. The Frankish kings of Gaul recognized his suzerainty. As head of the Eastern Empire, he was also Vicar of God on earth and champion of Orthodoxy. In an attempt to hold his reconstructed Empire together, he sought a close alliance with the Roman papacy. This concentration on the West, however, left the Eastern Empire vulnerable to forces from the East, who saw weakness and tried to exploit it in the following two centuries.

Justinian's greatest legacy lay not in his brief reconstruction of the Roman Empire, however, but in the enormous work he undertook of recodifying the outmoded and cumbersome apparatus of Roman law. The result was the *Corpus Juris Civilis*, which reduced a Roman lawyer's library of reference books from 106 volumes to 6 and greatly influenced Justinian's own and succeeding centuries.

Reorganization of the Eastern Empire

Justinian's death left the Eastern Empire severely weakened economically and militarily. The interest of the Persians and, shortly, the Arabs was aroused. First came the Persians whom Heraclius (610–641) was able to rebuff. He led his legions in triumph as far as Nineveh and Ctesiphon, earning for himself the title of the first Crusader. Before his death, however, the empire was already facing its next challenge from the Arabs, who conquered Syria,

Egypt, North Africa, and Armenia. The following decades were the darkest in Byzantine history. Threats on all sides from the Lombards, Slavs, Arabs, and Bulgars effectively reduced the empire to a Byzantine enclave centered in Constantinople. It was not until the advent of the Isaurian Emperors in 717 that Byzantium recovered. Critical changes resulted. All political power was invested in the military leaders. Latin was replaced by Greek, and literary forms began to take on Eastern characteristics. Christianity strengthened its hold on public affairs and in the development of monasticism, and the breach with the Roman legacy widened and deepened in all areas. Out of all this arose a truly Eastern and enduring empire, efficiently organized and militarily strong.

The Isaurian emperors

The task of stabilizing the Eastern Empire fell to the first oriental rulers to take control. The Isaurian emperors who ruled from 717 to 867 had originally come from the distant mountains of Anatolia. The first ruler of the Isaurian dynasty was Leo III, who finally repulsed the Arabs from Constantinople in 717. His successor, Constantine V, re-established control over important territories in Asia Minor, and fortified and consolidated the Balkan frontier. The Isaurians concerned themselves with administrative order and the general welfare of their subjects in an attempt to minimize internal strife. The bureaucracy of the empire became more closely associated with the imperial palace. A briefer legal code, called the Ecloga, replaced Justinian's complex Corpus. The Ecloga introduced a new concept in Christian society by limiting the traditional authority of the Roman paterfamilias by increasing rights for women and children. Marriage was no longer a dissolvable human contract, but, rather, an irrevocable sacrament. The oriental custom of mutilation as a criminal punishment replaced the death penalty, reflecting a somewhat crude concern for rehabilitation. The period of Isaurian rule saw violent conflict with the Christian Church, however, a conflict known as the iconoclastic controversy.

Interpretations of the causes of the iconoclastic controversy vary. In the preface to the Ecloga Leo III had cast his duties in terms of a divine mandate:

> Since God has put in our hands the imperial authority, according to His good pleasure...
> —bidding us after the manner of Peter, the head and chief of the apostles, to feed his most faithful flock—we believe that there is nothing higher or greater that we can do in return than to govern in judgement and justice those who are committed by Him to our care.[1]

Leo III, in his self-assumed role of king/priest, entered the controversy over the use of icons in the Eastern Church, favoring the iconoclasts.

Painted or mosaic icons depicting the saints, the blessed Virgin, and God himself occupied a special place in Orthodox churches. From the sixth century onward they were extremely important in Orthodox worship and teaching. In the eighth century their usage came into question. Those who opposed the use of icons called themselves iconoclasts. They maintained that icons were idols which perverted the worship of God by focusing on men. They demanded the removal of icons, and on many occasions used force and destruction to impose their will. For reasons we can only speculate upon, Leo III issued a proclamation in 730 which forbade the use of images in public worship. One reason for the edict appears to have been Leo's superstitious belief that the current Arab invasions and volcanic eruptions indicated God's displeasure with Orthodox practices. The iconoclast movement reached its peak under Constantine V and was given formal approval by the council of bishops in 754. Over the next century icons remained at the center of controversy and their use or persecution of those who used them ebbed and flowed depending upon the will of the current emperor. Gradually the iconophiles or lovers of icons gained ground, persecution was relaxed, and on the first Sunday of Lent in 843, a day still celebrated as an Orthodox feast day, icons were finally restored to their place in Eastern worship.

The iconoclastic struggle and the establishment of a united empire under Charlemagne in 800 in the West finally and irrevocably sealed Byzantium's future as part of the Eastern world. By the time of the Emperor Theophilus, who ruled from 829 to 842, the Byzantine court rivalled any in the world with its splendid architecture and brilliant culture. The University of Constantinople was reorganized in about 850 by Caesar Bordas, and became a great intellectual center. The solution of the iconoclastic struggle in 843 united the Orthodox Church, and strengthened its influence and character. The following one hundred and fifty years, until the middle of the

AD	GENERAL EVENTS	LITERATURE & PHILOSOPHY	VISUAL ART	THEATRE & DANCE	MUSIC	ARCHITECTURE
330	Constantinople founded by Constantine		Theodosian obelisk (6.13)		Christian Hymnody well established	
400	Fall of Rome		Narrative Christian art begins			
500	Reign of Justinian begins	History developed as High Art Procopius, *et al*	Barberini ivory (6.15) Mosaic floors Justinian and his court (6.25) *Abraham's Hospitality and the Sacrifice of Isaac* (6.23)			S Vitale, Ravenna (6.21) Hagia Sophia (6.27)
600	Isaurian rulers begin Leo III repulses Muslims		Silk textile art	Disappearance of formal theatre performance		
800	Charlemagne unifies Western Empire End of Iconoclast struggle		*Raising of Lazarus* (6.10) *Vision of Ezekiel* (6.11) Harbaville Triptych (6.14) *Virgin and Child* (6.16)			
1000		Recurrence of Platonic thought Michael Psellus Prodromic Poems	Emergence of hierarchical formula		Turkish *Orta Oinu*	St Theodosia (6.18) St Luke and the Virgin (6.20)
1200	Constantinople sacked by Frankish Crusaders					St Mary Pammakaristos (6.19)
1453	Fall of Constantinople to the Ottoman Turks					

6.2 Timeline of Byzantium.

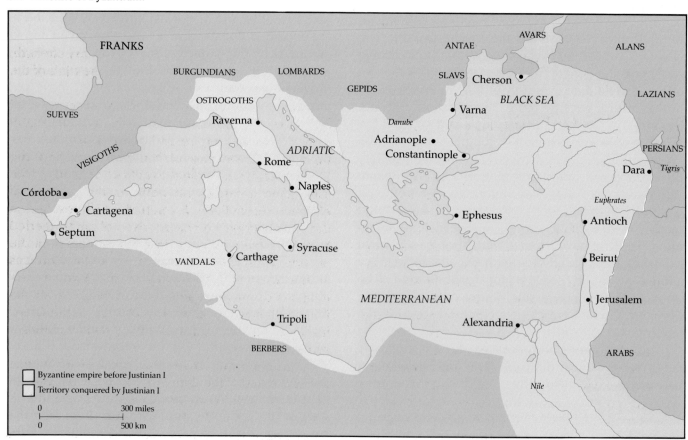

6.3 The Empire of Justinian I.

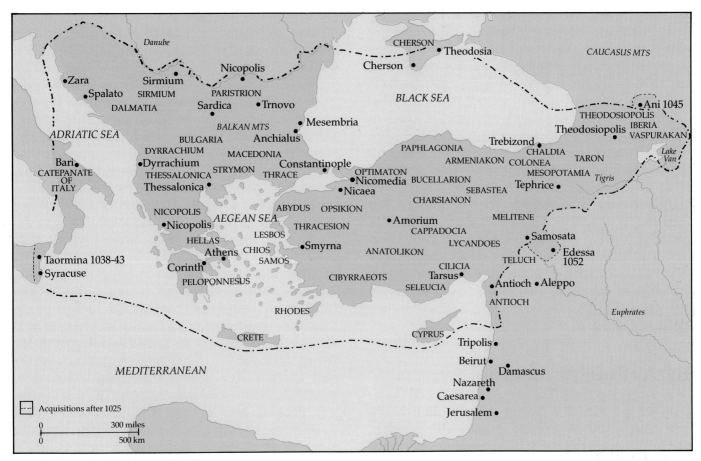

6.4 The Byzantine Empire c. AD 1025.

eleventh century, were a period of great prosperity and brilliance.

From Rise to Fall (867–1453)

Nothing in the West during this period remotely resembled the splendor and sophistication of Byzantium. Unlike in the West, the flavor of religious and secular life were closely intertwined in the Eastern Empire. There was a great deal of activity in the visual arts, and the subject matter was overwhelmingly religious. The church calendar was inseparable from the court calendar, and the spectacle of court and church ritual had a theatrical splendor which reinforced the majesty of the empire and the place of the emperor as God's viceregent. "Ritual sustained the rigid etiquette of the court, about which the characteristic evils of intrigue and conspiracy proliferated. The public appearance of the emperor was stage managed: he emerged dramatically from behind the last of several curtains raised successively."[2] Despite the strong economic and commercial base of the city and its military strength, however, it was not able to withstand the trials of the eleventh century.

First came internal troubles. A succession of feeble, short-lived emperors weakened the central authority of the empire and allowed disputes between the aristocracy of the provinces and the bureaucracy of the capital to get out of hand. At the same time a serious rift between the intellectual élite and the military developed, which resulted in the army and navy being deprived of funds needed to defend the empire against new threats from the outside. These new threats came from the Normans in the West and the Turks in the East. A new religious controversy arose in the empire over the Bogomil heresy, which drew on hatred of the Greek higher clergy, and led to the Bulgarians initiating a series of revolts.

The slide into chaos was checked for a time under the rule of the Comneni emperors, who lasted until 1185. The Comneni dynasty succeeded in ridding Greece of the Normans and defending the Empire against the Petchenegs, a group of southern

155

Russian nomads. Important commercial concessions had to be made to Venice, however, in return for her naval assistance. Venetian influence and power increased immensely. Byzantium could not recover its former strength. Internal struggles and conflicts proliferated. Finally, in 1203, a crusade set out from the West for the Holy Land, but was diverted to Constantinople by the Venetian contingent who were anxious to get their hands on the wealth of Constantinople. In 1204 a riot broke out, providing the Crusaders with an excuse for sacking the city, and delivering a fatal blow to the Empire. The treasures of the city—books and works of art centuries old—were almost all destroyed. Central organization collapsed. Parts of the empire broke away in acts of self-preservation. The Crusaders had brought the Empire to a mere shadow of its former self, and it was there for the taking by the Ottoman Turks in 1453.

Byzantine intellectualism

During the life of the Eastern Empire, Constantinople and Byzantium exerted considerable intellectual influence on the West. Nowhere in the medieval world was the classical tradition better preserved than in Byzantium. Although considered heir to the Roman Empire, the Eastern Empire was directly descended from classical Greece. The famed Hellenistic cities of Athens, Antioch and Alexandria all lay within its borders. Byzantium itself was to all intents and purposes a Greek city. Most of its citizens were Hellenes and spoke Greek. They were better versed in Greek classicism than any other nation, coming to classical literature as they did in their own tongue—though the language had changed somewhat over the centuries. No other nation of the Western Empire spoke Greek. Eastern libraries overflowed with classical texts, which were cherished as priceless treasures (Fig. **6.4**). Greek literature formed the basis of Byzantine education. Homer, Hesiod, Pindar, Aristophanes, Aeschylus, Thucydides, Demosthenes, Plato, Aristotle, and Plutarch, were widely read among the cultured classes. At the University of Constantinople the "consuls of the philosophers" and the "masters of the rhetoricians" found inspiration in classical traditions. It is also clear that the same love of antiquity permeated the ranks of private individuals. Even at its lowest ebb, Byzantium never fell into a cultural Dark Age.

The study of history took pride of place in Byzantine thought. In the sixth century we find such great historians as Procopius, Agathias, and later Psellus, Cinnamus, and Nicetas, who were without equal in the Western world. They understood politics and human psychology and wrote with superior composition and style. Although some, such as Anna Comnena, emulated the ancients to such a degree that their style became cramped and involved, she and others, such as Nicephorus Bryennius, were inspired to make the work of the historian into a true art rather than a sterile recitation of events. Their work displayed great individuality. They were meticulous, responsible, and anxious to maintain objectivity as far as possible.

Theology held the second highest place in Eastern intellectual pursuits. Undoubtedly the proliferation of theological literature was fuelled by the seemingly endless heresies which troubled Byzantium as Orthodoxy was defended and dogma established. Like the list of historians, the list of significant Eastern theologians is startling: Leontius of Byzantium, John of Damascus, Maximus the Confessor, Photius, and so on. Numerous works were devoted to scriptural commentary, and the development of monasticism produced a new genre of mystical literature. Religious eloquence founded in classical rhetoric was very popular. As the ninth century passed, creativity in theological study was lost, however, and only tradition remained. A period of stagnation had set in, and originality and freedom of thought disappeared.

In the realm of philosophy the University at Constantinople saw the first recurrence of Platonic thought in the eleventh century. Platonism spread through the proselytizing zeal of Michael Psellus who, often in conflict with the strict Orthodoxy of the Patriarchs, tells us how he worked his way from neo-Platonism and "the admirable Proclus" little by little to "the pure light of Plato".

Literature

The literature of Byzantium is often thought of as Greek. That is certainly accurate as far as Constantinople and the majority of Byzantine literary works go, but the Eastern Empire was not confined to Constantinople. The corpus of literature from the Empire encompasses works in Latin, Syriac, Coptic, Church Slavonic, Armenian, and Georgian.

Greek Byzantine literature, however, comprises

a massive quantity of works. Much from the early period has been lost, and much remains, unpublished, in manuscript form. Most of the body of Greek Byzantine literature treats religious subjects and much of it is hagiographic—biographies of saints and other religious figures. In addition, we find sermons, liturgical books, and poetry, theology, devotional works, scriptural commentaries, and so on. Of the thousands of extant volumes of Byzantine literature, only a few hundred are secular, and those include the histories mentioned earlier.

A key to the understanding of Byzantine literature is an understanding of Byzantine taste, which was quite different from our own:

> It would be unfair to judge Byzantine literature by the criterion of the aesthetic pleasure it affords to the modern reader. If we fail to be captivated or moved by it, this is largely because our literary taste is diametrically opposed to that of educated Byzantines. We appreciate originality, while they prized the cliché; we value conclusions, while they were naturally inclined to elaboration and verbiage.[3]

To follow this line of argument, we first turn to the development of the Greek language itself, which went through several stages: the epic (Homer and Hesiod), literary Attic (fifth and fourth centuries BC), and New Testament Greek (considered by scholars as decadent). These changes altered vowel quantity and quality, as well as rhythmic and metric qualities. "Many churchmen actively championed the use of lowly speech and rejected 'the fine style of the Hellenes' which they compared to the proverbial honey that drips from the mouth of a whore. They argued that to cultivate the epic and iambic meters was not only childish; it was an insult to Christ and the apostles."[4] As a result, Byzantine literature has a "timelessness" inasmuch as each generation of authors stood apart from the successive influence of their predecessors and went directly to "their distant models". Many Byzantine works, therefore, exist in a stylistic tradition without author, contemporary reference, or place.

Three genres can be identified in Byzantine literature. The first is historiography. The history we speak of in this context is not a chronicled record of events, which was a separate activity in Byzantium, but is rather a specific literary genre, written in ancient Greek, in imitation of ancient models, and interpreting events and their influence on each other. As Theophanes Continuatus wrote, "for the body of history is indeed mute and empty if it is deprived of the cause of actions." Historiography was also a branch of rhetoric "often shading into the laudation or the invective and normally including both the fictitious speech and the ethnographic excursus."[5] Probably the best known Byzantine historian was Procopius of Caesarea, known for his broad, sweeping narrative, objectivity, and accuracy. His model was the Athenian, Thucydides.

The second genre—hagiography—comprises the largest volume of Byzantine literature. A wide range of hagiographical texts exists, most of which were written in ecclesiastical Greek. This genre consisted for the most part of anecdotes and full life histories which emerged from Egyptian monasticism. The anecdotal accounts were first circulated by word of mouth, and then were collected in books called *paterica* or *gerontica*. Their contents dealt with the supernatural deeds of monks, and stressed moral precepts and the particular discipline pursued by the subject. The first Life concerns St. Antony and was written by Athanasius of Alexandria (*c.*360). Principally designed to laud the behavior of its subject, a Life usually followed a rhetorical format. The writer first states his embarrassment at undertaking a task so great; then comes a description of and praise of the subject's birthplace (if it is worthy of note) or the nation in which he was born; next comes a description of the family, but only if it was glorious; then comes a note of the birth and any miraculous signs accompanying it (if none existed, the author perhaps invented a few); finally, in carefully organized subdivisions, come descriptions of physical appearance, education, upbringing, characteristics, deeds, and so on. This *schema*—as this outline was called—made it easy to develop biographies of saints about whom little was known or who probably never existed. These Lives are interesting and readable accounts of spiritual progress, if somewhat predictable, and they provided heroes for the Medieval world. The Lives were written in simple language, intended for as wide an audience as possible, often bordering on the vernacular.

The third genre was literature actually written in the vernacular. Here the earliest works—the Prodromic poems—date to the first half of the twelfth century, and are attributed to the court poet Theodore Prodromos, although they may be the product of several authors. "Written in popular fifteen-syllable verse (*stichos politikos*), the poems take the

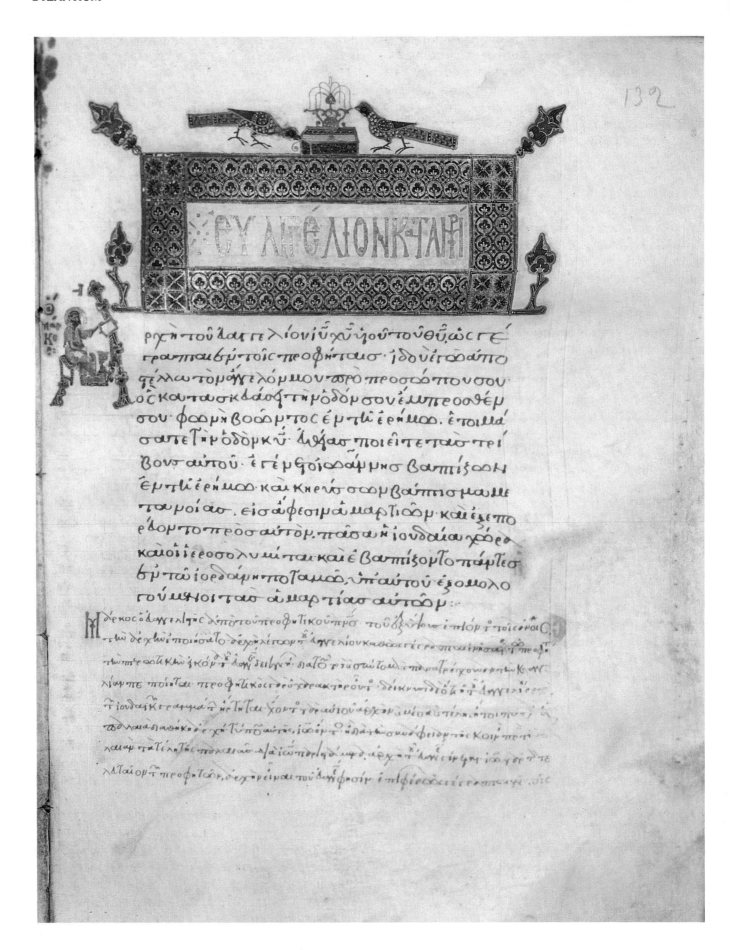

form of complaints addressed to the Emperors John II and Manuel I as well as to another member of the Comneni family. In one case we are introduced to a henpecked husband, in another to the father of a large family who cannot make ends meet on his modest stipend."[6] These works portray humor through slapstick and the coining of bizarre words, although their tendency to monotony and repetition often mars the effect. Popular in the late Byzantine period were romances of chivalry set in the contemporary world and peopled by knights, maidens, witches, and dragons in the fashion of the Western Empire. The epic based on heroic tales of the Eastern border between Byzantium and the Arabs in the ninth and tenth centuries was also popular.

Much of Byzantine literature, however, is solemn and even sombre in mood; its writers seem most at home with themes of calamity, death and the precariousness of human existence.

Intellectual influence

It is pertinent to examine briefly how the intellectual accomplishments of the empire influenced the West. The Byzantine conception of imperial power which derived from the Justinian Code was heavily influential in the emerging ideas of absolute monarchy. The law of Justinian was brought to Italy and by the eleventh century, law schools in Rome, Ravenna, and Bologna studied its doctrines. Justinian's concepts met with strong approval, especially in Bologna. Frederick Barbarossa turned to Bologna and found in their teachings of Justinian strong arguments for establishing his imperial claims in the middle of the twelfth century. The thirteenth-century Bologna Glossators provided the basis for the lawmakers of Frederick II Hohenstaufen to proclaim their emperor "law incarnate upon earth, [and] acknowledged his right to order ecclesiastical affairs as freely as the secular interests of his empire".[7] In the same tradition, the king of France was later declared "above the law". The great King Louis XIV was invested by divine right with limitless authority.

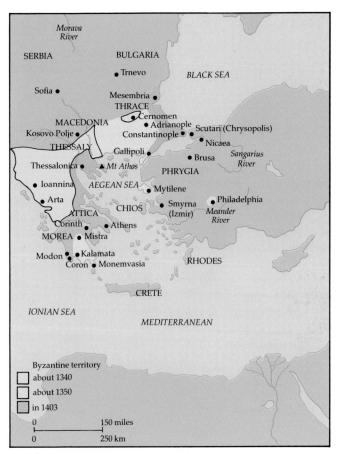

6.6 The Byzantine Empire 1340–1403.

Theological accomplishment in the Eastern Church proved superior to that in the West, at least until the twelfth century, and its influence can be seen in the works of Scotus Erigena, Peter Lombard, and St. Thomas Aquinas. French literature and legend display strong links with Byzantine sources, and particularly hagiography.

The promulgation of Aristotelian philosophy and a strong current of humanism, both of which figured prominently in the Renaissance of the mid-fifteenth century in Western Europe and especially Italy, were important Byzantine legacies. Platonic doctrine was established in a place of honor in the University of Constantinople in the eleventh century, and it was from Byzantium that Platonic thought spread to Italy, first to Florence, and then to the rest of Europe. The Greek scholars who came to Italy after the sack of Constantinople brought Byzantine humanism. It enjoyed a period of strong currency in the thirteenth and early fourteenth centuries. These scholars also brought many important manuscripts and an appreciation of Greek intellectual accomplishment was rekindled and invigorated the great humanist movement.

6.5 Headpiece from the Four Gospels with Commentaries, Byzantine illumination, 11th century. Ink, tempera and gold on parchment, 11 × 9ins (27.9 × 22.9cm). The Cleveland Museum of Art, Ohio (Purchase from the J.H. Wade Fund).

THE ARTS
OF BYZANTIUM

TWO-DIMENSIONAL ART

A fundamental characteristic of Byzantine visual art is the concept that in art exists the potential to interpret as well as to represent perceived phenomena. Byzantine art, like its literature, was conservative and for the most part, anonymous and impersonal. The artist was clearly subordinate to the work. Much of Byzantine art remains undated, and questions concerning derivation of styles, if not the styles themselves, lie unresolved. The physical expansion of artistic form from the constrained style of the late Roman and Roman Christian churches to the vast

wall surfaces of new Byzantine churches posed problems of style which took time to resolve. The development of narrative Christian art with its relatively new approach dates back to the mid-fifth century. Early attempts at

6.7 A seated "philosopher", early 6th century AD. Floor mosaic. Imperial Palace, Istanbul.

6.8 Eagle and serpent, early 6th century AD. Floor mosaic. Imperial Palace, Istanbul.

6.9 Head, in the border, early 6th century AD. Floor mosaic. Imperial Palace, Istanbul.

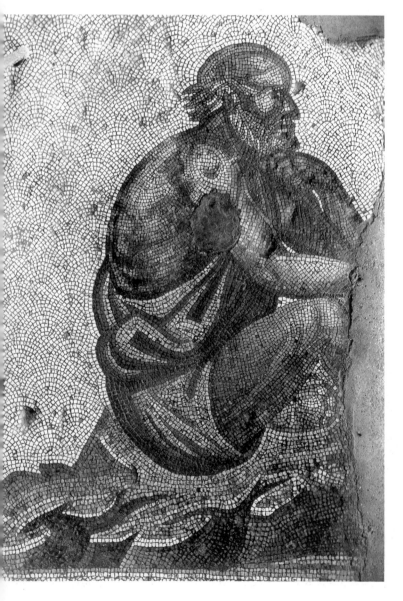

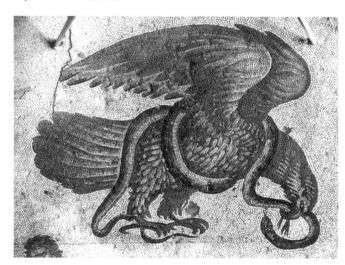

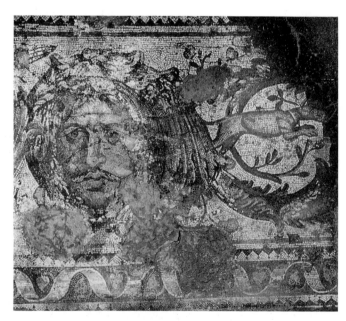

iconography can be traced to the third and fourth centuries.

The content and purpose of Byzantine art was always religious, although the style of representation underwent numerous changes. Classical standards subsided with a decline in enlightened patronage and skilled craftsmanship. The ostentation of the Imperial court influenced artistic style, with depictions of Christ and the saints frozen in immobile poses and garbed in regal purples. Lacy ornamentation corrupted classical standards in the sixth century. The period of Justinian marks an apparently deliberate break with the past. What we describe as the distinctly Byzantine style with its characteristic abstraction and focus on feeling rather than form began to take shape in the fifth and sixth centuries, although the classical Hellenistic tradition seems to have survived as an undercurrent. High realism in some works has led to occasional confusion among scholars over dating, where the style of a work appears to pre-date the work itself. Throughout the seventh century classicism and decorative abstraction intermingled in Byzantine art.

Certainly by the eleventh century Byzantine style had adopted a hierarchical formula in wall painting and mosaics, coupled with a reduced emphasis on narrative. The Church represented the kingdom of God, and as one moved up the hierarchy, one encountered figures changing in form from humankind to the divine. Placement in the composition depended upon religious, not spatial, relationships. Depiction is not illusionistic, but flat and antique. Here again, the Byzantine style is penetrated from time to time by several renaissance movements, mostly in the minor arts. By the eleventh century a strictly two-dimensional style appears which is elegant and decorative. Stylization and dramatic intensity characterize twelfth-century art, a style further intensified in the thirteenth century with turbulent movement, architectural backdrops, and elongated figures. The fourteenth century produced small-scale, crowded works of narrative content. Use of space is confused and perspective is irrational. Figures are distorted, with small heads and feet. A more intense spiritualization is obvious.

Stretching as it did over a thousand years, and influenced by turbulent history, Byzantine art represents a complex repertoire of styles. A few examples will suggest some of the changing characteristics of Byzantine two-dimensional art.

When Constantine established his capital at Byzantium, he found a cadre of artists and craftsmen already trained in other centers. These artists, when set to work to accomplish the artworks Constantine had in mind, naturally rendered their subjects in a manner quite different from those found in the Roman world. One of the earliest examples of two-dimensional art, which dates back to the formation period, is a mosaic floor of the Grand Palace. Mosaics were a distinctly Byzantine medium, and Figures **6.7** to **6.9** show examples of fine execution in a style which is essentially naturalistic. The mosaics depict individual figures, buildings, or scenes, which are unconnected with each other, composed on a white background. The picturesqueness, elegance, and grandeur of these works indicate Greek classical influence. Although the figures are fairly naturalistic, the compositions as a whole depart from naturalism in their absence of background and shadow. Each figure has about it a mystical, abstract feel, which seems to suggest a Medieval rather than antique style. As early examples of the Byzantine mosaic, these works display fine craftsmanship. The handiwork is very delicate and the colors are rich and varied. The palette explores almost the entire spectrum. An important development can be seen in Figure **6.9**, in which a portrait head forms part of the border. The colors of the hair intermingling with the foliage and the face depart from naturalism: the hair in places is green and the moustache is blue. Yet the overall effect remains highly realistic—a curious mix of vividness and stylization which would later typify Byzantine art.

6.10 *The Raising of Lazarus and the Entry into Jerusalem,* from the Homilies of Gregory Nazianzus, AD 867–886. 16.1 × 12ins (41 × 30.5cm). Bibliothèque Nationale, Paris.

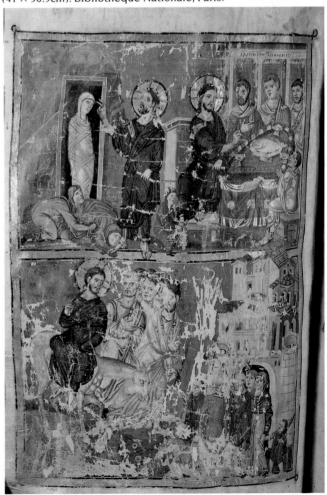

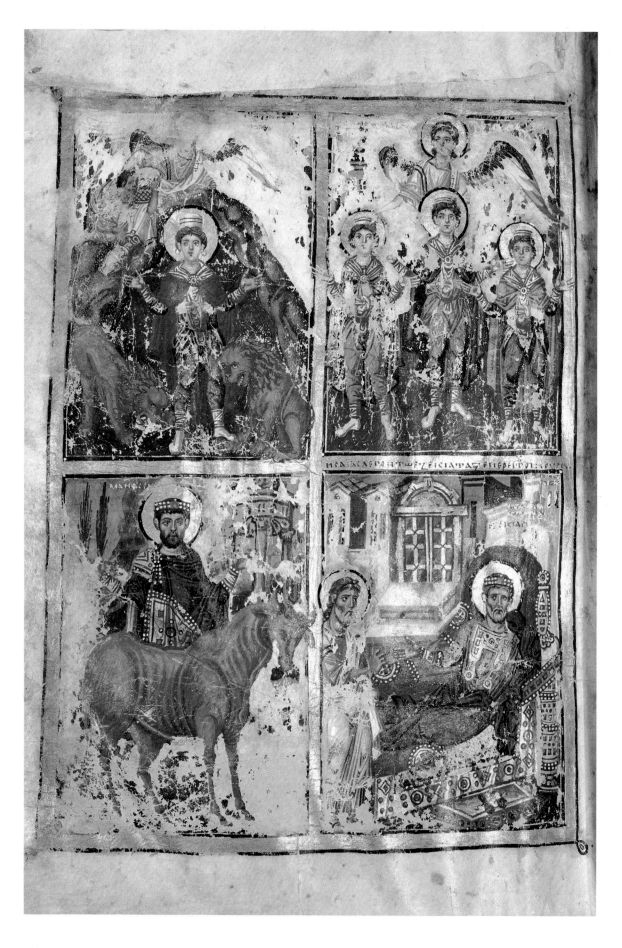

6.11 *The Vision of Ezekiel*, from the Homilies of Gregory Nazianzus. Bibliothèque Nationale, Paris.

6.12 A lion strangler, 8th century AD. Silk textile, 15.6 × 12.2ins (39.5 × 31cm). Victoria and Albert Museum, London.

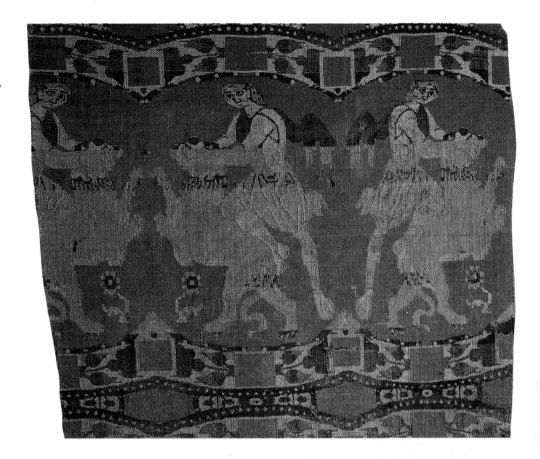

Hieratic style

By the middle centuries a style known as "hieratic"—holy or sacred—presented a formalized, almost rigid depiction intended not so much to represent men as to inspire reverence and meditation. One formula of the hieratic style ordained that a man should measure nine heads (seven heads would be our modern measurement). The hairline was a nose's length above the forehead. "If the man is naked, four noses' lengths are needed for half his width." By the thirteenth century mosaics display a return to more naturalistic depictions, but with a clear sense of spiritualism.

Manuscript illumination

In addition to the mosaics which decorated palaces and the wealthier churches, manuscript illumination and wall painting were also important features of Byzantine two-dimensional art. From the period immediately after the iconoclastic controversy we find exquisite manuscript illumination. The scenes shown in Figures **6.10** and **6.11** depict stories. Figure **6.10** unfolds its narrative in two registers. Much about these works seems classical in derivation, and yet the composition of space is Medieval in its crowding of figures, concentration on the surface plane, and lack of rational linear perspective. The execu-tion of detail is outstanding—the shading and detail exhibit control and delicacy. The colors are rich and varied.

Textile weaving was another important medium, and Figure **6.12** demonstrates characteristic Eastern design in rich color as a man, probably Samson, struggles with a lion.

SCULPTURE

The context in which the two-dimensional arts developed applies equally to sculpture. Early works include Roman-style sculptural vignettes, illustrating Old and New Testament themes of salvation and life after death. For two centuries or so the old art of Roman portrait sculpture held sway. By the end of the fourth century styles began to change. In Figure **6.13** we find the base of an obelisk, set up by Theodosius I, in which the frontal poses of figures, the varied ranks in which they are grouped, and the large accentuated heads reflect an oriental influence. Oriental and classically inspired works existed alongside each other in this period. The clear-cut, precise style of Greek inspiration later became an outstanding characteristic of Byzantine sculpture. As in painting, sculpture took a classical turn after the iconoclastic struggle, but with an harmonious infusion of a spiritualized ideal of human beauty.

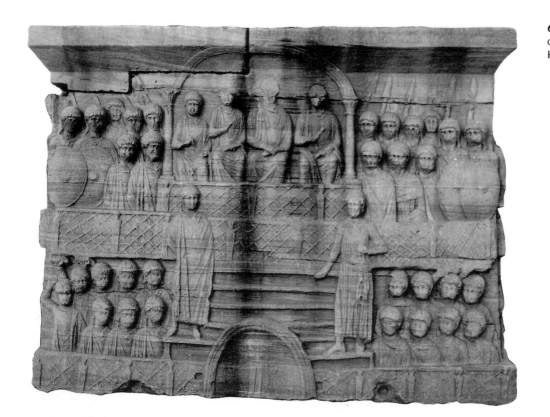

6.13 Base of the Theodosian obelisk, c. AD 395. The Hippodrome, Istanbul.

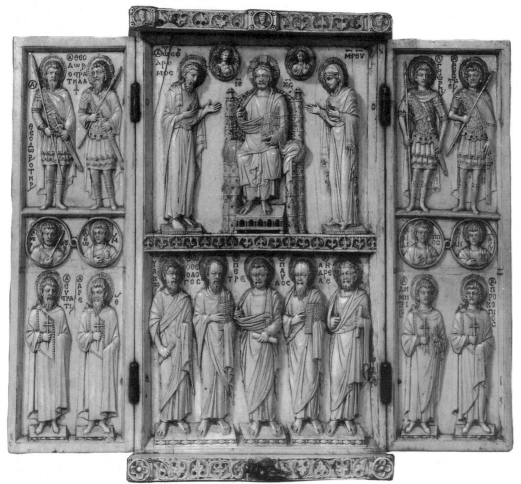

6.14 The Harbaville Triptych, interior, late 10th century AD. Ivory, 9½ins (24.2cm) high, central panel 5⅝ins (14.2cm) wide. Louvre, Paris.

6.15 The Barberini Ivory, showing a mounted emperor, c. AD 500. 13½ × 10½ins (34.1 × 26.6cm). Louvre, Paris.

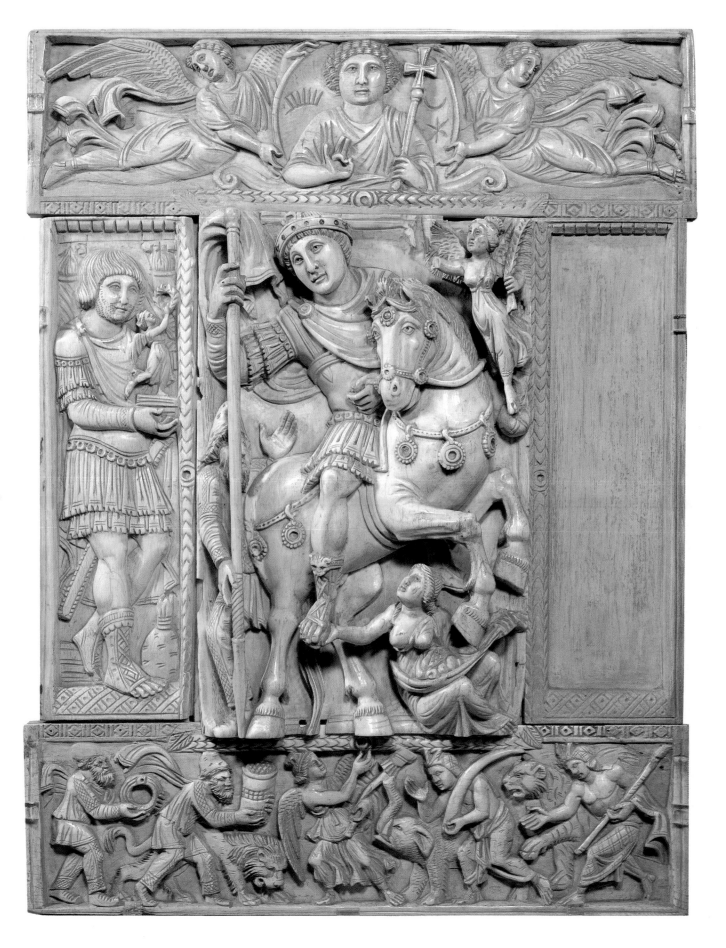

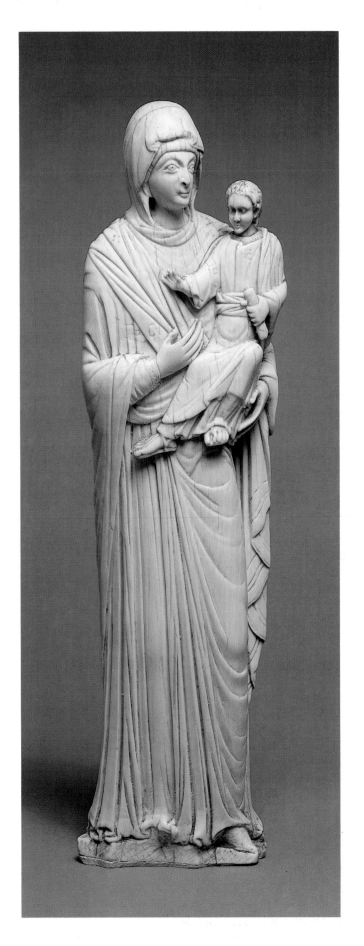

A number of carved ivory works of different styles provide evidence of the varying influences and degrees of technical ability prevalent in the Eastern Empire. Many of the ivories are consular diptychs and others are imperial diptychs, although not all ivories were in diptych form. In the *Barberini Ivory* (Fig. **6.15**) we find a work of five separate pieces, one of which is missing. At the center is an emperor on horseback. On one side is a consul in military costume, and at the top is a bust of Christ with winged victories on either side. The long panel at the bottom depicts Gothic emissaries on one side and an emissary from India on the other. Here we find qualities fairly typical of the time—brilliant technique, round features, and high relief. In addition, the emperor's head is individual and very recognizable. Later ivories of the tenth century show delicate elegance and a highly finished style. The *Harbaville Triptych* has been described as the most beautiful of all the Byzantine ivories (Fig. **6.14**). It represents the hieratic style in sculpture. The only known free-standing sculpture in ivory, the *Virgin and Child* (Fig. **6.16**), is in the same style. The drapery falls exquisitely and the surface is highly finished. The facial features, expression and hands, however, portray the typical hieratic elongation of proportion.

MUSIC

On its way to Europe, the Christian Church spread throughout Asia Minor accumulating musical elements on its way. Byzantium appears to have acquired much of its musical heritage from the monasteries and churches of Syria. Especially important in this heritage was the development of antiphonal psalmody and the use of hymns. Evidence of hymn singing can be found in the New Testament and in the writings of Pliny the Younger in the second century in Bithynia and Asia Minor. Some early Christian hymns were probably sung to folk melodies. There seems to have been both Eastern and Greek influence on early Christian music.

Although there are no surviving manuscripts of music, the strong traditions of the Greek Orthodox, Russian, and other Eastern churches still preserve what must be a flavor of the Byzantine chant which served as their model. Based on Syrian melodies and incorporating short responses between verses of the psalms, an independent hymnody gradually developed. Byzantine hymns had an elaborate structure which stood in contrast to the hymns of the Western Church. A hymn type developed in the eighth to tenth centuries based on

6.16 *The Virgin and Child.* 10th century AD. Ivory, 12⅞ins (32.5cm) high. Victoria and Albert Museum, London.

sixth-century hymns was called *kanones*. Its texts, not entirely original, were scriptural commentaries. Its melodies, also not original, were constructed on a principle common to Eastern music, quite different from Western ideas. Rather than building a melody from a series of notes in a scale, the Eastern singer constructed a melody from a series of short motifs, which the singer chose and combined. Some motifs were designed for beginnings, some for middles, some for endings, and some for connecting links. There were also standard ornamental formulas or melismas, and originality in performance depended on the combination, variation and ornamentation of the motifs. The motifs of a particular group express "the same quality of feeling, are congruous in melody and rhythm, and are derivable from the same musical scale."[8] Byzantine music had eight groups or *echoi*. These *echoi* played a fundamental part in the development of Western music. Our knowledge, however, is limited by the fact that music in the Byzantine Church was passed down by oral tradition for centuries before being written down.

Undoubtedly Eastern music contained a mystical or contemplative character and the presence of melismatic qualities created a complexity quite in keeping with the character of Eastern thought. The symbolic qualities of the *echoi* seem consistent with Eastern mysticism and the exploration of interpretation beyond the representational.

THEATRE

There is little question that the Byzantines were familiar with theatre. Ruins of Hellenistic theatres were found throughout the Eastern Empire. The philosophies of Plato and Aristotle included theatre, particularly, as we saw, in the *Poetics*. We know that Justinian's wife, Theodora, was an actress. References exist to the exodus of actors and playwrights from Byzantium at the time of the Turkish conquest. Theatrical spectacles surround the life of the imperial court. But what of theatre itself? The period between the fall of Rome and the late Middle Ages witnessed the virtual extinction of theatre in both East and West, except in its most rudimentary form. Certainly the Byzantine penchant for artistic anonymity might account for the absence of dramas. The literature of Byzantium excluded drama from its priorities. The kind of debased spectacles we found in the late years of the Roman Empire probably took place in Byzantium, but would have been frowned upon in a society dominated by the Christian Church. Senators were barred by law from marrying actresses. Justinian had to change the law so that he could marry Theodora. *Scaenici*, as theatre productions were called, continued into the sixth century in the West, and there are references to professional actors in Byzantium as late as the seventh century, but after that

formal theatre performances seem to have disappeared. "In the East problems more serious soon set people thinking of things sterner than merry supper-parties with groups of dancing girls".[9]

References throughout the Middle Ages indicating that it was "better to please God than the actors" and other critical remarks, however, suggest that some form of performance art continued, and it is not unlikely that such was also the case in Byzantium. The mime and some form of pantomime were probably the only forms of theatrical activity during this period. Theatre therefore existed in a non-scripted, non-literary form. To assist in our speculation about what may have existed in Byzantium, we can turn to evidence of twelfth-century Turkish theatre, undoubtedly of Byzantine influence. The Turkish *Orta Oinu* consisted of simple plays which

> were acted in the open, in a space thirty yards long and twenty wide, oval or quadrangular in shape. The women sat alone in a section opposite the single stage entrance and were shielded by a large veil from the vulgar gaze of the men. There were but two pieces of scenery, a chair or low screen stood near the entrance and a higher two-fold screen was placed at the opposite end of the stage. Doors, windows, gardens, woods, castles, or whatever the scene was supposed to depict, were painted on sheets of paper pasted on these screens. This was intended to inform the audience of the play's locale. The two principal actors were *Pishekiar*, the leader, and the comic *Kavuklu*; in addition there was a female character, *Zenne*, as well as other minor parts. All of the women of course were played by men.[10]

Perhaps this description could be applied to popular theatre in Byzantium, but we do not know. The aristocracy seems to have satisfied its dramatic inclinations with non-literary spectacles involving the actual *personae* of the imperial court.

DANCE

References to dance occur from time to time throughout this period. Whether we should consider Byzantine dance as an artistic form may be problematical. Two circumstances, at least, in which dance occurred are known. First, dancing often accompanied services in the Eastern churches. Second, the Roman dancing pantomime, "with all its subtlety of movement and expression deteriorated into a skilful, mostly fun-provoking means of entertainment. Either as solo performances at fairs and village festivals, or as little bands, these mimes appeared in the Byzantine Empire, where shows in the Roman style survived for some time."[11] Beyond this evidence of dance in Byzantium remains clouded.

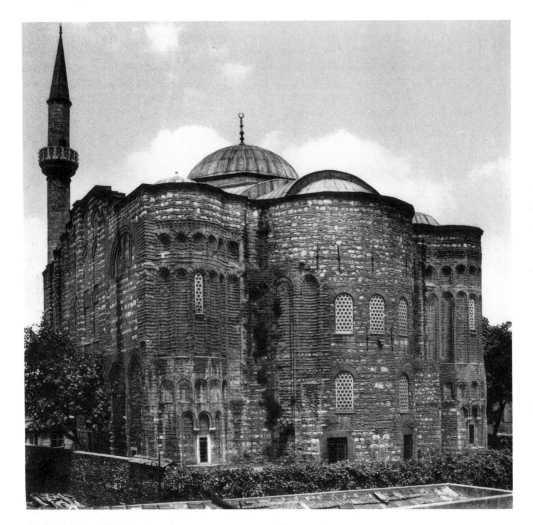

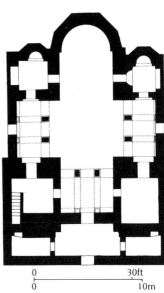

6.17 Ground plan of the church of St Clement, Ankara, Turkey.

6.18 St Theodosia, Istanbul, c. AD 1000.

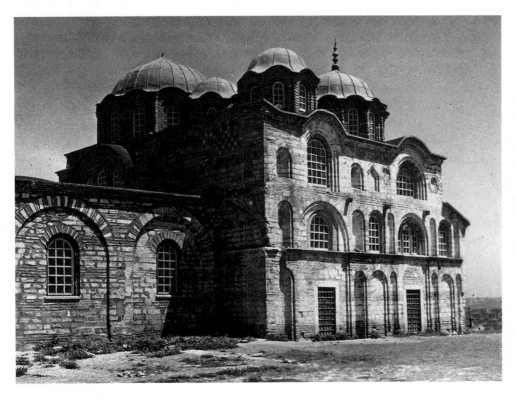

6.19 St Mary Pammakaristos, Istanbul, 13th century.

ARCHITECTURE

The architecture of the early years of the Eastern Empire was dominated by the personality and objectives of the Emperor Justinian. It was an age where royal patronage encouraged artistry, but artistry that clearly reflected the source of that encouragement. Justinian's purpose was to glorify Justinian, and, in a remarkably gifted and creative way, the arts and architecture of the age succeeded in doing just that. Results of his efforts can be found in both East and West.

The period from the sixth century until the beginning of the ninth was characterized by external and internal struggles. Out of this turbulence emerged a Byzantine state and, eventually, a high Byzantine culture. After Justinian's death the construction of public churches all but ceased. The Palace was the only important building. Yet, such churches as were built became models for later Byzantine architecture. The general plan of these early churches was made up of a dome and pendentive pavilion at the center with three apses grouped at the east end (Fig. **6.17**). The entire form probably described a cross-in-square plan which can be seen in later churches.

The churches constructed in the two or three centuries after St. Clement's employed classical principles of precise harmony of parts and suitability of composition to relate man to his aspirations. Elevated drums and vertical silhouettes became conventional, as shown in Figure **6.18**. Exteriors of brick or brick and stone project elegance and an emphasis on the rising line of the design. Exterior design and an individuality of expression appears to have been a priority in the tenth-century Byzantine style (Figs. **6.19** and **6.20**).

The effect was one of sumptuous elegance brilliantly and inextricably united with symbolic forms. Within this unity the flowing spaces, encased in an envelope of color, were functionally disposed for liturgical requirements. A deep, vaulted sanctuary and apse, communicating laterally with flanking side-chambers, housed the altar. A screen of painted icons stood athwart the main axis just beyond the eastern columns. Narthexes, and perhaps side porches, effected spatial and visual transition between the outer world and the jewel-like interiors. Incense, chant, ecclesiastical vestments, and ancient rites were combined with architecture and mosaic to evoke for the spirit and the senses that vision of another world around which Byzantine life revolved.[12]

6.20 Churches of St Luke and the Virgin, Stiris, Turkey, 11th century.

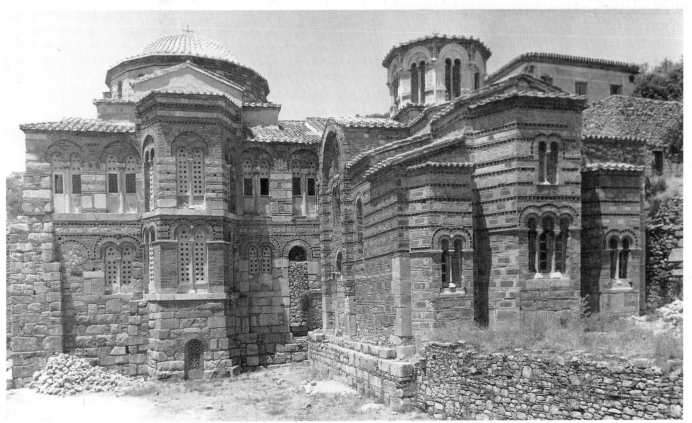

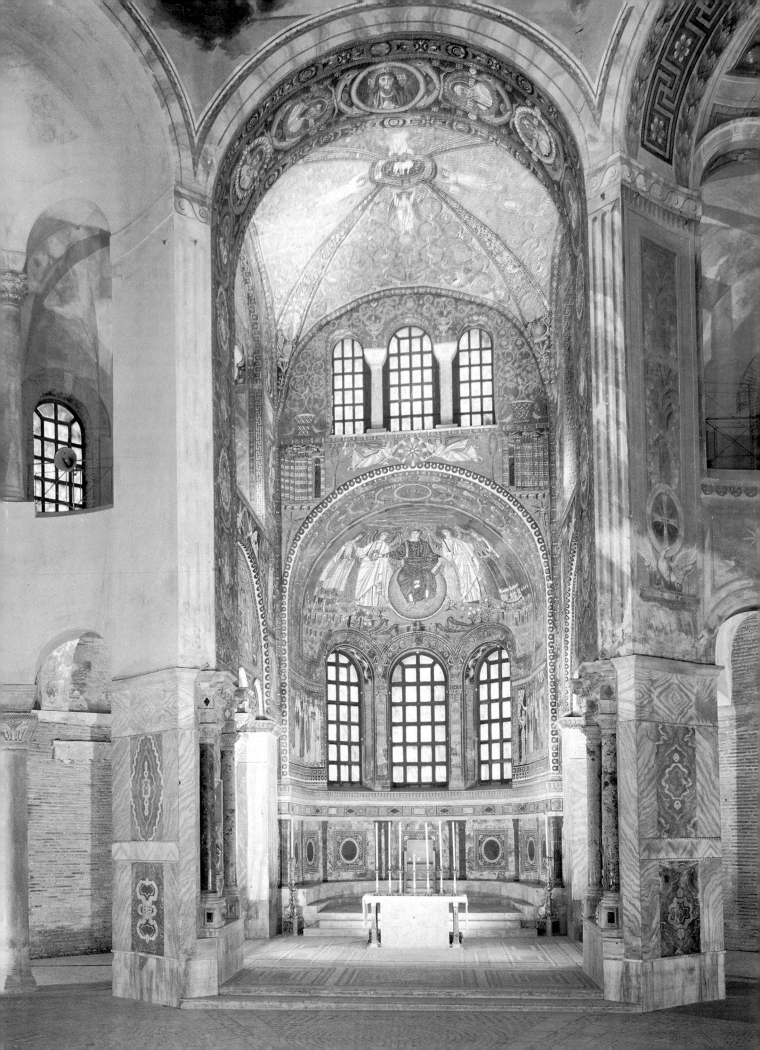

SYNTHESIS
In praise of the Emperor: the mark of Justinian

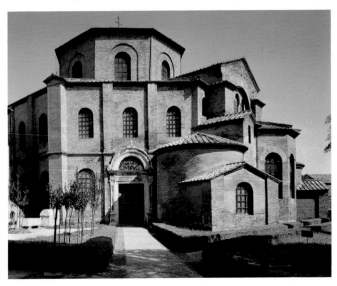

6.21 S Vitale, Ravenna, Italy, AD 526–547.

6.22 S Vitale, Ravenna, interior.

6.23 *Abraham's Hospitality and the Sacrifice of Isaac.* Wall mosaic. S Vitale, Ravenna.

Mosaic portraits of Justinian reveal a man who does not look like an emperor. He was of average height and build, with dark hair and ruddy complexion; his bland face was clean shaven and he seems to have worn a habitual faint smile. But this inconspicuous figure of a man was gifted with intelligence and talents such as few rulers possessed; and he played his role up to the hilt—with affability, arrogance and enormous vigor.[13]

San Vitale in Ravenna (Figs. **6.21**, **6.22** and **6.24**) is the major Justinian monument in the West, and was probably built as a testament to Orthodoxy in the declining kingdom of the Ostrogoths.

The prismatic geometry and warm brick texture of the exterior envelop an exhilerating, expanding well of strongly verticalized interior space. The key to the design is in the ingenious reciprocal manner in which volumenic parts are interlocked. For example, the eastern apse and its flanking spaces are composed of cylinders, prisms, and blocks which pile up dramatically against the outer octagonal shell, carrying the eye continuously across a concatenated play

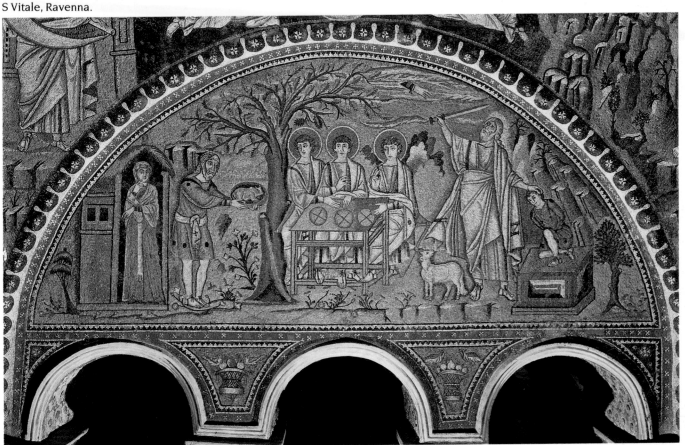

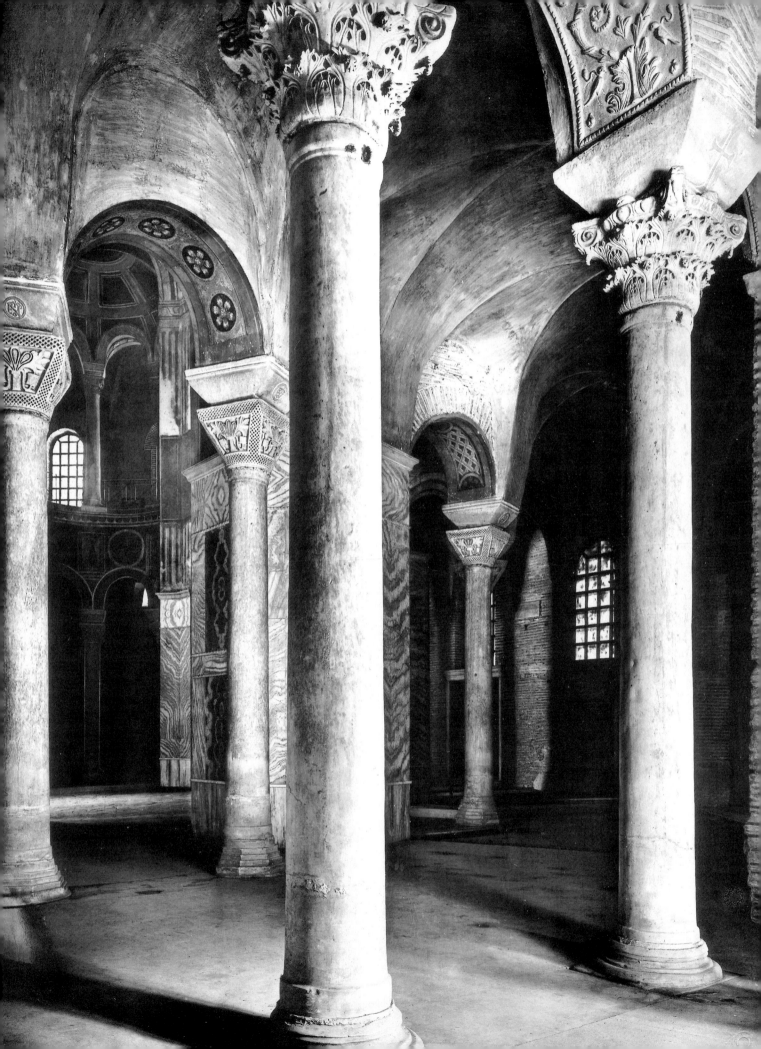

of surfaces. Each unit, delimited by the shadow lines of a sketchy terracotta cornice, can be read as an entity but is simultaneously joined and subordinated to the whole effect.[17]

The exterior composition defines precisely the interior space. The hemispheric dome rises one hundred feet above the floor. The aisles and gallery spaces around the outside contrast strikingly with the calm of the area under the dome. The relationships are complex in Byzantine spirit, and the entirety describes an organic unity of overwhelming proportion. On the inside we find a sanctuary alive with mosaics of the imperial court and sacred events. Figure **6.25** provides a vivid picture of the Emperor. What is fascinating here is the stylistic contrast

of two mosaics in the same church. *Abraham's Hospitality and the Sacrifice of Isaac* (Fig. **6.23**) demonstrates a relaxed naturalism whereas the mosaic depicting Justinian and his court demonstrates the orientalized style, more typically Byzantine, with the figures posed rigidly and frontally rather than naturalistically.

If San Vitale praises the emperor and Orthodoxy in the West, Hagia Sophia represents a crowning memorial in the East (Figs. **6.26–6.30**). Characteristic of Justinian Byzantine style, called *arcuate domicile*, Hagia Sophia uses well rehearsed vaulting techniques of Roman economy plus Hellenistic design and geometry. The result is a richly colored building in a style of orientalized antiquity. Basic to the conception is the elevated central pavilion with its domical image of heaven and large, open and

6.24 S Vitale, Ravenna, detail of aisle.

6.25 Emperor Justinian and his court, c. AD 547. Wall mosaic. S. Vitale, Ravenna.

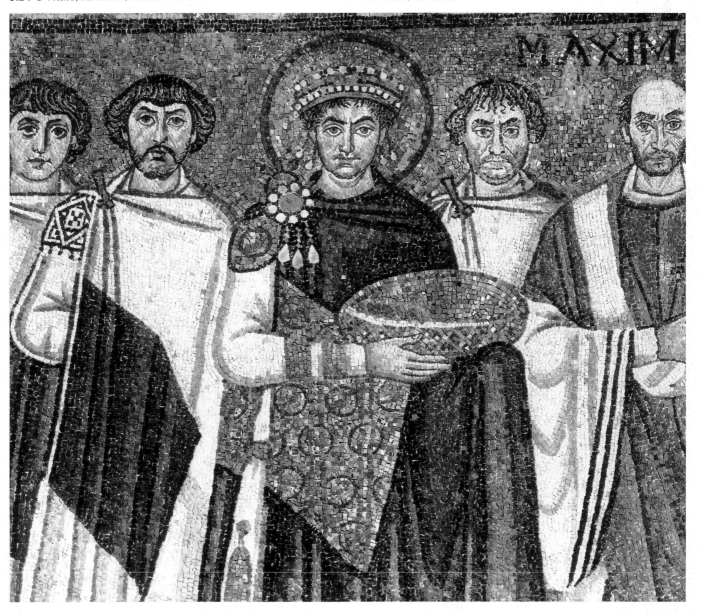

functional spaces. The magnificent Hagia Sophia provides us with a rare experience of Byzantine artistry. We know a little of its architect, Anthemius, who was a natural scientist and geometer from Tralles in Asia Minor. The church was built to replace an earlier basilica. This monument, which for a long time was the largest church in the world, was completed in only five years and ten months. The speed of the work, together with Byzantine masonry techniques in which courses of brick alternate with courses of mortar as thick or thicker than the bricks, caused great weight to be placed on insufficiently dry mortar. As a result arches buckled and buttresses had almost at once to be erected. Because of the rapid construction and the effects of two earthquakes, the eastern arch and part of the dome itself fell in 557. The flatness of a dome that large remains unique. Also remarkable is the delicate proportioning of the vaults which support such great weight. The building is intensely spiritual and yet capable of holding large numbers of worshippers; it creates a transcendental environment,

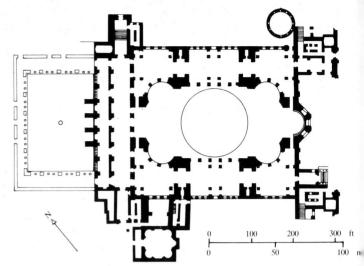

6.26 Plan of Hagia Sophia, Istanbul, AD 532–537.

6.27 Anthemius of Tralles and Isidorus of Miletus, Hagia Sophia, Istanbul.

6.28 Hagia Sophia, interior.

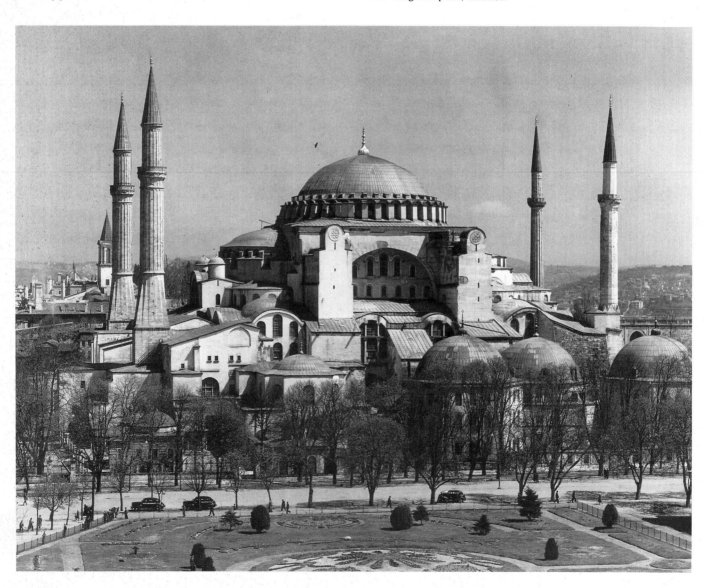

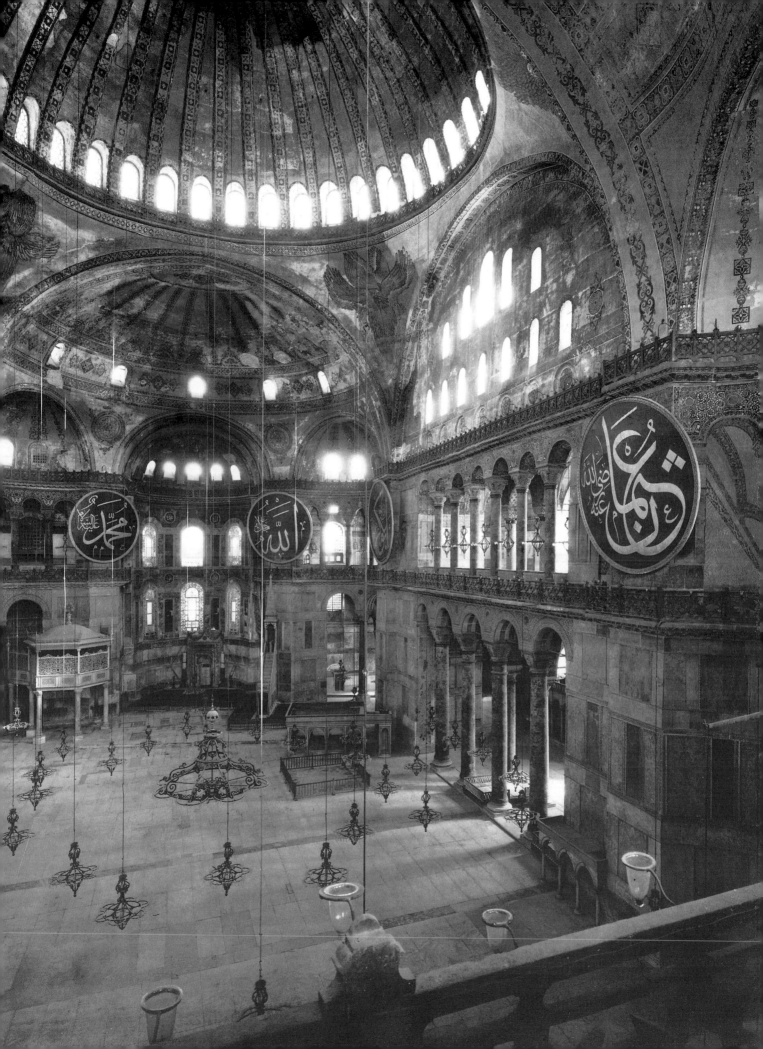

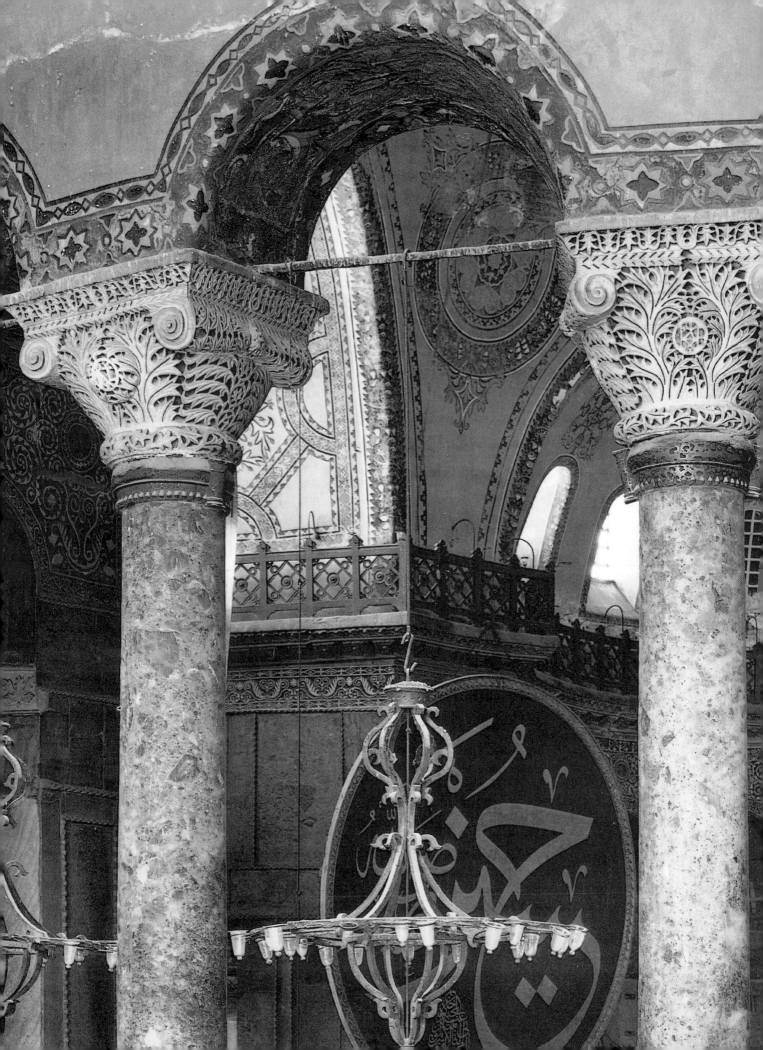

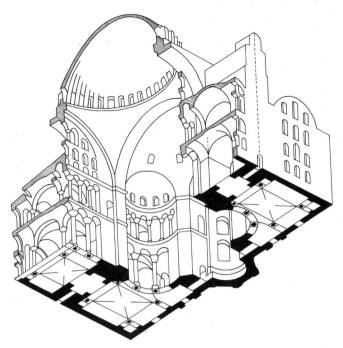

6.30 Axonometric section (worm's eye view) of Hagia Sophia.

where thoughts and emotions are at once wafted to a spiritual rather than a mundane sphere. "It seemed as if the vault of heaven were suspended above one," wrote Procopius.

The capitals of Hagia Sophia (Fig. **6.29**) illustrate marvelously the early works which typify an art that is totally Byzantine.

All traces of previous styles, Eastern or Western, blend together in a new style. At this point, "it is no longer to be described in any way as 'decadent', a term which could with justice be applied to some of the early Christian sculptures or capitals which are merely debased classical ones."[15] The "deeply undercut ornament" shows originality and achieves a uniquely effective result. Justinian's other buildings show work of the same type, but the Hagia Sophia represents the highest quality and achievement.

6.29 Capitals in Hagia Sophia.

SUGGESTIONS FOR THOUGHT AND DISCUSSION

Although Eastern in its tendencies, the Byzantine Empire played a significant role in the development of Western culture thoughout the last seven hundred years of the first millennium. It was the guardian of classical thought and style, even though it quickly developed its own characteristics. Justinian's rule marked a high point in Byzantine development, even though he sought above all to re-unify the Eastern and Western Empires. After Justinian, there came a new flourishing of splendor and artistic development which helped to consolidate the stylistic qualities which we clearly recognize as Byzantine.

Fundamental to Byzantine artistic style were the characteristics of the hieratic style, in which naturalism is replaced by mystical elongation of the human form. Painting, mosaic, and sculpture were infused with an obvious symbolism and spirituality clearly recognizable as Byzantine.

■ Icons are central to Byzantine art and religion. What was the inconoclastic controversy and what role did it play in the development of Byzantine religion and art?
■ Relate the characteristics of Byzantine literature to the characteristics of the other arts in Byzantium.
■ How does the Byzantine literary genre of history differ from our conceptions of history?
■ Discuss hagiography as a literary discipline.
■ How does the concept of "divine right", as we have noted it in previous chapters, take on new meanings in Justinian's Code and subsequent interpretations?
■ Discuss Byzantium and its rulers and arts as examples of theocratic authoritarianism. Is it possible to separate church, state, and art in this period?
■ What examples can you cite of Byzantine influence in the political, intellectual, religious, and artistic life of the West?

CHAPTER SEVEN

THE EARLY MIDDLE AGES

The Middle Ages is the name we have come to use for the thousand years centered upon the close of the first Christian millennium: the period that began with the Fall of Rome and closed with the "reawakening" of the Renaissance in Italy. The so-called Dark Ages comprise the early part of this period, when it came to seem that mankind had crept into a barricaded world of mental and physical isolation and self-protection. It was, for many, a time of fear and superstition: a "vale of tears" for the Christian, who had little to hope save the hope that beyond this life lay the possibility of heaven for those who obediently followed the teachings of the Church. But in monasteries and convents throughout Europe, literacy, learning and artistic creativity were nurtured, and the works of the period are in many cases filled with intuitive vision of rare and deeply moving quality. It was widely believed that the year 1000 would bring the Second Coming of Christ.

7.1 Scenes from the life of St Paul, from the Bible of Charles the Bald, c. AD 875–877. S Paolo fuori le Mura, Rome.

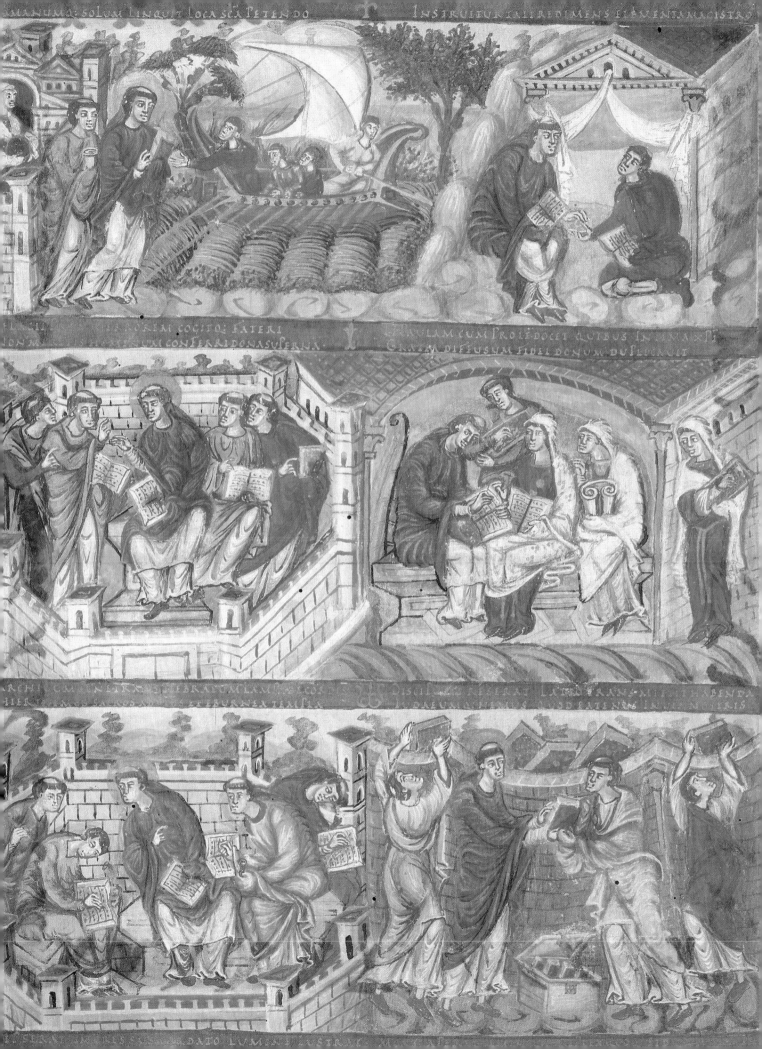

CONTEXTS AND CONCEPTS

If Periclean Athens was a culmination of diverse forces to create a cohesive civilization, then the early Middle Ages was a period of dissolution, as the Western world disintegrated into a chaotic jumble of confusion and, to a large degree, darkness.

The terms "Dark Ages" and "Middle Ages" were given to parts of the thousand years between the fifth and the fifteenth centuries, principally because this period was viewed as an age of darkness between the classical perfection of Greece and Rome and its revival in the fifteenth century. We continue to use the terms as convenient labels rather than as a statement of viewpoint. In an overview such as this, we must constantly remind ourselves that while certain aspects of an era may be summarized, specific exceptions did exist. This is especially true in a world as fragmented as that of the Middle Ages.

Pessimism and disillusionment increased in Rome over the centuries and continued into the Middle Ages. A well-known epitaph is often cited as evidence: "I was not; I was; I am not; I care not". Civic, secular government had all but ceased to exist. When Constantine I founded the second capital of the Roman Empire at Byzantium, he set in motion a division that became formal and permanent in AD 395. In the West the cloak of internationalism, which had loosely united the Mediterranean world since Alexander, became threadbare and fell apart. It was every locality and every people for themselves.

Since the turn of the Christian era the Roman Empire had been besieged from the outside while decaying from within. The Goths, the Huns, the Visigoths, the Vandals and, in the seventh century, the armies of Islam pressured and pierced the perimeters of the empire. The Western world was in a state of continual change. As one people pressed against another, the one pressed against turned upon its opposite neighbor. Nations as we know them did not exist. Borders changed from day to day as one people wandered and warred into the nebulous territory of its neighbors.

The barbarians

No specific date should be assigned to the fall of the Roman Empire. Throughout the third and fourth centuries a gradual Germanization of the western provinces accompanied a reciprocal Romanization of the Germanic peoples. The Germanic tribes constantly pressed against the borders of the Empire. Occasionally they would score a victory only to be pushed back by a fresh contingent of Roman troops. In the far north-west the Angles and Saxons raided the coasts of Britain. On the lower Rhine River the Franks fought amongst each other, with some Franks allied with Rome and others not. Frankish troops formed the backbone of Roman defenses along the upper Rhine against Germanic peoples there, while Germans were used to defend Roman territory along the Danube. By the end of the fourth century the Roman army had to a large extent become an army of barbarians, often led by barbarian officers.

Around the beginning of the fifth century entire populations of Germanic peoples, rather than raiding Roman territories, migrated into them and established permanent settlements. At the same time the Huns, a Mongolian people, "a race savage beyond all parallel" as one Roman historian put it, having been defeated on the borders of China, turned their attention to the Germanic peoples, and set off a further chain of migrations. The Visigoths, led by their greatest king, Alaric I, revolted in 396 and ravaged Greece. Pacified for a time by being given the office of *magister militum* of Illyrium, Alaric turned his Goths on Italy in 402 only to be repulsed by a defending army under a Vandal general. By 406 Roman defenses had deteriorated considerably and a mixed horde of Germanic peoples, mostly Vandals, surged into the Empire and made their way through Gaul into Spain. Capitalizing on the situation, Alaric again attacked Italy and succeeded in sacking Rome itself in 410. Alaric apparently had designs on Africa, but died before he could carry out his plans. His successor Ataulph returned to the policy of placing his armies as *foederati*, in the service of the imperial government. Ataulph married Galla Placidia, sister of the emperor Honorius, and took his Visigoths to southern Gaul and eventually attacked the Vandals in Spain. Between 425 and 455 Galla Placidia exercised imperial authority in the name of her son, Emperor Valentinian III, born of her second marriage, after Ataulph's death, to the Roman general Constantius. In response to further internal strife in Rome, the imperial government had moved its seat to Ravenna. In 455 the Vandals, under Gaiseric, looted Rome in a more vicious manner than had the Visigoths. Meanwhile in 452 the Huns led by Attila invaded along the Rhine. They penetrated into Italy, and threatened Rome in 453. Weakened by pestilence and, finally, the death of Attila in 453, the Hunnish threat dissipated, leaving the western borders in relative peace.

Valentinian III was assassinated in 454, and his successor, Maximian, was lynched by the Roman mob a few months later for failing to protect Rome from Gaiseric. From 456 onward the Germans ruled Italy, and in 476 the puppet Roman Emperor Romulus Augustus was deposed and not replaced. The Western Roman Empire had seen its last emperor. Two more invasions by the Franks and the Ostrogoths completed the picture, and in 489 Theodoric led the entire Ostrogothic people over the Alps and established himself as ruler of Italy. By the year 500 every part of what had been the Western Roman Empire was ruled by barbarian kings.

The early Christian Church

Meanwhile an infant Christianity was struggling to survive. As with any emerging entity it felt an intense need to create institutions. Christianity was a loosely organized, theologically divergent body, drastically different from the religions around it. It needed a united front in order to grow and to make its way in a pagan and suspicious world. In the first centuries of its existence the Christian Church shed its own blood as its various sects battled over questions of dogma which it was imperative to resolve if the Church was to be organized. However, in the thrust and counter-thrust so common to our existence, the emerging Church was a force in the process of coming together in a world in the process of coming apart.

There is much interesting speculation about why and how Christianity survived. In some ways it resembled the mystery religions. Its monotheism as an extension of the Jewish heritage, the immediacy of its founder and the doctrines he taught, all appealed to men and women of the late and post-Roman period. Christianity also had a multi-faceted appeal in its extreme simplicity on one hand and its subtlety on the other, making it acceptable to the most lowly and illiterate of individuals as well as those of sophisticated intelligence.

Although little is known about the spread of Christianity through the Roman Empire, by the end of the third century Christians were numerous enough to count as a political force. Converts from the aristocracy and upper classes enhanced its chances of survival substantially. Every city of consequence had a Christian community presided over by a bishop assisted by priests and deacons. Regarded as successors of the original apostles, bishops were chosen by the communities, and decided theological disputes in council. Christianity found varying degrees of tolerance from the Roman state. In general the Imperial government treated equally all of the various religious practices in its diverse and far-flung Empire. Occasionally, however, Christians suffered fierce persecution, mainly because they refused to worship the Emperor as a divine being. In addition, their secret meetings and rites became cause for concern for the authoritarian government. Christians also abhorred violence and refused to serve in the Roman army, a very difficult stance for the state to tolerate when beset by constant threats. The last great persecution occurred under Diocletian in 303. Shortly afterwards Constantine transformed Christianity into a favored religion of the Roman state. According to the bishop Eusebius, Constantine reported that he had had a dream prior to the Battle of Milvian Bridge, in which he was told to send his soldiers into battle with standards marked by Christian symbols. Constantine did so, won the battle, and was converted to Christianity. He later indicated that he was "brought to the faith by God to be the means of the faith's triumph". Christianity soon became the official religion of the Empire.

Numerous privileges resulted from this new status. The church could receive legacies, its clergy were exempt from taxation, and bishops were permitted to settle disputes of law in all civil cases in which a Christian was a party. In addition, the Church obtained the rights of sanctuary.

		GENERAL EVENTS	LITERATURE & PHILOSOPHY	VISUAL ART	THEATRE & DANCE	MUSIC	ARCHITECTURE
100							Basilica Ulpia (7.15)
200			Tertullian				
300		Barbarian invasions Council of Nicea Christianity becomes a State Religion	St Augustine St Jerome			Christian hymnody	Old St Peter's, Rome (7.18) St Paul's outside the Walls, Rome (7.19)
400		Pope Leo I Fall of Rome	St Benedict			Antiphonal psalmody	
500	Feudalism	Gregory the Great		St Luke from the presumed Augustine Bible (7.5)		Gregorian chant	
600			Troubadours	Lindisfarne Gospels (7.6) Purse lid–Sutton Hoo burial (7.7)			
700		Charles Martel repels Muslim invaders	Minnesänger Trouvères				Palace Chapel of Charlemagne
800	Feudalism	Charlemagne crowned Holy Roman Emperor	Song of Roland	Gospel Book of Godescale (7.27) Gospel book of St-Médard (7.28) So-called statue of Charlemagne (7.31) Ivory cover, Dagulf Psalter (7.32) Ivory cover, Lorsch Gospels (7.33)		Polyphony-Organa	Palatine Chapel – Aachen (7.20) Crypts at Auxerre (7.26)
900		Ottonian Empire begins (Otto I, II, III)		Gero Crucifix (7.8)	Tropes emerge		
1000				Bronze doors, Hildesheim Cathedral (7.11)	Professional dance apparent		St-Sernin (7.21) Abbey Church, Cluny III (7.25)
1100		Ottonian Empire ends					
1200			Nibelungenlied				
1300				Crucified Christ (7.10)			

7.2 Timeline of the Early Middle Ages.

After Constantine's conversion, the Church began to build up a more highly organized administration of its own, adopting a structure quite similar to that of the civil bureaucracy. By the fourth century each province was divided into bishoprics with an archbishop at its head. There was, however, no centralized administration for the whole Church comparable to the Imperial government. The bishops of the four great cities of Rome, Jerusalem, Antioch, and Alexandria claimed special privilege because the church in those cities was founded by the apostles. Rome claimed supremacy both because it was founded by Peter and because it was capital of the Empire.

Yet the opportunities presented by the conversion of emperors to Christianity were offset by problems stemming from the same source. In return for championing the faith, the Emperor expected the bishops to act as loyal servants of the imperial crown. When theological disputes arose, the Emperor often insisted on deciding the matter himself. For example, in the fourth century the Arianist controversy broke out over the nature of the Son in the Christian Trinity. In an attempt to quell the controversy, a new institution of church government was established—the General Council. The Council of Nicea in 325, its first convocation, agreed on a doctrine from which the Nicene Creed emerged, declaring that the Son was "of one substance with the Father". The issue continued to flame, and involved a succession of emperors—Constantine I, Constantius II, and, finally, Theodosius I, whose Council of Constantinople in 381 reaffirmed the doctrine of Nicea and put the issue to rest.

The Popes

Early reference to the primacy of Rome can be found in letters of St. Ignatus from AD 110 and of St. Irenaesis (c. AD 185). The claim of the medieval popes to exercise complete temporal authority over all of Christendom was developed slowly. The Bishops of Rome claimed supremacy because they were the heirs of St. Peter and because of the status of their city as capital. Other arguments included its sanctification by the blood of martyrs and its freedom from the contamination of the heresies which had touched other churches. Specific acknowledgement by a church council of Rome's supremacy first came in 344 from the Council of Sardica. The Council of Constantinople placed the Bishop of Constantinople second after the Bishop of Rome "because Constantinople is the New Rome". A series of strong and able Bishops of Rome consolidated the move toward supremacy over the next century. The argument put forward by the Bishops of Rome in support of their case came to be known as the Petrine theory. Perhaps its clearest formulation came from Pope Leo I (440–461). He had considerable administrative ability and played a significant role in civil affairs. He was twice called on by the Emperor to negotiate with the leaders of the barbarian armies which invaded Italy in 453 and 455. Pope Leo insisted that he was "heir" of St. Peter and that "Christ had appointed Peter to be head of the whole universal Church". He affirmed that all other apostles were subordinate to Peter, and, therefore, all other bishops were subordinate to the Bishop of Rome who had succeeded to Peter's See at Rome. In fact, nearly all Western Christians came to acknowledge the Pope of Rome as head of the whole Church, but what remained unclear was the actual extent of his authority in temporal affairs and in affairs of church governance.

Early Christian thought

Tertullian

The study of medieval thought of the first millennium is really the study of Christian thought. In order to understand the men and women of the early Middle Ages, how they might have seen the universe and how that viewpoint was translated into art form, it is important to examine some early Christian thought. Two of the most important figures were Tertullian and Augustine and our examination will focus on them. There were of course others of great stature

7.3 Europe and North Africa in the Late Roman period.

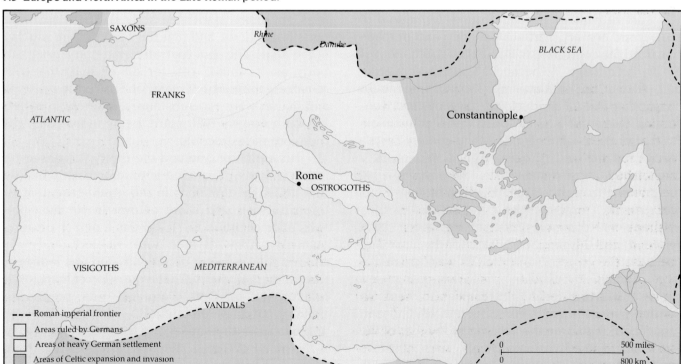

such as Cyprian, Arnobius, and Jerome.

In the early years of the Middle Ages the West was culturally dependent on the East. Its art, literature, and philosophy tended to be derivative rather than original. On the other hand, the prevailing interests of the West differed significantly from those of the East, reflecting its Roman heritage. They concentrated on the functional, practical and ethical. Law and government, the sovereignty of the state, tradition, and institutions were all preoccupations and all affected Western Christianity. The Church as an institution and its functions and authority were of prime importance. Humankind's duties, responsibilities, sin, and grace were all topics of great interest. The theistic and cosmological problems which took precedence in the East were of lesser importance in the West. The major theological conflicts occurred in the East, and in these matters the West almost automatically accepted the doctrinal decisions of the Eastern Church. In North Africa, however, in the Roman provinces of Africa, Numidia, and Mauritania, Greek influence was significantly less than in Gaul and Italy. Particularly in the province of Africa there were large numbers of Italian colonists with close ties to the provincial capital, Carthage, and thereby to Rome. By AD 200 Carthage boasted a strong and vital Christian Church, and from this community came Tertullian of Carthage, the first of the Latin Fathers. His writings demonstrate pointedly the differences between East and West.

Born of heathen parents around the middle of the second century, Tertullian studied and perhaps practiced law for a time in Rome, but spent most of his life in Carthage. He became a Christian convert in mid-life, but unlike Augustine, Tertullian seems to have been free of morbid self-consciousness concerning his moral pursuits prior to his conversion. Soon after the beginning of the third century Tertullian joined the sect of Montanism (a sect of early charismatics), and remained in that sect until his death sometime after 220. He was a prolific writer and covered a large number of themes. First writing in Greek, the common Christian language in both East and West, he switched to Latin, and was the first important theologian to do so. He also created a large Christian vocabulary, including many new words and giving technical meanings to words in current use. His major contributions to Christian thought are in two areas—he was the founder of the language of the Western Church, and of those aspects of its theology which marked a break with

the East. His writings were highly influential, and continued to be so even after his defection to Montanism destroyed his standing as a Catholic Father.

> His character and temperament are abundantly revealed in his writings. He was passionate, enthusiastic, restive and impatient, always at odds with himself and others, extreme in his views and in his expression of them, fanatical and intolerant, ascetic in his tendencies, a puritan of puritans, vigorous in his moral principles and uncompromising in his moral judgments, violent and vituperative in his denunciations of those that disagreed with him, in his polemics sophistical and unfair and not above personal slander and flagrant misrepresentation. . . . He looked at everything with the eyes of a lawyer . . . he gave the language and the theology of Western Catholicism a legal cast which they have never lost. . . . Practical duties and responsibilities were uppermost in his mind and the relationship between man and God which underlay them.[1]

Probably the most important of Tertullian's writings is an elaborate analysis of the soul, in which he explores human psychology, and concludes that corporeality determines the parameters of the soul. His arguments lean heavily on Stoicism. He believed that the soul had length, breadth, and thickness, not identical with the body, but permeating all parts of the body, and that the center of the soul lay in the heart. The soul controlled the body, using the body as it would. Yet, for all of that, the soul remained spiritual, not material. For Tertullian, spirit and matter were two substances, different in nature but both equally real; spirit, being indivisible, was therefore indestructible.

His notion of God and the trinity was based on legal concepts. "That God is triune means primarily that he is three persons in the legal sense, that is, three persons who share or own in common one substance or property."[2] God was a personal sovereign, to whom all men were subject, and who created the world out of nothing. God was independent and omnipotent. On the question of humanity's relationship to God, Tertullian was precise in defining God as an authority figure whom one approached with humility and fear. "The fear of man is the honor of God. . . . Where there is no fear there is no amendment. . . . How are you going to love unless you are afraid not to love?" Virtue, therefore, sprang from fear. It was obedience to divine law springing from fear of punishment if the law were broken. In this and so many other areas Tertullian's legal training was clear. He formulated an elaborate list of sins, including the Seven Deadly Sins of idolatry, blasphemy, murder, adultery, fornication, false witness, and fraud.

By the time of Tertullian the Church had begun to see this life as a mere probation for the life to come, without value in itself and possessing meaning only because in it rewards are laid up for the life beyond the grave. Tertullian believed the supreme virtues were humility and the spirit of other-worldliness, by which the Christian escaped the perils of this life sure of enjoying the reward prepared for the saints in heaven.

St. Augustine

St. Augustine (354–430) did not receive the sacrament of baptism until he was an adult because his mother, who was a Christian, believed that if he were baptized as a child the healing virtue would be destroyed by the lusts of youth. The vociferousness of his repentance may have exaggerated his profligacy. Nonetheless, after a period of skepticism and adherence to Manichaeism—a syncretic dualistic philosophy combining elements of Zoroastrianism, Gnosticism, and Christianity—he was baptized into the Christian faith. He later became Bishop of Hippo. A prolific writer, his works held great influence over developing Christian thought. *Confessions* and *City of God* are the best known of his works. His philosophy of art was also significant, and will be discussed later.

Apparently Augustine found great inspiration in the writings of Plotinus, but certainly he was also highly influenced by Platonic and neo-Platonic thought. As a result, he recoiled from Tertullian's emphasis on the senses and corporeal matters. He shared Tertullian's belief in intuition as the source of knowledge concerning God, but Augustine's concept of intuition had an intellectual cast. We should not trust the senses, which give us unreliable images of the truth. Augustine stated that intuition, our affective way of thinking, had a certainty which sprang from "the fact that it is of the very nature of reason to know the truth".[3] Knowledge was an inner illumination of the soul by God. Whatever we find intelligible is, therefore, certain. Knowledge, then, comes

from intuition and "confirms and amplifies the certainty of faith".[4]

Augustine's theory of creation followed Tertullian's in maintaining that the universe was created by God out of nothing. Creation occurred at a given moment which was the *first* moment, that is, the universe and time were created together. The context of this assertion countered the argument that if the universe were not eternal then God's creative power must have lain idle for some time before he used it, and also that God's will to create must have been an afterthought or sudden whim.

On the existence of the soul Augustine's arguments are similar to those of Descartes (see Chapter Ten). To doubt the existence of the soul is in fact to confirm its existence, because in order to doubt we must think, and if we think, we therefore must be thinking beings—souls. Unlike Tertullian, Augustine found the soul to be immaterial, that is, a spiritual entity. The spiritual character as well as the soul's immortality are demonstrated by our power to grasp eternal and immaterial essences. The question of where the soul comes from caused Augustine some difficulty. It was not, as Plato suggested, pre-existent. It did not emanate from God, but was created by Him. Augustine was uncertain whether the soul derived in each individual from the souls of the parents or was created by God and directly implanted in each new body. However, each soul was unique and contained three faculties—intellect, will, and memory.

His concept of original sin, as developed in *City of God*, led Augustine into a central role in the Pelagian Heresy. Pelagius and his followers opposed the concept of original sin. The doctrine of original sin, to which Augustine subscribed, held that all men are born to sin because of Adam's fall, and "are punished by being born to a state of sin and death, physical and spiritual, from which only Christ's passion and saving grace can redeem us". Pelagius rejected the doctrine of original sin, and insisted that sin was purely voluntary and individual and could not be transmitted. "Adam's fall affected neither the souls nor the bodies of his descendants." Every man creates his own character and destiny. Each soul enters the world sinless, and becomes sinful by individual act. Death is a natural event having nothing to do with the Fall. Whereas Pelagius argued that men were bad *if* they did bad things, Augustus held that men were bad *and therefore* did bad things. Before Christ's coming, therefore, there were men who lived without sin and attained salvation. Likewise, the souls of children who die unbaptized are not logically bound to go to Hell.

Augustine charged into the fray with an ardor that carried him even further than his objective—the formal condemnation of the heresy by the Council of Carthage in 411. For in fighting for original sin he asserted that God in his omniscience foresaw before the foundation of the world Adam's sin and its consequences, and therefore might be said to have elected from all eternity certain souls to be saved and others to be damned.[5]

Augustine also dealt with the question of Foreknowledge and Foreordination, in which he had difficulty maintaining the existence of free will in mankind. That question still bothers Christian theologians, and Augustine's position has been central, for example, to Luther's doctrine of justification by grace rather than good works, and Calvin's doctrine of predestination.

The Roman Church

In the sixth century Italy faced a very uncertain future. Although Rome no longer ruled a secular empire, the primacy claimed by its bishops gave Rome a potential position of great importance in the Christian world. Such a possibility, however, was clouded by two factors—the barbarism of the Western provinces and the complex theocracy of the East with its emperors *cum* sacred rulers. Without the Roman Empire, it would be difficult, indeed, for the Roman church to survive. The Acacian Schism led to an important development in Church history, the formulation by Pope Gelasius I (492–496) of the roles of priests and kings in the government of the Christian world. His central tenet was that the world was ruled by two powers, the sacred authority of the priesthood and the royal power, the responsibilities of the priesthood being the greater because they had kings within their pastoral charge. The problem was further complicated by Justinian's grand designs for a unified empire. Justinian had not the slightest intention of yielding to the Roman Bishops in matters of religion if it constituted a political inconvenience. By the middle of the sixth century it appeared likely that the Roman Church and its pope would simply become a tool of Byzantine imperial policy. Rome appeared to have been demoted to

the status of peripheral center of Catholic Christianity.

Rome was rescued from its potential demise by one of the greatest pontiffs in the history of the Roman Church, Gregory I (the Great). His abilities as a ruler and teacher significantly affected numerous aspects of the Church and its history, as well as many political and social matters in Rome. His land reforms and his administration of estates previously endowed to the Church revitalized church income, relieved famine, and provided money for churches, hospitals, and schools. His influence spread from Rome to the rest of Italy and beyond. One of the most important missions he undertook was the conversion of England in 597.

Undoubtedly the most important of his written works was the *Book of Pastoral Care*, "a treatise in the episcopal office that reflected the pope's high idealism in the way of life he laid down for a bishop and his profound understanding of ordinary human nature in the advice he gave on the care of the bishop's flock".[6] As a result of his efforts, Rome regained its position of primacy among the Western Christian churches. Despite the long-lasting results of Gregory's actions, he did not consider himself that he was building for the future. He believed that the Second Coming was near. He merely did what he thought had to be done in what little time remained. Unintentionally he built a base for an enduring Church and a dominant papacy of wealth and great prestige.

Feudalism

Europe during the sixth to ninth centuries was a place of dismal illiteracy and primitive living conditions. Death was a constant companion, and death-related superstition and fear flourished amidst general ignorance. A slowly emerging system of government called feudalism did little to elevate the lot of the common man; nor for that matter did the Church do much. Feudalism was a political division of territory into units, each one small enough to be governed by one man. It encouraged warfare and bloodshed since no ultimately powerful authority controlled the individual parts. Feudal lords continually raided each other in attempts to increase their wealth and property. Feudalism was based on a system of vassalage, and in that system were kings and barons, the latter supposedly responsible to, or a vassal of, the former. However,

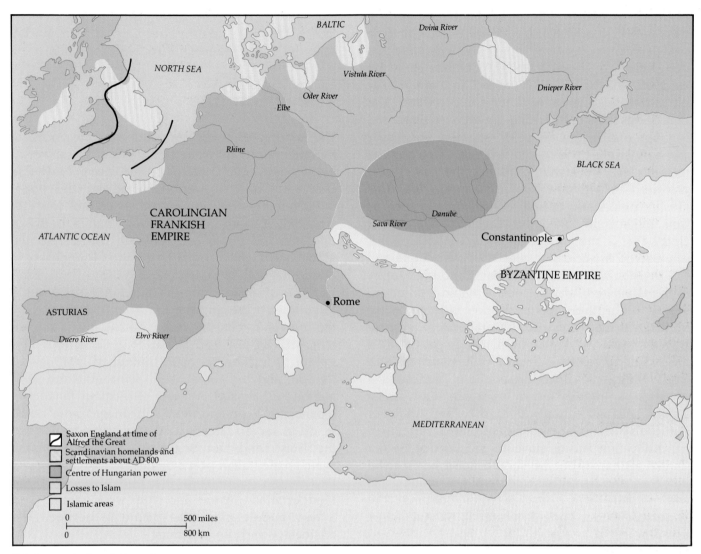

7.4 Europe in the ninth century.

very rarely did enough power exist at any level above the individual landholder to effect real control, and despotic rulers flourished. Trapped at the bottom of this rigid social structure (and often in the middle of the bloodletting) were the common people or serfs. Serfs were little more than slaves, attached to the land, working for the local lord, and subject to the lord's bidding. It was a life of ignorance and destitution. As Christianity spread, the terrors of "today" were endured in anticipation of reward in a life to come.

The devil as a symbol of the powers of darkness and evil was a strong force in medieval thinking and superstition, and the Church manipulated those fears and images as it sought, often fanatically, to convert the pagan world of the early Middle Ages. The promise of Heaven, and the prospect of the fires of Hell if a Christian life, as determined by the clergy, was not followed, were constant themes of the times. These ever-present devils and demons fostered a certain fascination as well as fear. As we shall see, in medieval theatre, for example, the devil often has the best part, and his role and popularity grew to staggering proportions. Stage portrayals of Hell were often fantastic technical achievements with flame, smoke, and gargantuan monsters—all of which enthralled the audience.

The Church, nevertheless, played an important stabilizing role in this desperate and frenzied world. It provided a source of continuity and, as its influence spread, medieval attention and philosophy turned from Man as the measure of all things to God as the measure of all things. The Western world slowly came to a belief that the demons could be escaped and that death promised an even greater life in the hereafter, at least for a selected few. The Church was itself divided and did little to reduce the isolation and ignorance of its followers. Very early the clergy were divided into two parts. One was the regular clergy consisting of monks and others who preferred to withdraw into a cloistered life. This lifestyle held strong appeal for many intellectuals as well. The second part of the Church was the secular clergy, that is, the Pope, bishops, and parish priests who served in society at large. The overall effect of this division was to confine learning and philosophy to the monastery, and thereby withhold intellectual activity from the broader world. In both cases inquiry was rigidly restricted. Detailed and unquestioned dogma was deemed essential to the Church's mission of conversion—and for its very survival. As a result, the medieval world was one of barricades—physical, spiritual, and intellectual. Each man, woman, and institution retreated behind whatever barricade he, she, or it considered most protective.

Education was a slave to the service of the Christian Church, but we should not minimize the influence and accomplishments of the theologians and scholars of the era, such as Boëthius, the Venerable Bede, Pope Sylvester II, St. Augustine, and others.

Charlemagne

As feudalism developed and life went on, the human spirit tried to free itself from these unbearable restraints and return to a broader sense of political order. Occasionally a ray of hope shone through. One such hope was Charlemagne. The expanding threat of Islam and the Moorish Conquest had been repelled by Charles Martel in AD 732. The succeeding Carolingian period, under Charlemagne, saw the first significant organized political centralization since the fall of Rome. Charlemagne united parts of Spain, France, western Germany, and northern Italy, and was crowned Holy Roman Emperor by the Pope in 800. He also revived an interest in art, antiquity, and learning. Charlemagne's renaissance had a different viewpoint from the Renaissance of six hundred or so years ahead, but it did rekindle some of the spirit of art and inquiry, if only in

cloistered circles. The Carolingian era lasted until late in the ninth century, but Europe then quickly reverted to a divided and troubled condition.

The Ottonians

The ninth and tenth centuries saw the focus of Europe shift to Germany in the guise of a universal empire under the Ottonians. The German Emperors Otto I, II, and III were crowned by the Pope. Subsequently they attempted to control the still struggling Church. The resulting conflict between Emperor and Pope, coupled with the developing feudal and monastic system, ensured Europe's continued fragmentation and isolationism.

The Ottonian Emperors failed in their attempts to subjugate the growing Christian Church, and by the eleventh century, the Church, especially its monastic orders, had come to great power and wealth. Christianity had triumphed throughout Europe, and the threat of invasion from the perimeters had ceased. A fervor of religious fanaticism resurfaced. More and more pilgrimages were being made to sacred sites, and the crusades to liberate the Holy Land had begun. Trade was beginning again as the Italian port cities of Venice, Genoa, and Pisa began to reclaim the trade routes of the Mediterranean. Towns and cities were growing, and a new middle class was emerging between the aristocracy and the peasants.

Literature

It seems clear that in the early Middle Ages, with the notable exception of the Carolingian court, the politically powerful cared little for culture, and for the most part they could neither read nor write. Thanks to the efforts of the monastic community, and particularly the Benedictine monks, important books and manuscripts were carefully preserved and copied. St. Benedict (c. 480–c. 550) was one of the few great scholars of the Dark Ages. Literature flourished in Spain, where Muslim contact with Greek scholarship, established when they invaded Egypt, led to the setting up of schools in Cordoba. Aristotle, Plato, and Euclid were on the curriculum alongside the Koran. Toledo and Seville were also centers of learning. It was biblical literature, however, which became the central focus of the period.

St. Jerome was a contemporary of St. Augustine,

and his scholarship and writings merited a position of primary importance in the last years of the Roman Empire. St. Jerome was familiar with the classical writers, and found the style of the scriptures somewhat crude. However, in a dream Christ reproached him and accused him of being more a Ciceronian than a Christian. As a result, Jerome resolved to spend the rest of his life in the study of the sacred books. From his dedicated work came his famous translation of the Bible into Latin. Assisted by Jewish scholars, he also translated the Old Testament from the Hebrew.

In addition to the works of Augustine, the major literary accomplishment of the early Middle Ages was the German *Nibelungenlied*. These primitive hero-stories of Northern peoples, which took their final shape in south-east Germany in about 1200, are a rich mixture of history, magic and myth. The title of this collection, written down by an unknown poet, translates as *Song of the People of the Mist*, meaning the Dead. They are folk stories which were later used by Wagner as a source for his operas. The *Nibelungenlied* comprises ten complete and twenty incomplete manuscripts and encompasses thirty-nine adventures, starting with that of the hero Siegfried, son of Siegmund, King of the Netherworld.

The literature of this period also included the poems of the troubadours, *Minnesänger*, and *trouvères* or court poets, who were popular throughout Europe. These professional story-tellers produced fantastic legends and romances, such as the *Song of Roland* and *Aucassin and Nicolette*. In the *Song of Roland*, an unknown poet tells, with fine but simple dramatic skills, the story of a great battle between Charlemagne and the Saracens of Saragossa in the Pyrenees. Charlemagne is deceived by the Saracens, draws his main army back into France and leaves Roland with a rearguard to hold the pass. The Saracens are aided by recreant Christian knights, and after a furious struggle, Roland and his entire army are killed.

St. Augustine's philosophy of art

The philosophy of art expounded by St. Augustine represents a radical shift from that of Plato and Aristotle in the principles of art evaluation. Plato and Aristotle approach art from political and metaphysical points of view, while Augustine approaches his analysis from a Christian point of view. Scripture, not philosophy, is his guide. Augustine considers the production and consumption of art to be of interest to the Church, whereas for Plato they were of interest to the *polis*. The degree to which an artist can be called a knower depends upon Christian doctrine. Yet here the Christian and the pagan face the same questions about the function and purpose of art, what creativity is, and how a work of art can be evaluated. For Augustine, however, the answers are to be found strictly in a Christian context, in the teachings of scripture and tradition, from an understanding of God's relationship with the world, from an understanding of our knowledge of God's design, and also from the mission of the Church. In dealing with art Augustine grappled with difficult conflicts, and his writings untiringly attempt to satisfy the requisites of faith and to do justice to the natural pleasure of art.

When the basic conflicts are resolved, Augustine still has a problem with the immediate sensuous gratification of art, because although the "Divine order and harmony" are reflected in nature and to a degree in art, "perceptual objects tie the senses down to earthly things and prevent the mind from contemplating what is eternal and unchanging".[7] Art and beauty ascend in their value as guides for the soul, according to their use of the sense of sight. Those arts which depend least upon the sense are the best mirrors of the Divine order. Therefore, music rates more highly than painting. The best teacher of all, however, is scripture. Scripture when properly interpreted provides the most direct knowledge of God's purpose and order, although music and painting can contribute to our understanding as well. As long as art agrees with the tenets of faith and reflects the harmony of divine Creation, it is justified.

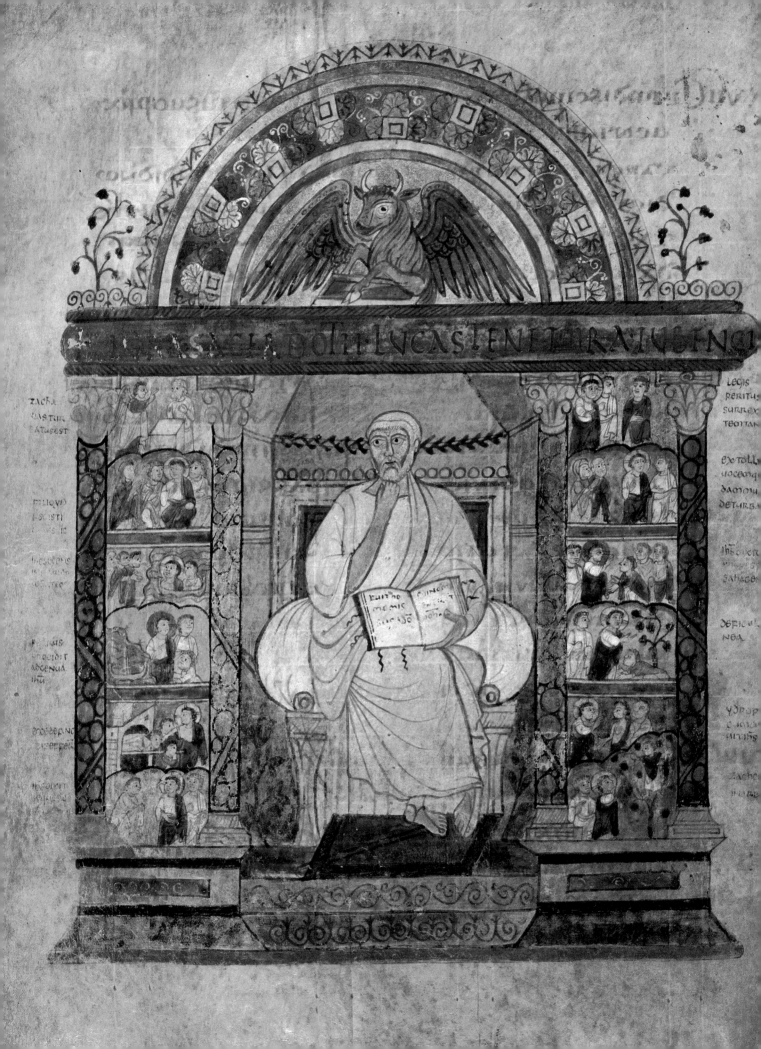

THE ARTS
OF THE EARLY MIDDLE AGES

TWO-DIMENSIONAL ART

Early Christian painting adapted local styles. For example, in the catacombs of Rome, the only safe haven for Christians, painting was Roman in style but incorporated Christian symbolism. Roman Christians were converted Roman pagans, and their paintings had a frankly practical intent. In its earliest phases, before Constantine, Christian painting was a secret art in a secret place; its function was to affirm the faith of the follower on his or her tomb. Early Christian painting was essentially burial art.

One often finds in early Christian painting a primitive quality, and this quality is probably more a reflection of technical inability than anything else. The need to pictorialize the faith was implicit. The presence or absence of artistic skill or ability was not important.

Christian painting developed in several stages. From the beginning it reflected the absolute belief in another existence in which the individual believer retained his or her identity. Painting was a tangible expression of the Christian's faith. Later, it was used to make the rites of the Church more vivid. Finally, its role was to depict and record Christian history and tradition. Inherent in Christian painting from the beginning was a code of symbolism whose meaning could only be grasped by a fellow Christian.

As the Roman world divided and the West plunged into chaos, painting became once again a private art, more an instrument of intellectualism than of inspiration to the faithful. So we find, outside of Byzantium, a new and exquisite form of two-dimensional art emerging, not on canvases or church walls, but on the beautifully illustrated pages of scholarly Church manuscripts. Figure 7.5 is a manuscript illustration telling the story of the gospels. It was sent by Pope Gregory the Great to St. Augustine in England. Its detail and symbolism attest to the presence and vitality of artistry in the West kept alive, albeit hidden, in the Church. The color and intricacy of this miniature, which borrows freely from pagan tradition to serve a new belief, rival the tremendous wall mosaics and decorations of Byzantium. It also typifies certain stylistic qualities which became more markedly characteristic of medieval painting and sculpture. Compositions of this age are close and nervous. Figures bump against

each other amid an atmosphere of frenetic energy. We feel a certain discomfort in these "walled-in" and crowded scenes, as the medieval illustrator must have felt in his own circumstances.

An Irish contribution to medieval manuscript illumination is illustrated in Figure 7.6. Here the figures are depicted in a flat and almost ornamental way. Technically the subjects are precisely and delicately rendered. Highlight and shadow give relief to the surface plane, as does the oblique treatment of the bench. Linear perspective is as yet an unknown quality. Colors are fairly subtle and figures are stabilized. Of note here is the frontal treatment of the eye, in contrast to the head, which is in profile. Outlining completes the stylized treatment of form. The picture is nonetheless carefully composed, with color and form controlled to achieve psychological balance.

During the period from the fifth to the eleventh

7.6 St Matthew, from the Lindisfarne Gospels, before AD 698. 13½ × 9¾ins (34.3 × 24.8cm). British Library, London.

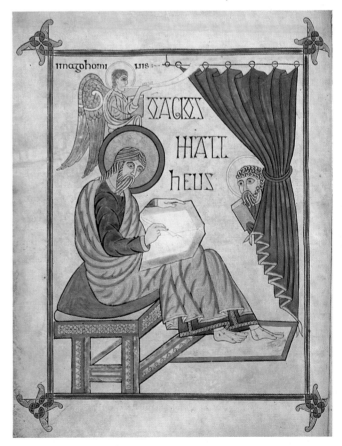

7.5 St Luke, from the presumed St Augustine Bible, 6th century AD. Corpus Christi College, Cambridge, England.

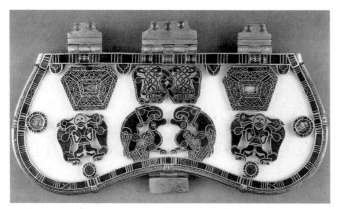

7.7 Purse lid from the ship burial at Sutton Hoo, England, early 7th century AD. Fittings of gold, garnets and millefiori glass, 7⅜ins (18.8cm) long. British Museum, London.

centuries, a tremendous wealth of artistic work emerged in non-traditional, two-dimensional areas of art. A fluid pattern of life was prevalent in the early Middle Ages throughout Europe and it was to very mundane and portable media that non-monastic, nomadic men and women turned much of their artistic energy. Clothing, jewelry, and shipbuilding, for example, all exhibited artistry among the Germanic, Irish, and Scandinavian peoples (Fig. **7.7**).

Emotionalism in art increased as the approach of the millennium sounded its trumpet of imminent doom. The fact that the world did not end on 1 January 1000 reduced emotionalism only fractionally. Emotionalism strengthened with an influx of Eastern art into the Ottonian Empire when Otto II married a Byzantine princess. A combination of Roman, Carolingian, and Byzantine characteristics typified Ottonian manuscript illustration. Despite an inherent appeal to feeling and medieval crowding, such work is evidence of the increasingly outward-looking approach of the early years of the second millenium after Christ.

Soon after the year 1000 a new style in painting began to emerge. It showed few characteristics to separate it immediately from its predecessors and was regionally fragmented. Because it was associated with a revolution in architecture, however, it took the name given to that style—Romanesque—and brought to a close the two-dimensional art of the early Middle Ages.

SCULPTURE

Sculpture played a very minor role in the centuries between the collapse of the Roman Empire and the rise of the Romanesque style in the eleventh century. This can probably be attributed to a rigid interpretation of the Old Testament prohibition of graven images. The association of statuary with pagan societies, notably Rome, was fresh in the memories of the Church, and so Christian sculpture

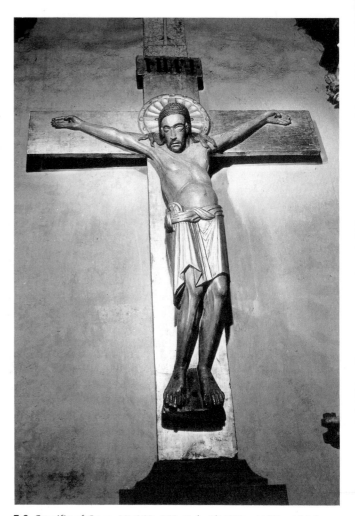

7.8 Crucifix of Gero, AD 969–976. Oak, 6ft 1⅝ins (187cm) high. Cologne Cathedral, Germany.

began in a less monumental style. Sculpture was largely funerary and the earliest examples are of sarcophagi.

Some of the most beautiful sculptural work of the Christian era after Constantine mirrors manuscript illumination in its small-scale, miniature-like detail. It reflects a restless, linear style with great emotion and is very precise in its compositional details.

Equally poignant is the *Gero Crucifix* (Fig. **7.8**). The realism and emotion of a crucified Christ whose downward and forward sagging body pulls against the nails is compelling indeed. Note the muscle striations on the right arm and chest, the bulging belly, and the rendering of cloth. There is a surface hardness in this work. The form is human, but the flesh, hair, and cloth do not have the soft texture we might expect. The face is a mask of agony and the total work full of pathos. The same subject matter and treatment is seen again in Figures **7.9** and **7.10**.

Of the Ottonian rulers, Henry II was the greatest patron of the arts, and in the church the honor belongs to Bernwald of Hildesheim, tutor to Otto III. During his years as Bishop (993–1022), Hildesheim became a center for

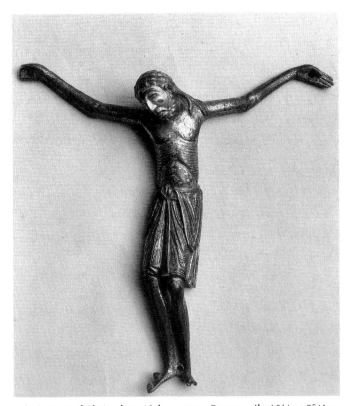

7.9 Corpus of Christ, late 12th century. Bronze gilt, 10¼ × 9⅝ins (26 × 24.5cm). The Metropolitan Museum of Art, New York (Gift of J. Pierpont Morgan, 1917).

7.10 Crucifix, early 14th century. Painted wood and gilt, 3ft 9ins (114cm) high, 3ft 5¼ins (105cm) wide. The Metropolitan Museum of Art, New York (Fletcher Fund, 1922).

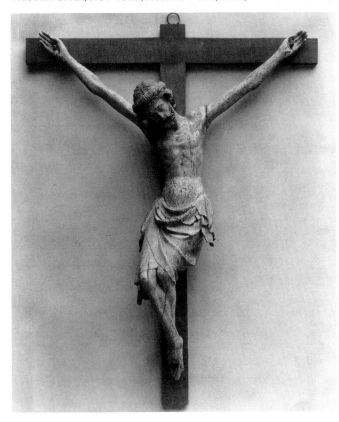

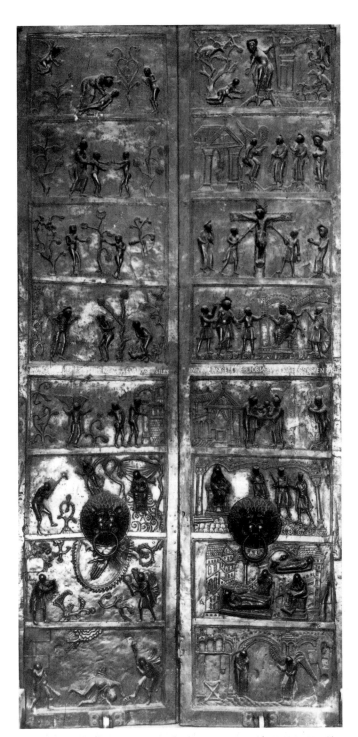

7.11 Doors of Bishop Bernward, 1015. Bronze, 16ft 6ins (5.03m) high. Hildesheim Cathedral, Germany.

manuscript painting and other arts. His patronage, however, was largely confined to the decoration of metal objects, and in particular the bronze doors of the Hildesheim Cathedral (Fig. **7.11**) which employed the *cire-perdue* technique, a lost-wax process that had been used for the casting of the bronze doors at Aachen, two hundred years earlier.

As with the painting, sculpture of the eleventh and

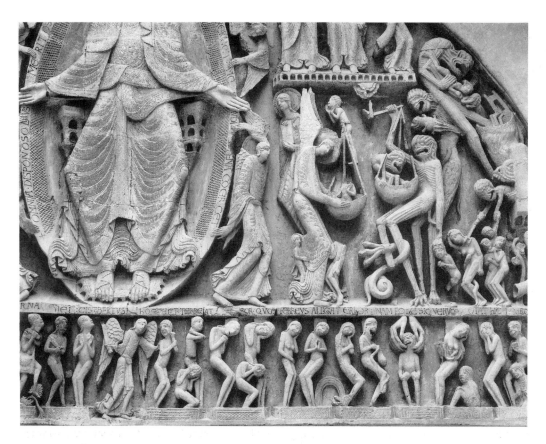

7.12 Gislebertus, Last Judgement tympanum, c. 1130–35. Autun Cathedral, France.

early twelfth centuries is called Romanesque. In the case of sculpture the title refers more to an era than to a style. Examples of sculpture are so diverse that if most sculptural works were not decorations attached to Romanesque architecture, we probably could not group them under a stylistic label. Unlike painting, however, we can draw some general conclusions about Romanesque sculpture. First, it is associated with Romanesque architecture. Second, it is heavy and solid. Third, it is stone. Fourth, it is monumental. These last two characteristics represent a distinct departure from previous sculptural style. Monumental stone sculpture had all but disappeared in the fifth century. Its re-emergence across Europe in such short time was remarkable. As we shall see, Church architecture was prolific during the Christian era, but the emergence of sculptural decoration indicated at least a beginning of an outward dissemination of knowledge from the cloistered world of the monastery to the general populace. Romanesque sculpture was applied to the exterior of the building, from where it could appeal to the lay worshipper. The relationship of this artistic development to the increase in religious zeal among the laity is not without significance. In such works as the Last Judgment tympanum (Fig. **7.12**) the illiterate masses could now read the message of the Church, an opportunity previously the prerogative of the clergy. The message here is quite clear. In the center of the composition, framed by a Roman style arch, is an awe-inspiring figure of Christ. Around him are a series of malproportioned figures in various degrees of torment. The inscription of the artist, Gislebertus, tells us that their purpose was "to let this horror appal those bound by earthly sin". Death was still central to medieval thought, and devils share the stage, attempting to tip the scales in their favor and gleefully pushing the damned into the flaming pit. A pair of demonic hands reaches down (lower right) to grasp a poor soul by the throat. So, although revolutionary in its material, scale, and scope, Romanesque sculpture retains the emotional, crowded, and nervous qualities of previous medieval works. The Romanesque style was a close cousin of its predecessors—the closing stages of an attitude or viewpoint about to be supplemented by another.

MUSIC

Most of the music from the Greek, Hellenistic, and Roman traditions was rejected by the early Christian Church. Music cultivated for enjoyment for its own sake and any music or instrument associated with spectacles or activities objectionable to the Church were unsuitable, as was the *hydraulos*, which we noted earlier. Disapproval of Roman or Greek music apparently did not reflect negativism toward music itself, but, rather, reflected a need to break existing or potential ties with pagan traditions.

We know that music played a role in Christian worship from earliest times, and since Christian services were modelled on Jewish synagogue services, it is likely that musical practices in the Church were closely linked to liturgical function. In the responsorial psalmody the leader sang a line of the psalm and the congregation sang a second in response. The melody for responsorial singing consisted of a single note for the first few words changing for the final words to a "half cadence". The congregation then sang the beginning of the response on the same note, concluding with a cadence (Fig. **7.13**). The early Church also used an antiphonal psalmody in which singing alternated between two choruses. Local churches in the West were relatively independent at first. So between the fifth and the eighth centuries AD several different liturgies and chants developed. Increasingly, after the eighth century, virtually all of these local variants were unified into a single practice under the central authority of Rome.

Early in the fourth century hymns were introduced into the Western Church. Some sources credit St. Ambrose for this innovation, while others credit Hilary, Bishop of Poitiers. Early hymns had a poetic text consisting of several verses, all of which were sung to the same melody, sometimes taken from popular secular songs. Mostly the hymns were syllabic, that is, each syllable was sung on a single note, and they were intended to be sung by the congregations, as opposed to a choir or a soloist. In style and content early Church hymnody tended to express personal, individualized ideas. Other sections of the liturgy were more formal, objective, and impersonal.

Another type of Church music at this time was the *alleluia*, which presented an interesting contrast in style to the hymn. The *alleluia* was melismatic in style and was sung after the verse of a psalm. The last syllable of the word was drawn out "in ecstatic melody, soaring phrase 'in gladness of heart and flowing, joy too full to be expressed in words'."[8] Eastern in influence and emotional in appeal, the *alleluia* came to the Christian service directly from Jewish liturgy.

Probably the most significant contribution to medieval music was made by Pope Gregory I. The tradition of the Gregorian chant is named after him, and he provided the driving force for codifying the diverse musical traditions of the early Church. Pope Gregory was not a composer, but rather an editor. He supervised the selection of melodies and texts he thought most appropriate for the musical setting of Church celebrations. Having organized Church music, he then became active in disseminating it throughout the West. The result of his efforts was not only to create an additional unifying force in and through the Church, but also to lay the foundations of a basic universal musical language.

In this same era, or perhaps slightly before it, came a significant change in tradition and practice, which stemmed from very practical considerations. Christian zeal for converting the pagan world created certain divisions in society and the Church that contributed to the unique character of the Middle Ages. The missionaries were spectacularly successful, nevertheless. As increasing numbers of converts strained the capacities of churches, monetary contributions created wealth which was, in turn, used to build larger sanctuaries. When these great buildings were filled, informal worship and antiphonal responses could no longer be conducted in an orderly fashion. So music became more the province of the choir or a chief solo singer, like the cantor in Jewish worship. Increased formality in the liturgy further divided cleric and congregation. Formal solo and choir music led to the establishment of a central training center, a *Schola Cantorum* for Church musicians in Rome. Some sources date the *Schola Cantorum* to before Pope Gregory, others, later.

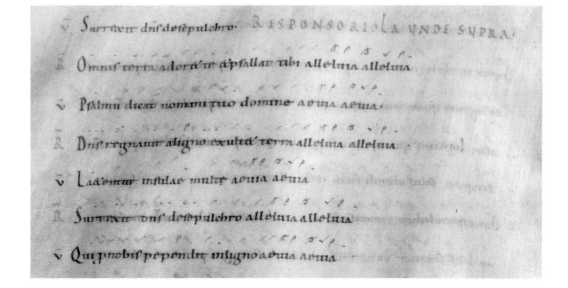

7.13 Responsorial psalmody, from the Hartker Manuscript, 980–1011. Vellum, 8.7 × 6.6ins (22.2 × 16.7cm). Stiftsbibliothek, St Gallen, Switzerland.

In addition to formalizing the training of church musicians, the *Schola Cantorum* also provided a means by which Gregorian reform could be universally introduced, inasmuch as *Schola*-trained musicians served congregations throughout Europe.

Chant melodies were passed on mostly by oral tradition from one generation of priests and monks to another. It seems likely that early chants had a simple, undulating, and haunting character. Their texture was monophonic, that is, a single melodic line. Chants were sung in a flexible tempo with unmeasured rhythms, which followed the natural accents of normal Latin speech. Melodic range probably did not exceed an octave, and chant melodies themselves consisted of groups of three or four notes related to one another. Medieval chants provided a unique and rich source of material for later composers, and are still used in Christian worship.

The Middle Ages also witnessed a growth in secular music. As might be expected, secular music used vernacular texts—the language of the common people as opposed to the Latin of Church music. Most secular music (like our own) concerned love, but other topics were also popular. Secular music probably owed much of its origin to the dance pantomime of Roman times, whose performers, as we noted, were forced out of the cities to become wandering bands of entertainers. A strong link has been suggested between the traditions of the pantomime and the poet-musicians of later medieval Europe called *trouvères* in northern France, *troubadours* in southern France, and *Minnesänger* in Germany. These wandering minstrels created and performed vocal music as they travelled throughout the countryside. Apparently most of their music was monophonic, like Church music, but they also sang with some form of musical accompaniment. Medieval secular song was probably strophic, that is, composed of several stanzas, all sung to the same melody.

Musical instruments of this era consisted of the lyre, the harp, and a bowed instrument called the *vielle* or *fiedel* (viola/fiddle). The *psaltery*, an instrument similar to a zither, the lute, the flute, the *shawm* (a reed instrument like an oboe), trumpets, horns, drums, and bagpipes, as well as the organ, were all popular. Small versions of the organ called *positives* and *portatives* were portable; a *portative* was played while held in the hands of the performer and a *positive* while placed on a table with a second individual working the bellows. Despite its Roman and unpleasant associations, the organ eventually found its way into the medieval Church.

While liturgical and secular traditions developed, a different philosophy of music emerged from the monastic community in the work of a scholar named Boëthius. Boëthius emphasized, as did the Greeks, the relationship of music to character and morals. He saw the value of music as an educational device, and noted its mathematical properties as a springboard to higher philosophical inquiry. Boëthius conceived of music as a form of study rather than an expression of feeling. The true musician for him was not the performer, but the composer/critic/philosopher who carefully examined "the diversity of high and low sounds by means of reason and the senses".

In the ninth or tenth century a new compositional and radically different texture appeared in music. Polyphony now brought more than one melodic line into musical composition. The earliest polyphony consisted of two parallel melodic lines at different pitch levels. When one line went up, so did the other, and so forth. Later, contrary motion separated the melodic lines so that, finally, the two lines became melodically independent. These early polyphonic compositions were called *organa* (*organum*). Polyphony is a textural component, and in the earliest polyphonic forms the rhythmic component of music remained free and unstructured. However, as melodic lines gained freedom from each other, necessity dictated that some form of rhythmic structure be employed to coordinate them. So at the very end of this era a new rhythmic notation emerged called mensural notation, which made possible an indication of the precise duration of each tone.

THEATRE

Some early scholars argued that theatre ceased to exist in the Western world for a period of several hundred years. That viewpoint is no longer widely held, and two pieces of evidence exist which suggest the existence of theatrical production. One is the presence of the wandering entertainers we have already noted. In this tribe of entertainers were mimists, jugglers, bear baiters, acrobats, wrestlers, and story-tellers. The mimetic propensity of human beings is too compelling to deny its existence amid the entertainments we know existed in this era. We do not know, however, the production characteristics. They may have consisted of simply miming a story or reading a play script, rather than the more formal presentations we prefer to call "theatre."

However, our second piece of evidence proves more conclusively that theatre existed. Writings from North Africa argue for the validity of the mimic stage, and logic indicates that what still existed in North Africa also existed in Europe in general. Sisebert, King of Spain in the seventh century, refers to the popularity of *ludi theatrici* at marriages and feasts, adding that members of the clergy should leave when these were performed. In the ninth century the Council of Tours and the Council of Aix-la-Chapelle ruled that the clergy should not witness plays and the obscenities of actors. We can infer that theatre existed from the railings of the Church against it. Charlemagne ruled that no actor could wear a priest's robe under penalty of corporal punishment or banishment. Charlemagne's edict has been taken by some as evidence of theatrical presentation and also, perhaps inaccurately, as evidence of the beginnings of liturgical drama. If this were the case, the prohibition would imply the use of actors other than the clergy in church drama. In the tenth century the German nun, Hrosvitha, is known to have written six plays based on the comedies of the Roman playwright, Terence. We do not know if Hrosvitha's plays were performed, but if they were, the audience would have been restricted to the other nuns in the convent.

We are sure, however, that liturgical drama began as an elaboration of the Roman Catholic Mass, probably in France. These elaborations were called *tropes* and took place on special ceremonial occasions, usually Easter, the dramatic highlight of the Church year. Records at Winchester in the late tenth century tell of a *trope* in which priests acted out the discovery of the tomb on Easter morning.

Thus theatre, along with the other arts, except dance, was adopted by the Church and became an instrument of God in an age of faith and demons.

DANCE

An outlet as natural as dancing, one which predates the theatre, and one which can be found at the religious and ritualistic center of nearly every culture in the world, did not surrender to the dictates of Christianity in the early Middle Ages. As with theatre, Church writings continually condemn it from Constantine's time to the eleventh century and beyond. St. Augustine complained that it was better to dig ditches on the Sabbath than to dance a "choric Reigen".

The age of expanding Church influence in a previously pagan world must have seen bitter conflict, as a religious philosophy in which all pleasures of the flesh were evil clashed with a pagan belief in the supernatural and superstition, to which wild fertility dances were central. History records many examples of masked pagan dancers attempting to invade churches. Even when Christianity gained a firm hold it was impossible completely to eradicate deeply rooted ritualistic dancing. It appears that a certain unspoken compromise was reached. Dancing continued since people will continue to do what gives them great pleasure, Church or not, damnation and the devil notwithstanding. But the pagan contexts of dance were put aside.

The Christian Church made many such compromises with life as it found it. Today we still celebrate ancient pagan festivals without a thought of their affecting our spirituality. Which child who has danced around a Maypole or gone trick-or-treating has considered such an indulgence a fertility dance or demonic mummery?

It is fairly clear, however, that most of the dancing to which various sources refer in the early Middle Ages was probably not in any way significant as artistic expression

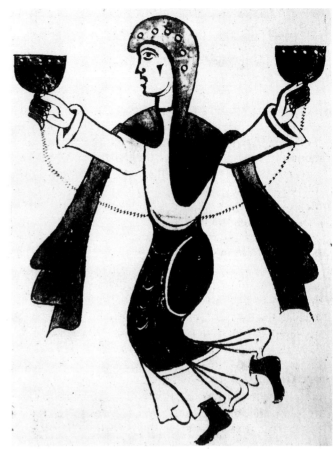

7.14 Professional dancer, from an illuminated manuscript of the 11th century. The New York Public Library.

or theatre dance. The frenzied outpouring of emotion which occurred in this period was largely spontaneous and took no account of a performer/audience relationship. Such dancing was the primordial response to a frenetic and frightening world in which man had been reduced, literally, to his basest self. Later, vestiges of demonic and death dances and animal mummeries would adopt a more formal, presentational character (death as a dancer was a frequent medieval image), but in these early years most dance is probably related to our survey in name only.

The same logic we applied to the circumstances of theatre in the previous section can apply here. We are fairly certain that theatre dance remained alive through successors to the pantomime called *joculatores* (jugglers). They performed at fairs and festivals, nearly always for the peasants, rarely for the nobility. Figure **7.14** depicts a professional dancer of the eleventh century. Some evidence suggests that a kind of undefined "hand dance" existed, as well as dances using the themes of Roman mythology.

ARCHITECTURE

When Christianity became a state religion in Rome, an explosion of building took place to accommodate the needs of worship. Previously small groups of the faithful had gathered as inconspicuously as possible wherever it was practical and prudent for them to do so. Even had it been safe to worship publicly, no need existed to construct a building of any consequence to house so few people. Respectability changed all that.

As with painting, early Christian architecture was an adaptation of existing Roman style. For the most part churches took the form of the Roman *basilica*. We tend to think of the term *basilica* as Christian in derivation, as in St Peter's Basilica in Rome. However, the term referred originally to Roman law courts whose form the first large Christian churches took. A *basilica* has a specific architectural design, and Christianity made some very simple alterations to this design. Roman *basilicae* had numerous doors along the sides of the building to facilitate entrances and exits. Church ritual required the altar to be the focal point. Entrance to the Christian basilica was therefore moved to the end of the building, usually facing west, so as to channel one's attention down the long, relatively narrow nave to the altar at the opposite end. Often the altar was set off by a large archway reminiscent of a Roman triumphal arch, and elevated to enhance sightlines from the congregation, which occupied a flat floorspace.

If we examine Figures **7.15** to **7.19** we can see clearly the underlying visual and physical structure of the basilican form as applied in different scales, proportions, and use of openings. The basic structure comprises two or

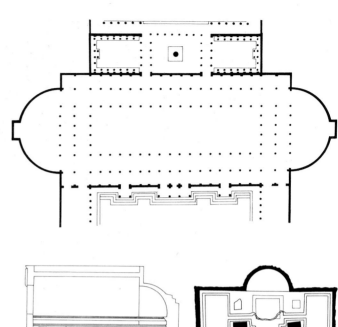

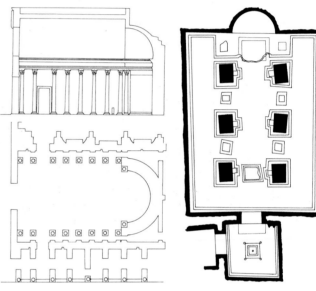

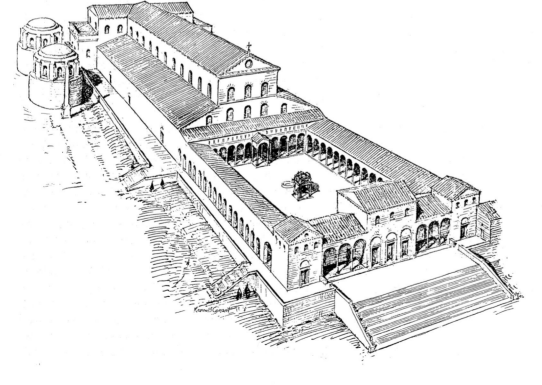

7.15 Plan of the Basilica Ulpia, Rome, c. AD 110.

7.16 Plan and section of a basilica in the Imperial Palace, Rome, c. AD 85.

7.17 Plan of an underground basilica near the Porta Maggiore, Rome, 1st century AD.

7.18 Old St Peter's Basilica, Rome, c. AD 333. Reconstruction by Kenneth J. Conant. Francis Loeb Library, Harvard University, Cambridge, Mass.

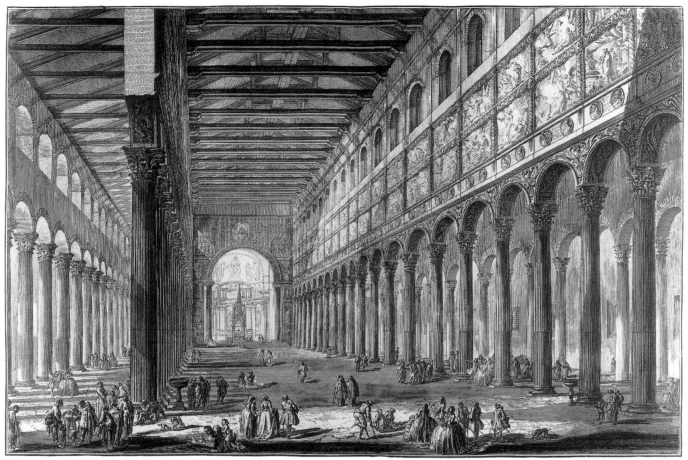

7.19 Interior of S Paolo fuori le Mura, Rome, late 4th century AD. Engraving by Giovanni Battista Piranesi (1720–78).

four long, parallel rows of columns or piers surrounded by an outer wall separated from the columns by an aisle. The central space, or nave, was heightened by clerestory walls and a beam or simple truss roof describing an isosceles triangle of fairly low pitch. Low-pitched roofs covered the side aisles. The basilica was reasonably easy to build, yielding a nave width of seventy or eighty feet. In contrast to later church styles, the basilica had no vertical monumentality, although its legal derivations did carry the connotation of social authority. In the basilican form, interior parts and spaces were clearly defined and self-evident. The form was stated in simple structural terms.

Another adaptation was the treatment of interior space as different from the exterior shell. This is one of two contrasting viewpoints in architectural design. In one case the exterior structure is apparent and reveals the nature and quality of interior space and *vice versa*. In the other case, as here, the exterior shell is just that—a shell, in many instances obscuring what lies inside. Whether intentionally or not, the basilica symbolizes the radical difference between the exterior world of the flesh and the interior world of the spirit.

Considering the nature of the medieval world, we might imagine that the fluid nature of the political situation would militate against anything so permanent as a significant work of architecture. However, as we noted, this was an era of cloisters and barricades, and despite their lack of artistry (or permanence), monasteries were built and so were fortresses. The purpose of a fortress in a world of war places the odds decidedly against its survival.

Not until the rule of Charlemagne do we find any consequential attempt at architectural design. Charlemagne's renaissance included architecture, and Charlemagne returned to his capital from visits to Italy with visions of Roman monuments and a belief that majesty and permanence must be symbolized in architecture of impressive character. Realization of his dreams was tempered by some of the difficult facts of life that often stand between an artist and the completion of his work. In this case Charlemagne's model was the church of San Vitale in Ravenna (Figs. **6.21**, **6.22** and **6.24**), built by Justinian in the Byzantine style. All Charlemagne's materials, including columns and bronze gratings, had to be transported over the Alps from Italy to Aachen in Germany. Likewise, skilled stonemasons were few and far between. The task, nevertheless, was accomplished, and Charlemagne's palace chapel stands today as a dominant design of compelling character (Fig. **7.20**). Charlemagne also encouraged the building of monasteries and apparently developed a standard plan for monastery design that was used, with local modifications, throughout his empire.

As Charlemagne's empire and the ninth and tenth centuries passed, a new and radical style in architecture emerged. Unlike its stylistic counterparts in painting and sculpture, Romanesque architecture was a fairly identifiable style, despite its diversity. The Romanesque style took hold throughout Europe in a relatively short period of time. It took its name from the Roman-like arches of its doorways and windows. To Renaissance men who saw these examples throughout Europe, the characteristics were clearly pre-Gothic and post-Roman (but Roman-like) and, therefore, they called them *Romanesque*. In addition to arched doorways and windows, characteristic of this style was a massive, static, and lightless quality in which we perceive a further reflection of the barricaded mentality and lifestyle generally associated with the Middle Ages.

The Romanesque style nonetheless exemplified the power and wealth of the Church Militant and Triumphant. If the style mirrored the social and intellectual system that produced it, it also reflected a new religious fervor and a turning of the Church toward its growing flock. Romanesque churches were larger than their prede-

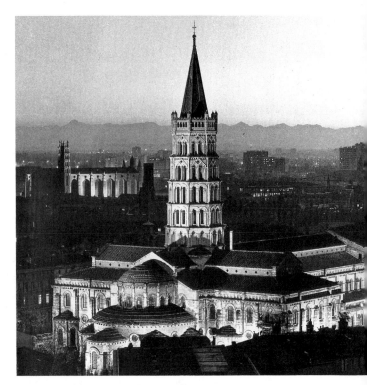

7.21 St-Sernin, Toulouse, France, c. 1080–1120.

7.22 St-Sernin, Toulouse, interior.

7.20 Palatine Chapel of Charlemagne, Aachen, Germany, AD 792–805.

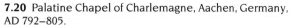

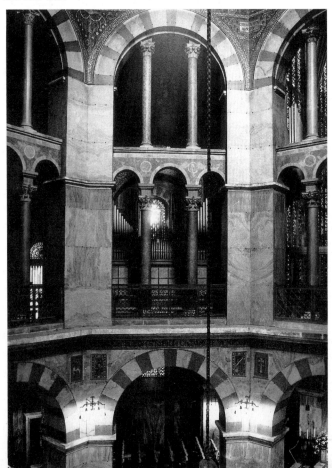

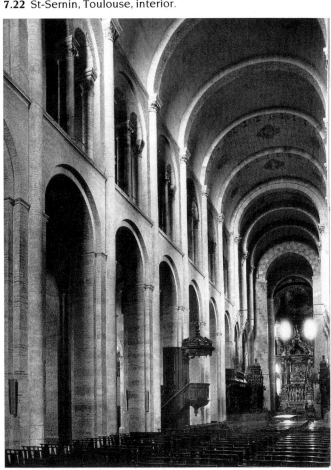

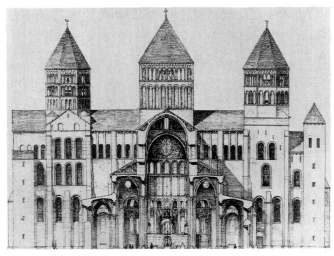

7.23 Transverse section of the nave and west elevation of the great transept of the Abbey Church Cluny III, France 1088–1130. Drawings by Kenneth J Conant (see **7.24**).

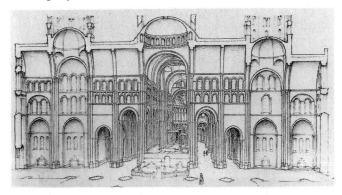

7.24 Transverse section of the great transept of the Abbey Church, Cluny III. Drawing by Kenneth J. Conant. Francis Loeb Library, Harvard University, Cambridge, Mass.

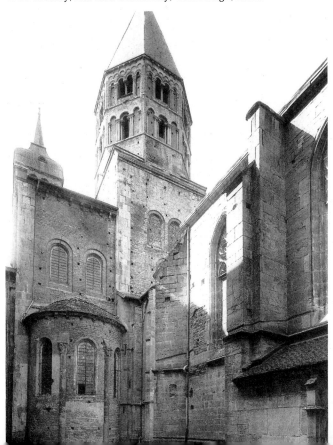

cessors, and we can appreciate their scale in Figures **7.21** and **7.22**. St. Sernin is an example of southern French Romanesque, and it reflects a heavy elegance and complexity we have not seen previously. The plan of the church describes a Roman cross, and the side aisles are extended beyond the crossing to create an ambulatory or walking space so that pilgrims who were mostly on their way to Spain could walk around the altar without disturbing the service. One additional change is worth noting. The roof of this church is stone, whereas earlier buildings had wooden roofs. As we view the magnificent vaulted interior we wonder how or whether the architect reconciled the conflicting forces of engineering, material, and aesthetics. Given the properties of stone and the increased force of added height, did he try to push his skills to the edge of practicality in order to create an interior of breathtaking scale? Were his efforts reflective of the glory of God or the abilities of Man?

Returning to the exterior view, we can see how some of the stress of the high tunnel vaulting was diffused. In a complex series of vaults, transverse arches, and bays, the tremendous weight and outward thrust of the central vault was transferred to the ground, leaving a high and unencumbered central space. If we compare this structural system with that of post and lintel and consider the compressive and tensile properties of stone, we can easily see the superiority of the arch as a structural device for creating open space. Because of the stresses and weight in this style, only very small windows were possible. So, although the fortress-like and lightless characteristics of Romanesque architecture reflect the historical context of the era, they also had a practical explanation.

The tenth-century church of Cluny, known as Cluny II, inspired numerous buildings throughout the West in the eleventh century. When it became too small, a new church, Cluny III, was begun in 1088. It remained the largest church in Christendom until St. Peter's in Rome was rebuilt in the sixteenth century. Cluny III (Figs. **7.23** to **7.25**) was demolished during the French Revolution. The nave with double aisles, the double transepts, and the choir with an ambulatory, were all enormous in scale. The nave arcades had pointed arches. Protruding apses and numerous towers adorned the exterior. The interior housed magnificent wall paintings, the most important of which was the huge Christ in Majesty in the main apse.

7.25 Exterior of south-west transept of Cluny III.

SYNTHESIS
The Carolingian Renaissance

When Pepin III died in 768 he was succeeded by his two sons, Charles and Carloman. Carloman died three years later and Charles, denying the succession of Carloman's infant sons, thus acquired the entire Frankish Empire. Carrying on the work of his father, Pepin, and grandfather, Charles Martel, Charlemagne, or Charles the Great, set about subduing the Frankish peoples and other tribes throughout Europe. He ruled over a vast empire of many nations. He became protector of Pope Leo III in Rome. On Christmas day, 800, as Charles knelt in prayer before the altar in the old church of St. Peter, Pope Leo suddenly placed a crown on his head, and the people acclaimed him as emperor.

7.27 St Mark and St Luke, from the Gospel Book of Godescale, AD 781–783. Vellum, 12¼ × 8¼ins (31.1 × 21cm). Bibliothéque Nationale, Paris.

7.28 St Mark, from the Gospel Book of St-Medard of Soissons, France, early 9th century AD. Paint on vellum, 14⅜ × 10¼ins (36.5 × 26cm). Bibliothèque Nationale, Paris.

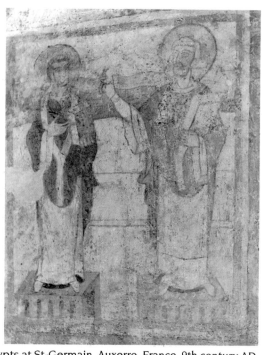

7.26 The crypts at St-Germain, Auxerre, France, 9th century AD.

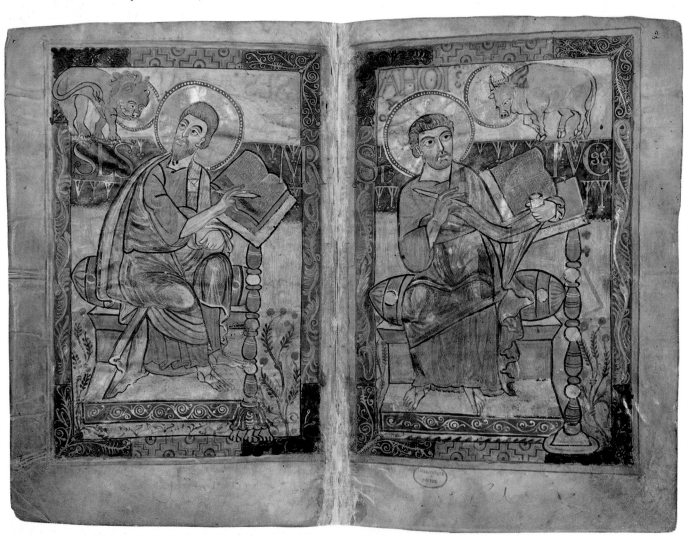

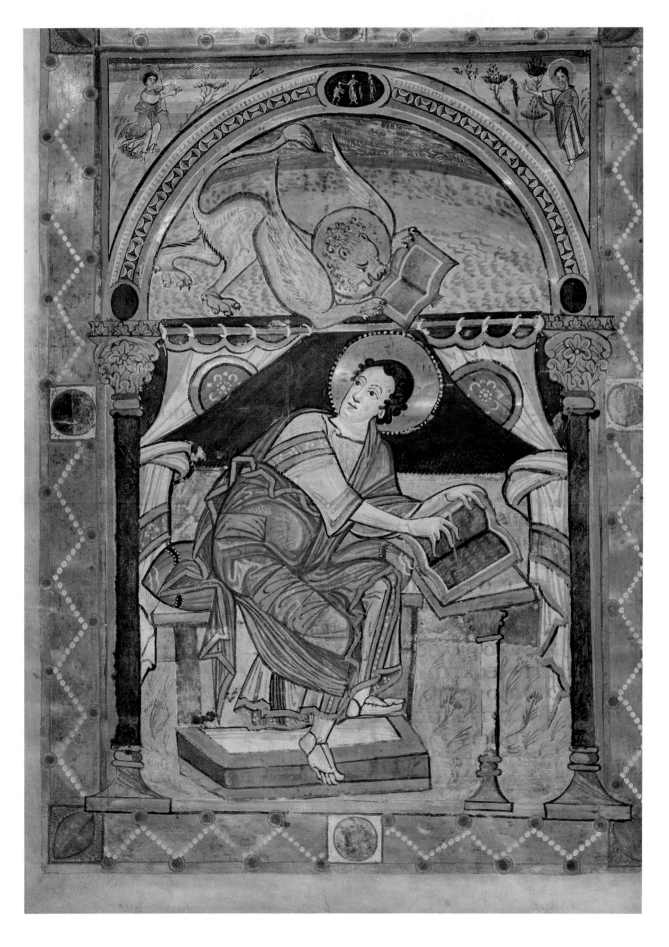

Perhaps his greatest contributions to European civilization lay in his support of education, reform of the Church, and cultivation of the liberal arts. Under the scholarly leadership of Alcuin of York, individuals were assembled from all parts of the West to reunite the scattered fragments of the classical heritage. The Carolingian renaissance—or *renovatio*, as it was called—represents the hinge, as it were, on which the ancient world turned into the Middle Ages. The classical revival initiated by Charlemagne was part of his attempt to revive the Roman Empire.

Carolingian manuscript illuminations are striking examples of early medieval painting. As an official court art, book illumination was promoted by the king, his descendants, relatives, associates, and officers of state. One exemplary product of the time was the *Gospel Book of Godescale* (Fig. **7.27**). The models for this work were probably Byzantine. The evangelists appear with lean, bearded faces. The cloth of their garments reveals a rudimentary *chiaroscuro*, with little attention to realism, merely light and dark stripes representing the highlight and shadow of the folds. Differing from the *Gospel Book of Godescale*, however, the *Gospel Book of Saint-Medard of Soissons* (Fig. **7.28**) displays a definite classicism in its arches complete with columns, intricate architecture, and frames adorned with cameos and pictures containing tiny figures.

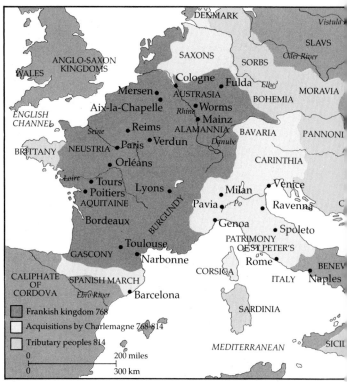

7.29 The Carolingian Empire.

7.30 *The Stoning of St Stephen at the Gates of Jerusalem*, 9th century AD. Wall painting. Crypts of St-Germain, Auxerre.

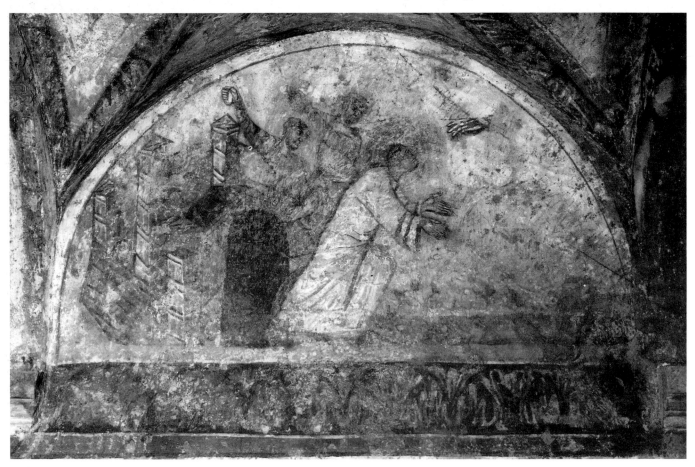

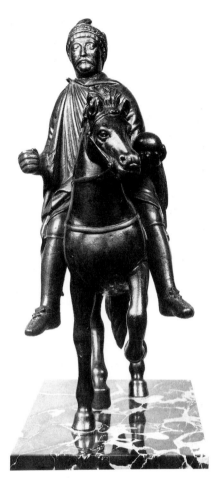

7.31 So-called *Statuette of Charlemagne*, c. AD 860–870. Bronze cast and gilt, 9¼ins (23.5cm) high. Louvre, Paris.

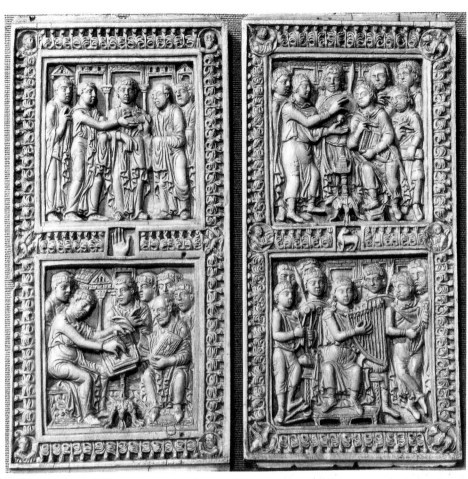

7.32 Cover of the Dagulf Psalter, showing David in various scenes, AD 783–795. Ivory, each leaf 6⅝ × 3¼ins (16.8 × 8.3cm). Louvre, Paris.

Nonetheless, there is characteristic confusion in the plethora of detail and a crowded nervousness.

Wall paintings were a highly original feature of Carolingian art and architecture. Although few examples remain, it seems clear that Carolingian palaces and churches were brightly painted in a style not unlike the Roman, with three-dimensional architectural detail presented in high verisimilitude on the two-dimensional surface. Also typical were large frescoes depicting the history of the Franks such as could be found in the Imperial Hall in the Palace at Ingelheim near Mainz. In many cases the inscriptions accompanying these frescoes reflect the elevated intellect of Alcuin and other scholars. The crypts at Auxerre show originality in their depiction of what appear to be life-size figures of several bishops of Auxerre (Fig. **7.26**). Clearly, the mural painters of the period possessed great skill and imagination. In the segment depicting the stoning of Saint Stephen (Fig. **7.30**), all "the most emphatic lines, both in the figures and in the architectural elements evoking Jerusalem, run parallel to the oblique lines of a grid easily reconstituted on the basis of the half-square in which the circumference of the arch is inscribed."[9]

The palace school at Charlemagne's court also reflected in its works an intention to revive classical style by copying sculpture from the late antique period. Classical influence continued to be nurtured. Charlemagne's political ambitions appear to have led to his rejection of the Byzantine style, demonstrating his opposition to the Byzantine Empire. We can see in the so-called *Statuette of Charlemagne* (Fig **7.31**) an imitation of a classical model. It is, however, the ivories of the period which show most clearly the classicizing trend and the artistry of the time. Although derived from antique models, these works are highly individual. The ivory covers of the *Dagulf Psalter* (Fig. **7.32**) have an amazing resemblance to Roman work. Commissioned as a gift for Pope Adrian I, the *Dagulf Psalter* reveals figures and ornamentation which are stilted and lifeless. There is little attempt at three-dimensional space, although the figures themselves appear in high relief. Composition appears to be organized around a central area to which the eye is directed through line and particularly through the eye focus of the figures themselves. Organization is crowded, but not frenetic. Figure depiction reveals strange proportions, almost dwarf-like, with heavy round-

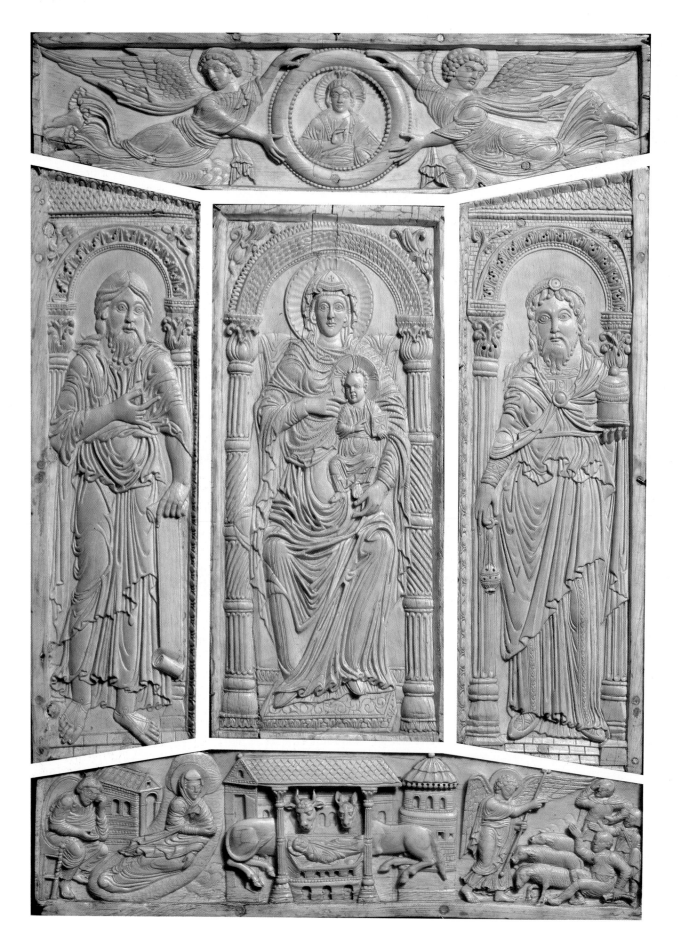

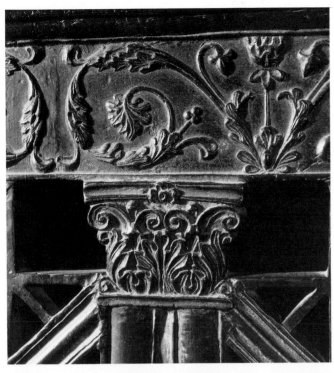

ed heads, long torsos, and short legs. Hairstyles reflect the late Roman Imperial period. The ivory cover of the *Lorsch Gospels* (Fig. **7.33**) is an exact replica of a sixth-century design.

Architecture, like painting and sculpture, was ruled by the political ideal of the Carolingian court. It is also clear that the artists of the period were capable of accurately reproducing capitals and friezes from classical antiquity, as Figure **7.34** illustrates. Large-scale building in the period was short-lived, however, despite its bold conception. Charlemagne carefully chose bishops for his kingdom to assist in the building program he envisaged. Almost immediately new construction began across the Empire. To the general characteristics of Carolingian architecture already noted we should add the specifics of

7.33 Back cover of the Lorsch Gospels, showing the Virgin and Child between Zacharias and John the Baptist, c. AD 810. Ivory, 15⅛ × 10⅝ins (38.4 × 27cm). Victoria and Albert Museum, London.

7.34 Detail of the parapet railings in the Tribune of the Palatine Chapel, Aachen, Germany, AD 792–805.

7.35 Tribune of the Palatine Chapel, Aachen.

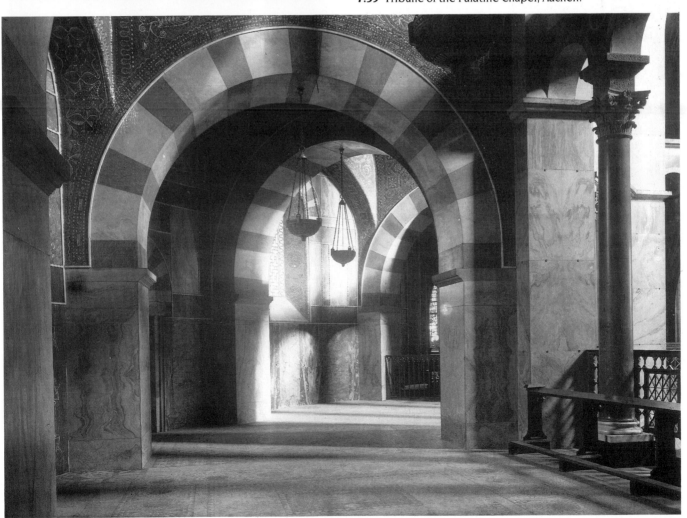

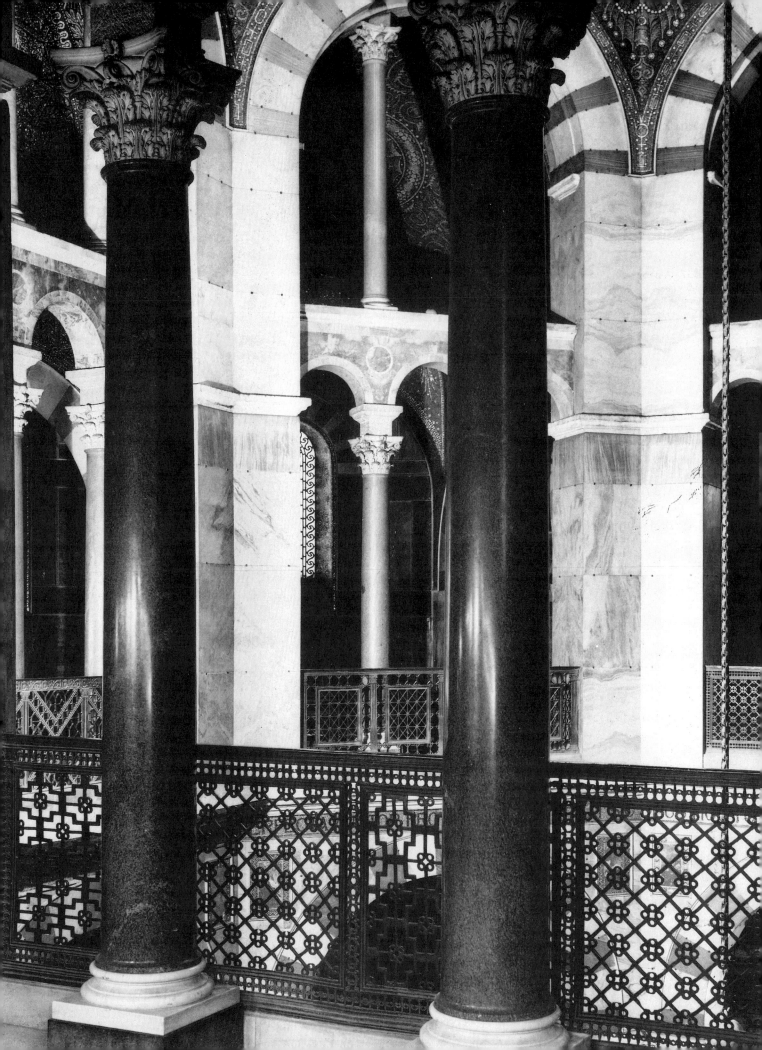

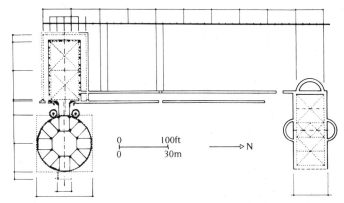

7.37 Reconstruction of the modular grid of the palace, Aachen.

a complete plan for a monastery drawn in ink on fine sheets of parchment sewn together and dated prior to 829. "The area covered by the projected building forms a vast rectangle over 700 feet long. The regularity of the layout, which recalls the *insulae* of Roman cities of the early Empire, may exemplify the chequer patterns of new cities projected by the Carolingians. All the buildings are arranged around the place of prayer, the church."[10] A totally new ground plan, internal and external configuration, and sense of the monastery and cathedral emerged from the Carolingian period. "The various elements that went to make up the Carolingian church existed singly in ancient architecture and in the early churches of Rome and Italy, but the bringing together and the calculated combination of these elements represented a genuine architectural achievement."[11]

It was, of course, the palace buildings at Aachen (see Fig. **7.20**) which became the jewel in Charlemagne's crown. Further illustration of the interiors (Figs. **7.35** and **7.36**) reveal the grandeur and style of this monument. The grid plan of the entire design (Fig. **7.37**) imposes a harmonious symmetry and rationality in its arrangement of buildings within an overall complex.

So here we find a true renaissance modified to serve the grand design of the emperor and his political ambitions. Recreation of antiquity in physical and intellectual form in the arts and humanities made visible and intelligible the dream of a resurrected Roman Empire with Charlemagne at its head.

7.36 View into the octagonal interior of the Palatine Chapel, Aachen, from the Tribune.

SUGGESTIONS FOR THOUGHT AND DISCUSSION

The early Middle Ages and the spread of early Christianity are essentially inseparable. Although we have not undertaken any lengthy discussion which directly applies the ideas of early Christianity to the arts, we need now, having completed the survey, to go back and try to relate the sections on the early Christian Church, Christian thought, and the Roman Church, as well as concepts of demons, sin, and Hell, directly to the arts.

Emotionalism in the arts may reflect a fragmented, frightening, and chaotic world such as prevailed in the early Middle Ages. Emotionalism may also reflect the changing thrust of faith from the cognitive intellectualism of the classical world to the intuitive abstractions of the Christian world. Emotionalism and symbolism seem to go hand in hand throughout the early Middle Ages, but their application or reflection in the arts is not always constant. In some cases emotionalism and symbolism are evidence of an inability to depict an unknowable, non-corporeal God, in contrast with the human gods of the classical world. In other cases symbolism is used to hide meaning from all but the intellectually initiated. In the case of the Roman Christians, symbolism was a purely practical device, which introduced Christians to fellow Christians and protected them from non-Christians, while emotionalism was strictly a sign of technical inability and the nature of the times. What ways can you find in which the arts manifested any or all of these considerations?

■ In what ways was the harsh judgement of God apparent in both Christian thought and the arts?
■ How does neo-Platonism relate to philosophy and art in the early Middle Ages?
■ What role did monasticism play in combining philosophy, tradition, and the arts?
■ How did the Christian Church provide for order and stability in the medieval world? How was the hierarchy of religious and state organization different from that of the Eastern Empire and a product of Western pragmatism?
■ How did Rome establish itself as the principal seat of Christianity?

CHAPTER EIGHT

THE LATE MIDDLE AGES

Humanity in the late Middle Ages seemed to experience a spiritual and intellectual revival which had a profound influence on the creative spirit. Perfectly expressed in the Gothic cathedral, the mystery of faith was embodied in the mystery of space. Stone was transubstantiated into ethereal tracery defining open space flooded by the colored light from stained-glass windows. The austere and fortress-like massiveness of the Romanesque style was thus transformed, and humanity's spirit, likewise, seemed to blossom as emphasis shifted from the oppressive wrath of God to the sweetness and mercy of the loving Saviour and the Virgin Mary. Meanwhile, the vigorous growth of towns and cities accelerated the pace of life and turned the focus of wealth and power away from the feudal countryside, and the new universities replaced monasteries as centers of learning.

8.1 Salisbury Cathedral from the south-west, begun 1220.

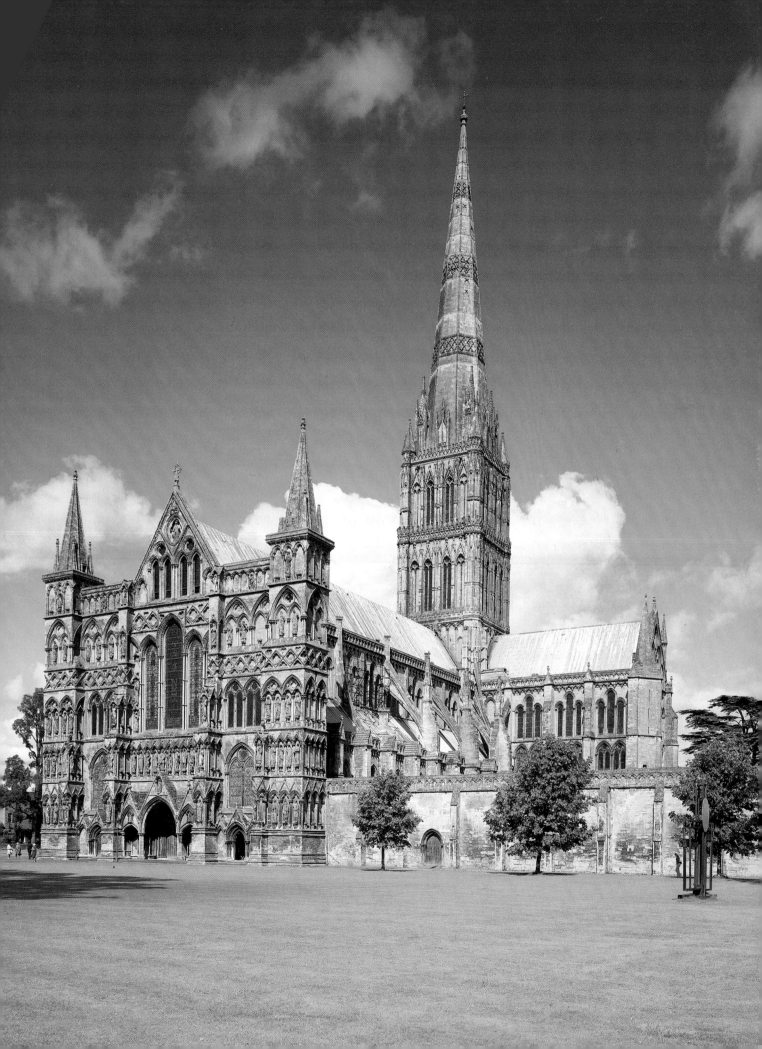

CONTEXTS AND CONCEPTS

The dramatic struggle of humankind's constant search for and defining of reality yielded some remarkable results in the twelfth to fifteenth centuries, bringing a new age to the Western world. Perhaps humankind possesses certain ideas of what ought to be, and no matter how oppressive the circumstances, these ideas struggle to be fulfilled. Perhaps life is, as some have called it, a search for personal freedom—whose freedom and under what conditions being subject to circumstances.

Circumstance plays an important role in humanity's image of reality, and the circumstances of the mid-Middle Ages were unique. The conversion of Europe to Christianity and the approach of the millennium (AD 1000) cannot be underestimated in their interrelationships. The desperate conditions of feudal society and faith in a life beyond this vale of tears led to a widespread belief that the Second Coming of Christ and the end of the world would occur at the close of the millennium. One might think that the Second Coming and the end of the world would be a joyous fulfilment for a Christian. However, when Europe awoke to discover that the world had not ended at the turn of the millennium, rather than disappointment there seems to have been a great sense of relief. Humankind had been granted a new lease of life on earth, and this was reflected in changes in the climate of feeling and thought.

Reform in the Christian Church

The development of Western culture and its artistic and other institutions in the late Middle Ages was undeniably affected, if not controlled, by the Christian Church. By the middle of the eleventh century the Christian Church had become very powerful. The tenth-century Church had become feudalized and corrupt, with many of its secular clergy seeking only wealth and power. But this corruption did not go unchallenged. Cries for reform came particularly from the monasteries. The founding of the Abbey of Cluny by William of Aquitaine in 910 signalled the start of a major movement for reform. The strict disciplines and high moral standards of Cluny's

Benedictine monks and abbots made Cluny a model of reform and its influence spread across Europe. While it succeeded in restoring monastic life to its original standards, however, it did little to reform the secular clergy.

Bishops and priests were appointed by feudal lords and the lesser nobility, with appointments often going to the highest bidder. Bishoprics were treated as family property, and the secular clergy, many of whose priests were married, did not consider their religious duties to be a high priority. Conditions were ripe for reform, and the reformers attacked the evils of the secular clergy with vehemence. Their objective was to free the Church from lay control and to reduce the secular interests of the clergy. The reform movement crossed national boundaries, and led by the papacy from the mid-eleventh century onward, transformed the structure of the medieval Church. Success depended on the re-establishment of the papacy as a central force in Christendom, a position it had not enjoyed for some time, despite recognition of the primacy of the Roman See.

Circumstances changed in 1046 under Emperor Henry III of Germany, who championed the cause of the reformers and in 1049 appointed Pope Leo IX, who ruled until 1054. During those five years Leo introduced a brilliant ecclesiastical reorganization, including the creation of a body of cardinals, making it possible for the papacy to exercise control over bishops named by lay rulers. Leo followed a series of synods in Rome with a personal tour of the Empire, during which he publicized and put into practice the reforms, and thereby both consolidated his program and rid the clergy of many of its most offensive bishops.

Conflict between papacy and laity over the investiture of ecclesiastical office could not be solved so easily, however, because at its heart lay the issue of the basis for royal authority. The resulting struggle has become known as the Investiture Conflict. Through a series of negotiated settlements with the various monarchs of Europe, the relationships between nobility and clergy, and clergy and papacy, were stabilized. The outcome was a compromise in which kings gave up their ancient theocratic claim to represent God's will in appointing senior clergy. Kings nevertheless continued to nominate bishops, but they found greater difficulty in presenting candidates who were considered unsuitable by the Church. From the twelfth century onward, ecclesiastical appointments were markedly better.

The papacy emerged from the conflict with greatly enhanced prestige and the importance of the Church in medieval affairs, artistic and otherwise, was increased.

Intellectual pursuits

The twelfth century has often been called an age of humanism. The wave of religious enthusiasm which swept Europe from the second half of the eleventh century to the middle of the twelfth coincided with a flourishing of cultural activity and a zest for learning. "The writers of the twelfth century reveal themselves to us as living personalities more vividly than those of the earlier Middle Ages. There was a revival of classical literary studies, a vivid feeling for nature in lyric poetry, a new naturalism in Gothic art."[1] There were exciting intellectual and ecclesiastical developments, the growth of new humanist or "personalist" elements in religious devotion, theology, and philosophy.

St. Bernard of Clairvaux

Particularly important during this period was the creation of new religious orders and the increase in status of women in religious and secular thought. The Virgin Mary assumed a new importance in religious life, and the cult of Mary Magdalene spread throughout Europe. A key figure in the changing religious thought was a young nobleman, Bernard of Clairvaux (1090–1153), who entered the order of Cîteaux, the most influential new monastic movement of the twelfth century.

Bernard was a religious enthusiast, in many ways a true fanatic, who had no doubt that his views were right and no inclination to avoid combat with those who disagreed with him. He waged bitter verbal battle against the scholar and theologian Peter Abelard; the monk and statesman Suger, abbot of St. Denis; and the whole order of Cluny. At the same time, he showed flashes of tolerance and practical good sense. He was gentle and kindly toward his monks, even the erring ones. When the duke of Burgundy asked to be accepted as a monk, Bernard told him to stay where he was. There were plenty of virtuous monks but few pious dukes. Because of his great reputation for holiness and eloquence, Bernard was often asked to intervene in the public affairs of his age—and his dynamic personality led him sometimes to intervene without being asked. He was an advisor to the French king, Louis VII. He helped to found the new military order of Knights Templars. He exercised a decisive influence during a disputed papal election of the 1130s by swinging public support to Pope Innocent II (1130–1143). He took a leading part in preaching the Second Crusade, and its dismal outcome was one of the few setbacks Bernard encountered in his public career. He was also horrified that his preaching of the crusade led to new massacres of the Jews, and he used all his great influence to check this unhappy byproduct of crusading zeal.

In his religious teaching, Bernard represented a whole new way of piety that was coming to characterize twelfth-century Christianity. It was both more mystical and more personalist than the religion of the early medieval centuries. In his treatises and letters on the religious life written for his fellow monks, Bernard described a way of "ascent to God", four stages of love by which a soul could attain to ecstatic, mystical union with the Divinity. These works are classics of religious literature. Bernard's sermons for the common people dealt with more homely themes. He would recreate the familiar Gospel stories with vivid word pictures. The central figures of the Christian story, Jesus, Mary, and the Apostles, had always been revered, but as remote hieratic figures. Bernard presented them as living, breathing personalities. He wanted to inspire in his audiences not just awe for a remote godhead but ardent, emotional love for the person of Jesus, and he emphasized the role of Mary as an intercessor who could lead men to her Son. A hardened sinner might feel too terrified by his own guilt to approach a stern, just God directly. Bernard drew for him the picture of a tender, gracious, infinitely merciful lady to whom he could turn for help. It was

	GENERAL EVENTS	LITERATURE & PHILOSOPHY	VISUAL ART	THEATRE & DANCE	MUSIC	ARCHITECTURE
1000	Henry III of Germany Pope Leo IX First Crusade	Abelard				
1100	Bernard of Clairvaux Muslim conquest of Edessa Second Crusade Muslim conquest of Jerusalem Eleanor of Aquitaine – Chivalry Third Crusade		Gothic style West portal jamb statues – Chartres Cathedral (**8.12**)	Courtly tradition Mystery, miracle, morality plays Mansion stages *Antecriste* *Adam Play* *Second Shepherd's Play*	Ars Antiqua Organa Cantilena Motet	Gothic style Abbey Church of St-Denis Chartres Cathedral (**8.22**) Notre Dame de Paris (**8.20**)
1200	Magna Carta	Thomas Aquinas Dante	South transept jamb statues— Chartres Cathedral (**8.14**) Psalter of St Louis (**8.8**) Nicola Pisano *David Harping* (**8.10**) Psalter of Alfonso (**8.24**) *St John on Patmos* (**8.9**)	Danse Macabre John Bodel of Arras		Amiens Cathedral (**8.23**) Exeter Cathedral (**8.26**) Westminster Abbey
1300	Hundred Years' War begins The Plague	Chaucer Froissart	Giotto Jean Pucelle Pietro Lorenzetti		Ars Nova	Ely Cathedral (**8.28**) Wells Cathedral (**8.27**) Lincoln Cathedral (**8.30**) Gloucester Cathedral (**8.31**)
1400		Villon Mallory		Confrérie de la Passion	International Style	

8.2 Timeline of the Late Middle Ages.

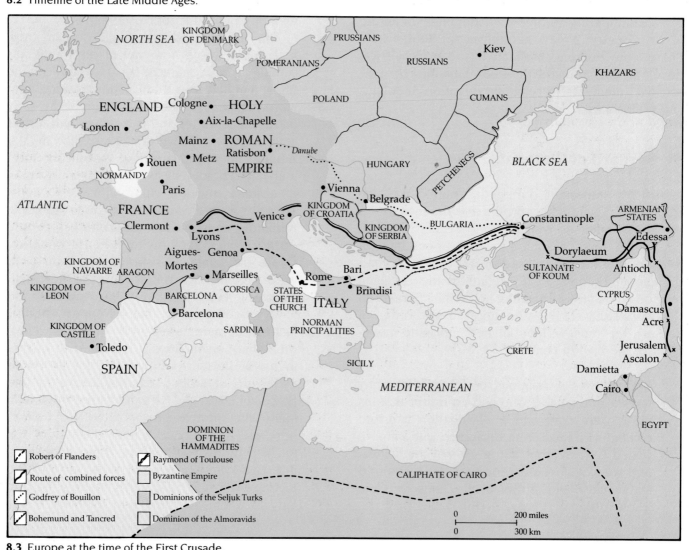

8.3 Europe at the time of the First Crusade.

about this time that collections of stories about Mary, known as *Miracles of the Virgin*, began to be popular. Bernard's preaching gave a powerful stimulus to the cult.

Bernard possessed a striking capacity to lead and inspire. His preaching and influence brought about an incredibly rapid expansion of the Cistercian order. In 1115 there were five Cistercian houses, Cîteaux, la Ferté, Pontigny, Clairvaux, and Morimond. When St. Bernard died in 1153, there were 343, and by the end of the thirteenth century this number was doubled. In their heyday the Cistercian houses were large as well as numerous. Rievaulx in England contained 650 monks in 1142, at a time when the largest of English Benedictine houses, Christ Church, Canterbury, could muster no more than 150.[2]

The Crusades

Our notion of the Crusades might well be of knights in shining armor setting out on glorious quests to free the Holy Land from the infidels. The Crusades were far from a romantic quest, however. They illustrate clearly the great energy and optimism of Europe in a new millennium and a new era. A strengthened Church leadership emerged from the period of the Crusades.

As early as the tenth century Popes had led armies against the Saracens in Italy, and by the end of the eleventh century, the Church was able to put forward several reasons why a Christian army might march against the Muslims. Byzantium had been rescued from the Turks and there was a possibility of healing the East-West schism. Pilgrimages to the Holy Land as a form of penance had become increasingly popular in this age of religious zeal. The safety of these pilgrims was seen as ample reason for interference by the Popes. A more practical benefit closer to home was the removal of troublesome nobles from the local scene. An opportunity came in 1095 at the Council of Clermont. Pope Urban II was supposedly asked for aid by the envoys of the Eastern emperor, Alexius Comnenus. Urban set about mounting a crusading army, and was astonished at the response to his call. Thousands came forward to take up the cross. Men, women, children, and cripples clamored to take part.

The reasons for the First Crusade went beyond its political and military objectives. It achieved its

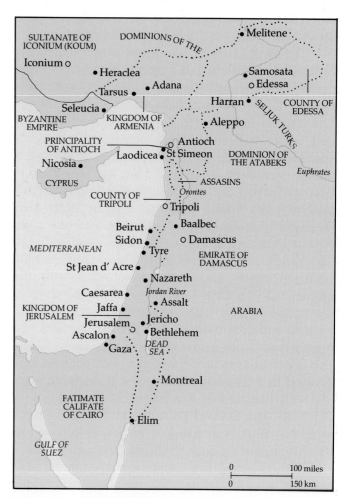

8.4 The Crusading States.

impetus from the religious enthusiasm of the individuals that made up the crusading army. Individuals were ready to make significant sacrifices for their faith. The idea of a crusade generated such a tremendous emotional response that even the Pope could not control it. Itinerant preachers heralded the crusade in their revival meetings. No one cared about the practical problems; it was an act of faith and piety: the infidels would scatter in fear before the banner of the cross. The walls of fortresses would tumble down like those of Jericho.

The most famous of these itinerant preachers was Peter the Hermit. At one point he was given credit for the entire movement, although we now know this not to be the case. Even if Peter did not initiate the idea of a crusade, he certainly contributed significantly to its popularization. Mounted on a mule, he wandered through France preaching crusade to any and all who would listen. His ascetic lifestyle and passionate oratory made many regard him as a saint. He drew enormous crowds, and by the time he reached Cologne in March 1096 thousands had taken up the cross and followed him.

The First Crusade, which ultimately led to the capture of Jerusalem and a bloody massacre, wound its way through Hungary, Greece, Constantinople, Syria, Nicaea, the southern coast of Asia Minor, Edessa, and Antioch (Fig. **8.4**). Beset with in-fighting and other self-inflicted problems, the crusaders stumbled onward. The final conquest of Jerusalem raised even more problems. What was Jerusalem to become? Was it to be a secular kingdom or Church property, like Rome? How was it to be defended? Most of the crusaders rushed home after the completion of their pilgrimage. The wide-ranging Christian conquests proved virtually indefensible. As time went on closer and closer association with the natives led the Christians to adopt the customs of the country. Very little was settled and no centralized authority existed. By 1144 the Muslims had reunited and the Christian state was under siege. The fall of Edessa sent shock waves through Europe and led to a clamoring for another crusade, coinciding with the reform movement of St. Bernard of Clairvaux. The Second Crusade set out in 1147, but ended in disarray and defeat. After that Europe lost its enthusiasm for such ventures for a generation.

In the interim the Muslims gathered their forces and set about driving out the Christians. On 3 October 1187 the Muslims led by Saladin conquered Jerusalem, ending eighty-three years of Christian rule. Again the news shocked Europe and again the Pope took the opportunity to make peace among warring nobles in Europe. Henry II of England and his son Richard, Philip Augustus of France, and Frederick Barbarossa of Germany all took up the cross. The Third Crusade, well planned, financed, and led by the most powerful rulers of Europe, set off in high spirits and expectations. One disaster after another befell the crusaders and by 1189 only Richard and Philip were still in the field. Their major accomplishment was the capture of Acre after a two-year siege. Philip then returned home to make trouble for Richard, now Richard I of England, as France and England resumed hostilities. Richard did succeed in agreeing a truce with Saladin which allowed pilgrims to enter Jerusalem safely. The final episode of this grand and romantic venture so familiar to us in legend was Richard's capture by the Emperor Henry VI and subsequent ransom. Another chapter in the conflict of politics and religion had come to a close.

The Third Crusade clearly demonstrated the limitations of the papal program. Although the ideal inherent in a crusade created a perfect excuse for the Pope to intervene in the temporal politics of Europe, their intervention was largely unsuccessful. The crusade failed to resolve the differences between France and England and failed to produce peace in Europe in general. The crusade itself failed precisely because its leaders could not forget old quarrels or refrain from new ones in the face of the enemy. Papal hopes for a united Christendom under its military leadership died with the end of the Third Crusade.

Chivalry

Society was organized in a feudal system throughout Europe over this period. The Carolingian and Ottonian Empires had suggested that a wider stability and order were possible. Life remained polarized in a rigid class system. The clergy and nobility ruled and the serf labored. In between there was a vacuum. This vacuum came to be filled by the town and the town guild, out of which a new age was formed.

At the same time, another medieval phenomenon flowered with a change in attitude that permeated society and the arts. Feudalism was a masculine, men-at-arms code of behavior. By the twelfth century a distinctly feminine point of view ruled ethics and personal conduct—that of chivalry and the courtly tradition. Men were away from the home or castle for long periods of time—whether trading or warring. It fell to women to control domestic matters and manners, and if Eleanor of Aquitaine (1122–1204) is any example, women controlled such enterprises very effectively. Courts of love emerged with codes of conduct and etiquette that thoroughly changed society's viewpoint to a softer, gentler tone than that of the rough code of feudalism.

We may speculate that the Code of Chivalry was a practical and euphemistic way of glossing over illicit love affairs while the husband was away. It was an age in which most aristocratic marriages were arranged for political convenience. Chaucer gives us an excellent view of the enigma of the medieval love triangle in the *Franklin's Tale* from the *Canterbury Tales*. The Franklin's solution illustrates the "civilized" code and its peculiar influence on the era.

More important than its impact on morals was the impact of the courtly tradition on religious philosophy. We described the early Middle Ages as an age of death and devils—notwithstanding its faith. Now, however, we find a warmer feeling, a quality of mercy. Christ the Savior and Mary the compassionate Mother became the focal points of the faith. This change in viewpoint is reflected very clearly in the arts of the time.

The middle class

Amid the changing points of view rose a new and important middle class, filling the vacuum between nobility and peasant and drawing thousands into emerging towns and cities, which offered a new hope of escape from slavery to the land. The Crusades had opened new horizons for Europe's barricaded mentality. Returning soldiers brought with them tales of the East and marvelous fabrics and goods that immediately caught the fancy of nobleman and commoner alike. All of this caused an explosion in demand for trade goods and services, not only for the import of desired materials, but also for a transformation of the physical world. Response was almost instantaneous, because the Italian trading cities such as Genoa, Pisa, and Venice, had never fully declined as commerce-oriented centers.

Within the newly emerging towns and cities very powerful guilds of artisans and merchants rapidly developed. No order gives up power easily, and struggles, sometimes violent, pitted burgher against nobleman. The Crusades had financially ruined many feudal landholders, and a taste of potential power and wealth strengthened the resolve of the new middle class. They needed a more dynamic society than feudalism could offer, and they threw their wealth and power behind strengthening monarchies. As a result administration became more centralized, society was stabilized, and a rudimentary democracy emerged. The thirteenth century witnessed the Magna Carta, which built upon twelfth-century English common law, and in 1295 the establishment of an English Parliament. Democracy began to emerge in Switzerland, and in 1302 the Estates General were founded in France, bringing a spark of democracy.

Intellectual life

Many universities gained their charters in the twelfth and thirteenth centuries, for example, Oxford University in England, the University of Salamanca in Spain, the University of Bologna in Italy, and the University of Paris in France. Many had existed previously in association with monasteries, but their formal chartering brought them out amid the public. Medieval universities were not as we know them today; they had no buildings or classrooms. They consisted of guilds of scholars and teachers who gathered their students together wherever space permitted. University life spawned a core of individuals who sought knowledge for its own sake and who could not accept a condition of society or a state of mind that walled itself in and rigidly resisted any questioning of authority. This environment bred new philosophy and thought. As we shall see, St. Thomas Aquinas built a philosophical structure which could accommodate divergent points of view. Dante suggested a new balance of viewpoints in the *Divine Comedy*. Aristotle was rediscovered and introduced throughout Europe, and Roger Bacon began a study of the physical world, on which he based all knowledge. Walls were collapsing, and light and fresh air flooded the Western world. New freedoms, comfort (both physical and spiritual), and potential affected every level of society. Thirteenth-century philosophy reconciled reason and revelation, the human and the divine, the kingdom of God and the kingdoms of man. Each were considered parts of a universal, harmonious order of thought.

Philosophy and theology

Abelard

"He that believes quickly is light minded." These words from Ecclesiasticus ... were quoted by Abelard in his so-called *Introduction to Theology* and they admirably represent his general attitude.... With a high regard for his own powers and a contempt for the abilities of others he combined a contentious temper which kept him constantly at war. He delighted in measuring wits with his teachers and exposing their weak points and when he disagreed with them no feelings of piety restrained him from attacking them publicly and in the most contemptuous terms.[3]

Abelard (1079–1142) has become a figure both of philosophy and romance. His life-long correspondence with and late-in-life love affair with Héloïse accounts for the romantic element. In the case of philosophy he was the pupil of both William of Champeaux and Roscellinus, but disagreed with the conclusions of both his masters. Abelard argued for the individual and concrete nature of substance, denying that particular objects were merely imperfect imitations of universal ideal models to which they owed their reality. That is to say, objects as we know them have *real* individuality which makes each individual object a substance "in its own right", and distinct from all other objects.

Abelard went beyond this point to argue that Universals do exist, and comprise the "Form of the universe" as conceived by the mind of God. Universals comprise patterns of type after which individual substances are created, and because of which these substances are the *kinds* of things they are.

Abelard was a Moderate Realist, or is sometimes labeled a Conceptualist, although conceptualism is usually related to later teaching. His viewpoint was adopted and modified by Thomas Aquinas, and in this revised form constitutes part of the philosophy of the Roman Catholic Church. Abelard believed philosophy had a responsibility to defend Christian doctrine and to make it intelligible. He also believed that philosophy should be free to criticize theology and to reject beliefs which were contrary to reason.

Abelard regarded Christianity as a way of life, and was very tolerant of other religions as well. He considered Socrates and Plato to have been "inspired". The essence of Christianity was not dogma, but the way of life exemplified by Christ. Those who lived prior to Jesus were, in a sense, already Christians if they followed the kind of life Christ practiced. An individual act was good or evil "solely as it is well or ill intended", he argued in his treatise *Know Thyself*. However, lest anyone excuse acts on the basis of "good intentions", Abelard insisted on some sort of standard for judging whether intentions were good or bad. Such a standard existed in a natural law of morality, "manifested in the conscience possessed by every man, and founded upon the will of God". When differences of opinion existed over the interpretation of the law of God, each person must obey his or her own conscience. Therefore, "anything a man does that is against his own conscience is sinful, no matter how much his act may commend itself to the consciences of others."[4]

St. Thomas Aquinas

The thirteenth century marked a new era in Christian thought in the West as Aristotle was rediscovered. With the exception of Aristotle's treatises on logic, the *Organon*, his writings were inaccessible to the West until the late twelfth century. Their reintroduction to Western consciousness created turmoil. In some centers of education, such as the University of Paris, Aristotle's metaphysics and physics were forbidden. Others championed Aristotelian thought, and asserted the eternity of the world and the denial of divine providence and fore-knowledge of contingent events. In the middle were men such as Albertus Magnus who, though orthodox in their acceptance of the traditional Christian faith, regarded the rediscovery of Aristotle in a wholly positive light. Magnus' first pupil was Thomas Aquinas (1227–74).

In his youth Aquinas joined the newly formed mendicant Order of Preachers (the Dominican Order), which led him to Paris to study with Magnus, who was the master teacher of the Dominicans. A prolific writer, Aquinas produced philosophical and theological works and commentaries on Aristotle, the scriptures, and Peter Lombard. His most influential works are the *Summa contra Gentiles* and the *Summa Theologiae*. Aquinas, like Magnus, was a modernist, and he sought to reinterpret the Christian system in the light of Aristotle, in other words to synthesize Christian theology and Aristotelian thought. He believed that the philosophy of Aristotle would prove acceptable to intelligent men and women, and further that if Christianity were to maintain the confidence of educated individuals, it would have to come to terms with and accommodate Aristotle. Aquinas was a very devout and orthodox believer, and had no wish to sacrifice Christian truth, whether to Aristotle or any other philosopher.

In dealing with God and the universe, Aquinas carefully defined the fields of theology and philosophy. Philosophy was limited to whatever lay open to argument, and its purpose was to establish such truth as could be discovered and demonstrated by human reason. Theology, on the other hand, was restricted to the "content of faith", or "revealed truth", which is beyond the ability of reason to discern or demonstrate, and "about which there can be no argument". There was, nonetheless, an area of overlap.

Aquinas concentrated upon philosophical proofs of God's existence and nature. The existence of God could be proved by reason, and Aquinas

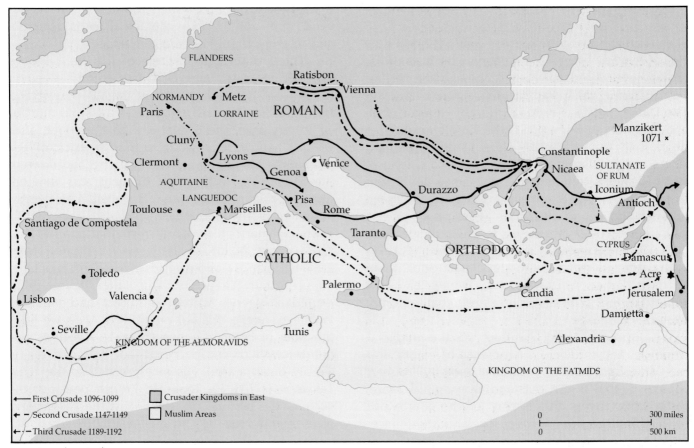

8.5 The Crusades.

believed that Aristotle had inadvertently done just that. The qualities to which Aristotle reduced all the activities of the universe become intelligible "only on the supposition that there is an unmoved . . . self-existent . . . form of being whose sheer perfection sets the whole world moving in pursuit of it".

Beyond this, Aquinas' conceptions of philosophical knowledge of God's nature move beyond and set aside the Aristotelian viewpoint, turning instead to Plato. Aristotle's view that God knows only His own Form is replaced with the idea that God's self-knowledge comprises a knowledge of the whole formal structure of the universe. On this point Aquinas follows the path of Augustine in his belief that the formal structure of the universe comprises in the divine mind a plan in accordance with which the world is created.

Secularism

By the fourteenth century revelation and reason, God and the state were considered separate spheres of authority, neither subject to the other.

Individual nations (in contrast to feudal states or Holy Empires) had arisen throughout Europe. Social and economic progress was disrupted by two events, however—the Plague (1348–50), which killed half the population of Europe, and the Hundred Years' War (1338–1453). Secular arts gained prominence, respectability, and significance. These changes, of course, were gradual, and they reflected a shift of emphasis rather than a reversal of values.

The terms "ebb and flow" and "shifting and sliding" can generally be used to describe the manner in which the arts have crossed the centuries. So far in our examination, lack of record has muddied the impact of that concept. From the twelfth century onward our understanding and examples of most of the arts are fairly clear and broadly based. We can determine whether characteristics of style may or may not adhere to all forms in all places in the same time. A major stylistic label may refer to a rather broad chronological period even though that style may have come and gone in some places without reference to the parameters of the period, or may never have arrived at all in other areas or art forms.

219

Literature

The greatest poet of the age was Dante (1265–1321). He wrote a few lyrics and the story of his passion for his lost love, Beatrice, in *La Vita Nuova*, but it was the *Divine Comedy* which was the major work of his life. The *Divine Comedy* is a description of Heaven, Hell, and Purgatory. It is a vision of the state of souls after death told in an allegory demonstrating humankind's need for spiritual illumination and guidance. Part of Dante's tremendous significance lies in the fact that he elevated vernacular Italian to the status of a rich and expressive language for poetry. It was no longer necessary for writers to use Latin. Petrarch (1304–74), who created the sonnet form, wrote in both Latin and his native Tuscan dialect. Soon poets all over Europe were following Dante's lead and exploring the poetic resources of contemporary everyday language.

A popular genre of literature was the medieval chronicle. The chronicle is a romance of history, and the *Chronicles of England, France, and Spain* by Froissart (*c.*1333–*c.*1400) is the outstanding example. Froissart's work covers the history of the fourteenth century and the wars between England and France. It was not written as a factual account but, in the words of its author, "to encourage all valorous hearts and to show them honorable examples".

Three other great writers of this period were Chaucer, Malory, and Villon. Geoffrey Chaucer (*c.*1340–1400) was the father of English poetry, and his *Canterbury Tales* are written in realist and humanist literary style. The *Tales* open with a prologue, after which Chaucer relates the stories of each of the pilgrims in his tale, much as Boccaccio had done in the *Decameron*, with which Chaucer was familiar. Chaucer was unprecedented, however, in his combination of cultivated irony and robust comedy. Sir Thomas Malory's *Morte d'Arthur*, completed in 1470, a year before Malory's death, was compiled from French romances, and comprises a collection of tales about Arthur, Launcelot, and other figures from Arthurian legend, written in direct and vigorous language. At the close of the Middle Ages, we have the work of François Villon (b. 1431). A robber and murderer, Villon escaped execution and, eventually, simply disappeared. His major work was the *Great Testament* (1461). He took old French poetic forms such as the *rondeau*, the *rondel*, and the *ballade*, and gave them a new life and melancholy beauty.

THE ARTS
OF THE LATE MIDDLE AGES

TWO-DIMENSIONAL ART

Gothic style

In the twelfth to the fifteenth centuries traditional paintings in the form of frescoes and altar panels returned to prominence. Two-dimensional art continued to illustrate the gradual flow of one style into another without the emergence of a clearly dominant identity. Because this period is so closely identified with Gothic architecture, and because painting found its primary outlet within the Gothic cathedral, we need to ask what qualities reflect a Gothic style in painting. The answer is not as readily apparent as it is in architecture and sculpture, but several characteristics can be identified. One is the beginnings of three-dimensionality in figure representation. Another is a striving to give these figures mobility and life within three-dimensional space. Space is the essence of Gothic style. The Gothic painter had not mastered perspective, and his compositions do not exhibit the spatial rationality of later works, but if we compare him with his predecessors of the earlier medieval eras, we discover that he has more or less broken free from the static, frozen, two-dimensionality of earlier styles. Gothic style also exhibits spirituality, lyricism, and a new humanism (mercy versus irrevocable judgement). Gothic painting is less crowded and frantic—its figures are less entangled with each other.

It was a changing style with many variations. An analysis of the work of any representative Gothic painter, whether Duccio, Simone Martini, Cimabue, Giotto, the Lorenzettis, the Limbourgs, or Broederlam, would be marked by influences of other styles on that painter's works, but within the broader framework of characteristics appropriate to the Gothic style.

Gothic style in painting could be found throughout

8.6 Giotto, *The Lamentation*, 1305–6. Fresco. Arena Chapel, Padua, Italy.

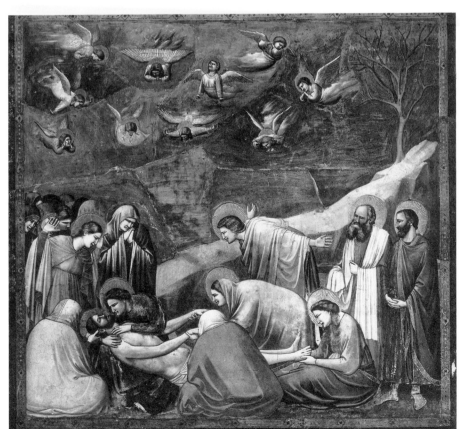

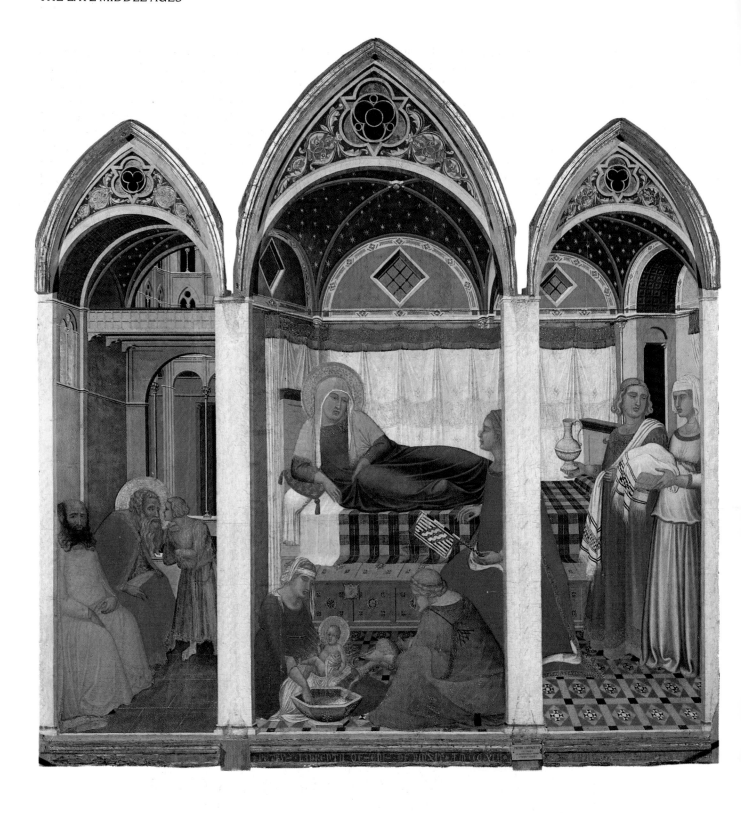

8.7 Pietro Lorenzetti, *The Birth of the Virgin*, 1342. Panel painting, 6ft 1½ins × 6ft ½in (1.87 × 1.84m). Museo dell' Opera Metropolitana, Siena, Italy.

continental Europe, but the center of activity and the area of greatest influence was Italy—Giotto, Duccio, Simone Martini, and the Lorenzetti brothers were the standard-bearers. By the turn of the fifteenth century Italian and northern European Gothic had merged into an international Gothic style typified by the works of Melchior Broederlam and the Limbourg brothers. Two examples serve to illustrate the several generalizations we made earlier. Pietro Lorenzetti's triptych, the B*irth of the Virgin* (Fig. **8.7**), shows a careful concern for three-dimensional space and figure depiction. The figures are lifelike and earthly; highlight and shadow give plasticity to faces and garments; the treatment of draping fabric in the gowns of the right panel shows precise attention to detail. We have a sense of a scene in progress in which we are participants, as opposed to a rendering frozen on a two-dimensional surface. A relaxed atmosphere pervades the scene and the eye travels across the work in a lyrical sweep with a pause here and there to observe important focal areas. Figure groupings are spaced comfortably; the composition spreads through the triptych, in a continuation behind the columns separating the panels. Giotto's *Lamentation* (Fig. **8.6**) illustrates the same concerns and many of the same solutions. Figures are given plasticity through highlight and shadow, although not as soft as Lorenzetti's because Giotto has hardened the edge of each form with an outline. His fabrics likewise do not drape freely. They retain an earlier decorative quality of

8.8 *Gideon's Army Surprises the Midianites,* from the Psalter of St Louis, 4¾ × 3⅝ins (12.1 × 9.2cm). Bibliothèque Nationale, Paris.

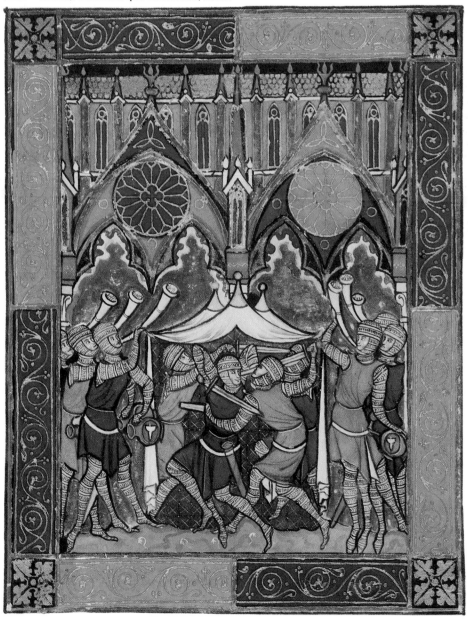

lower verisimilitude. Figures are crowded, but still free to move. Emotion permeates the fresco, and although it is frenetic to some degree, it is human, individualized, and controlled. What makes Giotto's fresco so compelling is his unique mastery of three-dimensional space. His background employs atmospheric perspective, but unlike other painters who created deep space behind the primary focal plane, Giotto brings the horizon to our eye-level. As a result, we participate in a three-dimensional scene that moves out to us. Space in the painting is contiguous with the space in front of it. Lorenzetti and Giotto had very different approaches, and a more detailed analysis would illuminate influences of other traditions in each work. Nevertheless, both examples contain clear general characteristics of the Gothic style.

Manuscript illumination

The Gothic style of two-dimensional art can also be seen in manuscript illumination. The Court Style of France and England produced some truly exquisite works. The Psalter of St. Louis (Fig. **8.8**) was produced for King Louis IX of France in about 1250. It was a lavish book containing seventy-eight full-page pictures of scenes from the Old Testament. The composition is elegant and lively. The figures exhibit graceful elongation and delicacy. Set against gold backgrounds, the depictions are carefully

balanced and, while somewhat crowded, show a relaxed comfort in their spatial relationships. Precision and control characterize the technique. Colors are rich. The overall composition blends human figures and architectural details in the same manner that church sculpture ornamented and became a part of its architectural environment.

The artists of these works were professionals living in Paris who were influenced by Italian style, and who clearly had a new interest in pictorial space, which begins to separate them from their medieval predecessors.

The influence of Paris can also be seen in English manuscript illumination. Figure **8.9** of *St. John on Patmos* was painted for Edward, son of Henry III, and his wife Eleanor of Castile. The elongated figures and small heads reflect the French court influence, as does the heavy drapery. "As in English sculpture, in painting also the English frequently transformed their French models by more angular treatment of the folds and by exaggerated poses and even expressions."[5] The same characteristics can be seen in Figure **8.10**.

In the later years of the Gothic period Italian experiment with three-dimensional space can be seen in manuscript illumination, such as that of Jean Pucelle, the Parisian illuminator and contemporary of Duccio. Figure **8.11**, Pucelle's *Book of Hours of Queen Jeanne d'Evreux*, graphically demonstrates this change.

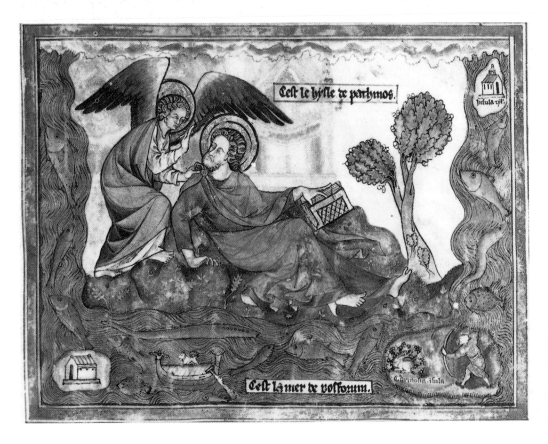

8.9 *St John on Patmos*, from the *Douce Apocalypse*, before 1272. 12½ × 8⅝ins (31.75 × 21.9cm). Bodleian Library, Oxford, England.

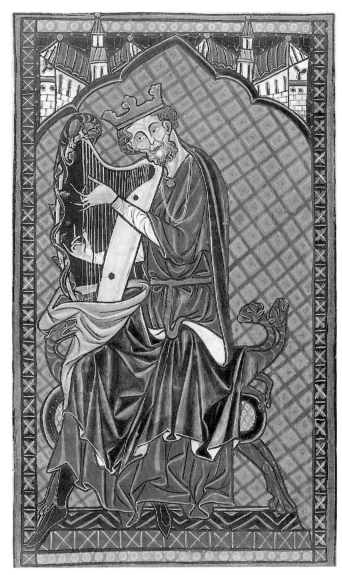

8.10 *David Harping*, from the Oscott Psalter, c. 1270. 7⅞ × 4⅜ins (20 × 11.1cm). British Library, London.

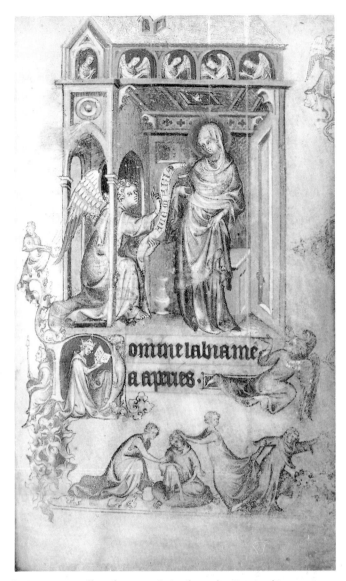

8.11 Jean Pucelle, *The Annunciation*, from the Hours of Jeanne d'Evreux, 1325–8. Grisaille and color on vellum. 3½ × 2⁷⁄₁₆ins (8.9 × 6.2cm). The Metropolitan Museum of Art, New York (the Cloisters Collection, 1954).

SCULPTURE

Gothic sculpture again reveals the changes in attitude of the period. It portrays serenity, idealism, and simple naturalism. Gothic sculpture, like painting, has a human quality, and takes a kindlier view of life. The vale of tears and death and damnation are replaced with conceptions of Christ as a benevolent teacher and of God as beautiful. This style has a new sense of order, symmetry, and clarity. Its visual images carry with greater distinctness over a distance. The figures of Gothic sculpture are less entrapped in their material and stand away from their backgrounds, almost as if they could be released with only a small amount of chiselling (Fig. **8.12**).

Schools of sculpture developed throughout France, and although individual stone carvers worked alone, their common links with a school gave their works a unified character. Rheims, for example, had an almost classical quality, while Paris was dogmatic and intellectual (perhaps a reflection of its role as a university city). As the period progressed, sculpture became more naturalistic. Spiritualism was sacrificed to everyday appeal, and sculpture took on a worldliness reflective of the increasing influence of secular interests, both middle class and aristocratic. Compositional unity also changed from early to late Gothic. Early architectural sculpture was subordinate to the overall design of the building. Later work lost much of that integration as it also gained in emotionalism (Fig. **8.14**). Restrained dignity and idealization gave way to individualized and emotionalized figure depiction.

Nothing illustrates this transition more clearly than the sculptures of Chartres Cathedral, which bracket nearly

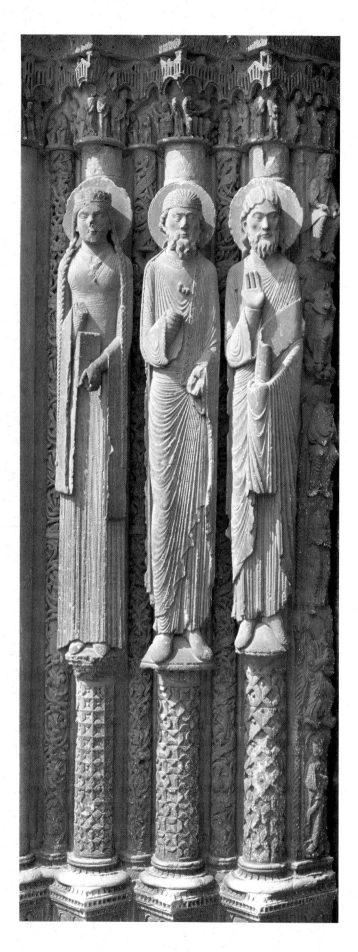

a century. The attenuated figures of Figure **8.12** display a relaxed serenity, idealism, and simple naturalism. They emerge from the portal columns of which they are clearly a part, in graceful and kindly spirit. Each is comfortable in its own space, and each has a human dignity despite idealized depiction. Cloth drapes easily over the bodies. Its detail is somewhat formalized and shallow, but we now see the human figure revealed beneath the fabric—in contrast to the previous use of fabric as mere compositional decoration. Warm and human as these saints may be, the warrior saints of one hundred years later are even more so (Fig. **8.14**). Proportion is more lifelike, and the figures have only the most tenuous of connections to the building proper. Notice especially the subtle S-curve of the figure on the extreme left. Fabric drapes much more naturally. Its folds are deeper and softer. In contrast to the idealized older saints, these young warriors have the features of specific individuals expressing qualities of spirituality and determination.

The Gothic style was fairly consistent in France, Germany, and Spain. In Italy, it was quite different. Italian sculpture had a classical quality partly due to the influence of the German Emperor Frederick II, who ruled southern Italy and Sicily (from where one of the major Italian sculptors of the period, Nicola Pisano, came). Pisano's works have both a Roman quality and a medieval quality in their crowded use of space (Fig. **8.13**).

By the turn of the fifteenth century the international

8.12 Jamb statues, west portal, Chartres Cathedral, France, c. 1145–70.

8.13 Nicola Pisano, T*he Crucifixion*, detail of Pulpit, 1259–60. Marble, whole pulpit c. 15ft (4.6m) high; relief 34ins (86cm) high. Baptistery, Pisa, Italy.

8.14 Jamb statues, south transept portal, Chartres Cathedral, c. 1215–20.

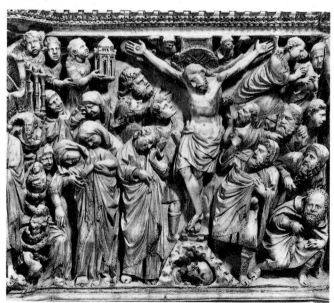

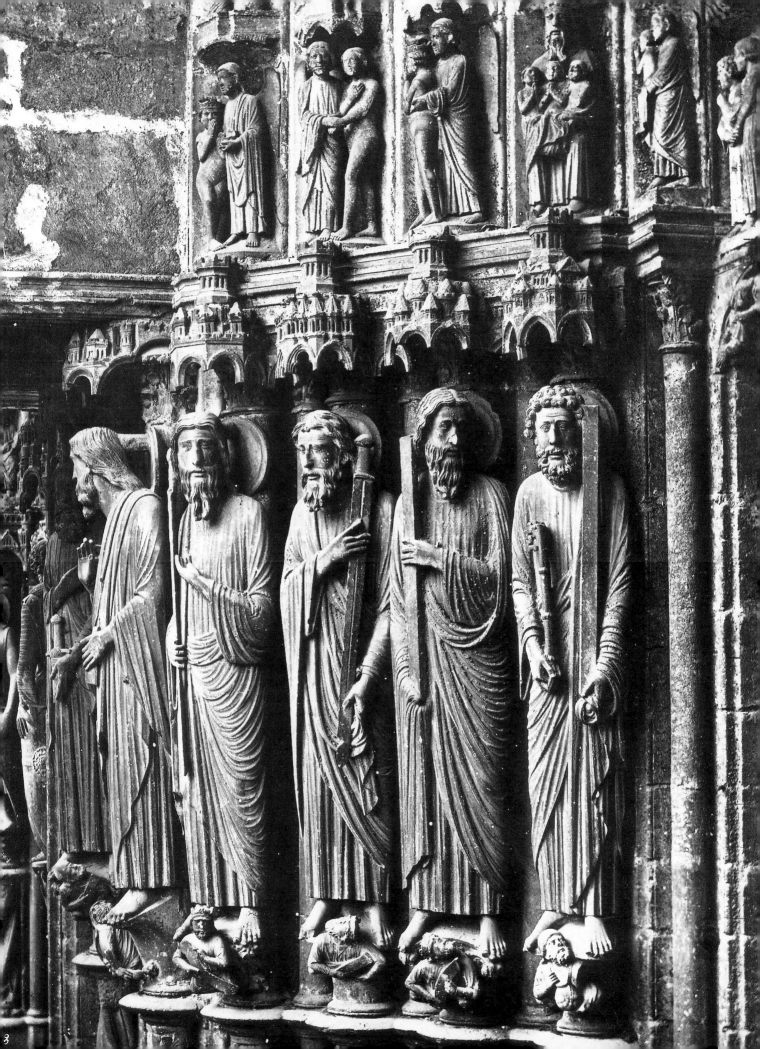

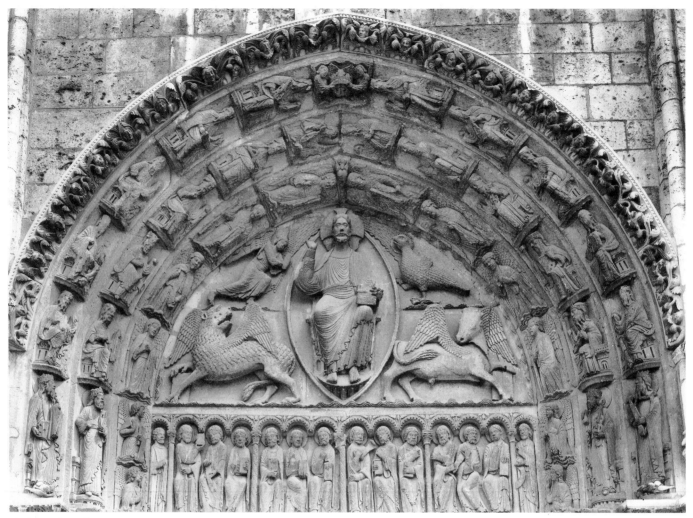

8.15 Central tympanum, west portal, Chartres Cathedral, c. 1145–70.

style noted in painting had virtually unified all of European Gothic, including Italian. This development in sculpture mirrored the deep space of Gothic painting and brought figures even further forward, not by detaching them from their background, but by making that background an empty space as opposed to a wall.

The content of Gothic sculpture is also noteworthy. Gothic sculpture, like most church art, was didactic—it was designed to teach. Many of its lessons are fairly straightforward, and can be appreciated by anyone with a basic knowledge of the Bible. Christ appears as a ruler and judge of the universe above the main doorway of Chartres Cathedral, with a host of symbols of the apostles and others (Fig. **8.15**). Also decorating the portals are the prophets and kings of the Old Testament, whose purpose is to proclaim the harmony of secular and spiritual rule by making the kings of France the spiritual descendants of Biblical rulers.

Other lessons of Gothic cathedral sculpture are more complex and hidden. According to some scholars specific conventions, codes, and sacred mathematics are involved. These factors relate to positioning, grouping, numbers, symmetry, and recognition of subjects. For example, the numbers three, four, and seven (which we often see in compositions of post-Gothic periods) symbolize the Trinity, the Gospels, the sacraments, and the deadly sins. The positioning of figures around Christ show their relative importance, with the position on the right being the most important. Amplifications of these codes and symbols are carried to highly complex levels. All of this is consistent with the mysticism of the period, which held to strong beliefs in allegorical and hidden meanings in Holy sources.

MUSIC

Paris was the center of musical activity in the twelfth and thirteenth centuries, and that one hundred and fifty years is often treated as a distinct period in musical style.

Perhaps in response to the relaxation, additional stability, and increasing complexity of life, music adopted formal composition, greater formalization of notation and structure, and in increased textural complexity. In earlier times improvisation formed the basis of musical composition. Gradually musicians felt the need to write down compositions—as opposed to improvising each piece anew on certain melodic patterns every time it was performed. As a result, in the late Middle Ages "musical composition" became a specific and distinct entity. Noteworthy composers included Leonin and Perotin.

Music was often transmitted orally from performer to performer or from teacher to student. Standardized musical notation made it possible for the composer to transmit ideas directly to the performer. The role of the performer thus changed, making him a vehicle of transmission and interpretation in the musical communication process.

The structure of musical composition also became more formal during this period. Conventions of rhythm, consonant harmony, and mode (similar to our concepts of key) were established. Polyphony began to replace monophony as the dominant musical texture. Monophony continued, with important examples of chant, hymns, and other forms emerging during this time.

Ars antiqua and ars nova

Each of these developments contributed so distinctly to music that modern scholars refer to the mid-twelfth and thirteenth centuries as *ars antiqua*, "old art", or the "old" method of composing. Very quickly in the fourteenth century music underwent another change, described as *ars nova*, "new art".

Music of *ars antiqua* shared the change of attitude that characterized two-dimensional art and sculpture—a more rational, as opposed to emotional, underlying approach and feeling. Increased formal structure and composer control, a reaction to society's increasing stability, were illustrated by triple groupings of beats, composition based on conventions of the chant, deliberate limitation of melodic range, strongly linear texture, and avoidance of characteristics of purely emotional appeal.

A number of forms typify twelfth- and thirteenth-century music, among them various types of *organum* (simple early polyphonic works, kinds of "singing together" as in early liturgy) and *cantilena* (monophonic and polyphonic secular songs). The most notable and typical forms, however, were the motet (from the French *mot*, meaning "word") and the madrigal. Motets developed from *organa* and employed a second set of words in the upper melodic voice. Later, a third and then a fourth voice were added. Usually a motet is considered as a sacred polyphonic work compared with Italian madrigals whose texts were secular. In their early form motets had sacred and secular texts. In the fourteenth century motets were more lengthy and elaborate than in the twelfth and thirteenth centuries, but they almost always retained two aspects of their earliest history—the lowest voice in the composition was taken from the chant, and the melodic range remained restricted.

Not unlike movements in the theatre and visual arts, the fourteenth century witnessed a distinct change in musical emphasis and general style. Music of the *ars nova* reflected greater diversity and freedom of rhythm. Harmonic organization changed to emphasize specific progressions focusing on tonal centers. Passages of parallel fifths, which we find characteristic of medieval music, were used less frequently than passages of parallel sixths and thirds. During this period the first complete Mass was composed by de Machaut. Other changes of considerable technical complexity occurred. The mysterious and haunting "open" sound of medieval chant was becoming a more "modern" sound. Music moved out of the Church, as did theatre, reflecting the philosophical separation of Church and state, and of revelation and reason. By the turn of the fifteenth century previously distinct French and Italian medieval musical styles converged in an international style such as occurred in the visual arts and architecture.

Secularism

Secular music flourished in the twelfth to fourteenth centuries. The tradition of the troubadour and the wandering entertainer continued, and the courtly tradition found in music and poetry an exquisite forum for its love-centered philosophy. Ballads of love and honor (on subjects such as Camelot and King Arthur) praising "m'lady's beauty" and the joys of loving her, even from afar, are typical. In Germany this tradition gave rise to *Minnesänger* (courtly love singers), poet-musicians who mingled love and religion and sang songs of sadness and death.

We still have much to learn about instruments and their timbre or tonal quality in this period. Timbres were probably clear and shrill, but about all we can add to the paragraph on early medieval instruments is the observation that performing ensembles, whether vocal or instrumental, were small in number. Although composition was formalized, composers apparently did not indicate on a score the instrument for a given part. Tradition was so entrenched that composers felt confident that performances of their music did not require specific directions to be adequate. Of quiet significance in the fourteenth century was the invention of the first keyboard instruments of the harpsichord variety. However, these did not come into common usage until a century later.

DANCE

Dance was part of medieval religious and secular activity, but with the exception of pantomime, examples of which have perished with the ages, theatre dance was less important than forms of group dancing. Fascinating illustrations survive such as the *ring dance* on the *Hymn of Jesus* in which twelve dancers representing the apostles and the zodiac danced in a circle. Amid the ravages of the plague, the *danse macabre* (dance of death) appeared—whipped by frenzy and hysteria, people danced until some dropped dead of exhaustion. *Choreomania*, an English version of the *danse macabre*, was characterized by group psychosis, dementia, and self-flagellation. Numerous folk and court dances also existed (Fig **8.16**).

Within the courtly tradition theatre dance found its rebirth. Court dance was expressive and restrained with instrumental accompaniment. A certain degree of spontaneity marked court dances, but increasingly they conformed to specific rules. Court theatrical dance also employed professional entertainers, and depended to a large degree upon the guiding hand of the dancing master, perhaps more like a square dance caller at that

8.16 Two dancing figures from German Minnesänger manuscript of the 14th century. The New York Public Library.

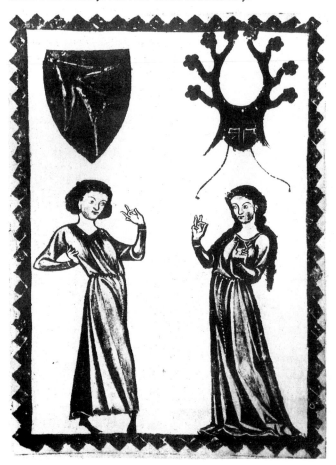

time than the ballet master and choreographer for whom he was the professional prototype. However, it remains for a later age to give us adequate documentation of theatre dance upon which to develop any detailed discussion.

THEATRE

Probably because of their relationship to the Church, major movements in the arts in the twelfth to fifteenth centuries were reasonably unified and widespread. Although local diversity was common, styles were generally alike. The theatre was no exception. As the Middle Ages progressed, drama associated with the Church followed the example of painting and included more and more Church-related material. Earliest church drama (the *trope*) was a simple elaboration and illustration of the Mass. Later, drama included Bible stories (mystery plays), lives of the saints (miracle plays), and didactic allegories (morality plays), with characters such as Lust, Pride, Sloth, Gluttony, and Hatred.

Theatrical development throughout Europe (including Germany, Italy, and Spain) appears to have followed a similar route, although the dates were different. *Tropes* were performed in the sanctuary, using niches around the church as specific scenic locations. On special occasions cycles of plays were performed, and the congregation moved from niche to niche to see part of the cycle. It is difficult for us to pinpoint specific developments even in specific churches, but clearly these dramatizations quickly became very popular

Over the years production standards for the same plays changed drastically. At first only priests performed the roles; later laymen were allowed to act in liturgical drama. Female roles were usually played by boys, but evidence exists to suggest that women did participate occasionally. The popularity of church drama soon made it impractical, if not impossible, to contain the audience within the church building. Evidence also suggests that as laymen assumed a greater role, certain vulgarities were introduced. Comedy and comic characters emerged, even from the Easter *tropes*. On their way to the tomb of Jesus the three Marys stop to buy ointments and cloths from a merchant. This merchant developed into one of the earliest medieval comic characters. Amateur actors never seem able to contain themselves when they discover something in their role that elicits laughter from the audience. The next performance inevitably sees the comic action expanded to prompt a bigger laugh. The most popular comic character of all was the Devil.

Church drama eventually moved outside the sanctuary and, like Church architecture and sculpture, opened itself more widely to the common man and woman, As medieval drama moved out of the Church, various production practices developed in different places. In France

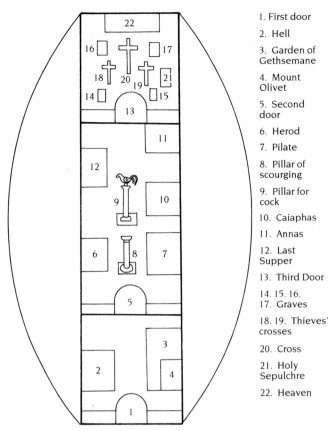

1. First door
2. Hell
3. Garden of Gethsemane
4. Mount Olivet
5. Second door
6. Herod
7. Pilate
8. Pillar of scourging
9. Pillar for cock
10. Caiaphas
11. Annas
12. Last Supper
13. Third Door
14. 15. 16. 17. Graves
18. 19. Thieves' crosses
20. Cross
21. Holy Sepulchre
22. Heaven

8.17 Plan of a medieval mansion stage, showing the mansions in the Donaueschingen Mystery Play, Germany.

8.18 The Valenciennes Mystery Play, 1547. Contemporary drawing. Bibliothèque Nationale, Paris.

and Italy the stationary stage decoration of the church interior became a mansion stage (Fig. **8.17**). The specific configuration of the mansion stage differed from location to location. In Italy it was rectangular and linear, designed to be viewed from one or two sides. In some parts of France arena staging, in which the audience completely surrounded the stage area, was introduced. Whatever the specific application, the mansion stage had a particular set of aesthetic conventions that made its style unique. The individual mansions depicted their locations realistically. At the same time, areas between the mansions were treated conventionally. They could serve as any location.

The most interesting depiction on the medieval stage was that of Hell or Hellmouth. If we knew more about exact dates, the development of Hellmouth could provide interesting comparisons with sculpture, for example, in charting changing attitudes toward death, Hell, fear, and mercy. Audiences demanded more and more realism and complexity in Hellmouth (compare with changes in Gothic sculpture), and descriptions of devils pulling sinners into the mouth of Hell (often depicted as the jaws of a dragon-like monster) amidst smoke and fire are common (Fig. **8.18**). One source describes a Hellmouth so complicated that it took seventeen people to operate it. Some plays, for example *Antecriste* and *Domes Daye*, were clearly intended to be frightening, but in the late Middle Ages even vividly depicted Hellmouths seem to have been comic in their intentions, rather than fearful. Plays such as *Abraham and Isaac* and the *Second Shepherd's Play* are humorous and compassionate, clearly reflecting the change in attitude of the age.

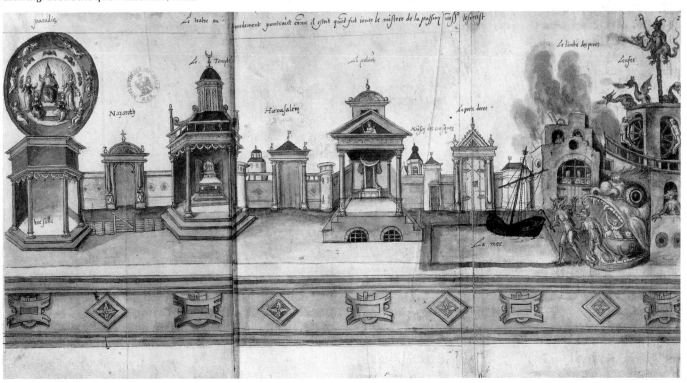

When the action of a play moved away from a specific mansion, the aesthetic became conventional such as we saw in classical Greek theatre. The text of the play told the audience where the action was supposed to occur and the audience then imagined that locale.

In England and parts of France and the Netherlands another staging style developed. Rather than move the audience or depict the entire set of locations on a multiscened mansion stage, theatre was brought to the audience on a succession of pageant wagons like the floats of a modern parade. Each wagon depicted a specific part of the play cycle. Many of these wagons were very elaborate, two storeys tall, and curtained for entrances and exits like a modern theatre. In some cases a flat wagon was combined with an elaborate background wagon to provide a playing area. This type of production was mostly used in cities where narrow wagons were needed to negotiate narrow streets. At intersections where there was more space wagons were coupled and crowds gathered to watch the play segment. When the segment finished, the wagon moved on, and was shortly replaced by another wagon that served as the setting for another short play in the cycle.

As time progressed theatrical production became more and more elaborate and realistic. Many productions were extremely complicated in detail and direction as well as in realistic depiction. Live birds, rabbits, and lambs gave life to the play, as did elaborate costumes that represented specific characters. Bloody executions, wounds, and severed heads and limbs were very common in later medieval drama.

When drama moved out of the church, local guilds began to assume responsibility for various plays. Usually the topic of the specific play dictated which guild was responsible. For example, the watermen performed the *Noah* play and cooks presented *The Harrowing of Hell* because it dealt with baking, boiling, and putting things into and out of fires. Increasing secularization and four-teenth-century philosophical division of Church and state gave rise to a separate secular tradition which led, in the fifteenth century, to French farce. Even religious drama came into professional secular control in France when King Charles VI granted a charter in 1402 to the *Confrèrie de la Passion*.

A typical mystery play was the *Adam* play of early twelfth-century France. It was performed in the vernacular and began by reminding the actors to pick up their lines, to pay attention so as not to add or subtract any syllables in the verses, and to speak distinctly. The play told the Bible story of Adam and was probably played in the square outside the church, with the actors retiring into the church when not directly involved in the action.

Illustrative of the expanding subject matter of Christian drama was a play of the thirteenth century, *Le Jeu de Saint Nicholas* by John Bodel of Arras. The play is set in the Holy Land amid the battles between the Christian Crusaders and the Infidels. In the battle all the Christians are killed except a Monsieur Prudhomme who prays to St. Nicholas in the presence of the Saracen King. The King is told that St. Nicholas would safeguard his treasure, and when St. Nicholas actually intervenes to foil a robbery attempt, the king is converted. Similar plays dealing with the conversion of historical figures (usually amidst attempts to ridicule Christianity or vilify Christians) were very popular, as were plays about the intercessions of Mary (called Mary-plays).

ARCHITECTURE

Gothic style in architecture took many forms, but it is best exemplified in the Gothic cathedral. The cathedral, in its synthesis of intellect, spirituality, and engineering, perfectly expresses the medieval mind. Gothic style was widespread in Europe. Like the other arts it was not uniform in application, nor was it uniform in date. It developed initially as a very local style on the Île de France in the late twelfth century, and spread outward to the rest of Europe. It had died as a style in some places before it was adopted in others. The "slipping, sliding, and overlapping" circumstances of artistic development were fully applicable to Gothic architecture.

The cathedral was, of course, a church building whose purpose was the service of God. However, civic pride as well as spirituality inspired cathedral building. Various local guilds contributed their services in financing or in the actual building of the churches, and guilds were often memorialized in special chapels and stained glass windows. The Gothic church occupied the central, often elevated, area of the town or city. Its physical centrality and context symbolized the dominance of the universal Church over all affairs of men, both spiritual and secular. Probably no other style has exercised such an influence across the centuries or played such a central role, even in twentieth-century Christian architecture. The Gothic church spins an intricate and fascinating story, only a few details of which we can highlight here.

Unlike any other architectural style, the beginnings of Gothic architecture can be pinpointed between 1137 and 1144 in the rebuilding of the royal Abbey Church of St. Denis near Paris. There is ample evidence that Gothic was a physical extension of philosophy, rather than a practical response to the structural limitations of the Romanesque style. That is, Gothic theory preceded its application. The philosophy of the Abbot Suger, who was advisor to Louis VI and a driving force in the construction of St. Denis, held that harmony, the perfect relationship of parts, is the source of beauty, that Light Divine is a mystic revelation of God, and that space is symbolic of God's mystery. The composition of St. Denis and subsequent Gothic churches perfectly expressed that philosophy. As a result, Gothic architecture is more unified than Romanesque. Gothic cathedrals use refined, upward-striving line to symbolize, both in exterior spires and the pointed arch, humanity's upward striving to escape (at the tip) from earth into the mystery of space (the Kingdom of Heaven).

The pointed arch is the most easily identifiable characteristic of this style, and it represents not only a symbol of Gothic spirituality but also an engineering practicality. The pointed arch completely changes the thrust of downward force into more equal and controllable directions, whereas the round arch places tremendous pressure on its keystone, which then transfers thrust outward to the sides. The pointed arch controls thrust into a downward path through its legs. It also adds design flexibility. Dimensions of space encompassed by a round arch are limited to the radii of specific semi-circles. Since the proportions of a pointed arch are flexible, dimensions may be adjusted to whatever practical and aesthetic parameters are desired. The Gothic arch also increased the sense of height in its vaults. Some sources suggest that this structure actually made increased heights possible. That implication is not quite correct. Some

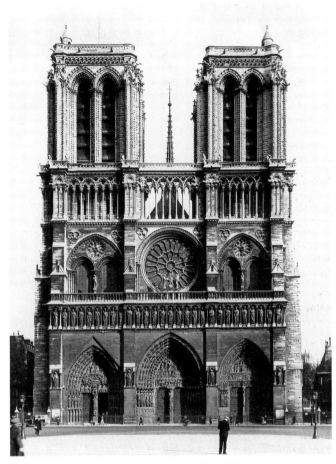

8.20 Notre Dame, Paris, west front, 1163–1250.

8.19 Flying buttresses, Notre Dame, Paris, 1163–1250.

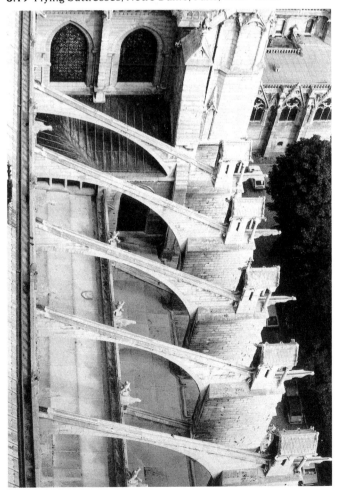

Romanesque churches had vaults as high as any Gothic churches, but the possibility for change in proportion of height to width did increase the apparent height of the Gothic church.

Engineering advances implicit in the new form made possible larger clerestory windows (hence more light) and more slender ribbing (hence a greater emphasis on space as opposed to mass). Outside, practical and aesthetic flying buttresses carry the outward thrust of the vaults through a delicate balance of ribs, vaults, and buttresses gracefully and comfortably to the ground (Fig. **8.19**). Every detail is carefully integrated into a unified whole. The severity of stone is transformed into a tracery of decoration emphasizing mysterious space. Three examples characterize Gothic style and illustrate the marvelous diversity that existed within it. The four-square power of Notre Dame de Paris (Fig. **8.20**) reflects the strength and solidity of an urban cathedral in Europe's greatest city of the age. Its careful composition is highly mathematical—each level is equal to the one below it, and its tripartite division is clearly symbolic of the trinity. Arcs (whose radii are equal to the width of the building) drawn from the lower corners, meet at the top of the circular window at the second level. Careful design moves the eye inward and slowly upward. The exterior structure clearly reveals the interior space, in contrast to the Romanesque buildings.

Chartres Cathedral (Figs. **8.21** and **8.22**) stands in remarkable contrast. Chartres is a country cathedral raised above the center of a small city. Just as its sculptures illustrate a progression of style, so does its architectural design. Our first encounter leads us to wonder why its cramped entry portal is so small in comparison with the rest of the building. The reason is that Chartres represents a cumulative building effort over many years, as fire destroyed one part of the church after another. The main entry portal and the windows above it date back to its Romanesque beginnings. The porch of the south transept (the portal holding the statues of the warrior saints) is much larger and more in harmony with the rest of the building. Finally, as our eyes rise upward, we wonder at the incongruity of the two unmatched spires. Fire was again responsible. The early spire on the right illustrates faith in a simple upward movement that

8.21 Chartres Cathedral, south transept porch, c. 1205–50.

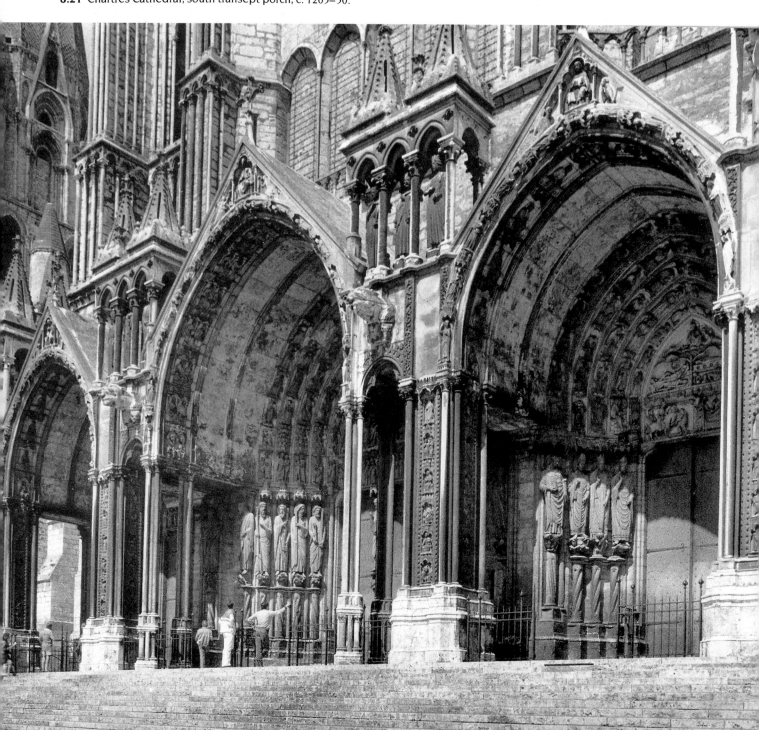

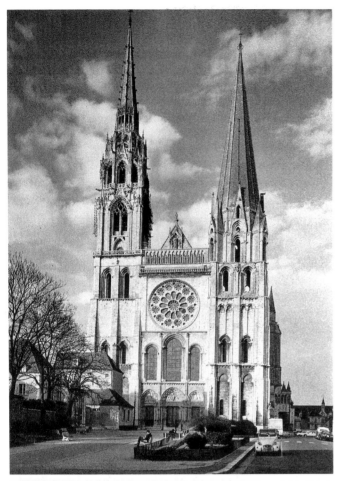

8.22 Chartres Cathedral, west front, 1145–1220.

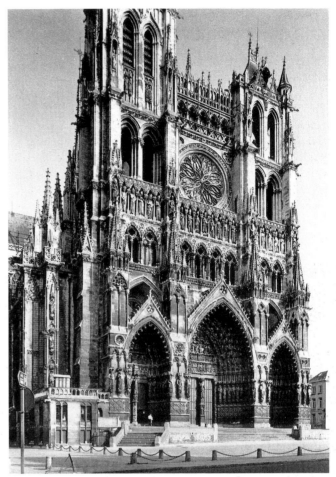

8.23 Amiens Cathedral, west front, c. 1220–59.

rises, unencumbered, to disappear at the tip into the ultimate mystery—space. The later spire, designed in psychological balance with the other, is more ornate and complex. The eye travels upward with increasing difficulty, its progress halted and held earthbound by decoration and detail.

The Cathedral at Amiens (Fig. 8.23) is similar in basic composition to Notre Dame, but rather than creating a sense of four-square power, it gives a feeling of delicacy. Amiens Cathedral illustrates a late development of Gothic style similar to the left spire of Chartres Cathedral. In scale and proportion, however, Amiens is more like Notre Dame. The differences between Amiens and Notre Dame provide an important lesson in the ways design can be used to elicit a response. Amiens is more delicate than Notre Dame, and this feeling is encouraged by the greater detail that focuses our attention on space as opposed to flat stone. Both churches are divided into three very obvious horizontal and vertical sections of roughly the same proportion. Notre Dame appears to rest heavily on its lowest section, whose proportions are diminished by the horizontal band of sculptures above the portals.

Amiens, on the other hand, carries its portals upward to the full height of the lower section. In fact, the central portal, much larger than the central portal of Notre Dame, reinforces the line of the side portals to form a pyramid whose apex penetrates into the section above. The roughly similar size of the portals of Notre Dame reinforces its horizontal sense, thereby giving it stability. Similarly, each use of line, form, and proportion in Amiens reinforces lightness and action, as compared with stability and strength in Notre Dame. This discussion does not imply that one design is better than the other. Each is different and displays a different approach. Perhaps the architects intended different messages. Nevertheless, both cathedrals are unquestionably Gothic, and we can easily identifiy the qualities that make them so.

The importance of stained glass windows in Gothic cathedrals cannot be overemphasized. They carefully controlled light entering the sanctuary, reinforcing a marvelous sense of mystery. They also took the place of wall paintings in telling the story of the gospels and the saints, the walls of the Romanesque style having been replaced by space and light in the Gothic.

SYNTHESIS
The Gothic temperament in England

In England as in the rest of the medieval world, the Catholic Church was the center of the spiritual community and, at least partially, the secular community as well. It was a time of expanding horizons, a time of greater openness as the Gothic mind let light into the barricaded darkness of the Romanesque. Into each corner of the European world crept individual national characteristics. And in England the changing styles and pervasive humor of the English peasant found its way into art.

Peasant restiveness led to a revolt against Richard II, which came to be known as Wat Tyler's rebellion. The attitudes behind that uprising are vividly expressed in the *Second Shepherd's Play*, whose folk spirit is typically English. Wonderful farce exudes from this part of the Wakefield Cycle, as we follow the journey of the shepherds to the manger, preceded by the invented story of Mak, who steals a sheep and hides it in his wife's bed. Amidst the farce we find social criticism. This one-act play is a masterpiece of English farce, full of comic

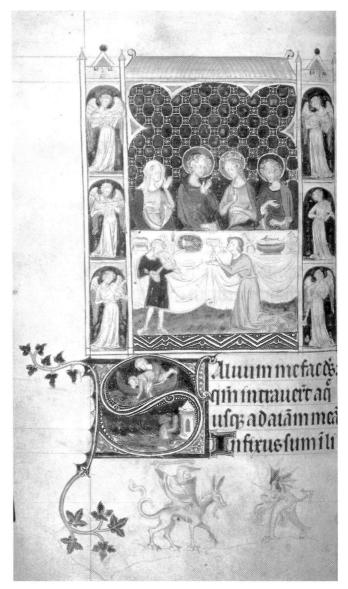

8.25 Page with main illumination, historiated initial text and *drôlerie*, from the Queen Mary Psalter, c. 1310. 7 × 4½ins (17.8 × 11.4cm). British Library, London.

8.24 *Drôlerie*, from the Psalter of Alfonso, 1284. British Library, London.

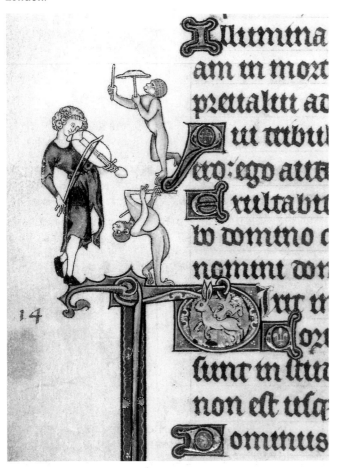

characterizations drawn very realistically. Mak, the sheep stealer, lives by his wits in the hard world and when under pressure simply brazens it out.

In the *Second Shepherd's Play* the New Testament references to the Nativity lead to pure invention until the last episode, in which the shepherds follow the star to Bethlehem, and even here their adoration of the Christ child is in character. The Biblical theme has given rise to variations that belong to folk drama and folk realism. The shepherds are not of Israel but of the English countryside, and Judea is not far from England.

Actually the realism of the play is profoundly medieval—that is, it exists side by side with a sense of wonder and with unquestioning faith. Only when we take note of this fact and also remember that this little drama is part of a Passion Play ... are we prepared to appreciate the remarkable artistry of the work. The grumblings of the shepherds over social injustice and domestic infelicity, Mak's complaints of poverty as well as his misbehavior, bad weather, gruff words—all dissolve into the mystery of the Nativity. Everything points to the necessity of redemption from suffering, sin and error.[6]

Medieval English humor found another outlet in manuscript illumination, in a form called the *droleries*, which began to appear in the margins of books in the thirteenth century. From these illuminations comes a wealth of information on contemporary costume, customs, social behavior, musical instruments, and even a few eccentricities. They show a taste for exaggerated, elongated forms and a love of lavish decorations. These marginalia also found their way into religious books, and we see the above-noted qualities nicely expressed in the *Psalter of Alfonso* (Fig. **8.24**) and the *Queen Mary Psalter* (Fig. **8.25**). In the latter, the figures are placed against architectural framework. The text begins with a historiated initial,

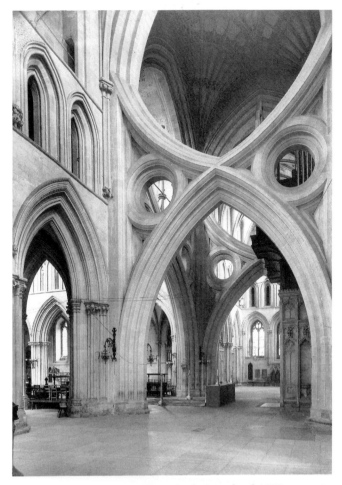

8.27 Arches of crossing, Wells Cathedral, England, 1338.

8.26 Interior towards the east. Exeter Cathedral, England, 1280–1350.

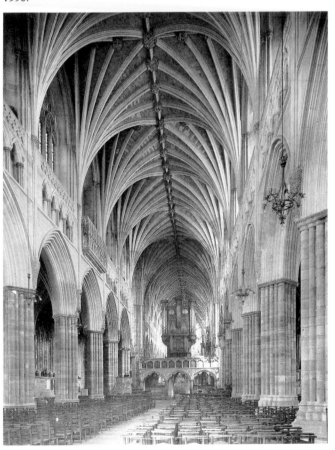

while the lower margin depicts a grotesque subject.

The English Gothic spirit also found expression in church building. The architecture of the period between 1280 and 1375 is called the Decorated style, during which English buildings evolved exuberant forms which anticipated the late Gothic in Germany and France.

Exeter Cathedral (Fig. **8.26**) illustrates an emphasis on the decorative effect of every detail. Moldings multiply, the ribs of the vaulting project boldly, and the number of ribs increases. At Wells Cathedral (Fig. **8.27**) eleven ribs spring from each bay boundary, giving the impression of an overwhelming richness of linear form and a complex interplay of light and shade. At Wells four so-called "strainer arches" appear between the crossing piers. This unusual feature serves a structural purpose and at the same time adds a harmonious and mysterious element to the design.

The crossing tower of Ely Cathedral (Fig. **8.28**) was rebuilt on an octagonal plan in 1323, and contrasts with the rectangular plan of the Romanesque transept and nave and also with the early Gothic choir. An octagonal lantern hangs above, seemingly suspended in mid-air.

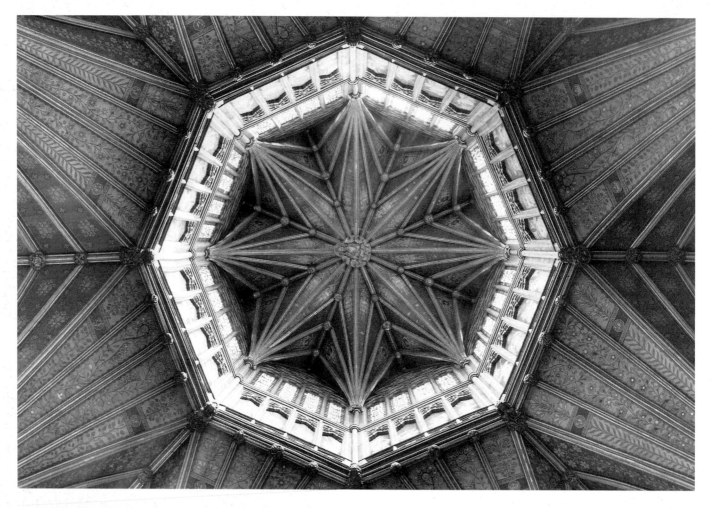

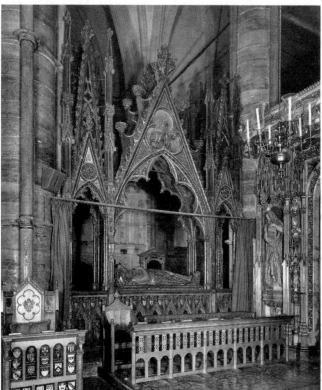

8.28 Interior of crossing-tower, Ely Cathedral, England, 1323–30.

8.29 Tomb of Edmund Crouchback, Earl of Lancaster, c. 1300. Westminster Abbey, London.

8.30 Rose window, south-west transept, Lincoln Cathedral, England, 1325–50.

A similar tendency toward richness and surprise exists in a series of English canopied tombs whose sculpture and architecture complement each other. This particular style originated in France and illustrates the influence of French sculpture in England. Figure **8.29** shows the tomb of Edmund Crouchback, Earl of Lancaster and youngest son of Henry III. This tomb and others like it comprise sculptures placed in rich architectural settings. Every possible surface is covered with lavish decorative sculpture. The sense of motion they impart is overwhelming.

Similarly we find increased complexity in English Gothic style in the window traceries at Lincoln Cathedral (Fig. **8.30**). In some cases window traceries extended to cover adjacent wall surfaces, and did so for strictly decorative reasons. English architects developed this decorative device into a highly original version of late

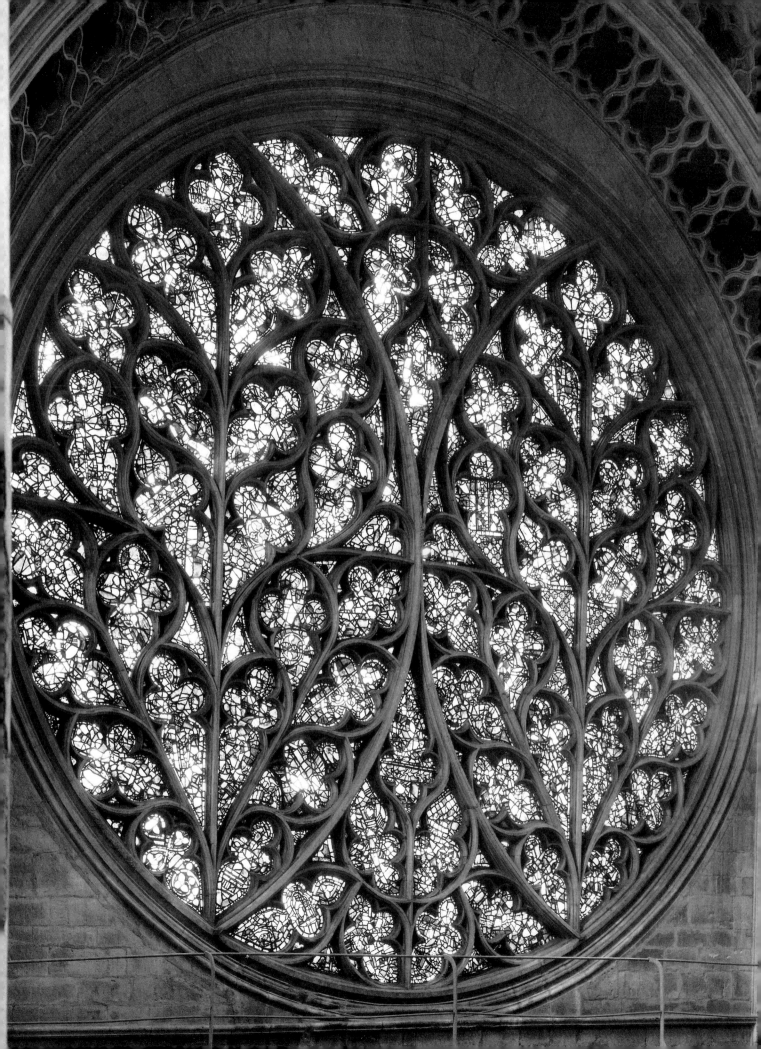

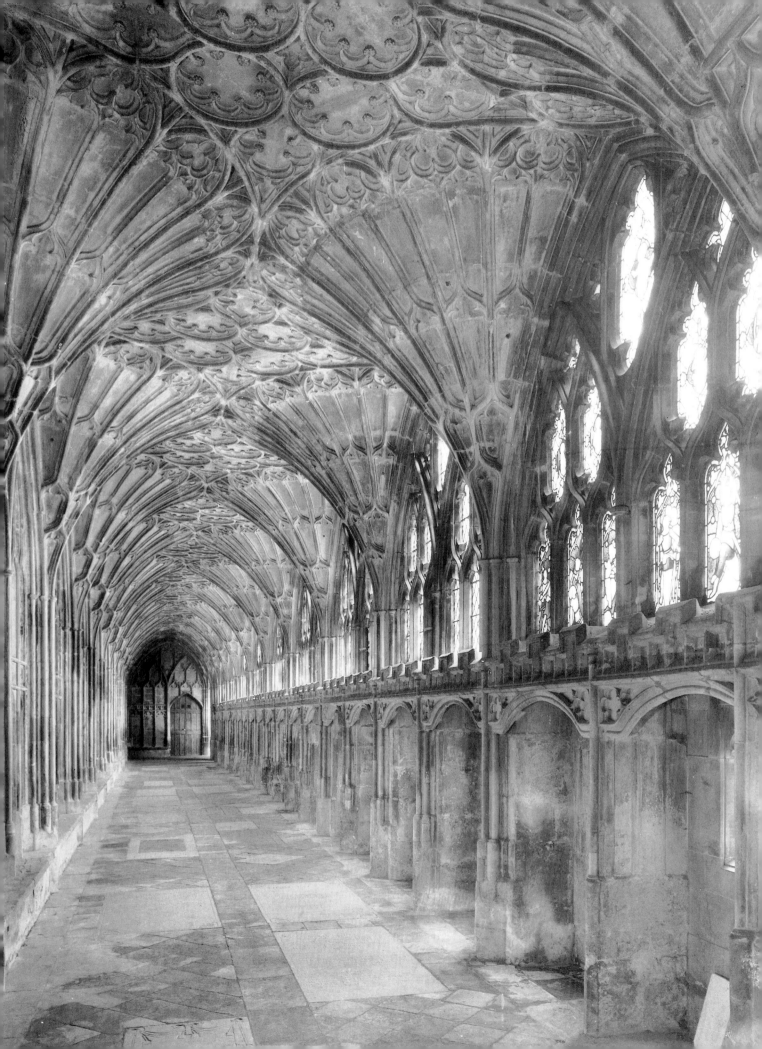

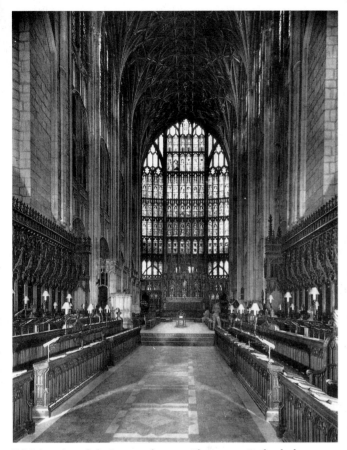

8.31 Interior of choir towards east, Gloucester Cathedral, England, rebuilt c. 1330.

Gothic style known as the Perpendicular Style. It began in London and spread elsewhere. The early Romanesque choir of Gloucester Cathedral (Fig. **8.31**) was reshaped in the 1330s according to the striking new style. The East wall was replaced by a huge window with vertical and horizontal traceries. The solid, Romanesque side walls were covered with thin, delicate traceries. The decorative effect of the new style extended up into the vaulting.

Further examples of the inventiveness of late English Gothic in fan vaulting can be found in the South Cloister of Gloucester Cathedral (Fig. **8.32**). Here the vault becomes more complex, employing cone-like forms. By the fifteenth century the fan vault had been perfected and was used in a number of late Gothic royal buildings.

8.32 South cloister, Gloucester Cathedral, before 1377.

SUGGESTIONS FOR THOUGHT AND DISCUSSION

The struggle for supremacy between Popes and monarchs in the late Middle Ages symbolizes the increasing division between things secular and things spiritual. The struggle was intensified as an increasingly international Church clashed with growing nationalistic claims. Yet a greater sense of stability and order was emerging, and a drastic change in attitude occurred with the transition from the code of feudalism to that of chivalry. The rise of the middle class became a balancing norm between aristocracy and clergy and serf.

Space and light replaced the cloistered barricades of the early Middle Ages, and an age of tolerance and rationalism was fuelled by the ideas of Bernard of Clairvaux, Abelard, and Thomas Aquinas. Revelation and reason were seen as alternative ways of knowing, and the synthesis of Platonic and Aristotelian thought and Christian theology dominated intellectual activity.

At the same time, mysticism, spirituality, and allegory complemented rationality, space, and relaxation in the arts, as those same characteristics permeated late medieval life in general. Sacred numbers dominated design. A new attempt to comprehend the infinite, to bring humanity together with deity in a comfortable relationship found expression in intellectual life, visual and performing art, and above all in the Gothic cathedral—the great symbol of medieval intellect, engineering, and spirituality.

■ What is the difference between cognitive truth and revealed truth?

■ What interrelationships can you find among the arts, chivalry, and the teachings of Bernard of Clairvaux?

■ How do these concepts differ from the concepts and artistic reflections of the early Middle Ages?

■ How does Thomas Aquinas further develop Augustine's neo-Platonic ideas? How do these contrast with Aristotelian philosophy?

■ How do the concepts of space and light illustrate the attitudes and arts of the late Middle Ages?

■ What further concepts relate Gothic arts to the history and philosophy of the times?

■ How did Gothic sculpture further Church and secular aims?

■ How does Gothic architecture reflect the theology and philosophy of the times?

241

CHAPTER NINE

THE EARLY AND HIGH RENAISSANCE

The Renaissance was explicitly seen by its leading figures as a rebirth of our understanding of ourselves as social and creative beings. "Out of the sick Gothic night our eyes are opened to the glorious touch of the sun" was how Rabelais expressed what most of his educated contemporaries felt. At the center of Renaissance concerns were the visual arts, whose new ways of looking at the world soon had their counterparts in the performing arts as well. Florence, the crucible of the Renaissance in Italy, was called the "New Athens", and it was here that there first emerged a redefinition of the fine arts as "liberal arts", in contrast to their lowlier status as crafts in the Middle Ages. Now, accepted among the intellectual disciplines, the arts became an essential part of learning and literary culture. Artists, architects, composers and writers gained confidence and independence from their new status and from the technical mastery they were achieving. For the first time, it seemed possible not merely to emulate the works of the Classical world, but to surpass them.

9.1 Andrea Mantegna, detail of the ceiling of the Camera degli Sposi, 1474. Fresco. Ducal Palace, Mantua, Italy

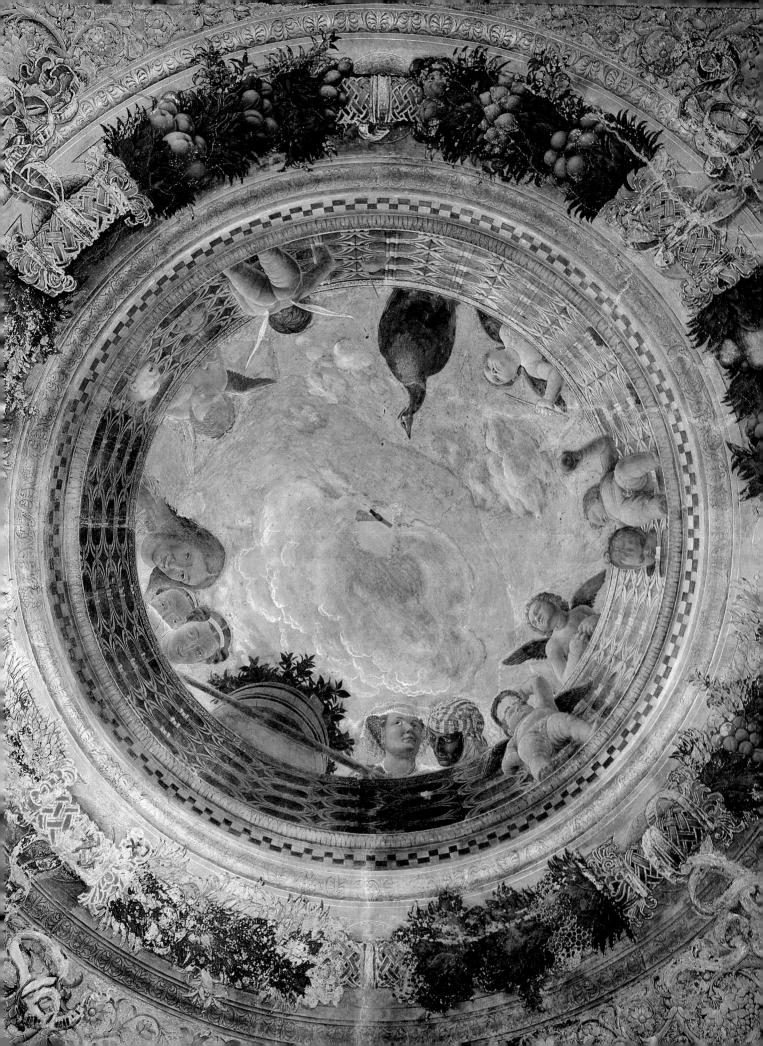

CONTEXTS AND CONCEPTS

The word Renaissance has many meanings. Its most literal translation is rebirth, but, when referring to a specific epoch in history, a rebirth of what? Does Renaissance, like Gothic, imply one artistic style or many similar styles? Is it a historical term or a philosophical one? Or is it all of these? Was it a unified period of consistent philosophical and artistic reflections, or was it merely a natural extension of medieval forces that quickly dissipated into diverse reflections? No precise, or more importantly, no universally accepted answers to these questions exist. The details and definitions surrounding the Renaissance have been debated for centuries. Certainly, *Renaissance* describes, in general, an attitude of self-awareness coined by individuals who had come to see themselves as no longer part of the Middle Ages, but where and how the Renaissance began and what specifically it was is as difficult to answer as is the question of where and how it ended—if it ended at all.

The approach in this work has been to use chronology loosely, as a touchstone, so that we can keep our historical bearings while we turn here and there amid politics, philosophy, and the arts. The period of the Renaissance in this work encompasses roughly three hundred and fifty years, from approximately 1400 to about 1750. During this time diverse styles developed, including a major style called baroque, and a new way of viewing the world emerged, which brought civilization out of the Middle Ages and toward an industrialized, modern world. Within the rough boundaries of this period we will discover vestiges of eras past, such as the Gothic era, which ended in some places before it began in others, a renewed interest in classical antiquity (often misunderstood), new explorations and scientific discovery, dramatic changes in religion and philosophy, and revolutionary developments in artistic styles. Some of these styles we can call very specifically, Renaissance and High Renaissance. In such cases the term has a much more specific meaning than it has in the title of this chapter or in its historical and philosophical applications. We can

call other artistic ventures within these historical parameters by other names such as mannerism or baroque. Some of these labels are traditional, some are debatable, and some do not refer to separate styles, but rather to aberrations or refinements of a style. Whatever the circumstances, the Renaissance as an historical or philosophical concept can be applied, as we have applied it, very broadly to an age whose horizons and enlightenment brought mankind to the threshold of a world view increasingly similar to our own.

Not unlike our own, the age of the Renaissance was one of innovation in technology, science, politics, and economics as well as the arts. It was an age of conflict and inquisitiveness, vitality, and change. There are difficulties in seeking comparisons with our own times, because viewing two or three centuries compressed into an age from the vantage point of history is significantly different from viewing our own time while we are still living in it. How do we define our age? How far back or into the future does it go? I offer these observations here because the Renaissance is often compared with the twentieth century, and also because some protagonists of the Renaissance, as they themselves called it, saw themselves in a particularly favorable light in comparison with those who preceded them in history. Rabelais, a French writer of the Renaissance period, assessed his age thus: "Out of the sick Gothic night our eyes are opened to the glorious touch of the sun."

Our view of the Renaissance, because it encompasses all the arts, must be a very broad and flexible one, and more objective than that of Rabelais. It must accommodate a fluid and three-dimensional mixture of time, place, attitude, and object. The epoch for our purposes is somewhat amorphous in shape, roughly three and a half centuries long. As in the Gothic era, Renaissance ideas and activities spread and receded differently in different places.

Humanism

The roots of Humanism can be traced back to the Gothic world of the fourteenth century to the slowly developing separation of religion and the state. Its specific origins can be found in the writings of Petrarch around 1341 in Italy, from where it spread throughout the Western world. Humanism as a philosophy is not, as some have ventured, a denial of God or faith, but rather an attempt to discover humankind's own earthly fulfilment. The biblical injunction "O Adam, you may have whatever you shall desire", became Humanism's liberating ideal. The medieval view of life as a vale of tears, that had no other purpose than preparing for salvation and the afterlife, was transformed by the Humanists into a view of humankind as men and women playing an important part in this world.

Concern for humankind's diversity and individuality did emerge in the late Middle Ages. Medieval Europe's expanding horizons and the increasing detail and complexity of life provoked new debate about man's responsibility for a stable moral order and for the management of events. Such discussion yielded a philosophy, perfectly consistent with Christian principles, that focused on the dignity and intrinsic value of the individual. Humankind was characterized by goodness and perfectibility and was capable of finding worldly fulfilment and intellectual satisfaction. Humanism developed an increasing distaste for intransigent dogma, and embraced a figurative interpretation of the scriptures and an attitude of tolerance toward all viewpoints.

Petrarch

Petrarch was born in 1304, and is a key figure, along with Dante and Boccaccio, in the transition from medieval to Renaissance thought. Petrarch's writings are very different from those of Dante and are filled with complaints about "the dangers and apprehensions I have suffered. . . . I was born among perils and among perils have grown old—if old I am, and there are not worse trials ahead." Most of the difficulties to which he refers, however, appear to have taken place before his birth or during his early childhood. Contrary to his description, he enjoyed the favor of the great men and women of his day. He writes, almost off-handedly, in his *Letter to Posterity*: "The greatest kings of this age have loved and courted me. They may know why, I certainly do not. With some of them I was on such terms that they seemed in a certain sense my guests rather than I theirs." Petrarch's unhappiness was a part of him. He was unable to reconcile his conflicting aspirations and interests into a workable existence. He desired solitude and quiet, but was continually active. He adored being a celebrity, yet at the same time attacked the veneer of the world around him and longed for the monastic life. On the one hand he would write love sonnets and pursue amorous adventures, while at the same time denouncing the sin of the flesh.

Petrarch's real love was learning, and in his pursuit of learning he earned the title Father of Humanism and made a significant impact on those who followed. Very narrow in his interests, he rejected medieval philosophy and declared that Aristotle "erred in the most weighty questions. [Although Aristotle] has said much of happiness both at the beginning and end of his *Ethics*, I dare assert, let my critics exclaim as they may, that he was so completely ignorant of true happiness that the opinions upon this matter of any pious old woman, or devout fisherman, shepherd, or farmer, would, if not so fine-spun, be more to the point than his." Petrarch also found science wanting as a way toward a "happy life". He had a passion for classical literature and Roman antiquity, but his classicism exhibited a new spirit of enthusiasm. He wrote, "O great father of Roman eloquence! Not I alone but all who deck themselves with flowers of Latin speech render thanks unto you. . . . In a word, it is under your auspices that we have attained such little skill in this art of writing as we may possess."

> Each of Petrarch's letters was, so far as he could make it, a polished Ciceronian essay obviously intended for publication, with all intimate or routine details which would mar the symmetry of the product, or which could not be described in classical language, relegated to a separate sheet, written in Italian or medieval Latin.[1]

Although Petrarch was a classical scholar, his religious thought was thoroughly medieval. He felt guilt at his admiration of things learned from pagan philosophers. He found Dante's connection between the good of this world and that of the next impossible. He rejected the intellectual tradition of the Middle Ages, but clung tenaciously to its moral code. He felt trapped by his love of fame, which he believed stood between him and salvation.

		GENERAL EVENTS	LITERATURE & PHILOSOPHY	VISUAL ART	THEATRE & DANCE	MUSIC	ARCHITECTURE
1300			Petrarch Boccaccio				
1400		Vitruvius' *De Architectura* Invention of the printing press Lorenzo de Medici Diaz Ferdinand and Isabella of Spain	Ficino Boiardo Poliziano Pulci	Flemish style Van Eyck Van der Weyden Fra Angelico Ghiberti Fra Lippo Lippi Gozzoli Della Botticelli Robbia Masaccio Donatello Uccello Mantegna Dürer	Sotties Mummeries Maître Pierre Pathélin Pisani Bruni Guglielmo Ebreo	Dufay Ockeghem Obrecht Isaac	Brunelleschi Alberti
1495 1527	High Renaissance		Sannazaro Erasmus Thomas More Rabelais Spenser Ariosto Bembo Cast Machiavelli Guicciardini	Leonardo da Vinci Michelangelo Bramante Raphael Giorgione Titian	Poliziano Trissino	Des Prez	Bramante Michelangelo Raphael

9.2 Timeline of the Early and High Renaissance.

Ficino

Among the influential Renaissance neo-Platonic Humanists stands Marsilio Ficino (1433–99). Our understanding of the originality of Italian Humanism and of the new direction it gave the arts is enhanced by study of his commentary on Plato's *Symposium*. It demonstrates the interest of the neo-Platonists in interpreting ancient texts, myths, and stories according to an elaborate allegorizing. Central to this tradition is the concept of love, which moves from God to the world and back to God. Intelligible beauty and visible beauty are divine beauty and human beauty, and are symbolized by the Celestial Venus and the Natural Venus, both of whom appear in Renaissance painting, as we shall see.

In Ficino's Second Speech from his commentary on Plato's *Symposium* he proposes that "God is Goodness, Beauty, and Justice, the Beginning, Middle, and End", as He is spoken of in Plato. God is Good when He creates, Beautiful when "He attracts to Himself", and Just when He "finishes according to the desert of each thing". Therefore, for Ficino, Beauty occurs between Goodness and Justice because its purpose is "to attract". Divine Beauty "creates everything in love", and inspires love. Love begins in Beauty and ends in Pleasure. Beauty is the radiance of the Divine Goodness. In Chapter XIII Ficino comments on Plato's assumption that differ-

ent gods bestow different arts upon men; for example, Jupiter bestows the art of ruling and the Muses bestow the art of music. Ficino concludes by asserting that the soul was endowed with the principle of music from the sounds of heaven. "Heavenly harmony is rightly said to be innate in anything whose origin is heavenly." We would therefore love God "because He is most beautiful", imitate Him because "He is good", revere Him because "He is most blessed", "so that by His bounty and mercy to us, He will grant us possession of His own Beauty, Goodness, and Bliss".

The Renaissance viewpoint

Attitudes and events in the age of the Renaissance affected each other in very complex ways. The fact that certain aspects of society—politics, religion, and the arts—are treated in separate paragraphs does not imply that any or all of these may be isolated from each other. All the characteristics found in any age and in its agencies and arts are very closely associated and interacting.

The revived interest in antiquity normally associated with the Renaissance was not the first revival. Charlemagne rekindled interest in antiquity. The German nun, Hrosvitha, had access to Terence and used his works as models for her plays. Aristotle was studied in the late Middle Ages. The fifteenth-century interest in classical antiquity was stronger and more widespread than before. Renaissance men and women found a kindred spirit in the Greeks and Romans. They were, after all, interested in the things of this world. Renaissance scholars found a practical resourcefulness, especially in Rome, which helped in recreating their social order. Of special interest was Roman emphasis on civic responsibility and intellectual competence. Intellectual drive led to a desire to reinterpret ancient writings, which many believed to have been corrupted by being manipulated in the service of Church dogma.

Aristotle provided an appealing balance of active living and sober reflection, and the Periclean Greeks offered an idealized conception of human-kind that could, for example, be expressed in painting and sculpture. Ideals of nobility, intellect, and physical perfection were stressed, and studies of classical art and philosophy led to new conceptions of what constituted beauty and proper proportion. In their pursuit of understanding classical art and architecture, in an age of new scientific inquiry, Renaissance scholars became enamored of measuring things. "True proportions" were believed to have been found when the Roman architect Vitruvius's treatise *De Archtitectura* was discovered in 1414. Scientific curiosity and concern for detail led to a fascination with anatomy. Scientific investigation discovered a system of mechanical perspective. All this measuring and codifying spawned a set of rules of proportion and balance. In the arts unity, form,

9.3 Map of Renaissance Europe.

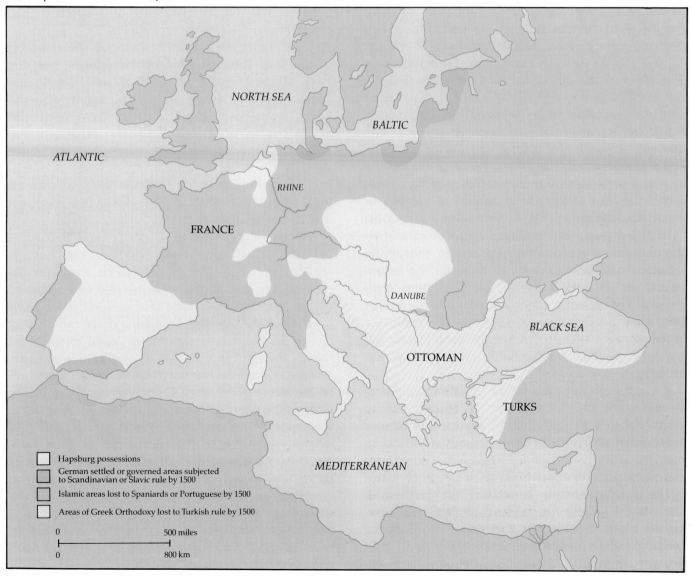

NORTH SEA

BALTIC

ATLANTIC

RHINE

FRANCE

DANUBE

BLACK SEA

OTTOMAN

TURKS

MEDITERRANEAN

☐ Hapsburg possessions
☐ German settled or governed areas subjected to Scandinavian or Slavic rule by 1500
☐ Islamic areas lost to Spaniards or Portuguese by 1500
☐ Areas of Greek Orthodoxy lost to Turkish rule by 1500

0 — 500 miles
0 — 800 km

and perfect proportion were codified as a set of laws.

Capitalism

In the arts as in all facets of society, the Renaissance placed new emphasis on the individual and on individual achievement. The rising middle classes with their new-found wealth and power were not long in discovering that, salvation or not, life was a great deal more comfortable if one had a good house, good clothes, good food, and reasonable control over one's own existence. Such control and satisfaction was seen to be directly related to material wealth, and so amid all other aspects of Renaissance life, and perfectly in tune with them, a new economic system of capitalism or mercantilism developed. To a large degree capitalism pursued wealth and power as its goals. In its broadest and perhaps lowest form, capitalism is a corporate pursuit with an insatiable goal. The corporation is an extension of the individual, but the corporation is not constrained by individual need or limitations concerning consumption of wealth. A corporation can therefore never be satisfied, regardless of the amount of wealth it attains.

Capitalism was in its early stages during the Renaissance and was not fully developed, but it was based on the fundamental tenets of pursuit of wealth and power as ends in themselves. In contrast to medieval agrarian feudalism, capitalism offered the individual reasonable freedom to pursue increased material standards of living to the extent of his or her wits and abilities. Capitalism challenged Renaissance men and women to pursue their own individual goals. There was an explosion of economic activity in the trading of goods and services previously unavailable or previously unthought of.

Capitalism depends on the creation of markets as well as the supply of markets, in contrast with the guild system, which produced only what was necessary. Capitalism, therefore, encouraged an increasing diversification of occupations and social situations, relying principally upon urban settlements for sustenance and essentially separating the home and workplace. Expansion of trade, capitalism, and commerce in the fourteenth and fifteenth centuries brought high prosperity to four locations in particular—northern Italy, southern Germany, what we now call the Low Countries (Belgium and Holland), and England.

Discovery

An additional ingredient in the already complex Renaissance social order came from a thirst for new discovery—scientific, technological, and geographic. Great visions illuminated even the possibilities for human flight in Leonardo da Vinci's remarkable designs for complex flying machines. Renaissance scholars sought the answers to all questions and began to develop empirical approaches to their inquiry in preference to the tools of faith and philosophy. As a result, conflicts between forward-looking science and backward-looking traditions and values were common in this era. Spirited and honest inquiry often raised more questions than it could answer, and these questions and conflicts had unsettling and destabilizing effects.

Technology significantly changed the character of this era. The invention of the printing press in 1445 allowed Humanist writings and Greek and Roman literature to be rapidly and widely disseminated throughout Europe. Availability of textbooks at reasonable prices revolutionized education and influenced the rise of *scholas* (similar to our public schools), thereby bringing a higher level of education now required for full participation in an increasingly complex world to a wider section of society, not just to the aristocracy.

Technology, science, curiosity, and individual self-confidence took humankind to the furthest reaches of the planet. Renaissance explorers increased the geographical knowledge of the age to global proportions. In 1486 Diaz ended the Mediterranean world's isolation by sailing down the coast of Africa. Six years later Columbus sailed to the West Indies. In 1499 Vasco da Gama completed a two-year voyage around the horn of Africa to India. At the turn of the sixteenth century, Balboa reached the Pacific Ocean. The full implications of the fact that the world was round crashed upon Renaissance men and women in 1522 with the completion of Magellan's three-year voyage around the world. It is easy for us to minimize the impact of these events on the general view of reality held at the time, but the discovery of an immense globate world in a heliocentric universe later proved catastrophic for many whose views of humanity and of God were compatible only with an earth-centered universe.

Political developments

Many of the circumstances and events as well as the arts of this period owed their shape to the political conditions of Europe's various regions. In the late Gothic period the Church had begun to lose its total authority over all social circumstances. Men and women were willing to render unto God that which they considered His, but they also wished to render something unto Caesar. The secular world began to drift toward the notion of national identity, although identities varied greatly. The feudal system retained its hold in Germany, while in Flanders we find a nascent democracy. France, England, and Spain moved toward governance by strong monarchies, for example, that of Ferdinand and Isabella of Spain (1474–1516). In Italy, whose geography is not unlike that of Greece, the independent city-states had retained their autonomy, and the seaports particularly had continued to grow even during the Middle Ages. Great rivalries, warfare, and intrigue existed, but the expanded commerce of the early Renaissance reinforced the dominant positions of these cities. Capitalism brought individual families to great wealth and power in most of the Italian port cities. The most important of these families, especially in the arts, was the Medici family under Lorenzo (the Magnificent) de' Medici (1449–92).

The arts suffered shifting fortunes during the years at the end of the fifteenth century in Italy. In Florence, which dominated Italian Renaissance culture during the fifteenth century, the tyrannical Medici family were also great patrons of the arts. But by 1498 Italy and Florence had seen the expulsion of the Medicis and the death of the reformer Savonarola. For a very brief time thereafter (but what a time!) the papacy again became a centralizing authority, champion of Italian nationalism, and great patron of the arts. Artists from diverse locations moved to Rome where schools of artists were established and artistic production proliferated, and spread throughout Europe. The High Renaissance was at hand. However, the merging of classicism and Humanism with Catholicism and inquiry resulted in events which unsettled the Western world for the last seventy years of the sixteenth century, and affected it irrevocably for all time.

The Reformation

Amidst the explosive cacophony of the Renaissance period came perhaps the most shattering and lasting blow the Christian Church has ever experienced, the Reformation. We can summarize by indicating that, like all other major turns of events, the Reformation was assisted by the peculiar circumstances of the times. We also must understand that it began not as an attempt to start a new branch of Christianity, but, rather, as a sincere attempt to reform what were perceived to be serious problems in the Roman Catholic Church at the time. The Roman Church had always been dominated by Italy, and, given the diverse and unique political climate of the Italian peninsula, the Catholic Church had responded to newly emerging Renaissance ideas with an increasing worldliness and political intrigue that was of great concern to many, especially in Germany. The selling of indulgences was widespread, and this practice of selling forgiveness was particularly repugnant to a monk named Martin Luther. In 1517 Luther summarized his contentions in his '95 Theses', which he tacked to the chapel door at Wittenberg, Germany. The resulting furor caused by the Church's response to Luther turned into a battle, public and royal, which eventually led to a complete split within the Roman Church and the founding of Lutheranism.

Luther's 95 Theses carried the subtitle of "Disputation on the Power and Efficacy of Indulgences". Their tone and intent can be grasped from the introduction: "Out of love and zeal for truth and the desire to bring it to light, the following theses will be publicly discussed at Wittenberg under the chairmanship of the reverend father Martin Luther, Master of Arts and Sacred Theology and regularly appointed Lecturer on these subjects at that place. He requests that those who cannot be present to debate orally with us will do so by letter. In the name of our Lord Jesus Christ. Amen." The Theses are a logical series of arguments relating to the primacy of repentance in Christian faith and how the Church deals with and should deal with that issue. Theology and canon law are scrutinized carefully, and where necessary Luther spared no words, as in Thesis 28: "It is certain that when money clinks in the money chest, greed and avarice can be increased", and in Thesis 33: "Men must especially be on their guard against those who say that the pope's pardons are that inestimable gift by which man is reconciled to him."

Clearly the Reformation at this stage was a political power struggle as well as a theological schism. Many people found Church dogma indefensible, especially in the light of widely disseminated opposing views. Popular resentment of central ecclesiastical authority was widespread, and even in areas still essentially feudal, there was enough political stability to resist domination by Rome. Later during the Reformation further breaks with Catholicism occurred. John Calvin's *Institutes of the Christian Religion* affected mid-sixteenth century Switzerland. Calvin's austere religious tenets were later carried to Scotland by John Knox. Finally a break with Rome occurred in England under Henry VIII. The political rather than religious nature of Henry VIII's battles with Pope Clement VII is well known and resulted in the confiscation of all Roman Church property in the Act of Dissolution. Bloody conflicts between Protestants and Catholics and Protestants and Protestants laid the groundwork for conditions which drove a certain set of emigrants to the shores of North America less than a century later.

Events in Germany and England reflected some of the Reformation's underlying economic, as well as spiritual and political, motivations. Throughout Roman Catholic Europe the huge body of clergy, through the sale of indulgences among other things, amassed considerable tax-free wealth. Secular governments and a growing number of their citizenry chafed under this economic burden. The injury was compounded by the fact that the civil sector, in return, was taxed by the Church.

The Reformation can be seen as a force that drastically affected artistic reflection from the second quarter of the sixteenth century onward. It marks a watershed of sorts, although a preoccupation with the relationship of reformation in the Church and emotional disarray in the visual arts overlooks the fact that secular and religious peace and stability were not necessarily the watchwords of life, especially in Italy, even in the fifteenth century. Nevertheless, the coincidence of the Reformation with the end of a significant style in the visual arts and the beginnings of Renaissance reflection in some of the performing arts, makes it a useful marker between this chapter and the next.

Literature

Early Renaissance literature concentrated largely on form and style. Early Italian writers such as Boccaccio and Petrarch in the fourteenth century began to develop the works of ancient writers in a new way. They borrowed ideas, stories, figures of speech, and general style, and tried to recreate ancient poetic and prose styles. Renaissance writers clearly achieved a more penetrating investigation and analysis of ancient literature and art than had their medieval predecessors. The result was an ordered plan, integrated structure, symmetry, and lofty style which fourteenth-century writers believed created a classical type of beauty. Various canons were laid down, for example, that the epic must begin in the middle of its plot, must contain supernatural elements, and must end with a victorious hero. The Italians were highly influential in Spanish, French, English, and German literature.

By the fifteenth century the philosophy of Humanism had spread throughout Italy with its goal of making life a work of art. From their influence came treatises on the perfect prince, the perfect family, the perfect gentleman and lady, the perfect poem, and the perfect work of art. Numerous Latin poems, histories, biographies, and orations were written and circulated, many in printed form. One result of Humanist Latin literature was the elevation of vernacular style. Vernacular literature such as that of Sannazaro (d. 1530) took the classical pastoral form. Boccaccio's romantic epic was improved upon by Boiardo (d. 1494), who is best known for his long work *Roland in Love*. Here the main characters have a variety of adventures in love and war. Marvelous gardens, islands of delight, strange lands, battles with giants and dragons, all appear.

The traditions of Boccaccio and Petrarch further influenced Poliziano of Florence (d. 1494) and his friend and patron Lorenzo de' Medici (d. 1492), as well as Pulci (d. 1484), who was much admired by later writers such as Byron. The Renaissance style combined seriousness, frivolity, irony, pathos, and "a love of dwelling in a beautiful dream world lighted by the golden sun of classical antiquity".

As was the case in the Early Renaissance, the first great achievements of the High Renaissance in verse and prose came from Italy. Great writers from other countries included Erasmus, the greatest Renaissance scholar of northern Europe and author of provocatively argumentative works like *In Praise of Folly* (1509); and Thomas More, English statesman, Humanist scholar and Roman Catholic saint and martyr, who created in his *Utopia* (1516) a vision of a perfect human society. The French writer Rabelais took a more earthy and rumbustious view of life in his comic masterpiece *Gargantua and Pantagruel* (1534). In all cases, High Renaissance literature nevertheless saw a growing attention to classical

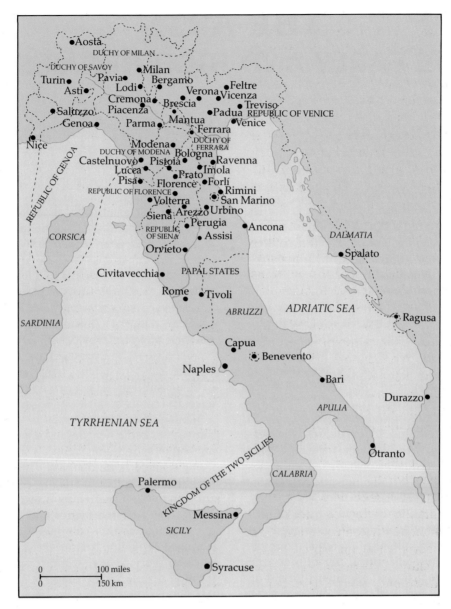

9.4 Map of Italy.

models. Classical comedy and tragedy, the ode and the epic were all revived.

The models used by Renaissance writers were mostly Latin rather than Greek.

Italian literary genius found its exemplar in Ariosto (d. 1533). In a series of *Satires*, modeled on those of Horace, Ariosto gives a revealing picture of himself, of his love of letters, and of the tedium of serving various members of the Estes family. The spirit of Ariosto here is close to that of Horace; his smoothness of style and its grace, its concise elegance, understatement, and its studied and sophisticated simplicity are all in the manner of Horace. Like Horace too he tries to make a friend of his reader, and has in what he says a charming note of intimacy.[2]

Ariosto's greatest work was his romantic epic, *Orlando furioso* (1515–1533), written in a verse form similar to that of Boccaccio. We are taken to fairy worlds filled with magic weapons, winged horses that fly through the clouds, men transformed into trees, and castles that disappear. He portrays a world of beauty, which allows the reader to escape the harsh realities of the time.

A fuller examination of the literature of the High Renaissance would include figures such as Cardinal Bembo (d. 1547), the great literary arbiter of the age, Castiglione (d. 1529), the first outstanding prose master of the High Renaissance, Machiavelli and Guicciardini (d. 1540).

THE ARTS
OF THE EARLY AND HIGH RENAISSANCE

TWO-DIMENSIONAL ART

Flanders

In the north of Europe lies a small area known as the Low Countries. In the fifteenth century the Low Countries included Flanders, and amid a dominant atmosphere of late Gothic architecture and sculpture, Flemish painters and musicians forged new approaches, which departed significantly from the international Gothic style, formed a link with their contemporaries in northern Italy, and influenced European painters and musicians for the next century. Many scholars believe that early fifteenth-century Flemish arts remained totally a part of the late Gothic style, but clearly the painters of this locale had significant contact with Italy, the heart of the Early Renaissance in art. Clearly, also, the Italians of this new Renaissance spirit admired Flemish painting.

Flemish painting of this period was revolutionary. In Gothic art painters attempted to create realistic sensations of deep space. For all their ingenuity, they essentially retained a two-dimensional feeling and a lack of continuity or rationality in their perspective. Gothic work contains a certain childish or fairy-tale quality. Giotto (Fig. **8.7**) attempted to bring us a three-dimensional world, but we are not for a moment convinced that his depiction is realistic. Flemish painters, however, achieved pictorial reality and rational perspective, and the sense of completeness and continuity found in Flemish works marked a new and clearly different style. Line, form, and color were painstakingly controlled to compose subtle, varied, three-dimensional, clear, and logically unified statements.

Part of the drastic change in Flemish painting stemmed from a new development in painting media—oil paint. Oil's versatile characteristics gave the Flemish painter new opportunities to vary surface texture and brilliance, and to create far greater subtlety of form. Oils allowed blending of color areas, because oil could be worked wet on the canvas, whereas egg tempera, the previous painting medium, dried almost immediately upon application. Gradual transitions between color areas made possible by oil paints allowed fifteenth-century Flemish painters to enhance use of atmospheric perspective, that is, the increasingly hazy appearance of objects furthest from the viewer, and thereby to control this most effective indicator of deep space. Blending between color areas also enhanced *chiaroscuro* (light and shade) by which all objects assume three-dimension-

ality—without highlight and shadow perceptible plasticity is lost. Early fifteenth-century Flemish painters used sophisticated exploration of light and shade not only to heighten three-dimensionality of form, but also to achieve rational unity in their compositions. Pictures which do not exhibit consistent light sources or which omit natural shadows on surrounding objects create very strange effects, even if their individual form depiction is high in verisimilitude. This new rational unity and realistic three-dimensionality separated fifteenth-century Flemish style from the Gothic style and tied it to the Renaissance.

Jan van Eyck's *Arnolfini Marriage* or *Giovanni Arnolfini and his Bride* (Fig. **9.7**) illustrates the qualities of Flemish painting, and also provides a marvelous range of aesthetic responses. Van Eyck used the full range of values from darkest darks to lightest lights and blended them with extreme subtlety to achieve a soft and realistic appearance. His colors are rich, varied, and predominantly warm in feeling. The only exception to the reds and red-brown derivatives is the rich green gown of the bride. The highly atmospheric bedroom creates a sense of great depth. All forms achieve three-dimensionality through subtle color blending and softened shadow edges. Natural highlights and shadows emanate from obvious sources, such as the window, and tie the figures and objects together. However, as real as this painting appears, it is a selective portrayal of reality. It is an artist's vision of an event, a portrayal very clearly staged for pictorial purposes. The location of objects, the drape of fabric, and the nature of the figures themselves are beyond reality. Van Eyck's work achieves what much art does, that is, it gives the surface appearance of reality while revealing a deeper essence of the scene or the subject matter—in this case, man, woman, marriage, and their place within Christian philosophy.

The case has been made many times that this work contains an elaborate symbolism commenting on marriage and the marriage ceremony. Two people could execute a perfectly valid marriage without a priest. The painting depicts a young couple taking a marriage vow in the sanctity of the bridal chamber and the painting is thus both a portrait and a marriage certificate. The artist has signed the painting in legal script above the mirror "Johannes de Eyck fuit hic. 1434". (Jan van Eyck was here. 1434). In fact, we can see the artist and another witness reflected in the mirror. The burning candle is part of the oath-taking ceremony and symbolizes marriage, the dog represents marital faith, the statue of St. Margaret invokes the patron saint of childbirth. There is considerable

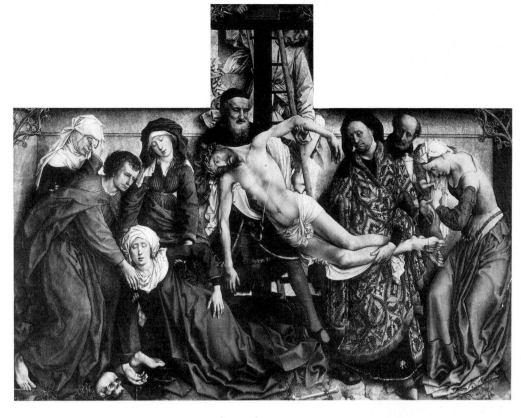

9.5 Rogier van der Weyden, *The Descent From The Cross*, c.1435. Oil on panel, 7ft 2⅜ins × 8ft ⅞ins (220 × 246cm). The Prado, Madrid.

9.6 Albrecht Dürer, *The Four Horsemen of the Apocalypse*, c.1497–8. Woodcut, 15.4 × 11ins (39.2 × 27.9cm). Museum of Fine Arts, Boston (Bequest of Francis Bullard).

debate about the accuracy or appropriateness of all these symbols and on whether the bride is pregnant or not. Most experts agree she is not—clothing design and posture of the period emphasized the stomach.

Every work of art tells a story to which we can respond at many levels. The more we know, the more we can discover of the messages and the human beings within the work. A full response requires investing a bit of effort.

Also illustrative of the same style, although slightly different from that of van Eyck, Rogier van der Weyden's deposition scene, the *Descent from the Cross* (Fig. **9.5**) has softly shaded forms, rational three-dimensionality, and surface realism quite unlike Gothic style. Carefully controlled line and form create soft, undulating S-curves around the borders and diagonally through the center. Colors explore the full range of the spectrum from reds and golds to blues and greens and the full extent of the value scale from dark to light. Composition, balance, and unity are extremely subtle. The figures are nearly statuary in depiction. Drapery folds are shallow and exhibit nervous, broken linearity.

The striking factor in this painting is its individualized human emotion. Dramatic power makes this work intensely appealing. Individualized character responses mark the people of this painting as they react to an emotion-charged situation. These figures are not types—they are individuals and so fully and realistically portrayed that we might expect to encounter them on the street. Van der Weyden's linear style was particularly influential

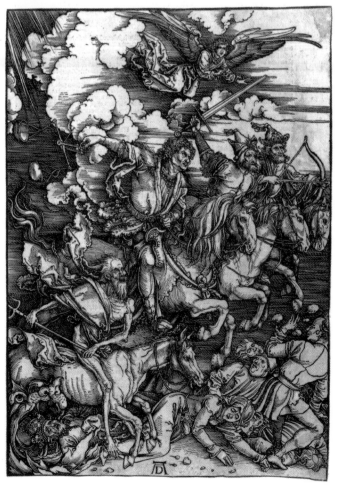

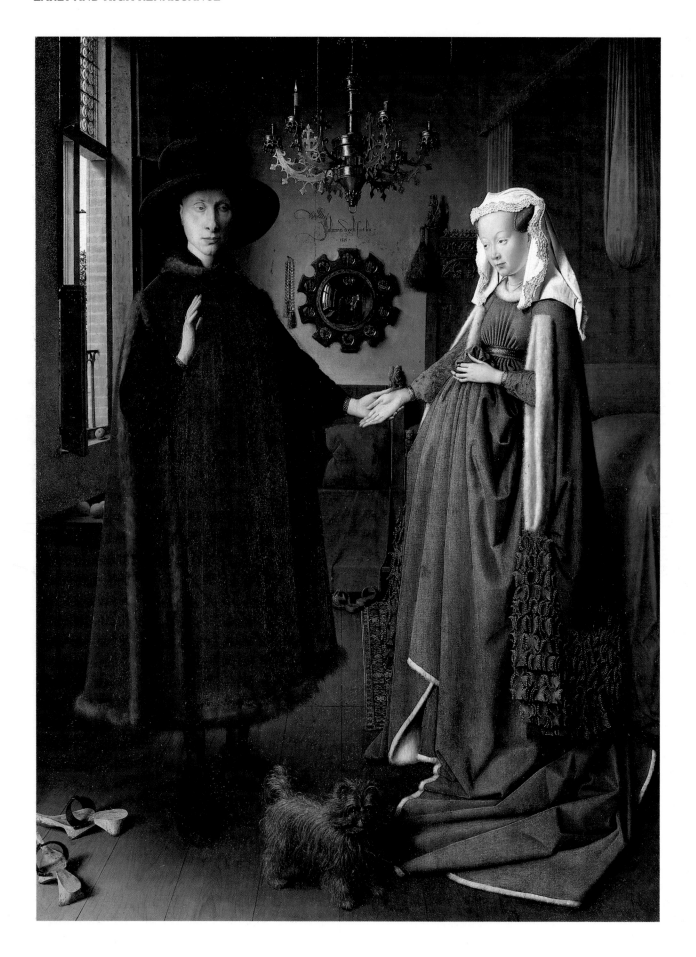

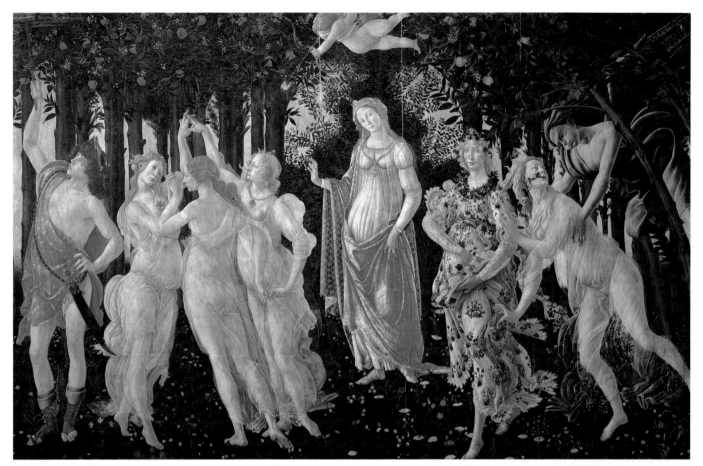

9.7 Jan van Eyck, *The Arnolfini Marriage* (*Giovanni Arnolfini and His Bride*), 1434. Oil on panel, 33 × 22½ins (83.8 × 57.1cm). The National Gallery, London

9.8 Sandro Botticelli, *La Primavera* (*Spring*), c.1478. Tempera on panel, 6ft 8ins × 10ft 4ins (2.03 × 3.15m). Galleria degli Uffizi, Florence.

in the masterly woodcuts and engravings of Albrecht Dürer. In contrast to the works of van der Weyden and van Eyck, Dürer's works reflect the tensions present in northern Europe at the end of the fifteenth and in the early sixteenth centuries. The emotion of the *Four Horsemen of the Apocalypse* (Fig. **9.6**), for example, and its medieval preoccupation with superstition, famine, fear, and death typify German art of this period.

Florence

It was in Italy, and more precisely in Florence, that the Renaissance, whatever connotations we attach to it, found its early spark and heart in about 1400. Florence was a wealthy port and commercial center and, like Athens, leapt into a golden age on a soaring spirit of victory as the city successfully resisted the attempts of the Duke of Milan to subjugate it. Under the patronage of the Medici family the outpouring of art made Florence the focal point of the early Italian Renaissance.

Two general trends in Florentine painting can be identified in this period. The first, more or less a

continuation of medieval tendencies, was lyrical and decorative. Its adherents were the painters Fra Angelico, Fra Lippo Lippi, Benozzo Gozzoli and Sandro Botticelli. This tradition is probably best expressed in the paintings of Botticelli. The linear quality of *Spring* (Fig. **9.8**) suggests an artist apparently unconcerned with deep space or subtle plasticity in light and shade. Rather, forms emerge through outline. The composition moves gently from side to side through a lyrical combination of undulating, curved lines, with focal areas in each grouping. Mercury, the Three Graces, Venus, Flora, Spring, and Zephyrus—each part of this human, mythical (notice the non-Christian subject matter) composition carries its own emotions, from contemplation to sadness to happiness. Beyond the immediate qualities there is deeper symbolism and emotion relating not only to the mythological figures, but also to the Medici family, the patron rulers of Florence.

Botticelli's figures further exhibit anatomical simplicity quite unlike the detailed muscular concerns we will find elsewhere in Florentine Renaissance painting. Although figures are rendered three-dimensionally and shaded subtly, they appear almost like balloons, floating

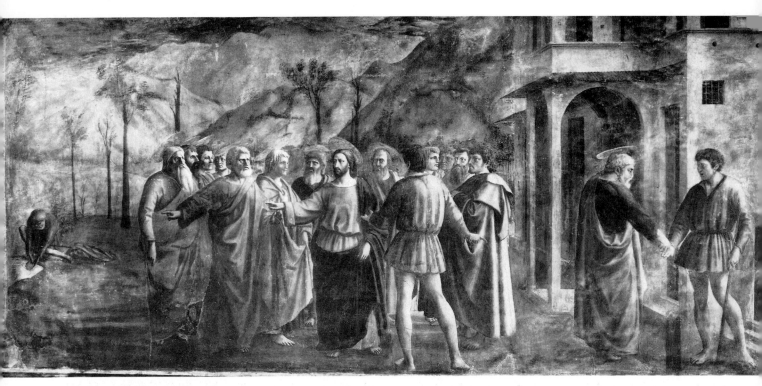

9.9 Masaccio, *The Tribute Money*, c.1427. Fresco. S Maria del Carmine, Florence.

9.10 Andrea Mantegna, *St James Led to Execution*, c.1455. Fresco. Ovetari Chapel, Church of the Eremitani, Padua, Italy (destroyed 1944).

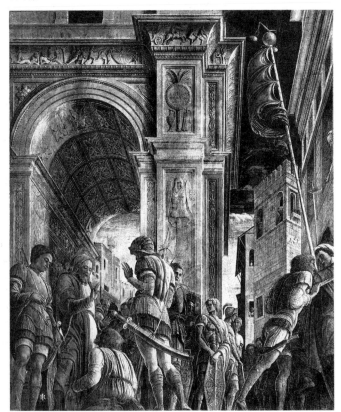

in space, without anatomical definition.

The second tradition in Florentine and other Italian painting of this period is much more clearly in the Renaissance style. Among the works of Masaccio, Uccello, Castagno, Veneziano and Baldovinetti exists a unifying monumentality, that is, paintings which are, or seem to be, larger than lifesize. When we compare Botticelli's *Spring* with the work of Masaccio (Fig. **9.9**) and realize that both were fifteenth-century Florentines, the differences between these two traditions strike us clearly. The *Tribute Money* illustrates concern for deep space and plasticity. Masaccio's emphasis on *chiaroscuro* creates dramatic contrasts, gives his figures solidity, and unifies the composition. He uses both atmospheric and linear perspective, and the building at the right exemplifies a new and significant scientific mechanization of single and multiple vanishing-point perspective (an invention that allowed the artist to plot foreshortened objects with photographic accuracy, thus enhancing deep, spatial realism). Masaccio's figures are warm, strong, detailed and very human. At the same time his composition carefully subordinates parts to the whole. Unlike many excessively detailed paintings this work does not lose us in detail or cause us to be overly aware of detail to the detriment of the whole.

Perhaps the most breathtaking example of early Italian Renaissance monumentalism is Mantegna's *St. James Led to Execution* (Fig. **9.10**). Here the forces of scale, *chiaroscuro*, perspective, detail, compositional unity and drama are overpowering. Much of the effect of this work is created by the artist's placement of the horizon line (eye level of the viewer) below the lower border of the painting.

The High Renaissance

As important and revolutionary as the fifteenth century was, both in Flanders and Italy, the high point of the Renaissance came in the early sixteenth century, as papal authority was re-established and artists were called to Rome. Its importance as the apex of Renaissance style has led scholars to call this period in the visual arts the High Renaissance. (Let us recall that our uses of the term Renaissance are flexible in this chapter. At this point we are dealing with a style in the visual arts, not with an historical era.) Painters of the High Renaissance included the titans and giants (terms very appropriate to their art as we shall see) of Western visual art: Leonardo da Vinci, Michelangelo, Raphael, Giorgione, and Titian.

Implicit in Humanistic exploration of the individual's earthly potential and fulfillment is a concept of particular importance to our overview of visual art in the High Renaissance style—the concept of genius. In Italy between 1495 and 1520 everything in visual art was subordinate to the overwhelming genius of two men, Leonardo da Vinci and Michelangelo Buonarroti. The great genius and impact of these two giants have led many to debate whether the High Renaissance of visual art was a culmination of earlier Renaissance style or a new departure.

By 1500 the courts of the Italian princes had become important sources of patronage and cultural activity now centered around them. Machiavelli found these centers and their societal leaders soft and effeminate. He accused them of deliberately living in an unreal world. In pursuit of their world of beauty, the Italian courtiers needed artists, writers, and musicians. The arts of the Early Renaissance now seemed vulgar and naïve. A more aristocratic, elegant, dignified, and exalted art was demanded, and this accounts, at least in part, for the new style found in the works of Ariosto, Castiglione, Raphael and Titian, for example. The new style is lofty. The wealth of the popes and their desire to rebuild and transform Rome on a grand scale also contributed significantly to the shift in style and the emergence of Rome as the center of High Renaissance patronage. Music came of age as a major art, finding a great patron in Pope Leo X. There was a revival of ancient Roman sculptural and architectural style. Important discoveries of ancient sculptures such as the *Apollo Belvedere* and the *Laocoön* were made. Because the artists of the High Renaissance had such a rich immediate inheritance of art and literature from the Early Renaissance period, and felt they had developed even further, they considered themselves on an equal footing with the artists of the antique period. Their approach to the antique in arts and letters was therefore different from that of their Early Renaissance predecessors.

High Renaissance painting sought a universal ideal achieved through impressive art, as opposed to overemphasis on tricks of perspective or on anatomy. Figures became types again, rather than naturalistic individuals—God-like human beings in the Greek classical tradition. Artists and writers of the High Renaissance sought to capture the essence of classical art and literature without resorting to copying, which would have captured only the externals. They tried to emulate, and not to imitate. As a result, High Renaissance art idealizes all forms and delights in composition. Its impact is one of stability without being static, variety without confusion, and clear definition without dullness. High Renaissance artists carefully observed how the ancients borrowed motifs from nature, and they then set out to develop a system of mathematically defined proportion and compositional beauty emanating from a total harmonization of parts. Such faith in harmonious proportions reflected a belief among artists, writers, and composers that a harmonious universe and the world of nature also possessed perfect order.

This carefully controlled human-centered attitude contained a certain artificiality and emotionalism reflective of the conflicts of the times. In addition, High Renaissance style departed from previous styles in its meticulously arranged composition, based almost exclusively on geometric devices. Composition was closed—line, color, and form or shape kept the viewer's eye continually redirected into the work, as opposed to leading the eye off the canvas. Organization centered upon a geometric shape, such as a central triangle or an oval.

Leonardo da Vinci

The work of Leonardo da Vinci (1452–1519) contains an ethereal quality which he achieved by blending light and shadow (called *sfumato*). His figures hover between reality and illusion as one form disappears into another, and only highlighted portions emerge. It is difficult to say which of Leonardo's paintings is the most popular or admired, but certainly the *Last Supper* (Fig. **9.11**) ranks among them. It captures the drama of Christ's prophecy, "One of you shall betray me", at the moment that the apostles are responding with disbelief. Leonardo's choice of medium proved most unfortunate because his own mixtures of oil, varnish, and pigments, as opposed to fresco, were not suited to the damp wall. The painting began to flake and was reported to be perishing as early as 1517. Since then it has been clouded by retouching, defaced by a door cut through the wall at Christ's feet, and bombed during World War II. Miraculously, it survives.

In the *Last Supper* human figures and not architecture are the focus. The figure of Christ dominates the center of the painting, forming a stable, yet active, central triangle. All line, actual and implied, leads outward from the face of Christ, pauses at various subordinate focal areas, is directed back into the work, and returns to the central figure. Various postures, hand positions, and groupings of

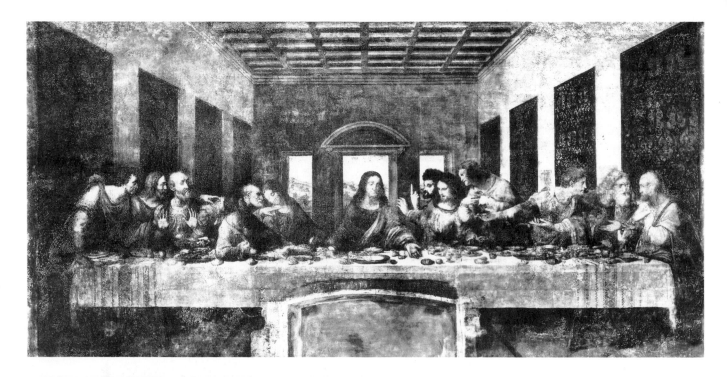

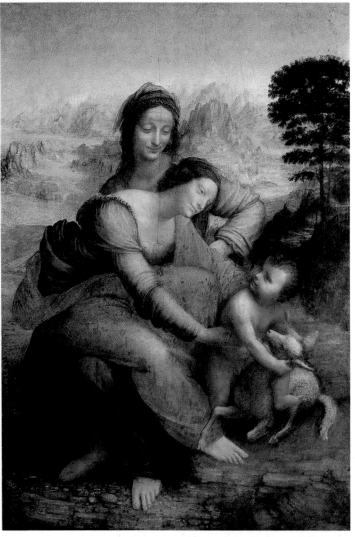

9.11 Leonardo da Vinci, *The Last Supper*, c.1495–8. Mural painting. S Maria della Grazie, Milan.

9.12 Leonardo da Vinci, *Virgin and Child with St Anne*, 1508–10. Panel painting, 5ft 6⅛ins × 4ft 3¼ins (168 × 130cm). Louvre, Paris.

9.13 Leonardo da Vinci, *The Virgin of the Rocks*, c.1485. Oil on panel, 6ft 3ins × 3ft 7ins (191 × 109cm). Louvre, Paris.

the disciples direct the eye from point to point. Figures emerge from the gloomy architectural background in strongly accented relief; nothing anchors these objects to the floor of the room of which they are a part. Although this is not the greatest example of Leonardo's use of *sfumato*, the technique is there. This typically geometric composition is amazing in that so much drama can be expressed within such a mathematical format. Yet, despite the drama, the mood in this work and others is calm, belying the conflict and turbulence of Leonardo's own life, personality, and times.

The *Madonna of the Rocks* (Fig. **9.13**) is Leonardo's interpretation of the doctrine of the Immaculate Conception, which proposed that Mary was freed from Original Sin by the Immaculate Conception in order to be a worthy vessel for the Incarnation of Christ. Mary sits in the midst of a dark world and shines forth from it. She protects the infant Christ, who blesses John the Baptist, to whom the angel points. The actions of gesture and eye direction create movement around the perimeter of a single, central triangle outlined in highlight. The portrayal of rocks, foliage and cloth displays meticulous attention to detail.

A pyramidal, compositional form is also the basis of Leonardo's *Madonna and Saint Anne* (Fig. **9.12**). St. Anne

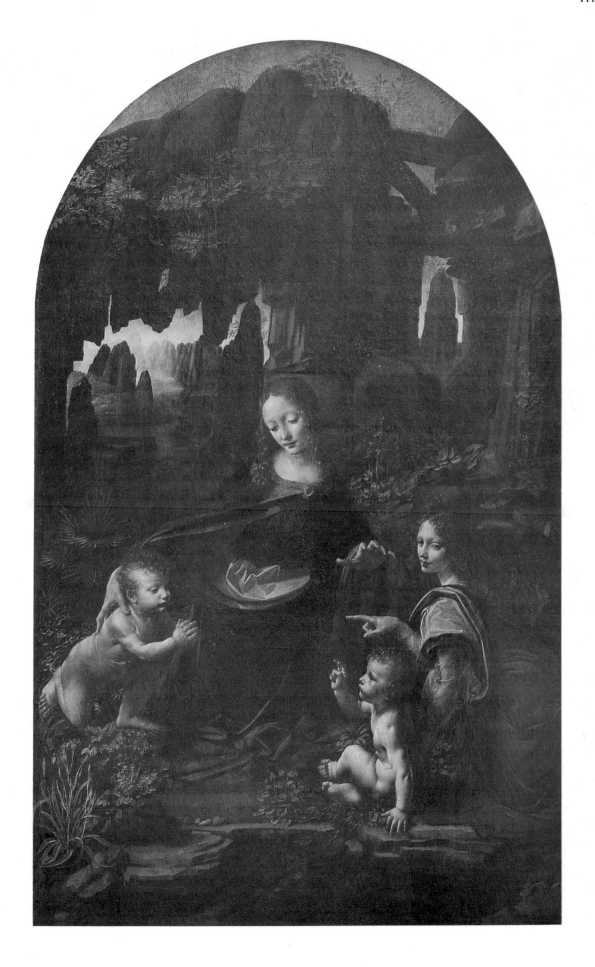

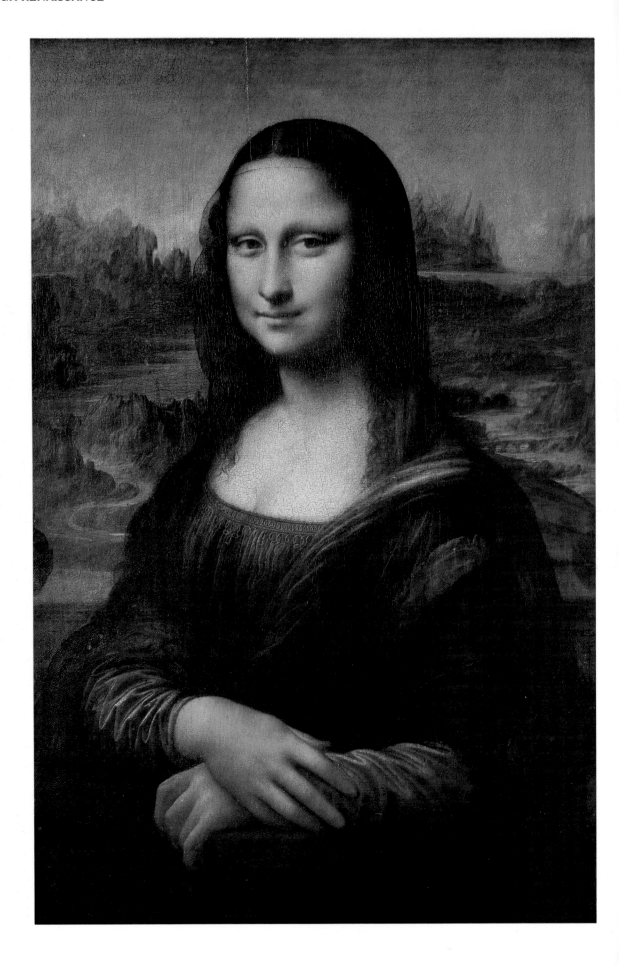

becomes the apex of the triangle whose right side flows downward to the Christ child, who embraces the symbol of the sacrificial lamb.

The mysterious *Mona Lisa* (Fig. **9.14**) was painted at about the same time as *Madonna and Saint Anne*. We are drawn to this work not by the obvious subject but by the background. As if to emphasize the serenity of the subject, and in common with *Madonna and Saint Anne*, there lies a wonderful and exciting mountain setting full of dramatic crags and peaks, winding roads which disappear, and exquisitely detailed naturalistic forms receding into the mists.

Michelangelo

Perhaps the most dominant figure of the High Renaissance, however, was Michelangelo Buonarroti (1475–1564), who was entirely different in character from Leonardo. Leonardo was a skeptic, while Michelangelo was a man of great faith. Leonardo was fascinated by science and natural objects; Michelangelo showed little interest in anything other than the human form.

Michelangelo's Sistine Chapel ceiling (Fig. **9.15**) is a shining example of the ambition and genius of this era and its philosophies. Some scholars see in this monumental work a blending of Christian tradition and a neo-Platonist view of the soul's progressive ascent through contemplation and desire. In each of the triangles along the sides of the chapel the ancestors of Christ await the

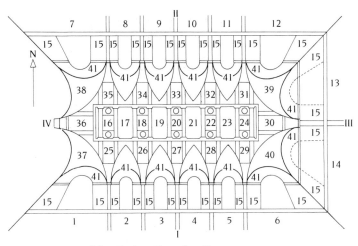

9.16 Diagram of the Sistine Chapel ceiling.

The Frescoes of the Sistine Chapel

I. South Wall with scenes from the life of Moses (1–6)
II. North wall with scenes from the life of Christ (7–12)
III. East wall with entrance (13–14)
IV. West wall with Last Judgment

15 Window niches with 24 portraits of the first Popes
41 Lunettes above the windows with portraits of the ancestors of Christ and scenes from the Old Testament

The Frescoes on the Ceiling
16 God Separates Light and Darkness
17 God Creates the Sun and the Moon and the Plants on Earth
18 God Separates the Water and Earth and Blesses his Work

19 Creation of Adam
20 Creation of Eve
21 Fall of Man and Expulsion from Paradise
22 Sacrifice of Noah
23 The Flood
24 The Intoxication of Noah
25 Jeremiah
26 Persian Sibyl
27 Ezekiel
28 Eritrean Sibyl
29 Joel
30 Zechariah
31 Delphic Sibyl
32 Isaiah
33 Cumaean Sibyl
34 Daniel
35 Libyan Sibyl
36 Jonah
37 The Punishment of Haman
38 The Brazen Serpent
39 Judith with the Head of Holofernes
40 David Slaying Goliath

9.14 Leonardo da Vinci, *Mona Lisa*, c.1503–5. Oil on panel, 30 × 21ins (76.2 × 53.3cm). Louvre, Paris.

9.15 Michelangelo, *The Creation of Adam*, detail from the Sistine Chapel ceiling, 1508–12. Fresco. The Vatican, Rome.

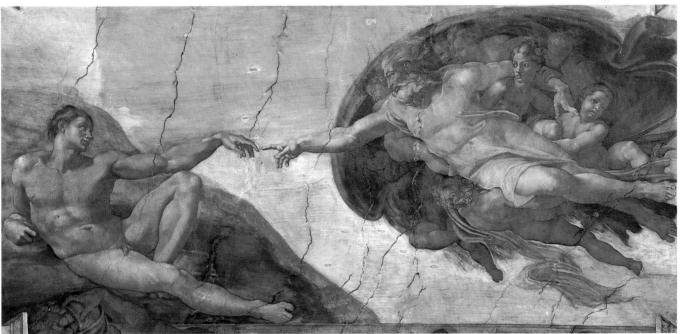

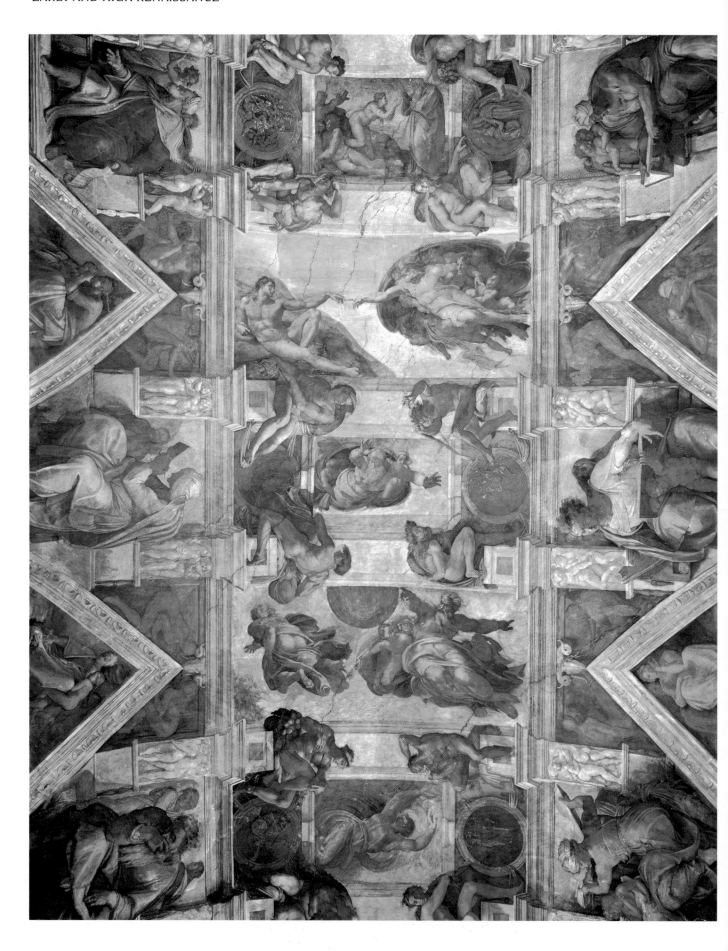

Redeemer. Between them, amidst painted pillars, are the sages of antiquity. In the corners Michelangelo depicts various biblical stories, and across the center of the ceiling he unfolds the episodes of Genesis. The center of the ceiling captures, at the moment of fulfilment, the Creation of Adam, and does so in sculpturesque human form and beautifully modelled anatomical detail. God, in human form, stretches outward from his matrix of angels to a reclining, but dynamic, Adam, awaiting the divine infusion, the spark of the soul. The figures do not touch, and we are left with a supreme feeling of anticipation of what we imagine will be the power and electricity of God's physical contact with mortal man.

The Sistine Chapel ceiling (Figs. **9.16** and **9.17**) creates a visual panoply of awesome proportions. It is not possible to get a comprehensive view of the entire ceiling, standing at any point in the Chapel. If we look upward and read the scenes back toward the altar, the prophets and sibyls appear on their sides. If we view one side as upright, then the other appears upside down. These opposing directions are held together by the structure of simulated architecture, whose transverse arches and diagonal bands separate vault compartments. Twenty nudes appear at intersections and harmonize the composition because they can be read either with the prophets and sibyls below them or with the Genesis scenes, at whose corners they appear. We thus see in action the basic High Renaissance principle of composition created by the interaction of the component elements.

Raphael

Raphael (1483–1520) is generally regarded as the third figure in the High Renaissance triumvirate, though it has been argued that he did not reach the same high level of genius and accomplishment as Leonardo and Michelangelo. In the *Alba Madonna* (Fig. **9.18**) the strong central triangle exists within the geometric parameters of a *tondo* (circular shape). The tendency of a circle to roll is counteracted by strong, parallel horizontal lines. The strong baseline of a central triangle is described by the leg of the infant John the Baptist (left), the foot of the Christ child, the folds of the Madonna's robes, and the rock and shadow (right). The left side of the central triangle comprises the eyes of all three figures and carries along the back of the child to the border. The right side of the triangle moves down the edge of the Madonna's robe to join the horizontal shadow at the right border. Within this intellectual formula, nevertheless, exists a comfortable, subtly and superbly modeled, idealized Mary and Christ child. Textures are soft and warm. Raphael's

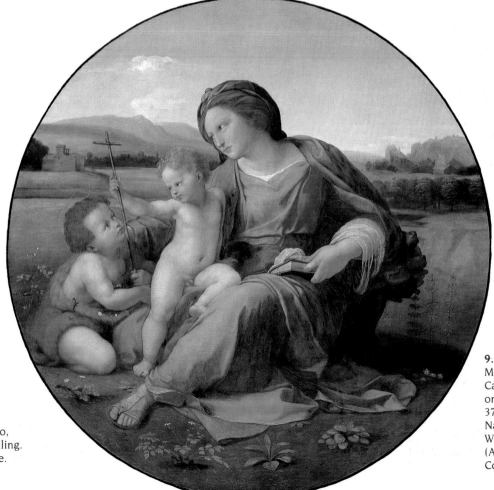

9.17 Michelangelo, Sistine Chapel ceiling. The Vatican, Rome.

9.18 Raphael, *The Alba Madonna*, c.1510. Canvas (originally oil on panel), diameter 37¼ins (94.5cm). National Gallery of Art, Washington DC (Andrew W. Mellon Collection).

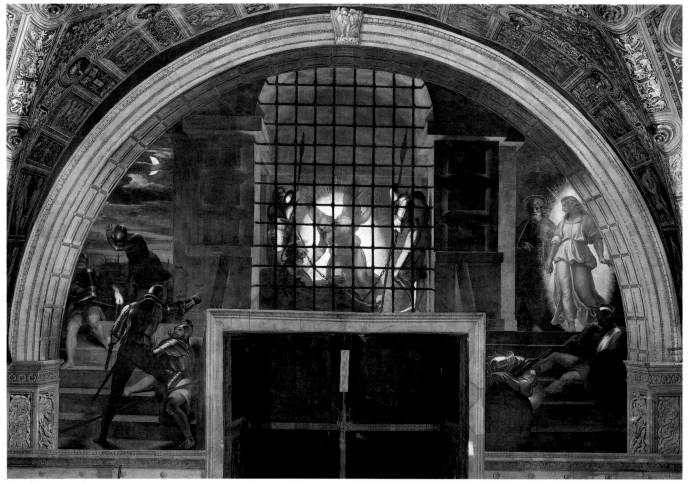

9.19 Raphael, *The Deliverance of St Peter*, 1512–14. Fresco. Stanza dell' Eliodoro, Vatican, Rome.

9.20 Lorenzo Ghiberti, *The Story of Jacob and Esau*, panel of the *Gates of Paradise*, c.1435. Gilt bronze, 31¼ins (79.4cm) square. Baptistery, Florence.

treatment of flesh creates a tactile sensation of real flesh, with warm blood flowing beneath it, a characteristic relatively new to two-dimensional art. Raphael's figures express lively power, and his mastery of three-dimensional form and deep space is without equal.

In the *Deliverance of Saint Peter* (Fig. **9.19**) Raphael again accepted the challenge of a constraining space. To accommodate the intrusion of the window into the lunette, Raphael divided the composition into three sections representing the three phases of the miracle. It is a highly expressive statement, with intense light shining particularly from the center section.

Papal patronage had assembled great genius in Rome at the turn of the sixteenth century and had ignited and supported a brilliant fire of human genius in the arts. The Spanish invasion and sack of Rome doused the flame of Italian art in 1527 and scattered its ashes to the far corners of Europe, contributing to the disillusionment and turmoil of religious and political strife that marked the next seventy years.

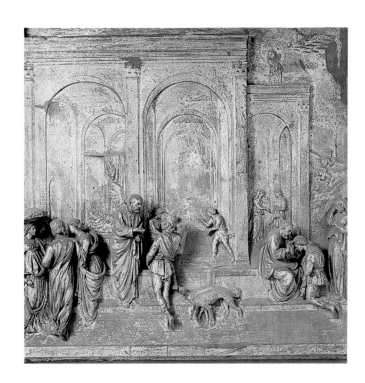

SCULPTURE

Florence

An attempt to capture the essence of European sculpture in the Early Renaissance can, again, best be served by looking to fifteenth-century Florence, where sculpture also enjoyed the patronage of the Medicis. The Early Renaissance sculptors developed the skills to create images of high verisimilitude. The goal, however, was not the same as that of the Greeks with their idealized reality of human form. Rather, the Renaissance sculptor found his ideal in Man as Man is. The ideal was the glorious individual—even if not quite perfect. Sculpture of this style presented an uncompromising and stark view of humankind—complex, balanced, and full of action. Relief sculpture, like painting, revealed a new means of representing deep space through systematic, scientific perspective. Free-standing statuary works, long out of favor, returned to dominance. Scientific inquiry and interest in anatomy were reflected in sculpture as well as painting. The nude, full of character and charged with energy, made its first reappearance since ancient times. The human form was built up layer by layer upon its skeletal and muscular framework. Even when clothed, fifteenth-

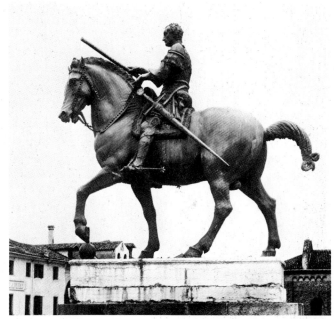

9.22 Donatello, Equestrian Monument to Gattamelata, 1445–50. Bronze, c.11 × 13ft (3.4 × 4m). Piazza del Santo, Padua.

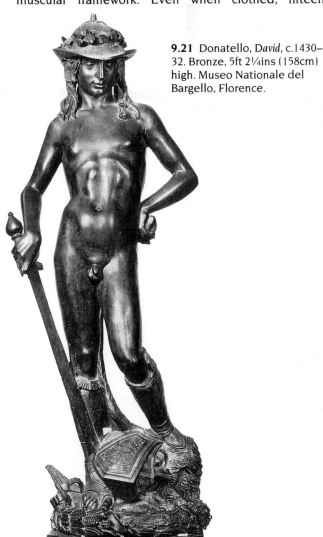

9.21 Donatello, David, c.1430–32. Bronze, 5ft 2¼ins (158cm) high. Museo Nationale del Bargello, Florence.

century sculpture revealed the body under the outer structure, quite unlike the decorative shell which often clothed medieval works.

Notable among fifteenth-century Italian sculptors were Ghiberti, della Robbia, Antonio Rosselino, Pollaiuolo, and Donatello. In Ghiberti's Paradise Gates (Figs. 9.20 and 9.23), we see the same concern for rich detail, humanity, and feats of perspective that we saw in Florentine painting. The bold relief of these scenes took Ghiberti twenty-one years to complete.

However, the greatest masterpieces of fifteenth-century Italian Renaissance sculpture came from the unsurpassed master of the age, Donatello (1386–1466). His magnificent David (Fig. 9.21) was the first free-standing nude since classical times. However, unlike classical nudes, David is partially clothed. His armor and helmet, along with bony elbows and adolescent character, invest him with rich detail of a highly individualized nature. David exhibits a return to classical contrapposto stance, but its carefully executed form expresses a new humanity whose individual parts seem almost capable of movement.

Perhaps Donatello's most famous work is the Equestrian Monument of Gattamelata (Fig. 9.22). In this larger-than-life monument to a deceased general we see the influence of Roman monumental statuary, and in particular the statue of Marcus Aurelius on Horseback, but with a unique concentration on both human and animal anatomy. Donatello skilfully directs the focus of the viewer not to the powerful mass of the horse, but to the overpowering presence of the human astride it. His triangular composition anticipates the geometric approach of the High Renaissance.

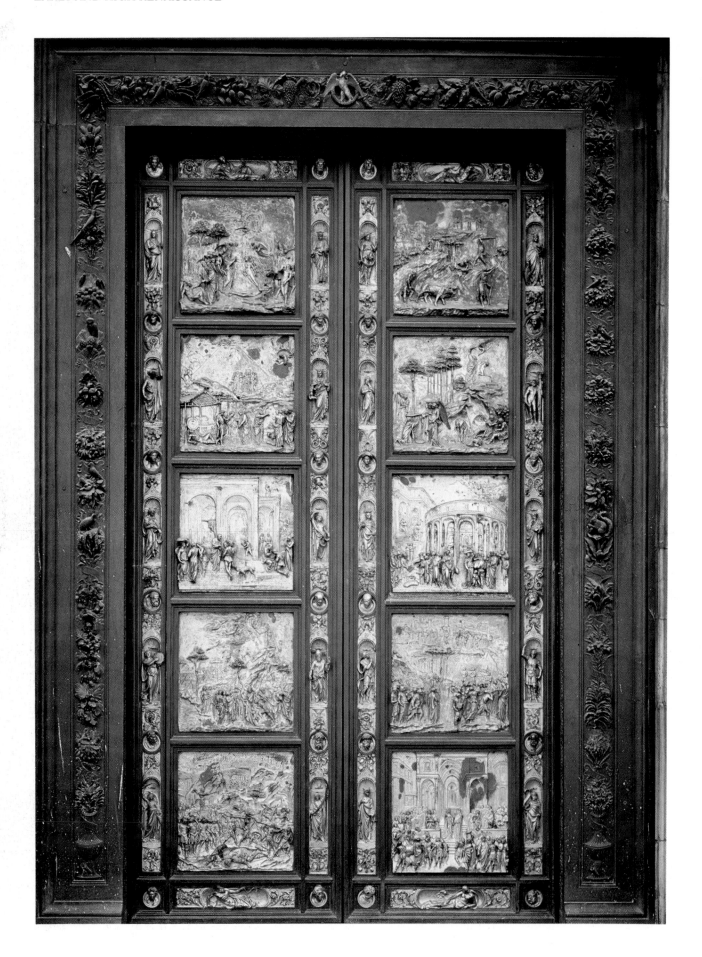

High Renaissance

The papal call to Rome gave impetus to a High Renaissance style in sculpture, as well as painting. High Renaissance sculpture, however, was Michelangelo Buonarroti. Michelangelo's ideal was the full realization of individualism—a reflection of his own unique genius. This ideal was expressed in a quality called *terribilità*, a quality of supreme confidence that allows a man to accept no other authority but his own genius. We find that characteristic in Michelangelo's gigantic *David* (Fig. **9.24**). In this nude champion there is a pent-up energy again reflecting the artist's neo-Platonic philosophy of the body as an earthly prison of the soul. The upper body seems to move in opposition to the lower portion (again in *contrapposto* position). Our eye is led downward through the right arm and left leg of the figure, and then upward along the left arm. The entire composition seeks to break free from its confinement through thrust and counterthrust. However, energy is contained and only potential.

In contrast we find the quiet simplicity of the *Pietà* (Fig. **9.25**). This is the only work Michelangelo ever signed, and it again reveals his neo-Platonist viewpoint.

9.23 Lorenzo Ghiberti, *The Gates of Paradise*, 1424–52. Gilt bronze, c.17ft (5.2m) high. Baptistery, Florence.

9.24 Michelangelo, *David*, 1501–4. Marble, 13ft 5ins (4.09cm) high. Academy, Florence.

9.25 Michelangelo, *Pietà*, 1498–9. Marble, 5ft 9ins (1.75m) high. St Peter's, Rome.

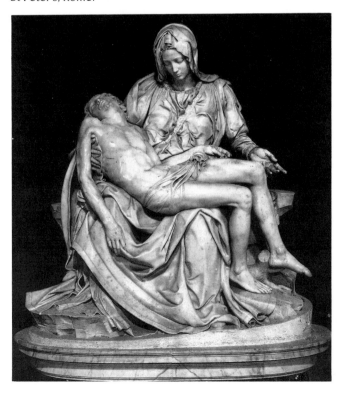

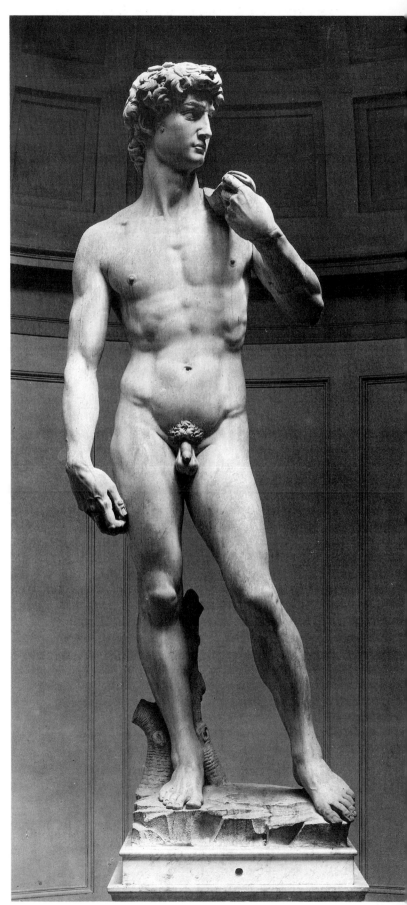

Here High Renaissance triangularity of composition contrasts with what many believe to be a late medieval subject matter and figure treatment. The size of the Madonna compared to the figure of Jesus reflects the cult of the Virgin characteristic of the late medieval period. Beyond these considerations, however, lies the absolute perfection of surface texture in this work. Michelangelo has polished the marble to such a degree that it assumes the warmth of real human flesh. Skin becomes even more sensuous in its contrast to rough stone. Cloth has exquisite softness, and the expressive sway of drape reinforces the compositional line of the work. Emotion and energy are captured within the contrasting forces of form, line, and texture.

MUSIC

The volatile courts of Renaissance northern Italy proved important patrons of the performing as well as the visual arts, but the *ars nova* of the fourteenth century found its most willing and significant successor in the Flemish school of composers, which developed parallel to the Flemish school of painters. Music historians are not of one mind in labeling the style of this locale and era. Some use the term Franco-Flemish, others reserve that term for a later, sixteenth-century development, preferring to call fifteenth-century Flemish composers the Burgundian School. The Dukes of Burgundy, like their Italian counterparts, were active patrons of the arts, and the painter Jan van Eyck, for example, benefited greatly from their patronage. As part of their courtly entourage the Dukes retained a group of musicians to provide entertainment and chapel music. Musicians were frequently imported from elsewhere, thus contributing to a cosmopolitan or international character in the Burgandian courts and disseminating Burgandian influence throughout Europe. Flemish composers were widely educated and thoroughly aware of the world around them. Writers of Masses and motets, they made specific contributions to the development of four-part harmony and in the use of only one text, usually sacred, for all voices. Flemish composers gave greater independence to the lower voices. The bass part was independent for the first time and became a typical feature of this style of composition. All parts were separated and were given consistent, measured rhythm, coming together only at cadences. Flemish music thus contained, for the first time in musical history, a true four-part harmony.

Four composers worked in this style—Guillaume Dufay, Johannes Ockeghem, Jacob Obrecht, and Josquin des Prez, with Dufay and Josquin being the most prominent. Dufay (1400–74) had been a member of the Papal Chapel at Rome and Florence and had traveled extensively throughout Europe, so he brought to Flanders a wealth of knowledge and experience. Within his lifetime he was heralded as one of the great composers of the era. He was a prolific composer and we have a wealth of his work in modern editions. His style intended each line to have a different timbre (tonal quality) with a separation of each of the parts clearly indicated. Dufay's sacred motets based on the chant, *Salve Regina*, formed the basis for numerous later polyphonic settings for the Mass.

Secular influence and patronage increased. The printing press made music, like the written word, more easily transmitted. More music than ever before was composed, and the individual identity and, in true Humanist spirit, the prestige of the composer became paramount. Composers strove to achieve an ideal sound. Ideal to them meant four or more voice lines of similar and compatible timbres, as opposed to contrasting timbres in earlier works. They concentrated on making the work a unified whole. More concern was given to the relationship of music and text, and clarity of communication became the objective of music. According to the philosophy of the day, the ideal means of communication was an unaccompanied vocal ensemble. All of these characteristics were highly developed in the works of Josquin des Prez (1450–1521).

Like Dufay, Josquin was trained in (among other places) Milan, Rome, and Florence and brought to Flanders an equally rich but somewhat later Renaissance heritage. He was compared to Michelangelo and called the "father of musicians". He wrote secular music of a light, homophonic nature similar to that popular in Italy at the same time, as this extract from the lyrics of his "El Grillo" ("The Cricket") shows:

> The cricket is a fine singer who can sing a long note. Sing, cricket, about carousels. The cricket is a fine singer, but he is not like other birds: as soon as they have sung a little while, they are off on business elsewhere; but the cricket always stays put. When the weather is at its hottest, then he sings only for love.

His chief contribution lay, like Dufay's, in the motet and in polyphonic development. Typically, his motets used individual musical motives in each phrase of the text, and for the first time in musical history a consistent use of motival imitation occcurred as the musical idea moved through each of the voices. Also typical and significant was a three-part form in which part one was recapitulated in part three, with those parts standing in contrast to part two (ABA form). Finally, as in all music of this school and era, there was a sense of harmonic progression to natural cadence. (Natural cadence has both mathematical and cultural/conventional characteristics. Chordal resolution on the tonic chord is based both on the relative ease with which certain proportions of a string are set into sympathetic vibration by another vibrating string and also on purely cultural conditioning.)

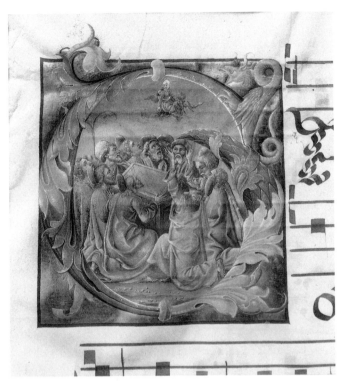

9.26 *The Assumption of the Virgin*, illuminated letter O, 15th century. Tempera on vellum, 12¼ × 13⅝ ins (31.1 × 34.6 cm). The Metropolitan Museum of Art, New York (Rogers Fund, 1911).

In Germany the Early Renaissance spirit, with its secular traditions, produced polyphonic *Lieder* (songs) in the mid-fifteenth century. These predominantly three-part, secular songs provided much of the melodic basis for the church hymns of Lutheranism after the Reformation. Heinrich Isaac (1450–1517) was probably the first and most notable German *Lied* composer of this era. He was a prolific musician and his diverse background, which included living at various times in Italy, the Netherlands, and France, gave his work an international flavor. He and other composers of *Lieder* adapted folk songs into polyphonic settings. The frequent usage and refashioning of this type of composition can be seen in one of Isaac's most famous works, "Innsbruck, I Must Leave Thee". Originally the song was a folk love song. Isaac notated the song into a polyphonic piece with words by the Emperor Maximilian. Later Isaac used the melody in his own sacred work, the *Missa Carminum*. The song then became widely known in another adaptation under the sacred title, "O World, I Now Must Leave Thee". Even Johann Sebastian Bach used the *Innsbruck Lied* in his *St. Matthew Passion*.

One final reference helps to give us a sense of the quality of Renaissance music of the early fifteenth century. Referring to the English composer John Dunstable, a French poem of about 1440 comments on the "English countenance" that helped to make European music so "joyous and bright" with "marvelous pleasantness". Humankind had found a note of optimism in a period devoted to vital earthly living. Certainly there were troubles, but God and humankind had a fairly comfortable and comforting relationship.

THEATRE

In the years corresponding to the Renaissance and High Renaissance in the visual arts, theatre retained the characteristics it had developed in the Middle Ages, and there is little to add to previous descriptions. Secular adaptation and production of mysteries and moralities flourished. The *Confrèrie de la Passion*, under license from Charles VI, continued to produce mystery plays in France throughout the fifteenth century. Their cycle of plays representing *Le Mystère du Vieil Testament* (*The Mystery of the Old Testament*) consisted of 44,325 verses and took twenty performances to complete. *Le Mystère du Nouveau Testament* (*The Mystery of the New Testament*) consisted of 34,574 verses. A third cycle, *Les Actes des Apôtres* (*The Acts of the Apostles*), rounded out the Confrèrie's repertoire and took forty days to present in its entirety.

But the French also developed a new secular form, the *sottie*, short theatrical entertainments woven into the yearly festivals of the Feast of the Ass and the Feast of the Fools. These festivals originated partly in pagan rites and were bawdy burlesques of the Roman Catholic Mass. A person called the Bishop, Archbishop, or Pope of Fools celebrated a mock Mass with a great deal of jumping around, buffoonery, and noise. Participants wore strange costumes (or nothing at all), and the entire affair was accompanied by much drinking. One of the most popular of the *sotties* written for the Feasts, Pierre Gringoire's *Jeu du Prince des Sots* (*Play of the Prince of the Fools*), was produced in Paris in 1512 at the request of King Louis XII to inflame the populace against Pope Julius II.

At the same time a more substantial French theatrical form also emerged—the farce. This secular genre was fully developed as a play form. The farce was performed as an independent production, in contrast to the *sottie*, which was an *entr'acte* entertainment. The most famous of the French farces of this period was *Maître Pierre Pathélin* (1470). It is still stageworthy and is occasionally produced.

Midway through the fifteenth century the Turkish conquest of Constantinople caused a mass exodus of scholars, artisans, artists, and actors to Italy. The impact of this emigration had little effect on Italian theatre, stimulating little more than a few stilted imitations of Greek tragedy, some sentimental pastorals based on Virgil, and some bawdy comedies that debased even Plautus and Menander. However, in contrast to medieval drama, which tended to be a group effort, with its texts fairly well established by tradition or biblical source, Italy witnessed a re-emergence of the individual playwright, whose themes characterized the Humanist and classical impetus of the period. These scholarly dramas in Latin

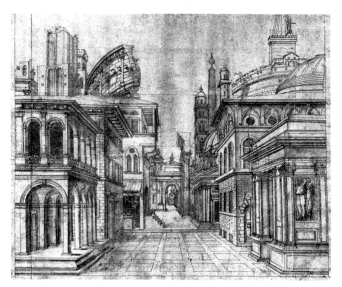

9.27 Baldassare Peruzzi, stage design, probably for *La Calendria*, 1514.

included *Philoginia* by Ugolino Pisani, *Philodoxius* by Leon Battista Alberti, and *Polissena* by Leonardo Bruni. In 1471 or 1472 the Italian stage witnessed a production of Angelo Poliziano's *Orfeo*, a kind of *sacra rappresentazione* (Italian mystery play) with Christian elements replaced by pagan mythology. *Orfeo* is significant for this era because it was written in vernacular Italian, rather than Latin.

Italian early Renaissance drama, like painting, tended not to reflect the discordant political cloak-and-dagger atmosphere of its surroundings. Italian playwrights chose mostly to write tender sentimental pastoral comedies in a graceful, witty, and polished style, rather like the music composed by John Dunstable. A few tragedies were written. The first Italian tragedy, *Sofonisba*, by Giovanni Trissino, was completed in 1515 and revealed the author's misconceptions of Aristotle's *Poetics* (a common occurrence in the Renaissance). However, the play was not produced until 1562, well into the next era.

For the most part, Italian drama was theatre of the aristocracy and was produced with elaborate trappings, usually at court (Fig. **9.27**), sometimes in public squares under courtly sponsorship. No permanent theatres existed at the time. Surviving Roman theatre buildings were in such disrepair that they were unusable.

Theatre tends to be institutionally moribund, and its forms and conventions come together slowly and hang on tenaciously. Writing a play, the creative act of an individual playwright, does not have impact until that script is produced for a public. Since production involves a number of problems and judgments affecting individuals other than the playwright, theatre often takes longer to reflect social and stylistic changes than do other disciplines. Theatre in the early years of the Renaissance had changed from medieval theatre, but real developments had to wait until the middle of the sixteenth century.

DANCE

Out of the same northern Italian courts that supported Renaissance painting and sculpture came the foundations of theatre dance. The point is well made that the visual and classical orientation of the Italian Renaissance was largely responsible for the primarily visual and geometric characteristics of dance as we know it. Line, form, repetition, and unity brought dance from a social to a theatrical milieu as the Italians, especially in Florence, began to create patterns in body movements. As in all the arts, there was an increasing concern for "rules" and conventionalized vocabulary.

Mummeries, pageants, and other dance-related activities dating to the traveling pantomimes of the Middle Ages emerged as formal dance in elaborate entertainments in the Italian courts of the fifteenth century. These entertainments were fashioned into spectacular displays, although they remained more social than theatrical. Concern for perfection, for individual expression, dignity and grace, created a vocabulary for dance steps and a choreography of patterns and design in the spirit of the Renaissance. Courtly surroundings added refinement and restraint, and the dancing master assumed greater importance and control as he coordinated and designed elegant movements. Dance was increasingly seen as something to be responded to as a visual display rather than to be experienced through participation.

An important milestone in theatrical dance occurred at this time. Guglielmo Ebreo of Pesaro wrote one of the first compilations of dance description and theory. His attempts to record a complex and visually oriented art led him to stress memory as one of the essential ingredients of the dancer's art. His observation isolated the most critical element of dance tradition, one which even today is responsible for keeping the dance alive and transmitted from generation to generation of dancers. Film and labanotation still have not replaced the personalized memory-form by which the traditions of dance are passed along. Guglielmo's work was a clear record of formal dance composition. He strove to bring dance out of the disrepute into which it had fallen in the bawdy pantomimes of previous eras. He sought to place dance above criticism and make it fully acceptable from an aesthetic standpoint. For Guglielmo, dance was an art of grace and beauty.

In the fifteenth century, dance left the floor of the courtly ballroom and moved to a stage to be participated in by only a skilful few (Fig. **9.28**). Movement was carefully coordinated with music. A dancer's ability to keep time supposedly afforded pleasure and sharpened the intellect. Through the influences of the Medici family, the emerging traditions of dance moved northward to France where, in the late Renaissance of the sixteenth century, the *ballet de court*, the French version of the Italian court dance, became the *ballet*.

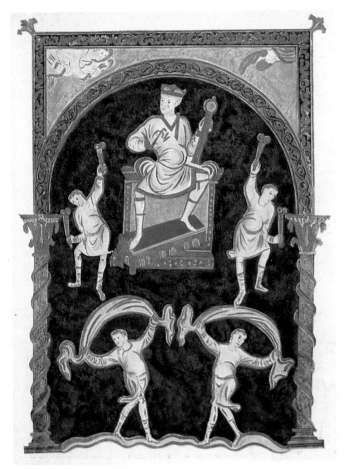

9.28 Social dancing, from a 15th-century English chronicle by Jean de Waurin in Vienna. The New York Public Library.

ARCHITECTURE

Early Renaissance architecture was centered in Florence and there were three significant stylistic departures from medieval architecture. First was its concern with revival of classical models along very mechanical lines. Ruins of Roman buildings were measured carefully and their proportions translated into Renaissance buildings. Rather than seeing Roman arches as limiting factors, Renaissance architects saw them as geometric devices by which a formally derived design could be composed. The second departure from the medieval was the application of decorative detail, that is, non-structural ornamentation, to the façade of the building. Third, and a manifestation of the second difference, was a radical change in the outer expression of structure. The outward form of a building was previously closely related to its actual structural systems, that is, the structural support of the building, for example, post and lintel, masonry, and the arch. In the Renaissance, these supporting elements were hidden from view and the external appearance was no longer sacrificed to structural concerns.

Early architecture of the period, such as the dome on the Cathedral of Florence (Fig. **9.30**) designed by Brunelleschi (1377–1446), was an imitation of classical forms appended to medieval structures. In this curious design, added in the fifteenth century to a fourteenth-century building, the soaring dome rises 180 feet into the air, and its height is apparent from both without and within. If we compare it with the Pantheon (Figs. **5.25** to **5.27**), Brunelleschi's departure from traditional practice becomes clearer. The dome of the Pantheon is impressive only from the inside of the building because its exterior supporting structure is so massive that it clutters the visual experience. That Brunelleschi's dome rises to a phenomenal height is apparent on the inside because the architect has hidden from view the supporting elements such as stone and timber girdles and light-weight ribbings. The result is an aesthetic statement, where visual appearance is foremost and structural considerations are subordinate.

The use of classical ornamentation can be seen in Brunelleschi's Pazzi Chapel (Fig. **9.29**). Small in scale, its walls serve as a plain background for a wealth of surface decoration. Concern for proportion and geometric design is very clear, but the overall composition is not a slave to pure arithmetical considerations. Rather, the Pazzi Chapel reflects Brunelleschi's sense of classical aesthetics. Brunelleschi's influence was profound in the first half of the fifteenth century, and he served as a model and inspiration for later Renaissance architects.

9.29 Filippo Brunelleschi, Pazzi Chapel, c.1440–61. S Croce, Florence.

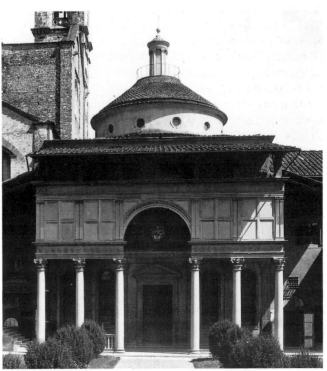

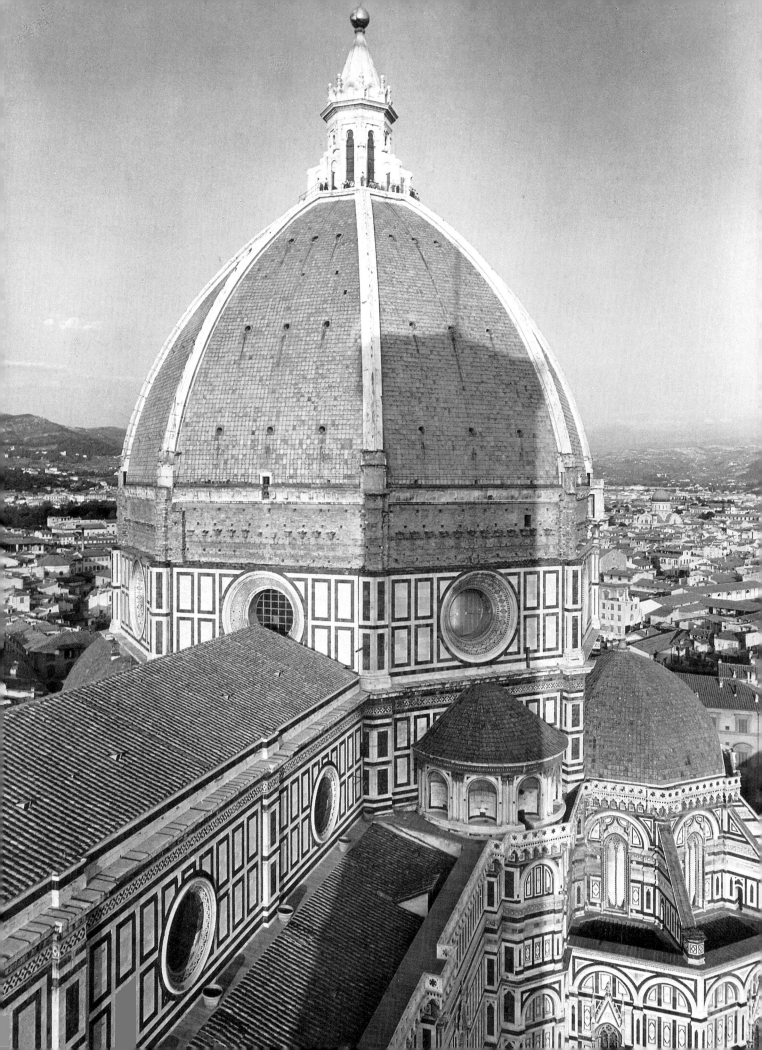

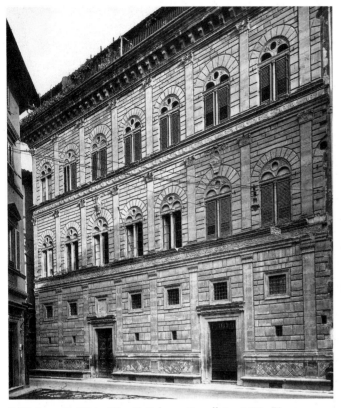

9.31 Leon Battista Alberti, Palazzo Rucellai, c.1452–70.

The second half of the fifteenth century was dominated by the Florentine scholar, writer, architect and composer Leon Battista Alberti. His treatise *Concerning Architecture* was based on Vitruvius and provided a scholarly approach to architecture that influenced Western building for centuries. His scientific approach to sculpture and painting, as well as architecture, encompassed theories on Roman antiquity that typified the reduction of aesthetics to rules.

However, the problems of Renaissance architects were different from those of their predecessors. Faced with an expanding range of types of building such as townhouses, hospitals, and business establishments, for which classical forms had to be adapted, the architect had to meet specific practical needs, which, apparently, the ancients did not. As a result, classical detail was applied to a wide range of forms and structures, many of which, like the Cathedral of Florence, were of non-classical origin. In his well-known Palazzo Rucellai (Fig. **9.31**), Alberti applied a detailed classical system to a non-classical building. His design reminds us of the Roman

Colosseum in its alternating arches and attached columns with upward progressing changes of order. However, the application of his systematic concept is rather academic, as opposed to individualistic.

At the turn of the sixteenth century, architecture witnessed a balancing of Christian and classical ideas and moved away from insistence and emphasis on decorative surface detail, to a greater concern for space and volume. The shift of patronage from the local rulers to the Roman Church, which brought the visual artist (painter, sculptor, and architect) to Rome, also changed the tone of architecture to a more formal, monumental, and serious style.

A perfect early example of High Renaissance architecture is Bramante's Tempietto or "little temple" (Fig. **9.32**). Pope Julius II wanted all Roman basilica-form churches replaced by magnificent monuments that would overshadow the remains of imperial Rome, and the Tempietto was built as part of this plan. The culmination of this style is Bramante's design for St. Peter's—later revised by Michelangelo and finished, later still, by Giacomo della Porta (Fig. **9.33**). St. Peter's was a geometrical and symmetrical design based on the circle and the square over which perched a tremendous dome surrounded by four lesser domes.

9.32 Donato Bramante, The Tempietto, 1502. S Pietro in Montorio, Rome.

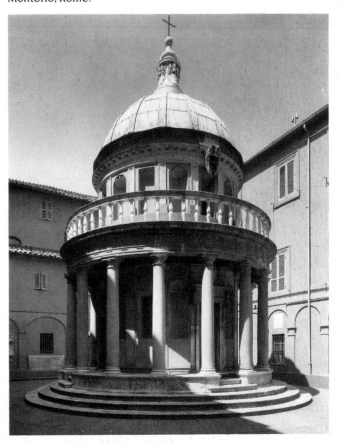

9.30 Filippo Brunelleschi, Dome of Florence Cathedral, 1420–36.

SYNTHESIS

Papal Splendor: The Vatican

Here for almost 2,000 years has been the center of a spiritual communion; in countries all over the world, Christians aspire to achieve a community of spirit with the succesor to St. Peter. By comprehending this significance of the Vatican, one can also understand what it was that led Roman Catholicism to embellish the center of its spiritual power with the diversity of human knowledge, including the arts.[3]

The Renaissance—and particularly the High Renaissance, when the papacy called all great artists to Rome—contributed most of the splendor of Vatican art and architecture. The papacy as a force and the Vatican as the

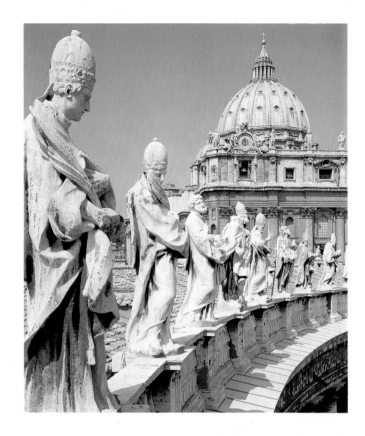

9.33 Michelangelo, St Peter's, Rome, from the west, 1546–64 (dome completed by Giacomo della Porta, 1590).

9.34 Gianlorenzo Bernini, statues on the colonnade of St Peter's Square, colonnade designed 1657.

9.35 Interior of the dome of St Peter's, Rome.

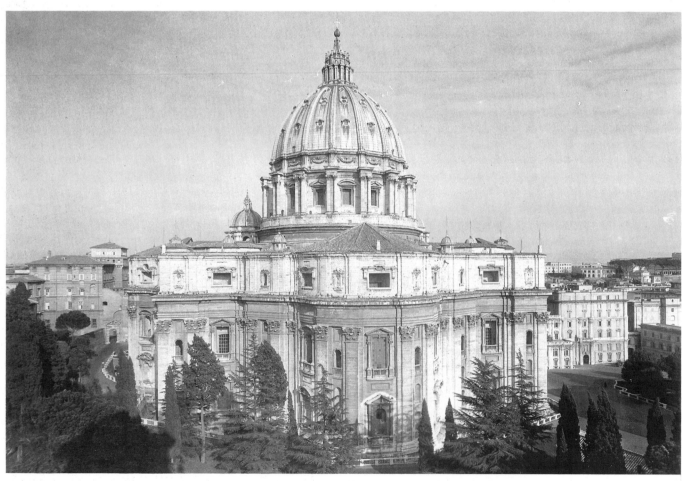

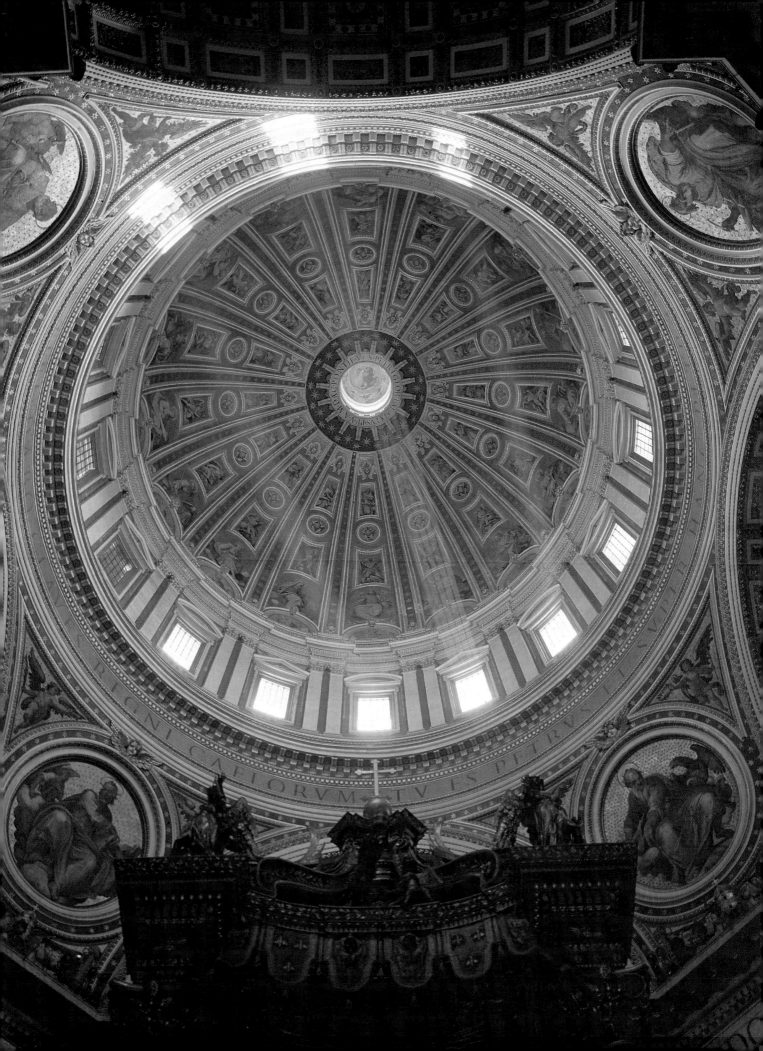

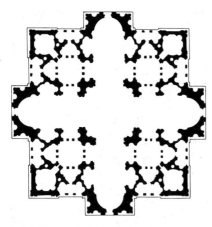

9.36 Bramante's design for St Peter's, 1506.

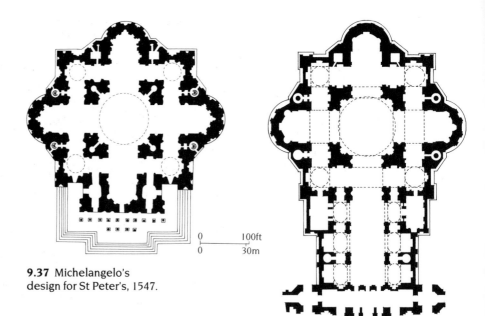

9.37 Michelangelo's design for St Peter's, 1547.

0   100ft
0   30m

9.38 Plan of St Peter's as built to Michelangelo's design with alterations by Carlo Maderno, 1606–15.

symbol of that force represent a synthesis of Renaissance ideas and reflections. Rome was the city of the arts in the fifteenth and sixteenth centuries. The artists of the age rediscovered classical antiquity and emulated what they found. Imitation was frowned upon, and the classical nature of Renaissance art lies in its expressiveness, which is indeed comparable to that of Greece and Rome. St. Peter's and the Vatican have earthly and heavenly qualities which reflect the reality of the Church on earth and the mystery of the spiritual church of Christ.

Part of the inspiration and reflection which we are about to examine will carry us into the second half of the sixteenth century, a time we will examine more fully in the next chapter. However, the roots of that expression lay in the Renaissance and High Renaissance, and so our examination properly becomes a part of this chapter.

Plans for replacement of the original basilica of Old St. Peter's (Fig. **7.19**) were made in the fifteenth century, but it was Pope Julius II (1503–13) who decided actually to put into effect the plans of Nicholas V (1447–1455). Julius commissioned Bramante to construct the new basilica. Bramante's design called for a building in the form of a Greek cross (Fig. **9.36**). The work was planned as "an harmonious arrangement of architectural forms" in an "image of bright amplitude and picturesque liveliness".

Bramante died in 1514 and was succeeded by two of his assistants and Raphael. Liturgical considerations required an elongated structure. Subsequent changes were made by additional architects, and these designs were severely criticized by Michelangelo. Following the death of the last of these architects, Pope Paul III (1534–49) convinced Michelangelo to become chief architect. Michelangelo set aside liturgical considerations and re-

turned to Bramante's original conceptions, which he described as "clear and pure, full of light ... whoever distances himself from Bramante, also distances himself from the truth" (**9.37**). Michelangelo's project was completed in May of 1590 as the last stone was added to the dome and a High Mass was celebrated. Work on the thirty-six columns continued, however, and was completed by Della Porta and Fontana after Michelangelo's death. Full completion of the basilica as it stands today was under the direction of yet more architects, including Maderna. Maderna was forced to yield to the wishes of the cardinals and change the original form of the Greek cross to a Latin cross (**9.38**). As a result, the Renaissance design of Michelangelo and Bramante, with its central altar, was rejected. It was replaced by Maderna's design of a travertine façade of gigantic proportions and sober elegance. His extension of the basilica was influential in the development of baroque architecture. The project was completed in 1614 (Fig. **9.33**).

The entire complex of the Vatican, with St. Peter's as its focal point, is a vast scheme of parks, gardens, fountains, and buildings (Fig. **9.39**). Its scale and style in the years 1585–1590 can be seen in Figure **9.40**. The colonnades of St. Peter's Square are decorated by 140 majestic statues of popes, bishops, and apostles by Bernini (Fig. **9.34**). Larger than life and harmonious in design, these works reach upward and create a finishing touch and *chiaroscuro* to the square, the façade, and the dome. The magnificence of the Vatican lies in its scale and its detail, and above all in the awesome dome (Fig. **9.35**).

Throughout the complex there are paintings and sculptures of the Renaissance, High Renaissance, Counter-

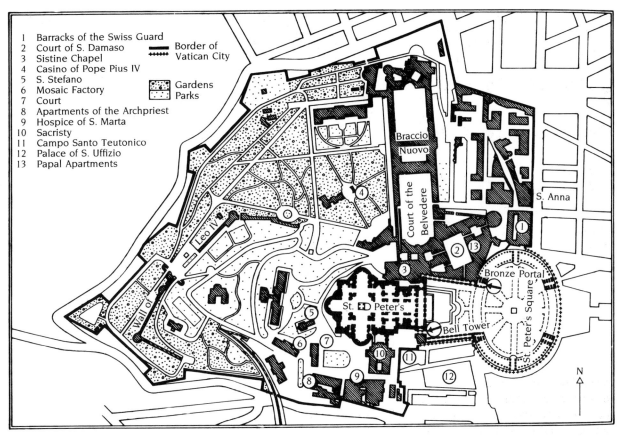

1 Barracks of the Swiss Guard
2 Court of S. Damaso
3 Sistine Chapel
4 Casino of Pope Pius IV
5 S. Stefano
6 Mosaic Factory
7 Court
8 Apartments of the Archpriest
9 Hospice of S. Marta
10 Sacristy
11 Campo Santo Teutonico
12 Palace of S. Uffizio
13 Papal Apartments

——— Border of
++++ Vatican City

Gardens
Parks

9.39 Plan of the Vatican and St Peter's.

9.40 View of the Vatican Palace, the Belvedere Court and the Belvedere Palace at the time of Pope Sixtus V (1585–1590). Contemporary engraving.

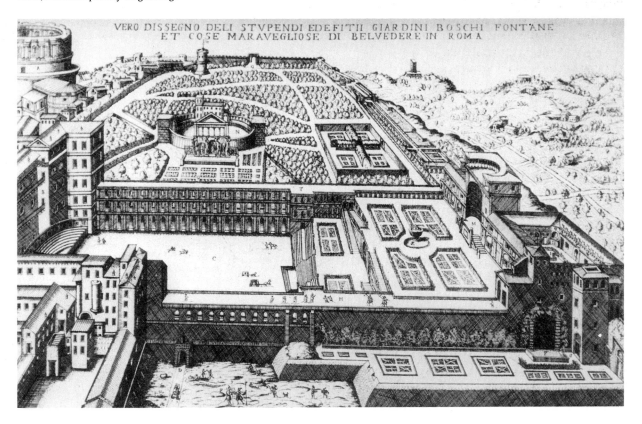

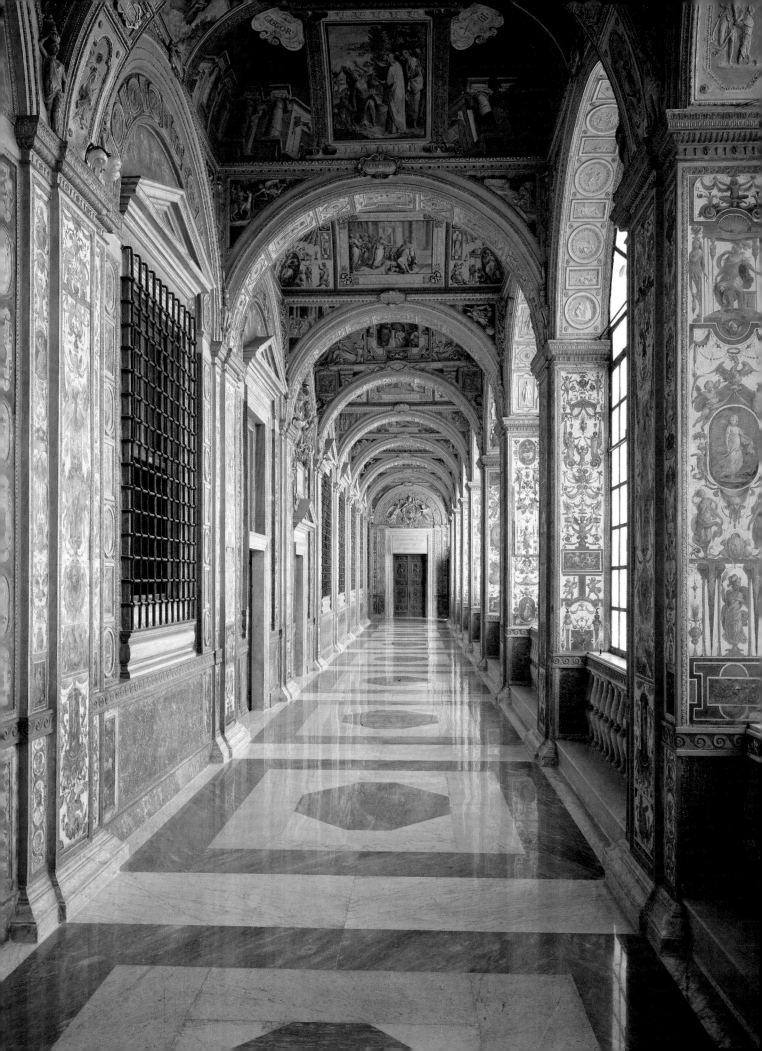

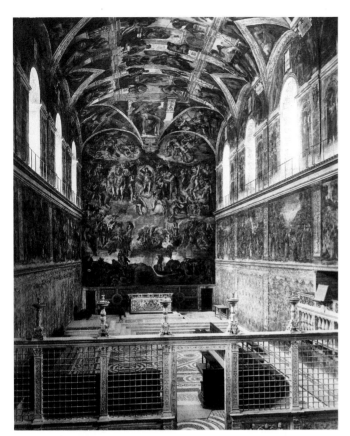

9.42 Michelangelo, Sistine Chapel, Rome, showing the ceiling (1508–12) and *Last Judgement* (1534–41).

Reformation, and baroque styles. Raphael's Loggia (Fig. **9.41**) forms part of the Vatican Palace apartments. Based on Raphael's study of ancient Rome and its buildings, the Loggia's theme is one of delight in seemingly inexhaustible inventiveness. Flowers, fruit, vegetables, bizarre animal figures and winged *putti* feature throughout. On the ceiling vault is a series of frescoes devoted to Old Testament themes, called *Raphael's Bible*. Raphael's work the *Deliverance of St. Peter* (Fig. **9.19**) is also found in these apartments.

The Vatican is a rich complex of artistry reflecting the times—the Church, the Papacy and their interrelationships with the world. Perhaps the crowning jewel is the Sistine Chapel (Figs. **9.15** to **9.17**) with its magnificent ceiling. But the ceiling is only a part. The entirety of the Sistine Chapel (Fig. **9.42**) is a supreme recreation of perfect classical harmony of form.

SUGGESTIONS FOR THOUGHT AND DISCUSSION

We have seen in this chapter that the Renaissance was made up of a vast array of concepts, styles, and attitudes. And yet in many ways it was a continuation of ideas present in the Middle Ages. Certainly interest in neo-Platonic thought continued in this period. We need to tie the thread of neo-Platonism as it was visually represented by Michelangelo and intellectually expressed by Ficino. What understandings can we draw from these examples, and how do they compare with neo-Platonism as we have seen it in previous chapters? What elements or ideas have we seen which were developments of medieval ideas?

The concept of Humanism and the emergence of the individual as a dignified, earthly entity is crucial to our understanding of this period. We have seen the rise of the playwright and composer and the emergence of the artist and the architect as individuals, rather than the anonymous artisans they had been in the Middle Ages. How does that fact, as well as thematic expressions in the arts, relate to the broader concepts of Humanism and specifically to the philosophies of Petrarch? Can you also suggest a relationship between all of these Renaissance concepts and the discoveries in science, exploration, and economics?

■ What events in the late Middle Ages may have contributed to political and other forces which caused the Reformation and split the Roman Catholic Church?
■ How were religious and practical concerns focused in this time of upheaval?
■ What major stylistic characteristics were common to the arts of the Renaissance?
■ What major stylistic characteristics linked the arts of the High Renaissance?
■ Why do we distinguish between the Early Renaissance and the High Renaissance as intellectual and artistic periods?
■ How does the Vatican as an expression of artistry reflect the ideas, ideals, and necessities of Roman Catholicism?

9.41 Raphael's Loggia, Vatican, Rome, c.1516–19.

CHAPTER TEN

THE LATE RENAISSANCE AND THE BAROQUE AGE

There was nervousness and unease in many leading minds in the decades following the close of the High Renaissance. The Reformation had challenged institutional Christian faith and its authority. The proposal of a heliocentric universe knocked humankind from its previously assured place at the center of all things. Harmony seemed once more to be an unattainable ideal as Europe was riven by wars and as philosophers and the new breed of scientists cast doubt on the certainties of the Renaissance. The modern age was in the making. Mannerism in art probed the borders of refinement and even perversity. The Baroque meant opulence, intricacy, ornateness and appeal to the emotions, and outdid its predecessors in reflecting the grandiose expectations of its patrons. Diverse and widespread, Baroque art took Renaissance clarity of form and recast it into intricate patterns of geometry and fluid movement.

10.1 Bernini, *Baldacchino* in St. Peter's, Rome, 1624–33. Gilded bronze, height c.100ft (30m).

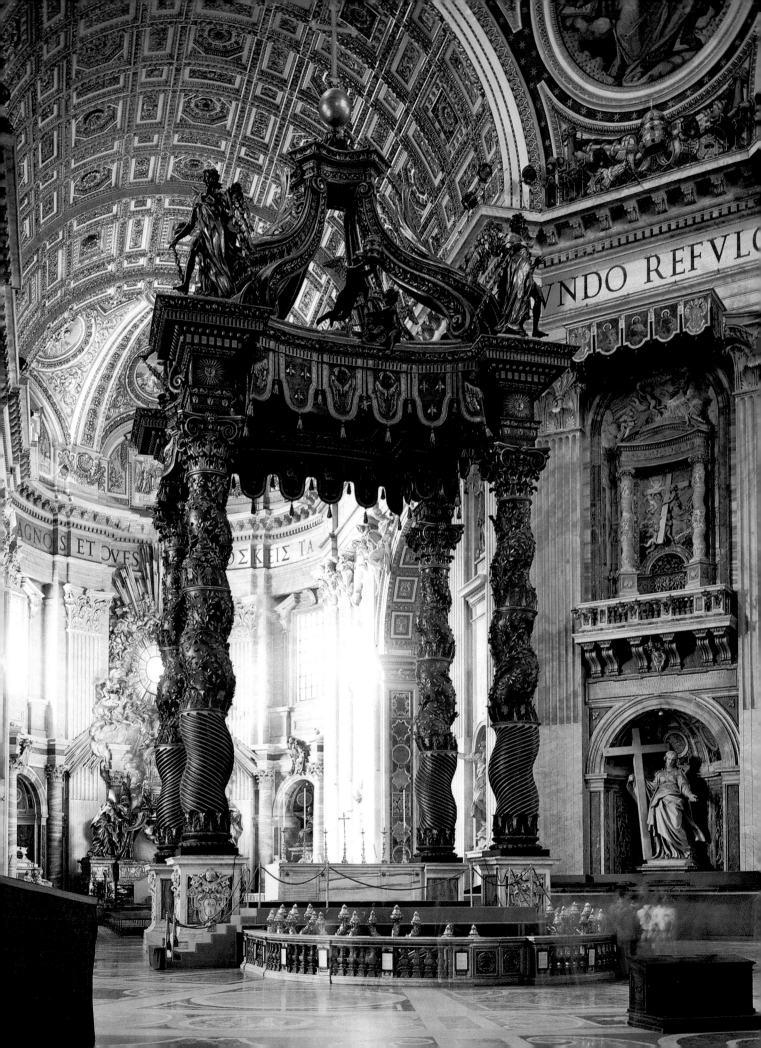

CONTEXTS AND CONCEPTS

The Reformation

"Luther," wrote Erasmus, "arose and threw the apple of discord into the world." The Reformation was in fact a climax of centuries of sectarian agitation. In the fourteenth century, English cries for reform and resentment of papal authority produced an English translation of the Scriptures, and caused John Wycliffe to pronounce that the corrupt clergy and even the Pope were "the damned limbs of Lucifer". But reform and separation are worlds apart. The effects of the Reformation contributed to profound turmoil in the Western world for the last three-quarters of the sixteenth century.

The discord of religious rebellion was rampant as various Protestant sects arose, some of them more dogmatic and intolerant than Roman Catholicism. Many of these sects had a significant effect on the arts. Zwingli, in Zurich, modeled his church on the New Testament and decreed that music was to put babies to sleep, not to praise God. He also persuaded the Zurich city council in 1524 to remove all works of art from the city's churches. Within Protestant sects there was persecution of other Protestants, and radical groups such as the Anabaptists suffered at the hands of Protestants and Catholics alike. In Geneva, John Calvin's revolt gave birth to a church-city and to a Protestant sect that quickly spread throughout Europe and eventually to North America. Geneva had just overthrown the Dukes of Savoy, but had not joined the Swiss confederation. Calvin's zealots gained political power and passed religious laws in the city council—church attendance became mandatory, and heresy was punishable by death or life imprisonment. Calvin called for a capitalistic spirit based on unceasing labor in gainful pursuits for the glory of God. Schisms and intolerance brought war, severing of commercial relationships, and frenetic and intense religious conviction. Protestant Reformation led to Roman Catholic Counter-Reformation. Religious wars were widespread, and in 1542 the Roman Catholic Inquisition was established in an attempt literally to destroy all non-Catholic belief.

Humanism and the Reformation

Although humanism was by no means identical with the Reformation and did not even lead directly to it, it did much to prepare the way. The most obvious contributions of the Humanists were their philological techniques and experience, acquired in the study of the classics, and their interest in and publication of patristic literature and Biblical texts. These in turn gave them a knowledge of primitive Christianity which they readily contrasted with the church of their own day. Many of them came to look upon the highly organized ecclesiastical hierarchy, the secular activities of the clergy, and the hair-splitting refinements of scholasticism as corruptions of Christianity. Thus they demanded reforms and urged that the church return to the preaching of the simple gospel of Jesus and promote morality and peace.

Although the Christian Humanists continued to believe in a higher and a lower plane of morality, one for the clergy and one for the laity, they were aware of the gulf which separated the Christian and the natural man and sought to narrow it. They attempted to apply to the society of their day the ethics of the Sermon on the Mount, supplemented by the ethics of the Stoics. Their criticism of immorality among the clergy did much to intensify the dissatisfaction of the Europeans with the church.

Equally important was the emphasis of the Christian Humanists upon the inwardness of religion, which led them to minimize such externals as images, music, church festivals, and the sacraments. Erasmus, for example, threw doubt on the doctrine of transubstantiation and imparted this doubt to Melanchthon, who attacked it before Luther. He also influenced Zwingli, who demanded a severely simple form of worship, and even the Illuminati of Spain. But Erasmus himself declined to draw the consequences of his religious views, primarily because this would threaten the unity of Christendom. It was this concern, more than anything else, which separated him from the Protestant reformers.

Christian Humanism as a predominantly intellectual movement could not present a common front or evoke a dynamic popular enthusiasm against the conservative and reactionary forces of that period of storm and stress. With but few exceptions, the Humanists remained aloof from the turmoil which accompanied the Reformation, preferred the contemplative life, and believed that they could best carry out their reforms within the framework of the traditional church. Although there were strong religious elements in Italian as well as northern Humanism, there was no one formula for binding together large numbers of people in a positive, dynamic religious movement.

Stressing the fundamental goodness of man and ignoring the Augustinian doctrine of original sin, the Humanists remained fundamentally optimistic with respect to what could be accomplished by combining the study of the classics with that of Christianity. This attitude contrasted sharply with the Lutheran emphasis upon faith and the Calvinist emphasis upon predestination. Submerged throughout most of Europe by the tumult accompanying the Reformation, Humanism appeared again in a new form in the movement of the Enlightenment, when the *philosophes*, basing their optimism to a large degree upon the scientific achievements of the sixteenth and seventeenth centuries, conjured up another "heavenly city".[1]

Practicalities

Into the religious upheaval of the Renaissance and its human-centered universe burst the frightening revelations of scientific discovery. The spirit of inquiry was particularly concerned with astronomy. In 1530 Copernicus transformed the world and humankind's perception of itself, its universe, and its God by formulating a heliocentric (sun-centered) theory of the universe (Copernican Theory). Although not immediately accepted, such an insight was devastating to those whose view of reality placed humankind as the ultimate being in an earth-centered universe. The visual arts, especially, reflected the changed perception of a universe of limitless, as opposed to tightly controlled, space.

Adding to the disturbance and disillusionment of the age was a new and critical approach to the basic questions of life. Montaigne in his *Essays* stated that every man "carries in himself the entire form of the human state" and injected disillusionment by emphasizing doubt and the contradictory nature of truth. Nicolo Machiavelli's *The Prince*, written early in the century, extolled the virtue of double standards, ultimate pragmatism, and the fundamental wickedness of all men.

None of this activity can be seen in isolation from political reality. In Paris on 15 February 1515, on the death of King Louis XII, Francis I assumed the French throne. Full of youthful vigor and power he and his army set out to conquer Milan. Bolstered by the Papacy, supported by Swiss mercenaries, and relieved by Venetian armies, however, Milan did not fall so easily. By 14 September 1515 Francis had nevertheless defeated the most renowned armies of Europe. A very frightened Pope Leo X made peace and granted Francis the right to nominate bishops, thereby strengthening French monarchical nationalism and further weakening papal authority.

In 1519 Emperor Maximilian died, leaving vacant the throne of the Holy Roman Empire, now a patchwork of kingdoms scattered across Europe. Three claimants sought the prize—Francis I, Charles (Carlos) I of Spain (then nineteen years old), and another young monarch, Henry VIII of England. The electorate of the Empire selected the Spanish monarch, who became Emperor Charles V. His succession began a bitter struggle among the three monarchs that tore at Europe for a generation. Francis I, meanwhile, was sympathetic to Humanist ideas. He saw the Protestant revolt as a threat to his own authority, and it became a fanatical preoccupation. He supported the strong tradition of Renaissance art and Humanism in France. Leonardo spent his last years at the court of Francis, and later Italian artists brought a changing style of art.

By the mid-sixteenth century Italy had been invaded not only by the French, but by the Spanish as well. Rome was sacked in 1527, and that date essentially marks the close of the era in the visual arts, which had seen under Papal patronage a remarkable, if brief, outpouring which we call the High Renaissance. Visual art, especially, then turned in a different direction to express the spiritual and political turmoil of its age.

	GENERAL EVENTS	LITERATURE & PHILOSOPHY	VISUAL ART	THEATRE & DANCE	MUSIC	ARCHITECTURE
1515	Francis I of France Charles I, Holy Roman Emperor					
1525	The Reformation begins Henry VIII of England Sack of Rome by Spain Copernicus – Heliocentricity		Bronzino El Greco Tintoretto Clouet	Machiavelli Tasso Cardinal Bibiena Commedia dell'Arte Sebastiano Serlio The Pleiade	Johan Walter	Lescot Palladio
1550	Council of Trent – Counter-Reformation Kepler – Laws of Planetary Motion Elizabeth I of England	Sir Philip Sidney Edmund Spenser Cervantes	Holbein the Younger Bologna Breughel the Elder	Catherine de Medici Balthasar Beaujoyeulx Teatro Olympico Fabrizio Caroso Cervantes De Vega	Palestrina Thomas Morley	Della Porta Borromini
1600	Galileo – Telescope Francis Bacon Henry IV of France Pope Paul V Descartes Thirty Years War Louis XIV of France	Montaigne Francis Bacon John Milton	Caravaggio Rubens Rembrandt Bernini	Marlowe Shakespeare Cesare Negri Beaumont and Fletcher Ben Jonson Inigo Jones Corneille Racine Molière	Caccini Jacopo Peri Monteverdi Buxtehude	
1650	Pope Innocent X Stradivarius Violins Oliver Cromwell	John Locke	Van Ruisdael Hals Puget Velázquez Coysevox Van Dyck Vermeer Poussin	John Dryden Wm. Wycherly Wm. Congreve French Academy of Dance	Rameau Corelli Lully Scarlatti Vivaldi Handel J.S. Bach	Le Vau Hardouin-Mansart Wren
1700		Alexander Pope Jonathan Swift				Neumann

10.2 Timeline of the Late Renaissance and Baroque Age.

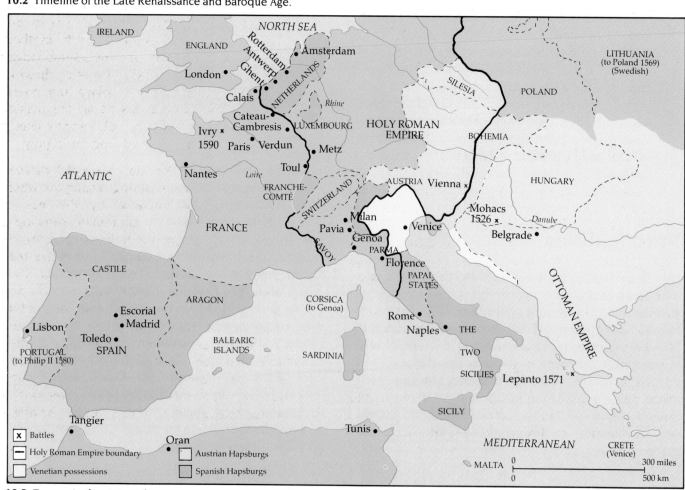

10.3 Europe in the sixteenth century.

The Counter-Reformation

The Roman Catholic response to Protestantism was the Council of Trent (1545–63) and the Counter-Reformation. Although little could be done to assuage the conflict and its social effects, conditions within the Catholic Church stabilized as a result of a determined attempt to prevent the Reformation spreading. The Council's decision to undertake a policy of attracting worshippers to the Church through art was of extreme significance to the arts. That momentous decision, humanitarian voices of restraint, and general fatigue closed the sixteenth century with a series of edicts of toleration and an impetus for a new, emotional art later called baroque that gave the seventeenth and early eighteenth centuries a quality unknown before or since.

The Bourgeoisie

Renaissance inquiry and exploration continued within a new framework. Magellan's global circumnavigation opened man's horizons fully. The "New World" was explored and pillaged, filling to overflowing the coffers of strengthened, independent European states, and to a large degree underwriting the cost of expensive artistic production. Colonialism and trade produced a growing and powerful middle class of wealthy merchants. Often the wealthy middle classes became enthusiastic patrons of the arts, anxious to acquire artistic works that reflected their perception of their own opulence.

Systematic Rationalism

The scientific inquiry of Copernicus was only the beginning of concern for orderly systems. Giordano Bruno (1548–1600) speculated upon a universe of infinite size, comprised of numerous solar systems and galaxies. As a reward for his trouble he was burned at the stake. Kepler (1571–1630) postulated the laws of planetary motion. Galileo (1564–1642) invented the telescope and anticipated the laws of motion. Sir Francis Bacon (1561–1626) proposed his *Novum Organum*, in which he established inductive reasoning as the basis for scientific inquiry. René Descartes (1596–1650) formulated scientific philosophy and Isaac Newton (1642–1727) discovered the laws of gravity. The effect of such inquiry and exploration was an irreversibly broadened understanding or awareness of the universe and humanity's place within it. That understanding permeated every aspect of Western culture. Its underlying philosophy was systematic rationalism that is, a seeking after logical, systematic order based on an intricate, moving, and changing universe subject to natural laws, and, therefore, relatively predictable. The artistic reflection of that philosophy was a widespread style called baroque. Consistent with the time, baroque arts sought rational order in intricate relationships and, like science and philosophy, held firmly in place by a Renaissance spirit, lifted branches into an atmosphere of emotional and unrestrained action.

Philosophy

Francis Bacon

Born with easy access to power and prestige, Francis Bacon studied law, entered politics, and became a member of Parliament. Under James I he became Attorney General, Lord Keeper of the Seal, and Lord Chancellor. In 1618 he was raised to the peerage as Baron Verulam, and in 1621 became Viscount St. Albans. Not above treachery and corruption, he fell from grace as rapidly as he had risen. His realism and perseverance, however, enabled him to produce his valuable enunciation of scientific method.

He was a prolific writer and his talents ranged from the scientific to the poetic. He is credited by some scholars as the author of plays and poems attributed to Shakespeare. His *Essays* are masterpieces of English literature. His philosophy used a methodology which anticipated modern inquiry.

> Bacon is a child of the new hope which dawned with the Renaissance, of discovering the whole truth about the universe by the use of reason.... Bacon ... is content to develop a method of discovery and to leave to others its utilization. His mind was less speculative than Leonardo's and more empirical than Descartes'. For him the great instrument to understanding is *invention*, or the abandonment of random discovery for deliberate research. So, too, the first purpose of *invention* is practical—the domination of nature by man. Knowledge, he tells us, is power. The condition of invention is acquaintance with and right interpretation of nature. Paradoxically, we conquer her by obeying her.[2]

Bacon's method was based on induction, the progression from specifics to generalities. Fundamental to this process is the examination of negative instances, and a critical spirit, which prevents one jumping to unwarranted conclusions. Verification of conclusions by continual observation and experiment is essential.

Bacon believed the task of science was to conquer nature by obeying her. The task of poetry, on the other hand, was to conquer nature by freeing the mind from obedience to nature and releasing it into its own world, wherein nature could be reshaped. In Bacon's own words in the *Advancement of Learning*, "Therefore, poetry was ever thought to have some participation of divineness, because it doth raise and erect the mind by submitting the show of things to the desires of the mind, whereas reason doth buckle and bow the mind unto the nature of things."

Montaigne

Michel de Montaigne (1533–92) derived his philosophy from the classical forms of self-discipline, which he found in Socrates and the Stoics. He found religions of worship and mystical revelation incomprehensible, whether Greek or Christian. On the other hand, he granted the mind and body "their ordinary comforts". Sobriety, control of the will, and bowing to reason were the basis of his outlook. Montaigne had an extraordinarily broad viewpoint, and he anticipated many of the ideas of the next two centuries. He was modest, truthful, and unprejudiced. He had a profound understanding of his own limitations and an admiration of excellence whether in literature or people. He concentrated primarily on reason. He separated theology and philosophy, and argued that scientific discoveries of the age, such as in astronomy, which were in conflict with Church teaching, could be accepted as a matter of reason and without theological conclusions.

Absolutism

One further important aspect of seventeenth- and early eighteenth-century life was absolutism. Although some democratic ideals existed, the major force in European life and art was the absolute monarch, who received his mandate from God, according to the theory of the divine right of kings. Strong dynasties of rulers controlled Europe. England passed its crown through the Tudors from Henry VIII to Elizabeth I (1558–1603). England experienced its own turmoil as Charles I and the monarchy were toppled by Cromwell, but the Restoration and Charles II quickly returned the country to continental European style and elegance. Style, elegance and opulence, the last of which, at least, was an undeniable characteristic of the age, were exemplified and personified by France's Louis XIV, the Sun King (1643–1715). His court and its splendors took further Roman Catholic encouragement of artistic development.

In the first half of the seventeenth century secular control over religious affairs was consolidated in the European states. The growth of absolutism based on divine right made it difficult for rulers to envisage any society other than one in which the people followed the religion of the sovereign. And as we have seen, it was politically advantageous for rulers to clothe themselves with divine right. The Protestant movement, which sought truth in the Bible alone, continued nonetheless in defiance of state churches. In states where monarchical power proved strongest, dissent was forced underground or into asylum elsewhere, and yet in all cases, dissent became a powerful religious force, especially in countries like Germany where it was coupled with social, political and economic forces.

Even where Catholicism remained as the state religion, clashes of power between absolute monarchs and Popes continued to rage. It seems clear that by 1650 the Papacy no longer exercised authority over international affairs. During the rule of Pope Innocent X (1644–55) representatives of the European states refused to comply with papal demands that no peace be made with the Protestants. Papal pretensions were quite simply ignored by the European states.

By the beginning of the seventeenth century the Papacy had shifted its focus once more to Rome and cultural activity in pursuit of its policy of encouraging religious devotion through great art. This gave rise to the religious baroque style. At the same time Catholic interests fell into other hands. The Society of Jesus—the Jesuits—effectively stirred Catholic rulers to take action against the Protestants in the Thirty Years' War. However, Jesuit zealousness also sparked a Protestant and Catholic backlash centering on Jesuit political philosophy, which opposed the growth of absolute monarchies, and on the Jesuit pursuit of a highly systematized moral casuistry.

France, however, provides the best example of

the triumph of the absolutist state over the Church. Jean Armand du Plessis, Duke of Richelieu, Bishop of Luçon, and a cardinal, held the post of chief minister to Louis XIII (1610–43) from 1624 to 1642. He sought to strengthen the monarchy, and after a bitter conflict succeeded in subduing the Huguenots in 1628. The Peace of Alais in 1629 concluded the last of the religious wars, and deprived the Huguenots of their political and military rights, although their civil and religious rights remained protected under the Edict of Nantes. Thereafter the Huguenots were strong supporters of the monarchy.

Royal absolutism continued to tighten its grip under Cardinal Mazarin, Regent of Louis XIV (1643–1715) from 1643 to 1661. The upper nobility tried to stem the tide of royal absolutism, but, partially because of the refusal of the Huguenots to participate, the revolts did not succeed. As a result, the Huguenots gained a special religious status. When Mazarin died in 1661 at the end of the war between Spain and France, Louis XIV assumed complete control of France. In a swift reversal and armed with the spirit of "one God, one king, one faith", he took the advice of the Jesuits and initiated a program of persecution against the Huguenots. In 1685 he revoked the Edict of Nantes, thereby forcing them either to become Catholics or leave the country.

Louis XIV came into conflict with the Papacy and there was a possibility that a national church would be created in France, similar to that established by Henry VIII in England. However, Louis found it to his advantage not to break with Rome and pulled back. Articles which had been drawn up to limit the authority of the Pope in France were not enforced, although they remained the law.

Humankind may have lost its ordinal role in the universe as a result of Renaissance inquiry, but, after a shaky initial reaction, gained a new confidence in its inter-dependence with a far-flung and perhaps infinite universe.

Literature

The last quarter of the sixteenth century and virtually the whole of the seventeenth saw a remarkable flowering of literature in England. This was the long golden age of English poetry and drama: it might be said that the Renaissance, which had been slow to cross the English Channel, took a new and unprecedented form. After the seemingly interminable Wars of the Roses and the turbulence of the

Reformation, England under Elizabeth I entered a period of political and social stability that was reflected in a mood of optimism and readiness to experiment in cultural matters.

Lyric poetry enjoyed wide popularity across the social scale. The ability to compose a sonnet or to coin an original and witty turn of phrase was regarded as essential in any courtier, while the growing and increasingly prosperous middle class—no longer confined to the large towns, but extending throughout the shires and country towns—demanded cultivated diversion. Significantly, there was a large and educated readership of gentlewomen. Writers and booksellers quickly responded to this new market and its discriminating demands.

An early and notable contribution to this upsurge of interest was Sir Phillip Sidney's *Defense of Poesie*, a brilliant and forceful polemic which laid claim to the cultural high ground for verse. Sidney (1554-86), in many ways the model English Renaissance courtier and man of letters, had read widely and judiciously in ancient, Italian and French literature, and his sonnets, best represented in *Astrophel and Stella*, embodied the best in the delicacy, elegance and expressiveness of the writing of the time. His friend Edmund Spenser (1552-99) "Englished" classical Roman models in his *Shepheards Calendar*, a collection of eclogues; and in his unfinished masterpiece, *The Faerie Queene*, celebrated Elizabeth in a long allegorical romance. The greatest literary genius of all, of course, was William Shakespeare (1564-1616), most of whose work was for the theatre, but who also left the remarkable Sonnets, in which the resources of the English language to express profound, passionate and contradictory feelings are pushed to breathtaking extremes.

The mood darkened noticeably after the death of Queen Elizabeth in 1603. Political instability and economic difficulties threatened, and the finest writing of the Jacobean years turned away from love—the almost exclusive theme of the Elizabethans—to an anxious and often anguished inner questioning. John Donne (1573-1631) represents this sea-change: his early love sonnets are among the most urgently erotic poems in the language, whereas the work of his later years—he became Dean of St. Paul's—relentlessly explores the meaning of an intelligent man's relationship with his soul and with his God. Donne was among the leading figures in a group that has since become known as the Metaphysical Poets, after their concern with "first and last things". Their often intensely

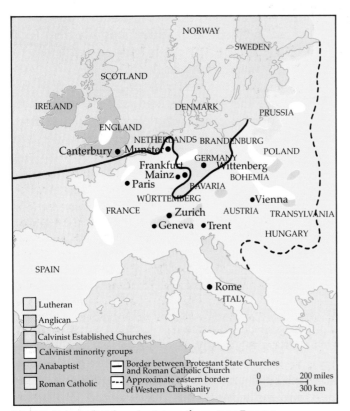

10.4 Religious divisions in sixteenth-century Europe.

private writing is characterized by deliberate and rich ambiguity of syntax and imagery. The poems of George Herbert (1593-1633)—never meant for publication—represent this movement at its best.

Many of the methods of the Metaphysicals were used and developed by Andrew Marvell (1621-78), a poet as public as they had been private. He wrote at the time of, and in the period immediately after, the Civil War, and his *Horatian Ode* in praise of Oliver Cromwell marks the return of poets and poetry to the political stage. His contemporary, John Milton (1608-74), was also deeply committed to the Parliamentarian cause, and his earlier works reflect his Humanistic education and his belief in the importance of the classical cultural and political heritage. In old age, blind, solitary and disappointed by the failure of his political ideals, he wrote his masterpiece, *Paradise Lost*. This monumental verse account of the Fall of Satan and of Adam and Eve has been described as the literary equivalent of the baroque. His richly Latinate language is deeply musical, confident and powerful; his themes are epic, tragic and uncompromisingly Protestant.

The Restoration of Charles II, which had so embittered Milton, saw a marked decline in the seriousness and quality of poetic output. Verse of cynical and easy licentiousness became typical of these culturally shallow years. The Glorious Revolution of 1688 marked a decisive change as the middle classes broke the power of the absolute monarch and the influence of the court. The confidence and pragmatism of the new Augustan age found its voice in John Dryden (1631-1700), whose satirical *Absolom and Architophel* marked a new role for the poet as a witty and entertaining critic of his age. Alexander Pope (1688-1744) filled and developed the part with consummate ease. The most brilliant satirist of the Augustan, and perhaps any, age, his devastatingly poised rhyming couplets hit home in the *Rape of the Lock*. Pope's acute sense of the importance of classical values and of the extent to which contemporary society fell short of honoring them led him first to develop a mock-heroic form, and then to fill it with profound moral anger in the *Dunciad*. Pope's name is often linked with that of Jonathan Swift (1667-1745), for this Anglo-Irish satirist and churchman shared many of his concerns. Swift was, if anything, more bitter: *Gulliver's Travels* mocked pomposity and woolly-headed idealism equally, while his other famous work in prose, *A Modest Proposal*, took satire to the very edge of horror with its chillingly deadpan suggestion that the English should solve the "Irish Problem" by eating the babies of the poor.

This period also saw the development of the novel. An early form of this genre had been in existence in Elizabethan England, but it was Miguel Cervantes (1547-1616) in Spain who first exploited its full potential in *Don Quixote*, which recounts the adventures of a comically self-deluded knight. The novel is a parody of the chivalric romances of an earlier age, but also an eloquent lament for a lost time of innocence and moral clarity. Writers in both France and England began to experiment with the versatile new form, which seemed ideally suited for the treatment of contemporary and everyday themes—though it would be a mistake to think of these works as "realistic". It was with Daniel Defoe (1660-1731) that the future direction of the European novel was established: his *Robinson Crusoe* is widely known and read to this day, and with *Moll Flanders* the novel found its voice and its audience. The form would henceforth be based on an imaginary biography or autobiography set in contemporary society; the central figure would be a man or woman (usually the latter) with whom the reader (generally female) would identify. So it was that the great age of poetry came to a close with the rise of the novel.

THE ARTS
OF THE LATE RENAISSANCE AND BAROQUE AGE

TWO-DIMENSIONAL ART

Mannerism

The turmoil of the last three-quarters of the sixteenth century is reflected in painting. Considerable debate exists about the nature of the period between the clearly developed style of the High Renaissance and the baroque style. The prevalent view today is a positive one, which regards this era in painting as a response to the conflicts of its time and not as a decadent and affected imitation of the High Renaissance. The name attached to the most significant trend, if not style, of the period is mannerism. The term originates from the mannered or affected appearance of the subjects in the paintings. These works are coldly formal and inward looking. Their wrongly proportioned forms, icy stares, and subjective viewpoint can be puzzling and intriguing if they are seen out of context. Nevertheless, we find an appealing modernism in their emotional, sensitive, subtle, and elegant content. At the same time, mannerism contains an intellectualism that distorts reality, alters space, and makes often obscure cultural allusions. Anti-classical emotionalism, abandonment of classical balance and form, conflict with its High Renaissance predecessors, and clear underpinnings of formality and geometry epitomize the troubled nature of mannerism's style and times.

Bronzino's *Portrait of a Young Man* (Fig. **10.5**) makes the point. A strong High Renaissance central triangle dominates the basic composition of this work. However, line has a nervous and unstable quality; incongruous, juxtaposed rectilinear and curvilinear forms create an uneasy and emotional feeling. The colors of the painting are very cold (greens and blacks), and the starkness of the background adds to the feeling of discomfort. Shadows are harsh, and skin quality is cold and stonelike. Although light and shade create some dimension, lack of atmospheric or linear perspective brings graphically clear background objects forcefully into the forward plane of the picture. The pose and affected stare of the young man are typical of the mannered artificiality that gave this movement its name. Finally, although less obviously in this work than in El Greco's *St. Jerome* (Fig. **10.6**), the human form is attenuated and disproportionate. The young man's head is entirely too small for his body and particularly for his hands.

El Greco (1541–1614), a Spanish painter born in Crete (hence the name E*l Greco*, the Greek), exemplified the strong, inward-looking subjectivity of his time. In *St. Jerome* we find alternation and compression of space. Forms are piled on top of each other in two-dimensional, as opposed to deep space. Rather than the closed composition of the High Renaissance, composition here, as in Bronzino's *Portrait of a Young Man*, escapes the frame, a comment on the disturbed centrality of humankind in its universe. Emotional disturbance is further heightened by the attenuated form of St. Jerome himself. In purely color terms, El Greco's work is not cold. The predominantly monochromatic shades of red-brown in this painting belong to the "warm" end of the color spectrum. However, the artist's characteristic use of strongly highlighted forms (the highlight is pure white, as opposed to a higher value of the base hue) sharpens contrasts and intensifies the emotional tone of the work. This non-verisimilar treatment (brushstroke is obvious in many places) allows the viewer to look beyond the surface reality of the painting to a special truth within.

The characteristics noted in these two works are typical. The tendencies of mannerism can be found in the works of other artists, such as Parmigianino, Tintoretto, and Pontormo (Italy), Morales (Spain), Clouet (France), Holbein the Younger (Germany), Mabuse and Brueghel the Elder (Flanders).

Baroque style

The seventeenth century was a period of relative stability. With that stability came an age of intellectual, spiritual, and physical action. Above it all stood wealth and strong personal emotion. Along with the new age came a new style, the baroque, which reflected the characteristics and concerns of its age, and did so in forms that acknowledged the presence of middle-class patronage in addition to that of the Church and the nobility. Painting appealed to the emotions and to a desire for magnificence through opulent ornamentation, but it also adopted a systematized and rational composition in which ornamentation was unified through variation on a single theme. Realism replaced beauty as an objective for painting. Color and grandeur were emphasized, as was dramatic use of light and shade. In all baroque art a

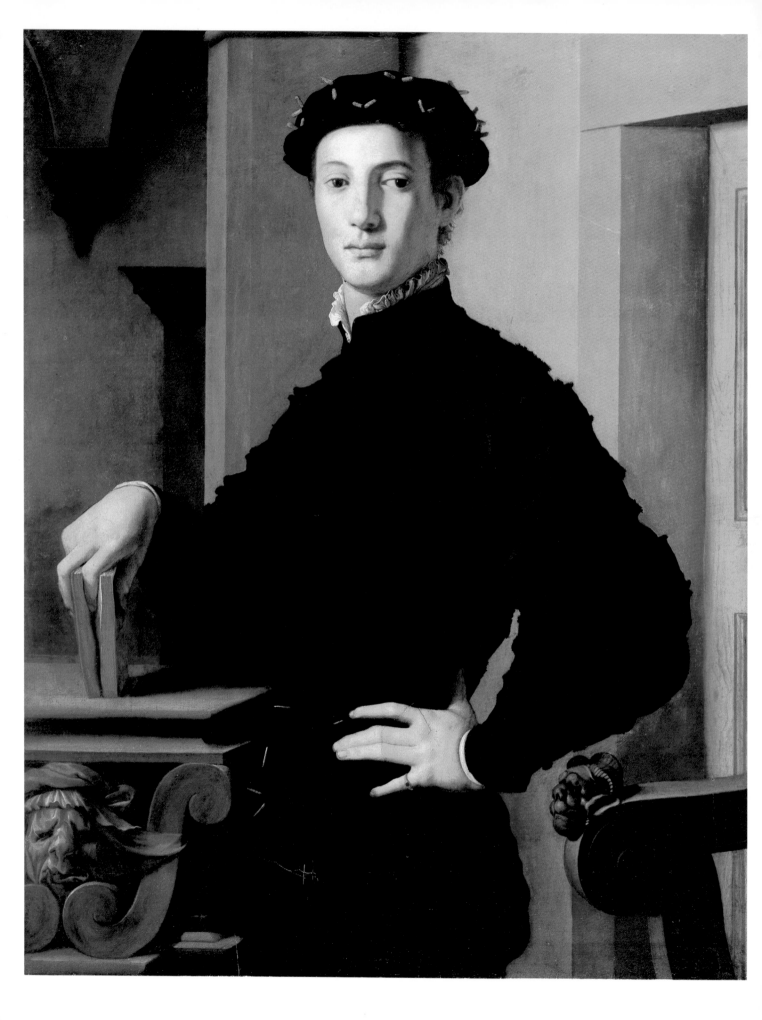

10.5 Bronzino (Agnolo di Cosimo di Mariano), *Portrait of a Young Man*, c.1535–40. Oil on wood, 37⅝ × 29½ins (95.6 × 75cm). The Metropolitan Museum of Art, New York (Bequest of Mrs. H.O. Havemeyer, 1929).

10.6 El Greco (Domenikos Theotokopoulos), *Saint Jerome*, c.1610–14. Canvas, 66¼ × 43½ins (168 × 110.5cm). National Gallery of Art, Washington DC (Chester Dale Collection).

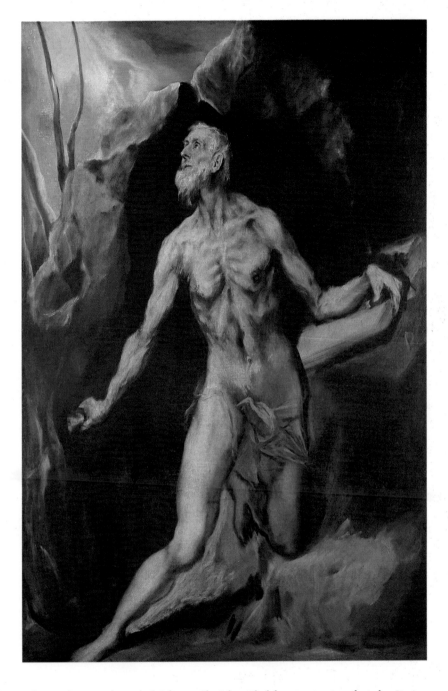

sophisticated organizational scheme subordinated a multitude of single parts to the whole and carefully merged one part into the next to create an exceedingly complex but highly unified design. Open composition was used to symbolize the notion of an expansive universe. The viewer's eye traveled off the canvas to a wider reality. The human figure, as an object or focus in painting, could be monumental in full Renaissance fashion, but could also now be a minuscule figure in a landscape, part of, but subordinate to, an overwhelming universe. Above all, baroque style was characterized by intensely active compositions that emphasized feeling rather than form, emotion rather than the intellect.

Baroque painting was diverse in application, although fairly easily identifiable as a general style. It was used to glorify the Church and religious sentiment—both Catholic and Protestant. It portrayed the magnificence of secular wealth, both noble and common, and it spread throughout Europe, with examples to be found in every corner.

The idea of absolutism dominated individual as well as collective psychology in the baroque age, each man governing his life like an absolute monarch. Balthasar Gracian advises the courtier: "Let all your actions be those of a king, or at least worthy of a king in due proportion to your estate." Every man was inwardly a king. The ego, or the superego, became an entity which recognized no limits beyond itself.... The baroque artist exercised this sovereignty "in due proportion to his estate" as Balthasar Gracian would have any man do; that is, his art. The seventeenth century produced artists who, if not solitaries, were at least independent men ... who considered their art, even if it depended upon commissions, as a personal activity, allowing no limits to be placed on their creative power.[3]

Individual paintings exhibit clear individuality. Virtuosity emerged as each artist sought to establish a style that was distinctly his own.

Caravaggio

In Rome—the center of early baroque—papal patronage and the Counter-Reformation spirit brought artists together to make Rome the 'most beautiful city of the entire Christian world'. Caravaggio (1569–1609) was probably the most significant of the Roman baroque painters, and in two of his works we can see his extraordinary style, in which verisimilitude is carried to new heights. In the *Calling of St. Matthew* (Fig. **10.7**) highlight and shadow create a dynamic portrayal of the moment when the future apostle is touched by divine grace. However, we find here a religious subject depicted in contemporary terms. Realistic imagery turns away from idealized and rhetorical form, and presents itself, rather, in a mundane form. The call from Christ streams, with dramatic *chiaroscuro*, across the two groups of figures via the powerful gesture of Christ to Matthew. This great painting expresses one of the central themes of Counter-Reformation belief: that faith and grace are open to all who have the courage and simplicity to transcend intellectual pride, and that the spiritual understanding is a personal, mysterious and overpowering emotional experience.

We see the same emotional dynamism in Figure **10.8**, the *Death of the Virgin*. Here again, idealized imagery gives way to naturalism. Caravaggio had frequent conflicts with the Church, and in the case of the *Death of the Virgin*, the Roman parish of S Maria del Popolo rejected the

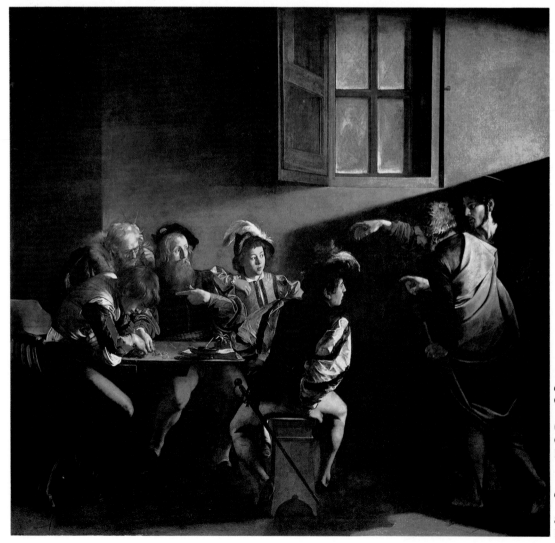

10.7 Caravaggio, *The Calling of St. Matthew*, c.1596–8. Oil on canvas, 11ft 1in × 11ft 5ins (338 × 348cm). Contarelli Chapel, S Luigi dei Francesi, Rome.

10.8 Caravaggio, *The Death of the Virgin*, 1605–6. Canvas, 12ft 1in × 8ft ½in (369 × 245cm). Louvre, Paris.

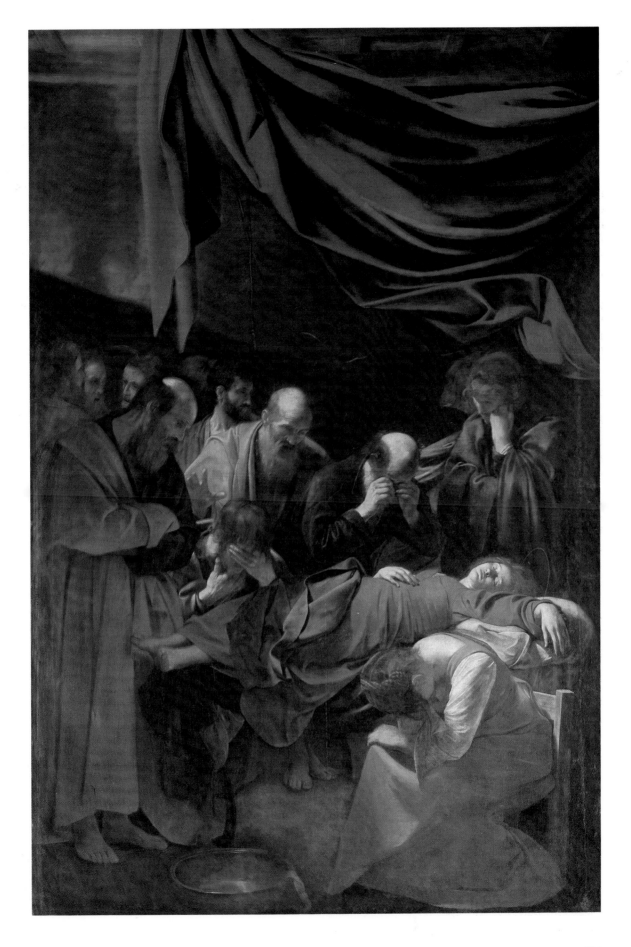

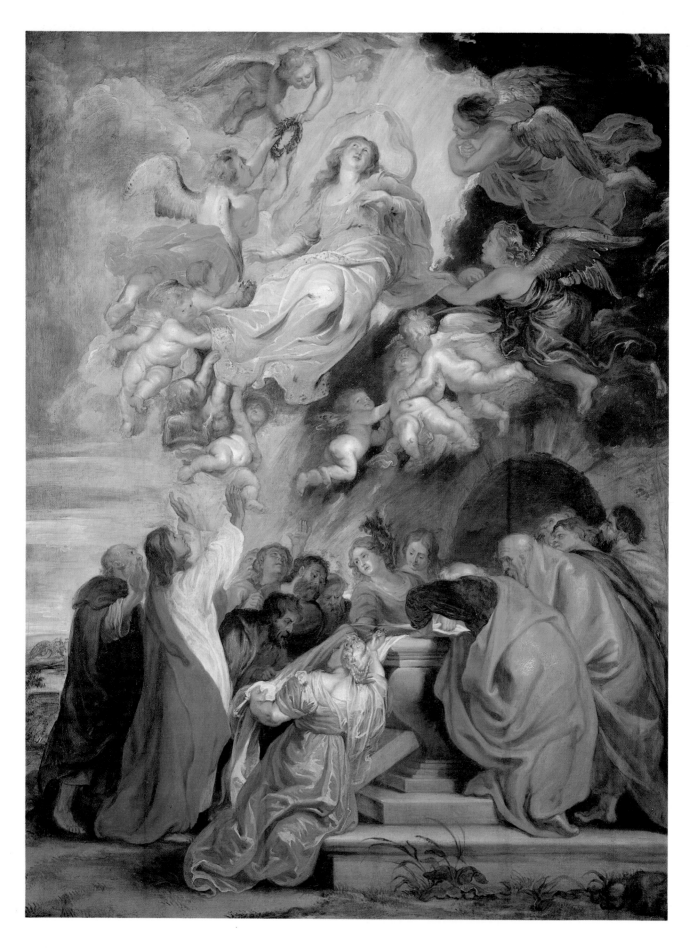

painting. Thereupon the Duke of Mantua purchased the work, on the advice of Rubens, who was then court painter. Before it was taken from Rome, however, it was put on public display for a week so that all Rome could see it.

Rubens

Peter Paul Rubens (1577–1640) painted in the baroque style with vast, overwhelming canvases and fleshy female nudes. His work also illustrates the use of art as religious propaganda. In the *Assumption of the Virgin* (Fig. **10.9**) Rubens presents a swirling and complex composition full of lively action, color, and curvilinear repetition. Typical of

Rubens are corpulent cupids and women whose flesh has a sense of softness and warmth we find in few other artists. Rubens' colors here are warm and predominantly limited to the red end of the spectrum. A diagonal sweep of green pulls through the figures in the upper left, but like all the low-value colors in this painting, it is subdued in brilliance. As a result the composition shows a strong contrast in light and dark and in lively and subdued tones. This work swirls comfortably through its uniformly curvilinear line. Detail is richly naturalistic, but each finely rendered part is subordinate to the whole. Rubens leads the eye around the painting, upward, downward, inward, and outward, occasionally escaping the frame entirely. Nevertheless, he maintains a High Renaissance central

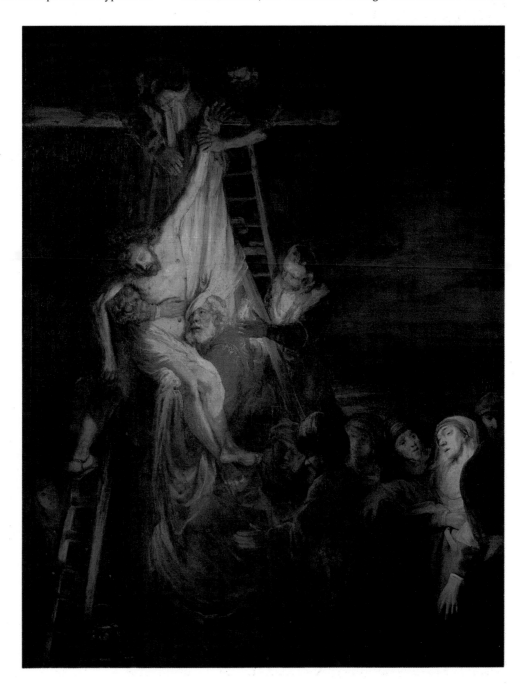

10.9 Rubens, *The Assumption of the Virgin*, c.1626. Wood, 49⅜ × 37⅛ins (125.4 × 94.2cm). National Gallery of Art, Washington DC (Samuel H. Kress Collection).

10.10 After Rembrandt van Rijn, *The Descent from the Cross*, c.1655. Canvas, 56¼ × 43¾ins (143 × 111cm). National Gallery of Art, Washington DC (Widener Collection).

triangle beneath the complexity, thus holding the broad base of the painting solidly in place and leading the eye upward to the lovely face of the Virgin at the apex. The overall feeling inspired by this painting is one of richness, glamor, decorativeness, and emotional optimism. Religious and artistic appeal is to worldly emotion and not to intellectualism or mystical asceticism.

Rubens produced works at a prolific rate, primarily because he ran what was virtually a painting factory, where he employed numerous artists and apprentices to assist in his work. He priced his paintings on the basis of their size and on the basis of how much actual work he, personally, did on them. We should not be overly disturbed by this fact, especially when we consider the individual qualities and concepts expressed in Rubens' work. His unique baroque style emerges from every painting, and even an untutored observer can recognize his works with relative ease. Clearly artistic value here lies in the conception, not merely in the handiwork.

Rembrandt

Rembrandt van Rijn (1606–69), in contrast to Rubens, could be called a middle-class artist. His genius lay not in producing glamorous and extravagant propaganda pieces, but rather in dramatically delivering the depths of human emotion and psychology. In contrast to Rubens, for example, Rembrandt suggests rather than depicts great detail. After all, the human spirit is intangible—it cannot be detailed, only alluded to. In Rembrandt we find atmosphere and shadow, implication and emotion. As in most baroque art, the viewer is invited to share in a feeling, to enter into an experience rather than to observe as an impartial witness.

Rembrandt's deposition scene *Descent from the Cross* (Fig. **10.10**) is at the opposite end of the emotional spectrum from Rubens' ascension scene, but it still conveys a feeling of richness. Colors are exclusively reds, golds, and red-browns. With the exception of the robe of the figure pressing into Christ's body, the painting is

10.11 Jacob van Ruisdael, *The Cemetery*, c.1655. Oil on canvas, 56 × 74¼ins (142 × 189cm). Detroit Institute of Arts (gift of Julius H. Haass, in memory of his brother Dr. Ernest W. Haass).

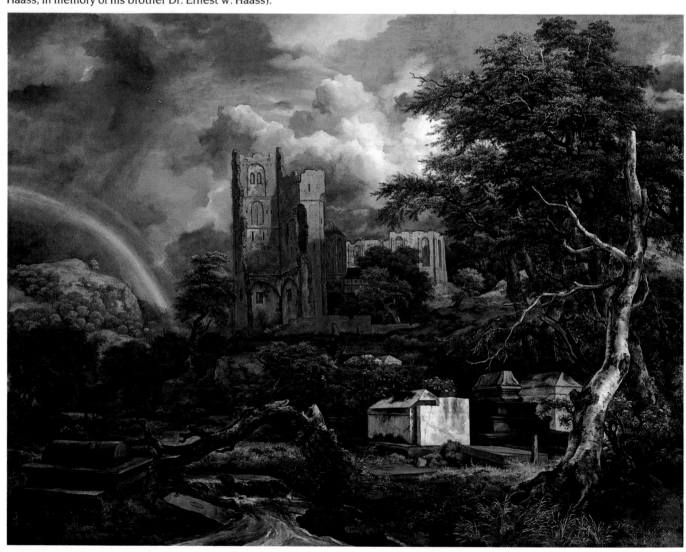

nearly monochromatic. Contrasts are provided and forms are revealed through changes in value. In typically open composition, line escapes the frame at the left arm of the cross and in the half forms at the lower right border. The horizontal line of the darkened sky is subtly carried off the canvas, middle right. A strong central triangle holds the composition together, growing from a darkly shadowed base, which runs the full width of the lower border, traveling upward along the highlighted form (lower right) and the ladder (lower left). Christ's up-stretched arm completes the apex of the triangle as it meets an implied extension of the ladder behind the cross. Drapery folds lead the eye downward and then outward in a gentle sweeping curve.

Van Ruisdael

Rembrandt's emotions were probably difficult for most collectors to cope with. More typical of the new, general marketplace and interests of the times were the emerging landscape painters. The painting by Jacob van Ruisdael (1628/9–82) called the *Cemetery* (Fig. **10.11**) provides another emotional experience of rich detail, atmosphere, light and shade, and grandiose scale. This painting is nearly five feet high and more than six feet wide. The graveyard and medieval ruins cast a spell of imagination and melancholy over the work. Humankind, by physical absence, at least in living form, is totally subordinated to the universe. The ruins suggest that even the physical effects of our presence shall pass away. Highlight and shadow lead the eye around the composition, but the path of travel is broken, or at least disturbed, by changes of direction, for example, in the tree trunk across the stream and in the stark tree limbs. Nature broods above the scene and we are led, again, outside the frame to an even wider, more diverse universe.

Baroque style was nearly universal in the period between 1600 and 1725, and further examples can be found in the paintings of Hals, Velázquez, Carracci, Van Dyck, Heda, Steen, Vermeer, Poussin, and Claude. Two-dimensional art stood at the doorway of the modern era.

SCULPTURE

The late sixteenth century witnessed relatively little sculpture production of major significance. However, the twisting, elongated form of *Mercury* (Fig. **10.12**) by Giovanni da Bologna (1529–1608) would be equivalent to the mannerist tendencies in painting of the same era. Affectation of pose, upward-striving line, linear emphasis, and nearly total detachment from earth suggest tension and nervous energy. Mercury races through the air seeking escape from the world and is supported by a puff of breath from a mask symbolizing the wind. The *Rape of the Sabine Women* (Fig. **10.13**) twists with frenetic fury. Line

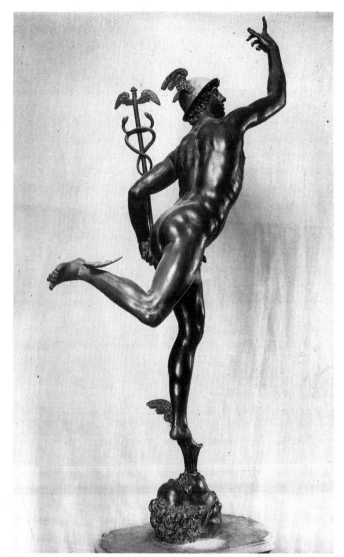

10.12 Giovanni Bologna, *Mercury*, c.1567. Bronze, height 69ins (175cm). Bargello, Florence.

and form fly off into space, violating Michelangelo's self-contained philosophies at every turn.

The splendor of the baroque was particularly noticeable in sculpture. Form and space were charged with energy, which carried beyond the limits of actual physical confines in the same sense as did Bologna's work. As did painting, sculpture appealed to the emotions through an inward-directed vision that invited participation rather than neutral observation. Feeling was the focus. Baroque sculpture also treated space pictorially, almost like a painting, to describe action scenes rather than single sculptural forms. The best examples we can draw upon are those of the sculptor Gianlorenzo Bernini (1598–1680).

David (Fig. **10.14**) exudes dynamic power, action, and emotion as he curls to unleash his stone at a Goliath standing somewhere outside the statue's frame. Our eyes

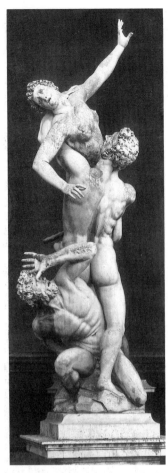

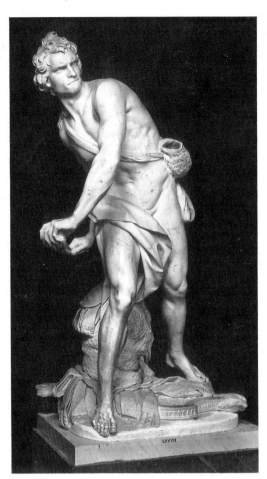

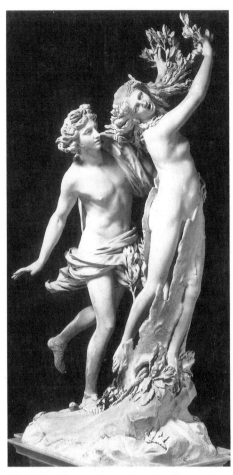

10.13 Giovanni Bologna, *The Rape of the Sabine Women*, 1583. Marble, height 13ft 6ins (411cm). Loggia dei Lanzi, Florence.

10.14 Bernini, *David*, 1623. Marble, height 67ins (170.2cm). Galleria Borghese, Rome.

10.15 Bernini, *Apollo and Daphne*, 1622-5. Marble, height 8ft (244cm). Galleria Borghese, Rome.

sweep upward along a diagonally curved line and are propelled outward by the concentrated emotion of David's expression. A wealth of detail occupies the composition. Detail is part of the work, elegant in nature, but ornamental in character. Repetition of the curvilinear theme carries throughout the work in deep, rich, and fully contoured form. Again the viewer participates emotionally, feels the drama, and responds to the sensuous contours of dramatically articulated muscles. Bernini's *David* flexes and contracts in action, rather than repressing pent-up energy as did Michelangelo's giant-slayer.

Apollo and Daphne (Fig. **10.15**) is almost whimsical or melodramatic by contrast to *David* but nevertheless exhibits the same active, diagonally moving upward curvature of line and ornamented detail. Every part of this complex sculpture is clearly articulated, but each part subordinates itself to the single theme of the overall work. Although statuary, *Apollo and Daphne* exudes motion, carrying itself beyond the confines of its actual form. Figures are frozen mid-stride—the next instant would carry them elsewhere. Daphne's hair flies in response to her twisting movement. Flesh is rendered sensuously.

This work is a pictorial description. More exists here than in previous works, whose forms barely emerge from their marble blocks.

The *Ecstasy* of St. *Theresa* (Fig. **10.16**) is a fully developed "painting" in sculptural form. It represents a statement by St. Theresa (one of the saints of the Counter-Reformation), describing how an angel had pierced her heart with a golden, flaming arrow: "The pain was so great that I screamed aloud; but at the same time I felt such infinite sweetness that I wished the pain to last forever." Amid richly opulent detail, accentuated by golden rays, the composition cries with the emotion of St. Theresa's ecstasy. Typical of baroque sculptural design, line swirls diagonally to create circular movement. Each detail merges easily into the next in an unbroken chain, however complex. Every aspect of the work is in motion. Figures float upward and draperies billow from an imaginary wind. Deep recesses and contours establish strong

10.16 Bernini, *Ecstasy of St Teresa*, 1645–52. Marble, height c.11ft 6ins (350cm). Cornaro Chapel, S Maria della Vittoria, Rome.

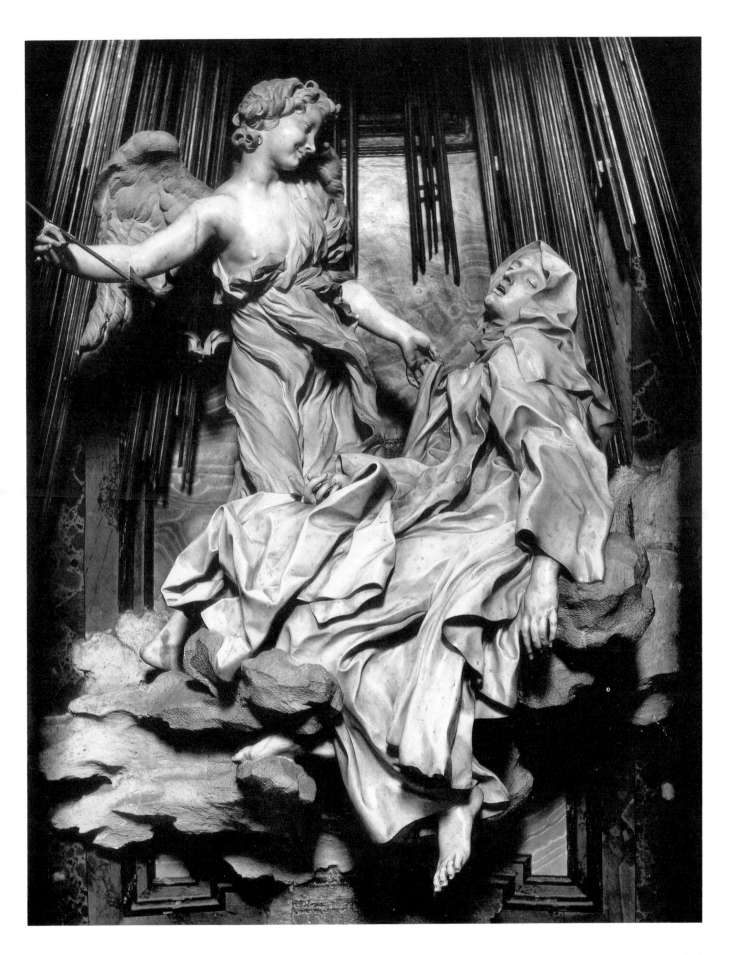

highlights and shadows, further heightening dramatic contrasts within the whole, in comparison with baroque painting and music. The drama of the "picture" forces involvement. Its intention is to overwhelm with an emotional and religious experience.

"Concentrating all their vital energy in a single supreme effort, the figures in baroque painting and sculpture seem to fragment their own personalities, to project the human soul beyond the corporeal husk in which it lies captive."[4] Pierre Puget's *Milo of Crotona* (Fig. **10.17**) seems possessed by a compulsive physical strength. Here power, in contrast to its usual interpretation in a style dominated by reason, remains raw and physical. Violent impulses spring forth under the stress of death and pain. In precisely the same sense, the portrait busts of Coysevox depict "character in the heat of action", as in the *Great Condé* (Fig. **10.18**).

MUSIC

The character of music in any given period derives not

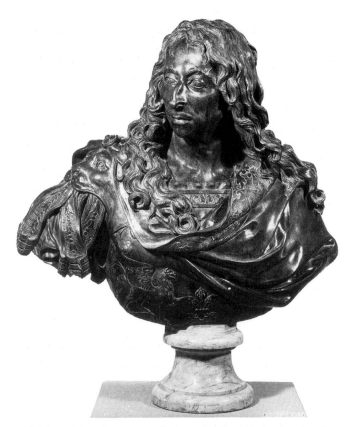

10.18 Antoine Coysevox, *The Great Condé*, 1688. Bronze, height 23ins (58.4cm). Louvre, Paris.

10.17 Pierre Puget, *Milo of Crotona*, 1671-83. Marble, height 8ft 10½ins (270.5cm). Louvre, Paris.

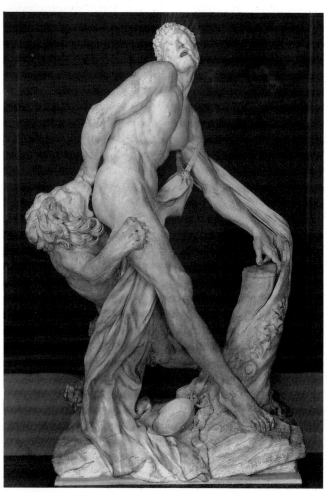

only from how melody, texture, and rhythm are used, but also from the timbres or tonal qualities of the voices and instruments used to produce musical sounds. Even the human voice has a diverse variety of colors, and the emotional or intellectual quality of sound can be enhanced or reduced by the way in which the singer employs vocal color and presentation. Musical instruments, while having a more limited range of timbres, likewise have their own individual tonal qualities. A violin and a trumpet sound quite unlike each other, and the same music played by a brass choir, as opposed to a string ensemble, is considerably different in its appeal to the listener's senses. We can only imagine, unless we have access to ancient instruments, the actual quality of musical sound in the baroque or any pre-modern era. In the Renaissance, instruments still adhered to the medieval concept of loud or soft instruments, basically the differences between the flute (recorder) and the violin (viol). Large ensembles such as orchestras, as we know them, were unheard of. Music sounded much "thinner" and less overwhelming.

In the courtly life of the sixteenth century dancing was widespread, and much instrumental music was composed with the dance in mind. Such works had clearly developed and consistent rhythmical patterns, and contrasts between dance pieces were important. Dance music also developed a theme and variation pattern.

Often a slow dance in duple meter preceded a fast dance in triple meter, both built on the same tune. Dance-related themes would later be fully developed by Bach in independent compositions called suites. In the latter part of the sixteenth century dance music for lute, keyboard instruments, and ensembles became increasingly popular. The introduction of the ballet of the French court (see section on Dance) brought forward a new outlet for musical composition.

In the same vein as Renaissance *commedia dell'arte* (see section on Theatre), improvization was popular and common in sixteenth-century music. Improvization usually took one of two forms—either the performer improvized ornamentation on a specific melody, or improvized a contrapuntal melody in harmony with an existing melody. Principal among improvized keyboard pieces was the *toccata*, a specialty of Venetian composers.

The Reformation brought many changes to Church music, from its complete absence in the services of the Calvinist sect, to new forms in Lutheran services. Even after the separation, Lutheran music maintained many of its Roman Catholic characteristics, including Latin texts and plainsong chants. The most important contribution of the Lutheran Reformation was the chorale. Contemporary hymns, many of which date back to Martin Luther for both text and tune, illustrate this form. Our four-part harmonies are of later modification, although the recent edition of the Lutheran Book of Worship attempts to return to the early chorale form. Originally the chorale was a single melody, stemming from the chant or folk song, and a text. Congregational singing was in unison and without accompaniment.

Lutheranism also contributed a considerable body of polyphonic choral settings, many from Luther's principal collaborator Johann Walter (1496–1574). These settings vary tremendously in style and source. Some were based on German *Lieder* and some on Flemish motets. However, polyphony, a complex texture, is not well suited for congregational singing, and polyphonic settings were uniformly reserved for the choir. By the end of the sixteenth century Lutheran congregational singing had changed again, with the organ being given an expanded role. Rather than singing unaccompanied, the congregation was supported by the organ, which played harmonic parts while the congregation sang the melody.

The Council of Trent and the Counter-Reformation also influenced music, fostering perhaps the most significant musical figure to emerge from the turbulent years of the late sixteenth century. Giovanni Pierluigi da Palestrina (1524–94) was choirmaster of St. Peter's in Rome, and, in response to the Council's opinion that sacred music had become corrupted by overly complex polyphonic textures, his compositions returned Roman church music to more simplified constructions. His works have great beauty and a certain simplicity but still retain polyphony as a basic compositional device. In Palestrina's works primary focus was on the text. He was successful in eliminating what the Council considered to be objectionable displays of virtuosity. He maintained the imitative qualities of his predecessors and provided clearly articulated sections marked by strong cadences.

In contrast to the purity and reduced complexity of Roman Church music and the martial solidity of Lutheran hymnody, secular music of the sixteenth century was bawdy, irreverent, and celebrated physical love. Often the same composers who wrote for the Church also wrote secular music. Probably more reflection of the nervous conflict of the age exists in such a dichotomy than first meets the eye. Illustrative of sixteenth-century secular music is the Italian madrigal, which also found its way to England, France, and Germany in slightly altered forms. The madrigal was an elaborate composition, usually in five parts, polyphonic, imitative, intense, and often closely linked to a text by word painting which attempted to equate musical sound with a literal interpretation. For example, water might be indicated by an undulating, wavelike melody.

In England the madrigal works of composers such as Thomas Morley (1557–1603), were called by a variety of names—songs, sonnets, canzonets, and ayres. In France the madrigal was called a *chanson*, and Clement Jannequin's *Chant des Oiseaux* (*Song of the Birds*) used word painting with singers imitating bird sounds. The frivolousness of such characteristics suggests an attitude not entirely unlike mannerism in the visual arts.

The word baroque originally meant a large, irregularly shaped pearl, and baroque music of the period from 1600 to 1750 complemented fully the ornate, complex, and emotionally appealing style of its performing and visual counterparts. The general characteristics used to describe baroque painting and sculpture are applicable in a non-visual sense to music, although it is important to remember that the term "baroque" is commonly applied to music of a somewhat later period than that occupied by baroque style in the visual arts. Reflective of the systematic rationalism of the era, baroque music stressed a refined systematizing of harmonic progression around tonal centers and led to tonal concepts of harmonic progression and major and minor keys that were basic to Western music for the next three hundred years.

Baroque composers also began to write for specific instruments or voices, in contrast to previous practices of writing music that might be either sung or played. They also brought to their music implicit forces of action and tension, for example, strong and immediate contrasts in tonal color or volume, and rhythmic strictness played against improvizatory freedom. The baroque era produced great geniuses in music: Monteverdi, Bach, Handel, Vivaldi, Scarlatti, Rameau, and others. The period also produced some new ideas, new instruments, and, most significantly, an entirely new form, opera.

Opera

In many ways opera exemplifies the baroque spirit. Whether one considers it music with theatre or theatre with music, opera is the systematizing of complex forms into one big, ornate, and even more complex design in which the component parts (the art forms it comprises) are subordinate to the whole. Some go so far as to call opera a perfect synthesis of all the arts. It combines music, drama, dance, visual art (both two- and three-dimensional), and architecture (since an opera house is a unique architectural entity). Likewise, in true baroque character, opera is primarily an overwhelming, emotional experience.

Opera was a natural elaboration of late fifteenth-century madrigals. Many of these madrigals, some called madrigal comedies and some called *intermedi*, were written to be performed between acts of a theatre production, and had a fairly dramatic character, including pastoral scenes and subjects, narrative reflections, and amorous adventures. Out of these circumstances came a new style of solo singing, as opposed to ensemble singing put to dramatic purposes. In 1600 two Italian singer-composers, Jacopo Peri (1561–1633) and Giulio Caccini (c. 1546–1618) each set to music a pastoral-mythological drama, *Eurydice*, by the playwright Ottavio Rinuccini (1562–1621). Peri's work is the first surviving opera. It was sparely scored, consisting primarily of recitative (sung dialogue) over a slow-moving bass. Musically and theatrically deficient, Peri's opera required a firmer hand to allow the new form to prosper.

That hand came from Claudio Monteverdi. In *Orfeo* (1607), Monteverdi expanded the same mythological subject matter of *Eurydice* into a full, five-act structure (five acts being considered classically correct) and gave its music a richer, more substantial quality. Emotionalism was much stronger in *Orfeo*. The mood swung widely through contrasting passages of louds and softs. (Throughout baroque music there is the musical equivalent of strongly contrasted light and shade in painting and sculpture. Almost instantaneous shifts from loud to soft, from activity to passivity, and from pleasure to pain, typify the baroque.) Monteverdi added solos (airs and arias), duets, ensemble singing, and dances. *Orfeo's* melodic lines were highly embellished with ornamental notation. The orchestra contained approximately forty instruments, including brass, woodwinds, strings, and continuo. Grandiose and spectacular staging characterized the production. The scenic designs of the great Bibiena family, one of which is illustrated in Figure **10.19**, suggest the treatment given to this and other baroque operas. Monteverdi's innovative and expansive treatment created the dramatic prototype of what we experience today, and he rightly is called the Father of Opera.

By the second half of the seventeenth century opera had become an important art form, especially in Italy, but also in France, England, and Germany. A French National Opera was established under the patronage of Louis XIV. French opera also included colorful and rich ballet and strong literary traditions using the dramatic talents of playwrights such as Pierre Corneille and Jean Racine. In England the court masques of the late sixteenth century led to fledgling opera during the suspension of the monarchy in the period of the Commonwealth. English

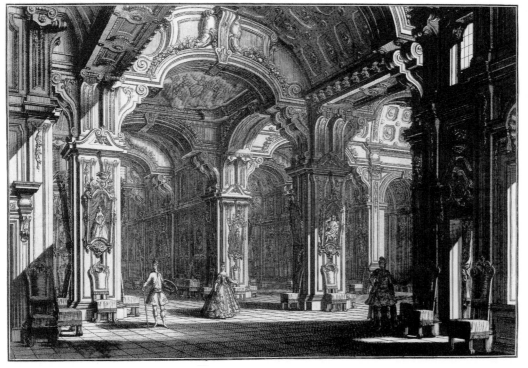

10.19 Giuseppe Galli da Bibiena, design for an opera, 1719. Contemporary engraving. The Metropolitan Museum of Art, New York (The Elisha Whittelsey Collection, The Elisha Whittelsey Fund, 1951).

opera probably stemmed more from a desire to circumvent the prohibition of stage plays than anything else. Spurred by a strong Italian influence, opera in the courts of Germany fostered a strong tradition of native composers, and the German tradition, thus established, led to one of opera's most astonishing eras in the mid-nineteenth century.

Cantata

Another important new musical form to emerge in the late seventeenth century was the Italian cantata. Like opera, it developed from monody, solo singing with the vocal line predominant and centering on a text to which the music was subservient; it consisted of many short, contrasting sections. Its proportions and performance were far less spectacular than opera, and it was designed to be performed without costumes or scenery. The high point of Italian cantata composition came in the works of Alessandro Scarlatti (1660–1725). Scarlatti composed more than six hundred cantatas. Typically, these begin with a short arioso section, somewhat slower in tempo and less highly organized, less rhythmically regular, and less emotional than an aria; a recitative follows, then a full aria, a second recitative, and a final aria in the opening key. Scarlatti's moods tended to be melancholic and tender, and his composition, elegant and refined. Most cantatas were written for solo soprano voice, although many used other voices and groups of voices. In Germany the cantata grew from the Lutheran chorale and found its most accomplished composers in Johann Sebastian Bach (1685–1750) and Dietrich Buxtehude (c. 1637–1707). Bach was under professional obligation as a choirmaster to compose a new cantata weekly. Between 1704 and 1740 he composed more than three hundred. His cantatas were primarily contrapuntal in texture, usually written for four soloists and four-part chorus, and often illustrative of the word-painting techniques mentioned earlier. They represent one of the great responses of Protestant art to the challenge of Counter-Reformation emotionalism: Bach's sacred music achieves extraordinary power in its ability to express a humane, heartfelt gesture of faith. Its drama is never theatrical; rather, it derives from an inner striving, a hard-won but triumphant victory over doubt and death.

Oratorio

A third major development in the same vein was the *oratorio*. Broad in scale like an opera, it combined a sacred subject with a poetic text, and, like the cantata, was designed for concert performances, without scenery or costume. Many oratorios could be staged and have highly developed dramatic content with soloists portraying specific characters. Oratorio began in Italy in the early seventeenth century, but all other oratorio accomplishments pale in comparison with the works of its greatest master, George Frederick Handel (1685–1759). Although Handel was German by birth, he lived in England and wrote his oratorios in English. His works continue to enjoy wide popularity, and each year his *Messiah* has thousands of performances around the world. Most of Handel's oratorios are highly dramatic in structure and contain exposition, conflict or complication, and *dénouement* or resolution sections. Many could be staged in full operatic tradition (except for two outstanding examples, *Israel in Egypt* and the *Messiah*). Woven carefully into the complex structure of Handel's oratorios was a strong reliance on the chorus. His choral sections (as well as his arias and recitatives) are carefully developed and often juxtapose complex polyphonic sections and homophonic sections. Each choral movement has its own internal structure, which, like the oratorio itself, rises to a climax and resolves to a conclusion. Most of the solo and choral sections of Handel's oratorios can stand on their own as performance pieces apart from the larger work. Nevertheless, as superb and individual as these may be, they fit magnificently together in a systematic development, losing their separate importance to the overall composition of the whole

Judas Maccabaeus, for example, tells the story of the Maccabaean wars between the Jews and the Syrians. Seven characters, Judas Maccabaeus, an Israelitish Man, two Israelitish Women, Simon the High Priest, an Israelitish Messenger, and a Priest, as well as a chorus of "The People of Israel" comprise the cast. In Part I the Jews lament the death of Mattathias, the father of Judas Maccabaeus and Simon, who had resisted attempts by the Syrian King to repress Jewish religion and liberties. They invoke divine favor and appoint Judas as leader. Judas appeals to the people's patriotism in the following air for tenor:

> Sound an alarm, your silver trumpets sound,
> And call the brave, and only brave around!
> Who listeneth, follow:—to the field again!
> Justice, with courage, is a thousand men.

The people respond; all acknowledge the value of liberty and prepare for war with pious trust in God and a heroic resolve to conquer or die. Part I ends on that high dramatic and emotional tone. Part II begins in celebration of recent victories under Judas' valorous leadership. However, news of a renewed war with Syrian armies out of Egypt brings despondency to the Israelites. Again Judas rouses their failing courage and sets out to battle while those who remain at home utter their detestation of the "heathen idolatries", by which the temple of Jerusalem had been desecrated. They resolve to worship only the God of Israel. Part III brings the work to triumphal climax amid the Feast of the Dedication of Jerusalem, recaptured and restored by Judas, with full liberties returned to the people of Israel. Judas returns in triumph from his final victory over his enemies. The oratorio is a powerful and complex emotional work of full baroque character.

Instrumental music

As baroque composers began to write specifically for individual voices and instruments, instrumental music assumed a new importance in contrast to its previous role as accompaniment for vocal music. Significant achievements were made in the exploration of the full range of possibilities for individual instruments and also in the technical development of the instruments themselves. Of particular significance was the need to create flexibility so that instruments could play in any key. For example, although we take equal temperament for granted, prior to the baroque era an instrument such as the harpsichord needed to be retuned virtually each time a piece in a new key was played. As a result, equal temperament established the convention we accept without question, that each half-step in a musical scale is equidistant from the one preceding or following. Such an advance was not perceived immediately as advantageous, and Bach composed a series of two sets of preludes and fugues in all possible keys ("The Well-Tempered Clavier," Part I, 1722; Part II, 1740) to illustrate the attributes of the new system.

Perhaps the most significant result of this focus on instruments and equal temperament was the wealth of keyboard music composed in this era. Most expressive of the complexity, ornamentation, and virtuosity of keyboard music was the fugue. Representing the highest point of the development in keyboard fugal music was the work of Bach, and nothing represents Bach better than the collection of twenty fugues and canons, *The Art of the Fugue*, published after his death.

Two other compositional forms added to baroque contribution to Western musical traditions: the *concerto grosso* (also the solo concerto) and the sonata. The master of the *concerto grosso* was Antonio Vivaldi (1669–1741). As was true not only of composers, but of baroque playwrights as well, Vivaldi composed for specific occasions and usually for a specific company of performers. Again like his performing arts contemporaries, he was prolific. He wrote approximately 450 concertos, 23 sinfonias, 75 sonatas, 49 operas, and numerous cantatas, motets, and oratorios. About two-thirds of his concertos are for solo instrument and orchestra, in contrast to *concerto grosso*, which uses a small ensemble playing as a solo instrument. Probably his most familiar solo concerto is *Primavera* (*Spring*), one of four works in Opus 8 (1725) representing the *Seasons*. The *Seasons* is program music, written to describe a text, in contrast to absolute music, which presents purely musical ideas. *Primavera* displays an interlocking development of interestingly shaped, indi-

vidual pieces joined to form an ornate whole. In the first movement (allegro) Vivaldi alternates an opening theme (A) with sections musically depicting the birds' song, the flowing brook, the storm, and the birds' return (ABACADAEA). This expanding and alternating pattern is called *ritornello*. Within this clear, but complex, structure there are ornamental melodic developments. For example, in a simple ascending scale of five notes, *do, re, mi, fa, sol*, the composer wrote additional notation near in pitch and surrounding each of the five tones; the resulting ascending scale comprises a melodic pattern of perhaps as many as twenty tones—a musical equivalent of the complex ornamental visual detail of painting, sculpture, and architecture.

The sonata in the baroque era often consisted of several movements (sections) of contrasting tempos and textures. It was written for a small ensemble of instruments, usually two to four, with a *basso continuo*. Considerable diversity existed in sonata composition, and many sonatas greatly vary from the definition just given. The trio sonatas of Archangelo Corelli (1653–1713) probably best illustrate the form. Corelli treated his instrument, usually the violin, as if it were a human voice—indeed the tonal and lyrical qualities are similar. In treating the violin like the human voice, Corelli did not explore the instrument's full range of technical possibilities, but he did create extremely diverse and sophisticated devices. He usually alternated four contrasting movements, in the same key, in slow-fast-slow-fast tempi. Corelli used essentially independent single themes that unfolded subtly, in a manner characteristic of the late baroque period.

Corelli's dependence and focus on the violin draws our attention to this major instrument, which developed considerably in the era. The violin was fully explored as a solo instrument and was also perfected as a physical entity. From the late seventeenth and early eighteenth centuries came the greatest violins ever constructed, the *Stradivari*. Made of maple, pine, and ebony by Antonio Stradivari (1644–1737) these remarkable instruments are priceless today, and despite the best scientific attempts of our age, have never been matched in their superb qualities, the secrets of which died with Maestro Stradivari. Not only is a violin similar to the human voice in timbre, but a well-made violin actually has an individual personality. It assumes certain qualities of its environment and of the performer. Its delicate nature responds like a human to external factors, and getting the best from it depends upon tender care and love from its owner.

The baroque age in music was a magnificent one. To all intents and purposes our contemporary music originated in baroque music and this legacy remains an integral part of contemporary experience.

THEATRE

Rather late in the day the theatre of the late Renaissance era caught the Renaissance spirit. When it did so it developed profound characteristics that had a great impact in every part of Europe. Although theatre can be and often is ephemeral, we have as clear a picture of its diverse character throughout Europe as we have of every other art discipline.

Italy

In Italy where Renaissance emphasis was visual, two important and influential developments occurred. One was a new form of theatre building, and the other was painted scenery. Both contributed to changed aesthetics and style in formal theatre production. Vitruvius, Roman architect and historian, was the source of Italian plans for a new physical theatre, but Renaissance scholars were quite inaccurate in their antiquarian enterprises. Nevertheless, Italian modifications of medieval mansion stages created compact, carefully designed theatres very similar to twentieth-century theatres. Palladio's Teatro Olimpico (Figs. **10.20** and **10.21**) was once thought to be the model for modern theatre, but scholars now believe that our theatre derived from the Teatro Farnese at Parma. The most significant change in the theatre of this era was a move to enclose the dramatic action within a "picture frame" or proscenium, so that the audience sat on only one side of the stage, watching the action through a rectangular or arched opening. The term "picture frame-stage" is particularly appropriate both in terms of its visual effect and the painting traditions of the era, which the theatre attempted to adopt.

The discovery of scientific, mechanical perspective found its way into the theatre in the sixteenth century, and the designs of Sebastiano Serlio (Fig. **10.22**) illustrate the new painted scenery. The visual and historical effect of these designs is impressive. These designs achieve their visual effect from falsified perspective "tricks" (just as did early Renaissance paintings) based on scientific, mechanical principles. From a point slightly upstage of the actual playing area, the size of the scenery physically diminishes to an imaginary vanishing point. The effect simulates a sense of great depth when, in reality, the set recedes only a few feet. Of course, the actors were restricted to a narrow playing area adjacent to the full-sized downstage wings. Were the actors to move upstage, they would have towered over the buildings. Stage settings became more and more elaborate, and a new "opening" usually brought out an audience to see not a new play, but, rather, the new accomplishments of the set designer. No end of magical devices was employed. Cities enveloped in flames, water and waves, scenery moving in and out, up and down, revolving stages, moving

10.20 Palladio, Teatro Olimpico, interior, Vicenza, 1580-84.

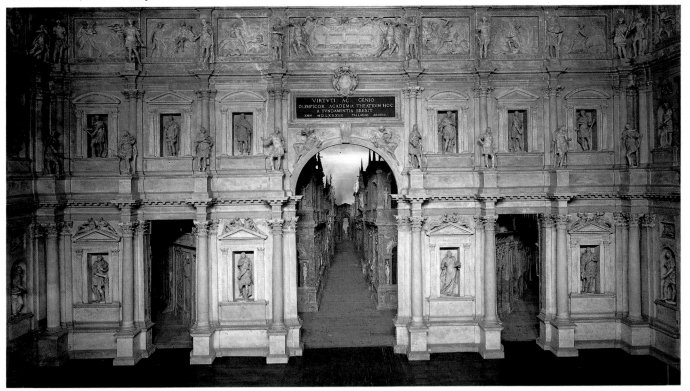

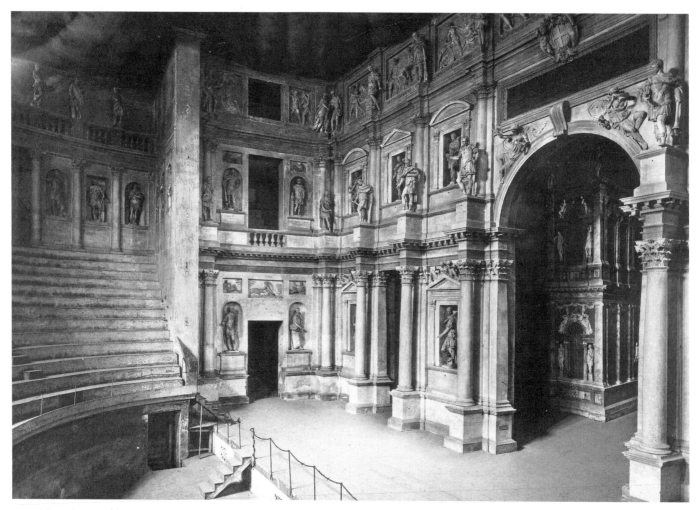

10.21 Palladio, Teatro Olimpico, stage, Vicenza, 1580-84.

10.22 Sebastiano Serlio, stage setting from D'*Architettura*, 1540–51.

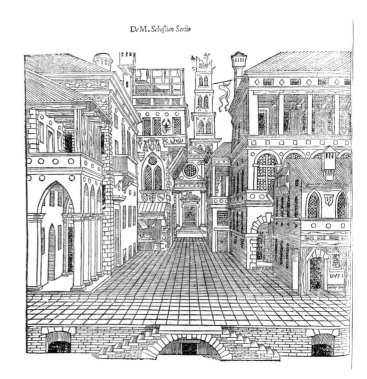

clouds, trap doors, rolling platforms, palaces and ships all captured the audience's fancy.

Stage and costume design was the major attraction of theatre in sixteenth-century Italy, far outstripping the meager plays of the period. The comedies of Ariosto, Cardinal Bibiena's *Calandria*, Machiavelli's *Mandragola*, Tasso's *Aminta*, and Bruno's *Il Candelaio* are the best representatives from the undistinguished playwriting of the age. Theatrical concerns were directed to opera, however, and the conflicting interests of that art form along with the visual orientation of the sixteenth century may be responsible for the literary vacuum on the Italian stage.

Also competing for the attention of the public was Italy's unique *commedia dell'arte*. *Commedia* developed parallel to the traditions of the theatre, and enjoyed tremendous popular support; it featured the actor rather than the script. *Commedia dell'arte* could be identified by four specific characteristics. The first was improvization. Even though fully fledged productions had plots and subplots, dialogue was completely improvized, depending only upon a plot outline or scenario. A few *commedia* works were serious, and some pastoral, but most were comic. We assume from information available that the acting style was highly naturalistic, calling for good entrance and exit lines as well as repartee. The second characteristic was the use of stock characters, for example, young lovers, old fathers, braggart soldiers, and comic servants (*zanni*). All wore stock costumes, which the audience could easily identify. (We have seen these character types previously in Roman comedy.) Actors portraying these roles required great skill, physical dexterity, and timing since much of the action was visual. The famous Scaramouche (Tiberio Fiorilli) could apparently still box another actor's ears with his foot at age eighty-three. Actors in the *commedia* also depended upon skills in dancing, singing, and acrobatics. Somersaulting without spilling a glass of wine seems to have gained an actor great adulation. A third characteristic was the use of mime and pantomime. Masks were worn by all roles except the lovers and the serving maid, and attitudes were communicated through gesture.

Commedia dell'arte had a fourth characteristic. Actors traveled in companies, and each member of the company played the same role over and over again. The practice was so pervasive and popular that actors often lost their own individuality to the role they played. Many actors changed their original name to that of the stage personage they portrayed. From the mid-sixteenth to the mid-seventeenth centuries troupes of *commedia* actors traveled throughout Europe. Their influence and popularity were tremendous, but *commedia* remained an Italian form, although its characters and situations found their way into the theatre of other nations. By the end of the seventeenth century, *commedia* had, to all intents and purposes, disappeared. One final fact must be noted. *Commedia dell'arte* introduced women into the theatre as equals. Their roles were as important as, and often more important than, those of men.

England

While late Renaissance Italy prepared the way for our modern theatre building and certain acting techniques, sixteenth-century England produced a new theatre of convention, and history's foremost playwright. In August 1588, a regal, red-haired, virgin Queen sat astride a horse amid some six thousand troops and proclaimed her resolve to rule among her subjects, to don armor and fight, if necessary, lest any "dishonor grow by me". The Queen was Elizabeth I, and under her aegis England and the English stage would rise to pre-eminence.

We must always be careful when we try to draw conclusions about why the arts developed as they did within a particular historical context. While Italy and France saw the arts prosper under varying forms of extravagant patronage, England saw a theatre of great literary consequence and conventional nature prosper under a monarch who loved the theatre only as long as it did not impose upon her financially. In other words, Elizabeth I encouraged the arts not by patronage of the kind provided by the Medicis, the Church, or Kings Francis I or Louis XIV, but, rather, by benign neglect.

England's drama in the mid to late sixteenth century was national in character, influenced undoubtedly by the severance of Church and state under Henry VIII. Nevertheless, literary influences in England in the sixteenth century were strongly Italian, and the theatre reflected these influences.

The Elizabethans had a seemingly insatiable appetite for drama, and the theatres of London saw prince and commoner together among its audiences. They sought and found, usually in the same play, action, spectacle, comedy, character, and intellectual stimulation so deeply reflective of the human condition that Elizabethan plays have found universal appeal through the centuries since their first production.

Shakespeare (1564-1616) was the pre-eminent Elizabethan playwright, and his and English sensitivity to and appreciation of the Italian Renaissance can be seen in the Renaissance Italian settings of many of his plays—*Romeo and Juliet, Othello, Two Gentlemen of Verona, The Merchant of Venice*, and so on. In true Renaissance expansiveness, Shakespeare took his audiences back into history, both British and classical, from *Henry VI* to *Hamlet*, from *Antony and Cleopatra* to *Richard II*, and far beyond, to the fantasy world of Caliban in *The Tempest*. We gain perspective on the Renaissance world's perception of their own or their fellows' condition when we compare the placid, composed reflections of Italian painting with Shakespeare's tragic portraits of Renaissance Italian intrigue.

Shakespeare, like most playwrights of his age, wrote for a specific professional company (of which he became a partial owner). The need for new plays to keep the company alive from season to season provided much of the impetus for his prolific writing, in the same sense that a required weekly cantata stimulated Bach and Scarlatti. A robust quality exists in Shakespeare's plays. His ideas have universal appeal because of his understanding of human motivation and character and his ability to probe deeply into emotion. He provided insights dramatically equivalent to Rembrandt's visual probings. Shakespeare's plays reflect life and love, action and nationalism; and they present those qualities in a magnificent poetry that explores the English language in unrivalled fashion. Shakespeare's use of tone, color, and complex or new word meanings give his plays a musical as well as dramatic quality, which appeals to every generation. Late Renaissance word painting in literature and music found a masterly peer in Shakespeare's use of musical sound in language. His characters can be as alive today as they were in his time, and the teenage troubles of Romeo and Juliet so accurately capture the complexities of life that even the most sophisticated audience members can be moved to tears by each new performance of a play they may have seen a dozen times or more.

Shakespeare was not the only significant playwright of the English Renaissance stage, however, and the plays of Christopher Marlowe (1564–93) and Ben Jonson (1573–1637) still captivate theatre audiences. Marlowe's *Tamburlaine the Great* rivals even Shakespeare and surges with a mighty use of language in blank verse. Marlowe's love of sound permeates his works, and if his character development is weak, his heroic grandeur has the classical qualities of Aeschylus and Sophocles. Ben Jonson's comedy stands in contrast to Marlowe's heroic tragedy. *Everyman in his Humor* documents the lives of a group of Elizabethan eccentrics. Jonson's wit and pen were sharp, and his tolerance was low. His plays were quarrelsome in nature and were often vicious caricatures of contemporary individuals. Even Shakespeare was a target. Jonson disparagingly referred to Shakespeare's "small Latin and less Greek". Jonson's eyes were on Renaissance ideas, however, and on Italian influences in particular. His most frequently produced comedy, *Volpone*, is set in Venice and satirically attacks the greed Jonson found throughout the world around him.

Most of us are at least vaguely familiar with the nature of Elizabethan theatre buildings, even though our documentation of their characteristics is fairly sketchy. In general we assume that the audience surrounded the stage on three sides, an inheritance from earlier times when stages were erected in the enclosed courtyards of inns. By 1576 professional theatre buildings existed in London. These were circular in shape ("this wooden O", according to Shakespeare's *Henry V*), and their performances were witnessed by a cross section of society from commoners in the "pit", the standing area around the stage, to nobility in the galleries, a sitting area under a roof. The stage, situated against one wall of the circular building, may or may not have been protected by a canopy, but the great spectacle of Elizabethan and Shakespearean drama was an "outdoor" event. Theatres were constructed of wood, and fire was a constant threat. Johannes de Witt, from whose accounts of a trip to London in 1596 we derive nearly all our knowledge of the physical theatre of the era, claimed that the Swan Theatre could seat three thousand spectators (Fig. **10.23**).

The scenic simplicity of Elizabethan theatre (no locales were depicted; all acting was done in front of an unchanging architectural façade) stood in strong contrast to the opulent spectaculars of English court masques during the reign of Charles I in the early years of the seventeenth century. Essentially the court masque was a toy for the nobility, an indoor extravagance which had developed earlier in the sixteenth century, probably influenced by its visually resplendent cousins in Italy. Short on literary merit, the English masque, nevertheless, was a dramatic spectacle *par excellence* and reflected monarchical splendor.

Banqueting halls in palaces were often redesigned to accommodate the scenic complexities of the masques. Stages often exceeded thirty-five feet in width and twenty-five feet in depth. Six feet high in front and seven feet high at the rear, these stages allowed manipulation of scenery from below and used a form of staging called forestage–façade, in which the actors played on a protruding area in front of (as opposed to amid) drops and wings. What is important about the English court masque is its direct tie to the scenic style of Palladio and Serlio in Italy. Inigo Jones (1573–1652), the most influential English stage designer of the time, freely imitated Italian perspective, using elaborate stage machines and effects, including the *periaktoi*, a three-sided, scene-changing device invented by the Greeks (Fig. **10.24**).

This baroque equivalent in English theatre was broken by the overthrow of the monarchy by Cromwell's zealots in 1642. Theatres were closed and productions forbidden (at least publicly) until the Restoration of the Stuarts under Charles II in 1660. Opera provided a handsome substitute, however. When Charles returned from exile in France he brought to the English theatre the continental style current in the French court. One result was a sophisticated comedy of manners called English Restoration Comedy. It was an era of great English acting

10.23 Interior of the Swan Theatre, Bankside, London (opened 1598). Contemporary pen drawing.

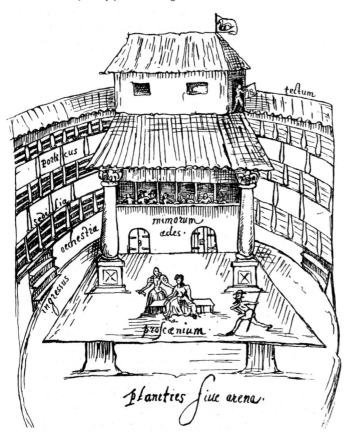

10.24 Inigo Jones, "The Whole Heaven" in *Salmacida Spolia*, 1640. Collection the Duke of Devonshire, Chatsworth, England.

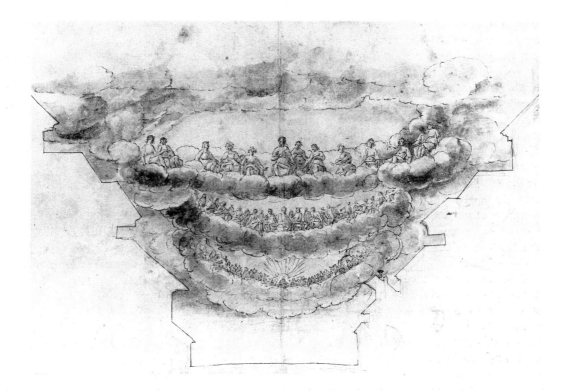

and a period of refinement in the forestage–façade style of physical theatre.

The Restoration theatre produced Nell Gwynn, Thomas Betterton, Elizabeth Barry, and Anne Bracegirdle, actors and actresses of fundamental importance in the emergence of a modern tradition in comic acting style. Playwrights such as John Dryden, William Wycherly, Sir George Etherege, *Love in a Tub* (1664), and William Congreve, *Love for Love* (1695), to name only a few, brought England and Western culture a comedy of high style and fashion.

Spain

Spain also shared a Renaissance, a golden age during the late sixteenth and early seventeenth centuries. Spanish Renaissance theatre developed parallel to the Elizabethan. Many playhouses were remarkably similar, notwithstanding the fact that there appears to have been little contact between the two countries. The greatest influence on Spanish theatre, however, came from Italy. The invasion of Italy by Charles V in 1527 brought Italian influence to Spain. Spanish Renaissance comedies played against street scenes similar to those of Serlio. Spanish theatre was also influenced by Italian *commedia dell'arte*, both in acting standards and in staging conventions.

Among those who wrote for an emerging Spanish classical or Renaissance theatre was Miguel de Cervantes (1547–1616). It was Lope de Vega (1562–1635), however, who brought Spanish drama to the fore. A Renaissance personality of intense vigor, he reportedly wrote over twelve hundred plays. Perhaps the most outstanding is *Fuente Ovejuna* (*The Sheep's Well*), which tells the poignant story of a peasant uprising against a tyrannical nobleman. Lope's contemporaries, Tirso de Molina, Juan Ruiz Alarcón, and Calderón de la Barca reflected the lyricism and Renaissance probing of individual human psychology we have seen so often in this era and gave Spain a brilliant moment in Western arts history.

France

The years from 1550 to 1720 in France parallel the years in Italian and English theatre just examined, and these years witnessed traveling *commedia* troupes and a cross-pollenization of theatre influences from France to England and vice versa, as exemplified by the English Restoration period. Within its own borders, France developed a unique and significant theatrical tradition scholars have called French neo-classicism. We must remember that labels are sometimes confusing; French neo-classicism is a part of the late Renaissance period and related, especially in its later years, to the baroque style in music and visual art. "Classicism" and "neo-classicism", as stylistic labels, will occur later in both music and the visual arts, and we must not let the differences from the periods of their original development confuse us.

Earlier we noted the Renaissance ideas and artistic encouragement of Francis I. Despite these facts French theatre remained essentially medieval until after his death in 1547. France lay in the midst of religious conflicts stemming from Francis' battles with Rome and his invasion of Italy. France also lay in the middle of the Protestant rebellion. The country was not under the thumb of Rome but it was essentially Catholic. So the Reformation and Counter-Reformation found France geographically and philosophically in the middle. The accession of Henry II to the throne in 1547–8 introduced Henry's wife Catherine de' Medici to France. Her influence was significant in bringing late Renaissance Italian ideas to the French court and was especially profound in the development of ballet.

Medieval religious drama had continued its strong traditions under the royal monopoly granted to the *Confrèrie de la Passion*, as we noted in the previous section. However, in 1548 a strange combination of Protestant and Catholic attitudes resulted in the legal suppression of all religious drama. Secular drama, freed from its religious competition, turned to Renaissance classicism. French rediscovery of Sophocles, Euripides, Aristophanes, and Menander provided a new impetus. As we have seen before in the arts, this turning back to the ancients had a tendency to foster specific rules for acceptable works of art. In the French theatre such attitudes formulated by the *Pléiade* forced plays to fit a structural and spatial mold called the Unities. As a result, the spirit and substance of classical drama was lost in attempts to bend it into artificial confines. The Unities of time and space became the masters of drama. No play was found acceptable by the academies unless it conformed to two specific rules— that the action occurred in a single location and that it encompassed no greater time span than twenty-four hours. Of course, had French antiquarians bothered to study actual classical Greek dramas, they would have discovered many violations of the Unities. Perhaps as a result of all this historically inspired rule making, little French tragedy of consequence was written during the period of England's great dramatic achievement. As in Italy and England (in the masque), this period witnessed scenic invention and extravagance.

Under the arbitrary conventions of misinterpreted classicism, Pierre Corneille (1606–84) managed to conform and to produce great plays. In 1635 he produced a masterpiece, *Le Cid*. His characterizations were original, his themes were grand and heroic, and his language was richly poetic. However, he violated the unities, and Cardinal Richelieu, France's official arbiter of taste, and his subservient *Académie Française* condemned the play. Corneille continued to write, and his late work *Andromède* was produced as a vehicle to spotlight Italian scenery and machinery imported by Torelli. Corneille's tragedies established a form and quality that strongly influenced a second important playwright of this era, Jean Racine (1639–99). *Phèdre*, perhaps his best work, illustrates the tragic intensity, powerful but controlled emotion, compressed poetry, subtle psychology and carefully developed plots that mark the best examples of French Renaissance or neo-classical drama.

Molière (1622–73) provided a comic counterpoint to the great achievements of the French tragedians. Early in his career he joined a professional company, a family of actors named Béjart. His earliest productions took place in what has come to be known as a "tennis court theatre", because the shape and size of the indoor tennis courts of the time made them easily adaptable to theatre. For over thirteen years the Béjarts and Molière toured France as an itinerant company. A fateful appearance before Louis XIV launched his career as a playwright, combining it with work as an actor and manager. *Tartuffe*, *Le Misanthrope*, and *Le Bourgeois Gentilhomme* brought French comedy to new esteem. For comedy to be so highly thought of is rare in the history of the theatre. Molière's instincts for penetrating human psychology, fast-paced action, crisp language, and gentle but nonetheless effective puncturing of human foibles earned him a foremost place in theatre history. Molière's comedies were not only dramatic masterpieces, they also stood up to the potentially overpowering baroque scenic conventions of Versailles. *Andromède* and *Psyché* challenged the painted backgrounds and elaborate machinery of Italian scene designers and emerged triumphant.

DANCE

European indoor court entertainments of the early and mid-sixteenth century often took the form of "dinner ballets". These entertainments were long and lavish and consisted of danced interludes called *entrées* between courses. Often the mythological characters of these *entrées* would correspond to the dishes served in the meal. Poseidon, god of the sea, for example, would accompany the fish course. In addition to mythology, danced depictions of battles in the Crusades, called *moresche* or *moresca*, were popular. Henry VIII of England found the tales of Robin Hood to his liking, and English court masques of the early sixteenth century often dealt with that folk theme. Theatre dance was closely connected, still, with social dancing, and social dances such as the *pavane*, *galliard*, *allemande*, *courante*, *sarabande*, *gigue*, and *minuet* played an important role not only in influencing theatre dance but also in influencing music, as we noted earlier. Purcell, Bach, Handel, and Couperin and, much later, Ravel, Schoenberg, Debussy, Respighi, and Prokofiev found inspiration in the dances of this era.

Courtly dancing in Europe, and especially in Italy, became more and more professional in the late sixteenth century. Skilled professionals performed on a raised stage and then would leave the stage to perform in the center of the banquet hall to be joined by members of court. During this period dancing technique improved and more complicated rhythms were introduced. All of these changes were faithfully recorded by Fabrizio Caroso

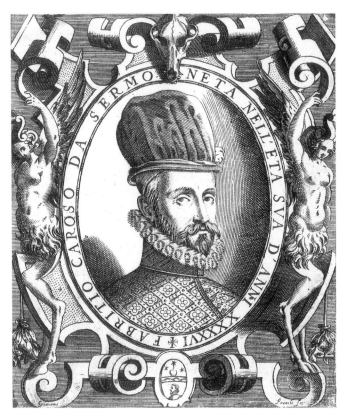

10.25 Fabrizio Caroso (born c.1553). Contemporary engraving, The New York Public Library.

(Fig. **10.25**) in *Il Ballerino* (1581) and Cesare Negri in *Nuove Inventioni di Balli* (1604).

Formal ballet came of age as an art form under the aegis of Catherine de Medici (1519–89), great-grand-daughter of Lorenzo the Magnificent. Catherine had left Italy for France to marry the Duc d'Orleans. However, on the death of Francis I she became Queen of France when her husband was crowned Henry II. Her Medici blood apparently endowed her with a love of pageantry and spectacle, and her political acumen led her to understand the usefulness of such pageantry in the affairs of state. After her husband's accidental death in 1559 (he was pierced through the eye at a tournament), she ruled France through her sons for the following thirty years. Love of spectacle permeated the French court, and lavish entertainments, some of which nearly bankrupted the shaky French treasury, marked important events such as the marriage of Catherine's eldest son, Francis II, to Mary, Queen of Scots. Although sources vary in attributing the specific development of these spectaculars into a balletic art form, we can be sure that either *Le Ballet des Polonais* (1572) or the *Ballet Comique de la Reine* (1581) marked the real beginning of formal Western ballet tradition.

Le Ballet de Polonais (The Polish Ballet) was produced in the great hall of the Palace of the Tuileries on a temporary stage with steps leading to the hall floor. The audience surrounded three sides of the stage and joined the dancers at the end of the performance in "general dancing". Music composed by Orlando di Lasso was played by thirty viols, and a text glorifying the King and Catherine was written by the poet Pierre Ronsard. Oversight of the entire production fell to Catherine's *valet de chambre*, Balthasar de Beaujoyeulx, an Italian who also produced the *Ballet Comique de la Reine*. This extravaganza was a mixture of biblical and mythological sources. It had original music, poetry, and song, and employed typically Italian Renaissance scenic devices to overwhelm the audience with fountains and aquatic machines. Over ten thousand spectators witnessed this costly "event", (*c.* 3.5 million francs) which ran from ten in the evening to four the next morning. Probably the most significant aspect of the *Ballet Comique*, and one that leads some scholars to mark it as the "first" ballet, was its use of a single dramatic theme throughout. Whatever the case, these ballets made France the center of theatrical dance for the next centuries. We can sense the Renaissance concept of this work from Beaujoyeulx' descriptions of ballet as "a geometric combination of several persons dancing together".

Especially at the turn of the seventeenth century dancing also formed a part of the court masques of England. However, given the presence of writers of the calibre of Ben Jonson and designers such as Inigo Jones, dance was a minor factor in these primarily theatrical productions. Newly emerging formal dance also provided part of the spectacle slowly becoming known in Italy as opera. But these were minor, peripheral episodes. The roots of theatre dance grew strong and deep in France.

During the reign of Henry IV (1589–1610) over eighty ballets were performed at the French court (Figs. **10.26** and **10.27**). In a ballet in 1615 "thirty genii, suspended in the air heralded the coming of Minerva, the Queen of Spain. . . . Forty persons were on the stage at once, thirty high in the air, and six suspended in mid-air; all of these dancing and singing at the same time."[5] Later, under Louis XIII, a fairly typical ballet of the period, the *Mountain Ballet*, had five great allegorical mountains on stage: the Windy, the Resounding, the Luminous, the Shadowy, and the Alps. A character, Fame, disguised as an old woman, explained the story, and then "quadrilles of dancers" in flesh-colored costumes with windmills on their heads (representing the winds) competed with other allegorical characters for the "Field of Glory". Such a work typically consisted of a series of dances dramatizing a common theme.

By the late seventeenth century baroque art had centralized in the court of Louis XIV. A great patron of painting, sculpture, theatre, and architecture, Louis also brought ballet into the full splendor of the era. Louis himself was an avid dancer, and studied for over twenty years with the dancing master Pierre Beauchamps, who is credited with inventing the five basic dance positions. Louis' title *Le Roi Soleil* (The Sun King) was certainly appropriate to his absolutist philosophies, but it actually

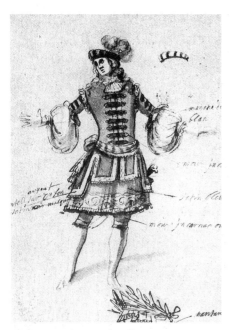
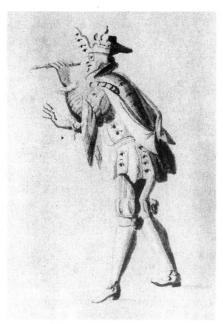
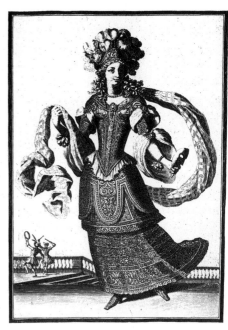

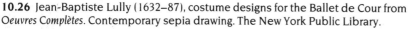

10.26 Jean-Baptiste Lully (1632–87), costume designs for the Ballet de Cour from *Oeuvres Complètes*. Contemporary sepia drawing. The New York Public Library.

10.27 Jean Louis Bérain (1638-1711), *Dame en Habit de Ballet*. Contemporary engraving. The New York Public Library.

derived from his favorite childhood role, that of Apollo the Sun god in *Le Ballet de la Nuit*, which he danced at the age of fourteen. Mazarin, Louis' First Minister, exploited the splendid role to promote the young monarch and to establish Louis' supremacy.

Louis employed a team of professional artists to produce ballet and opera at court, and the musician Jean-Baptiste Lully and the playwright Molière were active in these grand collaborative efforts. Usually the plots for French ballets came from classical mythology and the works themselves were a series of verses, music, and dance. The style of the dancing, at least in these works, appears to have been fairly simple, noble, and controlled. Gestures were symmetrical and harmonious. The theatrical trappings were elegant and opulent. Probably no conflict exists here even though we have described the baroque style as emotional in emphasis. An appeal to the emotion does not preclude formality, nor intricacy or restraint. One must also bear in mind that the costume of the era included elaborate wigs. Anything other than restrained movement, such as befitted the demeanor of a king, was probably impossible.

Finally, ballet became formally institutionalized when Louis XIV founded the *Académie Royale de Danse* in 1661. Thirteen dancing masters were appointed to the *Académie* to "re-establish the art in its perfections". Ten years later the *Académie Royale de Danse* was merged with a newly established *Académie Royale de Musique*. Both schools were given the use of the theatre of the Palais Royal, which had been occupied by Molière's company. Its proscenium stage altered forever the aesthetic relationship of ballet and its audience. Choreography designed

for an audience on one side only was developed and focused on the "open" position, which is still basic to formal ballet.

Establishment of the Academy of Dance led to prescribed "rules" for positions and movements. It also led to a fully professionalized artform in which women as ballerinas (career professionals) first took the stage in 1681 (Fig. **10.27**). The stage of the Palais Royal, which allowed no access to the auditorium, placed the final barricade between the professional artist and the "noble amateur" of the previous eras. As the baroque era came to a close in the early eighteenth century, ballet as a formal art discipline had its foundations firmly in place.

ARCHITECTURE

In the late sixteenth century architecture displayed mannerist tendencies, especially in France under Francis I. The Lescot wing of the Louvre (Fig. **10.28**) exhibits a discomforting design of superficial detail and unusual proportions, with strange juxtaposition of curvilinear and rectilinear line. If we compare this building with previous works from the Renaissance, we find a continuation of decorative detail applied to exterior wall surfaces. However, careful mathematical proportions are replaced by a flattened dome and dissimilar treatments of shallow arches. The helmet-like dome stands in awkward contrast to the pediment of the central section and wears a crown perched nervously on top. The relief sculptures of the top level of the central section are far too large to be comfortable in their architectural context.

In this same period there was another style of architecture of significant influence in later eras, but clearly of a different feeling from Lescot's. Andrea Palladio (1518–80) designed villas and palaces, which reflected his clients' individualism and desire for worldly possessions. The Villa Rotonda in Vicenza (Fig. **10.29**) shows strong classical influence, combining Greek and Roman details. The porticos carry freestanding Ionic columns, and the dome is reminiscent of the Pantheon. The rooms of the villa are arranged symmetrically around the central rotunda. Palladio's mathematical combination of cubes and circles is High Renaissance, but he has cleansed the exterior surfaces of detail, placing his decorative sculpture above, in anticipation of baroque treatments. Palladio explained his theories in *Four Books on Architecture*, which were highly influential in establishing canons later used in various "revival" periods, for example, in America, in Thomas Jefferson's Monticello.

In the seventeenth century baroque style emphasized the same qualities of light and shade, action, intricacy, opulence, ornamentation, and emotion exhibited in the other visual and performing arts. Architecture reflected all these qualities, but because of its scale, did so with amazing, dramatic spectacle. There were many excellent baroque architects, among them Giacomo della Porta (1540-1602) (Figs. **10.30** and **10.31**), Francesco Borromini (1599-1667) (Sant' Agnese and S. Carlo alle Quattro Fontane), Bernini (St. Peter's Plaza), Claude

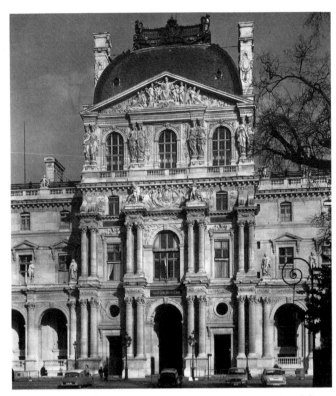

10.28 Pierre Lescot, exterior façade of the Square Court of the Louvre, Paris, begun 1546.

10.29 Palladio, Villa Rotonda, Vicenza, begun 1567-69.

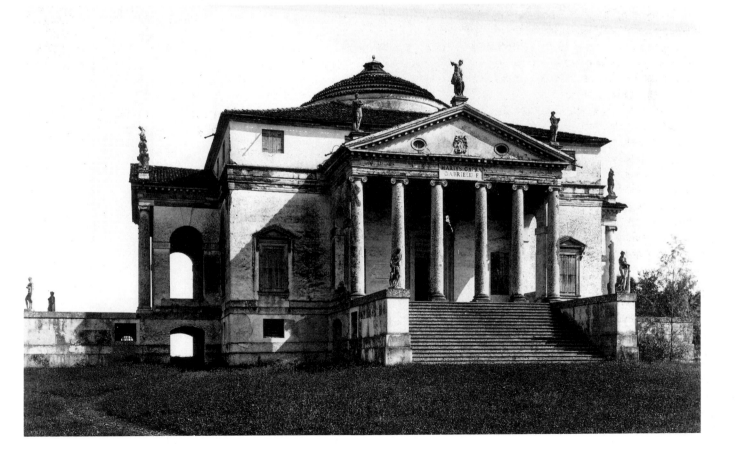

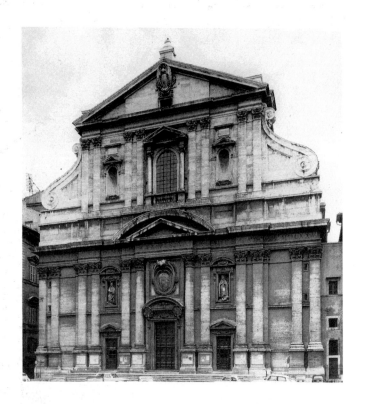

Perrault (East Front, the Louvre). Later, German baroque combined with the lightness and delicacy of rococo in the works of Balthasar Neumann (Figs. **10.32** and **10.33**). One certain summation of baroque style and its absolutist, imperial reflections is the Versailles Palace (Figs. **10.34** and **10.35**) of King Louis XIV of France. In a quite literal way the expanding nature of the baroque universe carried into the thousands of acres which surround the Palace and which, in their intricately related designs, comprise a monumental and complex architectural extravaganza. The palace itself is the central jewel in this elaborate, but nonetheless precise, setting. It would be somewhat repetitious to develop an elaborate analysis of either the exterior or interior of the palace. However, the properties of opulence, ornamentation, subordination of detail to

10.30 Giacomo della Porta, west front of Il Gesù, Rome, 1568-84.

10.31 Giacomo della Porta, interior of Il Gesù, Rome, 1568-84.

10.32 Balthasar Neumann, interior, pilgrimage church of Vierzehnheiligen, near Staffelstein, Germany, 1743-72.

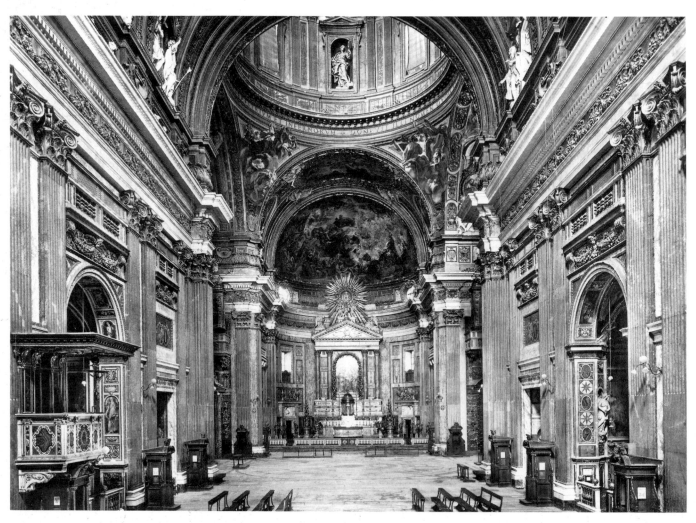

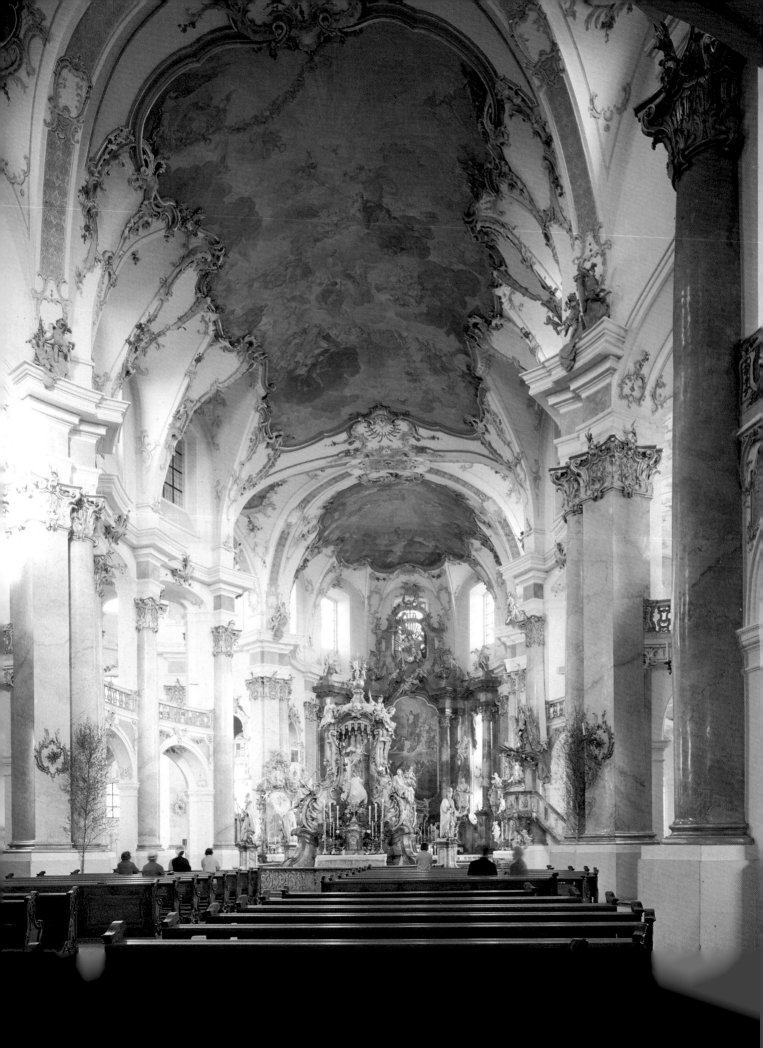

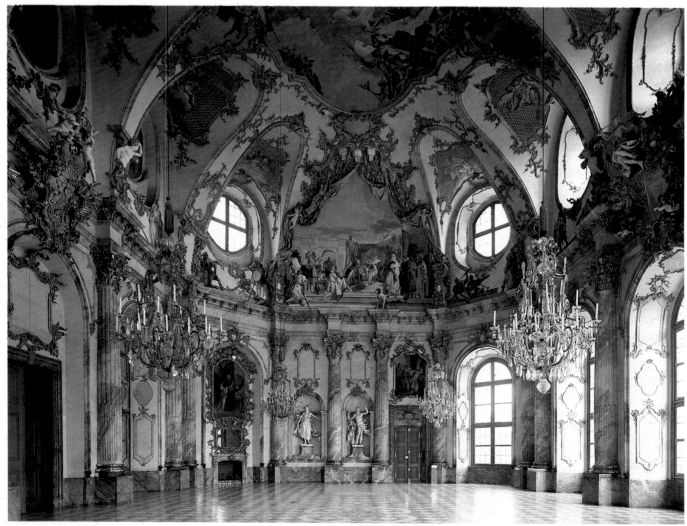

10.33 Balthasar Neumann, Kaisersaal, Residenz, Würzburg, Germany, 1719-44.

the whole, highlight, shadow, and emotion are all there. They are all baroque in the same sense noted in the other arts.

The Restoration of the monarchy under Charles II brought the baroque influence of the court of Louis XIV to England. Over a period of fifty years London witnessed numerous significant building projects directed by its most notable architect, Christopher Wren. Two of these projects, St. Paul's Cathedral and Hampton Court, illustrate the intricate but restrained complexity of English baroque style. The impact of Wren's genius, obvious in his designs, is attested to in an inscription in the crypt beneath St. Paul's: "Beneath is laid the builder of this church and city, Christopher Wren, who lived not for himself but for the good of the state." That statement gives us an important insight into nationalistic tendencies that were particularly prevalent in Protestant countries.

The influence of Renaissance geometric design and Greek and Roman detail mark St. Paul's Cathedral (Fig. **10.36**). The central area under the expansive dome is surrounded by auxiliary spaces. Wren's plan takes the shape of a Greek rather than a Latin cross, which helps to unify the design under the dome. The shorter arms and body of the Greek cross also eliminated the long nave of churches built on the plan of a Latin cross and had the practical effect of bringing worshippers closer to the altar and pulpit area. That concept is significant in Protestant worship, which places great emphasis on the sermon. Subtle elegance in the exterior façade keeps ornate detail in balance, without overstatement or clutter. Yet, at the same time, the awesomeness of the dome and the overall scale of the building is an overpowering emotional experience. The dome rises 275 feet above the ground

10.34 Louis de Vau and Jules Hardouin-Mansart, garden façade, Palace of Versailles, 1669-85.

10.35 Jules Hardouin-Mansart and Charles Le Brun, Hall of Mirrors, Palace of Versailles, begun 1678.

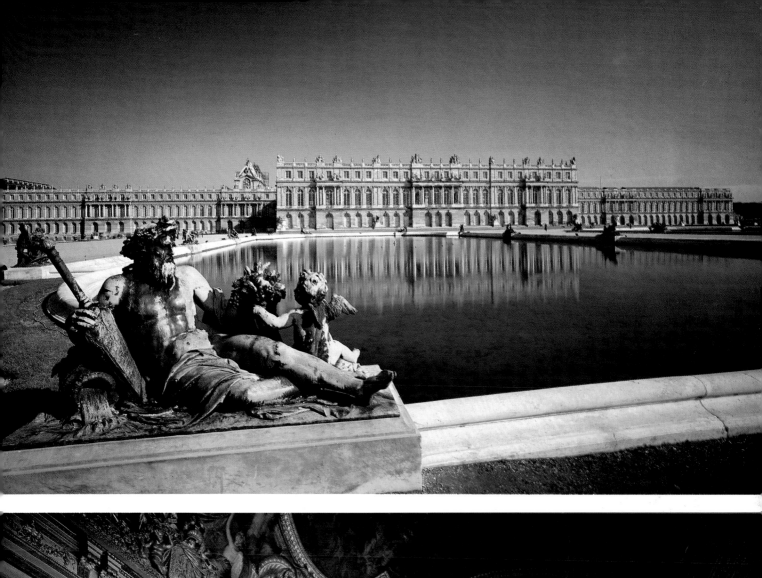

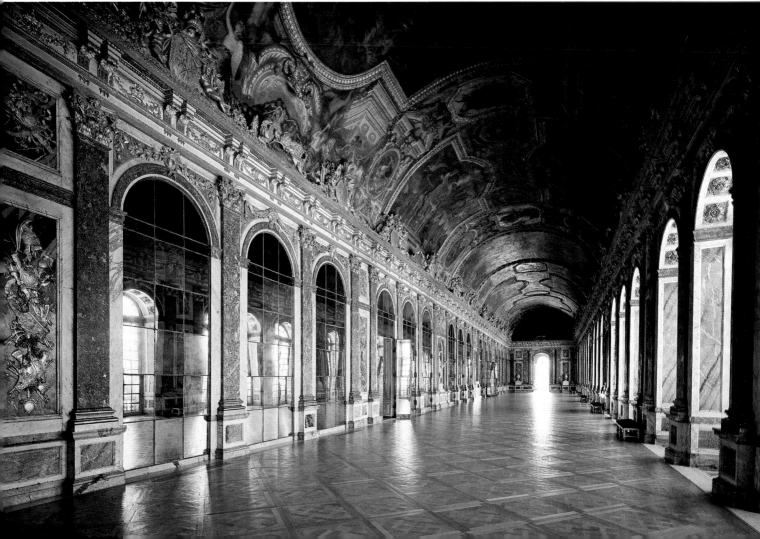

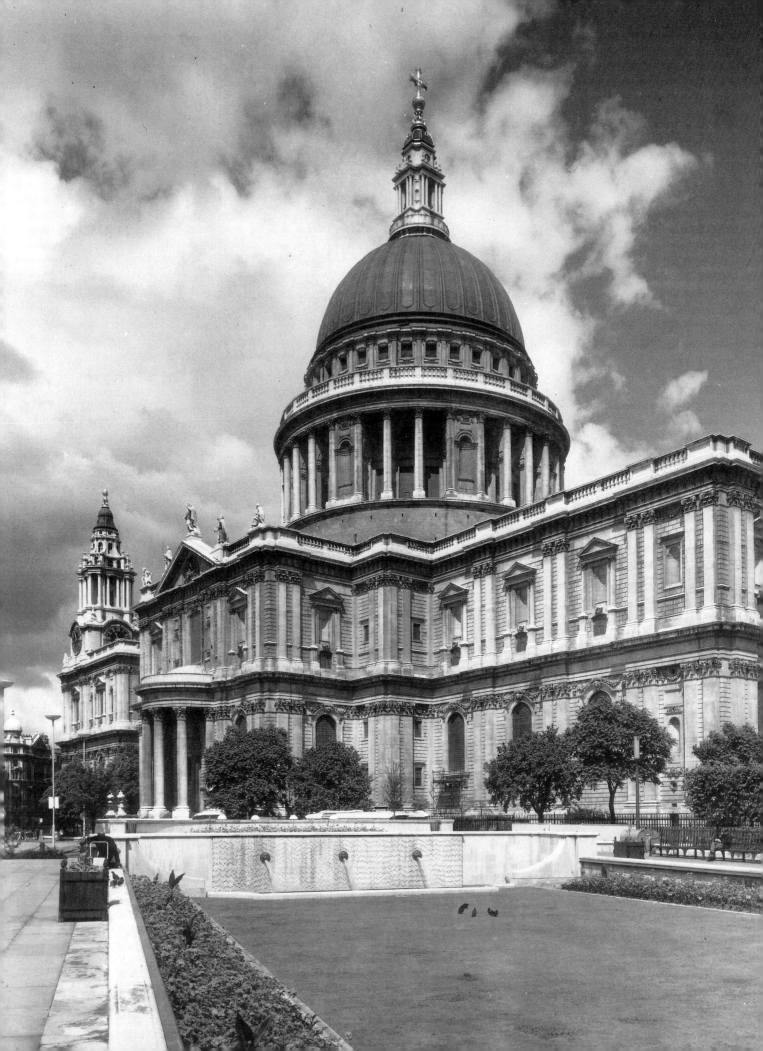

and in Renaissance fashion hides its structural components within a double sheaf of brick and timber coated with lead. On the top of the dome, to satisfy the clergy's call for a spire to dominate the city's skyline, rises a 90-foot lantern tower. The entire composition is a complex interaction of forces and details in which one part flows smoothly into another, losing itself in the overwhelming expression of the fully unified, total design.

On a smaller scale, but equally English baroque in expression, is Wren's garden façade for Hampton Court Palace (Fig. **10.37**), commissioned in the reign of William and Mary in 1689. With careful perception we can see how the seemingly straightforward overall design of this façade is a sophisticated and complex interrelationship of merging patterns and details. For example, in the center of the building are four attached columns surrounding three windows. The middle window forms the exact center of the design, with mirror-image repetition on each side. Now note that above the main windows is a series of relief sculptures, pediments (triangular casings), and circular windows. Now, return to the main row of windows at the left border of the photo and count toward the center. The outer wing contains three windows; then seven windows; then the central three; then seven; and finally the three of the unseen outer wing. Wren has established a pattern of three in the outer wing, repeated

it at the center, and then repeated it within each of the seven-window groups to create three additional patterns of three! How is is possible to create three patterns of three with only seven windows? First, locate the center window of the seven. It has a pediment and a relief sculpture above it. On each side of this window are three windows (a total of six) without pediments. So, we have two groupings of three windows each. Above each of the outside four windows is a circular window. The window on each side of the center window does not have a circular window above it. Rather, it has a relief sculpture, the presence of which joins these two windows with the center window to create a third grouping of three. Line, repetition, and balance in this façade form a marvelous perceptual exercise and experience.

SYNTHESIS
Versailles: Absolutism in Court Baroque

As we noted earlier, probably no monarch better represents the absolutism of the baroque era than Louis XIV, and no artwork better represents the magnificence and grandeur of the baroque style than does the Palace of Versailles and its sculpture and grounds—a grand design of buildings and nature to reflect man's systematic

10.36 Christopher Wren, St Paul's Cathedral, London, 1675-1710.

10.37 Christopher Wren, garden façade of Hampton Court Palace, England, c.1690.

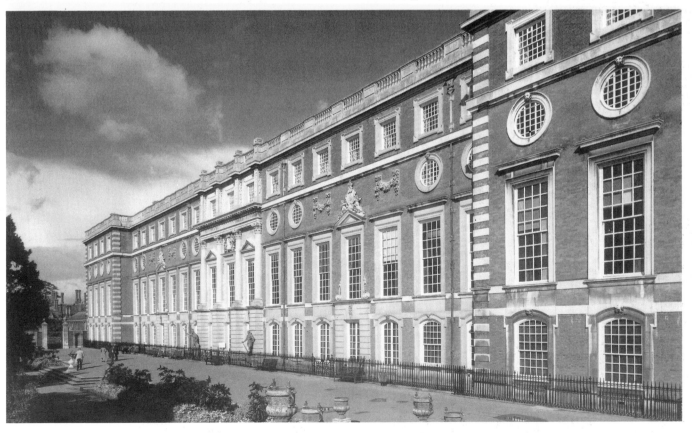

rationalism. The great Versailles complex grew from the modest hunting lodge of Louis XIII into the grand palace of the Sun King over a number of years, involving several architects and amid curious political and religious circumstances.

The Versailles château was rebuilt in 1631 by Philibert Le Roy. The façade was decorated by Louis Le Vau with bricks and stone, sculpture, wrought iron and gilt lead. In 1668 Louis XIV ordered Le Vau to enlarge the château by enclosing it in a stone envelope containing the king's and queen's apartments (Fig. 10.38). The city side of the château retains the spirit of Louis XIII, but the park side reflects classical French influence (Fig. 10.34). François d'Orbay and, later, Jules Hardouin-Mansart expanded the château into a palace whose West façade extends over 2000 feet. The palace became Louis XIV's permanent residence in 1682. French royalty was at the

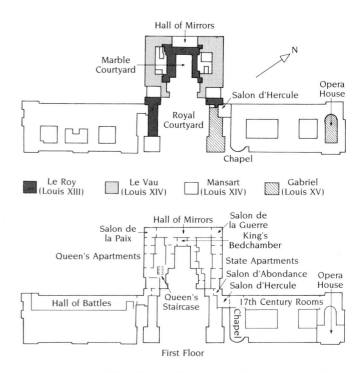

10.39 The *Salon d'Abondance*, Palace of Versailles.

10.38 Plans of the Palace of Versailles, 1669-85.

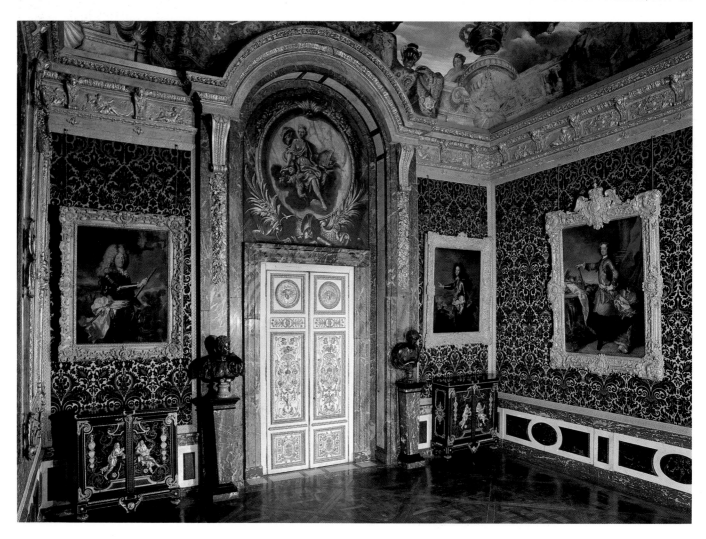

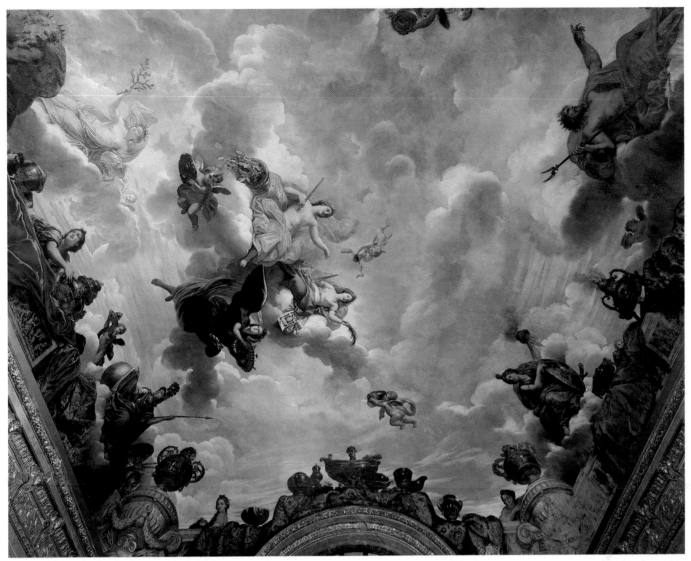

10.40 René-Antoine Houasse, *Royal Magnificence*, ceiling of the *Salon d'Abondance*, Palace of Versailles.

height of its power and Versailles was the symbol of the Monarchy of Divine Right.

As much care, elegance and precision was employed on the interior as on the exterior. With the aim of developing French commerce, Louis XIV had his court live in unparalleled luxury. He also decided to furnish his château permanently, something which was unheard of. The result was a fantastically rich and beautiful set of furnishings. Royal manufactories produced mirrors, tapestries, and brocades. The highest quality was required, and these furnishings became highly sought after in Europe. Le Brun coordinated all the decoration and furnishing of the royal residences, and kept a meticulous eye on anything for the State Apartments, such as the creation of statues, the design of ceilings and the carving of silver pieces of furniture.

The apartments of the Palace reflect a splendor and wealth previously unseen. Each room was dedicated to a Greek or Roman god whose planet is one of the sun's satellites. There is the additional brilliance of the *Salon d'Abondance* (figs. **10.39** and **10.40**) which was not considered a part of the State Apartments until the North Wing was built. The ceiling displays Magnificence, an allegorical figure representing, with the symbolism of scepter and cornucopia, the royal prerogatives of power and provision. Around her are Immortality and the Fine Arts, symbolized by a figure taking flight.

The Queen's Staircase (Fig. **10.41**) leads to a suite created by Le Vau for Queen Marie-Térèse and comprising four large rooms whose windows open to the flowers of the Parterre du Midi (Fig. **10.42**). The grounds are adorned throughout with fountains and statues. The Fountain of Apollo (Figs **10.43** and **10.44**) emphasizes the symbolism of the gardens, and sits astride the East-

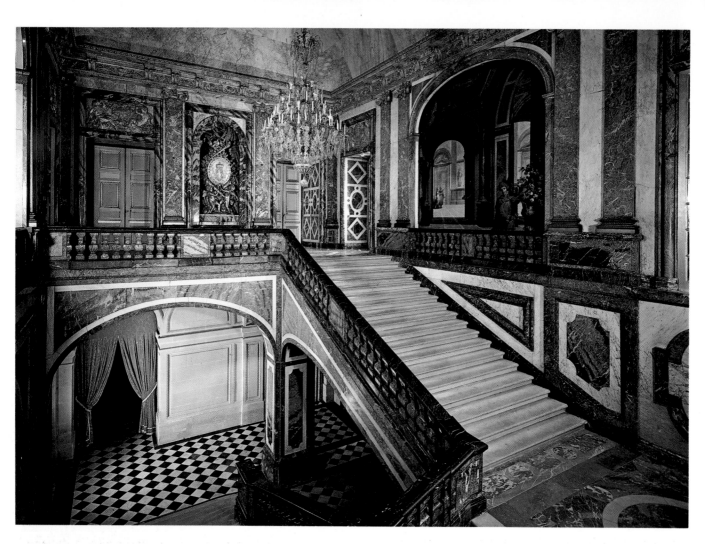

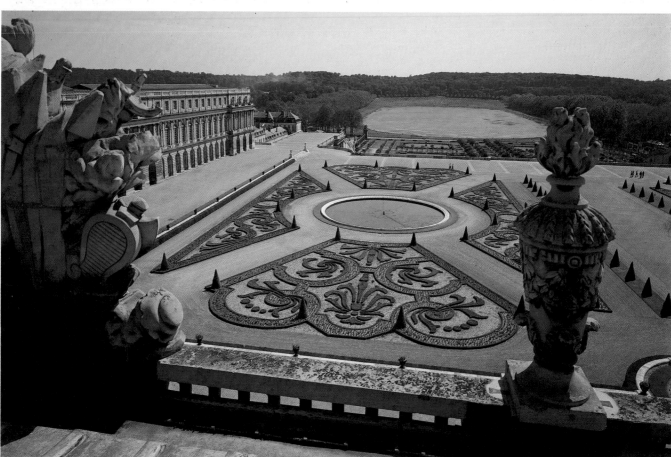

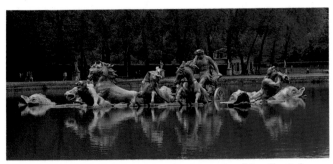

10.43 Apollo Riding his Horses, the Fountain of Apollo, Palace of Versailles.

10.44 The Fountain of Apollo, Palace of Versailles.

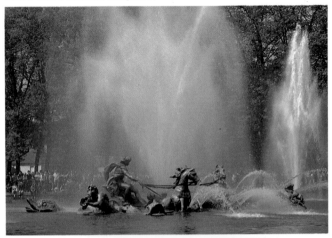

West axis of the grounds. This magnificent composition by Tuby was originally covered with gold. The sculpture was executed from a drawing by Le Brun and inspired by a painting by Albani. It continues the theme of allegorical glorification of *Le Roi Soleil* by representing the break of day, as the sun god rises in his chariot from the waters. Apollo was the perfect symbol for the Sun King, Louis XIV, whose absolutism shone in glorious baroque splendor, systematically rational, yet emotional in spirit, opulent in tone, and complex in design.

SUGGESTIONS FOR THOUGHT AND DISCUSSION

We have traced the late Renaissance through nearly two and a half centuries, from the end of the High Renaissance, approximately 1527, to the deaths of Bach and Handel in the mid-eighteenth century. As we have seen, the arts of the period were a product of the early Renaissance, most significantly the concepts of Humanism and the wrenching effects of the Reformation. As complex as the intricate designs of the baroque, this period shifted from the formal geometry and design of Renaissance classicism to the anti-classical and disturbed intellectualism of mannerism to the systematic rationalism of Court, Counter-Reformation, and Protestant baroque, with its base in Renaissance classicism and its intent in grandeur and emotion.

■ How did Humanism infuse the Reformation?

■ How did the upheaval of the Reformation and the discoveries such as heliocentricity manifest themselves in the arts and architecture?

■ What influence did the Roman Catholic Counter-Reformation have on the arts and architecture?

■ How did the concepts of systematic rationalism and absolutism affect life and the arts of the period?

■ Explain the impact of Francis Bacon on scientific methodology. How did his philosophy of art reflect classicism and Humanism?

■ Explain the major characteristics of baroque art and describe how each art discipline reflected those characteristics.

■ How did the sculptural works of Bernini, Puget, and Coysevox change the concept of space and action which we found in the sculptures of Michelangelo?

■ In what ways can opera be considered as a synthesis of baroque style?

■ In what ways does Versailles exemplify the concepts, contexts, and characteristics of the baroque period?

10.41 The Queen's Staircase, Palace of Versailles.

10.42 The *Parterre du Midi*, Palace of Versailles.

CHAPTER ELEVEN

THE ENLIGHTENMENT

The eighteenth century was an age of change and revolution in some areas and prosperous stability in others. The idea of the absolute monarch was challenged—though with varying success. The middle class rose to demand its place in society, and humanitarianism—social philosophy in action—attempted to make a place for all classes in the scheme of things. Knowledge, for the *philosophes*, was a transcendent and universal goal. The aristocracy found itself in decline, and the Rococo style reflected their increasingly superficial and delicate condition. The pendulum then swung back from exquisite refinement and artifice to intellectual seriousness, at least for a while. The structural clarity of Classicism returned in painting, sculpture and architecture, and above all in music, which found the culmination of a remarkable century of its history in works of emotional depth and formal inventiveness. The cult of "sensibility" with which the century closed presaged the upheavals of *Sturm und Drang* and the Romantics.

11.1 Jean-Honoré Fragonard, *The Swing*, c.1768–69. Oil on canvas, 32 × 25½ins (83 × 66cm). Wallace Collection, London.

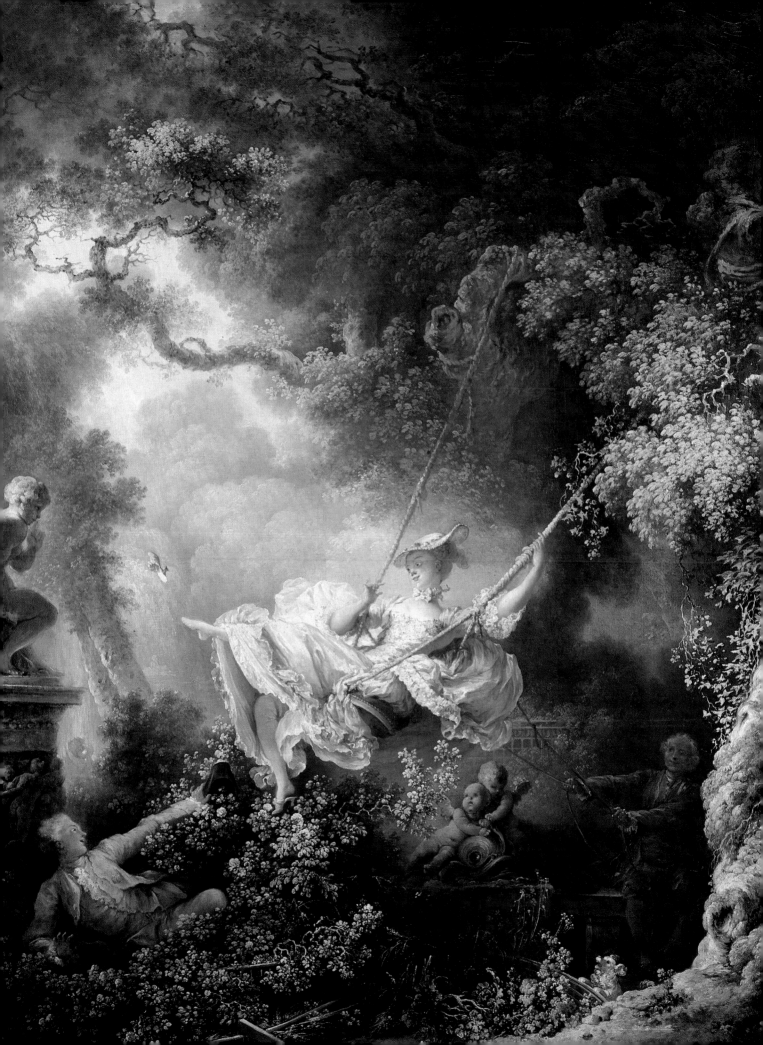

CONTEXTS AND CONCEPTS

The eighteenth century has often been called the Age of Enlightenment, but we have already witnessed too much shifting and sliding of styles, philosophies, and politics to take very seriously any arbitrary parameters, such as the turn of a century, regarding matters either of history or of art. In fact, we have already wandered freely in the early years of, and in some cases nearly half-way through, the eighteenth century without tripping over any natural barricades (Bach, for example, lived until 1750). The enlightenment of the eighteenth century thus grew out of seventeenth-century events and philosophies, which, like Gothic art or the Renaissance, made differing inroads at differing times in different places.

Seventeenth- and eighteenth-century thought held essentially that humankind consisted of rational beings in a universe governed by natural law. Some believed that law to be an extension of the law of God, and others, more secular in spirit, held that natural law stood by itself. Natural law was extended to include international law. International accords were formulated in which sovereign nations, bound by no higher authority, could work together for a common good.

Faith in science, in natural human rights, in human reason, and in progress, were touchstones of eighteenth-century thought. The notion of progress assumed that conditions of life could only improve with time and that each generation contributed to an even better life for those following. Some scholars ("ancients") held that the works of the Greeks and Romans had never been surpassed, while others ("moderns") held that science, art, literature, and inventions of their own age were better since they built upon the achievements of their predecessors.

Enlightenment, reason, and progress made the age one of secularism. Intellectual, social, and economic conditions combined to place politics and business outside religion and to wrest leadership and prestige away from the Church—of whatever denomination. Toleration of differences increased. Persecution and the imposition of inhumane corporal punishment for religious, political, or criminal offenses became less common as the era pro-gressed, particularly in Germany and Austria.

The rapid increase in scientific interest and discovery that followed Newton resulted in the development of new disciplines. Physics, astronomy, and mathematics remained the primary disciplines, but frenetic activity was replaced by quiet categorizing. The vast body of information gathered during the late Renaissance period needed codifying. The new sciences of mineralogy, botany, and zoology developed. First came classification of fossils, then classification of rocks, minerals, and plants. Linnaeus, the botanist, and Buffon, the zoologist, were pioneers in their fields. Chemistry struggled amid mistaken theories of combustion, but with the isolation of hydrogen and oxygen, the Frenchman Lavoisier assured chemistry its place as a science, first by correctly explaining the process of combustion and then by separating water into its two component elements. Finally, he postulated that although matter may alter its state, its mass always remains the same.

Technology

Science went hand in hand with technology. Telescopes and microscopes were improved. The barometer and the thermometer were invented, as were the air pump and the steam engine. By 1769 James Watt had patented a steam engine so reliable that it could drive a machine. The steam engine caused an acceleration in the invention of machines, and paved the way for the Industrial Revolution at the end of the century.

The seventeenth and eighteenth centuries saw significant improvement in agricultural technology. Although technology for mechanized seed planting had been developed in ancient Babylonia, it had disappeared from use, and planting in Europe was done by hand until the eighteenth century when Jethro Tull invented the seed drill. An important application of scientific observation in the agricultural field was the implementation of the four-course system of crop rotation. Other major eighteenth-century agricultural developments were the invention of the horseshoe and improvements in the plow.

The use of coal fuel in place of charcoal in the smelting of iron revolutionized metallurgy in the early eighteenth century. Strong coke enabled the capacity of blast furnaces to be increased tremendously. Coke-smelted iron initially proved to be more impure than charcoal-smelted iron, but the introduction of the puddling furnace solved the problem. Around 1740 Benjamin Huntsman contributed further to metallurgical development by inventing the crucible melting and casting process, which used hard coke as a fuel for achieving higher temperatures and tall chimneys instead of bellows for a greater blast. A new understanding of oxygen and chemical reagents made further advances possible. These improvements in metallurgy later led to the use of iron and steel as structural elements, first in bridges and later in buildings. They also made possible the development of new machinery for the manufacture of other machinery, tools, and finely constructed hardware and instruments.

Scientific and medical inquiry in the seventeenth and eighteenth centuries created a demand for precise instrumentation. It is important to note here that technology was the result of demand created by inquiry and not the other way around. A need for greater precision in observation and measurement led to the development of improved surveying, astronomical, and navigation instruments. The thermometer and the barometer were refined. Advances were also made in the skills and materials used in the manufacture of instruments, resulting in greater specialization and the creation of craft shops. These advances included more sophisticated optical glass making, leading to the development of lenses for use in telescopes and compound microscopes, and the ability to produce a precisely threaded screw.

Improvements in precision tooling affected clock-making and tools such as the lathe. The introduction of cams and templates allowed even greater accuracy and intricacy in production. An instrument called the dividing engine made it possible to graduate a circle by mechanical means, and to graduate scales on surveying and navigational instruments.

The field of engineering in the seventeenth and eighteenth centuries saw advances in hydraulics, road building, and bridge construction. Chézy's *formule d'hydraulique* ($v = C\sqrt{RS}$) for the measurement of flow enhanced earlier work by Pitot. The control of flow in canals was aided by the development of an extremely accurate bubble tube leveling device. A similar invention was the surveyor's level with telescopic sight. A new form of road building was developed by Trésaguet and adopted in Britain (known as the Telford base), which used a base of flat stones set vertically and which conformed to the shape of a rough arch. Bridge building was improved by modifications to the construction of pier foundations. The first iron bridge was erected at Coalbrookdale, England, in 1779.

The textile industry in England was revolutionized in the late eighteenth century by the introduction of power machinery, and the period from 1750 to 1830 really marks the beginning of the Industrial Revolution. The steam engine was undoubtedly the most significant invention of this period. It replaced human, animal, wind, and water power with machine power, and in so doing changed the course of history. The first full-scale steam engine was developed in England in 1699. Steam engines were first used to drain mine shafts. By the middle of the eighteenth century some wealthy individuals were using steam engines to generate water supply for domestic purposes. James Watt's invention of the separate condenser in 1769 brought steam engines to new levels of practicality and productivity. Further modifications primed the engine for its role as cornerstone of the Industrial Revolution. In 1800, when the patent for Watt's engine expired, new high-pressure steam engines were applied to a variety of tasks, most notably in the first successful steam locomotive in 1804. By 1820 the steam engine could generate an estimated 1000 horsepower, and the Industrial Revolution was at hand.

Philosophy

To understand the philosophy of the eighteenth century, we must retrace our steps to the Middle Ages. In the medieval period philosophy was closely linked with theology. In the seventeenth century Descartes (1596–1650) broke philosophy away from theology and allied it with the natural sciences and mathematics. Reason was supreme, and Descartes called for rejection of everything that could not be proved. Descartes's philosophy is called Cartesianism, and it is based on the contention that human reason can solve every problem facing humankind.

	GENERAL EVENTS	LITERATURE & PHILOSOPHY	VISUAL ART	THEATRE & DANCE	MUSIC	ARCHITECTURE
1700	Humanitarianism Frederick I William I Louis XV		Watteau	Colley Cibber Régnard Dufresny Alexander Pope J. Crébillon Marivaux Beginnings of American theatre	Couperin	
1725	Herculaneum excavated Frederick II Maria Theresa of Austria Crucible steel process		Hogarth Reynolds Copley Stuart	John Gay C. Gottsched C. Neuber		F. de Cuvilliés Knobelsdorff
1750	Pompeii excavated Beginnings of Industrial Revolution Watt's steam engine Adam Smith	Samuel Johnson Edmund Burke Robert Burns David Hume Immanuel Kant Denis Diderot Rousseau Voltaire G. Baumgarten Le Sage O. Goldsmith Prévost Henry Fielding J. Winckelmann Herder	Boucher Rigaud Nattier Chardin Falconet Gainsborough Clodion	David Garrick K. Ekhof Lessing Voltaire A.C. de Camargo M. Sallé O. Goldsmith Goldoni	C.P.E. Bach Haydn	Abbé Laugier G.B. Piranesi
1775	George III of England American Revolution First iron bridge - England French Revolution Louis XVI	Thomas Gray James Thomson Wm. Cowper	David Houdon	R.B. Sheridan Goethe J.G. Noverre Beaumarchais Royal Tyler Wm. Dunlop S. Vigano J. Dauberval C. Didelot	Mozart Stamitz	
1800		Jane Austen			Beethoven	T. Jefferson

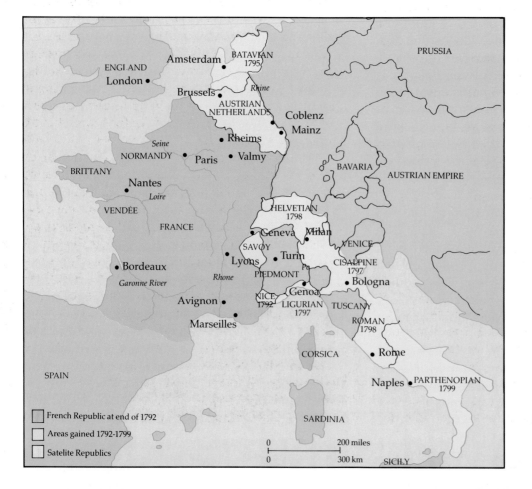

11.2 Timeline of the eighteenth century.

11.3 Europe in the eighteenth century.

Such rational philosophy was championed by Spinoza and Leibnitz, but late in the seventeenth century Cartesianism was challenged by John Locke (1632–1704), who argued that knowledge derives first from the senses. Locke redirected philosophical energies from the vast metaphysical systems of pure rationalism to a more practical, earthbound emphasis. Locke's philosophy was rationalistic, but because he stressed sensations and experience as the primary sources of knowledge, he is known as a sensualist or empiricist.

Empiricism became the predominant philosophy of the late eighteenth century, although it was not without its critics. Locke's approach formed the basis for the later philosophical thought of Hume and Kant. David Hume (1711–76), a Scotsman, differed from Locke by asserting that the mind is incapable of building up from sensations, and that in fact we live in a world of mere probabilities. Hume's philosophy was skeptical for the most part and maintained that not only philosophy, but also natural science, existed in a cloud of doubt. Mathematics was the only true and valid science.

Although Hume was not the only skeptic of the age, his philosophy might have ended in futility were it not for the German philosopher Immanuel Kant (1724–1804). Kant's major contribution to late eighteenth-century thought was the separation of science from philosophy and the attribution of separate functions and techniques to each. For Kant, science was concerned with the phenomenal world, the world of appearances, which it describes by general propositions and laws. Science must not go beyond the world of appearances to concern itself with the reality beyond those appearances. That reality, the noumenal world, was the realm of philosophy. Kant's division of science and philosophy succeeded in giving a much-needed justification and assurance to both philosophy and science and allowing both to move forward.

Kant's philosophy of art

Kant was thoroughly intrigued by the problems of art and aesthetics. An early work, *Observations on the Feeling of the Beautiful and the Sublime* (1764), prepared Kant for his later inquiry into beauty and art. His analysis of the problem in *Critique of Judgment* laid the foundation for much of our contemporary aesthetic theory. Kant's major contribution lies in his exploration beyond the realm of empirical analysis into the

realm of aesthetics as a legitimate domain of human experience. In the Introduction to the *Critique of Judgment*, he lists the three great domains of nature, freedom, and art. A full reading of the *Critique of Judgment* yields a thorough explanation of "the unique validity of judgments of beauty and sublimity".

The *philosophes*

The Enlightenment was not concerned only with philosophy and invention. Enlightened thought led to an active desire, called humanitarianism, to raise humankind from the low social circumstances into which superstition and tyranny had cast it. Men and women had a right, as rational creatures, to dignity and happiness. This desire to elevate humankind's social circumstances led to an examination and questioning of political, judicial, economic and ecclesiastical institutions.

The ideas of the Enlightenment spread largely through the efforts of the *philosophes*. Although the word appears to relate to philosophy, the *philosophes* were not philosophers in the usual sense of the word. Rather, they were popularizers or publicists. "Men of Letters", they culled thought from great books and translated it into simple terms which could be understood by a literate public. The most serious of all *philosophe* enterprises was the *Encyclopedia*, edited by Denis Diderot. The seventeen-volume *Encyclopedia* was a compendium of scientific, technical and historical knowledge, incorporating a good deal of social criticism. Voltaire, Montesquieu and Rousseau were among its contributors. It took twenty-one years (1751–72) to complete.

No *philosophe* undertook such a vocal or universal attack on contemporary institutions as Voltaire. Before we discuss Voltaire, however, we must return briefly to John Locke and the seventeenth century. In 1649 Charles I was deposed and beheaded by Cromwell's Commonwealth, and in 1660 Charles II was returned to England to re-establish the monarchy. Both Charles II and his successor, James II, attempted to rule in the absolutist manner of Louis XIV. However, the British Parliament intervened and in the 'Glorious Revolution' of 1688 removed James II and invited William of Orange and his wife, Mary, to assume the throne as joint monarchs. The new monarchs were forced as a condition of rule to accept a Bill of Rights, which later served as a basis for the United States Constitution. Immediately following the Glorious Revolution Locke wrote several treatises on government, asserting that the power of a nation came from its people as a whole. In a social contract between government and people, the people had the right to withdraw their support from the government whenever it used its power against the general will.

Voltaire (1697–1778) took Locke's ideas to France, and extolled them amidst his aggressive and vociferous skepticism. It is easy to cast Voltaire in the role of churlish negativist who had nothing positive to offer as a substitute for the ills he found in everything. In fact his championship of deism contributed greatly to improved religious toleration. His stinging wit broadened awareness of and reaction to witch-burnings, torture, and other abuses. Without question his popularizing of knowledge and broad program of social reform helped to bring about the French Revolution, which cast out the old order of absolutism once and for all.

Another influential figure in the mid-eighteenth century was Jean Jacques Rousseau (1712–72), who largely superseded Locke by propounding a theory of government so purely rationalistic that it had no connection whatever with the experience of history. To Rousseau, humans were essentially unhappy, feeble, frustrated, and trapped in a social environment of their own making. He believed humankind could be happy and free only in a small and simple community. Such a philosophy stands completely in contrast to that of Diderot, who held that only accumulated knowledge would liberate mankind. Indeed, it was an age of contrasts. Rousseau was an anarchist, and did not believe in government of any kind. He wrote on politics, therefore, not because he believed in government, but because he lived in an age of political speculation and believed he had the power to deal with every problem. His *Social Contract* (1762) was fully rationalistic and reasserted Locke's propositions of contract, the sovereignty of the people, and the right of revolution. More importantly, however, he took Locke's concept of primitive man and converted him into a noble savage who had been subjected to progressive degradation by an advancing civilization. In an age turning to rational, intellectual classicism, Rousseau sowed the seeds of romanticism, which were to flower in the next century. He also sounded the call for revolution. The opening sentence of the *Social Contract* reads, "Man is born free and everywhere he is in chains."

Economics and politics

In previous chapters we traced the development of trade and capitalism (often called mercantilism). The spirit of challenge and questioning was also applied to economics. Critics of mercantilistic government regulation and control were called physiocrats (from the Greek *physis*, meaning nature), because their philosophy held that the single source of all wealth was nature. Agriculture, forestry, and mining were of greater importance than manufacturing. Physiocratic theory also advocated a *laissez-faire* approach to economics—that production and distribution were best handled without government interference. Government supervision should be abandoned so that nature and enterprising individuals could cooperate in the production of the greatest possible wealth. General physiocratic ideas were systematized and altered in Adam Smith's *Wealth of Nations* (1776). Smith (1723–90), a Scotsman, argued that the basic factor in production was not nature, but human labor. He believed that enlightened self-interest without government intervention would be sufficient to allow individuals to produce wealth on an unheard-of scale.

On the political scene, the German states were in turmoil and flux in the eighteenth century (Fig. **11.5**). In 1701 Frederick I became King *in* Prussia (the word *in* rather than *of* was used to placate Poland, which occupied West Prussia). Frederick's major political stronghold was a small area called Brandenburg. However, Frederick's House of Hohenzollern soon came to dominate the whole of Prussia. Frederick's son, King Frederick William I (r. 1713–40), perfected the structure of the army and the German civil service, and went on, following Russia's defeat of Sweden in 1709, to occupy Swedish Pomerania, further expanding Prussian dominance. Frederick William had some strange eccentricities. For example, any man he suspected of being wealthy was compelled to build a fine residence to improve the appearance of the city. He also had a craze for tall soldiers, whom he recruited from all over Europe, thereby making his palace guard a cadre of coddled giants. Frederick William's son was given a rigorous training in the army and civil service.

When Frederick II (the Great) assumed the throne on his father's death in 1740, he brought to it a detailed knowledge of the Prussian service, together with an intense love of arts and literature. He was a man of immense ambition, and very quickly turned his sights on neighboring Austria. Austria's

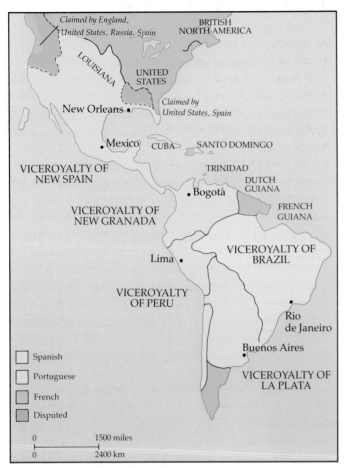

11.4 America in the eighteenth century.

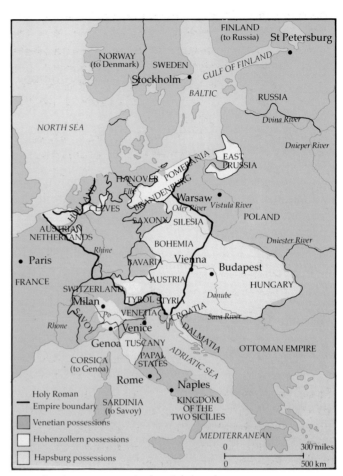

11.5 The German states in the eighteenth century.

House of Hapsburg was ruled by Charles VI, who died in 1740. His daughter, the Archduchess Maria Theresa, became ruler of all the Hapsburg territories, many of which were the subject of disputed claims of possession. Smelling opportunity, Frederick II of Prussia promptly marched into the Austrian territory of Silesia. What followed was a tug of war and peace between Austria and Prussia (and also between Austria and France, Saxony, and Bavaria over Bohemia). Austria and Prussia both emerged from hostilities strong and socially stable. Both countries became centres of artistic, literary, and intellectual activity in the second half of the eighteenth century.

Frederick the Great was an 'enlightened' and humanitarian ruler (a benevolent despot). He championed thinkers throughout Europe and reformed German institutions so that they were better able to render service to all classes of society, especially the poor and oppressed (in strong contrast to Louis XV and XVI of France). When he died in 1786 he left behind a strong and renowned Prussia.

Austria under the Hapsburgs, likewise, emerged strong and stable. Constant warfare did not interfere with internal order and enlightened reform. Maria Theresa's husband became Emperor Francis I in 1745, followed in 1765 by their son, Joseph II. Ruling jointly with his mother from 1765 to 1780 and alone until his death in 1790, Joseph II was an enlightened monarch; he unified and centralized the Hapsburg dominions and brought them into line with the economic and intellectual conditions of the day.

Meanwhile, George III, King of England (1760–1820), and Louis XV (1715–74) and his grandson, Louis XVI (along with Marie Antoinette) (1774–89), led England and France into revolution. We should already be familiar with the events and ramifications of the American Revolution. The complexities of the French Revolution (1789), which must remain outside the scope of our examination, led to wars throughout Europe, to a Second Revolution (1792), an "Emergency Republic", the "Terror", the Directory, to Napoleon's *coup d'etat* in 1799, and a new and explosive century for Europe.

Aesthetics and classicism

In order to set the stage for our discussion of the arts, we need to turn back a little for some additional information. The death of Louis XIV in 1715 brought to a close a magnificent French courtly tradition that had championed baroque art (German baroque continued well into the eighteenth century). The French court and aristocracy moved to more modest surroundings, such as intimate, elegant townhouses and salons, to an entirely different milieu from the vastness and opulence of the Palace of Versailles. Charm, manners and finesse replaced previous standards for social behavior. If the Enlightenment sought refinement of humankind, its society sought refinement of detail and décor, and delicacy in everything. "Sociability" became the credo of early eighteenth-century France and elsewhere.

Classical influences dating from the Renaissance continued to be important, principally because a "classical education" was considered essential for all members of the upper classes. The excavation of the ruins of the Roman city of Pompeii virtually intact in 1748 caused a wave of excitement. The ancient city of Herculaneum had been partly excavated in 1738. Amid this revived interest came Gottlieb Baumgarten's significant book, *Aesthetica* (1750–8). For the first time the word aesthetics was used to mean the study of beauty and theory of art. Then, in 1764 came Johann Winckelmann's *History of Ancient Art*, in which the author described the essential qualities of Greek art as "a noble simplicity and tranquil loftiness . . . a beautiful proportion, order, and harmony."

Refinement, grace, and delicacy brought the eighteenth century and its arts out of the baroque era—Pompeii, Herculaneum, aesthetic theory, and a return to antiquity or to "noble simplicity" (which was uniformly interpreted to mean nature) closed a century marked by war and revolution, rationalism, and skepticism.

Literature

Oliver Goldsmith (1730–74) was a prominent English eighteenth-century poet. He grew up in the village of Lissoy, where his father was vicar. The *Deserted Village*, written in 1770, describes the sights and personalities of his village.

Sweet Auburn! Loveliest village of the plain
Where health and plenty cheered the laboring swain;
Where smiling spring its earliest visit paid,
And parting summer's lingering blooms delayed,
Dear lovely bowers of innocence and ease,
Seats of my youth, where every sport could please;
How often have I loitered o'er thy green,
Where humble happiness endeared each scene!

His portrait of the old village parson includes a lovely simile.

To them his heart, his love, his griefs were given,
But all his serious thoughts had rest in heaven.
As some tall cliff that lifts its awful form,
Swells from the vale, and midway leaves the storm,
Eternal sunshine settles on its head.

Finally, we find great tenderness in his description of his unfulfilled dream of ending his life amid the scenes in which it had begun.

In all my wanderings round this world of care,
In all my griefs—and God has given my share—
I still had hopes, my latest hours to crown,
Amid these humble bowers to lay me down,
To husband out life's taper at the close,
And keep the flame from wasting by repose.
....
And as an hare whom hounds and horns pursue,
Pants to the place from which at first she flew,
I still had hopes my long vexations past,
Here to return—and die at home at last.

Other significant poets of the eighteenth century included Thomas Chatterton, Thomas Gray, James Thomson, and William Cowper.

The mid-eighteenth century is often called the Age of Johnson. Samuel Johnson (1709–84) began his literary career as a sort of miscellaneous journalist, writing for a newspaper. His principal achievement was as an essayist and the two hundred and eight *Rambler* essays covered a huge variety of topics including "Folly of Anger: Misery of a Peevish Old Age" and "Advantages of Mediocrity: An Eastern

Fable". The following extract is a famous passage from his last *Idler* essay.

There are few things, not purely evil, of which we can say, without some emotion of uneasiness, this is the last. Those who never could agree together shed tears when mutual discontent has determined them to final separation: of a place which has been frequently visited, though without pleasure, the last look is taken with heaviness of heart; and the Idler, with all his chilliness of tranquillity, is not wholly unaffected by the thought that his last essay is before him.

The secret horror of the last is inseparable from a thinking being, whose life is limited, and to whom death is dreadful. We always make a secret comparison between a part and the whole; the termination of any period of life reminds us that life itself has likewise its termination; when we have done anything for the last time we involuntarily reflect that a part of the days allotted to us is past, and that as more is past there is less remaining.

Edmund Burke, Edward Gibbon, and Robert Burns round out this circle of literary figures, and a list of eighteenth-century novelists would include the Frenchmen Le Sage (*Gil Blas*) and Prévost (*Manon Lescaut*), and the English writers Samuel Richardson and Henry Fielding.

One of the most influential of the pre-romantic writers was Rousseau, whom we have already mentioned. He laid a new emphasis on emotion rather than reason, on sympathy rather than rational understanding. Others included the novelists Horace Walpole and Mrs Radcliffe, who catered to the public taste for Gothic tales of dark castles and shining heroism in medieval settings. Lessing, Schiller, and Goethe, whom we discuss elsewhere, and Herder also contributed to the pre-romantic movement in Germany. Herder's essays, *German Way and German Art* (1773), have been called the "Manifesto of German Storm and Stress". In his greatest work, *Ideas on the Philosophy of the History of Mankind*, he analysed nationalism and prescribed a way of reviving "a national feeling through school, books, and newspapers using the national language".

The major thrust of romanticism outlasted the generation of the eighteenth century and continued well into the nineteenth. Offshoots of romanticism permeated every aspect of society, as we shall see in the next chapter.

THE ARTS
OF THE ENLIGHTENMENT

TWO-DIMENSIONAL ART

Rococo

The change from grand baroque courtly life to that of the small salon and intimate townhouse was reflected in a new style of painting called rococo. Often rococo is described as an inconsequential version of baroque. There is some justification for this description—some paintings of this style are characterized by fussy detail, complex composition, and a certain superficiality. To dimiss early eighteenth-century work with that would be a serious error. Rococo was a product of its time. Rococo art is, essentially, decorative and non-functional—like the declining aristocracy it represented. Its intimate grace, charm, and delicate superficiality reflect the social ideals and manners of the age. Informality replaced formality in life and in painting. The logic and academic character of the baroque of Louis XIV was found lacking in feeling and sensitivity. Its overwhelming scale and grandeur were too ponderous. Deeply dramatic action faded into lively effervescence and melodrama. Love, sentiment, pleasure, and sincerity became predominant themes. None of these characteristics conflicts significantly with the overall tone of the Enlightenment, whose major goal was the refinement of man. The arts of the period dignified the human spirit through social consciousness and bourgeois social morality, as well as through graceful gamesmanship

11.6 Antoine Watteau, *Departure for Cythera*, 1717. Oil on canvas, 51 × 76½ins (129.5 × 194.5cm). Louvre, Paris,

11.7 François Boucher, *The Toilet of Venus*, 1751. Oil on canvas, 42⅝ × 33½ins (108.3 × 85cm). The Metropolitan Museum of Art, New York (Bequest of William K. Vanderbilt, 1920).

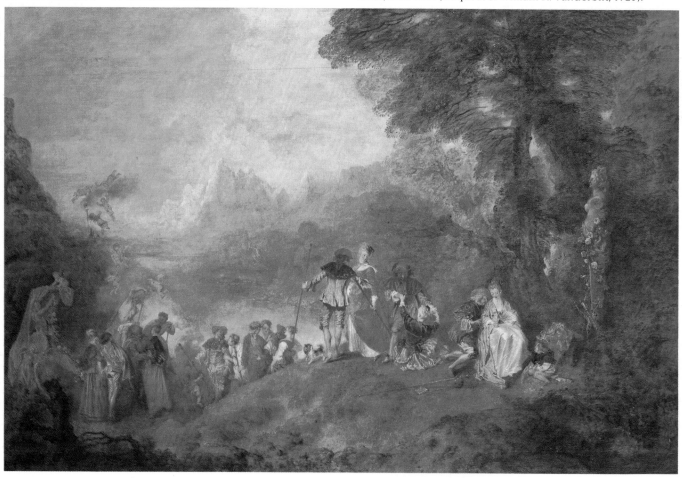

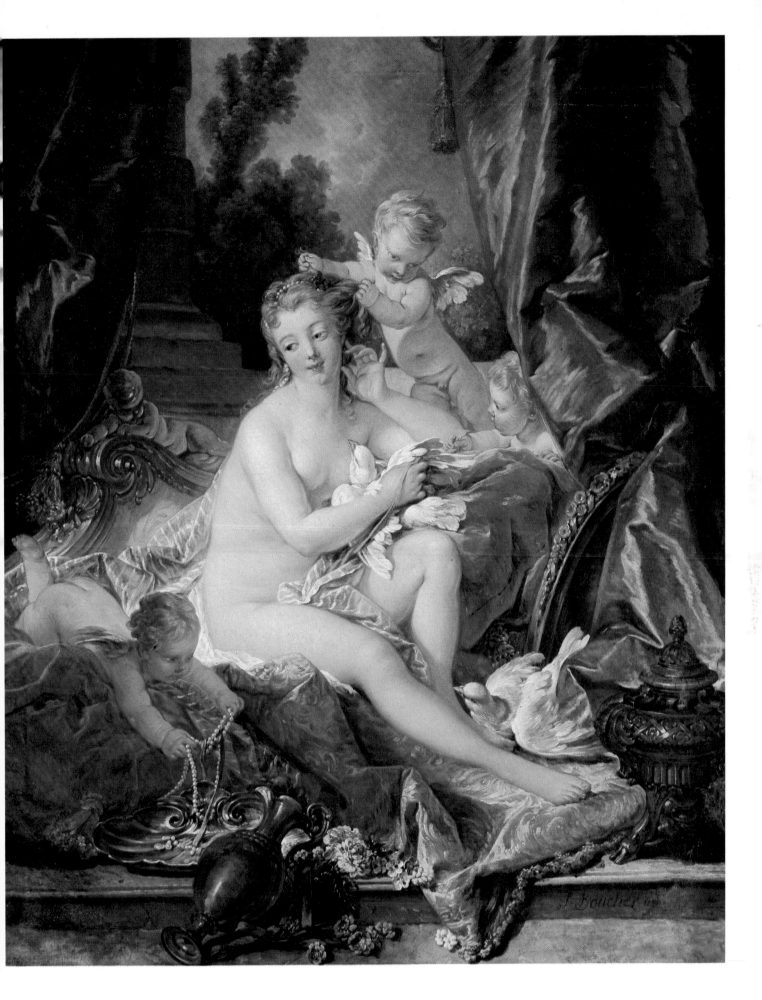

F. Boucher

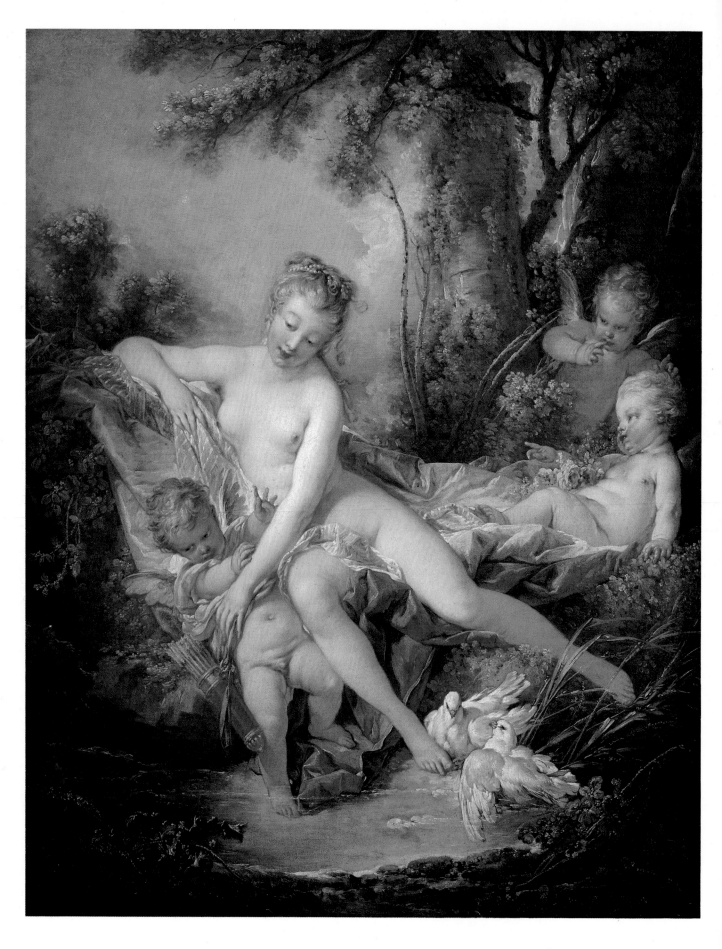

of love. Delicacy, informality, lack of grandeur, and lack of action did not always imply superficiality or limp sentimentality.

The transitional quandary of the aristocracy can be seen in the rococo paintings of Antoine Watteau (1683–1721). Although largely sentimental, much of Watteau's work refrains from gaiety or frivolousness. *Embarkation for Cythera* (Fig. **11.6**) illustrates idealized concepts of aristocratic social graces. Cythera is a mythological land of enchantment, the island of Venus, and Watteau portrays aristocrats as they await departure for that faraway place idling away their time in amorous pursuits. Fantasy qualities in the landscape are created by fuzzy color areas and hazy atmosphere. A soft, undulating line underscores the human figures, all posed in slightly affected attitudes. Watteau's fussy details and decorative treatment of clothing stand in contrast to the diffused quality of the background. Each grouping of couples engages in graceful conversation and love games typical of the age. Delicacy pervades the scene, over which an armless bust of Venus presides. Underlying this dreamlike fantasy there is a deep, poetic melancholy. These doll-like figurines, which are only symbols, engage in sophisticated and elegant pleasure, but the softness and affectation of the work counterbalance gaiety with languid sorrow.

The slightly later work of François Boucher (1703–70) continues the rococo tradition and gives us a taste of the decorative, mundane, and slightly erotic painting popular in the early and mid-eighteenth century. As a protégé of Madame de Pompadour, mistress of King Louis XV, Boucher enjoyed great popularity. His work has a highly decorative surface detail and portrays pastoral and mythological settings such as the *Toilet of Venus* (Fig. **11.7**). The consistency of Boucher's style can easily be seen by comparing *Toilet of Venus* with *Venus Consoling Love* (Fig. **11.8**). Boucher's figures almost always appear amidst exquisitely detailed drapery. His rendering technique is nearly flawless, and his displays of painterly virtuosity provide fussily pretty works whose main subjects compete with their decorative backgrounds for our attention. In comparison with the power and sweep of the baroque, Boucher appears gentle and shallow. The intricate formal design of the baroque, in which sophisticated ornateness created smooth articulation of parts is lost here in intricate and delicate details each of which takes on a separate focus of its own and leads the eye first in one direction and then another, nearly without control.

Humanitarianism

In strong contrast to the aristocratic frivolity of rococo style was the biting satire and social comment of enlightened humanitarians such as William Hogarth (1697–1764) in England in the 1730s. Hogarth portrayed dramatic scenes on moral subjects, and his *Rake's Progress* and

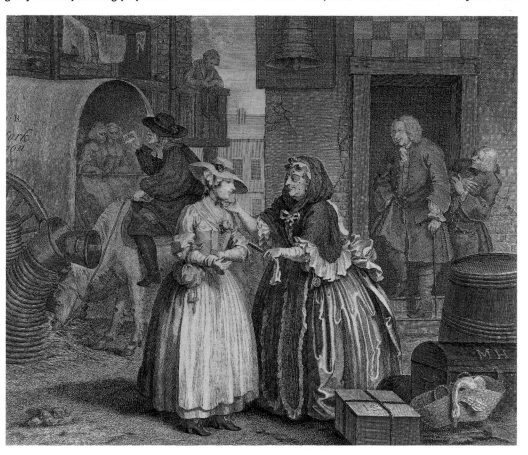

11.8 François Boucher, *Venus Consoling Love*, 1751. Canvas, 42⅛ × 33⅜ins (107 × 85cm). National Gallery of Art, Washington DC (Chester Dale Collection).

11.9 William Hogarth, T*he Harlot's Progress: Arrival in London*, 1731. Engraving. The Metropolitan Museum of Art, New York (Harris Brisbane Dick Fund, 1932).

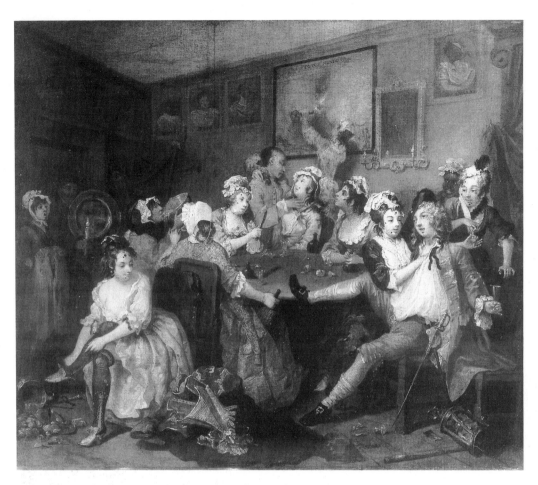

Harlot's Progress series are an attempt to instil solid middle-class values. He attacked the foppery of the aristocracy, drunkenness, and social cruelty. In the *Harlot's Progress* series (Fig. **11.9**) the harlot is a victim of circumstances. She arrives in London, is seduced by her employer, and ends up in Bridewell Prison. Hogarth portrays her final fate less as a punishment for her sins than as a comment on humankind's general cruelty. The same may be said of the *Rake's Progress* series, which portrays the unfortunate downfall of a foolish young man from comfortable circumstances. This series moves through several unusual and exciting incidents (Fig. **11.10**) to a final fate in Bedlam insane asylum. Hogarth's concern for and criticism of social conditions are expressed in his paintings and represent incitement to action characteristic of eighteenth-century humanitarianism. The fact that his paintings were made into engravings and widely sold as prints to the public illustrates the popularity of attacks on social institutions of the day.

Landscape

One of the most influential English painters of the eighteenth century was Thomas Gainsborough (1727–88), whose landscapes bridge the gap between the styles of baroque and romantic and whose portraits range from rococo to sensitive elegance.

> Although the elegant attenuation of his lords and ladies is indebted to his study of Van Dyck, Gainsborough achieved in his full-length portraits a freshness and lyric grace all his own. Occasional objections to the lack of structure in his weightless figures are swept away by the beauty of his color and the delicacy of his touch, closer to the deft brushwork of Watteau than to Boucher's enameled surface.... His landscapes ... exhale a typically English freshness.[1]

In the *Market Cart* (Fig. **11.11**) we find a delicate use of wash reminiscent of Watteau. We are caught up in an exploration of tonalities and shapes which express a deep and almost mystical response to nature.

Portraiture, sentimentality, genre

The popularity of portraiture also increased in the eighteenth century and the many fine exponents of portrait painting from this period include Gainsborough and Sir

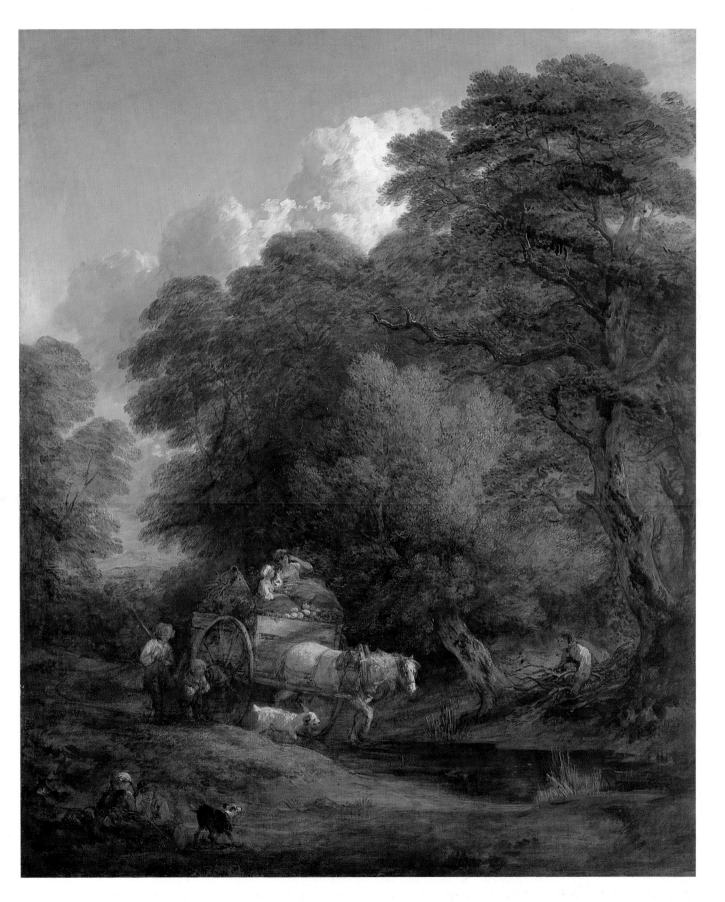

11.11 Thomas Gainsborough, *The Market Cart*, 1786-7. Oil on canvas, 72½ × 60¼ins (184 × 153cm). The Tate Gallery, London.

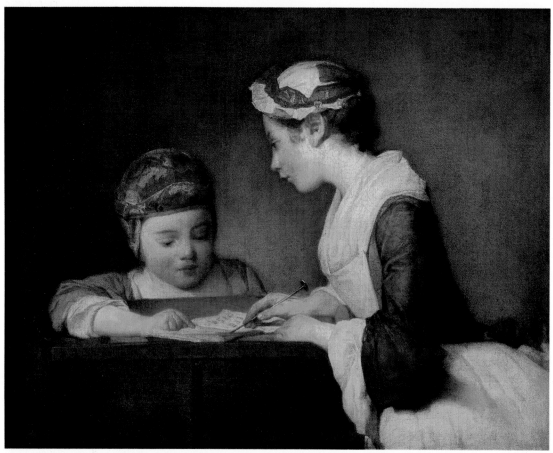

11.12 Jean-Baptiste Siméon Chardin, *The Young Governess*, c.1739. Oil on canvas, 22⅞ × 29⅛ins (58.3 × 74cm). National Gallery of Art, Washington DC (Andrew W. Mellon Collection).

11.13 Jean-Baptiste Siméon Chardin, *Menu de Gras*, 1731. Oil on canvas, 13 × 16⅛ins (33 × 41cm). Louvre, Paris.

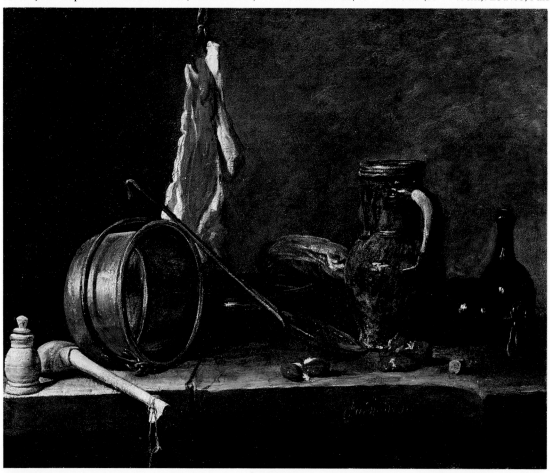

Joshua Reynolds in England, John Copely and Gilbert Stuart in America, and Rigaud, Latour, and the rococo portraitist Nattier in France. The spirit of sentimentality could be found in the paintings of Fragonard and Greuze. Italy's Tiepolo further developed the rococo style through unique palettes of blues, pinks, and yellows, while Canaletto and Guardi painted scenes of spectacle and architecture. A new bourgeois flavor could be found in the mundane (genre) subjects of France's Jean-Baptiste Chardin (Figs. **11.12** and **11.13**) and Italy's Pietro Longhi.

Neo-classicism

Discovery of the ruins of Pompeii, Winckelmann's interpretation of Greek classicism, Rousseau's Noble Savage, and Baumgarten's aesthetics sent the late eighteenth century whirling back to antiquity and in particular

to nature. A principal proponent of neo-classicism in painting was Jacques Louis David (1748–1825). His works illustrate the newly perceived grandeur of antiquity and its reflection in subject matter, composition, depiction, and historical accuracy. Although propagandist in tone (he sought to inspire patriotism and democracy), his neo-classical works show a Roman two-dimensionality and a strong, simple compositional unity. Accurate historical detail and antiquarian subject matter complete the works. In both the *Oath of the Horatii* (Fig. **11.14**) and the *Death of Socrates* (Fig. **11.15**) David exploits his political ideas amidst Greek and Roman themes. In both cases he implies a devotion to ideals so strong that one should be prepared to die in their defense. David's belief in a rational and ordered existence is reinforced by his sparse and classically simple composition. We must recognize, however, that the neo-classicism of David and others is not confined to copying ancient works. Classical detail

11.14 Jacques-Louis David, *The Oath of the Horatii*, 1784-85. Oil on canvas, c.14 × 11ft (427 × 335cm). Louvre, Paris.

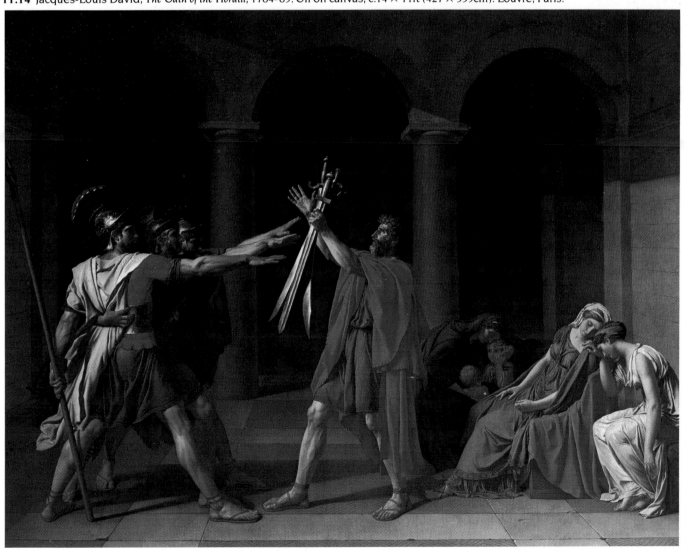

341

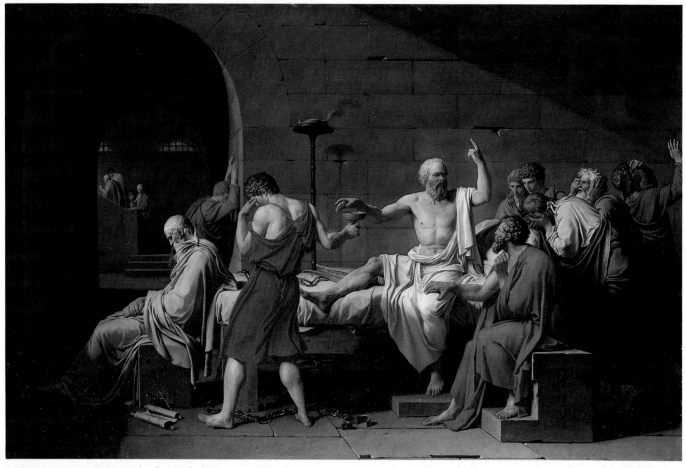

11.15 Jacques-Louis David, *The Death of Socrates*, 1787. Oil on canvas, 51 × 77¼ins (129.5 × 196.2cm). The Metropolitan Museum of Art, New York (Wolfe Fund, 1931. Catharine Lorillard Wolfe Collection).

and principles are treated selectively and adapted. The *Oath of the Horatii*, inspired by Corneille's play *Horace*, captures a directness and intensity of expression that would play an important role in romanticism. But the starkness of linear color edges, triangular arrangements parallel to the picture plane (like classical relief sculpture), strong, geometric composition (juxtaposing straight line in the men and curved line in the women), and smooth color areas and gradations hold it to the more formal, classical tradition. Curiously, David's work was admired and purchased by King Louis XVI, against whom David's revolutionary cries were directed and whom David, as a member of the French Revolutionary Convention, would sentence to death. David's career flourished; neo-classicism in painting increased in popularity and continued beyond the Revolution to the time of Napoleon and into the nineteenth century.

SCULPTURE

Sculpture struggled in the eighteenth century. The Academy of Sculpture and the French Academy in Rome encouraged the copying of antique sculpture, and resisted changes in style. Sculpture continued in the baroque style and lacked originality. Rococo style did find expression in the work of Falconet (1716–91), Pajou (1730–1809), and Clodion (1738–1814). In their works are myriad decorative cupids, nymphs, and so on, recurring motifs in painting of this style. Venus appears frequently, often depicted in the thinly disguised form of a prominent lady of the day. Madame de Pompadour, who epitomized love, charm, grace, and delicacy for the

11.16 Étienne-Maurice Falconet, *Madame de Pompadour as The Venus of the Doves*, 1782. Marble, height 29½ins (75cm). National Gallery of Art, Washington DC (Samuel H. Kress Collection).

11.17 Clodion (Claude Michel), *Satyr and Bacchante*, c.1775. Terracotta, height 23¼ins (59cm). The Metropolitan Museum of Art, New York (Bequest of Benjamin Altman, 1913).

11.18 Jean-Antoine Houdon, *Alexandre Brongniart*, 1777. Marble, height 15⅜ins (39.2cm). National Gallery of Art, Washington DC (Widener Collection).

11.19 Jean-Antoine Houdon, *Louise Brongniart*, 1777. Marble, height 14⅛ins (37.7cm). National Gallery of Art, Washington DC (Widener Collection).

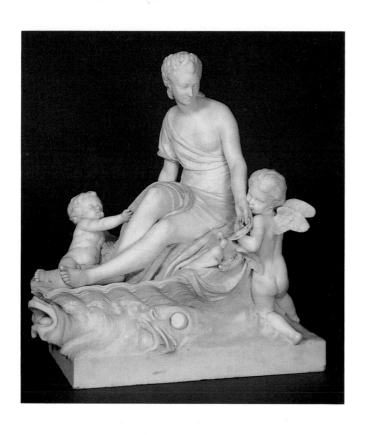

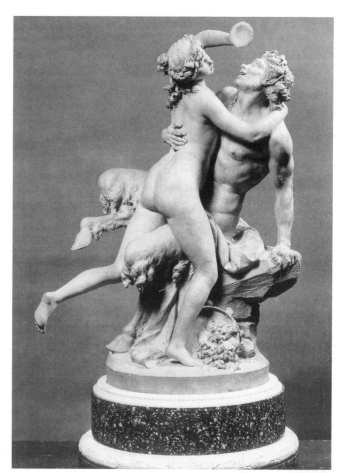

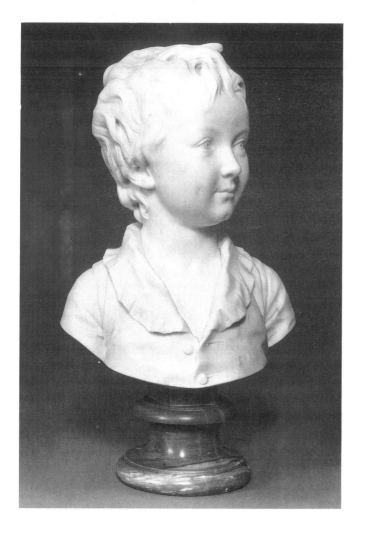

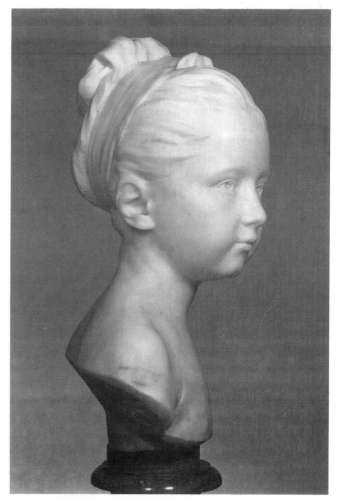

French, appears often as a subject in sculpture as well as in painting. Rococo sculpture was not on the monumental scale of its predecessors. Rather, in the spirit of decoration that marked the era, sculpture often took the form of delicate and graceful porcelain and metal figurines. Falconet's *Madame de Pompadour as the Venus of the Doves* (Fig. **11.16**) fully captures the erotic sensuality, delicacy, lively intelligence, and charm of the rococo heritage. The unpretentious nudity indicates the complete comfort and naturalness the eighteenth century found in love and affairs of the flesh.

Rococo sculpture exhibits masterful technique. Its surface textures, detail, and line all display superb delicacy and control of the medium. If this style and the society it exemplifies is found wanting in profundity, it must be admired for its technical achievement.

Claude Michel (1738–1814), best known as Clodion, reinforces the delicate themes of the time in dynamic miniatures such as the *Satyr and Bacchante* (Fig. **11.17**). "His groups of accurately modeled figures in erotic abandon are made all the fresher and more alluring by his knowing use of pinkish terracotta as if it were actually pulsating flesh, rendering each incipient embrace 'forever warm and still to be enjoyed'."[2]

In a more serious vein than much of eighteenth-century sculpture is the work of Jean Antoine Houdon (1741–1828) from the years just prior to the Revolution. His portrait busts, such as those of Alexandre and Louise Brongniard (Figs. **11.18** and **11.19**), exhibit penetrating psychological analysis coupled with delicate and accurate technical execution. Houdon's works marvelously express the personality of his subjects, and his portraits of American revolutionary figures such as Washington, Jefferson, John Paul Jones, and Benjamin Franklin are masterly projections of their characters. We should probably consider the work of Houdon as a part of the emerging eighteenth-century neo-classical style. The realistic truth Houdon expresses in individual character is much more akin to the ideals of neo-classicism than to those of the rococo. Sculpture, like society in the eighteenth century, was in transition. Academically rooted in the baroque, attempting to reflect the age of the rococo, and shadowing the aesthetic and antiquarian impetus of the last third of the century, sculpture slowly moved toward the nineteenth century and yet another stylistic shift.

MUSIC

Rococo

Rejection of French court society and its baroque arts brought ornamentation, delicacy, prettiness, and pleasant artificiality to a rococo style in music as well as painting and sculpture. Musicians improvized "decorations" in their performances, and the practice was so common that many composers purposely left their melodic lines bare in order to allow performers the opportunity for playful improvization. The purpose of music was to entertain and to charm.

François Couperin (1668–1733), more than any other composer, captured the musical spirit of his time, but he also managed to retain his baroque roots sufficiently to avoid excessive sentimentality or completely artificial decoration. Nevertheless, his works contain refinement appropriate for salon performance and avoid the emotional effects of his baroque predecessors. His compositions show a pleasant blending of logic and rationality with emotion and delicacy. He pursued allegory and mythological allusion in true rococo fashion.

Couperin was part of a uniquely French school of organ music from which came settings of popular airs and compositions similar to the overtures and recitatives of French opera. Many of Couperin's works were designed specifically to explore the tonal color possibilities of the organ, and his Masses, which comprised verses and interludes to be played in the Mass, exhibit ornamentation that can be associated with both baroque and rococo. His *passacaglias* and *chaconnes* (for example, the *Passacaille ou Chaconne* from the *First Suite for Viols*, 1728) show the same indefinitely repeated four- or eight-measure harmonic pattern found in music of the seventeenth century. However, his trio sonatas mark the earliest development in France of this musical form, which was to assume such an important role in the Classical Period to follow.

Expressive style

A second style of music—the "expressive style"—paralleling rococo, was a transitional stage between baroque and classical. This expressive style (more literally, sensitive style), or *empfindsamer Stil*, came from Germany and permitted a freer expression of emotions than the baroque, largely by allowing a variety of moods to occur within a single movement. Polyphonic complexities were reduced, and different themes with harmonic and rhythmic changes were introduced. Expressive style, therefore, was simple, and also highly original. Composers had the freedom to use new dynamic expressions, rhythmic contrasts, and original melodies. Yet the goal was a carefully proportioned, logical, unified whole, whose parts were clear and articulated to provide a definite demarcation between one part and the next.

The principal exponent of *empfindsamer Stil* was Carl Philipp Emanuel Bach (1714–88), son of J. S. Bach. His influence and position between baroque and classical styles caused many scholars to call him the founder of classical style. Although he wrote many different kinds of work, his most important compositions were for clavichord. The clavichord's soft, intimate tonal characteristics were well suited to C. P. E. Bach's delicate, dynamic shadings. His ornamentations stayed within the proportions of his melodic passages, assisting his desire to keep strong unity of modal and melodic materials. C. P. E. Bach's works often employ the element of surprise, with dramatic and swift changes in dynamics, harmonies, key, texture, and so on. Not the least of C. P. E. Bach's contributions to Western music was his *Essay on the True Way to Play Keyboard Instruments* (1753–62), which contains important information on ornamentation, musical thought, and practice in this period.

This expressive departure from the polyphonic emotionalism of the baroque was labeled as romantic at the time. What to some now appears sensible and restrained, witty and graceful, logical and reasoned, was thought then to be sentimental and whimsical. In less than a century the real romantics would rebel against this tradition, as it later developed, finding it too restrained and formal.

Classical style

In 1785 Michel Paul de Chabanon wrote, "Today there is but one music in all of Europe." The basis of this statement was music composed to appeal not only to the aristocracy but to the broad middle classes as well. Egalitarian tendencies and popularizing of ideas typical of the *philosophes* had also influenced artists, turning them toward a larger audience. Pleasure became a legitimate artistic purpose. Eighteenth-century rationalism regarded excessive ornamentation and excessive complexity (both baroque characteristics) as contrary to meeting a wide audience on its own terms. Those sentiments coupled with the discoveries of Pompeii and the works of Winckelmann and Baumgarten prompted a move to order, simplicity, and careful attention to form. We call this style in music classical (the term was not applied until the nineteenth century) rather than neo-classical or classical revival because although the other arts returned (more or less) to Greek and Roman prototypes, music had no known classical antecedents to revive, despite a fairly detailed understanding of Greek music theory. Music thus turned to classical *ideals*, though not to classical *models*.

One very clear characteristic of classical style was a definitely articulated structure. Each piece was organized into short statements called phrases, which recurred regularly and clearly. The most frequently cited example of this practice is Mozart's *Symphony No. 40 in G Minor*, whose opening movement is based on a three-note rhythmic pattern or motive organized into two contrasting phrases. These phrases are then grouped into themes which comprise sections in the movement. In contrast, for example, with the opening movement of Vivaldi's *Spring*, which we characterized as having an ABACADAEA structure, *Symphony No. 40*, typical of classical works, utilizes an AABA structure. Although it is part of a much longer

composition than Vivaldi's, it is much simpler and more clearly expressed. Classical music also avoided polyphony, depending instead upon a single, unobscured, melodic line that could be shaped into clear and expressive contours and brought to a definite cadence (conclusion).

A third change from the baroque lay in rhythmic patterns. Baroque's numerous ornamented parts flowing together in complex design fostered essentially unchanging rhythmic patterns. Classical phrase structure and melodic linearity allowed far more opportunity for rhythmic variety and also for rhythmic contrasts among or between lines. For example, the featured upper melodic line could carry one rhythmic impulse while the chordal supporting lines could carry another. Usually the chordal voices had more regular rhythms than the independent voice. Classical style also changed harmonic relationships, including more frequent use of modulation (key change).

Major musical forms such as the opera, oratorio, and concerto changed according to classical priorities. For example, Mozart's the *Marriage of Figaro* (1786), a comic opera on the theme of love and marriage, with a fast-paced plot, subplot, and dramatic conflicts, shows concern for simplicity and clarity. Haydn's oratorio, the *Creation*, reflects the Enlightenment's concepts of God and nature, reason and benevolence. The *Creation* also exhibits concern for simplicity and clear form. Operas and oratorios continued in popularity, but for the most part instrumental music became the dominant force. The concerto adapted smoothly from its baroque configurations into classical form and style. Chamber music also increased in popular appeal. Its small ensemble format was perfect for performance *en chambre*, in the small rooms of the eighteenth-century salon.

The most important forms in this period, however, were the symphony and the sonata. Sonatas were composed for virtually every instrument, and composers varied in their approach. Haydn, for example, employed a sonata-rondo form ((*rondo* was a classical variation of *ritornello*). The classical sonata, sometimes called sonata cycle, is a work of three or four movements, each of which consists of a specific structure. The most important structural configuration of the sonata is the typical configuration of the first movement. This structure is so important and specific that it is called sonata form or sonata-allegro form. It is used heavily not only in the first movement of sonatas, but also in the first movement of symphonies and chamber music. Using the traditional structural alphabet we would characterize sonata form as AABA. The A section begins with a thematic statement in the tonic key, followed by transitional materials called a bridge, a restatement of the opening theme or additional themes is then developed in a different key—usually the key of the dominant or the relative minor. The A section, called the exposition, closes with a strong cadence. Usually the entire exposition section is repeated (AA). In the next section (B), called the development section, the thematic material of the exposition undergoes numerous alterations called variations. The composer would restate thematic material in different rhythmic, harmonic, melodic, dynamic, and key configurations. Usually the composer strove to increase dynamic tension in the development section. Finally, tension is resolved in a recapitulation section (A). Although called a recapitulation section, it is not usually a strict repeat of the exposition. For example, in the recapitulation section of the allegro movement in *Symphony No. 40*, Mozart restated the opening theme in the original key to let the listener know he had finished the development section, but then he proceeded to finish the movement with a bridge and an extended coda. Not all classical sonatas, symphonies, or chamber music fits the textbook mold, but the characteristics just mentioned provide a fairly accurate guide for understanding classical sonata form.

The symphony, which used sonata-allegro form in its opening movement, also played an important part in the classical music tradition. Composers such as Stamitz, Cannabich, Wagenseil, Graun, C. P. E. and J. C. Bach, Gossec, and Boyce, in addition to the giants we will examine shortly, all contributed significantly to the development of this most important form. By the last quarter of the eighteenth century the symphony, as well as other forms of instrumental ensemble music, had largely eliminated use of *basso continuo*, and, thereby, the harpsichord. Primary focus, then, fell on the violin section, and classical symphonic compositions reflect that new focus. By the turn of the nineteenth century other sections, such as the woodwind, were given more important, independent material.

The timbre of an orchestra was fairly close to what we know today. The size, and therefore the overall volume of sound was not. The largest orchestra of the mid-eighteenth century, the Mannheim Orchestra, consisted of forty-five players, mostly strings, with six woodwinds, five brasses, and two timpani. Haydn's orchestra between 1760 and 1785 rarely exceeded twenty-five players, and the Vienna orchestras of the 1790s averaged thirty-five.

Haydn
The most illustrative symphonic literature of the classical style came from the minds and pens of Haydn, Mozart, and Beethoven (in his early years). Austrian-born Franz Joseph Haydn (1732–1809) pioneered the development of the symphony from a short, simple work into a longer, more sophisticated one. Haydn's symphonies are diverse and numerous (some sources indicate that he wrote more than one hundred and four). Some are light and simple, others are serious and sophisticated. Many of his early symphonies use the pre-classical, three-movement form. These usually consist of an opening *allegro* movement,

followed by an *andante* movement in a related key, and closed with a rapid *minuet* or *gigue*-like movement in triple meter. Other early works use four movements, the first of which is in a slow tempo. In contrast, *Symphony No. 3 in G Major* (c.1762) has a typical four-movement structure beginning with a fast tempo: I. allegro; II. andante moderato; III. minuet and trio; IV. allegro. *Symphony No. 3* emphasizes polyphony more than homophony, in contrast to the general classical trend, and the opening allegro movement does not use sonata-allegro form. The third movement, *minuet* and *trio*, is found in nearly every classical symphony and always has a two-part form. Haydn's minuets contain very charming music, emphasizing harmonic invention and instrumental color.

Haydn's middle symphonies from the early 1770s exhibit imaginative emotion and a larger scale than his earlier works. Exposition sections explore broadly expressed themes followed by contrasting ideas and restatement. The development sections are dramatic and employ sudden and unexpected changes of dynamics. The slow movements contain great warmth and emotion. Haydn frequently drew on Austrian folk songs and baroque dance music, and his modulations and changes of tonality contain great dramatic power.

Among his late works is his most famous, *Symphony No. 94 in G Major* (1792), commonly known as the "Surprise Symphony". Its second movement contains a charming theme and the dramatic "surprise" which gave the work its popular name. The tempo of the second movement is *andante*, and the orchestra begins with a very soft, clear statement of the theme. After presenting the quiet theme, Haydn inserts a tremendous, *fortissimo* chord. Its effect on those who are not familiar with the work is very amusing. This simple theme, constructed of triads, carries throughout the movement in a series of delightful variations. Melodies are disjunct, and phrase structure, highly symmetrical.

Mozart
Wolfgang Amadeus Mozart (1756–91), also an Austrian, had performed at the court of Empress Maria Theresa at the age of six. As was the case throughout the classical period, aristocratic patronage was essential for musicians to earn a living, although the middle classes provided a progressively larger portion of commissions, pupil fees, and concert attendance. Mozart's short career (he died at the age of thirty-five) was dogged by financial insecurity.

His early symphonies were simple and relatively short, like those of Haydn, while his later works were longer and more complex. His last three symphonies are generally regarded as his greatest masterpieces, and *Symphony No. 40 in G Minor* is often referred to as the typical classical symphony. This work and Nos. 39 and 41 have clear order and restraint and yet exhibit tremendous emotional urgency, which many scholars cite as the beginning of the romantic style. The opening movement of *Symphony No. 40* is cast in sonata-allegro form, and built, as we mentioned earlier, on a three-note motif. The second movement (*andante*) is also in sonata form. It begins with a comfortable motive in the viola section, but tension soon clouds the melody. The moderate tempo continues, but the rhythm changes from calm to agitated. The development section is very sombre and intense, and, as in the opening movement, the recapitulation returns subtly and creatively to the opening theme. The third movement explores the standard minuet and trio, and the fourth movement (*allegro*) closes the work in sonata form.

Beethoven

Ludwig van Beethoven (1770–1827) is often considered apart from the Classical Period and treated as a singular transitional figure between classicism and romanticism. Beethoven wanted to expand the classical symphonic form in order for it to accommodate greater emotional character. The typical classical symphony moves through contrasting movements; Beethoven changed that to accommodate a single thematic development throughout, and thereby achieved a unified, emotional work.

Beethoven's works are significantly different from those of Haydn and Mozart. They are more dramatic and use changing dynamics for emotional effects. Silence is used as a device in pursuit of dramatic and structural ends. Beethoven's works are also longer. He lengthened the development section of sonata–allegro form and did the same to his codas, many of which take on characteristics of a second development section. He also changed traditional thematic relationships among movements, especially in the Symphony No. 6 which has no break between the fourth and fifth movements. In the Symphony No. 5 no break occurs between movements three and four. In his four-movement works he changed the traditional third movement *trio* to a *scherzo* and *trio* of significantly different character. His symphonies draw heavily on imagery, for example, heroism in *Symphony No. 3* and pastoral settings in *Symphony No. 6*. *Symphony No. 5 in C Minor* begins with a motive even the non-musician knows well and which Beethoven described as "fate knocking at the door". The first movement (*allegro con brio*) develops according to typical sonata–allegro form, the second and contrasting movement (*andante con moto*) is in theme and variation form, and the third movement (*allegro*) is a *scherzo* in triple meter. Movement number four returns to *allegro* and to sonata form. Beethoven's nine symphonies become progressively more romantic, and the Ninth Symphony is a gigantic work of tremendous power. Its finale includes a chorus singing the text of Schiller's *Ode to Joy*.

Although classical style had a simpler character and used a more symmetrical structure than baroque, it did not sacrifice dynamic qualities in that pursuit. In the same sense that the simple qualities of Greek architecture, for example, did not lose their sophistication and interest in a slavish pursuit of apparently mathematical form and symmetry, so classical music maintained its dynamic and sophisticated character in its pursuit of form and reason. As classical style was shaped by its advocates it moved as comfortably toward romanticism as it had moved away from baroque.

THEATRE

If there was only one style of music throughout Europe in the last half of the eighteenth century, the same may not be said of theatre, which during the Enlightenment became more nationalist. In order to continue our story of theatre's history in this period we have no option but to continue to look at each country in turn. England, France, Germany, Italy, and the United States each contributed to eighteenth-century dramatic tradition.

Britain

We must remember that Britain preceded France in eliminating absolutism. The Restoration and its theatre, which began a new style in the late seventeenth century, carried England into the early eighteenth century. As was the case later in the rest of Europe, the character of English audiences was changing and its theatre changed accordingly. Queen Anne cared little for the theatre, and George I, being German and not speaking English well, could not understand it. Audiences in England tended more and more to be well-to-do, middle-class tradesmen. One effect of this was the shift in emphasis of Restoration comedy toward sentiment. Witty dialogue persisted, and English comedy in the Augustan age (in deference to George I) is well illustrated in the works of Colley Cibber (1671–1757).

Moderately clever plays such as *Love's Last Shift; or the Fool in Fashion* (1696), *She Wou'd and She Wou'd Not; or the Kind Imposter* (1702), and the *Careless Husband* (1704) delighted London audiences. The *Non-Juror* (1717) portrayed an English Catholic priest fomenting rebellion against the king, and it fomented its own furore among the Catholic community while earning Cibber the pleasure of the king. Cibber's final contribution to the theatre was a delightful and sharp-witted analysis of English acting called *An Apology for the Life of Colley Cibber, Comedian ... with an Historical View of the Stage during His Own Time* (1740). English comedy closed the century in high style with the plays of Oliver Goldsmith (1730–74) and Richard Brinsley Sheridan (1751–1816). Goldsmith's works, especially *She Stoops to Conquer* (1773), exhibit excellent humor and exceptionally well-drawn characters. Sheridan, probably the most

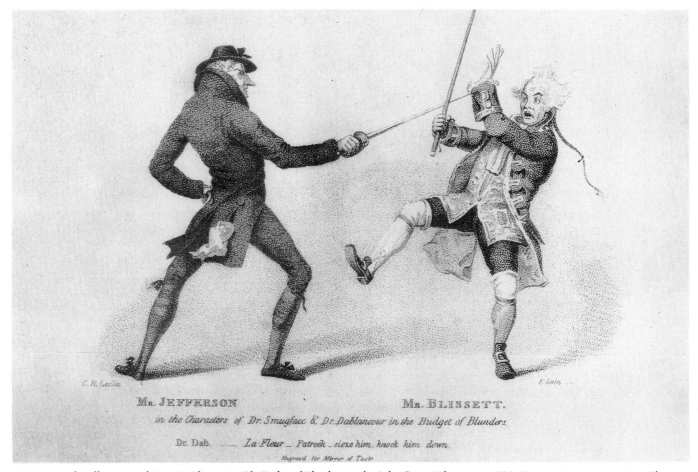

11.20 Joseph Jefferson and Francis Blissett in *The Budget of Blunders*, at the John Street Theatre, c.1796. Contemporary engraving. The New York Public Library.

famous British playwright of the period, created two masterpieces, the *Rivals* (1775) and the most brilliant comedy of the English stage, *School for Scandal* (1777), a biting satire with crisp, fast-paced dialogue.

Tragedy had been virtually non-existent in England since 1640 when all public theatres were closed by the Commonwealth. However, by the early eighteenth century the neo-classical traditions of seventeenth-century France and the pseudo-classical theories of essayist, critic, and poet Alexander Pope (1688–1744) made some inroads into British tragedy. A number of plays and playwrights followed these precepts. The most successful was James Thomson (1700–48) with *Sophonisba* (1729) and *Edward and Eleanora* (c.1735).

Undoubtedly the most popular theatre form in early eighteenth-century London was the ballad opera, and the best of these unquestionably was John Gay's *Beggar's Opera* (1728). It caricatured the bribery of Sir Robert Walpole and created a social scandal. The *Beggar's Opera* was not the only theatrical piece to burlesque the corruption of Walpole, and as a result of these theatrical attacks, Walpole successfully convinced Parliament to institute the Licensing Act of 1737, which limited legal theatrical production to three theatres, Drury Lane, Covent Garden, and Haymarket, and gave the Lord Chamberlain the right to censor any play.

Production style remained controlled, however, and as a result the physical theatre in London retained its elegant but intimate scale, in contrast to the mammoth opera houses that flourished elsewhere. The playing area consisted of a forestage, the sides of which contained doorways for entrances and exits by the actors, and above which were located boxes for spectators. Wing and drop scenery was placed upstage, behind a proscenium arch, and consisted of flat, painted pieces used strictly as a background. Lighting consisted of wax candles in chandeliers over the audience. As might be expected, fire was a constant danger, and smoke from the candles was an irritating nuisance.

The entire eighteenth century in England, and particularly the second half, was an age of actors rather than playwrights. The greatest of these, indeed the greatest theatre figure of this time, was David Garrick (1717–79). His genius significantly changed the style of English theatre and, as a result, that of America as well. Garrick began as an actor, attaining great fame after a sensational début performance in *Lethe; or Aesop in the Shades* (1740). He followed that with a tremendous success in Shakespeare's *Richard III*. However, he and his main rival Macklin changed the course of theatre history not by their acting, but by introducing antiquarian-inspired costume to the English stage. Macklin began by appearing in a costume described as "Old Caledonian habit", to which Garrick responded by playing King Lear in his own idea of "Old English" costume.

America

By briefly mentioning Gilbert Stuart, the American painter, earlier we finally acknowledged notable artistic enterprise in America. The arts, and theatre especially, came up squarely against unbending Puritan austerity. Sometime between 1699 and 1702, however, Richard Hunter gained permission from the acting Governor of the Province of New York to present plays in the city of New York. In 1703 an English actor named Anthony Ashton landed at Charlestowne, South Carolina. He was "full of Lice, Shame, Poverty, Nakedness, and Hunger", and to survive became "Player and Poet". Eventually he found his way to New York where he spent the winter "acting, writing, courting, and fighting". Perhaps as a consequence, the Province forbade "play acting and other forms of disreputable entertainment" in 1709. Notwithstanding an inauspicious start, American theatre struggled forward. The first recorded theatre was built in Williamsburg, Virginia, in 1716 and housed a performing company for the next several years. For the most part theatre in America was merely an extension of the British stage, and English touring companies provided most of the fare. Theatres themselves appear to have been small and closely modelled upon provincial English theatres with their raked stages, proscenium arches, painted scenery, and apron forestages flanked by entrance doors. Four hundred seats seems about average. The front curtain rose and fell at the beginning and end of each act. Numerous scene changes within the acts were executed in full view of the audience.

Companies from London, usually comedy troupes, came to Williamsburg annually for an eleven-month season. By 1766 touring British companies played the entire eastern seaboard from New York, Philadelphia, and Annapolis to Charleston. A milestone was passed on 24 April 1767 when the American Company, in fact British, presented Thomas Godfrey's *The Prince of Parthia*, the first play written by an American to receive a professional production. As the American Company prepared for its 1774–5 season, the Continental Congress passed a resolution discouraging "exhibitions of shows, plays, and other expensive diversions and entertainments".

Numerous American plays were written during the years of the American Revolution, most of which were never performed. Their titles, however, reflect the current of thought and the loyalist/rebel dichotomy: *The Americans Roused in a Cure for the Spleen* (1775), *Battle of Brooklyn* (1776), and *The Blockade* (1775). All of the former were loyalist satires against the revolutionary cause. Supporting the opposing cause were *The Adulateur* (1773), *The Group* (1775), and *The Blockheads* (1776), all aimed at the Tories, as well as *The Battle of Bunker's Hill* (1776), *The Fall of British Tyranny* (1776), and *The Patriots* (1776). Since there were no American professional actors, and since all the British professionals had fled back to England, the war years saw a flurry of amateur production throughout the colonies, including performances staged by the American troops themselves with the approval of George Washington.

The century closed with eighteen post-war years of production by the American Company, which returned from England in 1782. In 1787 Royal Tyler's *The Contrast* successfully launched a firm tradition of American theatre. Tyler was a Boston lawyer and American army officer, who had seen his first play only a few weeks before writing *The Contrast*. He presented a lively picture of New York society, with facile dialogue and well-drawn characters. The play satirizes Dimple, a young New Yorker who has turned into a fop because of his admiration of all things British. Although engaged to Charlotte, the daughter of a wealthy merchant, Dimple considers himself a European rake and makes advances to two of his fiancée's friends. One of the friends has a brother, Colonel Manly, the epitome of American plain manners, high principles, and patriotism. Manly falls in love with Charlotte, exposes Dimple, saves both Charlotte and his own sister from Dimple's duplicity, and ends up united with Charlotte. In the midst of this delightful comedy are two additional characters of extreme importance—Jessemy, Dimple's servant, every inch the mirror of his master, and Jonathan, Manly's servant, the prototypical "country bumpkin". The subplot of scenes between these two provides hilarious fun even for contemporary audiences.

Although *The Contrast* was successful, however, the first major American playwright was really British-trained William Dunlap, who wrote *The Father, or American Shandyism* (1789), which combined sentiment, wit, comic humor, and "the finer feelings of the human heart".

In 1794 the focus of American theatre turned to Philadelphia with the opening of the Chestnut Street Theatre. It had a handsome interior with boxes set in a semiellipse and a total seating capacity of either 1,200 or 2,000 (sources vary). The auditorium was gray with gold trim, including elegant gilt railings. The orchestra pit held thirty musicians, and the large forestage was flanked by walls representing the façades of handsome buildings. The large stage was lit by oil lamps, whereas the auditorium was lit by candles. A French traveler, whose descriptions detailed the theatre, indicated that "between the acts the pit is noisy and even indecent.... The women turn their backs on the pit during intermission."[3]

349

France

Ripples of the comic style of Molière and the neo-classicism of Racine extended well into the eighteenth century, but, essentially, the theatre of France underwent a barren period after the death of Molière. The recently established Comédie-Française produced fine actors and actresses in both comedy and tragedy, but its management appeared overly aware of its state patronage and held a backward-looking philosophy of production that stifled new directions. The Comédie-Française slipped into tragedies that were sentimental and melodramatic, and comedies caught up in contemporary triviality. A rival company at the Hôtel de Bourgogne (Fig. **11.21**) called themselves the *Comédie-Italienne*, to distinguish themselves from the *Comédie-Française* and to reflect the Italian nationality of the actors (although they played in French). Success for this company had begun in the closing years of the seventeenth century with productions of the playwrights Jean François Régnard (1655–1710) and Charles Rivière Dufresny (1654–1724). Briefly exiled for slighting Mme. de Maintenon, the *Conédie-Italienne* returned to successful seasons after the death of Louis XIV in 1715. Plays of the early years of the century often show a combination of neo-classicism, popularism, and rococo niceties. Tearful comedies called *comédies larmoyantes* satisfied the tastes of the salon set as well as an ever-increasing, middle-class audience, which demanded emotional plays in recognizably contemporary situations. The Enlightenment's egalitarianism brought tragedy to a curious state—the increasing numbers of women in theatre audiences seemed determined to cry, even in comedies, and they flocked to the well-equipped theatres in pursuit of such release. By the time of the Revolution, serious drama had become *drames bourgeois*, middle-class drama, of melodramatic proportion.

A few undistinguished tragedies of neo-classical bent were written, only to fall justifiably by the wayside. Of interest in this vein are the works of Jolyot de Crébillon (1674–1762) who wrote popular horror plays. His intention was to move an audience to pity and terror (cf. Aristotle) and never to offend their refinement or propriety. The plots of Crébillon's plays speak for themselves: a father kills his son (*Idoménée*, 1705); a father drinks his son's blood (*Atrée et Thyeste*, 1707); a man kills his mother (*Electra*, 1709). Crébillon continued to write tragedies well into the middle of the century, and his last two plays, *Catalina* (1742) and *Le Triumvirate* (1754), were written to compete with Voltaire, who dominated the first three-quarters of the eighteenth century.

The shifting character of French drama of the first half of the century can also be seen in the plays of Pierre Marivaux (1688–1763). Marivaux' style is difficult to classify, but is more in the rococo style than anything else. His plays are charming, sentimental, and meticulously written. *Les Fausses Confidences* (1732) described the efforts of a

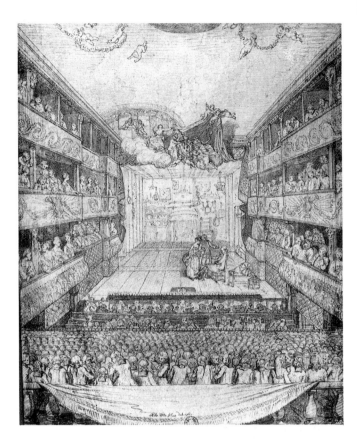

11.21 Interior of the Hôtel de Bourgogne, c.1765. Bibliothèque Nationale, Paris.

poor but handsome young man who sets out to make his rich mistress fall in love with and marry him. The questionable morality of his duplicity is assuaged when, in the end, the young man actually falls in love himself. Marivaux had his eye on the neo-classical "unities"—the entire action of the play occupies less than a day.

Perhaps nothing summarizes the first three-quarters of the eighteenth century better than the theatrical ventures of its most dominant personality, François Marie Arouet, known as Voltaire (1694–1778). His plays were diverse in style and genre. Curiously, given his critical, anti-establishment propensities, Voltaire's early plays, such as *Oedipe*, follow the rules of the French Academy (*Oedipe* is, in fact, a slavish imitation of Racine). An admirer of Shakespeare, Voltaire once called him an "inspired barbarian" because Shakespeare's dramatic structures were far too untidy for neo-classical tastes. In *Mérope* (1741) Voltaire declared that he had returned to first Greek principles. Most critics agree that what he meant by this was that he had eliminated any love scenes. His last play, *Nanine* (1778), had a gala première attended by most of the royal family, and by the time of his death two months later, he had received the greatest acclaim ever bestowed on anyone in the French theatre.

French drama had one final blaze of brilliance before the Revolution, in the plays of Beaumarchais. His two most famous plays, The Barber of Seville (1775) and The Marriage of Figaro (1784), are entertaining comedies built upon the traditions of neo-classicism dating back to Le Cid. In fact, at the last moment Beaumarchais expanded The Barber of Seville into a neo-classical five-act structure, adding only ponderousness to a fine play. Opening night criticism caused him to rewrite it into a four-act structure, which restored the sparkle and brilliance. Both The Barber of Seville and The Marriage of Figaro foretold the coming Revolution, and the nine years between the works saw a dramatically changed audience perception of the forecast. The Barber of Seville was enjoyed and received calmly, but by 1784 France was well aware of its circumstances. The criticisms directed against Figaro within the play were taken seriously as an indictment of society as a whole. The horrors and chaos of the Revolution left the French stage barren during the final ten years of the eighteenth century.

Germany

The mid-eighteenth century in Germany marked a determined attempt to develop a significant national theatre, even if the political concept of "Germany" remained somewhat nebulous. Chaos and a lack of any stable national boundaries or capital cities to act as cultural centers had previously prevented the development of a strong national theatre such as England, France, Italy, or even Spain had enjoyed. As we have seen, however, the late eighteenth century found both Germany and Austria with altered political circumstances.

Seeds planted by touring English, French, and Italian companies, nevertheless, had provided the basis for a "German" theatre. Johann Christoph Gottsched (1700–66) began a small literary renaissance at the University of Leipzig by translating numerous French neo-classical plays (some of dubious quality) into German. Gottsched turned from literary to production efforts primarily because of the acting talents of Carolina Neuber (1697–1760). In 1724 the troupe of which Neuber was a part came to the attention of Gottsched, and he joined forces with her. Their later collaborations to reform the theatre of Germany did much to improve circumstances and establish traditions. Konrad Ekhof (1720–78) followed Neuber's tradition with an acting style of earnestness, sincerity, and honest restraint that set the production standard of the era.

The literary values prominent in German theatre in the mid-eighteenth century were strengthened by a superb playwright, Gotthold Ephraim Lessing (1729–81). Lessing and Ekhof became part of the newly established Hamburg National Theatre. Lessing was offered the position of "stage poet", whose responsibilities included writing new plays, making translations, and composing prologues and epilogues for special occasions. Lessing

refused the position, indicating that he could not complete plays as frequently as required for such a position (recall the requirements for Bach and others to compose weekly cantatas as part of their employment conditions). Nevertheless, the Hamburg National Theatre was so eager to have Lessing associated with them that he was hired without this condition.

Lessing's first tragedy, written before his association with the Hamburg National Theatre, was Miss Sara Sampson (1755), a reworking of the Medea story in a middle-class English setting. A typical tragédie bourgeoise, it had great influence in Germany and replaced French neo-classical drama as a standard. His most remembered play, Minna von Barnhelm (1767) is often called the first German contemporary drama. It is a tender, serious comedy about womanhood. Lessing's final, and perhaps best play was Nathan the Wise (1779), which preached religious toleration, introduced blank verse, and employed strong symbolism. Nathan the Wise exemplified enlightened thought. As well as his plays Lessing provided important theoretical advancement in German theatre. In his Hamburgische Dramaturgie and other works, he argued that all art is but a reflection of nature, and that pseudo-classical rules interfering with that perception were false. Lessing considered Sophocles and Shakespeare as the dramatic models by which all playwrights should be measured.

Lessing made another contribution of consequence to German and Western theatre. He wrote plays that allowed for scene changes at the act break rather than between scenes so as not to impede the movement of the action. This change was significant. In a theatre using depictive scenic background, as opposed to theatre of scenic convention, such as the Greek or Elizabethan, pauses at any point in the dramatic action break the rhythmic and emotional flow of the production and elaborate scenic changes break the audience's involvement and attention. Clearly Lessing was a playwright of the theatre for which he wrote. His plays were written for the stage with theatre aesthetics in mind.

German theatre changed direction around 1770, and the years that follow introduced the romantic movement, which was to dominate the nineteenth century. Lessing's interest in Shakespeare and also his concern for unbroken action were shared by Johann Wolfgang von Goethe (1749–1832). For reasons that will become apparent in the next chapter, Goethe and others in Germany turned to Shakespeare, chivalry, and Elizabethanism for inspiration. In 1771 Goethe produced his Goetz von Berlichingen, a Shakespearean historical drama of German thought and concept. Complete with typically Shakespearean comic interludes amid the tragedy, Goetz von Berlichingen told the story of a Robin Hood-like robber-knight of the sixteenth century. Four years after the play, Goethe helped change the course of the next century with two monumental works, the novel Die Leiden des Jungen Werther (The Sorrows of Young Werther) and the first draft of the play

Faust. These two works and friedrich von Klinger's play *Sturm und Drang* (*Storm and Stress*) (1776) began a new revolt against classicism. *Sturm und Drang* drew much of its inspiration from the American Revolution. Its title became associated with a movement attracting young and free spirits everywhere, Goethe among them. Goethe's *Faust* draws most attention as the masterpiece of the age.

Part I of *Faust* is actually the theatrical masterpiece. Goethe began and partially completed it around 1774–5, but continued to rework the play until 1801. Part II occupied the remaining thirty years of his life and was not actually published until 1833, the year after he died. The Faust story was not original to Goethe, but his treatment of it was. There is some doubt whether Goethe even intended Part I to be a stage presentation, as opposed to a dramatic poem. It begins with a poetic dedication, followed by a "Prelude in the Theatre" and a "Prologue in Heaven". What follows is a series of twenty-six scenes ranging from Faust's study to a final prison scene. Nowhere does Goethe enumerate the scenes or give a list of characters. He does not even indicate passage of time. Rather, he provides absorbing speeches illustrating the struggles in Faust's mind and his commentary on life. The work is a dramatic mixture of passion and wisdom. Part II reflects idealism removed from the "conflict of conscience and love" of Part I. Part II is so formless that it is virtually impossible to stage. Goethe's Faust was a poet–dreamer and idealist, seeking the divine and the ability to understand the workings of nature and the mystery of life. He is the prototypical romantic hero, of great significance in the years to come.

Italy

Italian theatre in the eighteenth century is little more than a footnote compared to that of other countries, but it had some important aspects. First was its interaction with the French theatre. The traditions of France and Italy were continued in the *Comédie-Italienne* in Paris and in the plays of the Italian dramatist Goldoni, who wrote both in Italian and French. Carlo Goldoni (1707–93) settled in Paris in 1761, having made in Italy a significant but unsuccessful attempt to revive the *commedia dell' arte* by providing its actors with written texts. His plays have an eclectic style apparent, for example, in *Servant of Two Masters* (1740) and *La Locandiera* (*Mistress of the Inn*, 1751). In contrast to the more spectacular works of Gozzi, Goldoni's plays are intimate comedies of manners very much like Molière's, which served as Goldoni's models.

A second important aspect of Italian theatre in the eighteenth century was operatic production and specifically its magnificent scenic designs. Several schools of scenic design existed in Italy, each following a different tradition. Venice produced a school of light and graceful designs. Bologna, Parma, and Pisa, on the other hand, continued the opulent traditions of the baroque, especially through the work of the influential Galli-Bibiena family (Fig. **10.19**).

DANCE

"The only way to make ballet more popular is to lengthen the dances and shorten the *danseuses'* skirts." This opinion was attributed to the composer Campra. One of the most significant obstacles to the development of the ballerina's art was costume (Fig. **11.22**). Floor-length skirts were not conducive to freedom of movement, and as a simple result, *danseurs* (male dancers) played the prominent roles at the turn of the eighteenth century as the courtly splendor of Lous XIV's Versailles was left behind. In 1730 one of those curious accidents of history occurred, which helped to change the course of ballet and bring the ballerina into pre-eminence.

Marie Anne Cupis de Camargo (1710–70) (Fig. **11.23**) was a brilliant dancer, so much so that her mentor Mlle. Prevost (then Ballerina) tried to keep her hidden among the *corps de ballet*. During one particular performance, however, a male dancer failed to make his entrance, and Camargo quickly stepped forward to dance the role in his place. Her performance was superb and in a style that

11.22 Jean Baptiste Martin, *Apollon*, costume design for Apollo. Engraving. The New York Public Library.

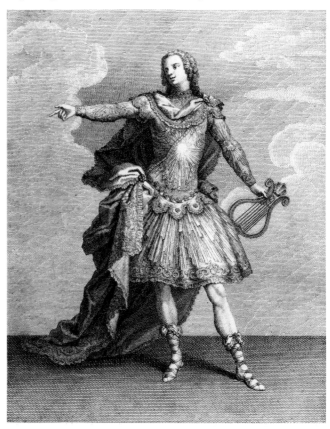

When emotion and expressiveness become melodramatic the pendulum can swing back to technique.

We have no way of identifying the actual characteristics of eighteenth-century ballet, but its mythological subject matter in the first half of the century is consistent with that of painting, sculpture, and music: *Les Indes Galantes* (1735), *Pygmalion* (1734), *The Loves of Mars and Venus* (1717), *Orpheus and Eurydice* (1718), *Perseus and Andromeda* (1726), and *The Judgment of Paris* (1732). Significant in earlier works, most of which were produced in London by the dancing master John Weaver, was the use of movement to communicate the story. These early attempts to integrate movement and dramatic content brought forth *ballet d'action* in the last half of the century.

The popularity of the *ballet d'action* helped to separate this form from the sprawling *ballet à entrée* and reinforce ballet's independence from the opera and drama. *Ballet d'action* contained an evolving classical concern for unity. Its emphasis on drama stood in contrast to focus on display of *ballet à entrée*. The primary moving force in this new form was Jean George Noverre (1727–1810). His influential *Letters on Dancing and Ballets* (1760) contended that ballets should be unified artworks in which all elements contribute to the main theme. For Noverre ballet was a dramatic spectacle, literally a play without words, whose content was communicated through expres-

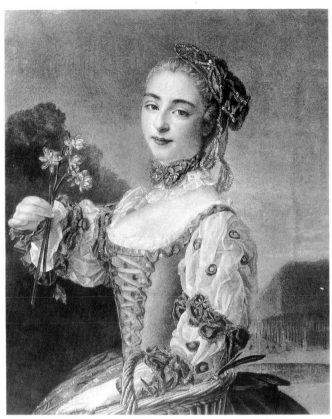

11.23 Portrait of Marie de Camargo (1710-70). The New York Public Library.

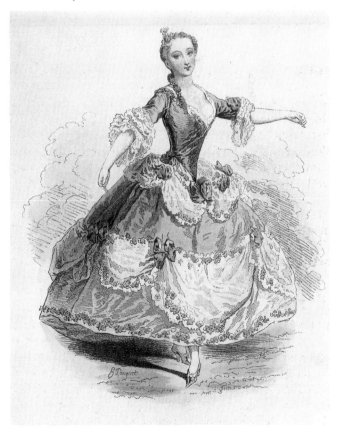

11.24 After Lancret, *Marie Sallé*, 1730. Engraving. The New York Public Library.

revealed ease, brilliance, and gaiety. Her footwork was so dazzling that, in order to feature it more fully, she raised her skirts to a discreet inch or two above the ankle! Her forte was the *entrechat*, a movement in which the dancer jumps straight up and rapidly crosses the legs while in the air. The move is still a technical achievement especially favored by male dancers. Voltaire indicated that Camargo was the first woman to dance like a man, that is, the first ballerina to acquire the technical skills and brilliance previously associated only with *danseurs*.

Another significant stylistic change came about through the individual accomplishments of a ballerina, Marie Sallé (Fig. **11.24**). Her studies in mime and drama led her to believe that the style prevalent in Paris was overly formal and repetitious. So in the early 1730s she broke her contract with the Paris Opera (an act punishable by imprisonment), and took up residence in London. Her style was one of expressiveness, as opposed to "leaps and frolics", and in 1734, in her famous *Pygmalion*, she wore simple draperies rather than the traditional *panniers*, and her hair flowed freely in contrast to the usual custom of piling it tightly on the top of the head. The contrast between the styles of Camargo and Sallé was an early example of the volatile nature of balletic style. A sterile emphasis on flashy technique can be quickly countered by emphasis on emotion and expressiveness.

sive movement. Technical virtuosity for the purpose of display was objectionable. He advocated music "written to fit each phrase and thought". In perfect harmony with Baumgarten and Winckelmann, Noerre insisted that ballet should study other arts and draw upon natural forms of movement, in order to be "a faithful likeness of beautiful Nature". He also argued for costumes that enhanced rather than impeded movement, and his ballets were considered excellent examples of "psychological realism".

Salvatore Vigano (1769–1821), another major figure of the period, followed Noverre's theories somewhat. Vigano's works moved from early choreography inspired by Shakespeare (specifically *Coriolanus*) to elaborate mime-dramas displaying neo-classical formulas. His *Creatures of Prometheus* (1801) had music by Beethoven. Vigano was highly influenced by the neo-classical painters Jacques Louis David and Jean Dominique Ingres. His ballets comprise a transition between classicism and romanticism, emphasizing heroic qualities. Works such as *Richard The Lion Hearted* and *Joan of Arc* were called *choreodrammi* and differ from *ballet d'action* in fervor and scale. Poses and groupings of solo dancers suggested classical sculpture and were used in contrast to sweeping ensemble movement.

Popularizing of ballet occurred along with other arts and philosophy, and by 1789 ballet themes, like those of painting, began to include subjects beyond mythology. Ordinary country life (as in Chardin's genre painting) provided topics for rustic ballets. These realistic portraits undoubtedly left much realism to be desired. They do serve, however, to illustrate trends toward egalitarianism in France and England, especially. Jean Dauberval (1742–1816), a student of Noverre, followed his teacher's example and accepted theories about nature as an inspiration for the dance and its gestures. His *La Fille Mal Gardée*, for example, showed ordinary folk in real situations.

Nevertheless, preoccupations with mythology persisted. A rare glimpse of late eighteenth-century choreography and mythical subject matter is available through the unbroken traditions of the Royal Danish Ballet, which still dances a fairly accurate production of Vincenzo Galeotti's *Whims of Cupid and the Ballet Master* (1786).

As the eighteenth century came to a close, Charles Didelot (1767–1837) changed the course of ballet forever. First, he simplified the line and form of dance costume by introducing tights. Next, he set the ballet world on its ear by attaching ballerinas to wires in *Zephyr and Flora* (1796) and flying them in and out of the scene. According to some sources, Didelot's wires allowed ballerinas to pause, resting effortlessly on the tips of their toes. As we well know, the line and form of the body created by that single effect constitutes a dramatic change in the aesthetic tone of a dance. That change was as obvious then as it is now. Soon ballerinas were dancing *en pointe* without using wires: an entirely new age in the dance had begun.

ARCHITECTURE

Rococo

Unlike most previous architectural styles, rococo was principally a style of interior design. Its refinement and decorativeness applied to furniture and décor more than to exterior structure or even detail. Even the aristocracy lived in attached row houses. Townhouses quite simply had virtually no exteriors to design. Attention turned to interiors, where the difference between opulence and delicacy was apparent. Figure **11.25** shows a polygonal music room characteristic of German rococo. Broken wall surfaces made possible stucco decoration of floral branches in a pseudo-naturalistic effect. In Venice curved leg furniture, cornices, and guilded carvings were *à la mode*. French designer François de Cuvilliés (1695–1768) combined refinement, lightness, and reduced scale to produce a pleasant atmosphere of grace and propriety (Fig. **11.26**).

English architecture of the early eighteenth century shared rococo refinement but in many ways was different from that of the continent. The late seventeenth and early eighteenth centuries in England produced a so-called "Georgian style" (referring to the Kings George I, II, III, whose reigns it partially encompassed). Georgian style was a kind of vernacular neo-classicism. Its relationship to

11.25 G. H. Krohne, The Music Room, Thuringer Museum, Eisenach, Germany, 1742–51.

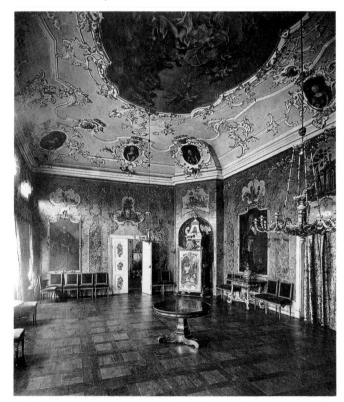

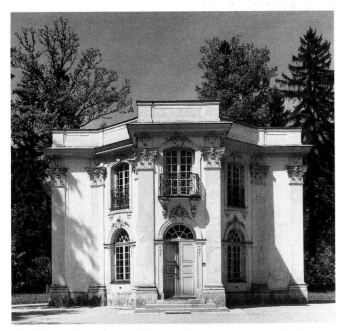

11.26 François de Cuvilliés, The Pagodenburg, c.1722. Schloss Nymphenburg, Munich, Germany.

rococo can be seen in its refinement and delicacy. Georgian architecture developed from the English baroque of Christopher Wren, which was much more restrained and classical than the florid baroque style of the continent.

Neo-classicism

In the mid-eighteenth century architecture's viewpoints changed entirely and embraced the complex philosophical concerns of the Enlightenment. The result was a series of styles and substyles broadly referred to as neo-classical. Excavations at Herculaneum and Pompeii, philosophical concepts of progress, the aesthetics of

Baumgarten, and the writings of Winckelmann combined to produce a new view of antiquity. Neo-classicism, as a result, was really a new spirit of examination of the past. Rather than seeing the past as a single, continuous cultural stream broken by a medieval collapse of classical values, theoreticians of the eighteenth century saw history as a series of compartments, for example, Antiquity, Middle Ages, Renaissance, and so on.

Three important concepts emerged as a result of this change in viewpoint. First was the archeological concept, which viewed the present as continually enriched by persistent inquiry into the past (progress). Second was the eclectic, which allowed the artist to choose among styles, or, more importantly, to combine elements of various styles. The third was the modernist concept, which viewed the present as unique and, therefore, possible of expression in its own terms. These three concepts profoundly influenced eighteenth-century architecture, had important bearing on the other arts and fundamentally changed the basic premises of art from that time forward.

Neo-classicism, as applied to architecture, encompasses these three concepts and reflects a variety of treatment and terminology. Basic to it, of course, are the identifiable forms of Greece and Rome. Neo-classicism in architecture took considerable impetus from the *Essai sur l'architecture* (Paris 1753) by the Abbé Laugier. Laugier's work was strictly rationalistic and expressed neo-classicism in a nutshell. He discarded the architectural language developed since the Renaissance. Rather, he urged the architect to seek truth in principles demonstrated in the architecture of the ancient world and to use those principles to design modern buildings that expressed the same logical limitations as the classical temple. Laugier's classicism descended directly from the Greeks, with only passing reference to the Romans.

In Italy, the architect Giambattista Piranesi (1720–78) was incensed by Laugier's arguments, which placed Greece above Rome, and he retaliated with an overwhelmingly detailed work that professed to prove

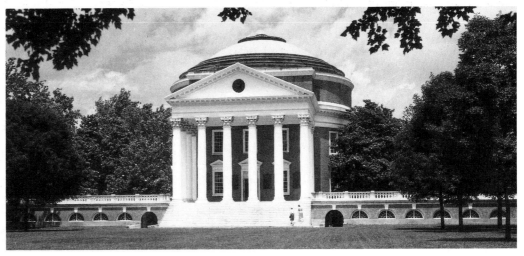

11.27 Thomas Jefferson, Rotonda of the University of Virginia, 1819-28.

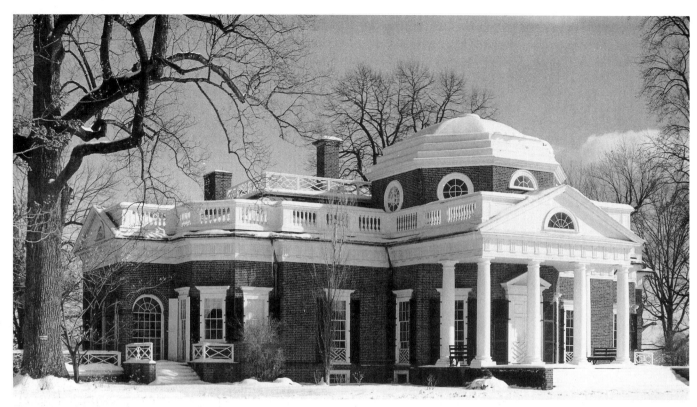

11.28 Thomas Jefferson, Monticello, Charlottesville, Virginia, 1770-84; rebuilt 1796-1800.

(perhaps by sheer weight of evidence) the superiority of Rome over Greece. Both Piranesi (*Della Magnificenza ed Architettura dei Romani*) and Laugier were instigators of the neo-classical tradition. The revival of classicism in architecture was seen in many quarters as a revolt against the frivolity of the rococo with an art that was serious and moral. In America neo-classicism had special meaning as the colonies struggled to rid themselves of the monarchical rule of England's George III. For revolutionary Americans classicism meant Greek and Greece meant democracy. The designs of colonial architect Thomas Jefferson (Figs. **11.27** and **11.28**) reflect the complex interrelationships of this period. Jefferson was highly influenced by Palladio, who enjoyed popularity in a significant revival in English villa architecture between 1710 and 1750. Jefferson, in a uniquely eighteenth-century way, considered architecture objectively within the framework of contemporary thought. His philosophy of architecture, of which Monticello and the Rotunda are illustrative, was founded on a belief that the architecture of antiquity embodied indisputable natural principles. He was strongly influenced by Lockean thought, natural law, and considered Palladian reconstruction of the Roman temple a foundation on which a theory of architecture could be built. Monticello contains a center with superimposed Doric and Ionic porticos (porches) and short, low wings attached to the centre by continuing Doric entablatures. The simplicity and refinement of Jefferson's statement here

goes beyond reconstruction of classical prototypes and appeals directly to the intellect.

Throughout the United States, and particularly in the South, the tenets of classical revival found numerous expressions. In Charleston, South Carolina, the Miles Brewton House provides us with one of the finest examples of American Georgian architecture (Fig. **11.29**). The pedimented portico supported by Ionic columns demonstrates the neo-classical emphasis of American architecture of this period.

11.29 Miles Brewton House, Charleston, South Carolina (architect unknown), c.1769.

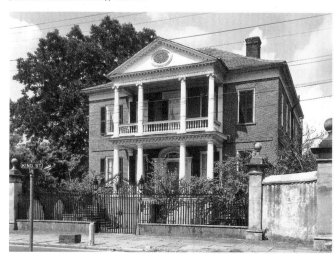

SYNTHESIS
The Enlightened Despot: Frederick the Great

In an age in which absolute monarchies began to lose their grip on Europe, Frederick the Great of Germany not only survived but also became an example of the spirit of the enlightenment which typified the century. As an absolute monarch his influence permeated Germany, and his interest in the arts had a profound impact on the emergence of a truly German art of significance. Frederick's contribution was sometimes inadvertent, but the results were undeniable.

Frederick the Great was probably the most important monarch of the period of European history called "Enlightened Despotism" or "Enlightened Absolutism". These labels imply that the rulers of the time governed "absolutely", that is, according to their will alone. This was in fact rarely the case and was certainly not so in Germany. The political circumstances themselves militated against absolute rule—Frederick governed a territorial state within the boundaries of the Holy Roman Empire of the German nation. Foreign policy, wars, and the realities of economics checked his freedom of action.

Frederick was also constrained by the law. Frederick II's father, Frederick William I, had begun an extensive codification of the laws and a thorough legal reform. "The philosopher of Sans Souci", as Frederick the Great was known, could hardly turn away from such a tradition in view of the expectations of an enlightened Europe and indeed he gloried in his reputation as a reformer. The result of his labors was the Prussian General Law, which sprang from practical administrative reforms. In all areas of Prussian life, whether in criminal law, agriculture, the church, schools, forestry, mining, manufacturing, trade, or shipping, his awareness and skilful manipulation of his administrators, he carried out reforms true to the enlightened spirit of the age. His insight, vision, and flexibility made his administration a dynamic and responsive process which kept abreast of politics and changing rules. Such genius undoubtedly kept Frederick from the troubles which beset Marie Antoinette and Louis XVI of France.

Frederick II began a long career of musical patronage as soon as he came to the throne. He sent Karl Heinrich Graun to Italy to hire singers, and he sent an envoy to Paris to hire dancers. He wrote to Voltaire in order to secure a troupe of French actors. While he was still a prince, Frederick had developed plans for a new opera house and had instructed the architect Knobelsdorff to begin designing it. Once he was king, work began on the Berlin Opera immediately. After a feverish start, work slowed because of difficulties with the site, which had to be leveled.

If an opera were to be produced fairly soon it clearly could not depend upon the completion of Frederick's

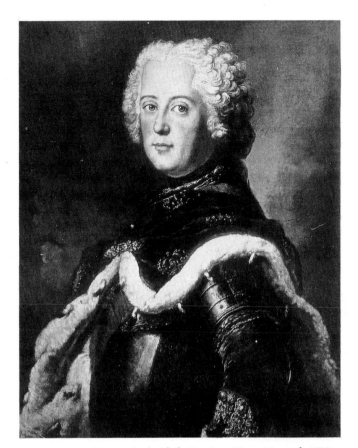

11.30 Antoine Pesne, *Frederick the Great as a Young Monarch*, 1739. Oil on canvas, 30¾ × 24¾ins (78 × 63cm). Gemäldegalerie, Berlin.

opera house. A temporary substitute was found and adapted. A theatre in the Stadtschloss called the *Kurfürstensaal*, which had been built in 1686 in imitation of the royal theatre at Versailles, was rigged up for the production of opera. On 13 December 1741 the first opera was produced. It was called *Rodelinda*. Written by Graun, it comprised twenty-four arias and virtually no choruses.

A comment from the time indicates that

> For the beginning there was a symphony in which fiery and gentle sections were opposed. This was such a masterpiece of full, pure harmony, such a many-sided, artful mixture of tunes, that it seemed as if the Muses and the Graces had united to draw Frederick out of his own heroic sphere and to themselves, where he could be held back from the rude cares of war. The bewitching voices of the singers, the naturalness and beauty of the action— everything was captivating to eye and ear. The whole spectacle, brought to such artistic perfection and executed with such skill, was received by the Monarch with high approval, and the public went forth from the theatre lost in enchantment.[4]

The opera house finally opened on 7 December 1742

with a production of Graun's *Cesare e Cleopatra*, but the building was not yet complete. Exterior decoration lay unfinished, and the audience had to pick its way through debris and piles of building materials. The building bore the inscription "FREDERICK REX APOLLONI ET MUSIS" ("King Frederick, Dear to Apollo and the Muses".) The immediate surroundings of the opera house were also magnificent. A large square next to the opera house could hold a thousand carriages. An intricate arrangement of plumbing planned around a nine-foot deep canal running under the theatre, provided the water for fountains and jets as well as for dousing the entire theatre in case of fire. At that time it was the largest theatre in the world.

By means of an elaborate system of pneumatic jacks, the entire floor of the theatre could be raised to stage level, and the scenery could be replaced by marble, sculptured fountains, thus creating a three-part, elaborate rococo ballroom. After dinner in a room adjacent to the theatre, the audience would return to participate in an extravagant opera ball.

On the instructions of the king, the audience was admitted free of charge to the operas, and anyone who was wearing acceptable clothing could get into the pit, where it was necessary to stand for the entire performance. Performances began with pomp and ceremony upon the king's entrance at six o'clock, and usually lasted until nearly eleven. The evening continued with the costume ball for some of the audience. It was, however, the members of Frederick's orchestra, poorly paid and out of the limelight, who made the most lasting contribution. Those local members of his musical entourage were quietly engaged in exciting artistic development, but went unnoticed, while the fanfare surrounding the stars of his imported opera heralded only tedious copies of tired works. Frederick's achievements are nonetheless significant, and with his enthusiasm and musical opinions he created an atmosphere in which music could flourish. He held auditions, commissioned composers, evaluated compositions and decided artistic policy. His spirit of *Aufklarung*, or enlightenment, set the intellectual tone in

11.31 Adolf von Menzel, *Frederick's Flute Concert at Sans Souci*, 1852. Oil on canvas, 57⅞ × 80¾ins (142 × 205cm). Staatliche Museen Preussischer Kulturbesitz, Nationalgalerie, West Berlin.

11.32 Georg Wenzelaus von Knobelsdorff, interior of Music Room, Sans Souci, 1745-47.

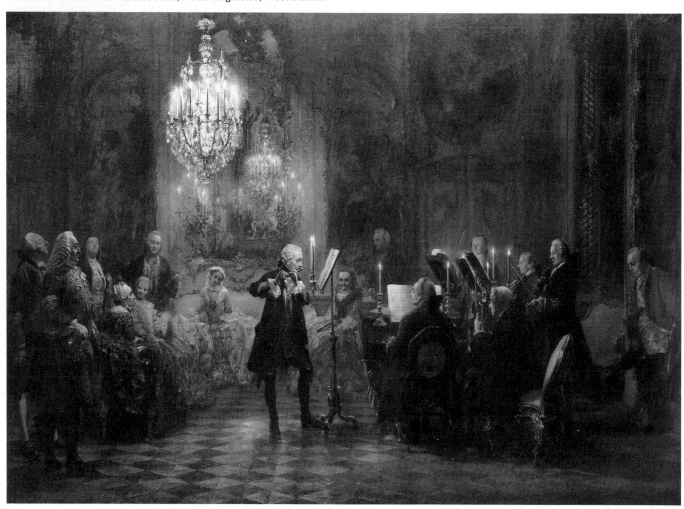

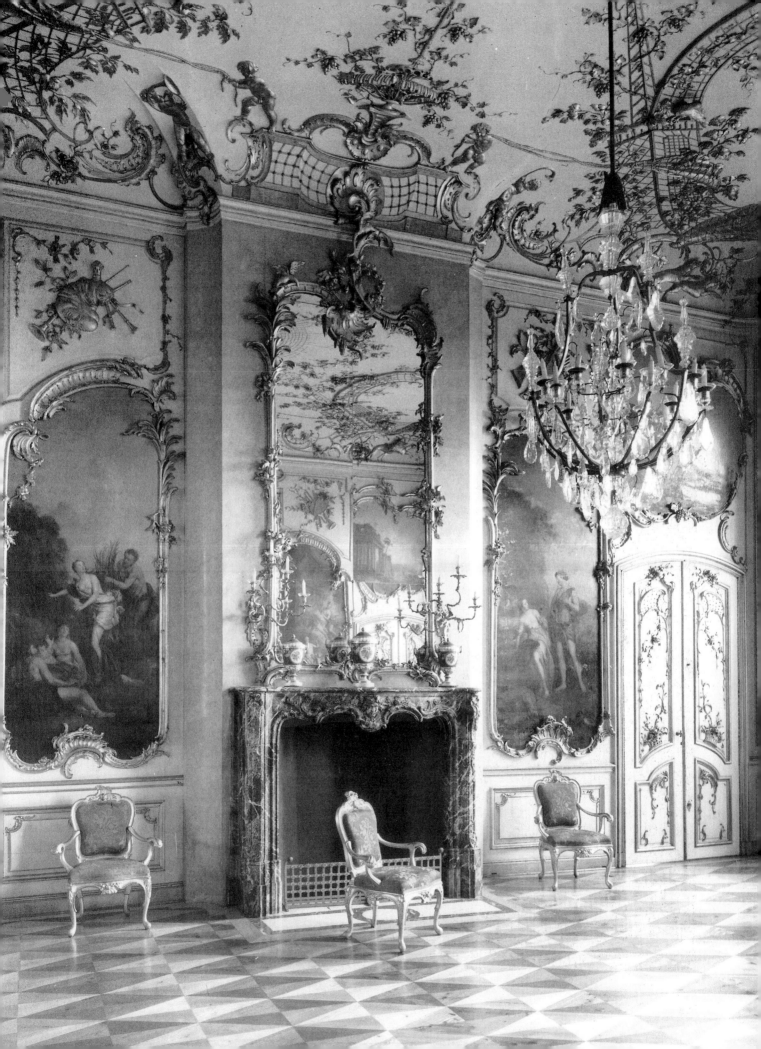

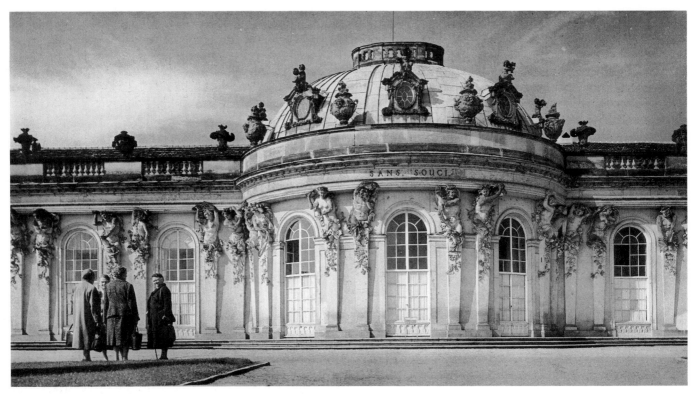

11.33 Georg Wenzelaus von Knobelsdorff, garden front of Sans Souci, 1745-47, Potsdam, East Germany.

11.34 Garden front of Sans Souci soon after completion. Contemporary engraving.

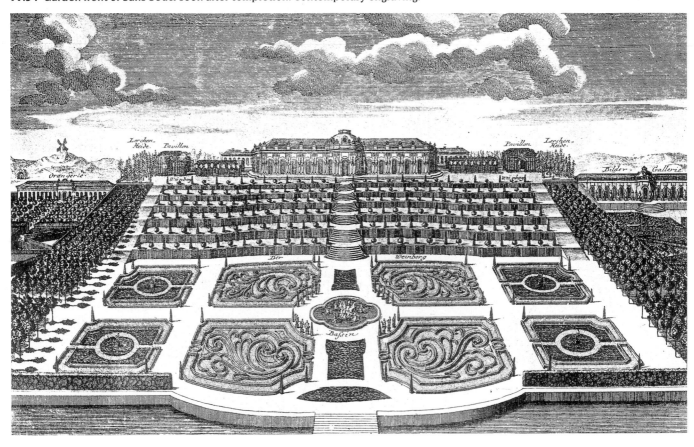

Berlin, and stimulated a tremendous quality and quantity of writing and discussion of music and musical theory. He also exerted considerable influence on composers such as J. S. Bach and C. P. E. Bach.

Frederick the Great often held musical concerts at his grand Sans Souci Palace (Fig. 11.31). The palace represents a new stylistic phase of eighteenth-century German art (Figs 11.32 and 11.33). Designed by Knobelsdorff, the architect of Frederick's opera house, the palace indicates both an increasing German receptivity to French rococo style and an amplification of Italian baroque style. Planned as a retreat for a philosopher-king, Sans Souci, which means "carefree", was the result of Frederick's desire for a summer palace where he could work, think, and entertain in seclusion and privacy the intellectual élite of Europe. Voltaire was one of his guests. Like Versailles, it had a formal design, as a drawing of the garden front illustrates (Fig. 11.34). The original plan was Frederick's, and included terraces faced with glass houses curved to catch the sun's rays from different angles. The entrance way and entrance hall of the palace interior show a return to classical tradition with their curving colonnades and Corinthian columns (Fig. 11.35), which provides a curious counterpoint to the richness and delicacy of the rococo interior. Sans Souci stands as a monument to the enlightened philosophies and vision of a monarch who reflected the ideas and ideals of the Enlightenment and, although a critic of contemporary German culture, nonetheless inspired and made possible a rich period of German artistry.

11.35 Georg Wenzelaus von Knobelsdorff, Entrance Hall, Sans Souci, 1745-47.

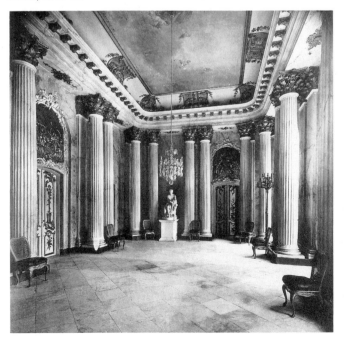

SUGGESTIONS FOR THOUGHT AND DISCUSSION

The eighteenth century was a period of transition, where some of the ideals and traditions of earlier eras and civilizations were continued and the foundations of the modern world were laid. The term "Enlightenment" can be applied to the philosophy, science, arts and political organization of the century, and it is important to understand the implications of the term in all of these contexts. What evidences can you find which substantiate the claim that the eighteenth century *was* a century of enlightenment?

Another important and related concept is that of humanitarianism, and we should be careful not to confuse humanitarianism with Humanism. What was humanitarianism and how did it manifest itself in society and the arts in the eighteenth century?

It was a century of contrasting styles. In the arts alone we have seen the overlapping of baroque, rococo, classicism, neo-classicism, and romanticism. What are the peculiar characteristics of each of these styles, and how are these characteristics manifested in each of the arts?

■ What impact did technology have on life in the eighteenth century? What is the difference between technology and science?

■ What other contrasts can you find in the concepts, contexts, and arts of the period?

■ The rococo style has been described as frivolous and superficial. Do you find any truth in this judgement?

■ In what ways did the neo-classicism of the eighteenth century resemble, and in what ways was it different from, the classicism of the Renaissance?

■ The concept of rationalism has occurred frequently in our discussion in this chapter. In what ways has this concept reinforced or differed from the concept of "systematic rationalism" which we used in the last chapter?

■ How did the concept of "progress" contribute to eighteenth-century architecture?

CHAPTER TWELVE

THE AGE OF INDUSTRY

With its roots in the eighteenth century, the Romantic movement entered the nineteenth with a force that matched the new engines of industrial progress. Again, in the arts, the pendulum had swung. Classical formality and restraint gave way to a relentless questioning and self-questioning, and in some cases an escapism, as the artist, a moral hero now liberated from patronage, was on his or her own, to rise or fall, to experiment and to protest. Caught between the institutionalized expectations of the Academy, the tastes of the public, and the artist's own vision of individual expression, each generation reacted more and more strongly against the style of its predecessor. The pace of change—social, technological, artistic—was quickening, and artists began to feel themselves increasingly marginalized within a materialistic society. The Impressionists and their successors tried to redefine their role and their art.

12.1 Caspar David Friedrich, *The Wanderer above the Mists*, c.1817–18. Oil on canvas, 29½ × 37¼ins (74.8 × 94.8cm). Kunsthalle, Hamburg.

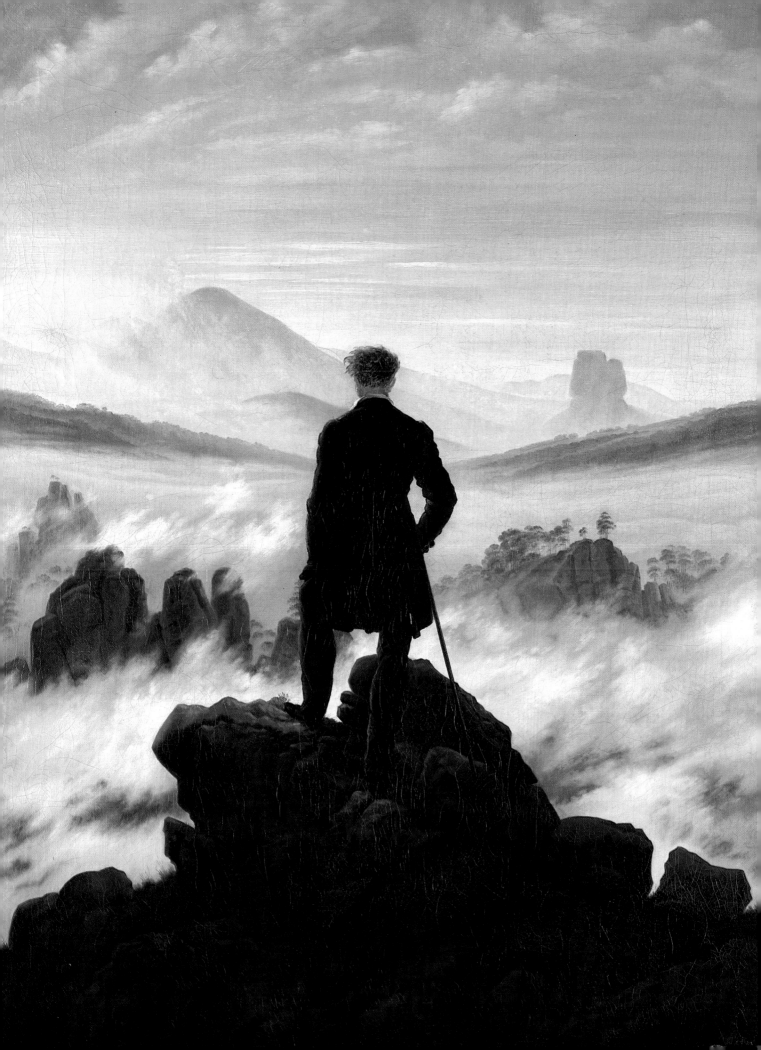

CONTEXTS AND CONCEPTS

The major social development since the Middle Ages was the rise of the middle class. Until the French Revolution it was in England that the middle class had reaped the greatest benefit from the changing circumstances. Capitalism had gradually replaced the guild system, and individual initiative fostered a spirit of invention. The first major industry to feel the thrust of invention was the textile industry, an industry fundamental to the requirements of society. Cumulative inventions revolutionized the English textile industry to the point where one worker, with a machine, could do as much work in a day as four or five men previously accomplished. Machines meant more cotton could be planted in the southern United States, and more cotton could be processed. Eli Whitney's cotton gin could do the work of a dozen slaves.

Technology

The early years of the nineteenth century saw wide experimentation with types of energy and energy usage. Gas was used as a fuel and for illumination. Coal gas was important in the pursuit of technological efficiency so characteristic of the period, an efficiency which would see gas outmoded by electricity before the century was over. Important developments in engine design took place in the first two decades of the nineteenth century. There was a need for a more efficient engine than the early steam engine, which was limited by the fact that it could generate only enough steam pressure to drive one cylinder at one pressure. Water turbines were much more efficient but could only be installed near to a moving water source. It took only a few years for the solutions to be found, however, and by the second decade of the century a successful compound engine had been developed. The principal use of the compound steam engine was in ocean-going steamships. The compound engine required less fuel, and the cargo capacity of the ships was proportionately increased. Later developments included steam turbines and internal combustion engines.

Mining production was increased by the introduction of new explosives based on nitroglycerine and more powerful hoisting and pumping equipment, while ore extraction and separation were made more efficient. These improvements were eclipsed, however, by the flotation method devised by the Bessel brothers in 1877. Significant improvements in smelting furnaces such as the blast furnace and the "wet process" of Joseph Hall combined with Nasmyth's steam hammer to improve production of iron and steel.

In America a new process for producing what became known as Bessemer steel soon made wrought iron obsolete and provided high quality steel for rails, shipbuilding and, late in the century, building construction. The further refinements of the "open hearth" steel process produced even higher quality, economical steel. The development of the rolling mill made possible more and more diverse applications, including cable for suspension bridges. The most famous example of suspension cable was in the Brooklyn Bridge in 1883.

The science of metallurgy was at the forefront of the technological revolution of the nineteenth century. Better understanding of metals and alloys led to more consistent and predictable products. Tests of materials and standards for strength and ductility were established. The relationship and importance of metallic microcrystals to surface fracture was demonstrated. The microscopic study of metals discovered the true nature of metallic structures, and practical explanations of the properties of metals were possible for the first time. Alloy steels came to be used for tools and structures, aluminium was introduced and new applications for copper came with discoveries concerning electric conductivity. The electric telegraph and the building of the first transatlantic cable revealed the relationship of small amounts of impurities to electrical conductivity and led to further investigation of alloys.

New machines and machine tools for application in all areas of industry were being invented and designed throughout the century. One of these was the milling machine (Fig. 12.2), which utilized rotary cutting edges and made possible the manufacture of

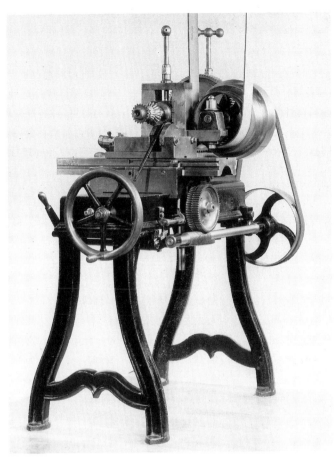

12.2 F.A. Pratt and Amos Whitney, the Lincoln Miller, 1855. Smithsonian Institution, Washington DC.

finish fabrics. After the invention of the power loom, further refinements improved the quality of power-woven cloth and increased output. Even greater sophistication was made possible by the invention of the Jacquard Loom, which was used to weave silk and for fancy weaving. By 1850 the Jacquard Loom had been applied to wool and to cotton. Other looms were designed for making lace and weaving carpet, as well as mechanisms to operate the thread guides of knitting machines (Fig. **12.3**). A final example of the machine to replace hand labor was the sewing machine, invented by Elias Howe (Fig. **12.4**).

Machine technology also invaded the home and the office, with a plethora of labor-saving inventions. The vacuum cleaner, carpet sweeper, telephone, telegraph, washing machine, typewriter, calculator, and cash register revolutionized domestic and office work.

Technology made tremendous impact on agriculture, which for the first time became an industry, not only increasing production capacity through mechanization, but also creating global markets via improved transportation. The farmer was no longer merely a local producer. Numerous developments can be listed. First came the McCormick Reaper in 1834, which was pulled rather than pushed by horses, followed by the horse-drawn hay rake in 1856. Improvements such as the self-sharpening

12.3 A.H. Dennett and G.H. Holmes, Mechanism to operate the thread guides of straight knitting machines, 1880. Smithsonian Institution, Washington DC.

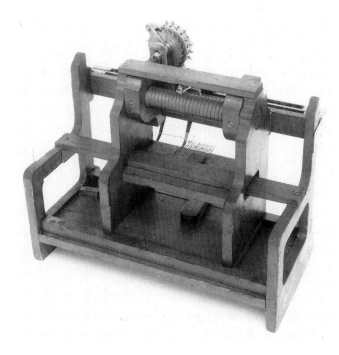

parts of exact tolerance which could be interchanged in a single product. This approach – called the "American System" – was developed in America and is generally attributed to Eli Whitney. The earliest application of interchangeable parts was in the manufacture of rifles such as the Sharpe's. The armaments industry also began to use a new grinding machine which enabled machinists to shape metal parts as opposed to merely polishing or sharpening. Further experiments refined the accuracy of grinding wheels and improved their abrasive surfaces. A new turret lathe made possible the application of several tools to a workpiece. This was an example of what has been called the "second generation" of machine tools in the industrialized West.

The first industry to benefit substantially from the Industrial Revolution was the British textile industry, which was revolutionized from top to bottom by mechanization and by improved transportation. The wool and cotton industries benefited from devices designed to prepare, spin, weave, and

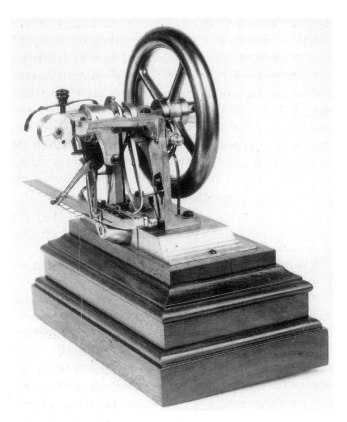

12.4 Elias Howe, sewing machine, c.1850. Smithsonian Institution, Washington DC.

plow blade and the steel plow, to which soil would not stick, clod-crushers and grain drills all made farming easier and more efficient. Next came the introduction of power-driven machinery, although horses continued to be the main source of power on the farm until the introduction of gasoline-powered tractors in the early twentieth century.

A major problem in food distribution was the shipment and storage of perishables. Natural ice was used world-wide for large-scale refrigeration early in the nineteenth century. The development of ice cabinets the size of railroad cars and improved tools for harvesting ice, shortly after the middle of the century, meant that perishable goods could be refrigerated, including frozen goods, and shipped across the American continent.

At the mid-point of the century the process of pasteurization was discovered, eliminating several milk-carried diseases. The use of heat in food preservation was applied to processing early in the nineteenth century, largely as a result of the experiments of Nicholas Appert. Hermetic sealing in the canning industry was widespread by the late 1840s.

Another major aspect of the technological revol-

ution was the harnessing of electricity. As early as the mid-seventeenth century Otto von Guericke of Magdeburg had developed a frictional electric motor. Contributors to this development had included Isaac Newton, Francis Hawksbee, Stephen Gray, and Charles F. Dufay. It was, however, barely more than a concept. By the nineteenth century the wet battery had introduced a source for the continuous flow of current. This was followed by experiments in electromagnetic induction, the electromagnet, the electric generator, and electric motors of usable capacity. Electrical energy was gradually applied to heating, lighting, and mechanical energy. Experiments produced a practical filament for an incandescent light bulb. The electric-powered streetcar rendered horsecars obsolete by 1888. By 1895 Niagara Falls had been harnessed for hydroelectric power, and long transmission lines and transformers carried electrical power throughout the Western world.

There were numerous technological developments in and before the nineteenth century which we have not mentioned, and all of these had wide-ranging effects, both good and bad, on the social structure world-wide. We have touched upon four major areas of technological development—advances in the production of metals; the development of machine-tool industries; the introduction of precision instruments leading to standardization; the development of efficient energy systems.

The first internal combustion engine to be sold in volume was the Lenois engine of 1860. It had one cylinder, and gas was ignited by an electric spark. It produced only one or two horsepower. Further experiment produced Otto's 1876 engine, which was the prototype for the modern automobile engine. It too had only one cylinder and produced three horsepower at 180 revolutions per minute. Significantly, it used a four-stroke cycle and compression of gas before ignition. It remained for Karl Benz and Gottlieb Daimler to perfect a light, fast engine which could power a horseless carriage. By the turn of the twentieth century the Western world had been fully mechanized.

Social changes

Watt's steam engine of 1769 heralded further invention in the textile industry and elsewhere. In 1807 Robert Fulton built the first practical steamboat, and in 1825 an Englishman, George Stephenson, built a steam locomotive, which led to the first English railroad. Such an explosion of steamboat and railroad building followed that by the middle of the nineteenth century the world's entire transportation system had undergone a complete revolution.

Soon steam engines ran sawmills, printing presses, pumping stations, and hundreds of other kinds of machinery, and further inventions and discoveries followed on the heels of steam. Electricity was recognized as a source of power, and before the century was over it was contributing significantly to a mechanizing world. The discovery of electricity brought with it the telegraph in 1832, which spanned continents and, in 1866, joined continents via the first transatlantic cable. The telephone was invented in 1876, and by 1895 radio-telegraphy foreshadowed twentieth-century developments.

The Industrial Revolution began in England and, at the conclusion of the Napoleonic wars, spread to France and the rest of Europe, gaining momentum as it spread, and irrevocably altering the fabric of civilization. By 1871, the year of the unification of Germany, major industrial centers had been established in Europe.

Coal and iron production gave Great Britain, Germany, France, and Belgium the lead in European industry. Vast resources of coal, iron, and other raw materials, exceeding the cumulative totals of all of

Europe, soon propelled the United States into a position of dominance. Industrialization increased wealth enormously, concentrated heavy industrial centers near the sources of raw materials and transportation routes, and increased colonial expansion to provide world markets for new goods. Capitalism as an economic system came to supremacy, spreading wealth through investment throughout the social strata but mostly centralizing economic control in the hands of a relatively restricted class of capitalists. Populations grew as the mortality rate among infants and the elderly decreased. A new class of machine workers—blue-collar workers—was created.

Drawn from pre-industrial home industries and farms, the new machine-worker class was cast into deplorable conditions, reduced from being their own masters to virtually slave status. They were almost helpless, subject to severe organizing restrictions, hampered by lack of education, and threatened constantly by the prospect of unemployment. Slums, tenements, and horrifying living conditions completed the degrading existence of this new class of workers, for whom the middle classes, caught in their own aspirations to wealth and political power, cared little.

Middle-class interests and outlook turned toward Liberalism, a political program with three

	GENERAL EVENTS	LITERATURE & PHILOSOPHY	VISUAL ART	THEATRE & DANCE	MUSIC	ARCHITECTURE
1800	Napoleon Bonaparte Fulton's steamboat Waterloo/Congress of Vienna Telegraph Stephenson's locomotive	Byron Shelley J. Fichte Keats Wordsworth Coleridge Scott G. Hegel	Ingres Géricault Daumier Goya Canova Constable	Kotzebue Goethe Von Kleist G. Buchner E. Scribe M. Taglioni J.S. Knowles	Bellini F. Schubert Donizetti F. Mendelssohn H. Berlioz F. Chopin	B. Latrobe J. Nash
1835	McCormick reaper	F. Schelling A. Schopenhauer	Turner Delacroix Pre-Raphaelites formed	V. Hugo A. Dumas (P.) C. Grisi Pixérécourt Petipa T. Gautier	Meyerbeer Rossini R. Wagner	
1850	Milling machine Pasteurization Internal combustion engine U.S. Civil War Transatlantic cable Vatican Council Unification of Germany	Karl Marx Charles Darwin Gregor Mendel	C. Corot D. Maclise Millet Courbet Manet J.E. Millais Renoir	C. Kean H. Beecher Stowe E. Augier Duke of Saxe-Meiningen	Offenbach A. Thomas F. Liszt C. Gounod G. Verdi J. Brahms Tchaikovsky	C. Barry
1875 1900	Flotation separation of ore Brooklyn Bridge Hydroelectric power Radio-telegraphy	H. Spencer	Cézanne Van Gogh Gauguin Rodin Monet Seurat Maillol Epstein	H. Ibsen E. Rostand A. Chekhov A.W. Pinero C. Stanislavsky Loie Fuller G.B. Shaw M. Maeterlinck	Mussorgsky G. Bizet C. Debussy R. Strauss Leoncavallo Mascagni	Louis Sullivan Burnham and Root F. Jourdain

12.5 Timeline of the nineteenth century.

goals: reducing the authority of a dominant church through religious toleration; reducing the power of a king and/or aristocracy through constitutional means; and removing economic barriers of a provincial nature through nationalism. In other words, Liberalism enshrined in its political program those things that would enhance middle-class power. Liberalism gained widespread support and became the political watchword of the age. Part of the middle-class program was a *laissez-faire* economic policy.

A new code of morality that stressed individual freedom and deliverance from bondage emerged. The *free man* was the goal of human endeavor. Men and women were to stand on their own feet, create their own destiny, and realize their inherent dignity. Individual freedom could only be achieved by struggle and survival, in which the unfit perished and the fit survived. The unfit were the degraded masses and the fit were rugged individuals, the chosen few.

The degraded masses, however, wanted to count. In order for them to do so, two conditions had to be met. First, they needed a basic education. Second, they needed basic self-confidence. Only in Prussia was there a public school system designed for mass education. Great Britain and France were delinquent in this regard until the 1870s and 1880s respectively. In the United States public education for the working classes had some localized impetus as early as the 1820s, but even the concept of mass education did not take root until mid-century. Compulsory elementary education was introduced toward the end of the nineteenth century.

Workers gradually acquired the right to form unions, a right which often required bloodshed to achieve. Not until the second half of the nineteenth century did laborers become free to unionize, and, thereby, to promote their own interests. Many different solutions to the working class problem were proposed—philanthropy, utopianism, and most important of all, the socialism of Karl Marx (1818–83).

Scientific attention turned to investigation of the atom and theories of evolution. Evolution as a unifying concept in science dated to the Greeks. However, Sir Charles Lyell became the first to coordinate earth studies, and his *Principles of Geology* (1830) provided an important base for evolutionary thinking. In 1859 Charles Darwin presented natural selection as the explanation of species development in his *Origin of the Species*. Darwinism was

modified by Gregor Mendel in 1866. By the end of the nineteenth century evolution was established as the framework within which scientific exploration of the universe took place.

The inevitable clash between evolution and Christianity occurred. Many Protestant denominations, after initially recoiling, were able to come to grips with the principles of evolution. This was easier for Protestants than Roman Catholics because, essentially, Protestants recognized the right of private judgment, as opposed to doctrinal control. At the same time that evolutionary doctrine was first being propounded, some Protestant scholarship was acknowledging the human elements of the Bible, that the Bible is a compilation of human writings over a period of time and was written under special circumstances. Of course, such biblical scholarship was (and still is) seen as equally diabolical to Darwinism by some Christian sects. Nevertheless, Protestantism, in general, gradually reconciled both doctrines to a modern outlook. Catholicism stated its rejection in Pope Pius IX's *Syllabus of Errors* (1864). Papal infallibility was declared by the Vatican Council of 1870 and maintained a position of intransigence on the subject of evolution throughout the papacy of Leo XIII (1878–1903).

Philosophy

In the late eighteenth century Immanuel Kant had tried to reconcile philosophical extremes through a dualism that distinguished between a knowable world of sense perceptions and an unknowable world of essences. His reconciliation led to a nineteenth-century philosophy which centered on the emotions. Such an idealistic appeal to faith was called romanticism, and this reaction against eighteenth-century rationalism permeated philosophy and the arts. Other German idealism, as evidenced by Fichte (1762–1814) and Schelling (1775–1854), rejected Kant's dualism, and developed an absolute system based on emotion that asserted the oneness of God and nature. However, nineteenth-century idealism (romanticism) culminated in the work of Hegel (1770–1831), who believed that both God and humankind possessed unfolding and expanding energy. Hegelian philosophy combined German idealism with evolutionary science and saw the universe from an optimistic viewpoint.

Hegel's aesthetic theory

Hegel's philosophy viewed "reality" as spirit or mind. Schelling, Hegel's immediate predecessor, regarded reason as a form of intellectual intuition "whose ultimate object is art". Hegel, on the other hand, believed art to be one ultimate form, but not the ultimate form of mind. Hegel regarded philosophy as the final form, while art was a previous "step toward truth". He called truth the Idea, which he defined thus: "The Idea is truth in itself and for itself—the absolute unity of the notion and objectivity ... the Idea is the truth; for truth is the correspondence of objectivity with the notion:—not of course the correspondence of external things with my conceptions—for these are only correct conceptions, held by me, the individual person."

According to Hegel, the objective of art is beauty, which is a means for expressing truth. He defined beauty as the "sensuous appearance of the Idea, or the show of the Absolute Concept. The Concept which shows itself for itself is art."[1] Hegel believed classical art was the format whereby the ideal content "reaches the highest level that sensuous, imaginative material can correctly express". Classical art comprises the perfection of artistic beauty, and the essence of classical art for Hegel is sculpture. Hegel conceived of sculpture in the same way as the classical Greeks, as the expression of the human form which alone can "reveal Spirit in sensuous fashion". This assertion goes back to the philosophies of Kant and Winckelmann. Kant maintained that man alone is capable of an ideal of beauty, and Winckelmann saw Greek sculpture as the perfection of beauty. Hegel went beyond Kant and Winckelmann to suggest that "Greek religion realized a concept of the divine which harmonized the ethical and the natural. Hence the Greek gods, the subject of Greek sculpture, are the perfect expression of a religion of art itself."

Finally, romantic art evolves content to such a degree that it contains "more than any sensuous imaginative material can expressly embody". Being subjective, the content of romantic art is the "Absolute that knows itself in its own spirituality". Identifying that concept with the God of Christianity, Hegel finds in romantic art three forms, each of which is progressively more spiritual—first is painting, second is music, and third is poetry, the most spiritual and universal of all, which includes within itself the totality of art.

The idealism of Schelling, Fichte and Hegel was challenged by Schopenhauer (1788–1860), who saw the world as a gigantic machine operating under unchanging law. Schopenhauer recognized no Creator, no benevolent Father, only a tyrannical and unfathomable First Cause. If Hegel was an optimist, Schopenhauer was a pessimist of the highest order.

Following Schopenhauer came Nietzsche, poet and philosopher. Nietzsche (1844–1900) accepted humankind's helplessness in a mechanical world operating under eternal law, but rejected Schopenhauer's pessimism. Rather, he preached courage in the face of the unknown and found in courage humankind's highest attribute. After a long selective process courage would produce a race of supermen and women.

Unlike the Germans, who were intent on coping with transcendental issues, the English and French focused upon philosophical explanation of the emerging, mechanized world. What was beyond this world was beyond knowledge and, therefore, inconsequential. For such philosophers as the Frenchman Auguste Comte (1798–1857), the nineteenth century was an era of science and it was the task of philosophy to sort out the factual details of worldly existence, rather than try to solve the riddles of the unknown universe. Comte's philosophy was called positivism, and his approach formed the basis for the science of sociology. Across the channel in Britain Herbert Spencer (1820–1903) expounded a philosophy of evolutionary materialism in which evolution provided the framework. He also believed that a struggle for existence and survival of the fittest were fundamental, and that the human mind, ethics, social organization, and economics were "exactly what they ought to be".

Internationalism

Philosophy and mechanization, especially in transportation and communications, made the nineteenth century an age of internationalism and social study. Humankind, particularly in Europe, sought to examine itself in a scientific manner, at the same time striving for nationalistic power. Communications networks bridged distances, and there were increasing numbers of international agreements. All this was set against fierce and imperialistic competition for raw materials and marketplaces. The Western world depended upon armaments to secure and protect all these advances. In the late nineteenth century various pragmatic alliances and treaties were forged, which in the guise of cooperation cast the die for war.

War was an ever-present specter in European existence. At the close of the eighteenth century, as France struggled to emerge from the chaos of its revolution, skillful maneuvering brought Napoleon Bonaparte to power. He stealthily planned his rise from first consul to dictator, behind a screen of hand-picked legislators. War with England and Austria persisted, and Napoleon set about resolving things in France's favor. The Battle of Marengo in 1800 gave France all of Italy and crushed the Austrians at a single stroke.

The Peace of Amiens with Great Britain in 1802 left Napoleon free to concentrate on rebuilding France. Again, space and scope prohibit us from pursuing Napoleon's endeavors, which included the creation of the Napoleonic Code and the establishment of a system of education. Nor can we detail the renewal of the Franco–British War (1803), Napoleon's rise to emperor (1804), his great sweep across Europe, or America's war with Britain in 1812.

After Napoleon's defeat at Waterloo in 1815 the Act of the Congress of Vienna, controlled by factions of the old aristocracy, attempted to arrange the affairs of Europe. In essence, the congress gave legitimacy to the restoration of dynasties displaced by the revolution and returned Europe to boundaries that existed prior to it. War and revolution continued to sweep through France and Europe in 1820, 1830, and 1848. A new Napoleon emerged in 1849—Louis, who later became Emperor Napoleon III. War raged around the edges of Europe in 1854, and returned to its heart in 1859.

The United States tore itself apart in civil war in the early 1860s as Europe continued its perennial fratricide. The Treaty of Versailles in 1871 brought hostilities to a halt for the time being, unified Germany, and ceded Alsace and Lorraine from France to Germany. Throughout all of this, Great Britain consolidated and extended an Empire that encircled the globe.

The tenor of the times created moods of turbulence and frustration. France, for example, had an entire generation of young men raised in an era of patriotic and military fervor under Napoleon. After his defeat they were left to vegetate in a country ruined by war and controlled by a weak, conservative government. Feelings of isolation and alienation increased. Suffering, downtrodden youth such as Goethe's Werther became romantic heroes. Curiosity about the supernatural was rampant. Escape to

Utopia became a common goal. A desire to "return to nature" fostered nature both as the ultimate source of reason, and also, conversely, as an unbounded, whimsical entity in which emotionalism could run freely, forming the basis of romanticism.

Patronage

The role of the artist changed significantly in the nineteenth century. For the first time art was able to exist without the support of significant aristocratic and religious commissions or patronage. In fact, patronage was deliberately resisted as an undesirable limitation of individual expression. Artists enjoyed a new place in the social order. Much of art became individualistic and increasingly critical of society and its institutions. The conflict between rebellious individual expression and established values, whether the values of a critic or of the public at large, created a chasm, which drove some artists into increasingly personal and experimental techniques. In many cases artists, particularly visual artists, were cut off from the world they viewed, reacted to, and needed to communicate with. They were prohibited from exhibition either by those with traditional standards, who controlled formal exhibitions, or by the vogue of public consumption, which controlled commercial galleries. As a result, many artists became the social outcasts, romantic heroes, and starving individualists of public legend.

Literature

The beginning of the main phase of romantic literature can probably be dated to around 1790. One characteristic was the tendency of writers to form groups or partnerships, an example of which was the close relationship between Goethe and Schiller. Britain again produced major literary figures such as Wordsworth, Coleridge, Scott, Byron, Shelley, and Keats. William Wordsworth (1770–1850) changed the commonplace and everyday with transcendental and often indefinable significance. He created a new world of beauty through his closeness to nature and in the harmony he felt existed between man and nature. In the *Prelude* Wordsworth writes of his early feelings. Invoking the "Wisdom of the spirit of the Universe", he says:

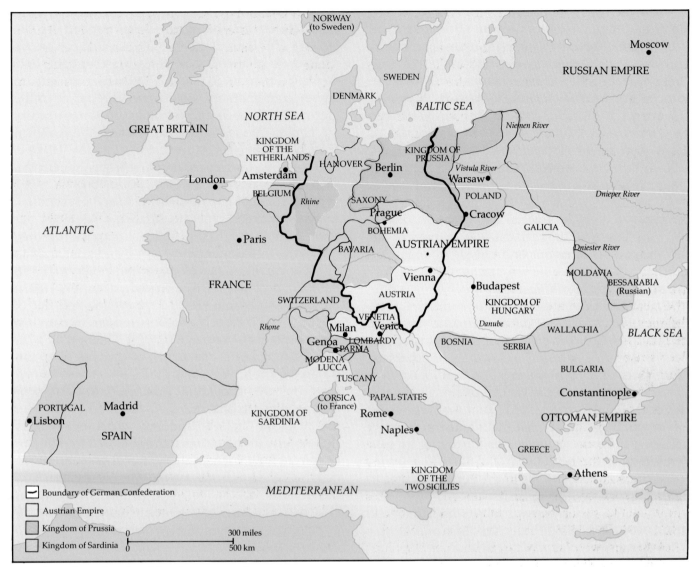

12.6 The industrialized world in the nineteenth century.

Not in vain
By day or star-light thus from my first dawn
Of childhood, didst thou intertwine for me
The passions that build up our human soul.

Recapturing his boyhood he describes skating
on a frozen lake:

So through the darkness and the cold we flew,
And not a voice was idle; with the din
Smitten, the precipices rang aloud;
The leafless trees and every icy crag
Tinkled like iron; while far distant hills
Into the tumult sent an alien sound
Of melancholy not unnoticed, while the stars

Eastward were sparkling clear, and in the west
The orange light of evening died away.

He creates from his college days at Cambridge a
picture of an ash tree near his room:

Often have I stood
Footbound uplooking at this lovely tree
Beneath a frosty moon. The hemisphere
Of magic fiction, verse of mine perchance
May never tread; but scarcely Spenser's self
Could have more tranquil visions in his youth,
Or could more bright appearances create
Of human forms with superhuman powers,
Than I beheld loitering on calm clear nights,
Alone, beneath this fairy work of earth.

371

Samuel Taylor Coleridge (1772–1834) reflected more the temperament of German romanticism. He is best remembered for his mysterious long poem, *The Rime of the Ancient Mariner*. This together with *Christabel* and *Kubla Khan* exemplify the romantic spirit of wonder. Walter Scott (1771–1832) was also influenced by German romanticism. His romances have an easy and fluent style, color, and a lack of depth. Like many Victorian painters and artists he delighted in the historical, evoking the splendors of the Middle Ages and the Renaissance.

Lord Byron (1788–1824) was the romantic poet *par excellence*, with his colorful and dramatic private life, his espousal of the nationalist aspirations of the Greeks, and his energetic and turbulent verse. *Don Juan*, a richly ironic ramble through human frailties, is probably his best work. Percy Bysshe Shelley (1792–1822) wrote in a quieter and more meditative vein, although the passions of romanticism are never far below the surface. The greatest of English romantics, however, was John Keats (1795–1821), the best of whose poems, such as *Ode on a Grecian Urn*, explore the tensions between classical grace and a romantic determination to experience life at its most intense.

It was in the novel that the nineteenth century achieved the most complete distillation of its concerns. In England, Jane Austen (1775–1817) delicately laid bare the private life of the middle classes in searching and ironical novels such as *Emma*. Emily Brontë (1818–48) wrote the stormily romantic *Wuthering Heights*, while her sister Charlotte (1816–55) produced the more sophisticated *Jane Eyre*. New possibilities for the novel were opened up by Honoré de Balzac (1799–1850) in France, whose great cycle of novels, part of his projected and only partially completed *Comédie Humaine*, sought to survey contemporary society from the palace to the gutter. The heroes and heroines of Balzac's works are figures through whose experiences the reality of social mechanisms is revealed. Charles Dickens (1812–70) had a comparable aim in his novels, the best of which, such as *Bleak House*, take a cross-section through the teeming society of Victorian England. Dickens' plots are dazzlingly ingenious, but their complexity has a serious purpose as they evoke the interdependency of rich and poor and the endless ramifications of every individual act. The naturalism of writers like Gustave Flaubert (1821–80) and Émile Zola (1840–1902) developed out of such novels; it closely parallels realism in painting. The heroine of *Madame Bovary* by Flaubert is a far from sympathetic character; the novel, like the poetry of Robert Browning (1812–89), Alfred Tennyson (1809–92), and Arthur Rimbaud (1854–91), concentrated more and more on the morbid and the pathological. Charles Baudelaire (1821–67) typifies this trend with his poems entitled *Les Fleurs du Mal* (*Flowers of Evil*). Poetry and the novel pursued divergent paths as the one moved into symbolism and the other, in the hands of writers like Henry James (1843–1916), applied a magnifying-glass to the psychology of refined human beings.

THE ARTS
OF THE AGE OF INDUSTRY

TWO-DIMENSIONAL ART

Classicism

The neo-classical traditions of the eighteenth century continued into the nineteenth, particularly in France, and the pursuit of physical and intellectual perfection initiated by David was taken up by Jean-Auguste Dominique Ingres (1780–1867). The work of Ingres, and perhaps David as well, illustrates the confusing relationships and conflicts that surrounded the neo-classical and romantic traditions in painting. Ingres' *Odalisque*, or *Harem Girl* (Fig. **12.7**), has been called both neo-classical and romantic, and in many ways represents both. Ingres professed to despise romanticism, and yet his proportions and subject exude romantic individualism and escape to the far away and long ago, to the exotic. His sensuous textures appear emotional, not intellectual. At the same time, his line is simple, his palette is cool, and his spatial effects are

geometric. The linear rhythms of his painting are very precise and calculated and, therefore, classically intellectual in appeal.

Romanticism

If Ingres believed himself to be a neo-classicist and not a romantic, there were those who willingly championed the banner of romanticism. The romantic style was diverse. It had an emotional appeal and tended toward the picturesque, nature, the Gothic, and, often, the macabre. Romanticism sought to break the geometric compositional principles of classicism. Compositions moved toward fragmentation of images. The intent was to dramatize, to personalize, and to escape into imagination. Romantic painting reflected a striving for freedom from social and artistic rules, a subordination of formal content to expressive intent, and an intense introversion. As the writer Zola said of romantic naturalism, "A work of art is

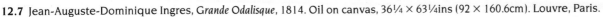

12.7 Jean-Auguste-Dominique Ingres, *Grande Odalisque*, 1814. Oil on canvas, 36¼ × 63¼ins (92 × 160.6cm). Louvre, Paris.

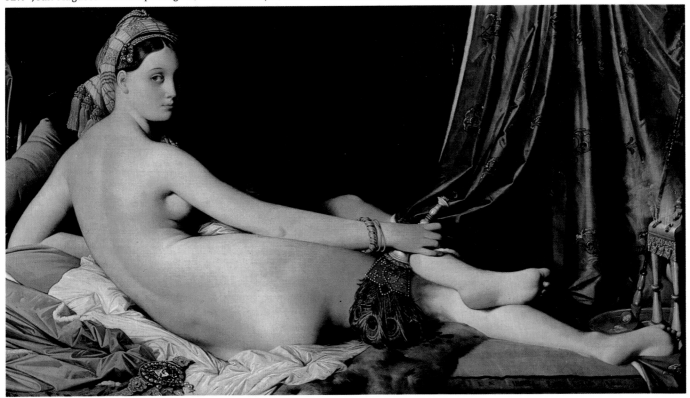

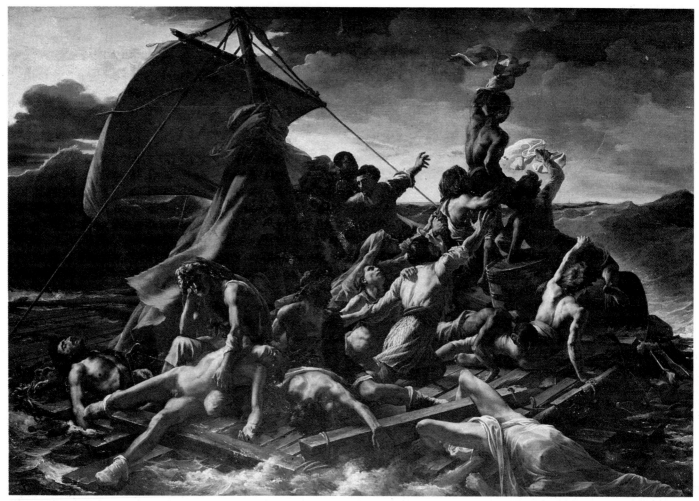

12.8 Théodore Géricault, *The Raft of the "Medusa"*, 1819. Oil on canvas, 16ft × 23ft 6ins (491 × 716cm). Louvre, Paris.

part of the universe as seen through a temperament." Closely associated with the critic and writer Baudelaire, romanticism dwelt upon the capacity of color and line to affect the viewer independently of subject matter.

Many romantic painters are worthy of note, for example, Daumier, Constable, Friedrich, Bingham, Gros, and Blake. A detailed look at Géricault, Goya, Turner, Delacroix, and Corot will suffice for our overview.

The *Raft of the Medusa* (Fig. **12.8**) by Théodore Géricault (1791–1824) illustrates both an emerging rebellion against classicism and criticism of social institutions. The painting tells a story about governmental incompetence, which resulted in tragedy. In 1816 the French government allowed the ship Méduse to leave port in an unsafe condition. As a result, it was wrecked. The survivors, aboard a makeshift raft, endured tremendous suffering, including cannibalism. Géricault captured that ordeal in his painting, and he did so in a manner that illustrates romantic style, as well as Géricault's classical and even High Renaissance training. Géricault was a pupil of David, and like David he achieved a firm modelling of

flesh, realism of figure depiction, and a very precise play of light and shade. He rendered powerful and expressive musculature reminiscent of Michelangelo. In contrast to David's two-dimensional, relief-like paintings, however, Géricault created complex three-dimensional patterns and a fragmented and disorderly compositional structure. He would draw two triangles rather than a strong central triangle. In the *Medusa*, the left triangle sweeps up the makeshift mast, signifying death and despair. The other triangle moving up to the right to the figure waving the fabric, signifies hope as a rescue ship appears, faintly, on the crest of a wave at the right border. The turbulence of the composition has a dramatic and climactic sense, fully charged with unbridled emotionalism, which extols the individual heroism of the survivors.

The Spanish painter and printmaker Francisco de Goya (1746–1828) used his paintings to attack abuses of government both Spanish and French. His highly imaginative and nighmarish works reveal subjective emotionalism in humanity and nature, often at their malevolent worst. *Execution of the Citizens of Madrid, 3 May 1808* (Fig.

12.9) also tells a story of an actual event. On 3 May 1808, the citizens of Madrid rebelled against the invading army of Napoleon. As a result, individuals were arbitrarily arrested and summarily executed. Goya captured a dramatic and climactic moment in the story and did so with a composition even more fragmented than that of Géricault. It is impossible to escape the focal attraction of the man in white, about to die. Goya's strong value contrasts force the eye to the victim; only the lantern behind the soldiers keeps the composition in balance. However, Goya leads us beyond the death of individuals, because these figures are not individuals—they are not realistically depicted. Instead Goya makes a powerful social and emotional statement. Napoleon's soldiers are not even human types. Their faces are hidden, and their rigid, repeated forms become a line of subhuman automatons. The murky quality of the background further charges the emotional drama of the scene and further strengthens value contrasts. Color areas have hard edges, and a stark line running diagonally from the oversized lantern to the lower border irrevocably separates executioners and victims. Goya has no sympathy for French soldiers as human beings in an ugly situation, perhaps only following orders. His subjectivity fills the painting. His portrayal is as emotional as the irrationality he wished to condemn.

The Englishman J. M. W. Turner (1775–1851) reflected subjectivity perhaps even beyond his romantic contemporaries and foreshadowed the dissolving image of twentieth-century painting. The romantic painter John Constable described Turner's works as "airy visions painted with tinted steam". The *Slave Ship* (Fig. **12.10**) visualizes a passage in James Thomson's poem *The Seasons*, which describes how sharks follow a slave ship in a storm, "Lured by the scent of steaming crowds of rank disease, and death." The poem was again based on an actual event, where the captain of a slave ship dumped his human cargo into the sea when disease broke out

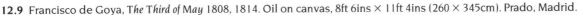

12.9 Francisco de Goya, *The Third of May 1808*, 1814. Oil on canvas, 8ft 6ins × 11ft 4ins (260 × 345cm). Prado, Madrid.

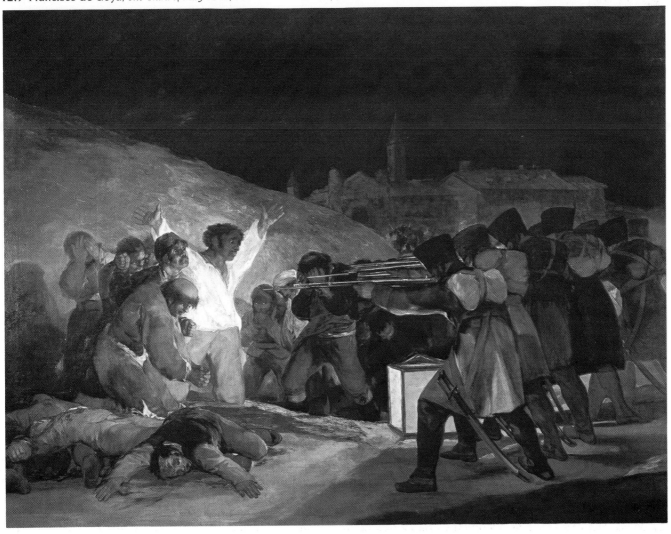

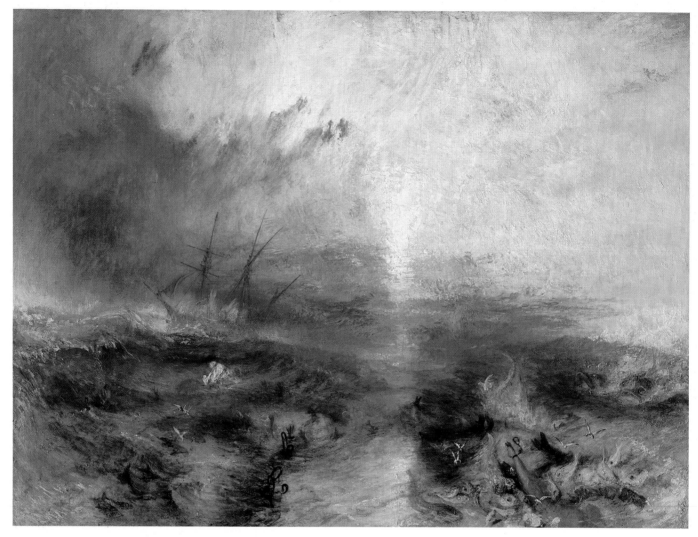

12.10 Joseph Mallord William Turner, *The Slave Ship (Slavers Throwing Overboard the Dead and Dying, Typhoon Coming On)*, 1839. Oil on canvas, 35¾ × 48¼ins (90.8 × 122.6cm). The Museum of Fine Arts, Boston (Henry Lillie Pierce Fund).

below decks. Turner's work demonstrates the elements of romanticism already discussed. He employs disjointed diagonals, which contribute to an overall fragmentation of the composition. His space is deeply three-dimensional. The turbulence of what is happening is reflected in the turbulence of painting technique. The sea and sky are transparent, and the brushstrokes reflect energetic spontaneity. Form and content are subordinate to expressive intent—a sense of doom prevails.

Eugène Delacroix (1798–1863) employed color, light and shade to achieve dramatic effects which capture climactic moments of high emotion. Delacroix has been described as the foremost "Neo-Baroque Romantic painter", and we can see the intricate and contrasting qualities of his painting which lead to such a conclusion. In *Liberty Leading the People* (Fig. **12.11**) Delacroix aims at a deeper symbolism as Liberty, championing the tricolor flag of France, inspires an emotional charge of the French people. Lights and darks provide strong and dramatic contrasts. The red, white, and blue of the French flag

provide symbolic references to patriotism, purity, and freedom, and as Delacroix carries these three colors throughout the work, they also serve to balance and unify the composition.

The approach of Camille Corot (1796–1875) is often described as romantic naturalism. Corot was among the first to execute finished paintings out of doors, as opposed to in a studio. His objective was to recreate the full luminosity of nature and to capture the natural effect of the perceptual experience, that is, how the eye focuses relative to detail and peripheral vision. His works strive for truthfulness of visual effect by reducing the graphic clarity of all details in favor of the clarity of the central objects (just as our eyes perceive clearly only those

12.11 Eugene Delacroix, *The 28th July: Liberty Leading the People*, 1830. Oil on canvas, 8ft 6ins × 10ft 7ins (259 × 325cm). Louvre, Paris.

12.12 Jean-Baptiste-Camille Corot, *Volterra*, 1834. Oil on canvas, 18½ × 32¼ins (47 × 82cm). Louvre, Paris.

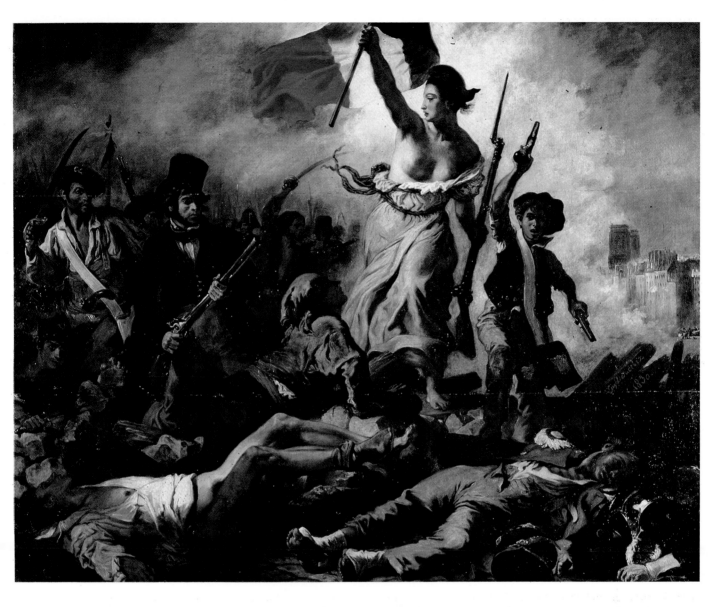

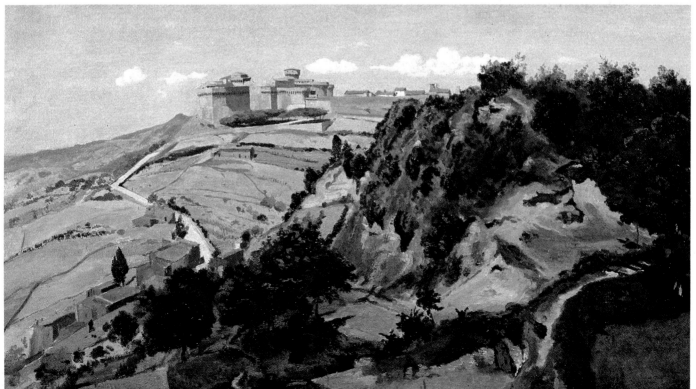

objects on which we focus in a moment, while the remaining objects in our field of vision remain relatively out of focus). Corot's works are spontaneous and subjective, but he retains a formal order to balance that spontaneity. *Volterra* (Fig. **12.12**) is a good example of this movement in the romantic tradition.

Realism

A new painting style arose in the mid-nineteenth century called realism. The term realism occurs in varying contexts in various sources. Some refer to social realism, and include painters such as Daumier. Social realism describes various styles which emphasize the contemporary scene, usually from a left-wing point of view and always with a strong thematic emphasis on the pressure of society on human beings. Others extend realism to include Manet. For others, the term appears to apply only to Courbet. Whatever the case, the term reality in the nineteenth century came to have special significance because the camera, a machine to record events, people, and locations, thrust itself into what previously had been considered the painter's realm. The style referred to as realism ran through the 1840s, 1850s, and 1860s, and its

central figure was Gustave Courbet (1819–77), whose aim was to make an objective and unprejudiced record of the customs, ideas and appearances of contemporary French society. He depicted everyday life and was influenced by the innovations of Corot in terms of the play of light on surfaces (Fig. **12.13**). Also a social realist, Courbet was more intent on social message than on meditative reaction and was therefore less dramatic and nostalgic than other romantics.

Jean François Millet (1814–75) was one of a group of painters called the Barbizon School who focused upon a realistic-romantic vision of landscape, and typically used peasants as their subject matter. The Barbizon School did not espouse socialism, but rather exalted honest, simple life and work on the land, as contrasted with the urban, bourgeois life. In Millet's *Woman Baking Bread* (Fig. **12.14**) these themes are applied and the peasant emerges as an heroic figure. Our vantage point is slightly from below, which gives the peasant woman a slight dominance over us, emphasizing her heroic grandeur.

Edouard Manet (1832–83) followed in the realist tradition, although often he is regarded as an impressionist (an association he denied). He strove to paint "only what the eye can see". Yet his works go beyond a mere reflection of reality to encompass an artistic reality, telling

12.13 Gustave Courbet, *The Stone Breakers*, 1849. Oil on canvas, 63 × 102ins (160 × 259cm). Formerly Gemäldegalerie, Dresden (destroyed 1945).

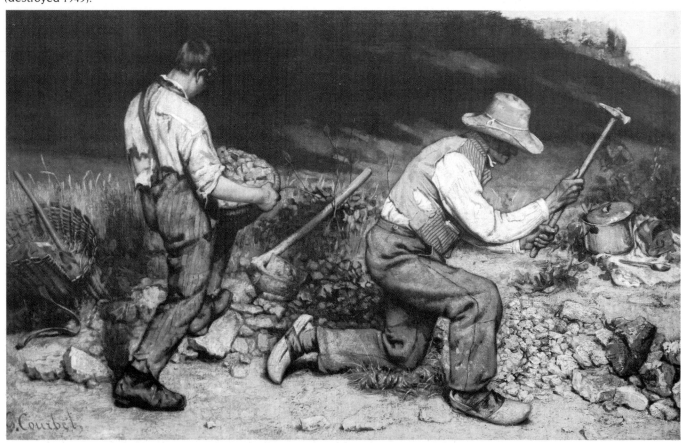

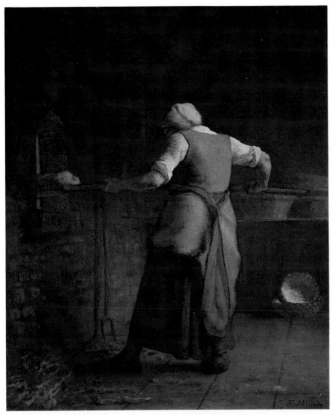

12.14 Jean-François Millet, *Woman Baking Bread*, 1853–54. Oil on canvas, 21¾ × 18ins (55 × 46cm). Collection: State Museum Kröller-Müller, Otterlo, The Netherlands.

us that a painting has an internal logic different from the logic of familiar reality. Manet liberated the canvas from competition with the camera (Fig. **12.15**). His search for spontaneity, harmonious colors, subjects from everyday life, and faithfulness to observed lighting and atmospheric effects led to the development of a style by a small group of painters in the 1860s described in 1874 by a hostile critic as impressionists.

Impressionism

Impressionism was as collective a style as any we have seen thus far. In an age as individualistic as the nineteenth century this style reflected the common concerns of a relatively small group of artists who met together frequently and held joint exhibitions. As a result, this painting style had marked characteristics, which applied to all its exponents. Impressionism suggested a new way of looking at things. Paintings of the style suggest an "on the spot" immediacy. They are impressions of landscapes, rivers, streets, cafés, theatres, and so on. *The River* (Fig. **12.16**) by Claude Monet (1840–1926) illustrates the concerns of the impressionists. It portrays a pleasant picture of the times, an optimistic view, in contrast to the

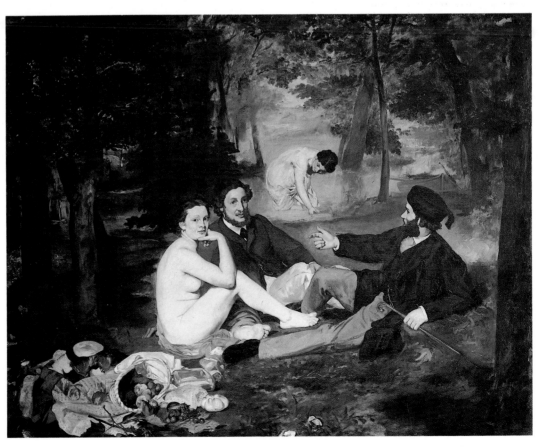

12.15 Edouard Manet, *Déjeuner Sur L'Herbe (The Picnic)*, 1863. Oil on canvas, 7ft × 8ft 10ins (213 × 269cm). Louvre, Paris.

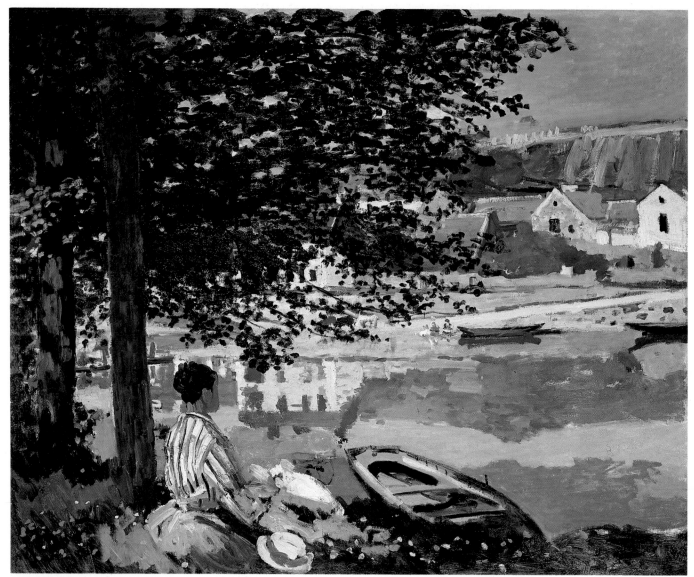

12.16 Claude Monet, *On the Seine at Bennecourt*, 1868. Oil on canvas, 31⅞ × 39½ins (78.5 × 100.5cm). Courtesy the Art Institute of Chicago (Potter Palmer Collection).

often pessimistic viewpoint of the romantics. It also suggests a fragmentary and fleeting image—a new tone in a new era. The tempo increases, and life's pace is more rapid. Monet, along with Degas, Renoir, and Mary Cassatt, among others, were central figures in the development of impressionism. *The Café* (Fig. **12.17**) by Auguste Renoir (1841–1919) further exemplifies the qualities of impressionism with its vibrancy and sense of shimmering immediacy.

Post-impressionism

In the last two decades of the nineteenth century impressionism evolved gently into a collection of rather disparate styles called, simply, post-impressionism. In

subject matter post-impressionist paintings were similar to impressionist paintings—landscapes, familiar portraits, groups, and café and nightclub scenes. The post-impressionists, however, gave their subject matter a complex and profoundly personal significance. Georges Seurat (1859–91), often described as a neo-impressionist (he called his approach and technique divisionism), departed radically from existing painting technique with experiments in optics and color theory. His patient and systematic application of specks of paint is called pointillism, because paint is applied with the point of the brush, one small dot at a time. He applied paint in

12.17 Pierre-Auguste Renoir, *The Café*, c.1876-7. Oil on canvas, 13¾ × 11ins (35 × 28cm). Collection: State Museum Kröller-Müller, Otterlo, The Netherlands.

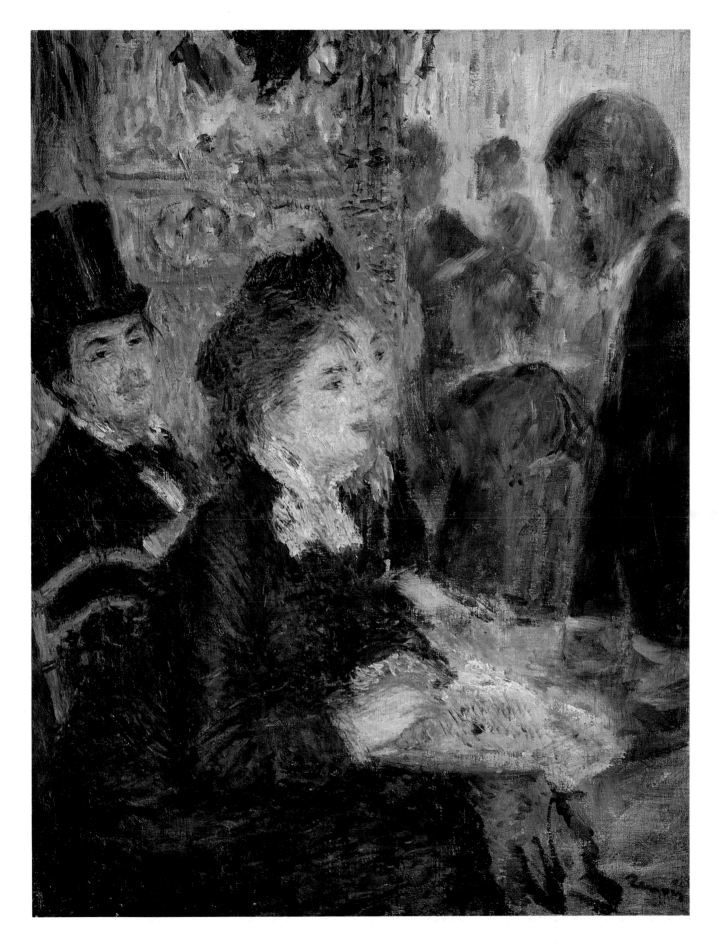

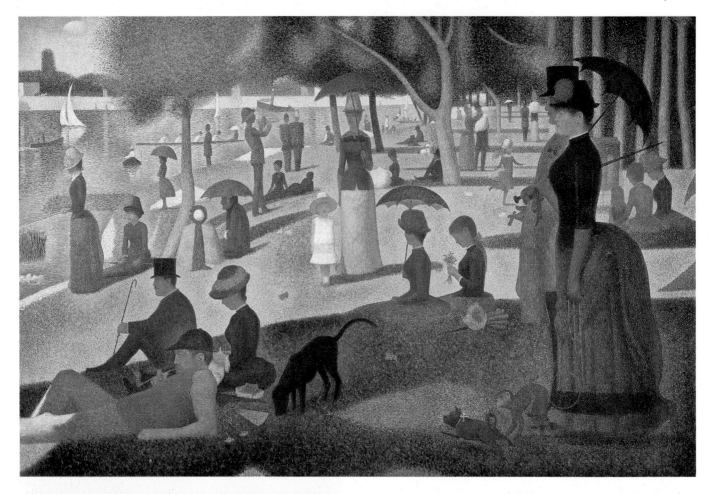

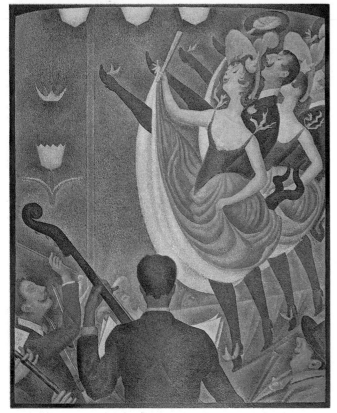

12.18 Georges Seurat, *Sunday Afternoon on the Island of La Grande Jatte*, 1884-86. Oil on canvas, 6ft 9½ins × 10ft ⅜in (205.7 × 305.8cm). Helen Birch Bartlett Memorial Collection, Courtesy of the Art Institute of Chicago.

12.19 Georges Seurat, *Le Chahut* (*The Hullabaloo*), 1889-90. Oil on canvas, 67⅛ × 55¼ins (171.5 × 140.5cm). Collection: State Museum Kröller-Müller, Otterlo, The Netherlands.

accordance with his theory of color perception, and *A Sunday Afternoon on the Grande Jatte* (Fig. **12.18**) illustrates his concern for the accurate depiction of light and colorations of objects. The composition of this work shows attention to perspective, and yet it wilfully avoids three-dimensionality. As was the case in much of post-impressionism, Japanese influence is apparent—color areas are fairly uniform, figures are flattened, and outlining is continuous. Throughout the work we find conscious systematizing. The painting is broken into proportions of three-eighths and halves, which Seurat believed represented true harmony. He also selected his colors by formula. Physical reality for Seurat was a pretext for the artist's search for a superior harmony, for an abstract perfection.

Le Chahut (Fig. **12.19**) reflects Seurat's experimentation with the aesthetic theories of Charles Henry—the scientific depiction of moods. Here we find the gaiety of

12.20 Paul Cézanne, *Mont Sainte-Victoire seen from Les Lauves*, 1902-4. Canvas, 27½ × 35¼ins (69.8 × 89.5cm). Philadelphia Museum of Art (George W. Elkins Collection).

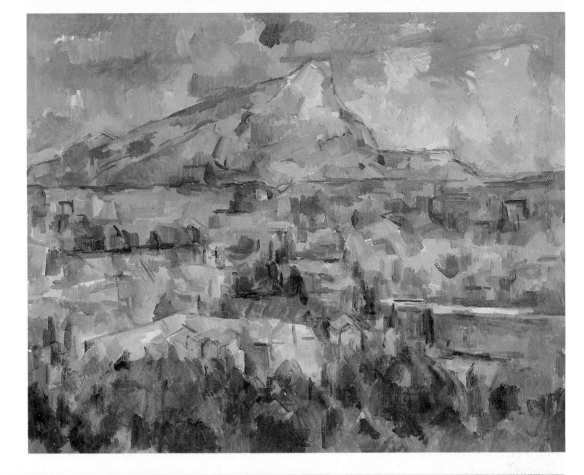

12.21 Paul Gauguin, *The Vision after the sermon*, 1888. Canvas, 28¾ × 36¼ins (73 × 92cm). National Gallery of Scotland, Edinburgh.

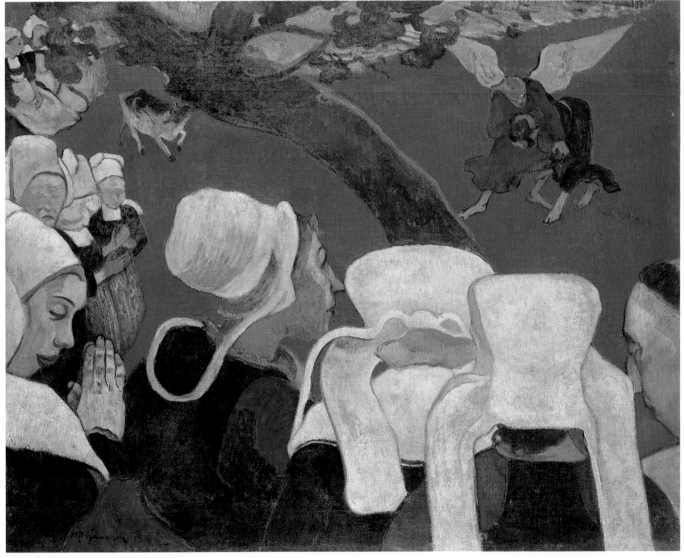

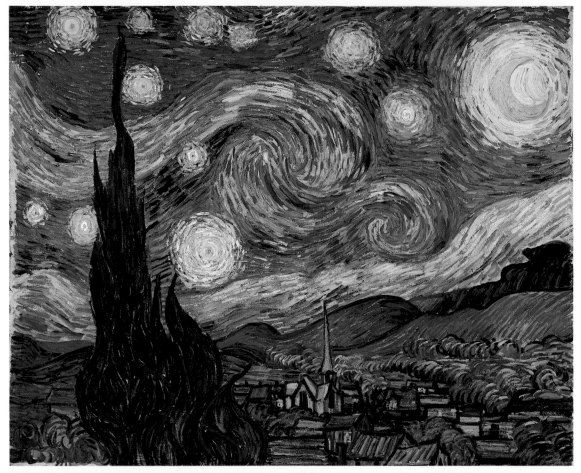

12.22 Vincent Van Gogh, T*he Starry Night*, 1889. Oil on canvas, 29 × 36¼ins (73.7 × 92.1 cm). The Museum of Modern Art, New York (acquired through the Lillie P. Bliss Bequest).

12.23 Vincent Van Gogh, T*he Potato Eaters* (2nd version), 1885. Canvas, 28½ × 37ins (72 × 93cm). Collection: State Museum Kröller-Müller, Otterlo, The Netherlands.

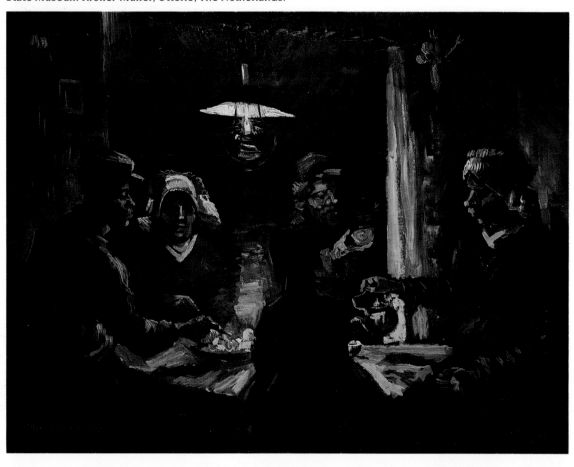

dance—the tone is light, the colors are warm, line and movement lead the eye upward. Reality takes a subordinate position to overall design, and the buoyant mood of the café and the singer is contrasted only slightly by the darker tones of the bass player (perhaps Seurat was trying to suggest the rich sonority of the instrument with this treatment).

Post-impressionism in painting called for a return to form and structure, characteristics the post-impressionists believed essential to art and lacking in the works of the impressionists. Taking the evanescent light qualities of the impressionists, Gauguin, Seurat, Van Gogh, and Cézanne brought formal patterning to their canvases, used clean color areas, and casually applied color in a systematic and almost scientific manner. The post-impressionists sought to return painting to traditional goals while, at the same time, retaining the clean palette of the impressionists.

Paul Cézanne (1839–1906), considered by many as the father of modern art, illustrates concern for formal design, and his Mt. Sainte-Victoire (Fig. **12.20**) shows a nearly geometric configuration and balance. Foreground and background are tied together in a systematic manner so that both join in the foreground to create two-dimensional patterns. Shapes are simplified and outlining is used throughout. Cézanne believed that all forms in nature were based on geometric shapes—the cone, the sphere, and the cylinder. Employing these forms, he sought to reveal the permanent reality that lay beneath surface appearance.

A highly imaginative approach to post-impressionist goals came from Paul Gauguin (1848–1903). An artist without formal training, and a nomad who believed that all European society and its works were sick, Gauguin devoted his life to art and wandering, spending many years in rural Brittany and the end of his life in Tahiti and the Marquesas Islands. His work shows his insistence on form, his resistance to naturalistic effects, and a strong influence of non-Western art, including archaic and "primitive" styles. Vision after the Sermon (Fig. **12.21**) has Gauguin's typically flat, outlined figures, simple forms, and the symbolism for which he and his followers were known—Symbolists or "Nabis" (from the Hebrew word for prophet). In the background of this painting Jacob wrestles with the Angel while, in the foreground, a priest, nuns, and women in Breton costume pray. The intense reds of this work are typical of Gauguin's symbolic and unnatural use of color, used here to portray the powerful sensations of a Breton folk festival.

A final approach to post-impressionism was that of Vincent Van Gogh (1853–90), whose emotionalism in the pursuit of form was absolutely unique. Although we have not dealt in much detail with biographical information concerning the art and artists we have examined, we must take note of Van Gogh's turbulent life, which included numerous short-lived careers, impossible love affairs, a tempestuous friendship with Gauguin, and, finally, serious mental illness. Biography here is essential because Van Gogh gives us one of the most personal and subjective artistic viewpoints in the history of Western art. Works such as the Starry Night (Fig. **12.22**) explode with frenetic energy manifested in Van Gogh's brushwork. Flattened forms and outlining reflect Japanese influence. Tremendous power and controlled focal areas exist, and we can sense the dynamic, personal energy and mental turmoil present in Van Gogh's art. The Potato Eaters (Fig. **12.23**) shows careful preparation in the style of Millet. This illustration is the last study before the final painting which hangs in the Van Gogh Museum in Amsterdam. The color and treatment are rough, suggesting the rough skin of the potato. The overall tone of the painting suggests the greyness of peasant life.

SCULPTURE

Neo-classicism

Neo-classical sculpture prevailed during the early years of the nineteenth century and consisted predominantly of a reproduction of classical works rather than a revising of them, as was the case in architecture. In France neo-classicism served its commemorative and idealizing functions as the political tool of Napoleon, who was glorified in various Greek and Roman settings, sometimes garbed in a toga and sometimes in the nude, as if granting him the status of a Greek god. Perhaps no style is free from outside influences, and nineteenth-century neo-classical sculpture often reveals aspects of rococo, baroque, and romantic style.

Antonio Canova (1757–1822) is recognized as the ablest of the neo-classical sculptors, and his works illustrate not only this style, but also influences of the rococo tradition. Venus Victrix (Fig. **12.24**), for which Napoleon's sister was the model, presents classical pose and proportions, similar in many ways to Ingres' Odalisque. Line, costume, and hairstyle reflect the ancients, but sensuous texture, individualized expression, and realistic and fussy detail suggest other approaches. At the same time, this work is almost two-dimensional. Canova appears unconcerned with the work when seen from any angle other than the front.

The Danish sculptor Bertel Torvaldsen (1768–1844) also pursued classical goals. His best known work, the Lion of Lucerne (1818–25) is carved out of the rock in a grotto near Lucerne and memorializes the Swiss Guards who died at Tuileries in 1792. The associations and implications of this monument, as well as the emotionalism which appears in the depiction itself, reflect romanticism nearly as much as they do classicism.

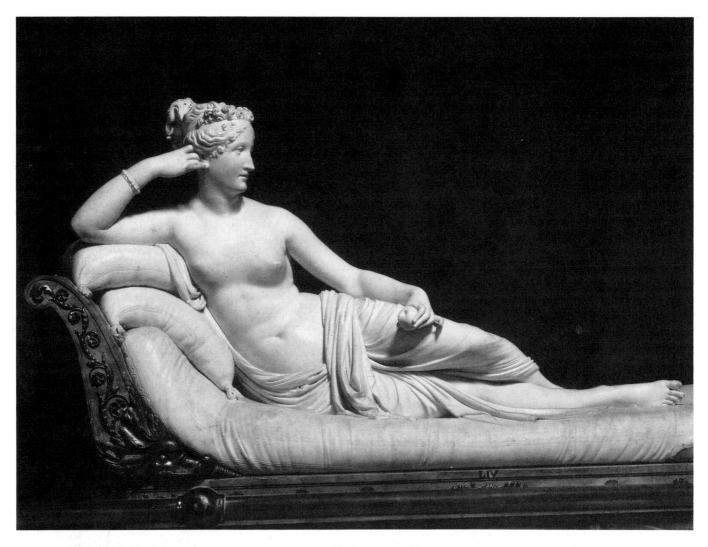

12.24 Antonio Canova, *Pauline Borghese as Venus Victrix*, 1808. Marble, life size. Galleria Borghese, Rome.

Romanticism

Romantic sculpture never developed into a uniform style. Those works not clearly of the traditions we have just mentioned show a generally eclectic spirit and a uniformly undistinguished character. There may be a reasonable explanation for such a phenomenon in that romantic idealism, whose strivings after nature and the far away and the long ago cannot be easily translated into sculptural expression. Certainly nineteenth-century devotion to landscapes does not. Of course, the term romantic is often applied to almost anything of the nineteenth century, as is the case with the most remarkable sculptor of this era, Auguste Rodin (1840–1917).

One can find ample room to apply idealism and social comment in Rodin's *Burghers of Calais* (Fig. **12.25**), which celebrates the noble, if humiliating surrender of the city. However, Rodin's textures, more than anything else, reflect impressionism; his surfaces appear to shimmer as

–light plays on their irregular features. The *Thinker* (Fig. **12.26**) provides a familiar example and shows the difficulty inherent in attempting to put into sculptural form what Monet, for example, tried to do with color and texture in painting. Rodin's textures, however, are more than reflective surfaces—they give his works dynamic and dramatic qualities. Although Rodin used a fair degree of verisimilitude, he nevertheless presented a subjective reality beyond the surface, a subjective viewpoint seen even more clearly and dramatically in *Balzac* (Fig. **12.27**). Rodin's style is of the nineteenth century, but it nearly defies description by any term other than modern.

Impressionism and Post-impressionism

Sculpture in the late nineteenth and early twentieth centuries sought a return to form combined with expressive emotional content. The works of Aristide Maillol

12.25 Auguste Rodin, *The Burghers of Calais*, 1886. Bronze, height 82½ins (209.5cm). Hirshhorn Museum and Sculpture Garden, Smithsonian Institution, Washington DC.

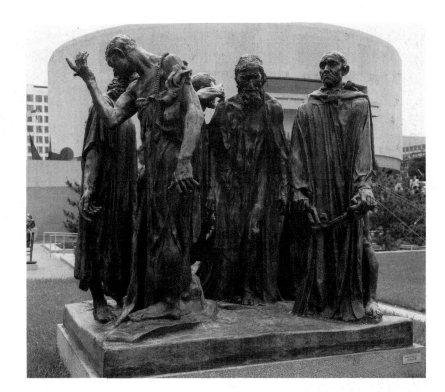

12.26 Auguste Rodin, *The Thinker*, first modelled c.1880, executed c.1910. Bronze, height 27½ins (70cm). The Metropolitan Museum of Art, New York (Gift of Thomas F. Ryan, 1910).

12.27 Auguste Rodin, *Balzac*, 1897. Bronze, height 43ins (109cm). Philadelphia Museum of Art (Rodin Museum, Gift of Jules E. Mastbaum).

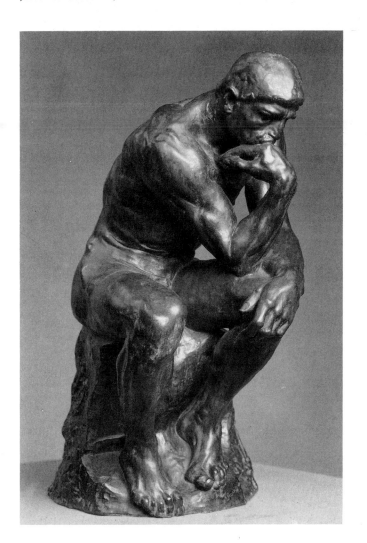

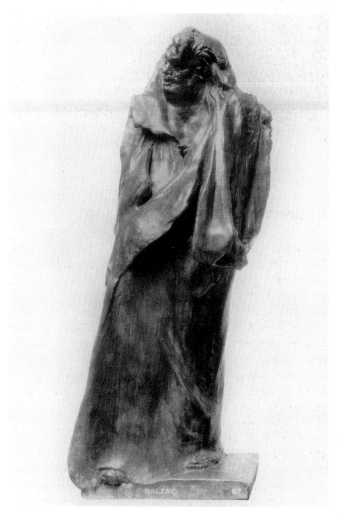

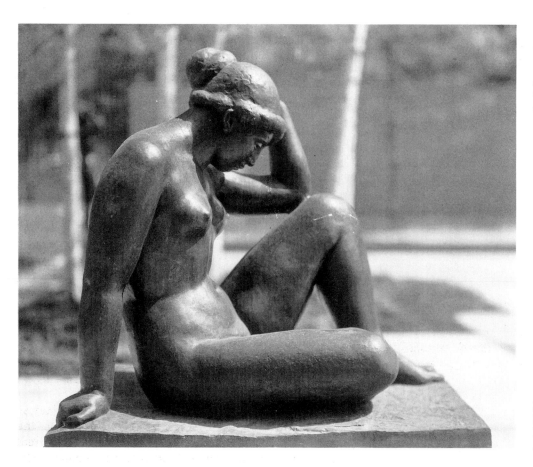

12.28 Aristide Maillol, *The Mediterranean*, 1902-5. Bronze, height 41ins (104cm). The Museum of Modern Art, New York (Gift of Stephen C. Clark).

12.29 Jacob Epstein, *Selina*, 1922. Bronze, height 22⅛ins (56cm). The Brooklyn Museum, New York (Gift of Adolph Lewisohn).

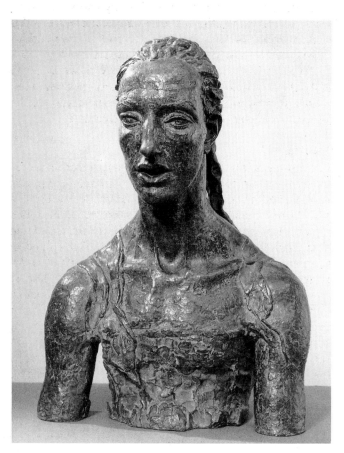

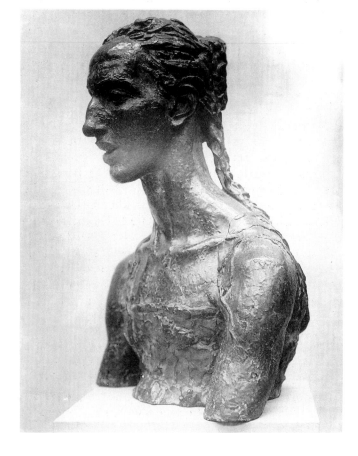

(1861–1944) point to these concerns and are occasionally classified as classical, a label appropriate in terms of the mythological sense and clear concern for formal composition. Many scholars, however, draw comparisions between Maillol and the post-impressionist painters, because he shared their desire not only for structure, but also for capturing emotional qualities. Maillol believed that a statue should exhibit rest and self-containment, and that belief emerged clearly in works such as *Méditerranée* (Fig. **12.28**). Finally, the poignant work of Jacob Epstein (1880–1959) (Fig. **12.29**) suggests post-impressionistic, emotive energy and subjective qualities similar to those found in the work of Van Gogh.

MUSIC

Richard Strauss claimed that by purely musical means he could convey to an audience the amount of water in a drinking glass. In an era of subjectivity music provided an artistic medium in which many found an unrivalled opportunity for the expression of emotion. All of the arts were closely related in the romantic period and drew inspiration from each other, but each art discipline offered its own unique qualities.

Romanticism

In pursuit of the expression of human emotion, romantic music made stylistic changes to classical music. Unlike some art disciplines where romantic tendencies amounted to a rebellion, romanticism in music was a more gradual change and natural extension of classical principles. The classical-romantic antithesis—the form versus feeling or the intellect versus emotion conflict—simply cannot be applied neatly to music of the eighteenth and nineteenth centuries. Subjectivity and emotion played a more important role in romanticism, and even if classicism sought sustenance in nature and antiquity, romanticism imbued nature with a strangeness that went beyond classical inspirations. Utopia, whether in the past or the future, and nature, whether malevolent or benevolent, were as obvious and influential in nineteenth-century music as in any other art discipline.

As in painting, spontaneity replaced control, but the primary emphasis of music in this era was on beautiful, lyrical, and expressive melody. Phrases became longer, more irregular, and more complex than in classical music. Melodic development nearly always had individual performance virtuosity as its object.

Rhythm varied from simple to complex. Much romantic rhythm was strictly traditional, but experiments produced new meters and patterns. Emotional conflict was often suggested by juxtaposing duple and triple meters, and rhythmic irregularity became increasingly common as the century progressed.

Harmony and tone color changed significantly. Harmony was seen as a means of expression, and any logic or restriction regarding key relationships was submerged by the need to achieve striking emotional effects. Form was clearly subordinate to feeling. Harmonic procedures became increasingly complex, and traditional outlines of major and minor keys were blurred in chromatic harmonies, complicated chords, and modulations to distant keys. In fact, key changes became so frequent in some composers' works that their compositions comprised virtually nothing but tonal whirls of continuous modulation. Chromaticism—the altering of normal whole- and half-tone relationships in a scale—gained increasing importance as composers sought to disrupt previously logical expectations. The result was a sense of uncertainty and of the bizarre. More and more dissonance occurred, changing in its role from that of a passing dissettlement leading to resolution to that of a principal focus. That is, dissonance was explored for its own sake, as a stimulant of emotional response, as opposed to its use merely as a device in traditional harmonic progression to resolution on the tonic. By the end of the romantic period, exploration (and exhaustion) of chromatics and dissonance led to a search for a wholly different tonal system.

Exploration of color as a response stimulant was as important to the romantic musician as it was to the painter. Interest in tonal color or timbre led to great diversity in vocal and instrumental performance. The technical and emotional limits of every aspect of music were probed with enthusiasm, and music literature of this period abounds with solo works and a tremendous increase in the size and diversity of the orchestra. In order to find our way through this complex era, we need to isolate some basic musical forms and explore them, their individual artworks, and their composers in relation to the general characteristics we have just described.

Lieder

In many ways "art songs" or *Lieder* characterized romantic music. A solo voice with piano accompaniment and poetic text allowed a variety of lyrical and dramatic expressions and linked music directly with literature, from which romanticism sprang. German lyric poetry provided the cornerstones for feelings in the period, and the burst of German romantic poetry encouraged the growth of *Lieder*. Literary nuances affected music, and music added deeper emotional implications to the poem. Such a partnership led to diverse results—some *Lieder* were complex, others were simple. Some were structured and strophic, others were freely composed. The pieces themselves depended upon an integral relationship between the piano and the voice. In many ways the piano was an inseparable part of the experience, and certainly it was more than accompaniment. The piano explored mood and established rhythmic and thematic material; occasionally it had solo passages of its own, fully rounding out the interdependency basic to *Lieder*.

The earliest, and perhaps the most important composer of *Lieder*, was Franz Schubert (1797–1828), whose troubled life epitomized the romantic view of the artist's desperate and isolated condition. Known only among a close circle of friends and musicians, Schubert composed almost one thousand works (from symphonies to sonatas and operas, to masses, choral compositions, and *Lieder*) but did not see his first public performance until the year of his death. His songs used a wide variety of poetry and poets, and he composed in strophic and through-composed form. Melodic contours, harmonies, rhythms, and structure were all determined by the poem. Schubert's *Die Forelle* (the *Trout*) is a well-known and frequently sung *Lied*, which clearly evidences romantic concern for nature.

In a limpid brooklet
Merrily speeding.
A playful trout
Shot past like an arrow.
I stood on the bank,
Watching with happy ease
The lively fish
Swimming in the clear brook.

A fisherman with his rod
Was standing there on the bank,
Cold-bloodedly watching
The fish dart to and fro . . .
"So long as the water remains clear,"
I thought, "He will not
Catch that trout
With his rod."

But at last the thief
Could wait no more.
With guile he made the water muddy.
And, ere I could guess it,
His rod jerked,
The fish was floundering on it,
And my blood boiled
As I saw the betrayed one.[2]

The first two verses share a simple melody and harmonic accompaniment. The mood is cheerful and calm. The third verse is excited and backed by a chromatic and agitated accompaniment. The song closes with a restatement of the opening melody. The popularity of *Lieder* cannot be overestimated, and drew such composers as Brahms, Wagner, Wolf, Mahler, Richard Strauss, Berlioz, and Fauré.

The growth of *Lieder* as an artform depended in no small manner upon nineteenth-century innovations and improvements in piano design. The instrument for which Schubert wrote had a much warmer and richer tone than earlier pianos. Improvements in pedal technique made

sustained tones possible and gave the instrument greater lyrical potential. Such flexibility made the piano perfect for accompaniment, and, more importantly, as a solo instrument. As a result, new works were composed solely for the piano, ranging from short, intimate pieces similar to *Lieder* to larger works designed to exhibit great virtuosity in performance. Franz Schubert also excelled in piano compositions, as did Felix Mendelssohn (1809–47) and Franz Liszt (1811–86). Liszt, influenced by the great violin virtuoso, Paganini, tried to bring to the piano the dazzling virtuosity of Paganini's violin. Liszt's performances and the demands of his compositions exhibited and encouraged theatricality, although less so than others, whose primary purpose was to impress audiences with flashy technical presentation. More restrained were the compositions of Frederic Chopin.

Frederic Chopin (1810–49), born in Warsaw of a Polish mother and French father, wrote almost exclusively for the piano. Each of his *études*, or technical studies, explored a single technical problem, usually around a single motive. More than simple exercises, these works explored the possibilities of the instrument and became short tone poems in their own right. A second group of compositions included, short intimate works such as preludes, nocturnes, and impromptus and dances such as waltzes, polonaises, and mazurkas. Polish folk dance tunes were particularly influential. A final class of compositions included larger works such as scherzos, ballades, and fantasies. Chopin's compositions were highly individualized, and many were without precedent. His style was completely opposed to classicism, almost totally without standard form and having little sense of balance of structure. His melodies were lyrical, and his moods varied from melancholy to exaltation.

Program music

The close relationship of musical composition to a text, such as occurred in *Lieder*, also surfaced in another area. When classical forms were not used, especially in longer works, significant problems arose in keeping compositions unified. As a result, romantic composers turned to building their works around a non-musical idea. When the idea was used in a general way, the music was called descriptive. When the idea was more specific and applied closely throughout, the music was called programmatic or program music. These techniques were not new to the romantic period, but they did offer a flexibility and variation, which the romantics found particularly attractive and employed with great gusto. A non-musical idea allowed the composer to rid himself of formal structure altogether. Of course, actual practice among composers varied tremendously—some using programmatic material as the sole structuring device, others continuing to subordinate program idea to formal structure. Nevertheless, the romantic period has become known as the "age of program music". Among the best known composers of program music were Hector Berlioz (1803–69) and Richard Strauss (1864–1949).

Berlioz' *Symphony Fantastique* (1830) employed a single motive, called an *idée fixe*, to tie the five movements of the work together. The text begins with an introduction, which familiarizes the audience with a hero who has poisoned himself because of unrequited love. However, the drug only sends him into semi-consciousness, in which he has visions, occurring as musical images and ideas. Throughout his visions is the recurrent musical theme symbolizing his beloved (the *idée fixe*). The first movement consists of "Reveries" and "Passions". Movement two represents "A Ball". "In the Country" is the third movement, in which he imagines a pastoral scene. In the fourth movement, "March to the Scaffold", he dreams he has killed his beloved and is about to be executed. The *idée fixe* returns at the end of the movement and is abruptly shattered by the fall of the axe. The final movement describes a "Dream of a Witches' Sabbath" in grotesque and orgiastic imagery.

Not all program music depends for its meaning or interest upon understanding its text. Berlioz believed that the audience did not have to know the text, that the work could be self-sufficient without it. We can enjoy and respond to most programmatic works, for example, *Pictures at an Exhibition* by Mussorgsky (1839–91), *Romeo and Juliet* by Tchaikovsky (1840–93), or *Academic Festival Overture* by Brahms (1833–97), without knowing the idea or text to which they refer, but our response is even greater if we do.

Many believe, however, that the tone poems (or symphonic poems) of Richard Strauss require an understanding of the program. His *Don Juan*, *Till Eulenspiegel*, and *Don Quixote* draw such detailed material from specific legends that program explanations and comments are integral to the works and help to give them coherence. In *Till Eulenspiegels Lustige Streiche* (*Till Eulenspiegel's Merry Pranks*) Strauss tells the legendary German story of Till Eulenspiegel and his practical jokes. Till is traced through three escapades, all musically identifiable. He is then confronted by his critics and finally executed. The musical references are so specific that it is difficult to imagine any meaningful relationship with the work apart from its program. Other program music encompasses concert overtures and incidental music and includes composers such as Bizet, Grieg and Mendelssohn.

Symphonies

At the same time as these relatively innovative directions were being pursued by romantic composers, a traditional direction continued in the romantic symphony and concerto. This direction, while employing the lyrical melodic tendencies of the period, retained classical form, and produced symphonic works based solely on musical information. That is, these symphonic works are built upon musical ideas such as motifs, themes and phrases, and maintain their unity through structure as opposed to non-musical ideas or texts. These works are known as abstract or absolute music. Their melodies, rhythms, and timbres reflect the characteristics noted at the beginning of the chapter, and include an increasingly dense texture and greatly expanded dynamic range. Although their form maintains tradition, their effect is emotional—the listener is bathed in an overwhelmingly sensual experience. Contrasts in dynamics and timbre are stressed, and, as in painting, form, although maintained, is subordinated to expressive intent. A synthesis of classical tradition and romantic spirit nonetheless occurred, and that synthesis was clearly present in the works of Brahms, Tchaikovsky, Mendelssohn, and Schumann.

We can also identify a new nationalistic trend in music of the romantic periods. The roots of such movements went deep into the past, but the political circumstances of the century prompted composers. Folk tunes and themes dominated this tendency, and localized experimentation with rhythms and harmonics created qualities, which, while still within romantic parameters, are easily associated with national identities. This was particularly the case in Russia, which for the most part has remained outside our examination of Western art, with the Russian composers Glinka, Balakirev, Cui, Borodin, Mussorgsky, Rimsky-Korsakov, Rubenstein, and, of course, Tchaikovsky. We find the same thing in Bohemia (Czechoslovakia) in the music of Smetana and Dvořák; in Spain with Albeniz and Falla; in England with Elgar and Vaughan Williams; in Scandinavia with Grieg; and in Germany and Austria with Wagner and Mahler.

Choral music

If instrumental music ranged from solo instrument to massive ensemble works, so did choral music, and the emotional tenets of romanticism were well served by the potential for diverse timbres and lyricism in the human voice. Almost every major composer of the era wrote some form of choral music, ranging from small pieces to huge ensemble works using soloists, massive choruses, and full orchestras. Franz Schubert is remembered for his Masses, the most notable of which was the *Mass in A Flat Major*. Felix Mendelssohn's *Elijah* stands beside Handel's *Messiah* and Haydn's *Creation* as a masterpiece of oratorio. Hector Berlioz marshalled full romantic power for his *Requiem*, which called for 210 voices, a large orchestra, and four brass bands.

Undoubtedly, the most enduring choral work of the romantic period, however, was Johannes Brahms' *Ein Deutsches Requiem* (*A German Requiem*). Based on selected texts from the Lutheran Bible, in contrast with the Latin of traditional requiems, Brahms' work is not a Mass for the dead as much as it is a consolation for the living. This is principally a choral work—the solos are minimal, two for baritone and one for soprano. Tonal colors in chorus and orchestra are very expressive. Melodic lines and harmonies weave highly pictorial textures. After the chorus sings "All mortal flesh is as the grass", the orchestra elicits strong feelings of fields of grass moving in the wind. The lyrical "How Lovely is Thy Dwelling Place" remains one of the favorite and most moving choral pieces ever written—for both performers and audience alike. An important factor in Brahms music is its lyricism and its vocal beauty. That is, Brahms explored the human voice as a human voice. His parts are written and his words chosen so that, while technically demanding, no voice is required to do what lies outside its tessitural or technical capacity. Such a fact is in strong contrast to many composers who treat the voice (and specific instruments for that matter) as if it were a mechanism unaffected by any restrictions. Brahms' Requiem begins and ends with moving passages aimed directly at the living: "Blest are They That Mourn". Hope and consolation underlie the entire work.

Opera

The spirit, style, and time of romanticism for many is summed up in the perfect synthesis of all the arts—opera. "I have written the opera with clenched fists, like my spirit! Do not look for melody; do not look for culture: in Marat there is only blood!" Such was the defiant statement of Pietro Mascagni describing his new opera Il Piccolo Marat in 1921. Mascagni's tantrum was the final burst of the end of an era. The preceding century and two decades produced almost our entire contemporary operatic repertoire. Three centers dominated operatic development—France (principally Paris), Italy, and Germany.

Paris occupied an important position in romantic opera during the first half of the nineteenth century. The spectacular quality of opera and the size of its auditoriums had made it an effective vehicle for propaganda during the revolution. As an artform opera enjoyed great popular appeal among the rising and influential middle classes. A new type of opera called grand opera emerged early in the nineteenth century, principally as a result of the efforts of Louis Veron, a businessman, Eugene Scribe, playwright and librettist, and Giacomo Meyerbeer, composer. Breaking away from classical themes and subject matter, these three staged spectacular productions with crowd scenes, ballets, choruses, and fantastic scenery, written around medieval and contemporary events and themes. Meyerbeer (1791–1864), a German, studied Italian opera in Venice and produced French opera in Paris. Robert The Devil and The Huguenots typified Meyerbeer's extravagant style and achieved great popular success, although Schumann called The Huguenots "a conglomeration of monstrosities". More musical and controlled, as well as classically based, was Berlioz' The Trojans written in the late 1850s. At the same time Jacques Offenbach (1819–80) brought to the stage a lighter style, which mixed spoken dialogue amidst the music. Called opéra comique this type of opera is serious in intent despite what the French word comique might suggest. It is a satirical and light form of opera, using vaudeville humor to satirize other operas, popular events, and so forth. In between Meyerbeer and Offenbach there was a third form of romantic opera called lyric opera. Works of Ambroise Thomas (1811–96) and Charles Gounod (1818–93) exemplified lyric opera. The composers turned to romantic drama and fantasy for their plots. Thomas' Mignon contains highly lyrical passages, and Gounod's Faust, based on Goethe's play, stresses melodic beauty.

Early romantic opera in Italy featured the bel canto style, which emphasizes beauty of sound. Illustrative of this substyle of romanticism were the works of Donizetti (1797–1848), Bellini (1801–35), and, above all, Rossini (1792–1868). Rossini's Barber of Seville takes melodic singing to tremendous heights and quality. His songs are light, ornamented, and very appealing, and his drama is exciting. Donizetti (Lucia di Lammermoor) and Bellini (the Sleepwalker) are much akin to Rossini in their pursuit of lyrical and expressive melodies.

Great artists often stand apart from or astride general stylistic trends, exploring on their own a unique or dominant theme. Such is the case with the Italian composer Giuseppe Verdi (1813–1901). Verdi combined earthy emotions and clear expression within a nationalistic philosophy. He refined opera into a human drama consisting of simple, beautiful melody.

His long career experienced different phases. The early phase saw works such as Rigoletto (1851), La Traviata (1853), and Il Trovatore (1853). In these works Verdi focused upon logic and structure, using recurring themes to provide unity. Out of the second phase came Aida (1871), a grand opera of spectacular proportion built upon a tightly woven dramatic structure. Finally, a third phase produced operas based on Shakespearan plays. Otello (1887) and Falstaff (1893) contrast tragedy and opera buffa. Both explore subtle balance among voices and orchestra, in concert with strong melodic development.

Nothing, however, represents romantic opera better than the works of Richard Wagner (1813–83) in Germany. At the heart of Wagner's prolific artistry lay a philosophy which was to affect the world of the musical and legitimate stage from the mid-nineteenth century to the present day. His ideas were laid out principally in two books—Art and Revolution (1849) and Opera and Drama (1851). Wagner's philosophy centered on the Gesamtkunstwerk, a comprehensive work of art in which music, poetry, and scenery are all subservient to the central generating idea. For Wagner the total unity of all elements reigned supreme. Fully expressive of German romantic philosophy, which confers upon music supremacy over all other arts, Wagner's operas placed music in the predominant role. Dramatic meaning unfolded through the use of Leitmotif, for which Wagner is famous, although he did not invent it. A Leitmotif ties a musical theme to ideas, persons, or objects. Whenever those ideas, persons, or objects appear or occupy thought, the theme is played. Juxtaposing *Leitmotifs* can suggest relationships between their subjects to the audience. These themes also provide the composer with building blocks, which can be used for development, recapitulation, and unification.

Wagner's operas are legendary. Beginning with *Die Feen* (*The Fairies*) and *Das Liebesverbot* (*The Ban on Love*), he rose to his first original, major grand opera, *Rienzi*. In 1843 he produced *Der Fliegende Holländer* (*The Flying Dutchman*), followed by *Tannhäuser* (1845). *Lohengrin, Tristan und Isolde* (1857–59), and the *Ring Cycle* (1852–74), consisting of *Das Rheingold, Die Walküre, Siegfried,* and *Die Götterdämmerung,* round out Wagner's operas. Each of these, and every work we have so casually treated, deserves detailed attention. Whatever we might say by way of description or analysis would be insignificant compared to the dramatic power these works exhibit in full production. Even a recording cannot approach the tremendous effect of these works in full production in an opera house.

Romanticism in the arts encountered many counter-reactions and opposing directions. The late nineteenth century in opera was no exception. In France an anti-romantic movement, called naturalism, developed. It opposed stylization and freely presented brute force and immorality, although it maintained exotic settings. The best operatic example of this movement was Georges Bizet's *Carmen* (1875), which tells the story of a gypsy girl and her tragic love (Fig. **12.30**). In contrast to earlier romantic works, the text for *Carmen* is in prose rather than poetry. Set in Spain, its scenes are highly realistic, and its music, colorful and concise. Bizet's naturalism was similar to the operatic style alluded to at the beginning of this section, Italian *verismo* opera, which emerged at the turn of the twentieth century.

Verismo

The spirit of *verismo* (verisimilitude or true to life), is a hot-blooded, slice-of-life vitality well characterized by Mascagni's earlier statement. The works of Mascagni, Puccini (Fig. **12.31**), Leoncavallo, Giordano, Refice, and others exemplify this tradition, which comprises a type of music drama that deals exclusively with the violent passions and common experiences of everyday people. Adultery, revenge, and murder are common themes. Mascagni's *Cavalleria Rusticana* and Leoncavallo's *Il Pagliacci* are the best known examples of this melodramatic form.

Impressionism

Elsewhere in music the anti-romantic spirit produced a style analogous to that of the impressionist painters. Even among the romantics a free use of chromatics marked later nineteenth-century style. However, a parting of the ways occurred, the effects of which still permeate contemporary music. On the one hand free use of chromatics and key shifts stayed within the parameters of traditional major-minor tonality. On the other hand, traditional tonality was rejected completely, and a new atonal harmonic expression occurred. Rejection of traditional tonality led to impressionism in music, a movement international in scope, but limited in quantity and quality. There was some influence from the impressionist

12.30 Georges Bizet, *Carmen*. Opera Company of Philadelphia.

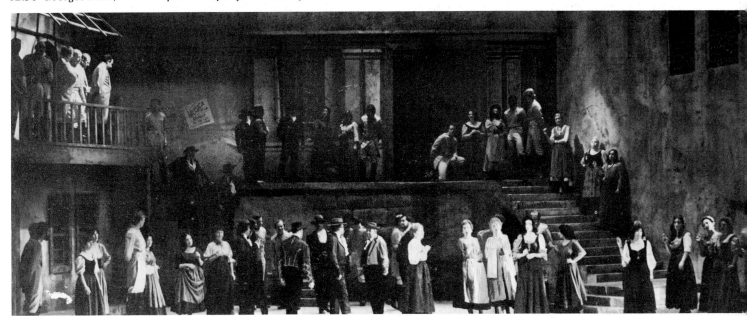

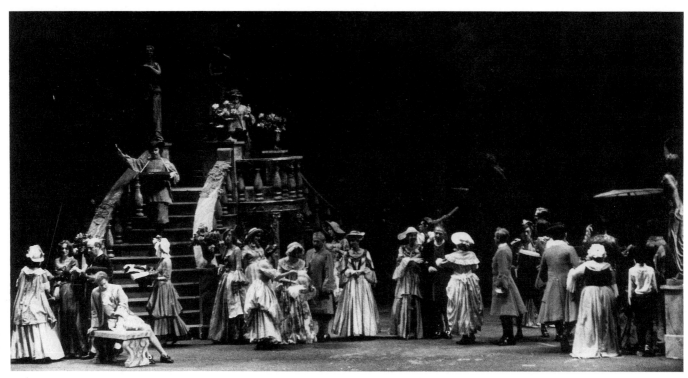

12.31 Giacomo Puccini, *Manon Lescaut.* Opera Company of Philadelphia.

painters, but mostly impressionism in music turned to the symbolist poets for inspiration.

Even though impressionist music was international, it is difficult, principally for want of significance or quality, to go beyond its primary champion, Claude Debussy (1862–1918), to find its substance. However, Debussy did not like to be called an impressionist, which is not surprising because the label was coined by a severe critic of the painters and was intended to be derogatory. He maintained that he was "an old romantic who has thrown the worries of success out the window," and he sought no association with the painters. However, similar motifs and characteristics can be seen. His use of tone color has been described as "wedges of color" applied in the same manner that the painters employed individual brushstrokes. Oriental influence is also apparent, especially in Debussy's use of the Asian five-tone scale. He wished above all to return French music to fundamental sources in nature and move it away from the heaviness of the German tradition. He delighted in natural scenes, as did the impressionist painters, and sought to capture the effects of shimmering light.

In contrast to his predecessors, Debussy reduced melodic development to short motifs of limited range and removed chordal harmony from traditional progression, perhaps his greatest break with tradition. For Debussy, and impressionists in general, a chord was considered strictly on the merits of its expressive capabilities and apart from any context of tonal progression.

As a result, gliding chords (repetition of a chord up and down the scale) have become a hallmark of musical impressionism. Dissonance and irregular rhythm and meter further distinguish Debussy's works. Here, again, form and content are subordinate to expressive intent. His works propose to suggest, rather than to state, to leave the listener with ambiguity, with an impression. Freedom, flexibility, and non-traditional timbres mark his compositions, the most famous of which is *Prélude à l'après-midi d'un faune,* based on a poem by Mallarmé. The piece uses a large orchestra, with emphasis on the woodwinds, most notably in the haunting theme running throughout. Although freely ranging in an irregular $\frac{9}{8}$ meter and having virtually no tonal centers, *Prélude* has a basically traditional ABA structure.

THEATRE

"The play-going world of the West End is at this moment occupied in rubbing its eyes, that it may recover completely from the dazzle of Thursday last, when, amid the acclamations of Queen Victoria's subjects, King Richard the Second was enthroned at the Princess's Theatre." Thus began the reviewer's comments in *The Spectator,* 14 March 1857. The dazzle of scenery, revivals, and a potpourri of uncertain accomplishments helped a stumbling theatre to keep up with its romantic brethren through the early years of the nineteenth century.

Romanticism

Romanticism as a philosophy was its own worst enemy in the theatre. Artists sought new forms to express great truths and strove to free themselves from neo-classical rules and restraints. Significantly, Shakespeare was seen as exemplary of new ideals and symbolic of freedom from structural confinement. Intuition reigned, and genius, being apart from everyday humankind, placed its holder above or beyond normal constraints. As a result, the romantic writer had no use for any guide but his own imagination. Unfortunately the theatre operates within some rather specific limits. So many nineteenth-century playwrights penned scripts that were totally unstageable and/or unplayable, that the era justly gained its reputation for dramatic barrenness. It seemed that great writers could not constrain themselves to the practicalities of the stage, and the hacks, yielding to popular taste, could not restrain themselves from overindulgence in phony romantic emotionalism, melodrama, and stage gimmickery. As a result, the best romantic theatre came from the pen of William Shakespeare, brought out of his Elizabethan "theatre of convention" into nineteenth-century antiquarianism. Be that as it may, the romantic period succeeded in shaking loose the arbitrary rules of neo-classicism, thus paving the way for a new era in the later years of the century.

The audiences of the nineteenth century played a significant role in what took the stage. Royal patronage was gone, and what was to be staged required box office receipts to pay its bills. A rising middle class swelled the eighteenth-century audience, changing its character. The nineteenth century witnessed the admission of the lower classes to its houses. The Industrial Revolution created larger urban populations, expanded public education to a degree, and sent feelings of egalitarianism throughout European and American social orders. All this enlarged theatre audiences, and prompted widespread theatre building. Audience diversity and capitalist entrepreneurial spirit caused theatre managers to program for the popular as well as sophisticated taste. In order to offer something for everyone, an evening's theatre program might contain several types of fare and last upwards of five hours. The consequence was predictable. Fewer and fewer sophisticated patrons chose to attend, and the quality of the productions declined in direct proportion.

By 1850 a semblance of order had returned, however, and theatres began to specialize, thus returning the sophisticated play-goer to the theatre with quality to suit the level of expectation. Nevertheless, the multiproduction evening remained a typical one until nearly the turn of the twentieth century. Audience demand was high, and theatre continued to expand. Theatre in continental Europe went quiet during the Napoleonic Wars and the depression which followed, but by 1840 prosperity had revived it considerably.

We noted in our examination of Athenian theatre that a playwright is always a man or woman of the theatre. In the early nineteenth century the theatre of which the playwright needed to be a part had particular characteristics. First of all there was the repertory company. These companies each comprised a set group of actors, including stars or leading actors and actresses, and arranged performances around a season. Each season several productions were staged. (That is quite unlike our contemporary professional theatre in which each play is produced and cast independently and runs for as long as it shows a profit.) Gradually, better known actors began to capitalize on their reputations (and sometimes were exploited by the same), and began to tour, starring in local productions and featuring their most famous roles. A virtual craze for visiting stars developed and the most famous began to make world tours. Along with the increase in touring stars came an increase in touring companies, and in the United States especially, these companies with their star attractions and complete sets of costumes and scenery became a regular feature of the landscape. By 1886 America could boast 282 touring companies. At the same time local resident companies became appreciably less popular, except in Germany, where a series of local, state-run theatres were established.

Theatre design was by now very diverse, but some generalities can be drawn. Principally, the changes in nineteenth-century stages and staging were prompted by increased interest in historical accuracy and popular demand for depiction rather than convention. Prior to the eighteenth century, history was considered irrelevant to art. Knowledge of antiquity through archeological excavation in Pompeii, however, aroused curiosity. The romantic

12.32 Charles Kean's production of William Shakespeare's *Richard* II, London, 1857. Between Acts III and IV, the Entry of Bolingbroke into London. Contemporary watercolour by Thomas Grieve. Victoria and Albert Museum, London.

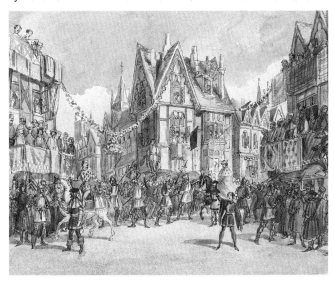

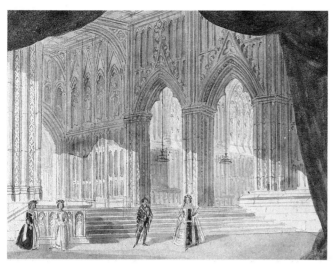

12.33 Charles Kean's production of William Shakespeare's *Richard* II, London, 1857. Act II, Scene 2, entrance into St Stephen's Chapel. Contemporary watercolour by Thomas Grieve, Victoria aand Albert Museum, London.

desire to escape to the far away and long ago decreed that the stage picture representing those places should be believable. At first such detail was used inconsistently, but by 1823 some productions claimed that they were entirely historical in every aspect. Attempts at historical accuracy took place as early as 1801 in the Berlin production of Schiller's *Maid of Orleans*, and Victor Hugo and Alexandre Dumas, *père*, insisted on historically accurate settings and costumes in France in the early years of the century. However, it remained for Charles Kean (1811–68) and the London theatre in the 1850s to bring the spectacle of antiquarianism fully to fruition (Figs. **12.32** and **12.33**).

The onset of realism as a standard for production led to three-dimensionality in settings and away from drop and wing scenery to the box set. The stage floor was leveled (since the Renaissance it had been raked, slightly upward sloped from downstage to upstage). New methods of shifting and rigging were devised to meet specific staging problems. Over a period of years all elements of the production became integrated in a total aesthetic unity, much in the spirit of Wagner's *Gesamtkunstwerk*. The distraction of scene changes (which were numerous) was alleviated by closing the curtain to hide stage-hands.

Stage space itself became clearly defined and separated from the audience. Rather than playing on the forestage between audience-occupied stage boxes, the actors moved upstage, within the confines of the scenery. Inventions in the use of gaslight made control of light possible so that the audience area could be darkened and the stage light controlled, creating an isolated and self-contained stage world (Fig. **12.34**).

All of this comprised the theatre of which playwrights were or were not a part, and there were many who were not. Goethe's *Faust Part* I was basic to romantic drama as

discussed in the last chapter. It was also virtually unstageable. In romantic philosophy art and literature were thoroughly entwined. Plays often were seen and studied as literature. The theatre-literature link of the nineteenth century brought writers to the theatre who were not of the theatre. Their inexperience was complicated by romantic disregard for practicality, and the result was problematic, to say the least.

Victor Hugo (1802–85) occupied an almost god-like position in the artistic community of Paris. After two abortive attempts (one at the hands of the state censor), he finally succeeded in producing his play, *Hernani*. An earlier diatribe which Hugo had directed against the neo-classicists succeeded in filling his audience with revenge-seekers who were determined that *Hernani* would fail. The production was a shambles, and in fact *Hernani*, though written by a master writer, is not a very good play. Characters violate their own integrity, honor is carried to ridiculous extremes, and the ending is totally contrived. The poetry remains nonetheless lyrical and charming, and Hugo's brave assault on the bastions of French neo-classicism did open a few doors for romantic dramatists, not least of whom was the novelist Alexandre Dumas, *père*

12.34 Gottfried Semper in collaboration with Richard Wagner, the Bayreuth Festspielhaus, opened 1876. Section and plan.

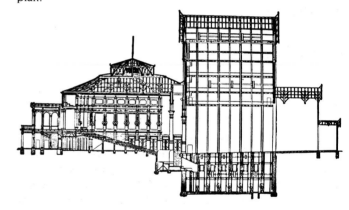

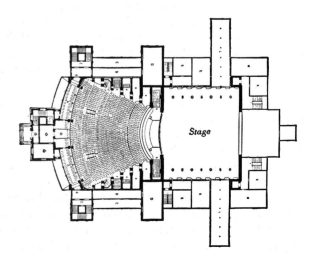

Stage

(1802–70). His prose work *Henry III et sa Cour* (1829) enjoyed success at the *Comédie-Française*, and it did much to popularize the romantic movement through its introduction of justified illicit love.

In England revivals of Shakespearean plays enjoyed more success than contemporary works. The Romantic poets Coleridge, Wordsworth, Byron, Keats, and Shelley attempted to write plays. A few of their works were produced, but all suffered from the maladies noted previously. James Sheridan Knowles (1784–1862), an actor, enjoyed some success as a playwright, mingling Shakespearean verse with melodramatic stories in *Virginius* (1820), *William Tell* (1825), and *The Hunchback* (1832).

Heinrich von Kleist (1777–1811) carried the German theatre into the nineteenth century along with Goethe and Schiller. His *Prince of Homburg* (1811) tells the story of a young officer so desirous of fame that he defies orders in an attempt to win a victory. His success does not excuse his endangering the entire army, and he is condemned to death. Only after realizing that his ego must be subordinate to service and the good of all is he spared. Another German playwright, Georg Büchner (1813–37) illustrates in *Danton's Death* (1835) the pessimistic side of romanticism. The dashing of hopes resulting from Napoleon's despotism and defeat is reflected in this story of idealism crushed by pettiness. *Woyzek* also expresses disillusionment, but in a remarkably modern and expressionistic psychological study.

Melodrama

The popular side of theatre production in the nineteenth century developed a romantically exaggerated form called melodrama. Typically this form of genre is characterized by sensationalism and sentimentality. Characters tend to be stereotyped and problems, solutions, and people tend to be all good or all evil. Plots are sentimental and the action is exaggerated. A strict moral code must also be observed. Regardless of circumstances, good must be rewarded and evil punished. Melodrama often employs some form of comic relief, usually through a minor character. The action progresses at the whim of the villain, and the hero is forced to endure episode after episode of superhuman trial. Suspense is imperative and reversal at the end obligatory. The term melodrama implies music and drama, and in the nineteenth century these plays were accompanied by a musical score tailored to the emotional or dynamic character of the scene. Actual practice was very similar to the use of contemporary film and television scores, but the music of the melodrama also often included incidental songs and dances used as curtain raisers and *entr'acte* entertainment.

Melodrama was popular throughout Europe and the United States, and playwrights such as Kotzebue (1761–1819) and Pixérécourt enjoyed great success. *Uncle Tom's Cabin*, based on the novel by Harriet Beecher Stowe (1852), took the stage by storm. The stage version was opposed by Mrs. Stowe, but copyright laws did not exist to protect her. The play does represent the same complex themes of slavery, religion, and love. The action involves a number of episodes, some of which are rather loosely connected. Characteristic of melodrama, *Uncle Tom's Cabin* places considerable emphasis on spectacle, the most popular of which at the time was Eliza's crossing the ice with mules, horses, and bloodhounds in pursuit.

Realism

In line with trends in philosophy and the other arts, a conscious movement toward realism in the theatre emerged around the middle of the century. This movement brought significant change, and by 1860 one could find in dramatic literature a striving for verisimilitude, or a truthful portrayal of the real world. Objectivity was stressed, and knowledge of the real world was seen as possible only through direct observation. Corot's approach to painting was based on a similar viewpoint. As a result, contemporary life, or life with which the playwright was directly familiar, became the subject matter of drama. Insight turned from the utopian past and exotic places to an investigation, and, to a large extent, idealization of human motives. Exposure to current and mundane topics on the stage was not particularly pleasant for many playgoers, and objection to turning the theatre into a "sewer or a tavern" came from many quarters. Playwrights responded by saying that the way to avoid such ugly depiction on the stage was to change it in society. The fault lay in the model, and not in the messenger.

Translating contemporary life realistically into dramatic form required a thorough knowledge of theatre practicality and presentation. A workable solution to that problem, which had plagued the romantics, came from Eugene Scribe (1791–1861). Scribe was a master of plot manipulation, and as a playwright was better able to mold a dramatic structure than the vague romantics. His early success came through well-plotted comedies of intrigue, and although his characterizations were very weak, his ability to put together a comprehensible action made him very influential both in his time and later. Scribe perfected a form known as the well-made play, and his formulaic approach to the writing of plays allowed him and his factory of collaborators to turn out plays in great numbers. His formula was straightforward—present a clear exposition of the situation; carefully prepare events that will happen in the future; provide unexpected but logical reversals; build suspense continuously; bring the action to a logical and believable resolution. The crux of the well-made play was logic and cause-to-effect relationships.

The realist movement in nineteenth-century theatre

found followers in Alexandre Dumas, *fils* (1824–95), and Émile Augier (1820–89), both of whom were greatly concerned with social problems. Dumas' *La Dame aux Camélias*, also known as *Camille*, was dramatized from his novel in 1849 (though not produced until 1852) and achieved phenomenal worldwide popularity. Its central character grew to legendary status. *Camille* is the story of a courtesan with a heart of gold who comes to a cruel fate. Although Dumas was probably only interested in painting a picture of French society, not in creating sentimentality, the play is sentimental and romantic. It is a sincere portrayal of youthful passion, and, unlike most melodrama, there is no rescue at the end—Camille dies in her lover's arms.

Another well-known late nineteenth-century romantic amid the realists was Edmond Rostand (1868–1918). Rostand wrote with excitement and passion, and his play *Cyrano de Bergerac* challenged the leading actors of the last century. Cyrano is a dashing, literate romantic, whose courage is unequalled, as is his one great flaw, his grotesque nose. Cyrano's death scene rivals any in the annals of theatre for passion, and for length!

The acknowledged master of realist drama was Norway's Henrik Ibsen (1828–1906). Ibsen took the format of Scribe's well-made play, eliminated many of its devices, and built powerful, realistic problem-dramas around careful selection of detail and plausible character-to-action motivations. His exposition is usually meticulous, and the play itself tends to bring to conclusion events that began well in the past. Ibsen's concern for realistic detail carries to the *mise en scène*, and his plays contain detailed descriptions of settings and properties, all of which are essential to the action.

Many of Ibsen's plays were controversial. Most still present pertinent and significant questions concerning social and moral issues and personal relationships. *A Pillar of Society*, *A Doll's House* (1879), *Ghosts* (1881), *An Enemy of the People* (1882), *The Wild Duck* (1884), *Rosmersholm* (1886) and *Hedda Gabler* (1890) all speak to a realist philosophy and form a cornerstone for contemporary drama. Ibsen's late plays, such as *The Master Builder* (1892) and *When We Dead Awaken* (1899) abandoned realism in favor of a symbolist quality. The haunting and dreamlike atmosphere was further developed by the Swedish playwright August Strindberg (1849–1912), whose almost Freudian approach is best represented in his *Dream Play* (1898).

Realism spread throughout the world, finding excellent reflections in the works of Arthur Wing Pinero, Henry Jones, John Galsworthy, and Anton Chekhov, although Chekhov departs from realism, as Ibsen did, to incorporate significant symbolism in his works. Anton Chekhov (1860–1904) is regarded by many critics as fundamental to modern realism. His themes and subject matter were drawn from Russian daily life, and they are realistic portrayals of frustration and the depressing qualities of mundane existence. His structures flow in the same apparently aimless manner as do the lives of his characters. Theatricalism and compact structure are noticeably absent. Nonetheless, his plays are skilfully constructed to give the appearance of reality.

The spirit of realism in England can have no better representative than George Bernard Shaw (1856–1950), whose wit and brilliance are without equal. Shaw's career overlapped the nineteenth and twentieth centuries, and illustrates how difficult it is adequately to categorize, even chronologically, the works and ideas of great artists. This great artist was above all a humanitarian. His beliefs (if they may be called that) were shocking to Victorian society. Considered a heretic and a subversive (because of his devotion to Fabian socialism), his trust and faith lay in humanity and its infinite potential.

Shaw's plays exhibit originality and the unexpected, and often appear contradictory and inconsistent in characterization and structure. His favorite device was the construction of a pompous notion only to destroy it. For example, in *Man and Superman* a respectable Victorian family learns that their daughter is pregnant, to which they react with predictable indignation. To the girl's defense comes a character who obviously speaks for the playwright. He attacks the family's hypocrisy and defends the girl. The girl, however, explodes in anger, not against her family, but against her defender. She has been secretly married all the time, and as the most respectable of the lot, she abjures her defender's free-thinking (and that of the audience, who thought they had understood the playwright's point of view).

Shaw opposed "art for art's sake" and insisted that art should have a purpose. He believed a play was a more effective means of transmitting social messages than were speakers' platforms and pamphlets. His pursuit of message through dramatic device is exceptionally skillful, and he succeeds, often despite weak characterizations, in pointing out life's problems through a chosen character in each play who acts as the playwright's mouthpiece. But he does more than sermonize. His plays show deep insight and understanding. His characters probe the depths of the human condition and often discover themselves through crisis, in a logical, reasonable, and realistic portrayal of life.

Naturalism, a style closely related to realism, occurred in the same period and can be found in the writings of Émile Zola (1840–1902), who was more a theoretician and novelist than he was a playwright. The essential differences between realism and naturalism are often debated. Both insisted on truthful depiction of life, but naturalism went on to insist on scientific methodology in the pursuit of art and the basic principle that behavior is determined by heredity and environment (behaviorism). Absolute objectivity, not personal opinion, dominated the naturalistic viewpoint.

Symbolism

Late in the nineteenth century, and very briefly, there was an anti-realistic movement called symbolism, also known as neo-romanticism, idealism, or impressionism. It erupted briefly in France, and has recurred occasionally in the twentieth century. It held that truth can be grasped only by intuition, not through the five senses or rational thought. Ultimate truth could be suggested only through symbols, which evoke various states of mind corresponding vaguely with the playwright's feelings. A principal dramatic symbolist, Maurice Maeterlinck (1862–1949) believed that every play contains a second level of dialogue, which seems superficial, but which actually speaks to the soul. He believed that great drama contains verbal beauty, contemplation, and passionate portrayal of nature and our sentiments, and an idea which the poet forms of the unknown. Therefore, plays (which contain human actions) only suggest through symbols higher truths gained through intuition. The symbolists did not follow the realists' path in dealing with social problems. Rather they turned to the past, and, like the neo-classicists, tried to suggest universal truths independent of time and place. Maeterlinck's *Pelléas and Mélisande* (1892) and *The Blue Bird* (1911) are excellent examples of symbolist plays.

Organic unity

The curtain fell on nineteenth-century theatre with two significant developments. First was the emergence of production unity as a principal aesthetic concern. To that end the production director was assigned the overriding responsibility of controlling unity. That consideration remains fundamental to modern theatre practice and owes its emergence principally to Georg II, Duke of Saxe–Meiningen (1826–1914). The second development was the emergence of the independent theatre movement in Europe, from which came France's *Théâtre Libre*, and Berlin's *Freie Bühne*, both champions of realism and naturalism; London's Independent Theatre, organized to produce theatre of "literary and artistic rather than commercial value", and the Moscow Art Theatre, founded by Constantin Stanislavsky, the most influential figure in acting and actor-training in the twentieth century. The significance of these theatres lay in the fact that they were private, open only to members. They therefore avoided the censorship that dominated public theatre, and nurtured free experimentation and artistic development, laying the foundations for a truly modern twentieth-century theatre.

DANCE

In a totally unrehearsed move, a ballerina leaped from the tomb on which she was posed and narrowly escaped a piece of falling scenery. That and other disasters plagued the opening night performance of Meyerbeer's *Robert the Devil* in 1831. The novelty of tenors falling into trapdoors, and falling stagelights and scenery, however, was eclipsed by the startling novelty of the choreography for this opera. Romantic ballet was at hand. In varying degrees all the arts turned against the often cold formality of classicism and neo-classicism. The subjective not the objective viewpoint, feeling rather than reason, sought release.

Since we cannot hold even part of an artwork up for examination in this discipline, we need to rely on other materials to gain an understanding of romantic ballet. Two sources are helpful—the writings of Théophile Gautier and Carlo Blasis. Gautier (1811–72) was a poet and critic, and his aesthetic principles held first of all that beauty was truth, a central romantic conception. He rejected Noverre and Vigano, who believed that every gesture should express meaning. Rather, Gautier believed that dance was visual stimulation to show "beautiful forms in graceful attitudes. The true, the unique, the external subject of ballet is dancing."[3] No deeper mean-

12.35 Illustrations from *The Art of Dancing*, 1820, by Carlo Blasis. The New York Public Library.

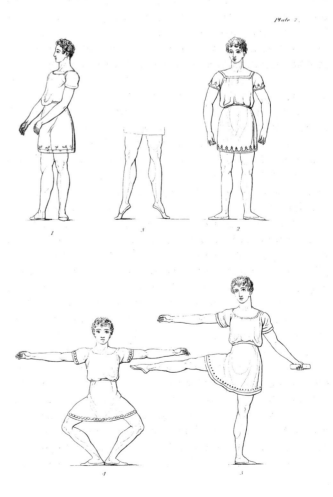

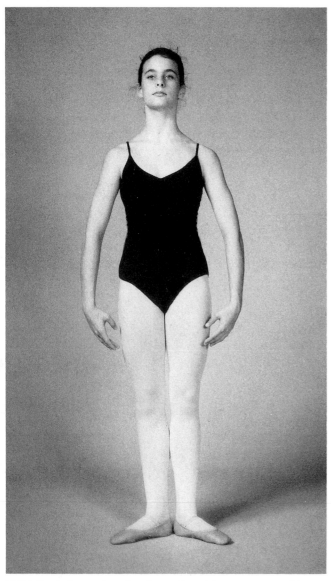

12.36 Basic "turned-out" or "open" position. Dancer: Kathleen Cantwell.

too experimental, revolutionary, and in bad taste. Much more systematic and specific than Gautier (Blasis was a former dancer), his principles covered training, structure, and positioning. All matters of ballet required a beginning, a middle, and an ending, and the basic "attitude" in dance (modelled on Bologna's statue *Mercury*, Fig. **10.12**) was that of standing on one leg with the other brought up behind at a ninety-degree angle with the knee bent. The dancer needed to display the figure with taste and elegance. To achieve the ends of ballet and to achieve proper position, the dancer was required to train each part of the body. The result was grace without affectation. From Blasis came the fundamental turned-out position, which rules ballet today (Fig. **12.36**). In contrast to Gautier's thinking, gesture and pantomime were seen as the "very soul and support" of ballet. Finally, Blasis, like Gautier, placed the female at the center of ballet, confining the male to the background. These broad principles, then, provided the framework and to a great extent a summary of objectives for romantic ballet: delicate ballerinas, lightly poised, sweetly gracious, costumed in soft tulle, and moving *en pointe*, with elegant grace.

Robert the Devil was probably the first truly romantic ballet. It told the story of Duke Robert of Normandy, his love for a princess, and an encounter with the devil. The ballet contains ghosts, bacchanalian dancing, and a spectral figure who was danced by Marie Taglioni (Fig. **12.37**).

Taglioni went on to star in perhaps the most famous of all romantic ballets, *La Sylphide* (1832). Here the plot centered on the tragic impossibility of love between a mortal and a supernatural being. A spirit of the air, a sylph, falls in love with a young Scot on his wedding day. Torn between his real fiancée and his ideal, the sylph, he deserts his fiancée to run off with the spirit. A witch gives him a scarf, and, unaware that it is enchanted, he ties it around the spirit's waist. Immediately her wings fall off and she dies. The sylph drifts away to some sylphidic Heaven, and the young man is left disconsolate and alone as his fiancée passes in the distance with a new lover on the way to her wedding. The Scottish setting was exotic, at least to Parisians. Gaslight provided a ghostly, moonlit mood enhanced by a darkened auditorium. Taglioni's dancing of the role of La Sylphide was unbelievably light and delicate, "a creature of mist drifting over the stage" (assisted by "flying" machinery). Taglioni's lightness, poetic delicacy, and modest grace established the standard for romantic style in dancing. The story, exotic design, and modal lighting completed the production style, a style which was to dominate for the next forty years—"moonbeams and gossamer", as some have described the era.

Choreographers of romantic ballet sought magic and escape in fantasies and legends. Ballets about elves and nymphs enjoyed great popularity, as did ballets about madness, sleepwalking, and opium dreams. Fascinating

ing was allowed. Passion was limited to love. Dancing for Gautier was like a living painting or sculpture—"physical pleasure and feminine beauty". Whether admirable, helpful, or not, his unbridled desire to focus on ballerinas placed sensual enjoyment and eroticism squarely at the center of his aesthetics. Gautier's influence was significant, and from his philosophy emerged the central role of the ballerina in romantic ballet. Male dancers were relegated to the background, strength being the only grace permissible to them. Gautier and his philosophy proved important as the inspiration for an 1841 work, *Giselle*, often called the greatest achievement in romantic ballet. *Giselle*, however, is a bit ahead of us.

The second general premise for romantic ballet was similar to Gautier's and came from *Code of Terpsichore* by Carlo Blasis (Fig. **12.35**). He found Noverre and Vigano subject matter came to the fore, for example, harem wives revolting against their oppressors with the help of the "Spirit of Womankind", in Filippo Taglioni's the *Revolt in the Harem* (possibly the first ballet about the emancipation of women). Not only did women come to prominence as ballerinas and in subject matter, but also as choreographers.

Romantic staging, especially in ballet, was aided significantly by improvements in stage machinery and lighting. Flickering gloom and controlled darkness and shadows added greatly to the mystery of stage scenes, achievements previously impossible when candles provided the light source. Gaslight, however, proved a mixed blessing. Its volatility and open flame made fire a constant danger, and the gauzy tutus, characteristic of the period and style, undoubtedly consisted of highly flammable material. During a performance of the *Revolt in the Harem*, a ballerina brushed an oil burner. Her dress caught fire, and she rushed around the stage in a blaze of flame. By the time a stagehand could extinguish the fire, she was

12.37 Marie Taglioni (1804–84). Engraving, c.1830. The New York Public Library.

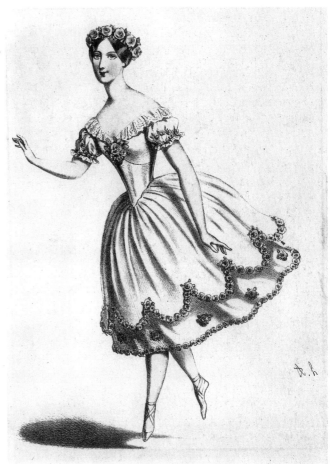

12.38 Carlotta Grisi, *Le Diable à Quatre*. Lithograph, 1845. The New York Public Library.

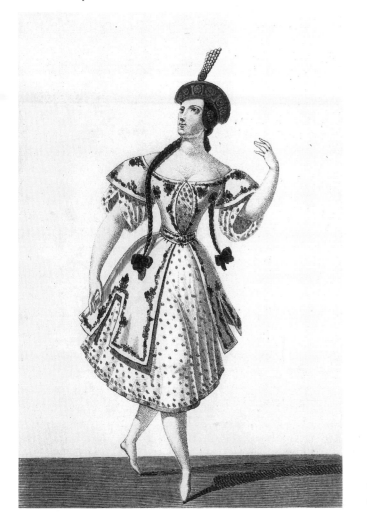

fatally burned and died two days later. Ironically, in rehearsal for *Le Papillon* (the *Butterfly*), another grotesque incident occurred. The story concerns a heroine, changed into a magic butterfly, who darts toward a torch until the flame shrivels her wings. The ballerina playing the role brushed against a gaslight fixture, her costume burst into flame, and she lingered in agony for eight months before dying of her burns. Only a day before, the management had insisted that the dancers dip their costumes in a flame-proofing solution. She had refused, insisting that the solution made her tutu look dingy.

With reference to the earlier comment concerning Gautier's influence on *Giselle* (1841), this ballet marks the height of romantic achievement. Adolphe Adam, known for his piece *O Holy Night*, composed the score. Heinrich Heine, the German poet, provided the legend—via a scenario by Gautier and a libretto by Vernoy de Saint-Georges. The prima ballerina was Carlotta Grisi (Fig. **12.38**). The choreography was created by Jean Coralli, ballet master at the Paris Opéra, although, apparently, Jules Perrot, Carlotta's teacher, choreographed all of her dances, and in them lies the essence of the ballet.

The ballet contrasts two typically romantic acts: one in sunlight (Act I) and one in moonlight (Act II). In a Rhineland village during a vine festival Giselle, a frail peasant girl in love with a mysterious young man, discovers that he is Albrecht, Count of Silesia. Albrecht is already engaged to a noblewoman. Giselle is shattered. In madness she turns from her deceitful lover, tries to commit suicide, swoons, and falls dead. In Act II Giselle is summoned from her grave, deep in the forest, by Myrthe, Queen of the Wilis (spirits of women who, having died unhappy in love, are condemned to lead men to destruction. The word "wili" comes from a Slavic word for "vampire"). When a repentant Albrecht comes to bring flowers to Giselle's grave, Myrthe orders her to dance him to his death. Instead Giselle protects Albrecht until the first rays of dawn break Myrthe's power.

Giselle contains many fine dancing roles for women and men and has been a favorite of ballet companies since its first production. Carlotta Grisi was acclaimed for her "tender melancholy".

Jules Perrot's characterizations and choreography do not concentrate entirely on the major dancers—he also gives the *corps* plenty to do. His ballets generally had skilfully drawn characterizations, which encompassed all social classes. His heroes were frequently men of humble birth, and he continued to provide good parts for male dancers even in an era dominated by Gautier's disdain for the *danseur*. One of Perrot's major accomplishments

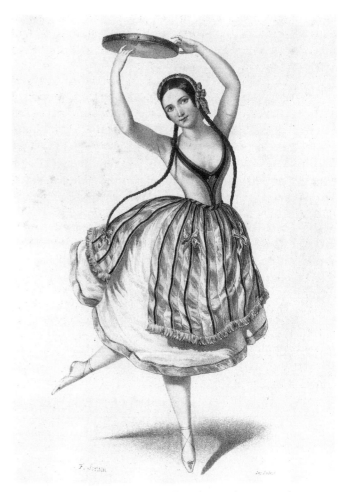

12.40 Fanny Cerrito (1817–1909). Lithograph, c.1845. The New York Public Library.

was the choreography for *Pas de Quatre* (1845) (Fig. **12.39**) at Her Majesty's Theatre, London. In an awesome gamble he brought together the four major ballerinas of the day, Taglioni, Cerrito (Fig. **12.40**), Grisi, and Grahn. His purpose was to allow each star to shine—without permitting anyone to upstage the others! A decision that the dancers would perform in order of age, with the oldest last, defused a raging conflict over who would perform in the place of honor (the last solo), and the ballet went forward to earn plaudits from Queen Victoria and London at large.

Russia

Traditionally Eastern in orientation, Russia had opened up to the West tentatively in the seventeenth and eighteenth centuries. By the nineteenth century the country had turned its attention more fully toward the rest of Europe and Russian artists began to take their place in Western arts. This was certainly true in dance. In St. Petersburg in 1862 an English ballet called the *Daughter of Pharaoh*, choreographed by Marius Petipa, sent

12.39 Le Pas de Quatre, Perrot. Lithograph, 1845. The New York Public Library.

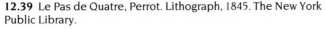
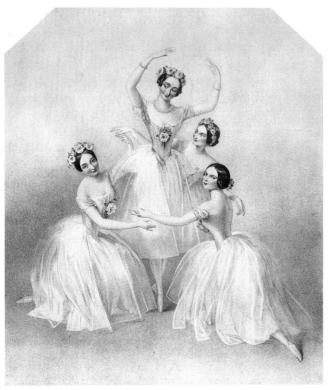

Russian audiences into rapture. Ballet was not new to Russia, however. As early as 1766 Catherine II had established the Directorate of the Imperial Theatres to supervise ballet, opera, and dance.

Petipa had come to Russia from France in 1842, and remained a central figure in Russian ballet for almost sixty years. By the middle of the nineteenth century, ballet companies were flourishing in Moscow and St. Petersburg. Dancers enjoyed positions of high esteem in Russia, in contrast to their lot in the rest of Europe. Petipa's influence carried Russia forward in a quasi-romantic style. He shared the sentimental taste of his time, but his ballets often contained very strange elements and numerous anachronisms. Minor characters might wear costumes suggesting period or locale, but the stars wore conventional garb, often of classical derivation. Prima ballerinas often appeared in stylish contemporary coiffures and jewels, even when playing the role of a slave. *Divertissements* were often inserted into a ballet. Lyrical and sustained movements predominated. Petipa included many different kinds of dance in his ballets—classical, character, folk, and demi-character dance. Mime played an important role as well. The inclusion of all

these various elements in a panoramic display gave Petipa's Russian choreography a variety and richness that was interesting and attractive. His creative approach and reliance on convention more than compensated for his anachronisms. As some have said on his behalf, "No one criticized Shakespeare for having Antony and Cleopatra speak in blank verse."

Petipa and his ballets demanded excellent dancers, and the Imperial School grew to include outstanding teachers, who produced outstanding pupils. From this close collaboration a Russian style evolved, which contained elements of French, Danish, and Italian traditions. Also from this Russian school, and choreographed by Petipa's associate Lev Ivanov, came the ever-popular *Nutcracker* and *Swan Lake* (partially choreographed by Petipa), the scores for both of which were composed by Tchaikovsky. *Swan Lake* was first produced in 1877 by the Moscow Bolshoi, and the *Nutcracker* in 1892. *Swan Lake* popularized the *fouetté* (a whipping turn), introduced by the ballerina Pierina Legnani in Petipa's *Cinderella* and incorporated for her in *Swan Lake*. She danced thirty-two consecutive *fouettés*, and to this day that number is mandatory. Balletomanes carefully count to be sure the

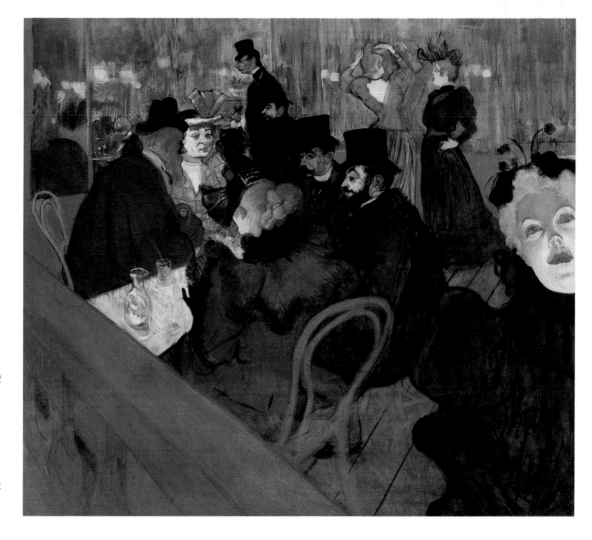

12.41 Henri de Toulouse-Lautrec, *At the Moulin Rouge*, 1892-95. Oil on canvas, 48½ × 55⅜ins (123 × 140.5cm). Courtesy of The Art Institute of Chicago (Helen Birch Bartlett Memorial Collection).

ballerina executes the required number. Russian ballet emphasized technique, and strong, athletic movements remain characteristic of its productions today.

Late in the century ballet declined in quality although not necessarily in popularity, because middle-class popularizing had a stultifying effect and turned dance efforts in a new, hedonistic direction. (Given Gautier's barely submerged eroticism, however, the direction probably was not all that new). The same sensual desires that brought many to the ballet also took them to the dance hall. The *Moulin Rouge* was the most famous dance hall, and the cancan the most famous dance. The posters of Toulouse Lautrec and Seurat capture the spirit of this age remarkably (Fig. **12.41**). It also was the age of the *Folies Bergère* to which a young American named Loie Fuller came in 1892. Probably not much of a dancer (she had only a few lessons), and certainly not a ballerina, nevertheless Miss Fuller created, in her "Butterfly Dance", "White Dance", "Violet Dance", and "Fire Dance", a new thrust and experimentation in theatre dance that was later to break the bonds of a sterile ballet

and point toward a new century of dance, which we know as "modern."

ARCHITECTURE

The nineteenth century was an age of increased individualism and subjective viewpoints. However, what is possible by way of experimentation for the painter, sculptor, musician, choreographer, and to some degree, the playwright, is not always possible for the architect. An architect's work involves a client who must be satisfied, and the results are public and permanent.

Classicism

The use of Greek and Roman forms after 1750 has been called classical revival or neo-classicism. Basically this revival can be broken into two general periods—Roman prior to 1815 and Greek from then on. Often the plethora

12.42 Benjamin H. Latrobe, interior, Basilica of the Assumption, Baltimore, Maryland, 1805-18.

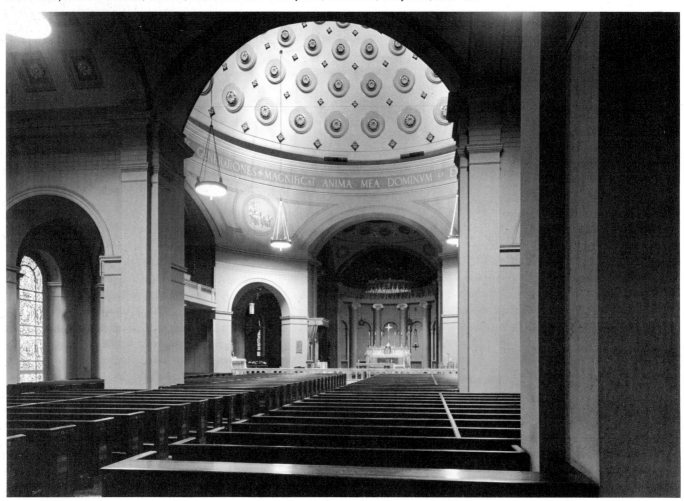

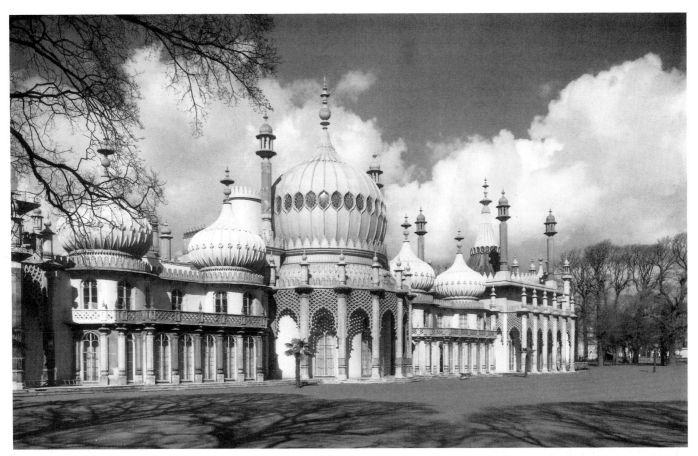

12.43 John Nash, Royal Pavilion, Brighton, England, remodeled 1815-23.

of terms describing this period can be confusing, and not the least of these is the term romantic classicism. However, such a label is not as contradictory as one might suspect if one considers "classical" as a description of architectural detail and "romantic" as a philosophy of individualized, intuitive creation, emphasizing, among other things, the far away and long ago, which, of course, Greece and Rome were. Other confusing terms occurring in relation to this era include federal style, which, essentially is a specific substyle of the resurrection of ancient prototypes in the romantic era.

Benjamin H. Latrobe's Catholic cathedral in Baltimore (Fig. **12.42**) illustrates many of the principles at issue here. In this view the Ionic orders of Athens are visible in the alcove behind the altar, while a Roman dome, like that of the Pantheon, dominates the nave. These basically "classical" forms are significantly modified and added to with numerous individualized details. Traditional Roman semicircular arches flank the central opening above the altar, yet that arch and its complements are flattened and also broken by cantilevered balconies. Whimsical, star-like decoration marks the dome, and a misty panorama of painted scenes winds over and through the modified pendentives.

Romanticism

Romanticism also borrowed styles from other eras and produced a vast array of buildings reviving Gothic motifs and reflecting fantasy, a style which has come to be known as picturesque. Eastern influence and whimsy abounded in John Nash's Royal Pavilion in Brighton, England (Fig. **12.43**). Picturesque also describes the most famous example of romantic architecture, the Houses of Parliament (Fig. **12.44**). The Houses of Parliament demonstrates a significant concept which can be described as a modern tendency in architectural design. The exterior walls function as a screen, and suggest nothing of structure, interior design or function. What we find inside has absolutely no spatial relationship to the outside. The strong contrast of forms and totally asymmetrical balance is also significant.

The nineteenth century was an age of industry, of experimentation and new materials. In architecture steel and glass came to the fore. At first it took courage for an architect actually to display structural honesty by allowing support materials to be seen as part of the design itself. England's Crystal Palace exemplified the nineteenth-century fascination with new materials and concepts. Built

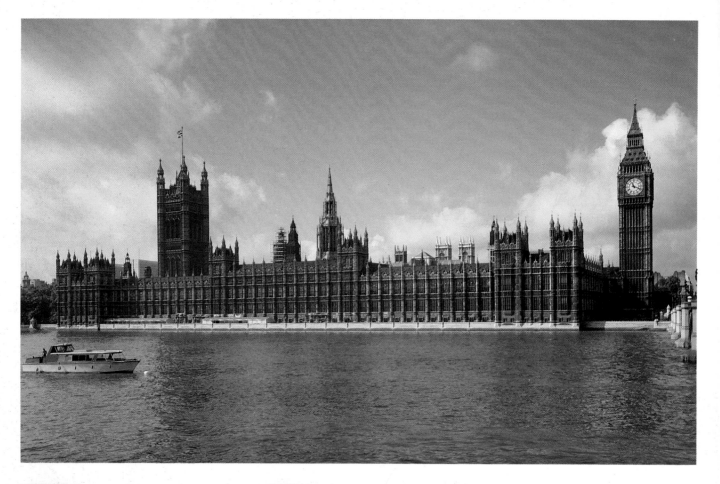

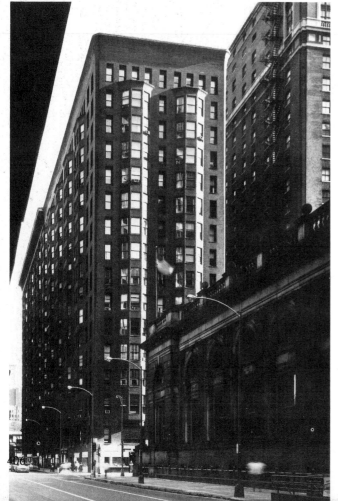

12.44 Sir Charles Barry and Augustus Welby Northmore Pugin, Houses of Parliament, London, 1839–52.

12.45 Daniel Hudson Burnham and John Wellborn Root, the Monadnock Building, Chicago, 1889–91.

12.46 Baron Victor Horta, Tassel House, Brussels, 1892–3.

for the Great Exhibition of 1851, this mammoth structure was completed in the space of nine months. Space was defined by a three-dimensional grid of iron stanchions and girders, designed specifically for mass production and rapid assembly (in this case, disassembly as well—the entire structure was disassembled and rebuilt in 1852–4 at Sydenham). Like the Houses of Parliament, the Crystal Palace was the product of the growing dichotomy between the function of a building as reflected in the arrangement of the interior spaces, its surface decoration, and its structure. A new style of building had arrived.

Experimentation and Art Nouveau

A new age of experimentation also took nineteenth-century architects in a different direction—upward. Late in the period the skyscraper was designed in response to

rubric for modern architecture by combining form and function into a theory in which the former flowed from the latter. As Sullivan said to an observer of the Carson, Pirie, and Scott Building (Fig. **12.47**), "It is evident that we are looking at a department store. Its purpose is clearly set forth in its general aspect, and the form follows the function in a simple, straightforward way."

In the final years of the nineteenth century a new style of architectural decoration evolved called Art Nouveau. It is not primarily an architectural mode but, like rococo, which it resembles, it provides a decorative surface (closely associated with graphic art) that imparts a unique character to the buildings it serves. These pages are not the place to argue Art Nouveau's heritage or significance. Rather they serve only to familiarize the reader with its easily recognized characteristics—characteristics which formed a part of Western artistic tradition. Art Nouveau is connected in some ways with the doctrines of nineteenth-century artistic symbolism, and its unique characteristic is the lively, serpentine curve, known as the "whiplash" (Fig. **12.46**). The style reflects a fascination with plant and animal life and organic growth. The influence of Japanese art, widely plundered late in

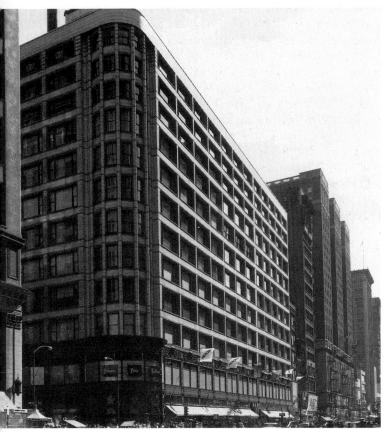

12.47 Louis Henry Sullivan, Carson, Pirie and Scott Department Store, Chicago, 1899–1904.

the need to create commercial space on limited property in burgeoning urban areas. Burnham and Root's Monadnock building in Chicago (Fig. **12.45**) was an early example. Although this prototypical "skyscraper" is all masonry—built completely of brick and requiring increasingly thick supportive walls toward its base—it was part of the trend to combine design, materials, and new concepts of architectural space. When all these elements were finally combined, the skyscraper emerged—almost exclusively in America. Architects were able to erect buildings of unprecedented height without increasing the thickness of lower walls by erecting structural frameworks (first of iron, later of steel) and by treating walls as independent partitions. Each story was supported on horizontal girders. The concept of the skyscraper could not be realized, however, until a man named Otis had invented a safe and reliable elevator.

A very influential figure in the development of the skyscraper and philosophies of modern architecture was Louis Sullivan, the first truly modern architect. Working in the last decade of the nineteenth century in Chicago, then the most rapidly developing metropolis in the world, Sullivan designed buildings characterized by dignity, simplicity, and strength. Most importantly, he created a

12.48 Frantz Jourdain, Samaritaine Department Store, Paris, 1905.

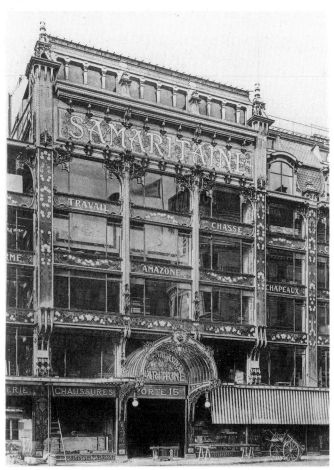

the nineteenth century, is evident in the undulating curves. Art Nouveau incorporates organic and often symbolic motifs, usually languid-looking flowers and animals, and treats them in a very linear, relief-like manner (Fig. **12.48**). The twentieth century had arrived.

SYNTHESIS
The Victorians:
The nineteenth century in Britain

We have called the nineteenth century the Age of Industry. It also has been described as the Age of Romanticism. It was both of these—we find industrialization and the philosophy and artistic aims of romanticism at the heart of the age. Yet the age was also significantly influenced by the indomitable spirit of England's great queen, Victoria, an influence reaching the continent of Europe and even America. A synthesis of artistic activities in the nineteenth century therefore yields no better subject than England and Victoria. Victoria's presence was not felt through her great patronage, as was the case with earlier European monarchs, but in the force of her personality and general social influence.

British confidence and complacency soared to great heights in the middle decades of the nineteenth century. At that time the British began to use the term 'Victorian' to describe the era they were living in, demonstrating their consciousness that their time was a distinctive period. New technology and a new approach to economics were combined with social stability and traditional values. Parliament and the monarchy symbolized continuity, stability and tradition in changing times. Designs for the new Parliament buildings reflected the antiquity of the institution of Parliament in their mock-medieval architecture. The revolutionary nature of the era was hidden behind a cloak of custom and tradition. When Victoria acceded to the throne in 1837, the British monarchy could trace its ancestry back further than any other European political institution apart from the Papacy. Victoria and Albert raised the monarchy to new heights of public esteem.

The character and essence of Victorianism can be clearly seen in the single discipline of painting, which reveals a remarkable complexity and scope. "There were contradictions, movements and countermovements; endless and labyrinthine courses were explored, false gods pursued.... If the period produced few artists of world stature, this was balanced by the cumulative effect of the

12.49 Daniel MacLise, *The Marriage of Eva and Strongbow*, first exhibited 1854. Oil on canvas, 10ft 2ins × 16ft 7ins (309 × 505cm). National Gallery of Ireland, Dublin.

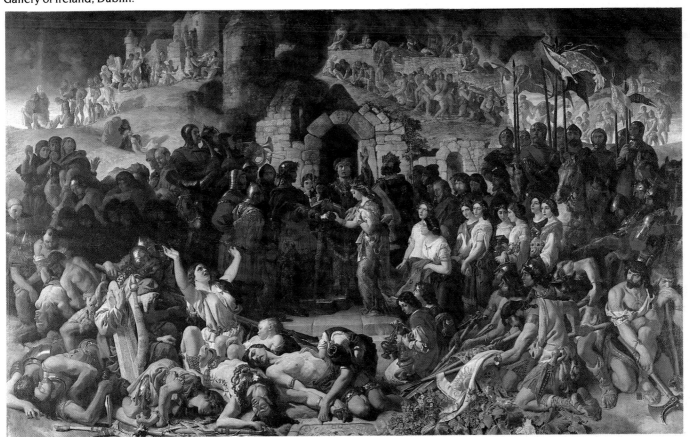

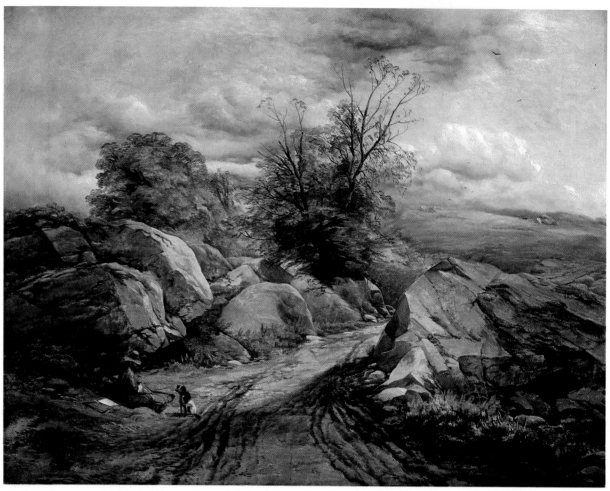

12.50 Thomas Creswick, *Landscape*, c.1851. Oil on canvas, 27 × 35ins (68.5 × 89cm). Royal Academy of Arts, London.

12.51 Sir John Everett Millais, *Ophelia*, 1852. Oil on canvas, 30 × 44ins (76 × 112cm). The Tate Gallery, London.

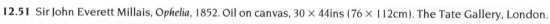

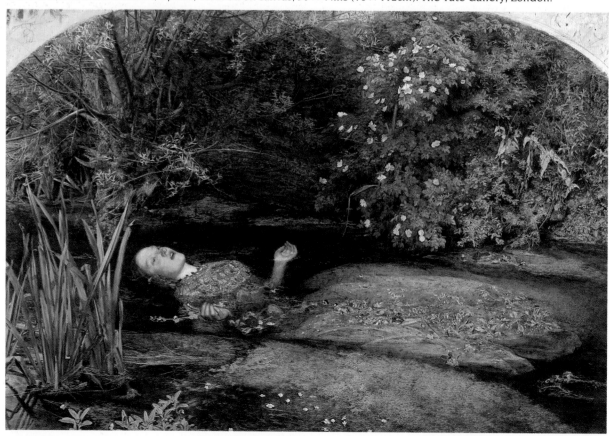

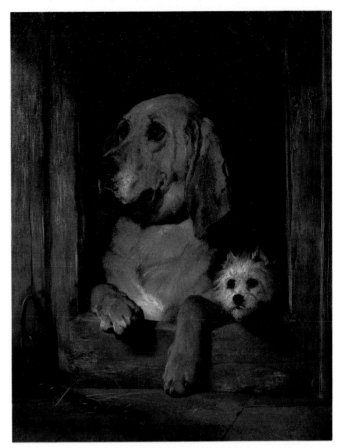

rich diversity of high talent, occasionally bordering on greatness."[4] The Victorian age had a profound interest in inter- and multi-disciplinarity. G. K. Chesterton described it as "a world in which painters were trying to be novelists, and novelists trying to be historians, and musicians doing the work of school-masters, and sculptors doing the work of curates." Although patronage had fallen from favor, state support of artists and an increase of private patronage did exist in England. Support groups for artists were first set up during this period, such as Morris and Company (1861), the Art Workers Guild (1884), and the New English Art Club (1885). The Royal Academy, which had been founded in 1768, also served artistic endeavors. On the one hand it provided a focus for artistic activity, and on the other it was seen as an established institution for rebelling artists to react against. The age produced historical painters, landscape painters, marine painters, sporting painters, animal painters, genre painters, fairy painters, nude and still-life painters, neo-classical painters, portrait painters, and the Pre-Raphaelites.

Interest in history both as a backdrop for Utopian escape and antiquarianism colored the arts as well as philosophy. Implications of sublimity and heroism caught the imagination of the Romantic painters. Scale as well as attitude found its way on to the canvas. *The Marriage of Eva and Strongbow* (Fig. **12.49**) by Daniel MacLise (1806–70) covers a canvas 122×199 inches, and depicts the twelfth-century marriage of Richard Strongbow, Second Earl of Pembroke and Strigul to Eva, eldest daughter of Dermot. Complex and busy, the work elicits an emotional thrust and captures a climactic moment. Strong contrasts in tonality compete with diverse focal areas for the viewer's attention. The central situation is played out while all about is in confusion. The coloring is harsh and the facial expressions are unreal.

Victorian landscape painters produced a prodigious quantity of "pretty, undisturbed scenes" which were designed for a growing picture-buying public. The themes were mostly superficial, emotional, and repetitive, and yet for the most part the genre is highly pleasing. Constable (1776–1837) was the guiding light as well as the shadow over other Victorian landscape artists. Constable's "chiaroscuro of nature" lent itself to easy adaptation, and his naturalistic style permeated the genre. Thomas Creswick's (1811–69) *Landscape* (Fig. **12.50**) has much in common with the work of Corot (Fig. **12.11**), displaying a careful treatment of rocks, trees, and foliage.

The Victorian love of animals is legendary, and the ownership of bizarre, wild, and exotic pets reached extremes during the age, a development perfectly consistent with the Romantic tendency and outlook. The Jubilee Year of 1887 was marked by the release of thousands of prisoners all over the British Empire. The exceptions were those convicted of cruelty to animals, which Queen Victoria regarded as "one of the worst traits of human nature". In *Dignity and Impudence* by Edwin Landseer (1802–

12.52 Sir Edwin Landseer, *Dignity and Impudence*, 1839. Oil on canvas, 35 × 27½ins (89 × 70cm). The Tate Gallery, London.

73) (Fig. **12.52**) we find an anthropomorphic treatment of the dog, who is given human sentiments.

The Pre-Raphaelites were highly controversial and appear to have exercised significant influence on the later movements away from naturalism. The Pre-Raphaelites formed themselves into a group in 1848.

The Pre-Raphaelites made artists see and paint what they saw with unprecedented skill, and they made a whole generation of designers and practitioners of the applied arts see anew and invest their work with an entirely new range of symbols.... By their resolute and enthusiastic return to the direct symbolism, frank naturalism, and poetic or romantic sentiment of medieval art, with the power of modern analysis superadded, and the more profound and intellectual study of both nature and art which the severity of their practice demanded, and last, but not least, their intense love of detail, turned their attention to other branches of design than painting.... By virtue of their complete distinction from the naturalistic school, [they] had a profound effect on the formative years of such twentieth-century figures as Picasso and Kandinsky.[5]

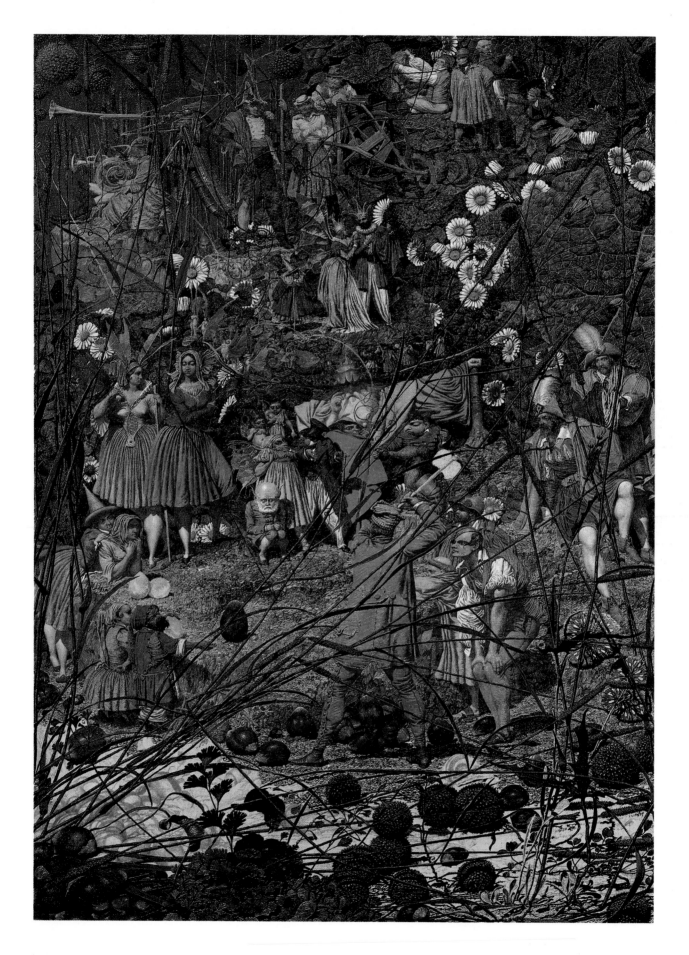

Sir John Everett Millais (1829–96) takes his subject from *Hamlet* in *Ophelia* (Fig. **12.51**), shows her in a weedy ditch and paints the detail of every floating petal with an obsessional, even morbid clarity.

Escape to legend and literature, and the fascination with the occult and spiritualism which accompanied romanticism led in England to a fascination with fairy tales. As Charles Dickens wrote in *Household Words* (Vol. 8), "In a utilitarian age, of all other times, it is a matter of grave importance that fairy tales should be respected." Fairy tales were subject matter understood and shared by artist and viewer alike. The resultant artworks represent a unique, Victorian contribution to art.

The fascinating painting *The Fairy Feller's Master Stroke* (Fig. **12.53**) took the artist, who was suffering from schizophrenia, nine years to complete. Richard Dadd (1817–87) had been among the founders of a group of painters called the Clique, and his early works had been undistinguished attempts at landscape, marine, and animal painting. After returning from an extensive trip to the Middle East and Italy, and after being rejected in the competition for the decoration of the Houses of Parliament, he stabbed his father to death. Fleeing to France, he planned to assassinate the Emperor of Austria. Captured after stabbing a passenger at Fontainebleau, he spent his remaining years institutionalized in Bethlam, or the Hospital of St. Mary of Bethlehem. He was provided with painting materials, and his subsequent works have a wonderful supernatural quality as we can see in Figure **12.53**. The flat coloring and obsessive detail has been explained as a reflection of the foreboding characteristic of schizophrenia. The drama of the painting is placed in the center, and the myriad details which surround it seem to be nothing more than highly imaginative decoration.

Victorian painting, with all its diversity, complexity, contradictions, somewhat less than stellar quality, and fascination with history, imagination, emotion, nature, animals, and unreality is representative or the remarkable romantics, realists, and multi-disciplinarians who rode the crest of the first wave which swept us into our industrialized world.

SUGGESTIONS FOR THOUGHT AND DISCUSSION

The Age of Industry was an uneasy age, torn by battles of ideas as well as armies. It was an age of technology, and the impact of technological innovation reduced the globe to an international neighborhood. The artist assumed an entirely new place in society, and wrestled with his or her own position, style, and persona. Individualism became supreme. Form became subservient to feeling, image to emotion. At the same time escapism rescued individuals from the complexities and pressures of the time. "To the far away and long ago" was the romantic's creed. Nature and the exotic called forth from every corner.

It was a time of change, and we have cautiously wandered through it from neo-classicism to romanticism to realism to naturalism to impressionism to post-impressionism to symbolism. We need to solidify our understandings of each of these "isms" as they apply to the arts and to nineteenth-century life.
■ How did one style affect another?
■ What relationships can you find between the aesthetics of Schelling and Hegel and the movements of the period?
■ How did the many technological inventions of the century transform life? Can you summarize the character of life, especially middle-class thinking, and apply that summary to directions and attitudes in the arts?
■ In what ways was the nineteenth century like our own? In what ways and in what attitudes was it different?
■ In what ways does Victorian painting symbolize nineteenth-century accomplishments or lack of accomplishments? What do its various directions tell us about life in nineteenth-century England?
■ Is it possible to trace in outline the changes in the role of the artist by examining the subject matter of the great paintings of the nineteenth century?
■ How would you compare the achievements of composers in the nineteenth century with those of composers in the eighteenth?

12.53 Richard Dadd, *The Fairy Feller's Master Stroke*, 1855–64. Oil on canvas, 21¼ × 15¼ins (54 × 38.5cm). The Tate Gallery, London.

CHAPTER THIRTEEN

THE TWENTIETH CENTURY

"Make it new" was the poet Ezra Pound's dictum, and the one constant in the arts of this turbulent and phenomenal century has been a seemingly inexhaustible quest for originality and freshness. Among the awesome contradictions of an age that has witnessed the worst and the best that humanity is capable of, our vision of ourselves and where we are going is as troublesome for us as it was for our Paleolithic ancestors. Under threat of being drowned out by the clamor of our machines, poisoned by our own waste, swamped by the inane, and extinguished by the wind of nuclear holocaust, we struggle to understand what it means to be human. It is in that spirit that we turn to the arts of the past as well as to that being created in our own time; for, as we strive from day to day coping with our finitude, it is there that we find the clues and pointers to our full potential as human beings.

13.1 Francis Bacon, *Study for Portrait on Folding Bed*, 1963. Oil on canvas, 78 × 58ins (198.1 × 147.3cm). The Tate Gallery, London.

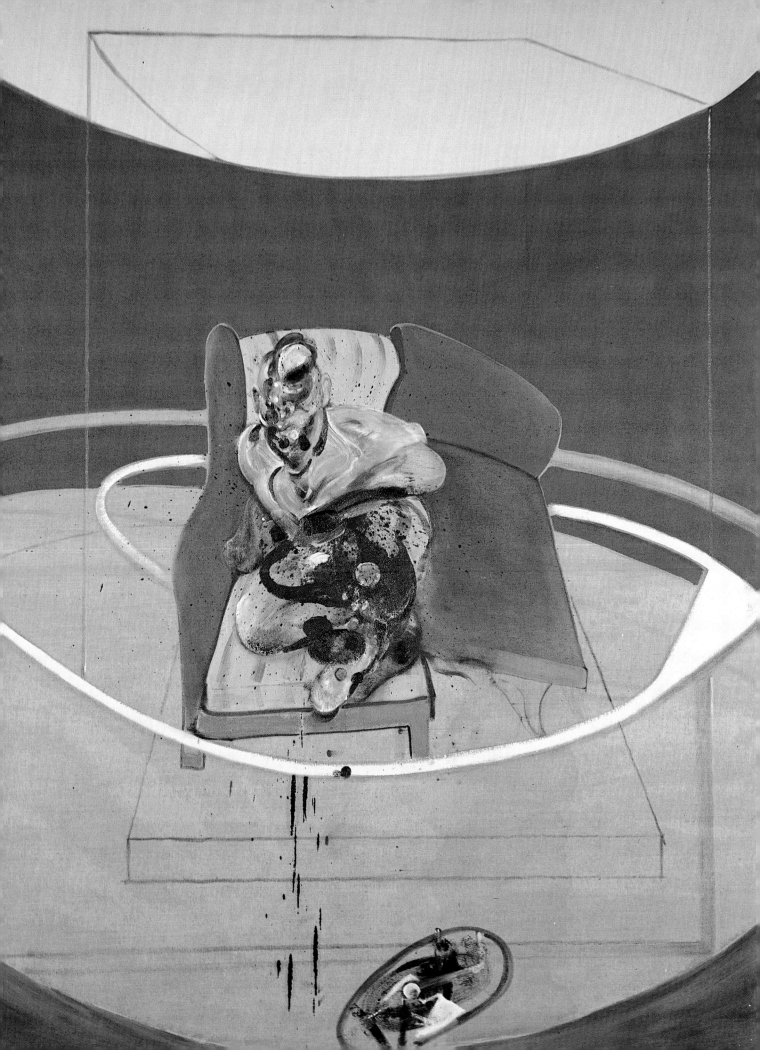

CONTEXTS AND CONCEPTS

How do we approach the world of our own century? Can we see it in a historical perspective, or are our observations obstructed like those of a tourist trying to gain a view of a large city while standing on a street corner surrounded by skyscrapers? Where does history end and first-hand personal involvement begin? How does one choose illustrations of trends and styles still in formation?

Such is the danger of attempting to bring history to one's own doorstep. Our century has produced more art than all the preceding centuries combined. Our society seems to crave works of art, and artistic expression permeates our existence. This final period is therefore difficult to deal with, but we shall try to be as objective as possible.

As Western culture approaches a new millennium the potential for cataclysmic demise hangs as heavily over us as it did over our predecessors of the tenth century. Our civilization has evolved from small, medieval beginnings to global commerce, economics, and government, and to global conflicts between Capitalism and Communism, Nationalism and Imperialism, and Christianity and innumerable other philosophies and religions.

Somewhere before 1914 Europe and the rest of the Western world seemed to go astray. Societies believed themselves headed toward the best that progress in science and invention could offer, and toward an era in which even competitive struggle would produce desirable, positive results. 1914 and the World War that defied logic changed all that.

Philosophy had lost credit in the nineteenth century. Compared to their former colleagues in the sciences, philosophers came to be regarded as a useless appendage to social progress. Greater and greater numbers of men and women began to believe that sensory and intellectual powers were not sufficient to solve the problems posed by philosophy. Although not entirely abandoned, philosophical questions, inherited from theology and relevant to humankind's relationship to the universe, slipped into irrelevance.

John Dewey

Early in the twentieth century a reorientation oc-

curred. Called pragmatism, a new philosophy emerged in America and found as its champion no less a figure than John Dewey (1859–1952). Vigorously defended and attacked, pragmatism frankly abandoned the search for final answers to great problems such as the nature of God and the existence of immortality. It contented itself with more modest goals stemming from social experience. Making use of scientific methodology, pragmatism pursued such issues as morals and aesthetic values in a democratic, industrialized society, and the means by which to achieve the highest personal fulfilment in education. Whether pragmatism is a philosophy or an adjunct of sociology, as some have claimed, and whether it can successfully address the problems it seeks to address must be judged by those of a later era.

Dewey's concept of "art as experience"—the title of his analysis of the aesthetic—is lengthy, but enlightening, challenging and sometimes frustrating. Experience is fundamental to Dewey's philosophy in all areas, but it appears most significant in his philosophy of aesthetics. Human experience, as interpreted by his aesthetics, presents a significant challenge to philosophy. According to Dewey the philosopher needs to go to aesthetic experience in order to understand experience in general. Only in aesthetic experience do we find experience "freed from the forces that impede and confuse its development as experience". Dewey is building on Hegel's concept of truth as a whole here. Dewey shares Schelling's belief that aesthetic intuition is "the organ of philosophy", that aesthetics is "the crown of philosophy". The following extract from *Art as Experience* is pertinent to our study.

> Every work of art has a particular medium by which, among other things, the qualitative pervasive whole is carried. In every experience we touch the world through some particular tentacle; we carry on our intercourse with it, it comes home to us, through a specialized organ. The entire organism with all its charge of the past and varied resources operates, but it operates through a particular medium, that of eye, as it interacts with eye, ear, and touch. The

	GENERAL EVENTS	LITERATURE & PHILOSOPHY	VISUAL ART	THEATRE & DANCE	MUSIC	ARCHITECTURE
1900	Triple Entente Balkan Wars Women's suffrage (USA) W.W. I Russian Revolution Treaty of Versailles S. Freud	John Dewey D.H. Lawrence J. Joyce	H. Matisse M. Beckmann De Chirico Rouault M. Duchamp Picasso J. Lipchitz G. Braque K. Malevich M. Ernst S. Davis F. Léger	I. Duncan C. Fitch A. Appia G. Craig S. Diaghilev W.V. Moody M. Reinhardt V. Nijinsky A. Strindberg M. Fokine E. Toller L. Pirandello E. Rice	I. Stravinsky A. Schoenberg Prokofiev F. Poulenc	A. Gaudí A. Perret C. Gilbert F.L. Wright
1925	A. Einstein Japanese Invasion of Manchuria W.W. II in Europe Pearl Harbor	A. Gide V. Woolf T.S. Eliot J. Dos Passos J. Steinbeck	Boccioni E. Barlach W. Zorach P. Mondrian S. Dali G. Wood J. Epstein H. Moore	V. Meyerhold E. O'Neill R. St. Denis D. Humphrey C. Odets G. Balanchine M. Anderson M. Graham	M. Ravel E. Satie B. Bartok C. Ives A. Copland W. Schuman	W. Gropius P. Behrens Le Corbusier
1945	Hiroshima Korean conflict Sputnik Vietnam War Martin Luther King	S. Kierkegaard J-P. Sartre A. Camus B. Pasternak	C. Brancusi J. Pollock W. de Kooning M. Rothko A. Giacometti Vasarely R. Lichtenstein F. Stella W. Calder	B. Brecht J. Limon M. Frisch J-P. Sartre A. Camus S. Beckett A. Miller E. Ionesco H. Pinter M. Cunningham E. Albee	P. Hindemith M. Babbitt B. Britten P. Boulez K. Stockhausen M. Davis V. Persichetti E. Carter L. Foss	G. Bunshaft M. van der Rohe P. Johnson P. Nervi R.B. Fuller
1980		R. Bradbury	C. Close D. Smith I. Noguchi C. Oldenburg J. Dubuffet G. Segal D. Hanson Christo	J. Cage L. Bernstein N.J. Paik	T. Williams P. Taylor D.L. Coburn J. Pielmeier B. Henley J. Waring	I.M. Pei

13.2 Timeline of the twentieth century.

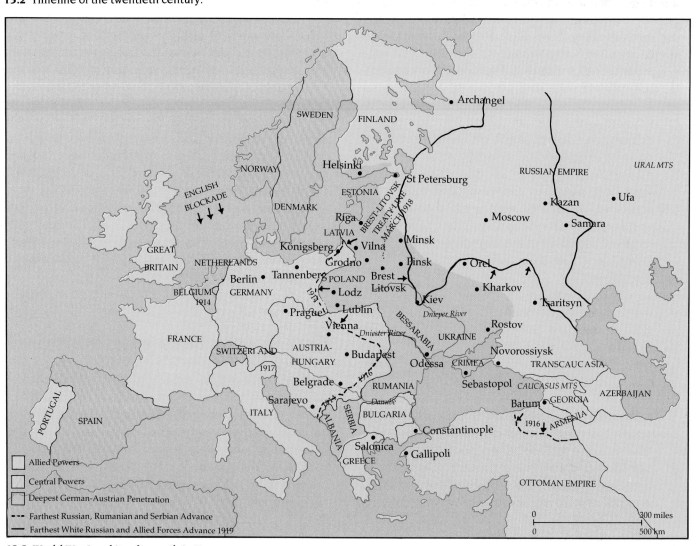

Allied Powers
Central Powers
Deepest German-Austrian Penetration
- - - Farthest Russian, Rumanian and Serbian Advance
—— Farthest White Russian and Allied Forces Advance 1919

13.3 World War I and its aftermath in Europe.

fine arts lay hold of this fact and push it to its maximum of significance. In any ordinary visual perception, we see by means of light; we distinguish by means of reflected and refracted colors: that is a truism. But in ordinary perceptions, this medium of color is mixed, adulterated. While we see, we also hear; we feel pressures, and heat or cold. In a painting, color renders the scene without these alloys and impurities. They are part of the dross that is squeezed out and left behind in an act of intensified expression. The medium becomes color alone, and since color alone must now carry the qualities of movement, touch, sound, etc., that are present physically on their own account in ordinary vision, the expressiveness and energy of color are enhanced.

Photographs to primitive folk have, so it is said, a fearful magical quality. It is uncanny that solid and living things should be thus presented. There is evidence that when pictures of any kind first made their appearance, magical power was imputed to them. Their power of representation could come only from a supernatural source. To one who is not rendered callous by common contact with pictorial representations there is still something miraculous in the power of a contracted, flat, uniform thing to depict the wide and diversified universe of animate and inanimate things: it is possibly for this reason that popularly "art" tends to denote painting, and "artist" one who paints. Primitive man also imputed to sounds when used as words the power to control supernaturally the acts and secrets of men and to command, provided the right word was there, the forces of nature. The power of mere sounds to express in literature all events and objects is equally marvelous.

Such facts as these seem to me to suggest the role and significance of media for art. At first sight, it seems a fact not worth recording that every art has a medium of its own. Why put it down in black and white that painting cannot exist without color, music without sound, architecture without stone and wood, statuary without marble and bronze, literature without words, dancing without the living body? The answer has, I believe, been indicated. In every experience, there is the pervading underlying qualitative whole that corresponds to and manifests the whole organization of activities which

constitute the mysterious human frame. But in every experience, this complex, this differentiated and recording, mechanism operates through special structures that take the lead, not in dispersed diffusion through all organs at once—save in panic when, as we truly say, one has lost one's *head*. "Medium" in fine art denotes the fact that this specialization and individualization of a particular organ of experience is carried to the point wherein all its possibilities are exploited. The eye or ear that is centrally active does not lose its specific character and its special fitness as the bearer of an experience that it uniquely makes possible. In art, the seeing or hearing that is dispersed and mixed in ordinary perceptions is concentrated until the peculiar office of the special medium operates with full energy, free from distraction. . . .

Fine art is sometimes defined as power to create illusions. As far as I can see this statement is a decidedly unintelligent and misleading way of stating a truth—namely, that artists create effects by command of a single medium. In ordinary perception we depend upon contribution from a variety of sources for our understanding of the meaning of what we are undergoing. The artistic use of a medium signifies that irrelevant aids are excluded and one sense quality is concentratedly and intensely used to do the work usually done loosely with the aid of many. But to call the result an illusion is to mix matters that should be distinguished. If measure of artistic merit were ability to paint a fly on a peach so that we are moved to brush it off or grapes on a canvas so that birds come to peck at them, a scare-crow would be a work of consummate fine-art when it succeeds at keeping away the crows.[1]

Carl Gustav Jung and intuition

The idea that artistic creativity goes to the root of our humanity has been expressed in various ways in the twentieth century. The theatre designer, Robert Edmund Jones, makes the connection between imagination and dreams in his book *The Dramatic Imagination*. His concepts were closely related to the concept of intuition propounded by Carl Jung (1875–1961). Jones sees the theatre as a place that deals with magic, not logic. The supernormal is normal, the imagination is the source of creativity, and imagination is "a special faculty ... by means of which we can form mental images of things not present in our senses". He cautions, however, that "Many people confuse imagination with ingenuity, with inventiveness. But imagination is not this thing at all. It is the power of seeing with the eye of the mind."

[Prior to Jung] various theorists had explored the role of imagination or intuition in creation. Friedrich Schelling in *The System of Transcendental Idealism* (1800) identified the phenomena of the imagination in terms of a half-metaphysical, half-psychological conception of artistic creativity. Samuel Taylor Coleridge then separated imagination and fancy, attributing to the former the transforming quality that Jung considered essential to intuition [*Biographia Literaria*, p. 167]. Early in the twentieth century Benedetto Croce differentiated between "intuitive knowledge" and "logical knowledge", the former "obtained through the imagination" and the latter "through the intellect", and proposed his central formula that "to intuit is to express". Henri Bergson contrasted intelligence with instinct and defined "intuition" as "instinct that has become disinterested, self-conscious, capable of reflecting upon its object and of enlarging it indefinitely".[2]

Jung, on the other hand, developed a working concept of intuition, which was "a function separate from thinking, feeling, and sensation which was characterized by the ability to see connections between things and find the potential inherent in a situation. ... [it was] an active creative process".[3] In *The Spirit in Man, Art, and Literature*, Jung describes intuition as "the source of [the artist's] creativeness". For Jung the universal unconscious related directly to art. There was a universal, as well as individual, unconscious in which lay a reservoir of primordial images upon which every individual could draw, but by which artists were especially influenced. "The creative urge lives and grows in him like a tree in the earth from which it draws nourishment. We would do well, therefore, to think of the creative process as a living thing implanted in the human psyche."

The creative process was the unconscious expression of archetypal images, that is, the characteristic in the unconscious which causes psychic material to be expressed in similar images and patterns throughout history (see C. G. Jung, *Man and His Symbols*).

Whether or not we wish to subscribe to Jung's concept of creativity, our intuitive or right brain function certainly seems to suggest that the very essence of being human contains the urge to create artistically and that qualities of banality, naïveté, sophistication or profundity can be applied to both technique and meaning in an artistic product. That is why we can find in some art, regardless of its age, superb craftsmanship which says nothing. In other art, profound meaning can be naïvely expressed. In yet other art, some of which dates to the earliest history of humankind, we find profound expression and superb craftsmanship.

Science and society

Science in the twentieth century has formulated and reformulated a series of fundamental concepts. Quantum Theory, the Theory of Relativity, and atomic theory are unique to our age. In Quantum Theory the German physicist Planck upset previous belief by suggesting that energy was released in spurts of small units called "quanta". Albert Einstein (1879–1955) overturned the physics of Newton by suggesting that the absolutes of space, time, and length, were not absolute, but, rather, relative. (In 1982 some researchers suggested that Einstein was in error and that the Theory of Relativity required re-examination). Atomic theory finally reduced the universe to units smaller than the atom—to positively and negatively charged particles, thereby revising previously held concepts about matter itself. The very creation of life has come within the possibility of twentieth-century science. Is Man, after all, the measure of all things?

Scientific methodology was applied also in the social sciences in the hope that organized approaches could yield the same precision and validity in concerns relating to humankind and society as occurred in studies of nature. Great bodies of data were amassed in attempts to understand economics, government, social classes, primitive cultures, and so on. Conclusions derived from social-scientific fact finding remain to be fully drawn.

Undoubtedly the most significant development in the social sciences, and one which had profound influence on the arts, occurred in psychology. Probes into the deep recesses of the human mind through psychoanalysis became dogma in the findings of Sigmund Freud (1856–1939). Variations on Freud, such as those of Jung, increased the popularity of psychoanalysis and gave birth to modern psychiatry. Earlier, John Watson argued that man was a machine operating in a stimulus and response environment. Watson's, as well as B. F. Skinner's behaviorism continues to enjoy credence as the millennium draws to a close.

Politics and war

As enticing as it may be, and as necessary to the consistent pattern of these chapters, an examination of the politics and economics of the twentieth century seems superfluous. I hope the century in which we live has enough intrinsic appeal and direct relationship to our daily existence for even the most phlegmatic of individuals to have taken the trouble to learn about it. Nevertheless, a few words are in order.

In the late nineteenth century, capitalism, colonialism, and competition for survival and expanding marketplaces left Europe in a state of fear of itself. The sun never set on the British Empire, and the Indian Ocean was called a British Lake. Every European nation maintained armed forces the equal of which the world had never seen. As many as three years of compulsory military service for young men was a general rule—not the exception. Behind burgeoning armies stood millions of reserves among the general population. Few wanted war, but it seemed that everyone expected war to come. European nations banded together in rival political alliances. The Triple Alliance of Germany, Austria-Hungary, and Italy was countered in 1907 by the formation of the Triple Entente of England, France, and Russia. The Balkan Wars of 1912–13 ignited the conflagration, which, upon the pretext of the assassination of the Austrian Archduke Franz Ferdinand, burst into world war.

The causes, the conflict, and the casualties of this catastrophe defy logic, and the resolution of affairs in the Treaty of Versailles (1919) served only to set the Western world on a course toward chaos. The treaty was supposed to protect Europe from Germany. It failed miserably to do so.

European society changed significantly as a result of the war. Capitalism in particular took a new direction. *Laissez-faire* liberalism had been prominent in nineteenth-century politics, but even before the war governments had begun increasingly to intervene in economic and other affairs. Governments erected tariffs, protected national industries, created colonial markets, and passed protective social legislation. The First World War made governmental control of nearly every aspect of society imperative. After the war the Western world experienced disruption of monetary traditions, inflation, taxes, and chaotic industrial output.

Between the Wars

Equally significant in the development of twentieth-century politics was the Russian Revolution. Boiling forth from a combination of old and new causes, the revolution shook Russia first in 1905 and then again in 1917 when Lenin came to power. This was followed by a bloody civil war in 1918, which lasted until 1922. When Lenin died in 1924, the communist die was cast. Stalin sent Russia through five-year plans and purges and established an adversarial struggle with the West that continues today, with only an uneasy abatement during World War II.

The years after World War I were troubled ones. Even the victors encountered difficulty in returning to peacetime conditions. Nonetheless, distinct advances in social democracy came out of it. Women now held the vote in Britain, Germany, the United States (as of 1913), and most of the smaller states of Europe. Social legislation proliferated. An eight-hour legal working day became common, as did government-sponsored insurance. All the participating nations suffered varying degrees of difficulty in economic, industrial and agricultural spheres. Inflation was rampant and credit was overextended. The Western economic system walked a delicate tightrope.

The 1920s was a decade of contrast. Struggling in its early years, the twenties experienced an apparent burst of prosperity. The mood was euphoric. But in 1929 came the economic crash, which sent the entire Western world into the deepest economic crisis it had ever known. Industry and agriculture collapsed.

Out of the crisis of the thirties came the forces that shaped World War II. The United States was offered a "New Deal" by Roosevelt. Britain and France struggled through trial and error to adjust their economies and institutions. Weak governments

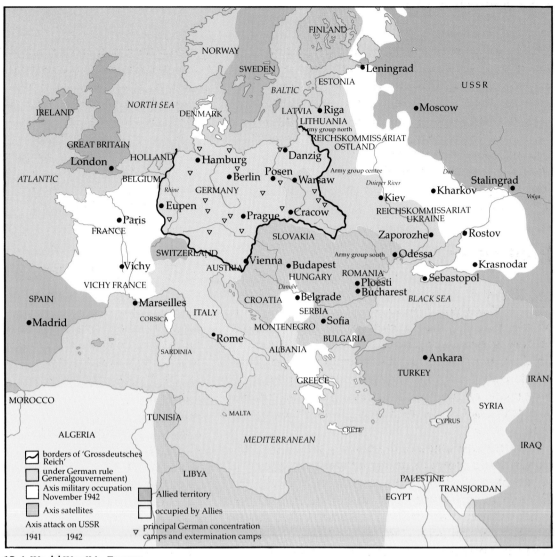

13.4 World War II in Europe.

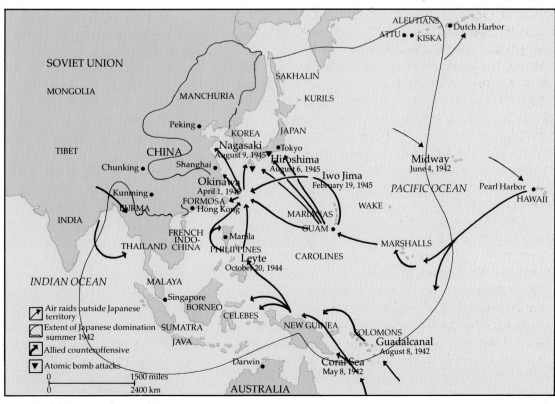

13.5 World War II in the Pacific.

in Germany and Italy capitulated to the totalitarianism of Hitler and Mussolini. Dictatorship and totalitarianism were not isolated occurrences. By 1939 only ten out of twenty-seven European countries remained democratic.

In the 1930s neither Germany, Italy, Russia, nor Japan was satisfied with the peace treaty that had ended World War I. Furthermore those countries which had instituted the peace were either too weak or unwilling to enforce it. From 1931 (when Japan invaded Manchuria) onward, Great Britain, France, and the United States stood aside and watched the boundaries they had established fall one after another. By 1939 Europe was fully at war, and three years later when Japan attacked Pearl Harbor, the entire world was again engulfed by hostilities.

On 6 August 1945 a nuclear explosion over the city of Hiroshima in Japan forever altered the state of the world and humankind's relationship to it. An old order had disappeared, and the approaching millennium was overshadowed by a specter even more discomforting than its predecessor in the tenth century.

Toward another millennium

The second half of the twentieth century is now well past its halfway point. The events of this era are well within the direct experience of my lifetime, and my perception is therefore journalistic rather than historical. Societies exist in a global environment in which the actions of even the smallest nation can have universal ramifications, often well beyond the importance of the original cause.

The optimism of democracy's victory over totalitarianism in World War II has been replaced by a more realistic, if less positive, appreciation of social inequities within democracy itself and with the struggle between capitalism and international communism. The peace of the late forties gave way to numerous regional conflicts, such as the Korean War (called by the United Nations a "police action"), the Arab-Israeli conflicts, the Vietnam conflict, and incessant Latin American struggles. The idealism of individual liberty has been forced to face the need for societal rights, and the question of where one ends and the other begins remains one of the most taxing problems of the era.

Elsewhere, multinational corporations rule the business world, and test-tube fertilization and DNA modification are scientific realities. Mechanization has assumed universal proportions, and computer-generated conclusions threaten to replace human reason as the source of problem solving. Technocrats threaten to rule a world of individuals whose education, if any, has consisted solely of job training. Philosophy in many quarters is considered unproductive speculation, and usefulness alone has become the touchstone of value. Many of our contemporaries have progressed to the point that they, like Oscar Wilde's cynic, "know the price of everything and the value of nothing".

Literature

Between 1914 and 1939 the novel came to the fore as a literary medium. As perhaps we have concluded from our survey of the inter-war period, it was a time of economic, moral, and intellectual chaos. The material with which writers had to deal was so complex that they needed a literary form capable of handling a multitude of ideas and experiences. They found that form in the novel: "A fiction in prose of a certain extent" as the French critic Abel Chevally and, later, the writer E. M. Forster called it. The novel became a catch-all form which replaced tighter mediums of expression such as the drama, the essay, and the epic poem. Improving standards of education created a new public which was receptive only to fiction in novel form. In an age of revolt against discipline and rigidity, the novel seemed immune to rules and restrictions.

As a result, subject matter was enriched and so was technique. Modern novelists challenged traditional methods of novel-writing, and attacked traditional concepts of time and space. Edouard, a character in the *Counterfeiters* (1925) by André Gide, says: "My novel hasn't got a subject . . . 'slice of life', the naturalistic school used to say. The great defect of that school is that it always cuts its slice in the same direction; in time, lengthwise. Why not in breadth? Or in depth? As for me I should not like to cut it at all. Police notwithstanding, I should like to put everything in my novel."

The inter-war period produced an Irish novelist of extraordinary quality, James Joyce (1882–1941). "Putting everything in my novel" could be used to describe Joyce's approach to *Ulysses*. In this particular case the police (as Edouard had said) were notwithstanding. The serial publication of *Ulysses* in the United States was stopped by the American courts, and although the finished work appeared in Paris in 1922, it was banned by the British authorities until 1941. Using methods often new to fiction, Joyce reveals in *Ulysses* actions and thoughts in great detail. The whole novel is the account of a single day in the life of Leopold Bloom. While the overall form is epic, virtually all other conventions of the novel are broken down, parodied, and recombined in extraordinary ways. Joyce also explored the unconscious mind in great depth in *Finnegans Wake* (1939), a work of dazzling originality and difficulty in which the English language is replaced by a polyglot punning.

The novels of D. H. Lawrence (1885–1930), such as *Women in Love*, were more traditional in technique, and his rejection of contemporary mass culture and the materialistic society that produced it, together with his messianic faith in all things "natural", links him strongly with the romantics of the nineteenth century. The novels and short stories of Virginia Woolf (1882–1941) painstakingly explore the inner landscape of feeling and emotion. In Germany, Thomas Mann (1875–1955), in his masterpiece, *The Magic Mountain*, created a richly symbolic picture of the fatal contradictions in European intellectual life between the wars. What all these writers had in common was a sense of dissatisfaction with, and alienation from, the values of their time and society. In America powerful, vital novels of social realism began to appear, making this an exciting period in American literature. Writers of these novels included John Dos Pasos, Thomas Wolfe and John Steinbeck.

Bold new directions were taken in poetry. T. S. Eliot's (1888–1965) most famous work, *The Waste Land* (1922) marked the full emergence of modernism in poetry as the traditional tools of meter and rhyme were cast aside. This new kind of writing needed to be read with great care if it was to make any sense at all. The *Cantos* of Ezra Pound took this tendency even further. Not all poets, however, chose to respond to the confusing complexity of their times by pursuing this strenuous route. W. H. Auden (1907–73) reflected the mood of the 1930s in a quite different way, with epigrammatic and satirical poetry that harked back to Alexander Pope.

Since World War II literature has, like the arts, taken many directions and developed many styles, particularly in America. Scanning the contents of Kiernan's *American Writing Since 1945* and Hoffman's *Harvard Guide to Contemporary American Writing* will give an impression of the enormous diversity. In fiction we find naturalism and realism, novels of manners, Southern fiction, Jewish fiction, Black fiction, Western fiction, the Beats, and Metafiction. In poetry we find formalist/academic poets, Black Mountainists, San Francisco/Beats, Confessionalists, the New York poets, Deep Imagists, Black poets and the Independents.

In literature, "schools, movements, and ideologies have not only proliferated but fragmented in the last decades, with a restlessness born of a nagging dissatisfaction with the reigning modes."[4] Modernism versus Romanticism is a continuing battle. Whether we turn to Hemingway (1899–1961), James T. Farrell (1904–1979), Sinclair Lewis (1885–1951), Gore Vidal, Norman Mailer, John Gardner, John Cleever, William Faulkner (1897–1962), Kenneth Rexroth (1905–1982), or Alan Ginsberg, to scratch only the surface, American literature provides a deep well of sources exploring our humanity and our vision of reality.

THE ARTS
OF THE TWENTIETH CENTURY

Two-Dimensional Art

The first half of the twentieth century exploded with new styles and approaches to the visual arts, including expressionism, fauvism, cubism, abstract art, dada, and surrealism.

Expressionism

Expressionism traditionally refers to a movement in Germany between 1905 and 1930, but its broad applications include a variety of specific approaches, essentially in Europe, that focused on a joint artist/respondent reaction to composition elements. Any element (line, form, color, and so on) could be emphasized to elicit a specific response in the viewer. The artist would consciously try to stimulate a response that had a specific

13.6 Max Beckmann, *Christ and the Woman Taken in Adultery*, 1917. Oil on canvas, 58¾ × 49⅞ins (149.2 × 126.7cm). The Saint Louis Art Museum (Bequest of Curt Valentin).

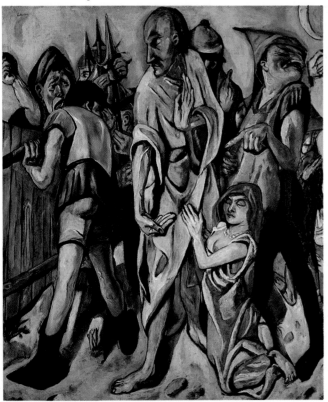

relationship to his or her feelings about or commitment to the subject matter. Subject matter itself mattered little; what counted was the artist's attempt to evoke in the viewer a similar response to his or her own. In Max Beckman's *Christ and the Woman Taken in Adultery* (Fig. **13.6**), the artist's revulsion against physical cruelty and suffering is transmitted through distorted figures crushed into shallow space. Linear distortion, changes of scale and perspective, and a nearly Gothic spiritualism communicate Beckman's reactions to the horrors of World War I. In this approach, meaning relies on very specific non-verbal communication.

Fauvism

Closely associated with the development of the expressionist movement were the *fauves* (wild beasts). The label was applied by a critic in response to a sculpture (exhibited in 1905), which seemed to him "a Donatello in a cage of wild beasts". Violent distortion and outrageous coloring mark the subjective expression of the fauves. Their two-dimensional surfaces and flat color areas were new to European painting. The best-known artist of this short-lived movement was Henri Matisse (1869–1954). Other fauves included Albert Marquet, Raoul Dufy, Othon Friesz, André Derain, and Maurice de Vlaminck. Matisse tried to paint pictures that would "unravel the tensions of modern existence". In his old age he made a series of very joyful designs for the Chapel of the Rosary at Vence, not as exercises in religious art, but, rather, to express the joy and nearly religious feeling he had for life. *The Blue Nude* (Fig. **13.7**) illustrates the wild coloring and distortion of Matisse and fauvism. The painting takes its name from the energetically applied blues, which occur throughout the figure as darkened accents. For Matisse color and line were indivisible, and the bold strokes of color in his work comprise coloristic and linear stimulants, as well as revelations of form. Matisse literally "drew with color". Underlying this work, and illustrative of the fauves' relationship to expressionism, is Matisse's desire, not to draw a nude as he saw it in life, but rather to express his feelings about the nude as an object of aesthetic interest. Expressionism was very diverse and was associated with a number of trends, including the Bridge and Blue Rider groups and artists such as Kandinsky, Rouault, Corinth, Kollwitz, Marce, Klimt, and Kokoschka.

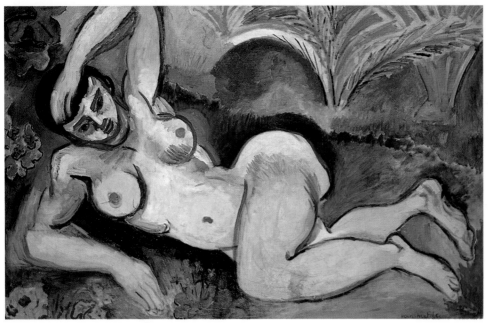

13.7 Henri Matisse, *Blue Nude* (*"Souvenir de Biskra"*), 1907. Oil on canvas, 36¼ × 55¼ins (92.1 × 140.4cm). The Baltimore Museum of Art (The Cone Collection, formed by Dr. Claribel Cone and Miss Etta Cone of Baltimore, Maryland).

13.8 Pablo Picasso, *Les Demoiselles d'Avignon*, 1907. Oil on canvas, 8ft × 7ft 8ins (244 × 234cm). The Museum of Modern Art, New York (acquired through the Lillie P. Bliss Bequest).

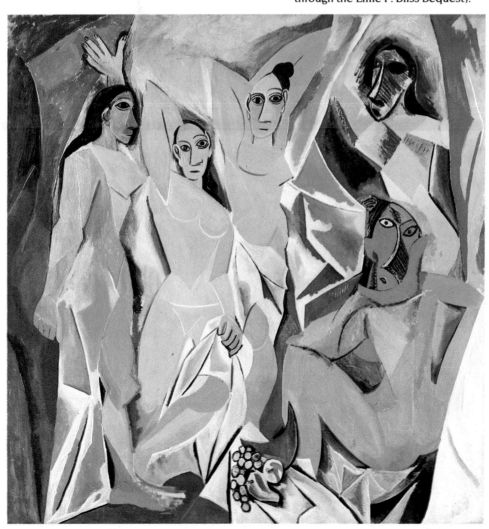

Cubism

Between 1901 and 1912 an entirely new approach to pictorial space emerged to which the term cubism was applied. Cubist space violates all concepts of two- or three-dimensional perspective. In the past the space within a composition had been thought of as separate from the main object of the work. That is, if the subject were removed, the space would remain, unaffected. Pablo Picasso (1881–1973) and Georges Braque (1882–1963) changed that relationship to one in which the artist tried to paint "not objects, but the space they engender". The area around an object became an extension of the object itself. If the object were removed, the space around it would collapse. Cubist space is typically quite shallow and gives the impression of reaching forward toward the viewer, thereby intruding into space outside of the frame. Essentially the style developed as the result of independent experiments of Braque and Picasso with various ways of describing form. Newly evolving notions of time-space continuum were being proposed by Albert Einstein at this time. We cannot be sure whether the Theory of Relativity influenced Picasso and Braque, but it certainly helped to make their works more acceptable. The results of those experiments brought them to remarkably similar conclusions. Picasso's *Demoiselles d'Avignon* (Fig. **13.8**) illustrates concern for spatial construction, expressive powers, and formal properties, especially in the exaggeration of certain features of the face, head, and body. These exaggerations resulted from Picasso's interest in primitive African sculpture, which showed similar distortions. The *Demoiselles* portrays an aggressive and harsh expression. Forms are simplified and angular, and colors are restricted to blues, pinks, and terracottas. Cubism uniformly reduced its palette range to nearly monochromatic parameters, thereby allowing emphasis to fall on spatial exploration, without the distraction of other elements.

Braque (1882–1963) showed similar concerns for spatial construction, and reduced objects to geometric shapes. It was in response to Braque's geometric forms

13.9 Fernand Léger, *Three Women*, 1921. Oil on canvas, 6ft 1¼ins × 8ft 3ins (183.5 × 251.5cm). The Museum of Modern Art, New York (Mrs. Simon Guggenheim Fund).

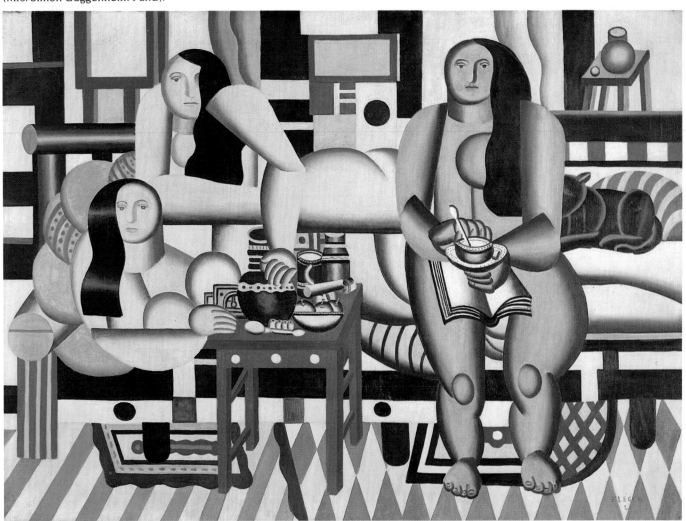

that the term cubist was first applied. Unfortunately, such a term has led many observers to look for opaque cubical shapes rather than for a new kind of space "which was only visible when solid forms became transparent and lost their rigid cubical contours".[4]

The complexities of cubism, of course, go beyond these brief remarks. Diverse subject matter, disciplinary experiments (for example, collage), evolving depiction, and applications such as those of Fernand Léger (1881–1955) (Fig. **13.9**), Juan Gris, and numerous others, carried cubism throughout the first half of the twentieth century. The cubists had a brief association with a movement in Italy called futurism, which denounced contemporary culture and sought more adequately to express and reflect the mechanistic and dynamic qualities of twentieth-century life. Balla, Severini, Boccioni, Carrà, and Russolo exemplify futurism in painting and in sculpture.

Abstraction

In the last chapter we used the words "dissolving image" to describe tendencies in visual art that appeared to be moving away from recognizable or objective reality. Undoubtedly the approach most recognizable or most illustrative of what many people would call modern art is abstract art. A more precise term would be non-representational art. All art is abstract, that is, an abstraction of, or standing apart from, the object it purports to reveal. Paintings, sculptures, plays and symphonies all are abstractions regardless of the degree of verisimilitude they contain. However, abstract or non-representational art contains minimal reference to natural objects, that is, objects in the phenomenal or natural world (see paragraphs on philosophy in Chapter Twelve). In many ways abstract art stands in contrast to impressionism and expressionism in that the observer can read little or nothing in the painting of the artist's feelings about any aspect of the universe. Abstract art seeks to explore the expressive qualities of formal design elements in their own right. These elements are assumed to stand apart from subject matter. The aesthetic theory underlying abstract art maintains that beauty can exist in form alone, and no other quality is needed. Numerous painters have explored these approaches, among them Hölzel, Kandinsky, Gabo, Larionov, and Kupka. Several subgroups such as de Stijl, suprematists, constructivists, and the Bauhaus painters have pursued its goals. The works of Piet Mondrian and Kasimir Malevich illustrate many of the principles at issue in abstract painting.

Mondrian (1872–1944) believed that the fundamental principles of life consisted of straight lines and right angles. A vertical line signified active vitality and life, and a horizontal line signified tranquility, rest, and death. The crossing of the two in a right angle expressed the highest possible tension between these forces, positive and negative. *Composition in White, Black, and Red* (Figure **13.10**) explores Mondrian's philosophy in a manner characteristic of all his linear compositions. The planes of the painting are close to the surface of the canvas, creating, in essence, the thinnest space possible, in contrast to the deep space of other styles. The palette is restricted to three hues. Even the edges of the canvas take on

13.10 Piet Mondrian, *Composition in White, Black and Red*, 1936. Oil on canvas, 40¼ × 41ins (102 × 104cm). The Museum of Modern Art, New York (Gift of the Advisory Committee)

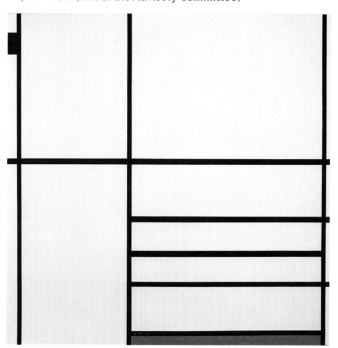

13.11 Kasimir Malevich, *Suprematist Composition: White on White*, c.1918. Oil on canvas, 31¼ × 31¼ins (79.4 × 79.4cm). The Museum of Modern Art, New York.

expressive possibilities as they provide additional points of interaction between lines. Mondrian believed that he could create "the equivalence of reality" and make the "absolute appear in the relativity of time and space" by keeping visual elements in a state of constant tension.

A movement within the non-representational tradition was suprematism, whose works puzzle many individuals. A work such as *White on White* (Fig. **13.11**) by Kasimir Malevich (1878–1935) seems simple and confusing even by abstract standards. For Malevich these works go beyond reducing art to its basic common denominator. Rather, he sought basic pictorial elements that could "communicate the most profound expressive reality".

Dada

The horrors of World War I caused tremendous disillusionment, and gave birth to a movement called dada. During the years 1915–16 numerous artists gathered in neutral capitals in Europe to express their disgust with the directions of all Western societies and, especially,

their cultures. Dada was a political protest. Considerable debate exists about when and how the word dada (the French word for hobby-horse) came to be chosen, but the dadaists themselves accepted the word as two nonsense syllables, like the first sounds uttered by a baby. In many places the dadaists produced more left-wing propaganda than they did art. By 1916 a few works began to appear. These comprised many experiments in which chance played an important factor. For example, Jean Arp produced collages constructed by dropping haphazardly cut pieces of paper onto a surface and pasting them as they fell. A large dadaist exhibit in 1920 featured the compositions of George Grosz, John Heartfield, and Raoul Hausman. Max Ernst (1891–1976), inspired by de Chirico,

13.12 Max Ernst, *Woman, Old Man and Flower*, 1923–24. Oil on canvas, 38 × 51¼ins (96.5 × 130.2cm). The Museum of Modern Art, New York.

13.13 Marcel Duchamp, *The Bride*, 1912. Oil on canvas, 35¼ × 21¾ins (89.5 × 55.3cm). Philadelphia Museum of Art (Louise and Walter Arensberg Collection).

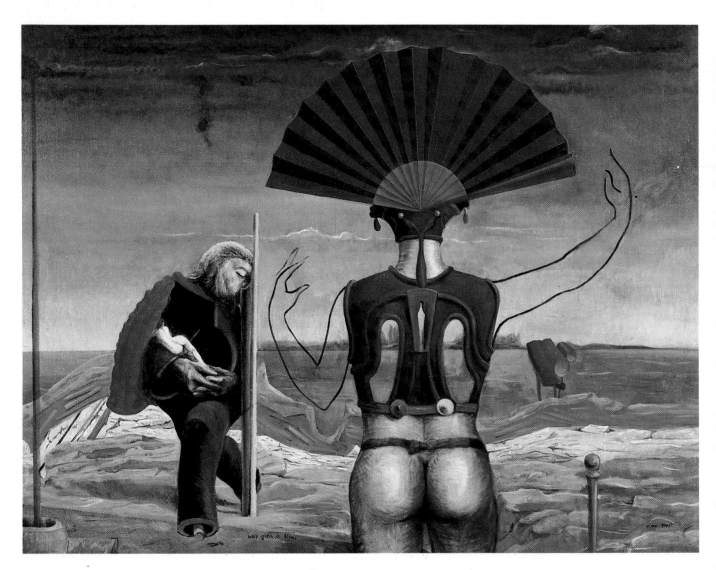

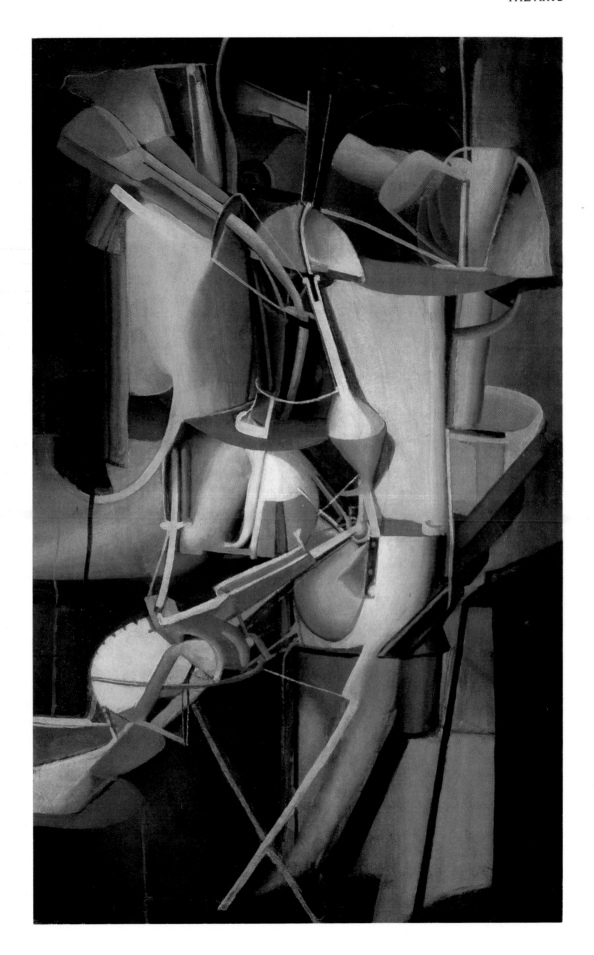

juxtaposed strange, unrelated items to produce unexplainable phenomena. Such usage of conventional items placed in circumstances that alter their traditional meanings is characteristic of dadaist art. Irrationality, meaningless malevolence, and harsh, mechanical effects are typical, as in Figure **13.12**.

Themes dealing with mechanism proved to be popular in the early twentieth century, as life became more and more dominated by machines. Mechanistic themes can be seen in the works of Marcel Duchamp (1887–1968), who often is associated with the dada movement and is sometimes called protodadaist, especially regarding his famous *Nude Descending a Staircase* (Philadelphia Museum of Art). The *Bride* (Fig. **13.13**) is a mechanistic diagram of contrasting male and female forces whose organs bear a striking resemblance to a flesh-colored internal-combustion engine. Duchamp apparently saw men and women as no more than machines. Human passion comprised the fuel on which men and women moved. Many of Duchamp's works exploit chance and accident.

Fascination with the subconscious mind, as popularized by the psychologist Sigmund Freud, stimulated explorations in psychic experience such as is found in the automatic writings of the poet Philippe Soupault. By 1924 a surrealist manifesto had developed and tied the subconscious mind to painting. "Pure psychic automatism" described surrealist works. Surrealism was seen by its advocates as a means for discovering the basic reality of psychic life through automatic association. A dream was supposedly capable of transference directly from the unconscious mind to canvas without control or conscious interruption by the artist.

Surrealism

The metaphysical fantasies of Giorgio de Chirico and Paul Klee have surrealist associations. The works of de Chirico (1888–1978), such as *Nostalgia* (Fig. **13.14**), contained no rational explanation for their juxtaposition of strange objects. They reflected a dream-like condition, how strange objects come together in a dream. These works are not rational and reflect a world humankind does not control. In them "there is only what I see with my eyes open, and even better, closed".

Surrealism is probably more accurately described by the paintings of Salvador Dali and Joan Miró, as well as by Magritte, Delvaux, Brauner, and some of the works of Ernst (especially the *frottages*—rubbings). Dali (b. 1904) called his works, such as the *Persistence of Memory* (Fig. **13.15**), "hand-colored photographs of the subconscious", and the high verisimilitude of this work coupled with its nightmarish relationships of objects makes a forceful impact. The whole idea of time is destroyed in these "wet watches" (as they were called by those who first saw this work) hanging limply and crawling with ants.

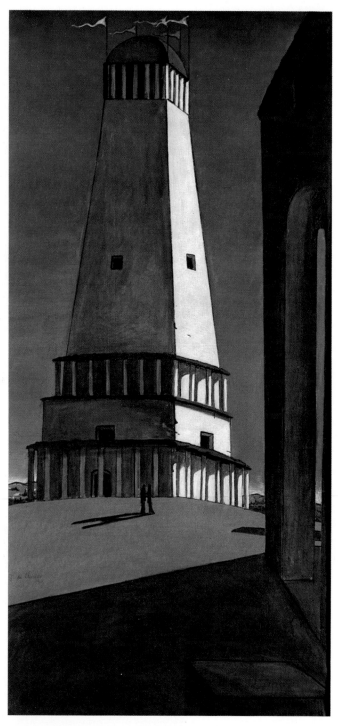

13.14 Giorgio de Chirico, *The Nostalgia of the Infinite*, c.1913–14, dated on painting 1911. Oil on canvas, 53¼ × 25½ins (135.2 × 64.8cm). The Museum of Modern Art, New York.

American painting

Until the early twentieth century, painting in the United States had been little more than a translation of European trends to the American experience. However, since the early twentieth century, a strong and vigorous Ameri-

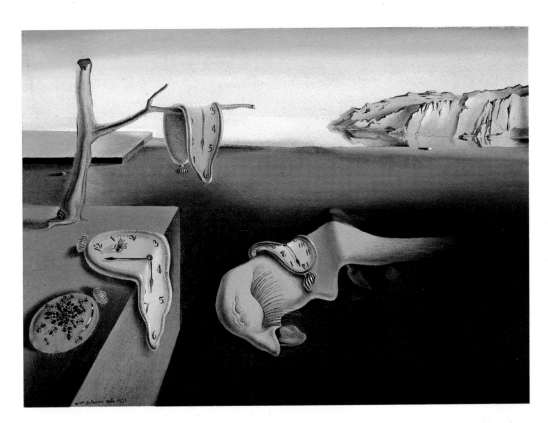

13.15 Salvador Dali, *The Persistence of Memory*, 1931. Oil on canvas, 9½ × 13ins (24 ×33cm). The Museum of Modern Art, New York.

13.16 Stuart Davis, *Lucky Strike*, 1921. 33¼ × 18ins (84.5 × 45.7cm). The Museum of Modern Art, New York (Gift of the American Tobacco Company, Inc.).

can painting has emerged. It encompasses many individuals and diverse styles and approaches. As usual, our discussion will be an overview with only a few examples.

An early group called the Eight emerged in 1908 as painters of the American "scene". These included Robert Henri, George Luks, John Sloan, William Glackens, Everett Shinn, Ernest Lawson, Maurice Prendergast, and Arthur B. Davies. They shared a warm and somewhat sentimental view of American city life and presented it both with and without social criticism. Although uniquely American in tone, the works of the Eight often revealed European influences, for example, impressionism in the works of Ernest Lawson. Modernism in America was effectively furthered in the aesthetically adventurous works of Arthur Davies and Maurice Prendergast.

The modern movement also owed much to the tremendous impact of the International Exhibition of Modern Art (called the Armory Show) in 1913, in which rather shocking European modernist works, such as Duchamp's *Nude Descending a Staircase* and the cubist work of Braque and Picasso, were first revealed to the American public. Following thereafter came Marsden Hartley, Arthur G. Dove, Alfred Maurer, John Marin, and Georgia O'Keeffe. Max Weber, a Russian-born Jew, brought an ethnic cultural heritage to American painting through works that explored and manipulated many of the current European styles such as cubism and fauvism.

Precisionists, such as Stuart Davis (1894–1964), took natural objects and arranged them into what amounts to abstract arrangements, as in *Lucky Strike* (Fig. **13.16**). Also characteristic of these paintings is a use of strong and

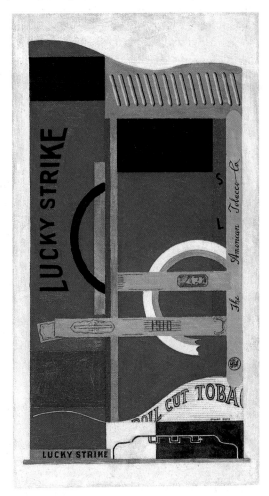

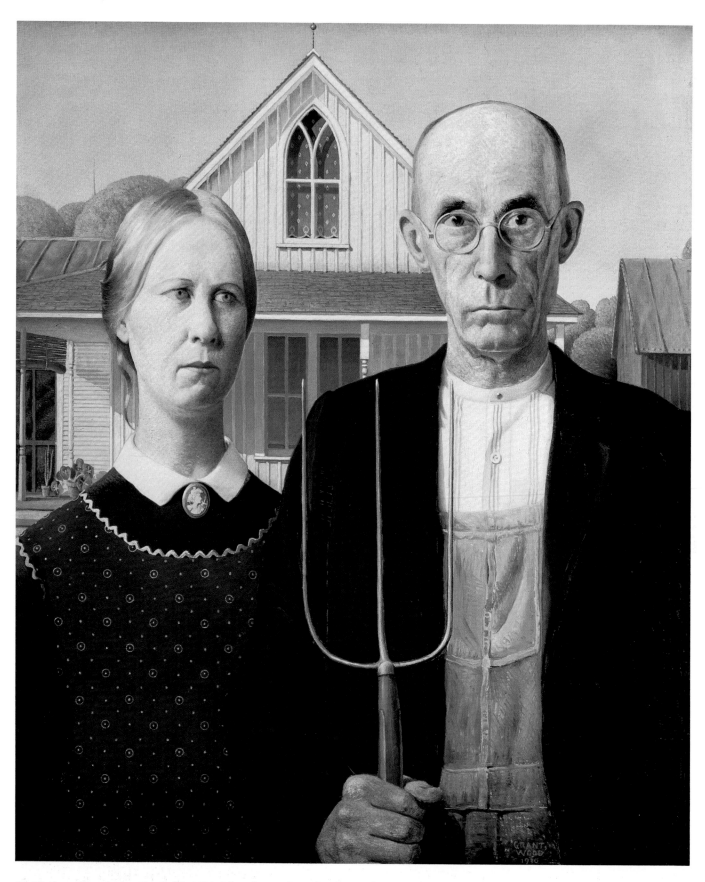

13.17 Grant Wood, *American Gothic*, 1930. Oil on beaver board, 29⅞ × 24⅞ins (79 × 63.2cm). Friends of American Art Collection, Courtesy of Art Institute of Chicago.

vibrant color appropriate to commercial art and much like the pop art of the 1960s.

Pictorial objectivity was continued in the realist tradition in the works of Edward Hopper, Reginald Marsh, Thomas Hart Benton, John Steuart Curry, and Grant Wood (1892–1942), as in his work *American Gothic* (Fig. **13.17**). The era closed to the frustrating tunes of the Depression and World War II. The Federal Arts Project of the Works Progress Administration (WPA) was established at this time and made a significant contribution to the arts, not because it produced great art but because it provided Federal funding and moral encouragement to artists and the arts.

Abstract expressionism

The first fifteen years following the end of World War II were dominated by a style called abstract expressionism. Beginning essentially in New York, abstract expressionism spread rapidly throughout the world on the wings of our modern mass-communication networks. Like most modern styles, which include great variation among individual artists, abstract expressionism is difficult to define in specific terms, although some scholars believe it to be self-explanatory. Two characteristics can be identified. One is a freedom from traditional use of brushwork, and the other is the exclusion of representational subject matter. Complete freedom of individual expression to reflect inner life gave rein to create works of high emotional and dynamic intensity. Absolute individual freedom of expression and freedom from rationality underlie this style. There appeared to be some relationship to the optimistic post-war feeling of individual freedom and conquest over totalitarianism. By the early 1960s, when life was less certain and the implications of the nuclear age had sunk in, abstract expressionism had all but ceased to exist.

The most heralded artist of this style was Jackson Pollock (1912–1956). A rebellious spirit, Pollock evolved this approach to painting only ten years before his death. Although he insisted that he had absolute control, his compositions consisted of what appeared to be totally unfettered dripping and spilling of paint on to huge canvases placed on the floor. His work (Fig. **13.18**), often called action painting, elicits a sense of tremendous energy, actually transmitting the action of paint application to the respondent through a new concept of line and form.

13.18 Jackson Pollock, N*umber* 1, 1948. Oil on canvas, 68 × 104ins (172.7 × 264.2cm). The Museum of Modern Art, New York.

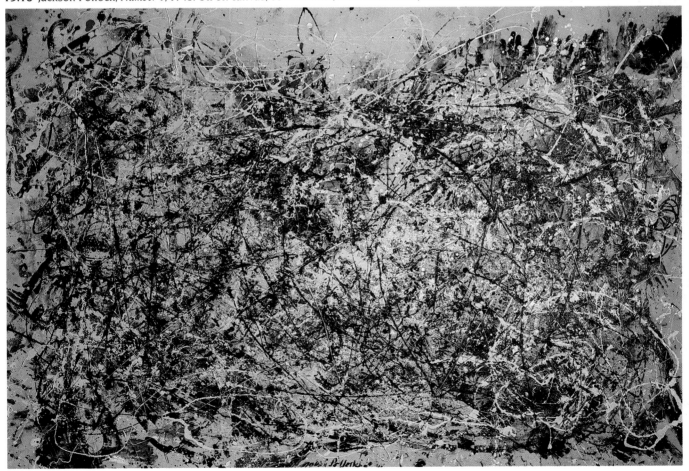

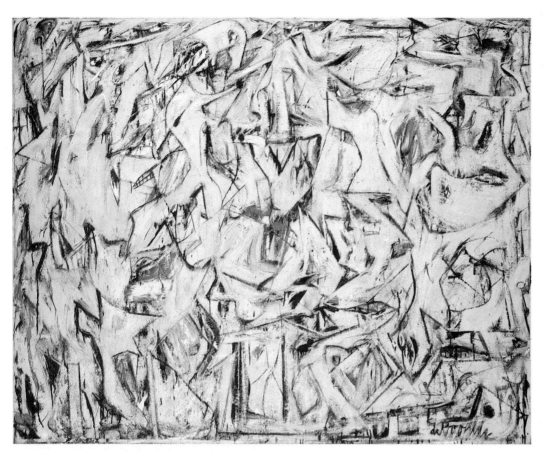

13.19 Willem de Kooning, *Excavation*, 1950. Oil on canvas, 80⅛ × 100⅛ins (203.5 × 254.3cm). Courtesy the Art Institute of Chicago (Collection Mr. and Mrs. F. C. Logan Prize, Gift of Mr. and Mrs. Edgar Kaufmann Jr. and Mr. and Mrs. Noah Goldowsky).

A different approach to abstract expressionism can be seen in the work of Willem de Kooning (b. 1904). Sophisticated texture and focal areas (Fig. **13.19**) emerged from de Kooning's practice of reworking, scraping off, repainting, and repainting again. Yet his laborious approach produced works that display spontaneity and free action. Underneath rest a ferocity and dynamic passion, which tend to build in intensity as the eye moves from one focal area to the next.

Included also among the abstract expressionists is the color-field painting of Mark Rothko (1903–70), whose highly individualistic paintings follow a process of reduction and simplification (Fig. **13.20**). He removed from his canvases all of "memory, history, and geometry". He referred to these as "obstacles between the painter and the idea". Rothko's works are intensely personal and appear to reflect an expression from deep within the mind of an extremely sensitive experience. Other abstract expressionists include Arshile Gorky, Hans Hoffman, Franz Kline, Clyford Still, Richard Diebenkorn, and Jean Dubuffet.

After, and in some instances as a reaction against, the emotionalism of abstract expressionism came an explosion of styles: pop art, op art, hard edge, minimal art, post-minimal art, environments, body art, earth art, video art, kinetic art, photo realism, and conceptual art. We have space to note, however briefly, only some of these.

Pop art

Pop art evolved in the 1950s, and concerned itself above all with image in a representational sense. Subjects and treatments in this style come from mass culture and commercial design. These sources provided pop artists with what they considered to be essential aspects of today's visual environment. The pop artists traced their heritage to dada, although much of the heritage of the pop tradition continues to be debated. However, pop is essentially an optimistic reflection of the contemporary scene. The term "pop" was coined by the English critic Lawrence Alloway and related to the images found in popular culture that marked this approach. Jasper Johns, Robert Rauschenberg, Robert Indiana, Andy Warhol, and James Rosenquist all illustrate the pop style, but probably the compelling depictions of Roy Lichtenstein (b. 1923) are the most familiar (Fig. **13.21**). These magnified cartoon-strip details use the Ben-Day screen of dots by which colored ink is applied to cheap newsprint. Using a stencil about the size of a coin, the image is built up into a stark and dynamic, if sometimes violent, portrayal.

Op art

Op art concerns itself with optics and perception. Emerging from the 1950s, op art was an intellectually oriented and systematic style, very scientific in its applications. Based on perceptual tricks, the misleading images of these paintings capture our curiosity and pull us into a conscious exploration of what the optical illusion does and why it does it. Victor Vasarély (b.1908) bends line and form to create a very deceiving sense of three-dimensionality. Complex sets of stimuli proceed from horizontal, vertical, and diagonal arrangements. Using nothing but abstract form, Vasarély creates the illusion of real space. Vasarély's lead was followed by other op artists, among whom Richard Anuzkiewicz is probably the most notable.

Hard edge

Hard edge or hard edged abstraction also came to its height during the 1950s. In this style, which the work of Ellsworth Kelly and Frank Stella best illustrate, flat color areas have hard edges which carefully separate them from each other. Essentially, hard edge is an exploration of design for its own sake. Stella abandoned the rectangular format in favor of irregular compositions to be sure his paintings had no relationship to windows. The shape of the canvas was part of the design itself, as opposed to being a frame or a formal border within which the design was executed. Some of Stella's paintings have iridescent metal powder mixed into the paint, and the metallic shine further enhances the precision of the composition.

Photo-realism and conceptualism

Photo-realism is an offshoot of pop art concerned with photographic images. Using photographic images as a

13.20 Mark Rothko, *Number* 10, 1950. Oil on canvas, 7ft 6⅜ins ×57⅛ins (229.6 × 145.1cm). The Museum of Modern Art, New York (Gift of Philip Johnson).

13.21 Roy Lichtenstein, *Whaam!*, 1963. Acrylic on canvas, 68 ×160ins (172.7 × 406.4cm). The Tate Gallery, London.

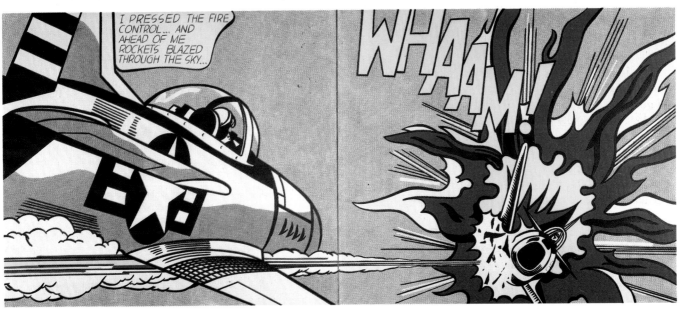

basis, photo-realist works are usually extremely complex. The works of Chuck Close are examples.

Finally, conceptual art challenges the relationship between art and life, and, in fact, the definition of art itself. Essentially anti-art, like dada, conceptual art attempts totally to divorce the imagination from aesthetics. It insists that only the imagination, not the art-work, is art. Therefore, artworks can be done away with. The creative process needs only to be documented by some incidental means such as a verbal description, a photograph, or a simple object like a chair. The paradoxes adhering to conceptual art are many, including its dependence on a physical something to bridge the gap between artist's conception and respondent's imagination.

SCULPTURE

Sculpture revived significantly in the twentieth century. Interest in cultures other than European (for example, African and Polynesian), in which sculpture played a dominant role, added new dimensions to the search for expressive elements owing nothing to the classically idealized human body. However, as if to illustrate that new styles do not replace old ones, classicism continued as a style as Figures **13.22** and **13.23** suggest. Maillol's *Air* creates parallels of arms and legs and a compelling gesture of the hand which is accentuated by the positions of the head and the supporting arm. The total composition elicits a severity which is exceptional in Maillol's work. The self-contained form and symbolic mythology of MacNeil's *Into the Unknown* again demonstrate a return to classical form and subject matter. Both Maillol and MacNeil focus on simplicity of form, clear line and structure, and maintain the intellectual appeal we have seen throughout history in works of the classical spirit.

Futurism

New concerns for space turned, logically, to three-dimensional space and the potential relationships it presented. Technological developments and new materials also encouraged the search for new forms characteristic of the age. Futurists in the visual arts searched for dynamic qualities, representative of the times (Fig. **13.24**), and believed that many of the new machines of the era had sculptural form. Some sculptures followed mechanistic lines and also included motion.

Expressionism and other departures

German expressionist themes were pursued in sculpture by Ernst Barlach (1870–1938). Man's loneliness and

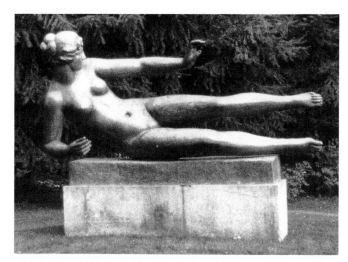

13.22 Aristide Maillol, *Air*, 1938–9. Lead, 55⅛ × 100¼ins (140 × 254.6cm).

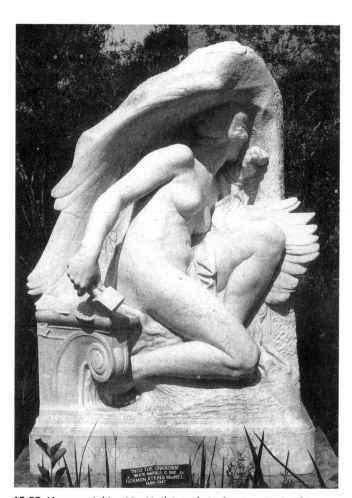

13.23 Hermon Atkins MacNeil, *Into the Unknown*, c.1912. White marble, c.48ins (120cm) high. Brookgreen Garden, South Carolina.

13.24 Umberto Boccioni, *Unique Forms of Continuity in Space*, 1913. Bronze (cast 1931), height 43⅞ins (111.2cm). The Museum of Modern Art, New York (acquired through the Lillie P. Bliss Bequest).

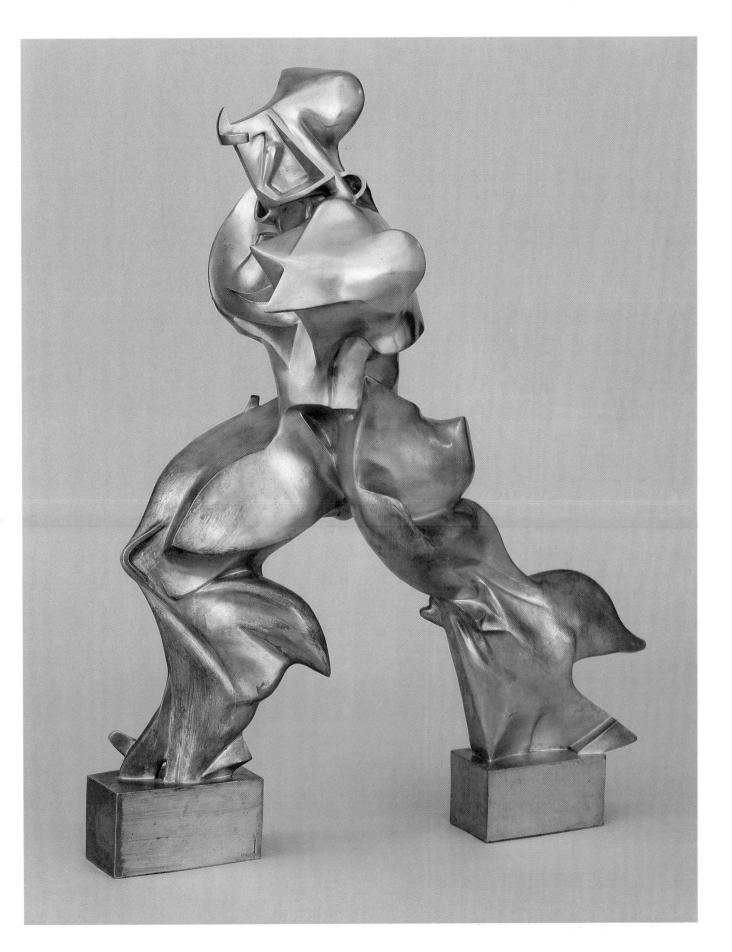

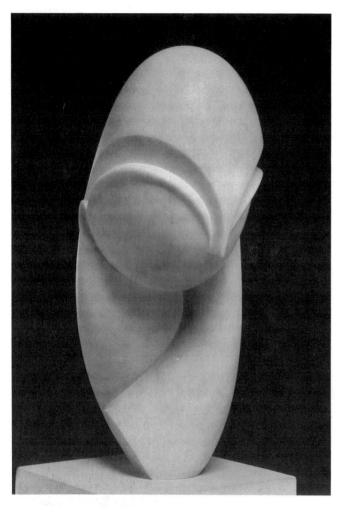

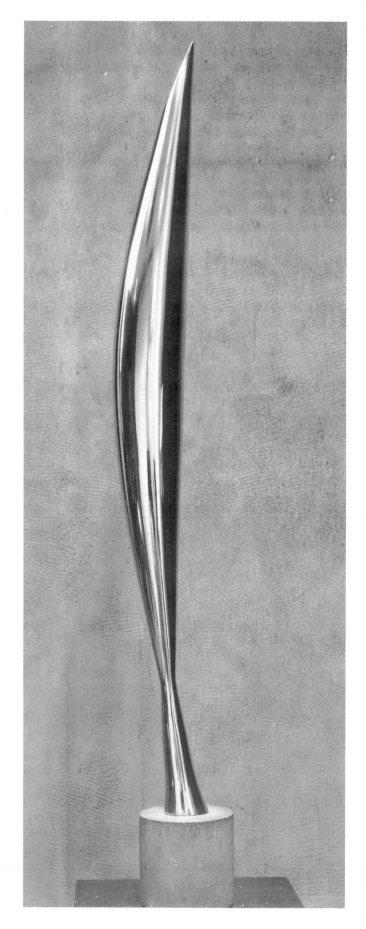

13.25 Constantin Brancusi, *Mlle. Pogany*, 1931. Marble on limestone base, height 19ins (48cm). Philadelphia Museum of Art (Louise and Walter Arensberg Collection).

13.26 Constantin Brancusi, *Bird in Space*, c.1928. Bronze (unique cast), height 54ins (137cm). The Museum of Modern Art, New York.

search for God formed much of the somber symbolism of Barlach's work. The direct influence of African art can be seen in the sculptures of Constantin Brancusi (1876–1957) (Fig. **13.25**). Yet beyond this, the smooth, precise surfaces of much of his work seem to have an abstract, mechanistic quality. Brancusi's search for essential form led to very economical presentations, often ovoid and simple, yet animate. Certainly, great psychological complexity exists in *Bird in Space* (Fig. **13.26**). Brancusi greatly influenced the works of the English sculptor Henry Moore (1898–1986), whose *Recumbent Figure* (Fig. **13.27**) carries forward the theme of figure depiction in a most untraditional manner. Primitive objects, especially the Chacmool figures of Mexico, appear repeatedly in his works. References to nature abound in these unique sculptural presentations which span the last forty years (Figs. **13.28** and **13.29**). African influence can also be seen in the work of Amedeo Modigliani (1884–1920) and Jacob Epstein (1880–1959) (Fig. **13.30**).

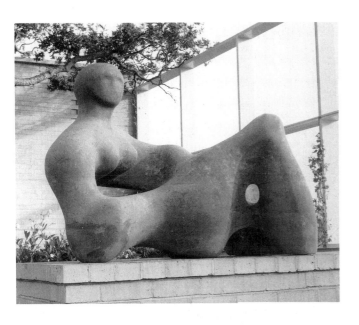

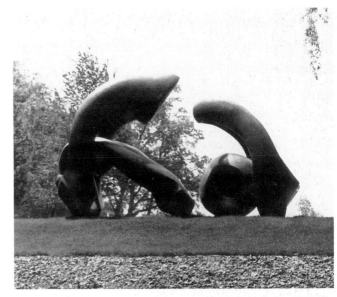

13.27 Henry Moore, *Recumbent Figure*, 1938. Green Hornton stone, length 55ins (139.7cm). The Tate Gallery, London.

13.28 Henry Moore, *Hill Arches*, 1973. Bronze, length 18ft (5.49m). Hyde Park, London.

13.29 Henry Moore, *Three Piece Reclining Figure*, 1975. Bronze, length 15ft 6ins (4.72m). Hyde Park, London.

13.30 Sir Jacob Epstein, *The Visitation*, 1926. Bronze, height 5ft 5ins (165.1cm). The Tate Gallery, London.

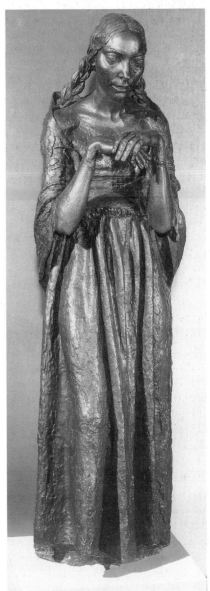

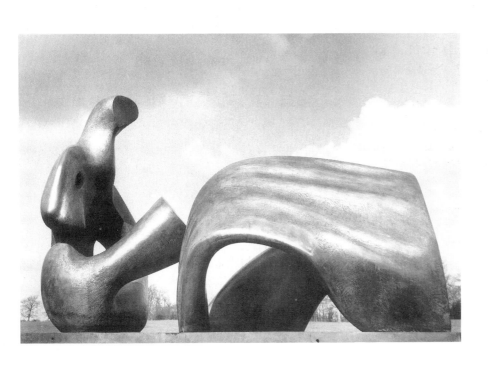

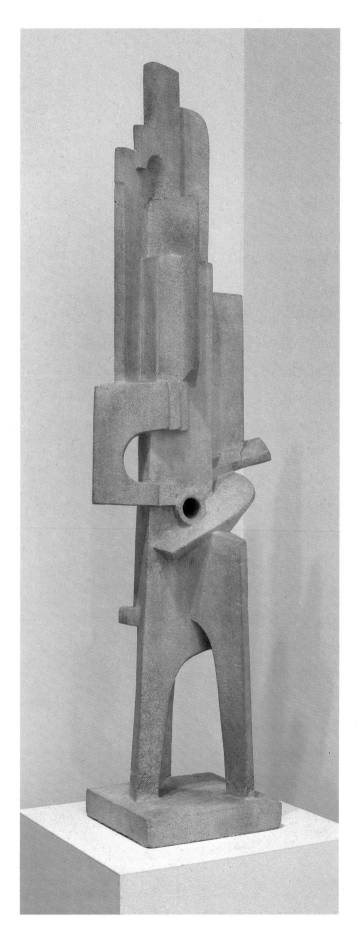

In 1925 Jacques Lipchitz (1891–1973) created a series of transparents cast from cardboard cut and bent to approximate Picasso's paintings. When he opened the interiors of these works, he discovered a radical new understanding of space. Interior spaces need not be voids, but, rather, could become integral parts of the sculptural work itself. From this understanding came the concept of negative space, which played an important role in sculpture, especially that of Henry Moore. Many of

13.31 Jacques Lipchitz, *Man with a Guitar*, 1915. Limestone, height 38¼ins (97.2cm). The Museum of Modern Art, New York (Mrs. Simon Guggenheim Fund).

13.32 William Zorach, *Child with Cat*, 1926. Bronze, height 17½ins (44.4cm). Museum of Art, The Pennsylvania State University.

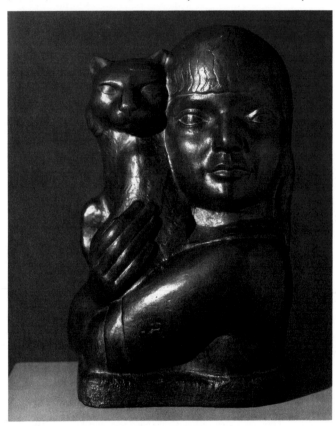

13.33 Alexander Calder, *Spring Blossoms*, 1965. Painted metal and heavy wire, height 52ins (132.1cm). Museum of Art, The Pennsylvania State University.

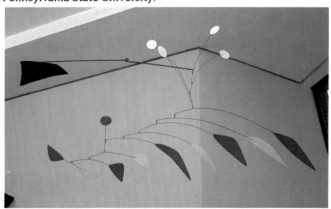

Lipchitz's works, such as Figure **13.31**, reflect his interest in primitive and archaic art and cubism.

In the United States between the two world wars, the carvings of William Zorach (1887–1966) came to prominence. His work displays a forthright attitude and avoids academic idealism. Soft curvilinear line and form hold works such as Figure **13.32** together in a comfortable, if conventional composition. At the same time, the original mobiles of Alexander Calder (1898–1976) (Fig. **13.33**) put abstract sculpture into motion. Deceptively simple, these colorful shapes turn at the whim of subtle breezes or by motors. Here is the discovery that sculpture can be created by movement in undefined space.

Contemporary sculpture

Much contemporary sculpture resembles abstract expressionist painting, especially in its rejection of tra-

13.34 David Smith, *Cubi* XIX, 1964. Stainless steel, height 9ft 5ins (287 cm). The Tate Gallery, London.

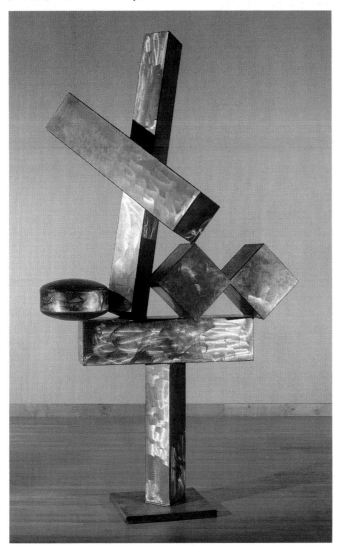

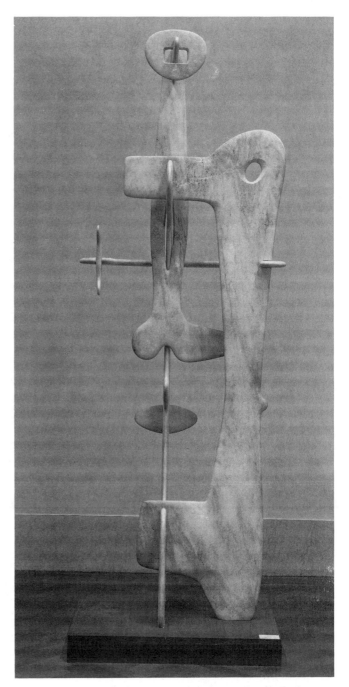

13.35 Isamu Noguchi, *Kouros* (in nine parts), 1944–45. Pink Georgia marble, slate base, height c. 9ft 9ins (297.2cm). The Metropolitan Museum of Art, New York (Fletcher Fund, 1953).

ditional materials in favor of new ones, notably materials which do not require molds or models. Individualized shapes and action-stimulants have severed sculpture, as far as is possible, from the natural world. Yet, even in such a context, abstract sculpture often has a title by which the sculptor links his or her non-objective expression to objective associations. The range of variation in works of this approach is immense and encompasses artists such as David Smith, Theodore Roszak, Seymour Lipton, Ibram

Lassaw, and Isamu Noguchi. The simplicity of shape characteristic of the work of David Smith (1906–65) (Fig. **13.34**) has been called, among other things, primary structure and environmental sculpture, names which forge a strong link with architecture. Here the respondent encounters an experience in three-dimensional space in which he or she can walk through as well as around the sculptural form.

Isamu Noguchi (b. 1904), perhaps less concerned with expressive content than others, has continually experimented with abstract sculptural design since the 1930s. His creations have gone beyond sculpture to provide highly dynamic and suggestive designs for the choreography of Martha Graham, with whom he was associated for a number of years. Noguchi's *Kouros* figures (Fig. **13.35**) contain abstract relationships with archaic

13.36 Alberto Giacometti, *Man Pointing*, 1947. Bronze, height 70½ins (179cm). The Museum of Modern Art, New York (Gift of Mrs. John D. Rockefeller III).

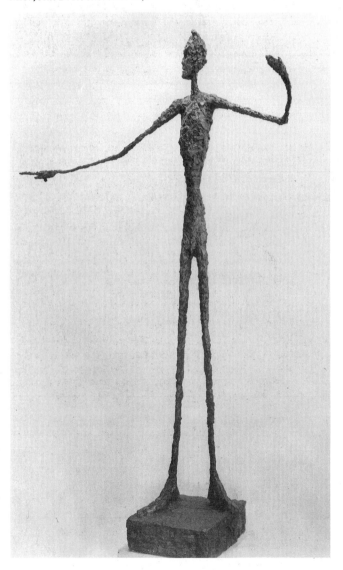

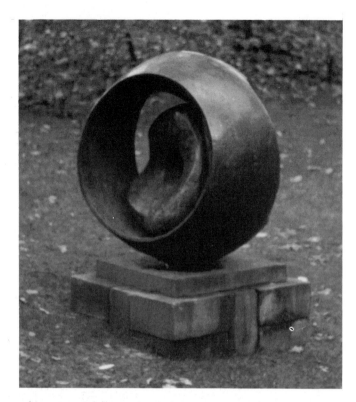

13.37 Dame Barbara Hepworth, *Sphere with Internal Form*, 1963. Bronze, 40ins (101.5cm) high. Collection: State Museum Kröller-Müller, Otterlo, The Netherlands.

Greek sculpture and also exhibit exquisitely finished surfaces and masterly technique.

Objectivity returns in the unique approaches of Alberto Giacometti (1901–1966). He was a surrealist sculptor in the 1930s but continued to explore the reality of the human figure and surface depiction and meaning, as can be seen in Figure **13.36**. Here form is reduced to its essence in a tortured fragmentation that appears to comment on the nature of humankind in the contemporary world.

Another search for an abstraction of the human form can be seen in *Sphere with Internal Form* (Fig. **13.37**). Here Barbara Hepworth (1903–75) incorporates two themes—a small form resting inside a large, enclosing form, and the piercing of the form. The piercing of form suggests sculptural and mental activity. Light is admitted into the form and provides tonal contrasts.

Yet another approach which has emerged since World War II is found sculpture, that is, objects taken from life and presented as art for their inherent aesthetic, communicative value. In the same sense, and perhaps a development from cubist collages, is the movement called junk culture. Here natural objects are assembled and/or joined to create a single artwork. Philosophies or interpretations of this kind of assemblage art vary widely and may or may not have significant relationship to or reflection upon a social scene in which obsolescence and throw-away materials are fundamental.

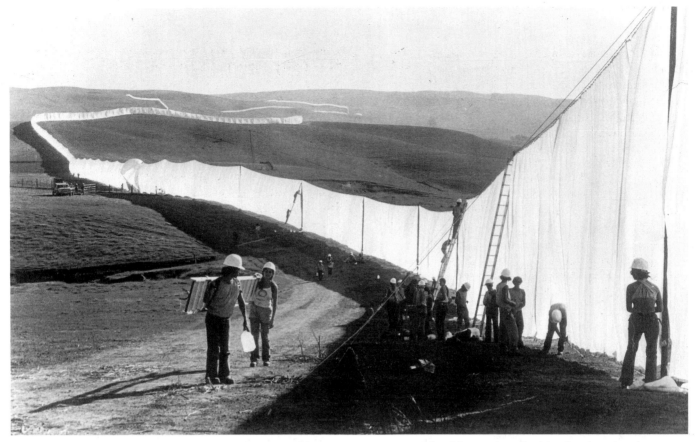

13.38 Christo, *Running Fence, Sonoma and Martin Counties, California, 1972–76*. Woven nylon fabric and steel cables, height 18ft (5.49m), length 24½ miles (39.2km). September 1976, two weeks.

13.39 Jean Dubuffet, *Jardin d'Email*, 1973–74. Concrete, epoxy paint and polyurethane, 66ft 8ins × 100ft (20 × 30m). State Museum Kröller–Müller, Otterlo, The Netherlands.

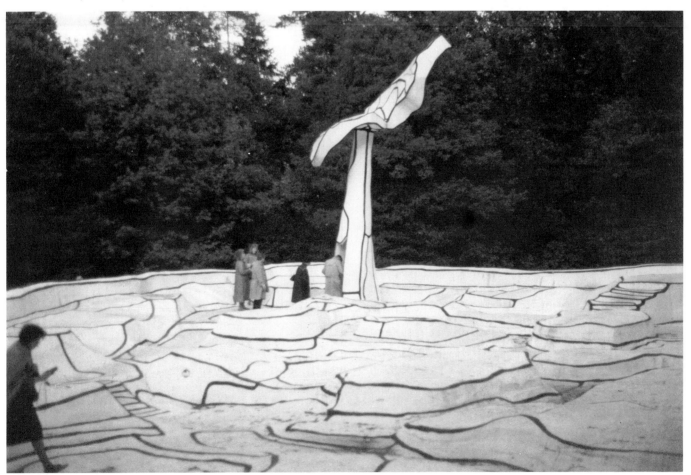

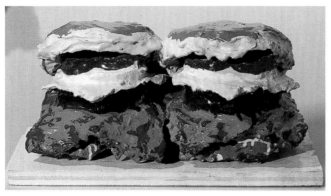

13.40 Claes Oldenburg, *Two Cheeseburgers, with Everything* (*Dual Hamburgers*), 1962. Burlap soaked in plaster, painted with enamel, height 7ins (17.8cm). The Museum of Modern Art, New York (Philip Johnson Fund).

Pop objects serve as source materials for Claes Oldenburg (b. 1929). *Dual Hamburgers* (Fig. **13.40**) presents an enigma to the viewer. What are we to make of it? Is it a celebration of the mundane? Or is there a greater comment on our age implicit in these objects? Certainly Oldenburg calls our attention to the qualities of design in ordinary objects by taking them out of their context and changing their scale. The influence of the Pop Movement can also be seen in the plaster figures of George Segal (b. 1924). Working from plaster molds taken from living figures, Segal builds scenes from everyday life with

13.41 George Segal, *The Bus Driver*, 1962. Figure of plaster over cheesecloth; bus parts including coin box, steering wheel, driver's seat, railing, dashboard etc. Overall height 6ft 3ins (190.5cm). The Museum of Modern Art, New York (Philip Johnson Fund).

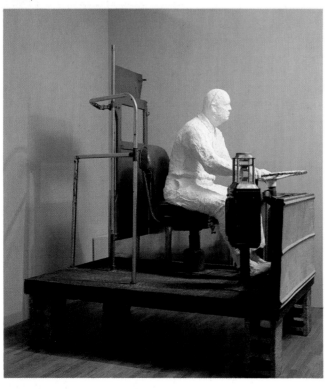

unpainted plaster images (Fig. **13.41**). These unpainted ghosts remove the sculptural environment from reality to a different plane altogether. Similar in a way, but in stark contrast are the photo-realistic sculptures of Duane Hanson (b. 1925), whose portrayals, including hair and plastic skin, are often displayed in such circumstances that the respondent does not know for sure at first sight if he or she is viewing a sculpture or a real human. Hanson's portrayals express a tragic quality and are an exposé of crassness and bourgeois tastelessness. They often portray the dregs of American society.

In the late 1950s and 1960s a style called minimalism in painting and sculpture sought to reduce design complexity to a minimum by concentrating on non-sensual, impersonal, geometric structures. No communication was intended between artist and respondent. Rather artists such as Tony Smith present these neutral objects without interpretation to stimulate whatever the viewer wishes.

Ephemeral art has many possible implications, including the works of the conceptualists, who insist that what is revealed is that "art is an activity of change, of disorientation and shift, of violent discontinuity and mutability". Designed to be transitory, ephemeral art makes its statement and then, eventually, ceases to exist. Undoubtedly the largest work of sculpture ever designed was based on that concept. Christo's *Running Fence* (Fig. **13.38**) was an event and a process, as well as a sculptural work. In a sense, Christo's works, such as this and *Valley Curtain*, are conceptual in that they call attention to the experience of art in opposition to its actual form. At the end of a two-week viewing period, *Running Fence* was removed entirely and ceased to be.

Environmental art creates an inclusive experience, and in *Jardin d'Email* by Jean Dubuffet (b. 1901) (Fig. **13.39**) we find an area made of concrete, which is painted with white paint and black lines. It is capricious in form and surrounded by high walls. Inside the sculptural environment we find a tree and two bushes of polyeurethane. We might conclude that Dubuffet has pushed the essence and the boundaries of art to their limits. He has consistently opted for chaos, for *art brut*—the art of children, psychotics, and amateurs. The *Jardin d'Email* is one of a small series of recent projects in which he has depicted the chaotic, disorienting, and inexplicable in three-dimensional form.

What comes next? Was the recent German *Documenta* VI, with its diverse examples of transitory art, a harbinger of the future? Is television our next art medium? Nam June Paik's *Video Composition X* was a sensational display in which a large room was turned into a garden of shrubbery, ferns, and small trees, scattered among which, and looking up from the greenery were thirty television sets, all repeating the same program in unison. Bill Viola's *He Weeps for You* featured a drop of water forming at the end of a tiny copper pipe and then falling on a drumhead. The image was blown up on a large television screen, and the sound of the falling drop was amplified into a thunderous boom. MIT's *Centerbeam* was a 220-foot long contraption using holograms, video, colored stream, and laser beams—art or a science fair project?

MUSIC

Non-traditional transitions

Music took no less a radical path from its nineteenth-century heritage than did painting and sculpture. Nevertheless, contemporary concert programs illustrate for us the unique phenomenon that response to works of art is always in the present tense. Our own experiences with and responses to the meanings in works of art are those of today, whether the artwork was created this morning or twenty thousand years ago. So we have the luxury of sharing experiences directly with Michelangelo, William Shakespeare, Leonardo da Vinci, J. S. Bach, and the architects of Athens, as well as with those men and women of our own era who illuminate and comment upon the events and circumstances surrounding us. Our contemporaries may and do choose to follow the traditions of the past or invent new ones.

Twentieth-century music took both paths. New directions in twentieth-century music differed from past traditions essentially in three ways. The first was rhythmic complexity. Prevailing tradition since the Middle Ages, when composition began to formalize its structures and conventions, emphasized grouping beats together in rhythmic patterns called meter. The characteristic accents of duple and triple meters helped to unify and clarify compositions, as well as to give them certain flavors. For example, triple meter with its *one-two-three, one-two-three* accent patterns created lilting dance rhythms, of which the waltz was characteristic. Duple meter's alternating accents could, for example, stimulate a marching regularity. The modern composer did away with these patterns and regularity of accents, choosing instead to employ complex, changing rhythms in which it is virtually impossible to determine meter or even the actual beat.

The second change consisted of a focus on dissonant harmonies. Prior to the late nineteenth century, musical convention centered upon consonance as the norm to which all harmonic progressions returned. Dissonance was used to disturb the norm, so as to enable the music to return to consonance. All art requires some disturbance of an established stasis in order to elicit the respondent's interest, in the same sense that a play must have a complication in order to move it forward, and then (using traditional approaches) have something to resolve. Dissonance in music fulfilled much the same role. Dissonances were expected to be brief and passing in nature and to return to consonance. As we saw, the late

nineteenth century witnessed significant tampering with that concept. By the twentieth century composers were using more and more dissonance, focusing on it, and refraining from consonant resolution.

The third major change from the past comprised the rejection of traditional tonality or sense of key altogether. Traditional thinking held that one note, the *doh* or tonic of a scale, was the most important. All music was composed with a specific key in mind. Modulations into distant or related keys occurred, but even then the tonic of the key was the touchstone to which all progression related. Many composers rejected that manner of systematizing musical sound and chose, instead, to pursue two other paths. One was to reject any sense of tonal center and importance of one tone over the other. All twelve tones of the chromatic scale became equal. The systems that resulted from this path were called twelve-tone composition and serialism. Less radical approaches were also used in which traditional major/minor tonality was denied, but in which some sense of tonal center still existed.

In order to capture the flavor of the diverse approaches occurring in the first half of the twentieth century, we need to move forward in a fairly irregular manner. We shall pause to examine kinds of music as well as composers and events as the first five decades of the century unfolded.

Transition from the nineteenth to the twentieth centuries rode primarily on the works of one major composer, the impressionist Claude Debussy, whom we discussed in the previous chapter. Several other traditions were current. One, of German–Italian influence, built upon the works of Richard Wagner and was called the cosmopolitan style. The principal composer in this group was César Franck. A classically oriented style came into the century in the works of Camille Saint-Säens, Jules Massenet, and Gabriel Fauré.

Debussy's style linked him closely with the French composer, Maurice Ravel (1875–1937), who began as an impressionist, but became more and more classical in orientation as years went by. However, even in his earlier works, Ravel did not adopt Debussy's complex sonorities and ambiguous tonal centers. Ravel's *Bolero* (1928) exhibits strong primitive influences and the unceasing rhythm of Spanish dance music. More typical works of Ravel, for example, his *Piano Concerto in G*, use Mozart and traditional classicism as their models. As a result of Ravel's tendencies and the similar concerns of composers such as Eric Satie, Arthur Honegger, Darius Milhaud, and Francis Poulenc, the early twentieth century witnessed a neo-classical direction, which stayed completely within the established conventions of Western music, but rejected both romantic and impressionistic developments.

Traditional tendencies continued throughout this period and can be seen in various quarters, one of which is the music of the American, William Schuman, in the 1930s and 40s. His symphonies exhibit bright timbres and energetic rhythms and focus on eighteenth- and nineteenth-century American folklore. The eighteenth-century American composer William Billings figures prominently in the works of Schuman in the *William Billings Overture* (1943) and the *New England Triptych* (1956), based on three pieces by Billings. *American Festival Overture* (1939) is perhaps his most famous work. Traditional tonality can also be found in the works of England's Benjamin Britten and Russia's Shostakovich and Prokofiev. Notwithstanding traditional tonality, Prokofiev's *Steel Step* reflected the encroachment of mechanization of the 1920s. The machine as a symbol for tremendous energy and motion found its way into music, and in the *Steel Step* Prokofiev intentionally dehumanized the subject in order to reflect contemporary life.

Hindemith

Experimentation and departure from traditional tonality marked the compositions of Paul Hindemith (1895–1963). Concerned with problems of musical organization, he systematized his approach to these problems and theorized solutions in the *Craft of Musical Composition*. Hindemith's work was extremely chromatic, almost atonal. His system of tonality was based on the establishment of tonal centers, but did not include the concepts of major and minor keys. He hoped that his new system would become a universal music language, but it did not. He was, however, extremely influential in twentieth-century music composition, both as a composer and a teacher. His works are broad and varied, encompassing nearly every musical genre, including ten operas, art songs, cantatas, chamber music, requiems, and symphonies. *Kleine Kammermusik für fünf Blaser* is a delightful composition for five woodwinds in five contrasting movements. Its overall form is very clear, as are its themes. Its dissonant harmonies and untraditional tonalities typify Hindemith's works. Part of Hindemith's approach to composition embraced the concept of functional music or *Gebrauchsmusik*. This approach was a reaction to what Hindemith considered "esoteric isolationism in music". Rather, he (and others) tried to write music that the general public could easily understand and also that the amateur musician could play.

Bartók

Another non-traditional approach to tonality was the unique style of the Hungarian composer Béla Bartók (1881–1945). He was interested in folk music and is often considered a representative of a nationalistic school of composition. Whether or not that is true, Bartók's interest in Eastern European folk music is significant, because much of that music does not use Western major/minor tonalities. So Bartók's interest in it and in non-traditional tonality in general went hand in hand. Bartók invented his own type of harmonic structure, which could accommodate folk melodies. As non-traditional as some of his work is, however, he also employed traditional devices and forms. His style was precise and very well structured. He often developed his works from one or two very short motifs. His larger works were unified by repetition of thematic material throughout. He even used sonata-allegro form. Textures in Bartók's works are largely contrapuntal, which gives them a melodic emphasis with little concern for harmony. Dissonances occur freely.

However, Bartók's employment of traditional devices was always bent to his own desires and nearly always lay outside the traditional tonal system. Bartók contributed significantly to string quartet literature, and his quartets, in a way not dissimilar to Chopin's *études*, each set out a particular problem, which it then proceeded to solve, combining simple melody with complex tonality. One characteristic of his melodic development was octave displacement, in which successive notes of a melody occur in different octaves. Apparently this characteristic also came from the folk music in which he was so interested. He had discerned that when peasants found the notes of a melody too high or low, they simply jumped up or down an octave so as to sing them comfortably.

In addition to melody, rhythm was very important to Bartók. His works tended to focus on rhythmic energy, employing many different devices, such as repeated chords and irregular meters (always to generate dynamic rhythms). His use of polyrhythms, that is, various juxtaposed rhythms, created a non-melodic counterpoint of unique quality.

Stravinsky

Nontraditionalism was followed in other quarters, and with the *Firebird* (1910) Igor Stravinsky (1882–1971) came to prominence. The *Rite of Spring* (1912–13) created an even greater impact. Both works were scores for ballets. The *Firebird* was a commission for the Russian impresario, Diaghilev, and premièred successfully at the Paris Opéra, while The *Rite of Spring* created a near riot and a great scandal because of revolutionary orchestrations and driving primitive rhythms. These were Stravinsky's early works. On the whole his works display a variety of styles and forms, but of whatever nature, he was a significant composer who was as prolific as he was diverse.

The effect of the *Rite of Spring* was so cataclysmic that a closer look is necessary. It was the third of his ballet commissions for Diaghilev, and is subtitled *Pictures of Pagan Russia*. It depicts the cruel rites of spring which culminate in the sacrifice of a virgin who dances herself to death accompanied by frenetic, primitive music. The compelling rhythms of the work give it its unique character. Rapid, irregular, and mechanical mixtures of very short note values create unbelievable tension. Melodic material is quite unconventional, consisting of short driving motifs, which are cut short of thematic fulfillment. Melodies are short and fragmentary. Every musical element is experimentally treated in order to achieve expressive ends. After World War I Stravinsky embraced neo-classicism in a series of works with classical and baroque references. His flexibility ranged even to the creation of serial compositions toward the end of his life.

Schoenberg

The movement which drew the most attention in the first half of the twentieth century grew out of German romanticism and took a radical turn into atonality. The composer at the root of the movement was Arnold Schoenberg (1874–1951). Between 1905 and 1912 Schoenberg turned away from the gigantic postromantic works he had been composing to a more contained style, in works for small ensembles and in orchestral works, which treated instruments individually. In orchestral works his timbres alternate swiftly, contrasting with large blocks of tone colors characteristic of earlier works. They also display rhythmic and polyphonic complexity together with fragmented melodies.

Although the word atonality (without tonality) is used to describe Schoenberg's works, he preferred the term pantonality, that is, inclusive of all tonalities. His compositions sought freedom to use any combination of tones without the necessity of having to resolve chordal progressions. He called that concept "the emancipation of dissonance". Prior to World War I, Schoenberg created one of his most famous works, *Pierrot Lunaire* (*Moonstruck Pierre*, 1912). This cycle of twenty-one songs is based on French surrealist poems translated into German and use a female solo voice accompanied by various instruments. Important in this work is the use of the speaking voice (*Sprechstimme*) and a very stylized declamation.

At times in their careers Schoenberg, Alban Berg, and Anton Webern represented expressionism in music. Similar to the movement of the same name in painting, expressionism (sometimes called the twentieth century's neurotic form of romanticism) approached humanity in terms of its psychological relationship to the modern world. Humankind was helpless in a world beyond its control and governed by subconscious forces in rebellion against established order. *Erwartung*, in which Schoenberg utilized complex rhythms, dissonance, strange orchestration, and fragmented melodies, evokes great intensity of feeling. As with many of his works, it sought, by all means available to him, to portray the complex thoughts and emotions of the composer relative to his subject matter.

By 1923 Schoenberg was composing in a twelve-tone or dodecaphonic technique, in which a row or series of the twelve tones in an octave was used in various ways—as melodies and harmonies, with rhythmic considera-

tions, upside down, backward, upside down and backward, that is, in whatever predetermined form the composer desired. The logical structure of this technique is fairly mathematical and somewhat formalized, but it does maintain a balance between emotion, accident, and mechanization. The important thing for a listener to understand about these apparently strange works, or works which stand outside conventional tonal organization, is the fact that they contain specific organization and logical order. When the listener knows the guideposts to look for, Schoenberg's music progresses just as comfortably as does that of traditional tonality. Schoenberg regarded pantonality as a logical step forward from a situation in which all the possibilities of the older system had been exhausted.

Ives and Copland

Ives and Copland were both Americans with experimental and highly personal styles. Charles Ives (1874–1954), was so experimental and ahead of his time that many of his compositions were considered unplayable and did not receive public performances until after World War I. Content to remain anonymous and unmotivated to shape his experiments into a system, as Schoenberg did, Ives went unrecognized for many years. Complexity underlies his compositions. His melodies spring from folk and popular songs, hymns, and other, often familiar, material, which he treated in most unfamiliar ways. His rhythms are hopelessly irregular and often without measure delineation except for an occasional bar line to indicate an accent beat. Textures involve such dissonant counterpoint that frequently it is impossible to distinguish one melodic line from another. Some of the tone clusters in his piano music are unplayable without using a block of wood to depress all the necessary keys at once. Ives' experiments, such as the *Unanswered Question* (1908), also employ ensembles placed in various locations to create stereophonic effects. For Ives all music related to life's experiences and ideas, some of which were consonant and some dissonant, and his music reflected that philosophy accordingly.

Aaron Copland (b.1900) integrated national American idioms into his compositions. Jazz, dissonance, Mexican folksongs, and Shaker hymns all appear. The latter of these figure prominently in Copland's most significant work, *Appalachian Spring* (1944). First written as a ballet, later it was reworked as a suite for symphony orchestra. Copland also used a variety of approaches, some reserved and harmonically complex, and some simple. He often used all tones in the diatonic scale, such as in the opening chord of the work. Despite a diversity of influences, he achieved a very personal and individual style, which is traditionally tonal. His unique manipulation of rhythms and chords has been highly influential in twentieth-century American musical composition.

Jazz

American in its origins, although debatable as to its classical or baroque qualities, is the musical phenomenon called jazz. Undoubtedly the most significant Black contribution to American music, jazz began near the turn of the century and went through many changes and forms. Jazz comprises sophisticated and complicated styles focusing on improvized variations on a theme. The earliest form—blues—went back to the music of the slaves and consisted of two rhythmic lines and repeat of the first line (AAB). Performers at the end of the nineteenth century such as Bessie Smith gave the blues an emotional quality, which the accompanying instruments tried to imitate. At approximately the same time came ragtime, a piano style with a strict, two-part form. Syncopation played an important role in this style, whose most famous exponent was Scott Joplin. New Orleans, the cradle of jazz, also produced traditional jazz, which featured improvizational development from a basic, memorized chordal sequence. All this was followed in the thirties and forties by swing, bebop, and cool jazz.

After World War II[6]

After World War II, several distinctly different directions began to develop which tended further to polarize schools of music along lines which had begun before the war. Two general tendencies have been taken. First, toward control and formality, and second toward less control of all elements to the point of random occurrences and total improvization by performers. The post-Webern serialism of Milton Babbitt in America and Pierre Boulez in France are clear examples of a move toward tighter control and predetermination of events. The improvizational works of Earl Brown and the many and varied approaches taken by John Cage exemplify a move away from composer control and predetermination, leaving decisions to performers or to chance. At the same time a number of composers continued in more traditional styles, which stemmed from the musical principles of Hindemith, the neo-classicism of Stravinsky, Prokofiev, and Shostakovich, and the nationalistic styles of Bartók, Copland, and Ernest Bloch.

Serialism

Post-Webern or postwar serialism reflects a desire to exert more control and to apply a predetermined hierarchy of values to all elements of a composition. Before the war, twelve-tone technique involved the creation of a set or row of twelve pitch classes arranged in a specific order. Although the order could be manipulated in a number of ways, certain relationships between the

pitches of the tone-row were constant and provided the underlying structure and much of the flavor of this style. To a certain extent structural decisions were made before the composer actually began writing the composition itself. The composer was then subject to fairly strict limitations regarding the selection of pitches as the work progressed, since all pitch order was pre-established. Proponents of the technique argued that composers have always worked within limitations of some kind and that the discipline required to do so is an essential part of the creative problem-solving process. Opponents argued that writing music in this fashion was more a matter of mathematical manipulation appealing to the intellect and less the function of a composer's ear and basic musical instincts.

Three Compositions for piano by the American composer Milton Babbitt, written in 1947–8, is one of the earliest examples of serial technique applied to elements other than pitch. In this work, rhythm and dynamics are also predetermined by serial principles. Olivier Messiaen was largely responsible for the post-war revival of serial principles in Europe, and two of his students, Pierre Boulez and Karlheinz Stockhausen, both produced works in the 1950s which were totally serialized—for example, *Structures* for two pianos by Boulez, and *Kreuzspiel* (*Crossplay*) for oboe, bass clarinet, piano, and percussion by Stockhausen. Both of these composers later moved away from these techniques. A group of Italian composers, including Luciano Berio, Luigi Nono, and Bruno Maderna, also began as post-war serialists, and later moved in other directions.

Aleatory music

While some composers were developing techniques and even systems of highly controlled composition in the late 1940s, others went in the opposite direction. John Cage has been a major force in the application of aleatoric or chance procedures to composition with works such as *Imaginary Landscape* No. 4 for twelve radios and *The Music of Changes* (1951). Cage relied on the I *Ching* or *Book of Changes* for a random determination of many aspects of his works. The I *Ching* dates from the earliest period of Chinese literature and contains a numerical series of combinations based on the throwing of yarrow sticks (not unlike the throwing of a dice or coins). The ultimate example of chance music is Cage's *4'-33"* (1952) in which the performer makes no sound whatever. The sounds of the hall, audience, traffic outside, that is, whatever occurs is the content of the composition.

Cage toured Europe in 1954 and 1958 and is thought to have influenced composers such as Boulez and Stockhausen to incorporate aspects of chance and indeterminacy into their music. Examples of this influence are Boulez's *Third Piano Sonata* and Stockhausen's *Klavierstück*, both dating from 1957. These works, however, only go so far as to give options to the performer concerning the overall form of the work or the order of specific musical fragments, which are, for the most part, conventionally notated, and thus controlled. Other composers who experimented with indeterminacy are Earl Brown, Morton Feldman, and Christian Wolff.

Improvization

An open, improvizatory tradition was carried on by composers like Lukas Foss with the Improvization Chamber Ensemble of which he was founder. A number of other improvization groups, many funded by granting organizations and universities, sprang up in the United States during the 1960s along with the intense exploration of new sound possibilities from both conventional and electronic instruments.

Mainstream

What is often referred to as a mainstream of musical composition also continued after the war. The source of much of this music is a combination of nineteenth-century romantic tradition, the folk styles of Bartók and Copland, quartet harmonies of Hindemith, the modality of the impressionists Ravel and Debussy, and the neo-classicism of Prokofiev and Stravinsky. To some degree, both serialism and indeterminacy can be found here as well as popular or jazz elements. American composers of the so-called mainstream include Aaron Copland, Samuel Barber, Elliott Carter, William Schuman, William Bergsma, Vincent Persichetti, Roger Sessions, and Leonard Bernstein, to name only a few. In Europe such composers as Benjamin Britten, Luigi della Piccola, Geoffredo Petrassi, and Hans Werner Henze would be called mainstream by most. The only similarity in the music of these composers is that none of them gravitates toward the extremes of total predetermination or total randomness, and their music generally relies upon traditional musical principles.

Postwar jazz

Styles stemming from traditional jazz proliferated after the war. There was a gradual move away from the big bands to smaller groups and a desire for much more improvization within the context of the compositions. The term bebop was coined as a result of the characteristic long-short triplet rhythm which ended many phrases. The prime developers of this style were alto-saxophonist Charlie "Bird" Parker and trumpeter Dizzie Gillespie. Pianists, Thelonius Monk, Earl "Bud" Powell, and "Todd" Dameron were also innovative and influential in develop-

ing this style. The cool jazz style developed in the early 1950s with artists like Stan Getz and Miles Davis. Although the technical virtuosity of bebop continued, a certain lyric quality, particularly in the slow ballads, was emphasized and, more importantly, the actual tone quality, particularly of the wind instruments, was a major distinction. Third Stream was a term used by composer Gunther Schuller to describe his own attempt to blend Euro-American art music techniques such as serialism with elements of the bebop and cool jazz styles. Other composers rooted in the jazz tradition such as Charles Mingus, Ted Macero, and Lee Konitz were employing techniques similar to the avant-garde composers previously discussed as aleatoric or indeterminate.

Electronic music

The development of the RCA synthesizer and the establishment of the Columbia-Princeton Electronics Music Center provided an opportunity for composers such as Milton Babbitt to pursue the application and further development of primarily serial techniques. Composers such as John Cage found electronics a logical means to achieve their musical goals of indeterminacy as in *Imaginary Landscape* No. 5. Mainstream and jazz composers were not seriously affected by the electronic medium until the 1960s.

We need to note that electronic production and alteration of sound does not imply, in itself, a specific musical style. However, electronic sound production led to two new approaches during the 1950s. First, *musique concrète*—the use of acoustically produced sounds, and, second, electronically generated sound. In recent times this distinction has become less meaningful due to the major advances in technology since that time.

Composers such as Edgard Varèse, Otto Luening, and Vladimir Ussachevsky used *musique concrète* techniques, and Pierre Schaeffer in Paris is also well known for developing *musique concrète* in his early experiments and works such as *Étude aux Objects* (1954). *Musique concrète* by its nature is less controlled than the synthesized music of Babbit and later composers such as Mario Davidovsky and Charles Wuorinen, who tended to use only electronically produced sine waves, square waves, and so on.

The 1960s and 1970s

The 1960s and early 1970s saw even further extremes in the "ultrarational" and "antirational" directions in addition to an even stronger desire constantly to create something new. At times this desire for newness superseded most other considerations. Many composers, such as Donald Martino, Henry Weinberg, and Peter Westergard, continued to use strict serial techniques often involving a total control concept in the tradition of Babbitt. The serialism of the European composers, however, evolved into something quite different. Stockhausen, for example, became more interested in the total manipulation of sound and the acoustic space in which the performance was to take place. His work *Gruppen* (1957) for three orchestras is an early example. As he became more and more interested in timbre modulation, his work encompassed a greater variety of sound sources both electronic and acoustic in an interesting combination of control and noncontrol. An example of this is *Microphonie* I (1964). Igor Stravinsky, one of the most influential composers of the early part of this century, developed his own serial style in the late fifties and early sixties.

Elliott Carter, although not a serialist, developed a highly organized approach toward rhythm often called metric-modulation, in which the mathematical principles of meter, standard rhythmic notation, and other elements are carried to complex ends. The pitch content of Carter's music is highly chromatic and exact, and his music requires virtuoso playing both from the individual and the ensemble. A number of other composers such as Wolpe, Shapey, and Chou Wen-Chung also stressed complex rhythmic subdivisions and virtuoso instrumental technique to some degree or other.

Virtuoso playing produced an important composer-performer relationship in the 1960s, and many composers, such as Luciano Berio, wrote specifically for individual performers, such as trombonist Stewart Dempster. In the same vein percussionist Max Neuhaus was associated with Stockhausen, and pianist David Tudor, with John Cage.

Experimentation with microtones has been of interest to music theorists throughout history and many non-Western cultures employ them routinely. Microtones can be defined as intervals smaller than a half step. Our system divides the octave into twelve equal parts. There seems to be no reason why the octave cannot be divided into 24, 53, 95 or any number of parts. The possibilities are limited only by our ability to hear such intervals and a performer's ability to produce them. Alois Haba experimented in the early part of the century with quarter tones (24 per octave) and sixth tones (36 per octave), as did Charles Ives. Composer Harry Partch developed a number of instruments designed to produce microtones. Since the war, experimentation and composition in the area of microtones has been carried on by Ben Johnston, John Eaton, Julian Carrillo, Lou Harrison, and others.

In an atmosphere of constant searching and experimentation, composers often questioned the validity of traditional concepts of art in general and specifically the limitations of the traditional concert hall. The earlier work by Cage and others led in a number of directions including theatre pieces, multi-media or mixed media, so-called danger music, biomusic, soundscapes, happenings, and total environments which might include stimula-

tion of all the senses in some way. Thus the definition of a composer as opposed to playwright, filmmaker, visual artist, and so on was often obscured.

Since the early 1960s electronic instruments which could be used in live performance have been highly influential in music composition. Live performance mixed with prerecorded tape occurred in the 1950s, and by the 1960s it became common to alter the sound of live performers by electronic means. Computer technology has been added to the composition and performance of music, and the options available through computer application are now endless.

Theatre music, sometimes called experimental music, ranges from relatively subtle examples of performers playing or singing notated music and moving to various points on the stage, as in Berio's *Circles* (1960), to more extreme examples, such as the works of La Monte Young, in which the performer is instructed to "draw a straight line and follow it" or react to the audience just as an audience was to react to the performers, that is, exchange places. A more active example is Nam June Paik's *Homage to John Cage* in which the composer ran down into the audience, cut off Cage's tie, dumped liquid over his head, and ran from the theater, later to phone and let the audience know the composition had ended. Needless to say, such compositions contain a high degree of indeterminacy.

Some works were never intended to be performed, but only conceptualized, such as Nam June Paik's *Danger Music for Dick Higgins*, which instructs the performer to "Creep into the vagina of a living whale" or Robert Moran's *Composition for Piano with Pianist*, which instructs the pianist to climb into the grand piano.

There was also a return to minimal materials exemplified by Stockhausen's *Stimmung* (*Tuning*), dating from 1968, for six vocalists singing only six notes. Minimal music generally can be defined as music which uses very little musical material, but often for an extended length of time, such as *One Sound* for string quartet by Harold Budd and the electronic piece *Come Out* (1966) by Steve Reich. Works such as *In C* or *Rainbow in Curved Air* by Terry Riley and *Drumming* by Steve Reich are also minimal, but stress a periodic rhythm; thus they have been termed periodicity music.

Many mainstream composers continued writing throughout the 1960s and early 1970s. However, a noticeable element of controlled indeterminacy has found its way into the music of many of them. The late sixties and seventies brought greater tolerance and acceptance on the part of composers for each other's varying aesthetic viewpoints and musical styles. Thus a blending of avant-garde (largely indeterminant) techniques with the traditional values of the mainstream has resulted in music produced by composers such as George Crumb, *Ancient Voices of Children* (1970); Donald Erb, *The Seventh Trumpet* (1969); and Karel Husa, *Apotheosis of this Earth* (1970).

Just as indeterminacy and aleatoric procedures had been developed during the 1950s by composers of the Western European music tradition, freedom from melodic, rhythmic, and formal restraints in jazz led to the free jazz style of the 1960s. Saxophonist Ornette Colman was one of the earliest proponents of such freedom. Others, such as John Coltrane, developed a rhythmically and melodically free style based on more modal materials, while Cecil Taylor developed materials which were more chromatic. In the mid-to-late sixties a mature blend of this freedom, with control and sophistication, was reached in Miles Davis's *Bitches Brew* album of 1967. A number of musicians, such as Wayne Shorter, Bill Evans, Herbie Hancock, Ron Carter, Chic Corea, and Keith Jarrett, who originally worked with Miles Davis, became leading artists in the 1970s, developing a style called jazz-rock, or fusion.

The post-war period has been one of rapid change due to the constant quest for something new. Whether it be new sounds, the application of new technology, new notation, new formal parameters, entirely new ways of presenting music, or combining music with visual and other stimuli, aesthetic viewpoints and styles have been both numerous and varied. Extremism and intolerance from both the conservative and avant-garde have not been uncommon. An insatiable appetite for something new affected composers of almost all music styles since World War II. The influence of music composition for film and television has made the era an interesting one, bringing together varying styles for dramatic purpose and proliferating new sounds and applications to a wide audience, occasionally gaining acceptance for a form which, in a traditional concert hall, would be unacceptable.

There is no doubt that the extremism beginning after the war and culminating gradually during the 1970s has given way in the 1980s to a re-evaluation and acceptance of all styles as containing valid material upon which to draw for a composition.

THEATRE

Toward the New Stagecraft

Two important theorists bridged the turn of the century. Adophe Appia (1862–1928) and Gordon Craig (1872–1966) had symbolist leanings and tried to articulate new ideas and ideals about theatre production. Appia attempted to find a new means for unifying theatre action among the diverse visual forms and conditions of the theatre—moving actors, horizontal floors, and vertical scenery. In 1899 Appia, a Swiss, published his influential work *Die Musik und die Inscenierung* (*Music and Staging*), setting forth his suggested reforms. Beginning with the actor, he maintained that the stage design must be in harmony with the living presence of the performer. Accurate depictive reality was unnecessary. Rather, there should

be an atmosphere of a man or woman amidst the setting. The audience's attention should be focused on the character, not on scenic details. Appia believed that two-dimensional painted scenery was incompatible with the live actor because of the extreme and distracting contrast between flat scenic elements and a plastic, three-dimensional human form. For Appia the human body was reality itself, and the stage floor should only set the human body in relief. Scenic reality was the living presence of the actor, and the stage should be cleared of everything that "is in contradistinction with the actor's presence".

The Englishman Gordon Craig was more a visionary and a theorist than an actual man of the theatre. He found the theatre lacking in artistic purpose and direction and believed in a unity of production elements under the aegis of a superdirector. He sought to replace scenic imitation or depiction with suggestion and insisted upon a spiritual relationship between setting and action. Theatre was "a place for seeing". Moving figures, light and shadow, and dramatic color all had tremendous potential, which Craig tried to explore. For the most part Craig's theories remained just that. His designs proved impractical, and in many cases, disastrous to the production. He had some successes, however, and managed to convince many theatre artists of the significance of his viewpoint.

Appia and Craig were important proponents of eclecticism, sometimes called artistic realism and sometimes called organic unity, which drastically changed theatre style at the turn of the twentieth century. Previously, all plays were held to a single standard—whatever was the vogue of the day. For example, in the mid-nineteenth century, when antiquarian realism was the fashion, all plays—melodramas, Greek tragedies, or Shakespearean comedies—would have been staged in the same style. However, artistic realism or eclecticism held that the stage environment must be appropriate to the given play. Style was largely seen to be reflective of the style appropriate to the period in which the play was written. Therefore, the twentieth century became, and still is, an era of stylistic diversity, of eclecticism, in which each play and each production of each play determines the actual style the audience witnesses.

The organic approach to theatre grew principally from the work of Max Reinhardt (1873–1943). He treated each play as an aesthetic problem and saw the physical environment of the production (the *mise en scène*) as a vital part of stylistic communication. Also, to enforce organic unity, since numerous separate artists may contribute to one production, he, like Craig and others, cast the director as the supreme theatre artist, ultimately responsible for all aspects of production—actors, lighting, costumes, scenery, props, sound, and even the final version of the script itself. When this approach finally reached the United States around 1910, it was called the New Stagecraft, and was carried forward primarily by the efforts of two influential designers, Robert Edmond Jones and Lee Simonson. For the most part, artistic realism (and also realism as a depictive style) has remained the dominant approach to the theatre in the twentieth century, especially in the United States.

American theatre came of age in the twentieth century, the early years of which were dominated by Clyde Fitch (1865–1909). Broadway epitomized the height of theatrical success, and in 1901 Fitch had four plays running concurrently on the "Great White Way". The *Truth* and the *Girl with the Green Eyes* were more theatrical than realistic, but they did advance the cause of American theatre, as did William Vaughn Moody (1869–1910) in the *Great Divide*, which contrasted New England refinement and its narrow moral codes with the rough honesty and freedom of the West.

Expressionism

Expressionism brought to the theatre ideas which reflected disillusionment more than they did realism. But here we must tread carefully, because the theatre is both visual and oral. The painter's revolt against naturalism came to the theatre in visual form in scenic design. Settings which followed expressionism in painting occurred often. For the playwright, expressionism was merely an extension of realism and naturalism and allowed the playwright a more adequate means to express his own reaction to specific items in the universe around him. August Strindberg, for example, had turned inward to the subconscious in expressionistic plays such as the *Dream Play* and the *Ghost Sonata*. In so doing, he created, as did Leonid Andreyev in *He Who Gets Slapped* and Frank Wedekind in *Spring Awakening*, a presentational rather than representational style.

The disillusionment of German expressionism after World War I typified the plays of Ernst Toller (1893–1939) and Georg Kaiser (1878–1945). Toller's personal struggles, his communistic idealism, and his opposition to violence and revolution are reflected in the heroine of *Man and the Masses*. Sonia, a product of the upper class, leads a strike for peace. Her desire to avoid violence and bloodshed is opposed by the mob Spirit (the Nameless One), who seeks just those results and an abrogation of the peace the strike intended to achieve. For leading the disastrous strike, Sonia is imprisoned and sentenced to death. Kaiser's *From Morn until Midnight* traces its way through the nightmarish life of a bank clerk whose pursuit of happiness is shattered at every turn.

Expressionism also found its way to America. Elmer Rice's *Adding Machine* (1923) depicts Mr Zero, a cog in the great industrial machinery of twentieth-century life, who stumbles through a pointless existence. Finding himself replaced by an adding machine he goes berserk, kills his employer, and is executed. Then, adrift in the hereafter,

he is too narrow-minded to understand the happiness offered to him there. He becomes an adding machine operator in Heaven and finally returns to earth to begin his tortured existence all over again.

Social action

The early years of the twentieth century witnessed numerous production experiments aimed at creating social action. Typical of the devices used by social-action advocates were subjective attitudes toward subject matter, fragmentary scenery, and generally distorted visual elements. For the most part they sought to combine the traditional goals of theatre, to entertain and to teach, so that by entertainment they could teach and thereby motivate the spectator into action outside the theatre. An excellent example came from the Moscow Art Theatre in the late nineteenth century and involved the work of Vsevolod Meyerhold (1874–1942). Meyerhold's plays were a product of the Russian Revolution and its attempts to transform society. For Meyerhold a revolutionized society required a revolutionized theatre. His approach led him to difficulty on two counts, however. First, his mechanized treatment of the actor was not acceptable to Constantin Stanislavsky, the dominant force in the Moscow Art Theatre. Second, Meyerhold was considered too formalistic to appeal to the masses. Nevertheless, by the time he was removed from his post in the 1930s, he had made a significant contribution to the theatre and had earned fame and influence throughout Europe and America.

Meyerhold shared the belief that the director was the supreme artist in the theatre and freely rewrote scripts to suit his own ends. He devised a system of actor training called biomechanics, the object of which was to make an actor's body an efficient machine for carrying out the instructions of its operator (the director). Meyerhold's actors were often required to swing from trapezes, do gymnastic stunts, and spring up through trap doors.

Central to Meyerhold's viewpoint was the concept of theatricalism. Rather than striving to imitate or depict life, he wished the audience to be fully aware that they were in a theatre and never to confuse theatre with life. He wished to stir the audience to desirable social action outside the theatre. As a result, he removed many of the devices that theatre uses to hide its theatricality. Curtains were removed so that backstage areas and lighting instruments were fully visible. He also introduced a practical and theatrical style of staging called constructivism. The settings used in this approach were called constructions and consisted of various levels and playing areas of a completely non-objective nature. Scenery was not a background, but rather a series of structures on which the actors could perform and with which they could be totally integrated. Ultimately, the stage, the actor, and all aspects of performance were parts of a machine to be manipulated by the director.

Social action and protest also found a home in the American theatre during the first half of the twentieth century. The spiritual and economic collapse of the Great Depression prompted many playwrights to examine the American social fabric. Maxwell Anderson had questioned America's values earlier, but the most poignant protest came from the pen of Clifford Odets (1906–63). In 1935 he produced a one-act play concerning New York's bitter taxicab strike. *Waiting for Lefty* removed audience-actor separation by making the audience part of the auditorium portion of a labor hall. At the front, on the traditional stage, several characters waited for the appearance of Lefty, so that the meeting could begin. As the play progressed, actors rose from seats in the audience to voice their complaints. Tension mounted, and when it was discovered that Lefty had been assassinated, actors began to chant "strike, strike, strike . . ." The involvement of the audience within the aesthetic environment of the action actually caused the audience to take up the chant themselves. During the Depression, when the play was produced, its impact was significant. However, even today productions of *Waiting for Lefty* often have the same effect on an audience.

Odets followed with *Golden Boy* and *Awake and Sing*, and was joined by other notable social-action writers such as Lillian Hellman with the *Children's Hour*, the *Little Foxes*, *Another Part of the Forest*, and *Toys in the Attic*. At the same time came the social criticism of John Steinbeck's *Grapes of Wrath* and his masterpiece, *Of Mice and Men*, although these were staged in a more traditional, realistic style.

Independent Art Theatre Movement

The Independent Art Theatre Movement, mentioned in the last chapter, produced one of America's greatest playwrights, Eugene O'Neill. The first two decades of the twentieth century saw an intense struggle for theatre monopoly between the theatrical Syndicate and the Schubert Brothers. Unions were formed, the movies drained theatre audiences, and little attention was paid to nurturing the soul of any vital theatre, the playwright. However, one independent theatre led the way. The Provincetown Players consisted of a group of young actors and writers who spent their summers together on Cape Cod. Banding together, they opened the Wharf Theatre in Provincetown and later moved to New York, where their commitment to playwright development led to productions of young Eugene O'Neill (1888–1953). Son of the famous actor James O'Neill, Eugene knew the theatre well and was influenced especially by the expressionist works of August Strindberg as well as the sea stories of Joseph Conrad. The prolific output of O'Neill's pen covered wide-ranging subjects, styles, and a restless search for new

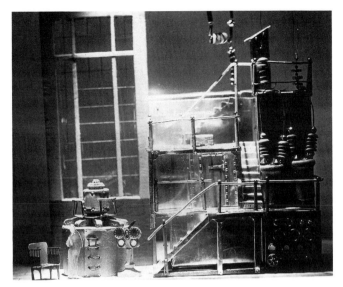

13.42 Lee Simonson, constructivist set for Eugene O'Neill's *Dynamo*, 1929. The New York Public Library.

approaches. The *Emperor Jones*, the *Hairy Ape*, and *Dynamo* (Fig **13.42**) employed expressionistic techniques. The *Great God Brown* used masks to contrast internal and external reality. *Strange Interlude* employed soliloquies and was so long that the production started at 5.30 p.m. and broke for an hour and a half for dinner before resuming and running until 11.00 p.m. *Mourning Becomes Electra* was based on a Greek tragedy and set in New England. *Ah, Wilderness!* was a warm, realistic comedy. The list goes on and on.

Pirandello

Finally came a playwright who spread new roots, out of which grew the Theatre of the Absurd. A product of disillusionment, Luigi Pirandello (1867–1936) had lost faith in religion, realism, science, and humanity itself. Still searching, however, for some meaning or basis for existence, he found only chaos, complexity, grotesque laughter, and perhaps, insanity. His plays were obsessed with the question "What is real?" and he pursued that question with brilliant variations. *Right You Are If You Think You Are* presented a situation in which a wife, living with her husband in a top-floor apartment, is not permitted to see her mother. She converses with her daily—the mother is in the street and the daughter is at a garret window. Soon the neighbors' curiosity demands an explanation from the husband. A satisfactory answer is forthcoming, but the mother has an equally plausible, although radically different explanation. Finally, the wife, who is the only one who can clear up the mystery is approached. Her response, as the curtain falls, is loud laughter! Pirandello cried bitterly at a world he could not understand, but he did so with mocking laughter directed at those who purported to have the answers or were sure that they soon would. As *You Desire Me*, *Henry IV*, *Naked*, *Tonight We Improvize*, and perhaps his most popular play, *Six Characters in Search of an Author*, all reflect the confusion and suffering Pirandello found in the early twentieth century.

After World War II

A breaking point such as World War II is an arbitrary guidepost. World War II, however, falling nearly at mid-century, is more than merely convenient—it was a time when the world nearly ceased all peaceful activity. Nevertheless, many playwrights whom we have yet to examine began their careers before the war, and our neglect of them until this point is a matter of convenience and not a commentary on their pre-war significance.

Epic theatre

Theatre of social action, of which Meyerhold was an example, found a very successful exponent in the Epic Theatre of Bertolt Brecht (1898–1956). Although most of Brecht's plays were written before the war, they were not produced until after. With his Berliner Ensemble, Brecht brought his theories and productions to a wide audience and acclaim. Drawing heavily on the expressionists, Brecht developed complex theories about theatre and its relationship to life, and he continued to mold and develop those theories until his death. Brecht called his approach epic, because he saw it as a revolt against dramatic theatre. Essentially, he strove to move the audience out of the role of passive spectator and into a more dynamic relationship with the play. To this end, Brecht postulated three circumstances—historification, alienation, and epic. Historification removed events from the life-like present to the past in order to make strange the actions presented. According to Brecht, the playwright should make the audience feel that if they had lived under the conditions presented, they would have taken some positive action. Having seen this, the audience should recognize that, since things have changed, they can make changes in the present as well. Alienation was part of the goal of making things strange, part of histori-fication. Many devices could be used, such as calling the audience's attention to the make-believe nature of the production or by inserting songs, film sequences, and so on.

Like Meyerhold, Brecht believed the audience should never confuse the theatre with reality. The audi-ence should always see the play as a comment on life, which they must watch critically. Therefore, alienation meant that the spectator should judge what he or she sees in the theatre and apply it to life outside—the spectator must be alienated from the play's events, although he or she may become emotionally involved. Brecht did not subscribe to the unified approach to production. Rather, he saw each element as independent, and, thereby, as a device to be employed for further alienation. Theatricality characterized the production ele-ments of scenery, lighting, costumes, and properties. Finally, Brecht called his theatre epic because he be-lieved that his plays resembled epic poems more than they did traditional drama. His plays presented a story from the point of view of a storyteller and frequently involved narration and changes of time and place, which might be accomplished with nothing more than an explanatory sentence. *Caucasian Chalk Circle*, the *Good Woman of Setzuan*, the *Threepenny Opera*, *Mother Courage*, *Galileo*, and *Mahagonny* are some of Brecht's more impor-tant works.

Following in the Brechtian tradition were German playwrights such as Max .Frisch (the *Chinese Wall*, *Bieder-mann and the Firebugs*, and *Andorra*), whose works deal with the general question of guilt, and Friedrich Dürrenmatt (the *Visit*, the *Physicist*), dealing with moral responsibility. Later came Peter Weiss (the *Persecution and Assassination of Jean-Paul Marat as Performed by the Inmates of the Asylum of Charenton under the Direction of the Marquis de Sade*).

Absurdism

Luigi Pirandello's non-realistic departures created the mold from which emerged a movement called absurdism. Existentialism, a philosophy which questioned the nature of existence, placing a meaningless present amid a guilt-ridden past and an unknowable future, also contributed to absurdist style. From such antecedents came numer-ous dramas, probably the best known of which were written by the French philosopher and playwright Jean-Paul Sartre (1905–80). Sartre's existentialism held that there were no absolute or universal moral values and that humankind was part of a world without purpose. There-fore, men and women were responsible only to them-selves. His plays attempted to draw logical conclusions from "a consistent atheism". Plays such as the *Flies* (1943), *No Exit* (1944), the *Devil and the Good Lord* (1951), and the *Condemned of Altona* (1959) translate Sartre's philosophies and existential viewpoint into dramatic form.

Albert Camus (1913–60) was the first playwright to use the term absurd, a state which he considered to be a result of the dichotomy between humankind's aspirations and the meaninglessness of the universe in which indi-viduals live. Finding one's way in a chaotic universe, then, became the theme of Camus' plays, such as *Cross-Purposes* (1944), *Caligula* (1945), and the *Just Assassins* (1949).

After these two playwrights came a series of absur-dists who differed quite radically from both Sartre and Camus, both of whom strove to bring order out of absurdity. The plays of Samuel Beckett, Eugene Ionesco, and Jean Genet all tend to point only to the absurdity of existence and to reflect the chaos they saw in the universe. Their plays are chaotic and ambiguous, and the absurd and ambiguous nature of these plays make direct analysis purely a matter of interpretation. *Waiting for Godot* (1958), the most popular work of Samuel Beckett (b. 1906) has been interpreted in so many ways to suggest so many different meanings that it has become an eclectic experience in and of itself. Beckett, like the minimalist sculptors, left it to the audience to draw whatever conclusions they wished about the work confronting them. The works of Ionesco (b. 1912) are even more baffling, using nonsense syllables and clichés for dialogue, endless and meaningless repetition, and plots that have no development. He called the *Bald Soprano* (1950) an antiplay, and his other works, among them the *Chairs*, the *Lesson*, and *Rhinoceros*, reflect virtually the same approach. The absurdist movement has influenced other playwrights and production approaches, from Harold Pinter to Edward Albee.

Realism continued its strong tradition throughout the post-war era and owed much of its strength to the works of Tennessee Williams and Arthur Miller. However, realism has expanded from its nineteenth-century definition to include more theatrical approaches and devices such as fragmentary settings. Realism has also become more eclectic in its inclusion of many non-realistic devices such as symbolism. Undoubtedly the theatre has concluded that stage realism and life's realism are two different concepts entirely. Tennessee Williams (1912–83) skilfully blended the qualities of realism with whatever scenic, structural, or symbolic devices were necessary to meet his goals. The *Glass Menagerie*, A *Streetcar Named Desire*, *Summer and Smoke*, and the *Night of the Iguana*, among others, dealt sensitively and poignantly with the problems and psychology of everyday people. His character development is thorough and occupies the principal focus in his dramas as he explores the mental and emotional ills of our society. Arthur Miller (b. 1915) probed the social and psychological forces that destroy contemporary men and women in plays such as *All My Sons*, *Death of a Salesman*, the *Crucible*, A *View From the Bridge*, *After the Fall*, and *Incident at Vichy*.

The last twenty-five years

The great social turmoil of the late 1960s and early 1970s made its impression on the arts. It was a revolutionary period, and the theatre was deeply affected. Happenings, group gropes and participatory performances were a new kind of theatre, performed not in traditional theatre buildings, but in streets, garages, on vacant lots and so on. Convention was ignored and traditional theatre split at the sides. Life began to imitate art, and scenes of

ritualized madness seemed more like a synthesis of Brecht, Artaud, Genet and Ionesco than real life.

Theatre since the 1960s has remained vital because of its diversity. Unfortunately that diversity makes it impossible to do more than quickly scan the landscape. The social distress of the 1960s spawned a reaction against the traditional commercial theatre in the United States. Called the New Theatre, this somewhat limited movement appeared in coffee-houses and off-off Broadway theatres. Participants in the movement stressed creativity and non-traditional production standards and forms, and sought new kinds of theatrical materials. Ellen Stewart's La Mamma Experimental Theatre Club, Joe Cino's Café Cino, Julian Beck's Living Theatre, and the Open Theatre experimented with hundreds of plays, techniques, and styles. Outside of the groups just mentioned, many other individuals should be noted in these contemporary approaches—Jerzy Grotowski, Peter Brook, Robert Wilson, and Richard Schechner, to name a few.

Theatre still requires that the playwright bring to the theatre new works for production—in whatever style. The commercial limitations of theatre production cause great difficulty in this regard. Significant efforts, such as those of the Actors' Theatre of Louisville, are greatly responsible not only for helping new playwrights, but also for bringing new works to production, and for keeping theatre vital in areas of the United States not next door to New York City and Broadway. The significance of these efforts can be seen in two productions, the *Gin Game* and *Agnes of God*. D. L. Coburn's the *Gin Game* emerged from the Actors' Theatre's First Festival of New Plays in 1976–7. Its story evolves around an elderly man and woman who meet in a retirement home. The vehicle for their reviews, debates, and intimacy is an on-going card game (Fig. **13.43**). The

13.43 D. L. Coburn, *The Gin Game*, The Actors' Theatre of Louisville. 1978. Georgia Healslip (left), Will Hussung (right).

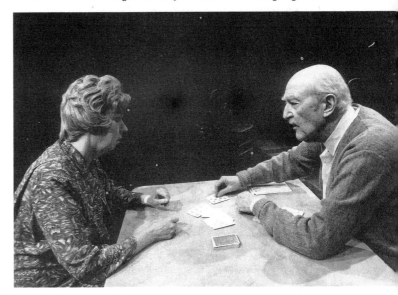

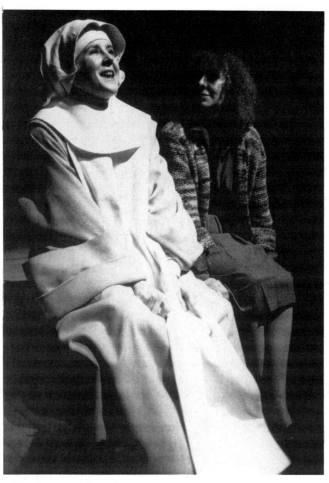

13.44 John Pielmeier, *Agnes of God*, 1980. The Actors' Theatre of Louisville. Mia Dillon (left), Adale O'Brien (right).

Gin Game won a Pulitzer prize in 1978 and enjoyed a successful Broadway run. John Pielmeier's *Agnes of God* (Fig. **13.44**) was produced as part of the Fourth Festival of New American Plays, 1979–80. It deals with a psychiatrist who becomes obsessed with an unusually mystical nun who has been charged with murdering her child at birth. These and other Actors' Theatre of Louisville plays, such as Beth Henley's *Crimes of the Heart* (1978–9), Marsha Norman's *Getting Out* (1977–8), and William Mastro-simone's *Extremities* (1980–1), continue to make a signific-ant contribution to the contemporary theatre, often finding their way to the commercial forum of Broadway.

Theatre today is a mix of modernists, who still believe that theatre requires a representation of an action, and post-modernists, who, in Robert Palmer's words, believe theatre to represent "an archeological shift in the presuppositions of our thinking". Playwrights as such seem unnecessary to the post-modernists. Rather they are makers of theatre—people such as Richard Foreman and Robert Wilson, who call performance art "the theatre of images". Theatre, like the other arts, has entered an age of pluralism.

FILM

Beginnings

On 23 April 1896, at Koster and Bial's Music Hall in New York, the Leigh Sisters performed their umbrella dance. Then, waves broke upon the shore. This was the exciting subject shown at the launch of a new process for screen projection of movies, the Vitascope. Invented by Thomas Armat, although Thomas Edison has received much of the credit, the Vitascope was the result of centuries of experimentation in how to make pictures move. Relying on the principle of persistence of vision and the basics of photography, the Vitascope could capture real objects in motion and present them on a screen for a mass audience.

Technological experiments in rapid-frame photo-graphy were numerous in the last half of the nineteenth century, but it remained for Thomas Armat and others to perfect a stop-motion device essential to screen projec-tion. Two Frenchmen, the Lumière brothers, are usually credited with the first public projection of movies on a large screen in 1895. By 1897 the Lumières had success-fully exhibited their *Cinématographie* all over Europe and listed a catalogue of 358 films. They opened in America three months after the première of the Vitascope. Later that year the American Biograph made its début using larger film and projecting twice as many pictures per minute, creating the largest, brightest, and steadiest picture of all.

At that point movies were nothing more than a recording of everyday life. George Méliès in France and Edwin S. Porter in the United States would demonstrate the narrative and manipulative potential of the cinema. Between 1896 and 1914 Méliès turned out more than one thousand films. Edwin S. Porter, in charge of Edison Company Studios, studied the narrative attempts of Méliès, and, acting as his own scriptwriter, cameraman, and director, spliced together old and freshly shot film into the *Life of an American Firefighter*. In 1903 Porter made the *Great Train Robbery*, the most popular film of the decade. It ran a total of twelve minutes. The popular audience was entranced, and flocked to electric theatres to see movies that could engross, excite, and thrill them with stories of romance and adventure. The movies were a window to a wider world for the poor of America.

By 1910 the young film industry counted a handful of recognized stars, including the Danish actress Asta Nielsen and the French comedian Max Linder, who had made more than four hundred films for the screen's first mogul, Charles Pathé. Short films remained the staple of the industry, but especially in Europe there was a growing taste for more spectacular fare. The Italian film, *Quo Vadis*, was produced in 1912, complete with lavish sets, chariot races, Christians, lions, and a cast of hundreds. A full two hours in length, it was a landslide success.

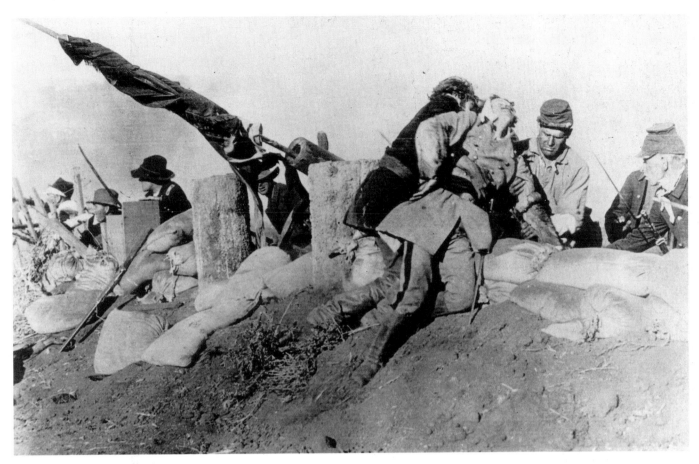

13.45 D. W Griffith, *The Birth of a Nation*, 1915.

Lawsuits regarding patents and monopolies marked the first decade of the century, and in order to escape the constant badgering of Thomas Edison's lawyers, independent film makers headed West to a sleepy California town called Hollywood, where among other things, weather and exotic and varied landscape were much more conducive to cinematography. By 1915 over half of all American movies were being made in Hollywood.

That year also witnessed the release of D. W. Griffith's *Birth of a Nation* (Fig. **13.45**), three hours in length, popular, controversial, and destined to become a landmark in cinema history. It unfolds the story of two families during the Civil War and the Reconstruction Period. Roundly condemned for its depiction of leering, bestial blacks rioting and raping white women, and for the rescue of whites by the Ku Klux Klan, the film nonetheless contains great artistry and a refinement of film making techniques. Griffith is cited as defining and refining nearly every technique in film: the fade-in, fade-out, long shot, full shot, close-up, moving camera, flash-back, crosscut, juxtaposition, editing, and preshooting rehearsals.

As if the *Birth of a Nation* were not colossal enough, Griffith followed it in 1916 with *Intolerance*, a two-million dollar epic of ancient Babylon, biblical Judea, sixteenth-century France, and contemporary America. As the film progressed, brilliant crosscutting increased in frantic pace to heighten suspense and tension. However, audiences found the film confusing. It failed miserably at the box office and ruined Griffith financially.

The same era produced the famous Mack Sennet comedies, which featured the hilarious antics and wild chase scenes of the Keystone Kops. Sennet was one of Griffith's partners in the Triangle Film Company. A third partner was Thomas Ince, who brought to the screen the prototypical cowboy hero, William S. Hart, in such works as *Wagon Tracks*. However, nothing better represents the second decade of the twentieth century than the work of the baggy pants comedian and true film genius, Charlie Chaplin, the Little Fellow. Chaplin represented all of humanity, and he communicated through the silent film as eloquently and deeply as any human ever has. In an era marked by disillusionment, Chaplin presented resilience, optimism, and an indomitable spirit that made him the love of millions. By the end of World War I, Chaplin shared the limelight with that most dashing of American heroes, Douglas Fairbanks.

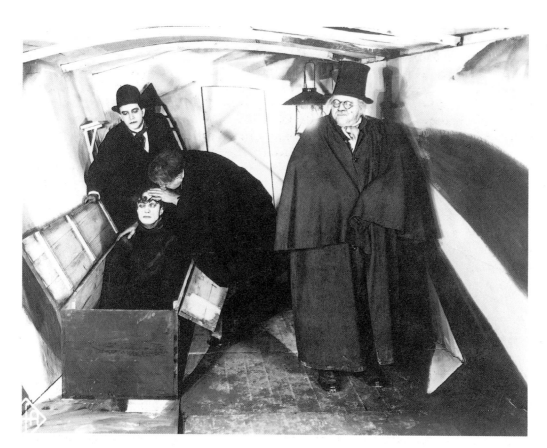

13.46 Robert Wiene, *The Cabinet of Dr. Caligari*, 1919.

Expressionism

German expressionism made its mark in film as well as in the visual and other performing arts, and in 1919, its most masterful example, Robert Wiene's the *Cabinet of Dr. Caligari* (Fig. **13.46**), shook the world. Macabre sets, surrealistic lighting effects, and distorted properties, all combined to portray a menacing post-war German world.

Europe

A film-making revival engulfed Europe after the war, led by talented film makers such as Carl Mayer, F. W. Murnau, G. W. Pabst, and Fritz Lang. Lang's futuristic *Metropolis* told the story of life in the twenty-first century. Critics called the plot ludicrous, but marveled at the photographic effects. In France, film found its first real aesthetic theorist in Louis Delluc and came to be regarded as a serious art form.

Russian film making theory can be seen in the concepts and expressions of Sergei Eisenstein in *Battleship Potemkin* (1925). This cruel story of the crew of the ship *Potemkin* contains one of the most legendary scenes in cinema. A crowd of citizens are trapped on the great steps of Odessa between the Czar's troops and mounted Cossacks. The editing is truly amazing. The scene comprises a montage of short, vivid shots—a face, a flopping

arm, a slipping body, a pair of broken eye glasses—all deftly combined into a powerful whole.

The glorious twenties

The 1920s were the heyday of Hollywood, and its extravagance and star system dazzled the world with Gloria Swanson and legions of other starlets. It was the era of the big studios, such as MGM, Paramount, Universal, Fox, and Warner Brothers, accompanied by a wave of construction of fantastic movie houses, which rivaled the opulence of baroque absolutism. The scandals, the intrigues, and the glamor, mostly immoral, were the stuff of legends. Out of such decadence came Cecil B. DeMille and the *Ten Commandments* and the *King of Kings*.

Twenty thousand movie theatres existed around the country, and to keep apace of demand, movie studios turned out one film after another—mostly on a formula basis. The decade, nevertheless, produced some great artistry, for example, Erich von Stroheim's *Greed* (1924). Although cut from nine hours to two by MGM employees, the film was a brilliant story of a boorish dentist, practicing without a license, who murders his greedy wife.

The twenties was the era of Fairbanks and Pickford and an immigrant Italian tango dancer, called Rudolph Valentino, who made millions of American women swoon in movies such as *Four Horsemen of the Apocalypse*, the *Sheik*,

Blood and Sand, and *Son of the Sheik*. After Valentino's death, John Gilbert set feminine hearts fluttering, and his co-star on three occasions, Greta Garbo, did the same for American men. The Talmadge and Gish sisters, along with Pola Negri, helped fuel the amorous fires of the roaring twenties. The lighter side of movie making featured Harold Lloyd, Harry Langdon, Buster Keaton, and Laurel and Hardy.

Although the technological breakthrough had come many years earlier, and short talking films had been released, the *Jazz Singer* in 1927 heralded the age of talkies, with Al Jolson's famous line "You ain't heard nothin' yet!" As eager as individuals usually are to present new technological advances, the film industry was not particularly enthusiastic about introducing talking films. The public was very satisfied with silent movies. Profits were enormous, and the new invention required a vast capital investment to equip movie theatres with sound projection equipment. However, the die was cast. For some it meant continued stardom, while for others, whose voices did not match their visual appearance, it meant obscurity. Early successes in using sound as an aesthetic component of the film came from directors King Vidor in *Hallelujah* and Rouben Mamoulian in *Applause* (1929). Lewis Milestone's *All Quiet on the Western Front* used sound to unify visual compositions in a truly remarkable and unforgettable anti-war statement.

The thirties

The early thirties produced films of crime and violence. Films such as *Little Caesar*, with Edward G. Robinson, kept Hollywood's coffers full during the Depression. The gangster genre fell out of favor amid public cries that American youth were being harmed by the glorified violence of the cinema. The earthier side of films also showed itself in the mid-thirties in the sexually explicit dialogue of Mae West. Again amid public outcry, the Production Code was strengthened, and Miss West was toned down. From the mid-thirties on, new types of film emerged, including the musicals of Fred Astaire and Ginger Rogers, in a Busby Berkeley world of glitter and tinsel that attempted to bolster sagging attendances and salve the sores of a Depression-weary populace. The screen overflowed with Jeanette MacDonald and Nelson Eddy, Maurice Chevalier, Shirley Temple, and a new star, Judy Garland, in the *Wizard of Oz* (1939). The tawdry faded, and wholesomeness abounded. Happiness poured forth in the *Thin Man* (1934). A new genre of comedy films was heralded by Clark Gable and Claudette Colbert in Frank Capra's *It Happened One Night* (1935).

But there was more to the thirties. Dozens of new stars arose (MGM boasted "more stars than there are in heaven")—Bette Davis, Henry Fonda, Spencer Tracy, Jean Harlow, Joan Crawford, Katherine Hepburn, Leslie Howard, Norma Shearer, Robert Taylor, Tyrone Power, Errol Flynn, Frederick March, James Cagney, Will Rogers, Wallace Beery, Mickey Rooney, Gary Cooper, James Stewart. The list seems endless, as do the films. The most popular and unusual star of the thirties, however, was a product of the artistic genius of Walt Disney. Mickey Mouse led a genre of animated films whose popularity and creativity persists to this day. The western continued, and in 1939 John Ford's classic, *Stagecoach*, made John Wayne the prototypical cowboy hero. This superbly edited film exemplified the technique of cutting within the frame, which became a Ford trademark (and also prohibited others from re-editing and tampering with the product). At the other end of the spectrum, the thirties sent the Marx Brothers crashing through slapstick comedies and popping pompous bubbles and produced W. C. Fields's ill-humor, which stemmed from bubbles of an alcoholic nature.

Chaplin continued to produce comedy into the thirties. *City Lights* (1931) was a silent relic in an age of sound, but its consummate artistry made it a classic nonetheless. It depicts the story of Chaplin's love for a blind girl, who erroneously believes he is rich. He robs a bank and pays for an operation that restores her sight. He is apprehended and sent to prison. Years later she happens across a tramp being chased by a group of boys. Amused and yet saddened, she offers the tramp a coin and a flower. At the touch of his hand she recognizes him but is stunned by the realization that her imagined rich and handsome lover is really nothing more than a comical tramp. The film ends with the awareness that their relationship cannot be. *City Lights* is a moving film containing touching scenes and great comedy, including a society party scene in which Chaplin swallows a whistle, and in a fit of hiccups, destroys a musical performance and calls a pack of dogs and several taxicabs.

The epic of the decade was David O. Selznick's *Gone with the Wind*, a four-million-dollar, three-and-three-quarter-hour, eternally popular extravaganza with an improbable plot and racial stereotypes. Nonetheless, Clark Gable, Vivian Leigh, Leslie Howard, and Olivia De Havidland, along with the magnificent cinematography made the film a lasting piece of entertainment.

The rise of Nazism in Germany had virtually eliminated the vigorous German film industry by the late thirties, but not until Fritz Lang had produced his psychological thriller M, which employed subtle and deft manipulation of sound, including a Grieg leitmotif. Peter Lorre's performance as a child-murderer was significant. From Europe during the thirties also came the master of suspense and shot manipulation, Alfred Hitchcock, whose the *Man Who Knew Too Much*, the *Thirty-Nine Steps*, *Sabotage*, *Secret Agent*, and the *Lady Vanishes* were only a prelude to decades of further artistry. Throughout this era Hollywood film was unabashedly non-didactic. Entertainment was its primary goal, but that did not preclude artistry and virtuosity in shaping a celluloid strip into an aesthetically articulated series of forms and images.

The forties and neo-realism

World War II and its aftermath brought radical change to the form and content of the cinema. A film came out in 1940 that stunned even Hollywood. Darryl Zanuck and John Ford's version of John Steinbeck's *Grapes of Wrath* artistically visualized the social criticism of Steinbeck's portrayal of the Depression through superb cinematography and compelling performances. Theme and social commentary burst forth again in 1941 with two outstanding works, *How Green Was My Valley*, which dealt with exploited coal miners in Wales, and *Citizen Kane*, about wealth and power, and thought by some to be the best film ever produced. The cinematic techniques of *Citizen Kane* forged a new trail. Orson Welles, director and star, and Greg Toland, cinematographer, brilliantly combined deep-focus photography, unique lighting effects, rapid cutting, and moving camera sequences.

The forties also saw Van Johnson, Alan Ladd, Humphrey Bogart, Lauren Bacall, Gregory Peck, Cary Grant, and Ingrid Bergman in such works as the *Philadelphia Story*, *Notorious*, and *Casablanca*. But as the war ended and Italy revived from the yoke of Fascism, a new concept set the stage for the years ahead.

In 1945 Roberto Rossellini's *Rome, Open City* graphically depicted the misery of Rome during the German occupation. It was shot on the streets of Rome using hidden cameras and mostly non-professional actors and actresses. Technically, the quality of the work was deficient, but the effectiveness of its objective viewpoint and documentary realism changed the course of cinema and inaugurated a style called neo-realism.

McCarthyism and message movies

The early years after World War II were extremely profitable, but the era of the big studio was on the wane. The strengthening of labor unions and anti-trust rulings on theatre ownership completely changed the nature of the film industry. In addition, the House Un-American Activities Committee hearings produced a decade in which all liberal thought was stifled. Any subject or individual that might in any way be considered controversial was cast aside. Hundreds of careers and lives were destroyed, and films turned almost exclusively to safe and escapist fare. Message movies became virtually nonexistent in the United States. Even the most daring film of the period, *On the Waterfront*, obfuscated the facts when it came to revealing the higher-ups who were manipulating corrupt unions. At the same time television made it possible for the public to have moving pictures in the living room. Hollywood's immediate response to television was a series of technological spectaculars such as CinemaScope, Cinerama, and 3-D. Soon, it became clear that good movies, not special effects, were needed to stimulate attendance. John Ford's westerns such as *Red River*, Billy Wilder's *Sunset Boulevard*, and Alfred Hitchcock's *North by Northwest* were forthcoming, as was the blockbuster success *Ben Hur*, in 1959. Fred Zinnemann's *High Noon* and *From Here to Eternity* earned high plaudits. Elia Kazan, a theatre entrepreneur, turned to film in 1944 and produced outstanding dramas, such as *A Tree Grows in Brooklyn*, *A Streetcar Named Desire* (with Marlon Brando repeating his famous Broadway role), and *On the Waterfront*.

The demise of the studio

The forties and fifties saw a revival of musical comedies, more John Wayne, and an unforgettable genre of forgettable Saturday matinée series from *Captain Video* to *Buck Rogers*. Elvis Presley first gyrated across the screen in 1956, and the tragic fall of Judy Garland captured the American heart. Elizabeth Taylor and Audrey Hepburn came to stardom in *National Velvet* and *Roman Holiday* respectively. However, the most unforgettable actress of the fifties was Marilyn Monroe, movie sex symbol and tragic off-screen personality. The *Misfits* (1962), an appropriately titled work, brought her and Clark Gable together for their last film appearances.

The sixties was an era of international film and of the independent producer. No longer did the studio undertake programs of film production, not did they keep stables of contract players. Now each film was an independent project whose artistic control was in the hands of the director. A new breed of film-maker came to prominence—Rossellini, De Sica, Kurosawa, Fellini, Antonioni, Bergman, Godard, and Truffaut. Neo-realism predominated in the foreign film tradition, which saw such superb works as Fellini's *La Strada* (1954) and *La Dolce Vita* (1960). Film art was universal, and the stunning artistry of Kurosawa's *Rashomon* (1951) and *Seven Samurai* (1954) had tied East and West in an exploration of the human condition that could penetrate to great depths or slide across the surface in inane superficiality. Imagery, symbolism, and an unusual vision marked the films of Sweden's Ingmar Bergman. *Wild Strawberries*, the *Virgin Spring*, and *Persona*, among others, creatively and often horrifyingly delved into human character, suffering, and motivation.

The last twenty-five years

The seventies and eighties have seen curious directions in film. Devotees have come to regard film as an art form with a significant enough heritage to provide for historical and scholarly study and analysis. More and more films are being made to appeal to a very specific and sophisticated clientèle, and even movies made for and achieving wide commercial success have levels directed at an in-group of film buffs. For example, the tremendously popular *Star Wars* consisted of a carefully developed series of repetitions and satires of old movies. Lack of knowledge of old films did not hamper one's enjoyment of the film and its tremendous visual accomplishments, but awareness of the parodies enhanced the response of those who were knowledgeable.

Questions remain to be answered regarding whether cable television and pay TV, in which first-run films are released not to movie theatres but to television outlets, will doom the theatre film. Certainly such an approach has and will have a significant effect on the basic aesthetics of film making. Films shot for theatre screens are basically long-shot oriented, because the size of the screen enhances broad visual effects. Television, on the other hand, is a close-up medium. Its small viewing area cannot manage wide-angle panoramas. Details are simply too small. Television must rely mostly on the close-up and the medium shot. Television movies must be written to hook an audience in the first few minutes to prevent viewers from changing channels. A theatre movie can develop more slowly since the audience is unlikely to go to another theatre if something exciting does not happen in the first few moments. Compromises with film aesthetics already influence some film making, where directors have one eye on the theatre box office and the other on the lucrative re-release to television. As a result, this perspective produces films which try to meet the aesthetic parameters of both media. It is clear, however, that as the twentieth century draws to a close, only the mass marketplace will decide what the art of the cinema will be, because whether art, entertainment, or both, cinema depends upon commercial success for its continuation.

DANCE

Diaghilev and the ballet tradition

Dance revolutionaries leaped through two different doors in the early twentieth century. The first door was not only held open by Sergei Diaghilev (1872–1929), but was mostly built by him. Diaghilev arrived in St. Petersburg, Russia, in 1890 to study law. Through his cousin he soon became friends with several artists, among them, Alexandre Benois, Walter Nouvel, and Leon Bakst. Not particularly interested in ballet, Diaghilev studied music (with Rimsky-Korsakov, who dissuaded Sergei from attempting a musical career) and also painting. His artistic interests distracted him so that he took six years instead of four to get his law degree. In 1898 Diaghilev's artistic

friends launched a new magazine, *World of Art*, and appointed him as editor. His entrepreneurial and managerial talents made the venture a success and launched him in a career of artistic management which shaped the ballet world of the twentieth century. His love of the arts, his associations with ballet, and his social contacts made it possible for him to produce outstanding works employing the finest choreographers, dancers and designers of the age. Diaghilev played a tremendously important role in bringing the art of Paris and Munich to Moscow and Leningrad and vice versa. The *World of Art* had a wide impact on the arts in general, as did Diaghilev himself.

Having successfully produced opera outside of Russia, Diaghilev was encouraged by designer Benois to take Russian ballet to Paris. In 1909 he opened the first of his many *Ballets russes*. The dancers included the greatest dancers of Russia, among them Anna Pavlova and Vaslav Nijinsky (Fig. **13.47**). For the next three years Diaghilev's ballets were choreographed by Mikhail Fokine, whose

13.47 Vaslav Nijinsky as Petrushka, 1911. The New York Public Library.

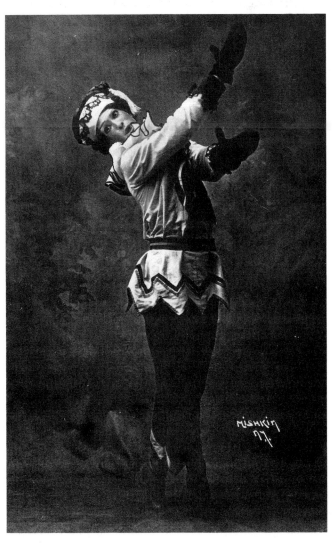

originality of approach stood quite in contrast to the evening-long spectaculars of Petipa. Fokine was in tune with theatrical and musical theories stemming from Wagner, Reinhardt, Appia, and so on, which insisted on artistic unity of all production elements—costumes, settings, music, as well as dancing. Dancing, in turn, he felt, should blend harmoniously with the theme and subject of the production. Fokine was to leave Diaghilev's company in 1912, but probably the great contribution made by their association, in addition to the aesthetic unity just mentioned, was the reintroduction of the male dancer as a premier performer.

The first production of the *Ballets russes* in Paris was a resounding success and almost immediately revived the stagnant and debased Parisian entertainment which ballet in France had become. Invited to return in 1910, Diaghilev included in his program for that appearance a work commissioned from the young composer Igor Stravinsky, the *Firebird*. By the advent of World War I, the Russian ballet had conquered London, Berlin, Rome, Monte Carlo, Vienna, and Budapest, and a decaying ballet tradition had been rescued.

The success was due as much to the superb integration of outstanding music, costume, and set design as it was to Fokine's choreography. The consummate artistry of Alexandre Bakst's costumes and sets must be acknowledged, and a glimpse of their exquisite line and style can be seen in Figure **13.48**. His vibrant colors and rich textures greatly influenced fashion and interior decoration of the period.

In one of those twists of fate and personality, Diaghilev was not content to allow Nijinsky to remain his *premier danseur*. He insisted that Nijinsky be a choreographer as well, which partially accounted for Fokine's departure. In 1912 Nijinsky choreographed the controversial *Prelude to the Afternoon of a Faun* with music by Debussy. The choreography was latent with sexual suggestion, and the performance caused an uproar over its obscenity. Nijinsky's choreography was strangely angular in contrast to Debussy's music. The dancing suggested the linear and geometric qualities of a Greek frieze or vase painting. A year later Nijinsky caused an actual riot when his choreography of Stravinsky's *Rite of Spring* was unveiled. Although the controversy had more to do with the music than with the dancing, the choreography was also controversial, hinting at deep primordial forces, especially in the scene we noted in the music section, wherein a virgin dances herself to death to satisfy the gods. Nijinsky's decision to marry in 1913 caused a rift with the homosexual Diaghilev, resulting in Nijinsky's dismissal from the company.

Diaghilev's new choreographer, Léonide Massine, took the company (and ballet in general) in new directions. Previously the *Ballets russes* had featured picturesque Russian themes. Now it turned to tastes emerging in the visual arts, to cubism and surrealism. *Parade* in 1917

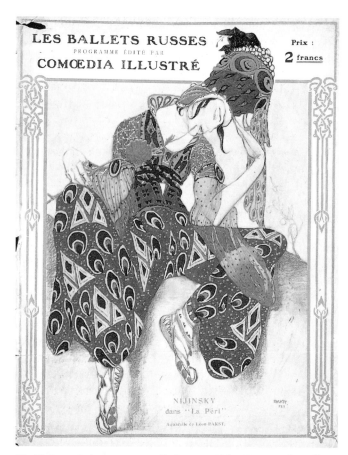

13.48 Leon Bakst, costume design, *Les Ballets Russes – Comœdia Illustré*, "Nijinsky dans *La Péri*", 1911. Victoria and Albert Museum, London.

found dancers in huge skyscraper-like cubist costumes designed by Pablo Picasso. The music, by Satie, included sounds of typewriters and steamship whistles.

In 1924 Diaghilev hired a new choreographer who was to be a force in ballet for the next sixty years. George Balanchine came to Diaghilev from St. Petersburg and choreographed ten productions for him over the next four years. Two of these continue to be danced—the *Prodigal Son*, composed by Prokofiev, and *Apollo*, composed by Stravinsky. When Diaghilev died in 1929 his company died with him, and an era ended. Ballet had been reborn as a major art form with elegance and excellence, a blending of choreography, dancing, music, and visual art—a rival to opera in claiming "perfect synthesis of the arts".

Duncan and the modern dance movement

In the previous chapter our discussion closed by noting the revolutionary approaches of Loie Fuller. These were indicative of dissatisfaction with the formal conventions and static qualities into which ballet had fallen, and against which even Diaghilev responded. However, while Diaghilev continued within balletic traditions, others did not, and the most significant of these was the remarkable and unrestrained Isadora Duncan (1878–1927). By 1905 she had gained notoriety for her barefoot and deeply emotional dancing. She was considered controversial among balletomanes and reformers alike, but even Fokine saw in her style a confirmation of his own beliefs.

Although an American, Isadora Duncan achieved her fame in Europe. Her dances were emotional interpretations of moods suggested to her by music or by nature. Her dance was personal. Her costume was inspired by Greek tunics and draperies and she danced in bare feet, a strictly unconventional and significant fact, which continues to be a basic quality of the modern dance tradition she helped to form.

The personalized emotion and unstructured form of Duncan's approach to dance certainly differed from established dance tradition, its novelty alone proving noteworthy. However, it was as much Duncan herself who accounted for the impact of her style. Unabashedly forward, she maintained, "I have discovered the art which has been lost for two thousand years." Outgoing and eccentric, she gained entrance to numerous circles which would have been closed to anyone of lesser steel, and, as a result, she was able to raise untold funds for her numerous projects. She was a curiosity, and, as it turned out, a tragic one, but her ability to keep the spotlight on herself, coupled with her undeniable performance magnetism, made her and her dancing style a significant force in the era. She died of a broken neck when the fringe of her shawl caught in the tire spokes of a car in which she was riding. Only moments before she called to friends, as she stepped into the car, "Goodbye, my friends. I go to glory."

Despite the notoriety of the young feminist Isadora, it remained for her contemporary, Ruth St. Denis, and her husband, Ted Shawn, to lay more substantial cornerstones for modern dance. Much more serious than Duncan, Ruth St. Denis numbered among her favorite books Kant's *Critique of Pure Reason* and Dumas' *Camille*. Her dancing began as a strange combination of exotic, oriental interpretations, and Delsartian poses. (Delsarte is a nineteenth-century system originated by François Delsarte as a scientific examination of the manner in which emotions and ideas were transmitted through gestures and posture. His system came from overzealous disciples who formed his findings into a series of graceful gestures and poses, which supposedly had specific denotative value. To us, it all may look rather foolish.) Ruth St. Denis was a remarkable performer with a magnificently proportioned body. She manipulated it and various draperies and veils into graceful presentations of line and form, in which the fabric became an extension of the body itself.

St. Denis' impact on dance was solidified by the formation with her husband of a company and a school to carry on her philosophies and choreography. The Denishawn school and company were headquartered in Los Angeles and took a totally eclectic approach to dance. Any and all traditions were included, from formal ballet to Oriental and American Indian dances. The touring company presented tremendously varied fare, from Hindu dances to the latest ballroom crazes. Branches of the school were formed throughout the United States, and the touring company occasionally appeared with the *Ziegfeld Follies*. By 1932 St. Denis and Shawn had separated, and the Denishawn Company ceased to exist. Nevertheless it had made its mark on its pupils, if not always positively.

First to leave Denishawn was Martha Graham, probably the most influential figure in modern dance. Although the term modern dance defies accurate definition and satisfies few, it remains the most appropriate label for the non-balletic tradition Martha Graham has come to symbolize. Graham found Denishawn unsatisfactory as an artistic base, but her point of view, essentially, maintained that artistic individualism is fundamental. "There are no general rules. Each work of art creates its own code." Even modern dance has come to include its own conventions, however, principally because it tried so hard to be different from formal ballet. Ballet movements were largely rounded and symmetrical. Therefore, modern dancers emphasized angularity and asymmetry. Ballet stressed leaps and based its line on toework, while modern dance hugged the floor and dancers went barefoot. As a result, the early works of Graham and others tended to be rather fierce and earthy, as opposed to graceful. But beneath it all was the desire to express emotion first and foremost. The execution of conventional positions and movements, on which ballet is based, was totally disregarded. Martha Graham described her choreography as "a graph of the heart".

As her career progressed, Martha Graham's work has emerged, through her own dancing and that of her company, as a reaction to specific artistic problems of the movement. Early works were notorious for their jerks and tremblings, which Graham saw as based on the natural act of breathing. The dynamics of contraction and release fundamental to inhalation and exhalation created a series of whiplash movements in which energy and effort were expressly revealed (in contrast to ballet, in which effort is concealed). Gradually her style became more lyrical in line and movement, but passion was always the foundation.

After the Depression, when social criticism formed a large part of artistic expression, Graham pursued topical themes (unusual for her) concerning the shaping of America: *Frontier* (1935), *Act of Judgement*, *Letter to the World*, and, finally, her renowned work to the music of Aaron Copland, *Appalachian Spring* (1944). *Appalachian Spring* dealt with the effects of Puritanism and depicted the overcoming of its fire-and-brimstone by love and common sense.

Another influential modern dancer to leave Denishawn was Doris Humphrey, for whom all dance existed on "the arc between two deaths", that is, between absolute motionlessness and complete collapse. Her choreography stressed the dynamic tension between balance and imbalance, between fall and recovery. She and her partner, Charles Weidman, who was famous as a pantomimist, developed their modern dance techniques from elementary principles of movement. Various treatments of conflict and resolution were fundamental and led to such works as the *Shakers* (1931) and the *New Dance* trilogy (1935–6). From the Humphrey–Weidman company came two significant additional forces in the modern dance exploration of individualism in artistry—Anna Sokolow and José Limon.

Ballet in the thirties

Ballet, of course, did not succumb to obscurity with Diaghilev's departure. Strong national traditions were developed and maintained throughout Europe. Attention turned in the United States to establishing an American ballet. In 1933 Lincoln Kirstein and Edward Warburg combined forces to create the School of American Ballet, which opened on 1 January 1934 with George Ballanchine as its head. Elsewhere in the country the thirties witnessed the establishment of the San Francisco Ballet and the Philadelphia Ballet.

Attempts to develop artistically significant ballet companies in the United States found themselves continually in competition with a company which stressed its Russian character, the new *Ballets russes de Monte Carlo*, an attempt to perpetuate the traditions of Diaghilev. Its American tours in the thirties were greeted by sensational responses from the American public. If the *Ballets russes de Monte Carlo* was competition for young American companies, it was also a blessing, because its tours introduced many Americans to ballet. It fostered positive public response to an art form which was struggling against modern dance experiments and was also wrapped in unfortunate stereotypes of sissy stuff and of lunatic local teachers who forced young dancers *en pointe* before their feet had matured sufficiently to withstand such strain.

World War II brought an end to the American Ballet Company and provided a watershed for exciting new efforts, which would occur when peace returned.

After World War II

Much of what we said of dance in the early years of the century applies to the years since 1945. José Limon and

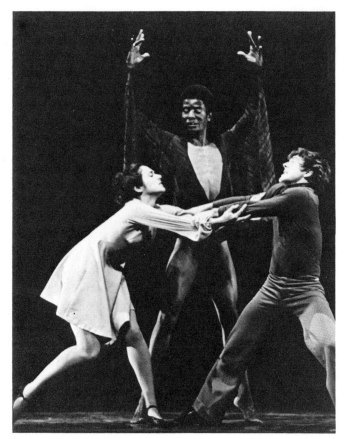

13.49 Choreographer: Jean Sabatine, *Nameless Hour*. Jazz Dance Theatre at Penn State, The Pennsylvania State University.

Martha Graham, as well as George Balanchine, continued to influence dance well into the second half of this century. Limon's *Moor's Pavane* used Purcell's *Abdelazer* for its music. Based on Shakespeare's *Othello* and structured on the Elizabethan court dance, the *Pavane* is an unusual dramatic composition that sustains tension from beginning to end.

Martha Graham's troupe produced a radical and controversial choreographer who broke with many of the traditions of modern dance (as flexible as those traditions have been). He incorporated chance or aleatory elements into his choreography and has often been associated with the composer John Cage. Merce Cunningham uses everyday activity as well as dance movements in his works. His concern is to have the audience see the dance in a new light, and, whatever the reaction may be, his choreography is radically different from anyone else's. His works show elegance and coolness, as well as a severely abstract quality. Works such as *Summerspace* and *Winterbranch* illustrate Cunningham's use of chance, or indeterminacy. His object is to keep the dance fresh, and he thoroughly prepares numerous options and orders for sets, which then (sometimes by flipping a coin) can be varied and intermixed in different order from performance to performance. The same piece may appear totally different from one night to the next. Cunningham also treats stage space as an integral part of the performance and allows focus to be spread across various areas of the stage, unlike classical ballet which tends to isolate its focus on center stage or downstage center alone. So Cunningham allows the audience member to choose where to focus, as opposed to forcing that focus. Finally, he tends to allow each element of the dance to go its own way. As a result, the direct, beat-for-beat relationship that audiences have come to expect between music and footfalls in ballet and much modern dance simply does not exist.

Since 1954, another graduate of Martha Graham's troupe (and also of Merce Cunningham's) has provided strong direction in modern dance. Paul Taylor's work has a vibrant, energetic, and abstract quality that often suggests primordial actions. Taylor, like Cunningham, often uses strange combinations of music and movement in highly ebullient and unrestrained dances such as *Book of Beasts*. Interestingly, Taylor's music often turns to traditional composers, such as Beethoven, and to specialized works like string quartets. The combination of such a basically esoteric musical form with his wild movements creates unique and challenging works for the viewer to grasp.

In a tradition which encourages individual exploration and independence, there have been many accomplished dancer/choreographers. Alwin Nikolais was among these. His works (he designs the scenery, costumes, and lights and composes the music, as well as the choreography) tend to be mixed-media extravaganzas, which celebrate the electronic age with spectacles that many have compared to early court masques. Often the display is so dazzling that the audience loses the dancers in the lighting effects and scenic environment. Another figure of importance is Alvin Ailey, a versatile dancer whose company is known for its unusual repertoire and energetically free movements. Twyla Tharp and Yvonne Ranier both have experimented with space and movement. James Waring has incorporated Bach and 1920s pop songs, florid pantomimes and abstractions, as well as romantic point work.

Another form of dance, which has its roots in the black musical heritage, but which draws upon the broad experiments of modern dance is jazz dance. Its forms are not universally agreed upon, and like modern dance, its directions are still in flux. Nevertheless, stemming from sources as diverse and yet as allied as "primitive" Africa and the urban ghetto, this discipline has seen significant activity and experimentation throughout the United States (Fig. **13.49**). Choreographers such as Asadata Dafora Horton in the 1930s and Katherine Dunham and Pearl Primus in the 1940s were the pioneers in this approach, which has seen contemporary works from choreographers such as Talley Beatty and Douglas McKayle.

Contemporary ballet is so universal that it is virtually impossible even to name the plethora of excellent companies and dancers around the world. If modern communication and travel have made our world a global neighborhood, they have also made it possible for individuals in the hinterlands to have access to fine experiences in ballet and modern dance through international tours of the world's great companies. The Bolshoi, the Stuttgart, Royal Danish, and so on have made occasional trips to the United States. Often large numbers of American tourists are found in the ballet houses of London, Moscow, and Vienna. In the United States and Canada fine professional regional companies keep ballet traditions alive and fresh. Dance has become one of this country's most popular and growing art forms, with the availability of quality works growing each year.

ARCHITECTURE

Art Nouveau continued into the early years of the twentieth century, with one of its greatest exponents, Antoni Gaudí (1852–1926), designing town houses such as the Casa Batlló (Fig. **13.50**) in Barcelona. At the same

13.50 Antoni Gaudí, Casa Batlló, Barcelona, 1905–7.

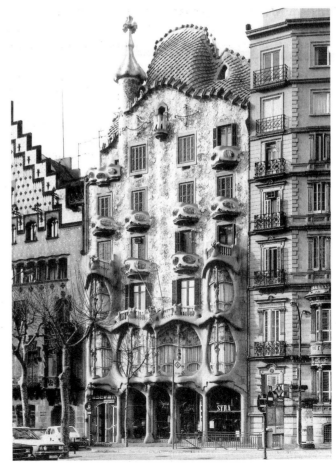

time widespread experimentation with new forms and materials continued. Descriptive terminology has been applied to many of the directions taken by individual architects, and attempts have been made to categorize more general tendencies, in order to bring the period under some kind of stylistic label. As was the case with modern dance, attempts at far-ranging categorizing have not met with universal acceptance. Terms such as rational, functional, international, and modern have been suggested. Some have quite specific application to some tendencies, but perhaps only the vague term modern can cope with them all. We will leave such discussion to others and will focus as much as possible on individual attempts. Individualism, as we have seen, has been the hallmark of the arts in our century.

Experimentation

Structural expression and preoccupation with building materials dominated the early twentieth century, as it had

13.51 Auguste Perret, Garage Ponthieu, Paris, 1905–6.

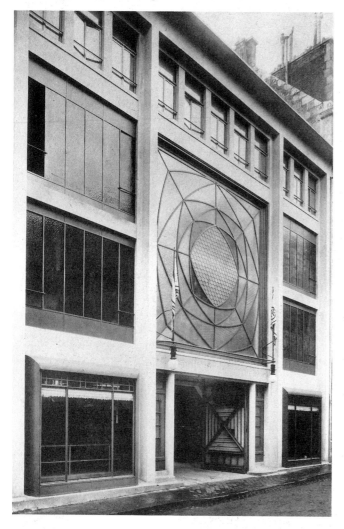

dominated the nineteenth. Of vital importance to the new century and its approaches was reinforced concrete or ferro-concrete. Ferro-concrete had been in use as a material since around 1849, but it had taken nearly fifty years to emerge fully as an important architectural material. Auguste Perret (1874–1954) single-mindedly set about developing formulas for building with ferro-concrete, and his efforts were influential in the works of those who followed. We can grasp some of the implications of this approach in Perret's Garage Ponthieu (Fig. **13.51**). The reinforced concrete structure emerges clearly in the exterior appearance. The open spaces were filled with glass or ceramic panels. The result achieved a certain elegance and logical expression of strength and lightness.

If Perret was single-minded in his approach to problems in structure and materials, his contemporary (and assistant to Louis Sullivan), Frank Lloyd Wright (1867–1959), was one of the most innovative and influential of twentieth-century architects. Perret summarized and continued earlier tradition, but Wright wished to initiate new ones. One manifestation of Wright's pursuits was the prairie style, developed around 1900 and drawing upon the flat landscape of the Midwest for its tone (Fig. **13.52**). The prairie houses reflected Japanese influence in their simple horizontal and vertical accents. Wright was also influenced by Sullivan in his pursuit of form and functional relationships. Wright attempted to devise practical arrangements for his interiors and to reflect the interior spaces in the exterior appearance of the building. He also tried to relate the exterior of the building to its context or natural environment and took great pains to suggest an interrelationship of interior and exterior space.

Wright also designed some of the furniture for his houses—comfort, function, and design integration were the chief criteria. Textures and colors in the environment were duplicated in the materials, including large expanses of wood both in the house and its furniture. He made a point of giving his furniture several functions, for example, tables that also served as cabinets. All spaces and objects were precisely designed to present a complete environment. Wright was convinced that houses profoundly influenced the people who lived in them, and he saw the architect as a "molder of humanity". Wright's works ranged from the simple to the complex, from the serene to the dramatic (Fig. **13.53**), and from interpenetration to enclosure of space. He always pursued experimentation, and the exploration of various interrelationships of spaces and geometric forms mark his designs.

As we mentioned, the early twentieth century was a time of individual experimentation in form and materials. The United States produced Purcell and Elmslie. George W. Maher, Schmidt, Garden and Martin, as well as Charles and Henry Green, Irving Gill, and Bernard R. Maybeck. Germany produced Peter Behrens, Bonatz and Scholer, Max Berg, and Fritz Höger. Other European architects

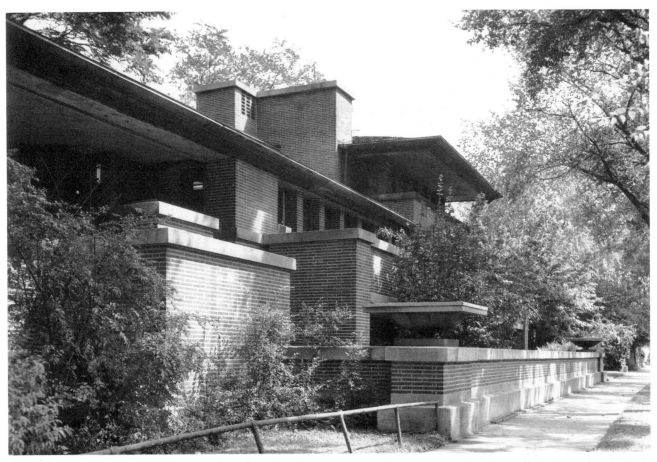

13.52 Frank Lloyd Wright, Robie House, Chicago, 1907–9.

13.53 Frank Lloyd Wright, Kaufmann House, ''Falling Water'', Bear Run, Pennsylvania, 1936–37.

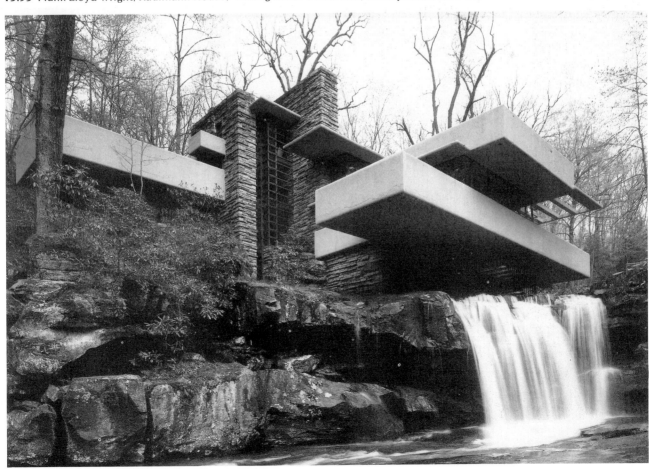

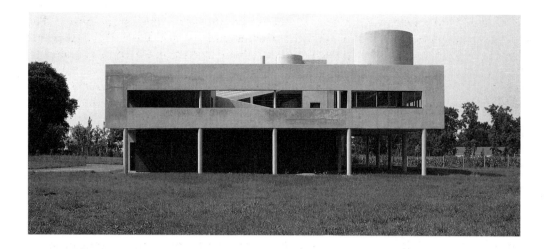

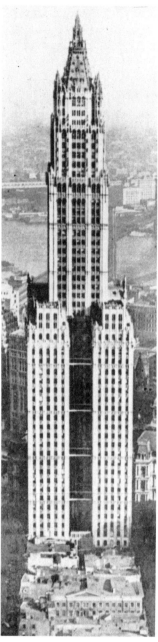

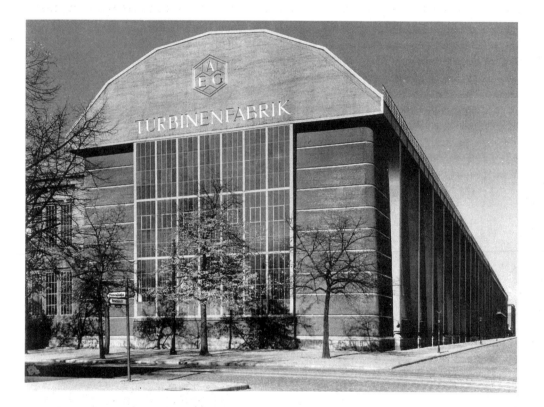

included Otto Wagner, Josef Hoffmann, Adolf Loos, H. P. Berlage, Michael de Klerk, and Piet Kramer. There were, of course, many others, all reflecting individualized concepts and approaches.

Use of poured concrete and exposed steel, both of whose textures contributed to the external expression of a building, can be seen in the A. E. G. turbine factory designed by Peter Behrens (1868–1940) (Fig. **13.54**). Apart from supporting girders, the side walls of the factory are totally of glass and create an expressly open feeling. The façades have no decoration whatsoever, but the front corners of poured concrete are striated as if to suggest masonry blocks. The flat plane of the façade is broken by the overhanging gabled roof and the forward-reaching window panels.

13.55 Le Corbusier, Villa Savoye, Poissy, France, 1928–30.

13.54 Peter Behrens, AEG turbine factory, Berlin, 1908–9.

13.56 Cass Gilbert, The Woolworth Building, New York, 1913.

Poured concrete and new concepts in design can also be seen in the works of Le Corbusier (1887–1965) in the 1920s and 30s. Le Corbusier was concerned with integration of structure and function, especially in poured concrete. His belief that a house was "a machine to be lived in" was demonstrated by several residences in these two decades. The machine concept did not imply a depersonalization, as much machine-related art in the first half of the century did. Rather, it implied efficient construction from standard, mass-produced parts, logically designed for usage as the parts of an efficient house-machine. Le Corbusier had espoused a domino system of design for houses, using a series of slabs supported on slender columns. The resulting building was box-like, with a flat roof, which could be used as a terrace. The Villa Savoye (Fig. **13.55**) combines these concepts in a design whose supporting structures freed the interior from the necessity of weight-supporting walls. In many ways the design of the Villa Savoye reveals classical Greek inspiration, from its delicate columns and human scale to its precisely articulated parts and totally coherent and unified whole. The design is crisp, clean, and functional.

In addition, this period continued many traditional approaches, which we need not dwell upon in any detail, but which must be noted. Cass Gilbert's Woolworth building (Fig. **13.56**), is illustrative, stimulating not only considerable discussion, including the appellation Woolworth Gothic, but also a wave of Gothic skyscrapers including Howells and Hood's Chicago Tribune Tower (1923–5).

The Bauhaus

Probably the most philosophically integrated approach to architecture came from Germany in the mid-twenties. Under the aegis of Walter Gropius and Adolph Meyer, the Bauhaus School of Art, Applied Arts, and Architecture approached aesthetics from a spirit of engineering. Experimentation and design were based on technological and economic factors rather than on formal considerations. The Bauhaus philosophy sought to establish links between the organic and technical worlds and thereby to reduce contrasts between the two. Spatial imagination, rather than building and construction, became the Bauhaus objective. The design principles Gropius and Meyer advocated produced building exteriors completely free of ornamentation. Several juxtaposed, functional materials form externally expressed structure, and such an expression clearly marks the fact that exterior walls are no longer structural, merely a climate barrier. Bauhaus buildings evolved from a careful consideration of need and reflect a search for dynamic balance and geometric purity.

Modern architecture

Architecture affords no relief from the problem of trying to sample or overview an era still in the making. In a sense, the task is more difficult here, because the human element of artistic creation has been blurred by architectural corporations, as opposed to individual architects. There is also a tendency for the contemporary observer to see a sameness in the glass and steel boxes that dominate our cities and to miss the truly unique approach to design that may comprise a housing project in an obscure locale.

World War II caused a ten-year break in architectural construction and, to a certain extent, separated what came after from what went before. However, the continuing careers of architects who had achieved significant accomplishment before the war bridged that gap. Geographical focus shifted from Europe to the United States, Japan, and even South America. The overall approach still remained modern or international in flavor, which helps us to select a few examples to illustrate general tendencies.

As a type, the skyscraper saw a resurgence of building in the fifties, in a glass-and-steel box approach that continues today. Illustrative of this type and approach is Lever House in New York City (Fig. **13.57**). A very important consideration in this design is the open space surrounding the tower. Created by setting the tower back from the perimeter of the site, the open space around the building creates its own envelope of environ-

13.57 Gordon Bunshaft (Skidmore, Owings and Merrill), Lever House, New York, 1950–52.

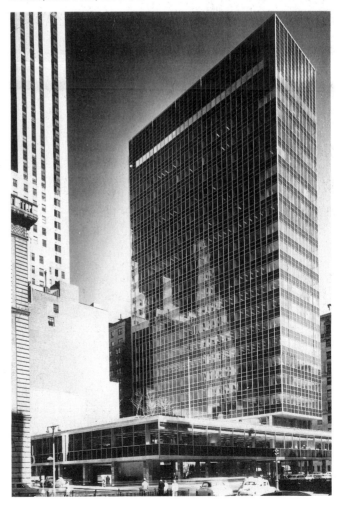

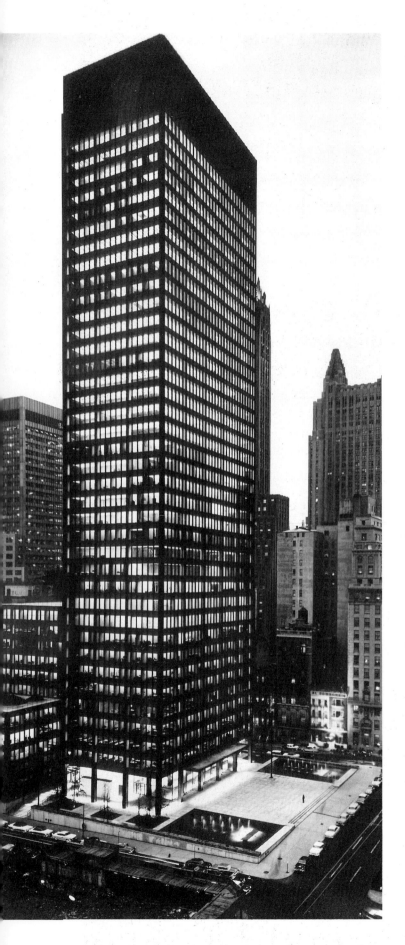

ment or context. Reactions against the glazed appearance of the Lever Building have occurred throughout the last thirty years, with surfaces such as aluminium pierced by small windows, for example. In the same sense, an intensification of the glazed exterior has occurred, wherein metalized windows, rather than normal glass, have formed the exterior surface. Such an approach has been particularly popular in the Sun Belt, because metalized glass reflects the sun's rays and their heat. In any case, the functional, plain rectangle of the international style has continued as a general architectural form regardless of individual variation.

The rectangle, which has so uniformly and in many cases thoughtlessly, become the mark of contemporary architecture leads us to the architect who, before World War II, was among its advocates. Mies van der Rohe insisted that form should not be an end in itself. Rather, the architect should discover and state the function of the building. His pursuit of those goals and his honesty in taking mass-produced materials at face value, that is, bricks, glass, and manufactured metals, and outwardly expressing their shapes was the basis for the rectangularization that is the common ground of twentieth-century architecture. His search for proportional perfection can be traced, perhaps, to the German Pavilion of the Barcelona Exposition in 1929 and was expressed in projects such as New York's Seagram Building (Fig. **13.58**).

The simple straight line and functional structure basic to Mies' unique insights were easily imitated and readily reproduced. However, such commonplace duplication, although overwhelming in numbers, certainly has not overshadowed exploration of other forms. Differing reflections in contemporary design ultimately have pursued the question formulated by Louis I. Kahn, "What form does the space want to become?" In the case of Frank Lloyd Wright's Guggenheim Museum (Fig. **13.59**), space has become a relaxing spiral that reflects the leisurely progress one should make through an art museum. Eero Saarinen's Trans-World Airline Terminal takes the dramatic shape of flight in curved lines and carefully designed spaces, which accommodate large masses of people and channel them to and from waiting aircraft. (Such shapes could only be executed by modern construction techniques and materials such as reinforced concrete.) Flight has also been suggested by Le Corbusier's dynamic church, Notre-Dame-du-Haut (Fig. **13.60**). However, this pilgrimage church appears more like a work of sculpture than a building. Here function cannot be surmised from form. Rather, the juxtaposed rectilinear windows and curvilinear walls and the overwhelming roof nestled lightly on thin pillars above the walls all appear as a "pure creation of the spirit".

The simple curvilinearity of the arch and the dome is

13.58 Mies van der Rohe and Philip Johnson, Seagram Building, New York, 1958.

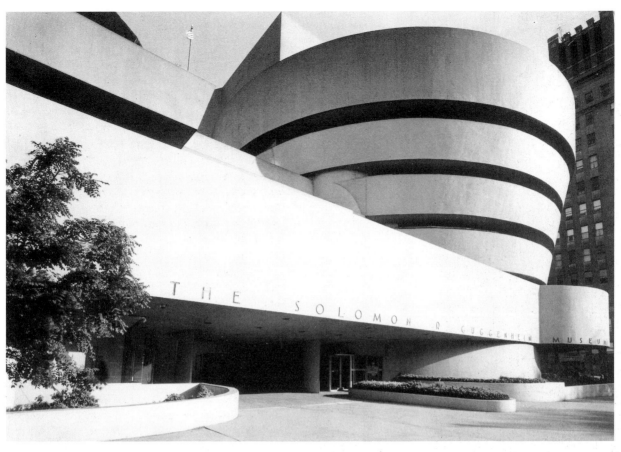

13.59 Frank Lloyd Wright, Solomon R. Guggenheim Museum, New York, 1942–59.

13.60 Le Corbusier, Notre-Dame-du-Haut, Ronchamp, France, 1950–54, from the south east.

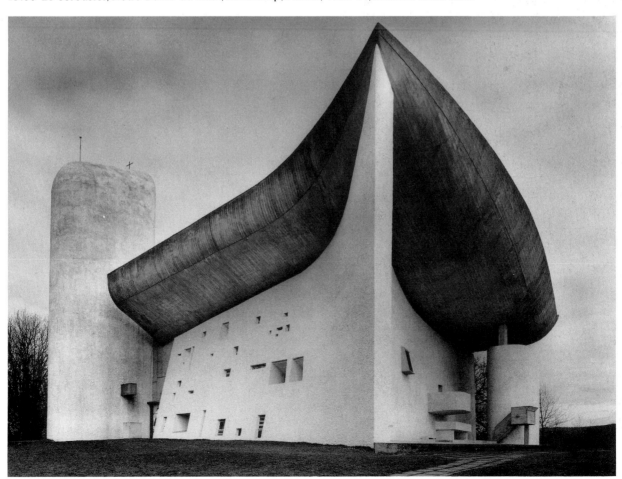

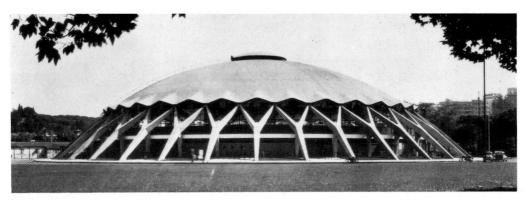

13.61 Pier Luigi Nervi, Small Sports Palace, Rome, 1957.

13.62 Richard Buckminster Fuller, Climatron, St. Louis, 1959.

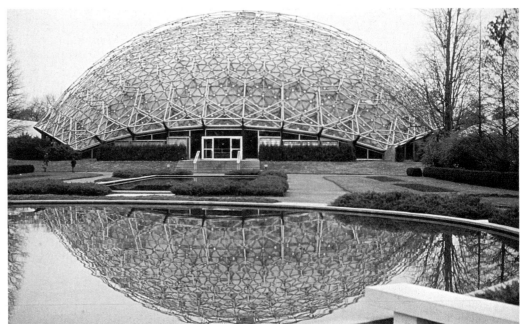

the mark of two different and noteworthy architects. The unencumbered free space in their projects represents a contrast to the self-contained boxes of the international style. Pier Luigi Nervi's Small Sports Palace (Fig. **13.61**) and R. Buckminster Fuller's Climatron (Fig. **13.62**) illustrate the practical need for free space, but they also suggest the trend toward spansion architecture which stretches engineering to the limits of its materials, and which, in the case of the Kansas City Hyatt Regency Hotel, took design tragically beyond practicality.

Post-modernism

Contemporary architecture also has turned in pluralistic directions. Post-modern or "revisionist" architecture puts new manifestations on past styles. The Spanish architect Ricardo Bofill (b. 1939) and the Italian, Aldo Rossi, both derive much of their architectural language from the past. As Bofill remarked, his architecture takes "without copying, different themes from the past, but in an eclectic manner, seizing certain moments in history and juxtapos-

ing them, thereby prefiguring a new epoch." We see this eclectic juxtaposition in his public housing development called, with typical grandiosity, Le Palais d'Abraxas (Fig. **13.64**). Here columnar verticality is suggested by glass and by cornice/capitals, which dynamically exhibit the characteristics of classicism. In Japan, post-modern architects such as Arata Isozaki, Kisho Kurakawa, and Minoru Takeyana portray in their buildings the restrained elegance and style of traditional Japanese art. In the United States, Michael Graves (b. 1934) has reacted to the repetitive glass, concrete, and steel boxes of the International style, which dominates modern cities, by creating a metaphorical allusion to the keystone of the Roman arch (Fig. **13.63**). The bright red pilasters suggest fluted columns, and fibreglass garlands recall both art deco and the rococo. Post-modern architecture focuses on meaning and symbolism: The past and ornamentation are acceptable; functionalism no longer controls. The post-modernist seeks to create buildings "in the fuller context of society and the environment". Social identity, cultural continuity, and sense of place become foundations for the art.

SYNTHESIS
The Bauhaus: Integration of the Arts

In 1919 Walter Gropius (1883–1969) wrote what has been called the Bauhaus Manifesto. He contends that "all the arts culminate in architecture". He continues:

> In the past, the ornamentation of buildings was considered to be the major function of the visual arts. They played a vital role in the creation of great architecture. Today these arts stand in self-sufficient isolation from which they can be redeemed only by conscious co-operation and mutual understanding between all those involved. Architects, painters and sculptors must rediscover and understand the many-sided aspects of building, both as a whole and in all its parts; only then will their work be informed with that architectonic spirit which was lost in salon art.

Gropius was inspired by a vision of buildings as a new type of organic structure "created by the integration of all the arts and perfectly expressing the totality of the contemporary situation". The challenge was directed not so much at architects, as at painters and sculptors who had once worked in close collaboration with architects and master builders, but who, by the twentieth century, were virtually isolated from the crafts. Gropius sought in "art and technology—a new unity". He did not wish to return to the styles of the past. In fact, he decided to abandon the "sterile vocabulary of an artistic language which had lost its meaning". He sought the evolution of a new architectonic outlook.

> This idea of the fundamental unity underlying all branches of design was my guiding inspiration in founding the original Bauhaus. During the war I had been summoned to an audience with the Grand Duke of Sachsen-Weimar-Eisenach to discuss my taking over the Weimar School of Arts and Crafts (*Grossherzogliche Kunstgewerbeschule*) from the distinguished Belgian architect, Henri Van de Velde, who had himself suggested that I should be his successor. Having asked for, and been accorded, full powers in regard to reorganization I assumed control of the Weimar School of Arts and Crafts, and also of the Weimar Academy of Fine Art (*Grossherzoghliche Hochschule für Bildende Kunst*), in the spring of 1919. As a first step towards the realization of a much wider plan—in which my primary aim was that the principle of training the individual's natural capacities to grasp life as a whole, a single cosmic entity, should form the basis of instruction throughout the school instead of in only one or two arbitrarily "specialized" classes—I amalgamated these institutions into a *Hochschule für Gestaltung*, or High

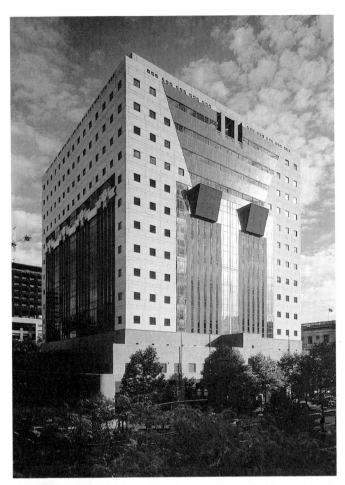

13.63 Michael Graves, Portland Public Office Building, Portland, Oregon, 1979–82.

13.64 Ricardo Bofill, The Palace of Abraxas, Marne-la-Vallée, near Paris, 1978–83.

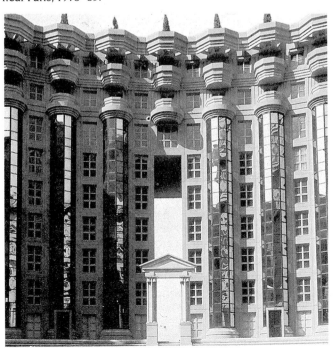

School for Design, under the name of *Das Staatliche Bauhaus Weimar*.

In carrying out this scheme I tried to solve the ticklish problem of combining imaginative design and technical proficiency. That meant finding a new and hitherto non-existent type of collaborator who could be molded into being equally proficient in both. As a safeguard against any recrudescence of the old dilettante handicraft spirit I made every pupil (including the architectural students) bind himself to complete his full legal term of apprenticeship in a formal letter of engagement registered with the local trades council. I insisted on manual instruction, not as an end in itself, or with any idea of turning it to incidental account by actually producing handicrafts, but as providing a good all-round training for hand and eye, and being a practical first step in mastering industrial processes.

The Bauhaus workshops were really laboratories for working out practical new designs for present-day articles and improving models for mass-production. To create type-forms that would meet all technical, aesthetic and commercial demands required a picked staff. It needed a body of men of wide general culture as thoroughly versed in the practical and mechanical sides of design as in its theoretical and formal laws. Although most parts of these prototype models had naturally to be made by hand, their constructors were bound to be intimately acquainted with factory methods of production and assembly, which differ radically from the practices of handicraft. It is to its intrinsic particularity that each different type of machine owes the 'genuine stamp' and 'individual beauty' of its products. Senseless imitation of hand-made goods by machinery infallibly bears the mark of a makeshift substitute. The Bauhaus represented a school of thought which believes that the difference between industry and handicraft is due, far less to the different nature of the tools employed in each, than to subdivision of labor in the one and undivided control by a single workman in the other. Handicrafts and industry may be regarded as opposite poles that are gradually approaching each other. The former have already begun to change their traditional nature. In the future the field of handicrafts will be found to lie mainly in the preparatory stages of evolving experimental new type-forms for mass-production.

There will, of course, always be talented craftsmen who can turn out individual designs and find a market for them. The Bauhaus, however, deliberately concentrated primarily on what has now become a work of paramount urgency: to avert mankind's enslavement by the machine by giving its products a content of reality and significance, and so

saving the home from mechanistic anarchy. This meant evolving goods specifically designed for mass-production. Our object was to eliminate every drawback of the machine without sacrificing any one of its real advantages. We aimed at realizing standards of excellence, not creating transient novelties.[7]

In his integrative efforts Gropius assembled a group of painters at the Bauhaus, and when the Bauhaus was founded in 1919 there were more painters than architects on its teaching staff. We have already described and examined some of these artists and their works. Nonetheless,

There is a common bond between the painters who taught at the Bauhaus. This is most evident when one considers the notable painters of that period who did not belong to the Bauhaus, such as the Brücke artists, or Emil Nolde and Oscar Kokoschka. This kind of Expressionism—wild, ecstatic, sensational—had no representation in the Bauhaus. The choice made by Gropius betrays the architect. Most of the painters who taught at the Bauhaus came from southern and western Germany, or at least, like the foreigners—Wassily Kandinsky and Lyonel Feininger—received their artistic education there. This common background may help to explain a basic stylistic homogeneity. All the painters working at the Bauhaus, without exception, wrestled with the same creative problems as arise in architecture, and this "elective affinity" with architecture is far from accidental. This is true both of Lyonel Feininger's transcendental dream buildings and of Oskar Schlemmer's space-dividing sets for his imaginary puppet theatre. Johannes Itten's system of art education is permeated by the spirit of analysis and organization, as are his paintings. The same can be said for the screen-like scaffoldings characteristic of many of George Muche's early compositions. In Paul Klee's drawings and watercolors, basic architectural principles, such as supports, loads, equilibrium, stress, mass and space, and repetition and contrast, are applied to create playful anecdotes, fairy tales, and whimsical fantasies, while Wassily Kandinsky's paintings express these same principles as moods and symbols of human experience. In the Constructivist works of Laszlo Moholy-Nagy and Josef Albers, architectural laws are applied in the pictorial projection on a flat plane.[8]

Gropius himself summed up the aims of the Bauhaus thus:

During the all too few years of its existence, the Bauhaus embraced the whole range of visual arts: architecture, planning, painting, sculpture, industrial design, and stage work. The aim of the Bauhaus was

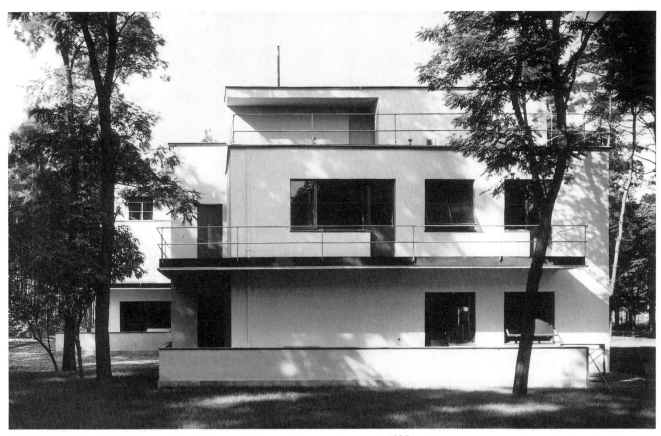

13.65 Walter Gropius, Professor Gropius's own house at Dessau, Germany, 1925.

13.66 Walter Gropius, a Pair of semi-detached houses for the staff of the Bauhaus, Dessau, 1925.

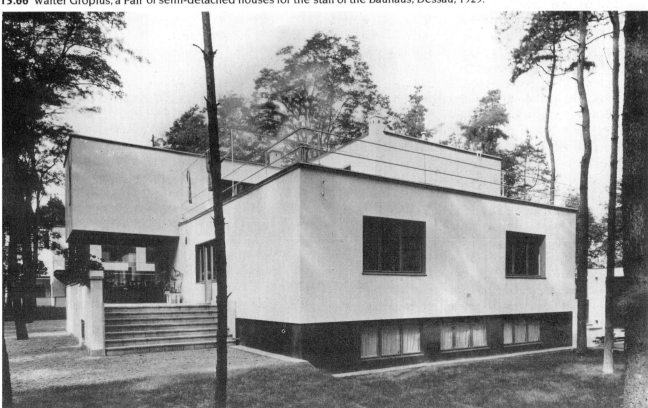

to find a new and powerful working correlation of all the processes of artistic creation to culminate finally in a new cultural equilibrium of our visual environment. This could not be achieved by individual withdrawal into an ivory tower. Teachers and students as a working community had to become vital participants of the modern world, seeking a new synthesis of art and modern technology. Based on the study of the biological facts of human perception, the phenomena of form and space were investigated in a spirit of unbiased curiosity, to arrive at objective means with which to relate individual creative effort to a common background. One of the fundamental maxims of the Bauhaus was the demand that the teacher's own approach was never to be imposed on the student; that, on the contrary, any attempt at imitation by the student was to be ruthlessly suppressed. The stimulation received from the teacher was only to help him find his own bearings.[9]

SUGGESTIONS FOR THOUGHT AND DISCUSSION

In the fall of 1984 I was prvileged to be one of one hundred participants from North and South America and eastern and western Europe gathered in Amsterdam for a conference entitled *New Directions in the Arts*. We spent a week listening to contemporary artists, visiting Dutch museums and conservatories, and discussing the state and future of the arts and what we as artists and arts administrators could do about these conditions.

The week was taxing and exhilarating. The conclusion most of us reached as a result of our experiences was that probably the conference was wrongly titled. There seemed to be no new directions in the arts. Rather, the new seemed to be a vital pluralism in which various styles and approaches crossed paths which previously were isolated or unapproachable. New understandings, tolerances, and appreciations were established which encouraged broadened horizons rather than defences of the previously established or institutionalized. Exciting things await us, the artist and the non-artist alike. The fact that in 1986 in the United States more people attended arts events than attended sports events speaks positively for the future.

Predicting the future is more or less pointless, however. Understanding the present and the past is essential. I hope our journey in this text has made our humanity and our creative impulses more understandable and more meaningful.

■ Can you make a direct relationship between the artistic styles we have studied in this chapter and the events and attitudes you may have experienced or heard about from your parents and friends?

■ Are you disturbed or bored by the non-objectivity of the art you see around you? Why do you think you react as you do?

■ What is the most positive or negative association or reaction you have had relative to contemporary art?

■ Have the attitudes and concerns of the first half of the twentieth century changed much?

■ Do you feel more comfortable with the art of our time or with the art of centuries past?

■ Do you relate to film more readily than you do to other arts? Why do you think this is so?

■ Do you think the arts have progressed over the centuries, or have the arts existed without progress or development?

■ What relationship do the arts have to our humanity? If we removed all the arts from our environment, would you want to live in such surroundings?

NOTES

See **Further Reading** for full bibliographical details of cited works:

Introduction
1 Roger Sperry, *Science and Moral Priority: Merging Mind, Brain, and Human Values*

Chapter 1
1 Marshack, *The Roots of Civilization*
2 Marshack, op. cit., p.34
3 Marshack, op. cit., p.275
4 Marshack, op. cit., p.276
5 Marshack, op. cit., p.274
6 Marshack, op, cit., p.220

Chapter 2
1 Garraty and Gay, *A History of the World*, p.49

Chapter 3
1 Frankfort, *Kingship and the Gods*, p.37
2 Frankfort, op. cit.
3 Frankfort, op. cit.
4 M. A. Murray, *Egyptian Sculpture*, p.23
5 Lange and Hirmer, *Egypt*
6 Freedly and Reeves, *A History of the Theatre*, pp.5–6
7 Montet, *Lives of the Pharaohs*, pp.38–40
8 Sachs, *The Rise of Music in the Ancient World*, p.33
9 W. S. Smith, *The Art and Architecture of Ancient Egypt*, p.20

Chapter 4
1 Hofstadter and Kuhns, *Philosophies of Art and Beauty*, p.4
2 Ibid.
3 B. A. G. Fuller, *A History of Philosophy*, p.172
4 Hofstadter and Kuhns, op. cit., pp.78–9
5 Ibid.
6 In each Greek tragic contest a playwright was required to present four plays in succession—three tragedies and a satyr play
7 Arnott, trans., in *An Introduction to the Greek Theatre*, pp.76–7
8 The chorus was a distinctive feature of Greek drama, portraying the dual function (in the same play) of narrator and collective character—responding to the actors
9 McLeish, *The Theatre of Aristophanes*
10 Lawler, *The Dance in Ancient Greece*, p.12
11 Robertson, *A shorter History of Greek Art*, p.123

12 Hamilton, trans., in *Three Greek Plays*
13 Wm Arrowsmith, trans., in *The Complete Greek Tragedies* Vol. VI (New York, Random House, 1958)

Chapter 5
1 Fuller, op.cit., p.266
2 Ibid.
3 Garraty and Gay, op. cit., p.203
4 Hofstadter and Kuhns, op. cit., pp. 140–1
5 Garraty and Gay, op. cit., p.209
6 Andreae, *The Art of Rome*, p.71
7 "Rings around the Pantheon", *Discover* (March 1985), p.12
8 Andreae, op. cit., p.109
9 Ibid.
10 Andreae, op. cit., p.118

Chapter 6
1 Garraty and Gay, op. cit., p.431
2 Roberts, *History of the World*, p.321
3 Mango, *Byzantium*, p.234
4 Mango, op. cit., p.235
5 Mango, op. cit., p.242
6 Mango, op. cit., p.251
7 Diehl, *Byzantium*, p.286
8 Grout, *A History of Western Music*, p.14
9 Nicoll, *The Development of the Theatre*, p.48
10 Freedly and Reeves, op.cit., p.177
11 Sorell, *The Dance Through the Ages*, p.5
12 MacDonald, *Early Christian and Byzantine Architecture*, p.43
13 Sherrard, *Byzantium*, p.56
14 MacDonald, op. cit., p.32
15 Rice, *The Art of Byzantium*, p.300

Chapter 7
1 McGiffert, *A History of Christian Thought*, p.7
2 McGiffert, op. cit., p.10–12
3 Fuller, op. cit., p.353
4 Ibid.
5 Fuller, op. cit., p.357
6 Tierney and Painter *Western Europe in the Middle Ages*, p.87
7 Hofstadter and Kuhns, op. cit., p.172
8 St Augustine, quoted in Grout, op.cit., p.19
9 Hubert et al., *The Carolingian Renaissance*, p.11
10 Hubert et al., op. cit., p.40
11 Hubert et al., op. cit., p.50

Chapter 8
1 Tierney and Painter, op. cit., p.257

2 Tierney and Painter, op. cit., pp.259–60
3 McGiffert, op. cit., p.201
4 Fuller, op. cit., p.377
5 Zarnecki, *Art of the Medieval World*, p.406
6 Gassner, ed., *A Treasury of the Theatre*, p.187

Chapter 9
1 Strayer and Munro, *The Middle Ages*, p.539
2 Artz, *From the Renaissance to Romanticism*, p.84
3 Campos, ed., *Art Treasures of the Vatican*, p.7

Chapter 10
1 Grimm, *The Reformation Era*, pp.85–7
2 Fuller, op. cit., p.42
3 Bazin, *The Baroque*, p.30
4 Bazin, op. cit., p.176
5 Père Menestrier, in Vuillier, *A History of Dance* (New York, D. Appleton and Co., 1897), p.90

Chapter 11
1 Hartt, *Art*, pp.292–3
2 Hartt, op. cit., p.283
3 Hewett, *Theatre USA*, p.40
4 Helm, *Music at the Court of Frederick the Great*, p.94

Chapter 12
1 Hofstadter and Kuhns, op. cit., p.381
2 G. Mackworth-Young, trans., *Schubert, 200 Songs* Vol. I (New York, International Music Co.) pp.xxi–xxii
3 Sorell, op. cit., p.138
4 Maas, *Victorian Painters*, p.10
5 Maas, op. cit., p.16

Chapter 13
1 *Art as Experience*, Ch.IX, 'The Common Substance of the Arts'
2 McDermott, 'Creative Evolution', *Theatre Journal*, 1984, pp.217–18
3 McDermott, op. cit., p.218
4 Kiernan
5 Hamilton, *Nineteenth and Twentieth Century Art: Painting, Sculpture, Architecture*, p.211
6 The text for this section was prepared by David Kechley. I have edited where necessary to conform to the rest of the chapter
7 Gropius, *The New Architecture and the Bauhaus*, pp.51–5
8 Roters, *Painters of the Bauhaus*, p.6
9 Gropius, *The Theatre of the Bauhaus*, p.1

GLOSSARY

a cappella. Choral music without instrumental accompaniment.

abacus. The uppermost member of the capital of an architectural column; the slab on which the architrave rests.

absolute music. Music that is free from any reference to nonmusical ideas, such as a text or program.

abstract. Non-representational; the essence of a thing rather than its actual appearance.

academy. From the grove, the Academeia, where Plato taught; the term has come to mean the cultural and artistic establishment which exercises responsibility for teaching and the maintenance of standards.

accent. In music, a stress that occurs at regular intervals of time. In the visual arts, any device used to highlight or draw attention to a particular area, such as an accent color. See also *focal point*.

acoustics. The study of sound and its character.

action theatre. A contemporary phenomenon in which plays, happenings, and other types of performance are strongly committed to broad moral and social issues with the overt purpose of effecting a change for the better in society.

aerial perspective. The indication of distance in painting through use of light and atmosphere.

aesthetic. Having to do with the pleasurable and beautiful as opposed to the useful.

aesthetic distance. The combination of mental and physical factors that provides the proper separation between a viewer and an artwork; it enables the viewer to achieve a desired response.

aesthetics. A branch of philosophy dealing with the nature of beauty and art and their relation to human experience.

affective. Relating to feelings or emotions, as opposed to facts. See *cognitive*.

aleatory. Chance or accidental.

allegory. Expression by means of symbols to make a more effective generalization or moral commentary about human experience than could be achieved by direct or literal means.

altarpiece. A painted or sculptured panel placed above and behind an altar to inspire religious devotion.

ambulatory. A covered passage for walking, found around the apse or choir of a church.

animism. The belief that objects as well as living organisms are endowed with soul.

anthropomorphic. Human characteristics attributed to nonhuman beings.

apse. A large niche or niche-like space projecting from and expanding the interior space of an architectural form such as a basilica.

arcade. A series of arches placed side by side.

arch. In architecture, a structural system in which space is spanned by a curved member supported by two legs.

architrave. In post-and-lintel architecture, the lintel or lowest part of the entablature, resting directly on the capitals of the columns.

aria. An elaborate solo song found primarily in operas, oratorios, and cantatas.

art song. A vocal musical composition in which the text is the principal focus.

articulation. The connection of the parts of an artwork.

atonality. The avoidance or tendency to avoid tonal centers in musical compositions.

atrium. An open courtyard within or related to a building.

avant-garde. A term used to designate innovators, "the advanced guard", whose experiments in art challenge established values.

balance. In composition, the equilibrium of opposing or interacting forces.

ballad. A narrative song usually set to relatively simple music.

barrel vault (tunnel vault). A series of arches placed back to back to enclose space.

bas-relief. *see relief*

basilica. In Roman times a term referring to building function, usually a law court, later used by Christians to refer to church buildings and a specific form.

beats. In music, the equal parts into which a measure is divided.

binary form. A musical form consisting of two sections.

biomorphic. Representing life forms, as opposed to geometric forms.

bridge. A musical passage of subordinate importance played between two major themes.

buttress. A support, usually an exterior projection of masonry or wood, for a wall, arch, or vault.

cadence. In music, the specific harmonic arrangement that indicates the closing of a phrase.

canon. A body of principles, rules, standards or norms; a criterion for establishing measure, scale, and proportion.

capital. The transition between the top of a column and the lintel.

caryatid. A sculptured female figure standing in the place of a column.

cast. see *sculpture*.

catharsis. The cleansing or purification of the emotions through the experience of art, the result of which is spiritual release and renewal.

chamber music. Vocal or instrumental music suitable for performance in small rooms.

chiaroscuro. Light and shade. In painting, the use of highlight and shadow to give the appearance of three-dimensionality. In theatre, the use of light to enhance plasticity of human and scenic form.

chord. Three or more musical tones played at the same time.

choreography. The composition of a dance work; the arrangement of patterns of movement in dance.

classical. Adhering to traditional standards. May refer to Greek and Roman art in which simplicity, clarity of structure and appeal to the intellect are fundamental.

clerestory. A row of windows in the upper part of a wall.

coffer. A recessed panel in a ceiling.

cognitive. Facts and objectivity as opposed to emotions and subjectivity. See *affective*.

collage. An artwork constructed by pasting together various materials, such as newsprint, to create textures or by combining two-and three-dimensional media.

colonnade. A row of columns usually spanned or connected by lintels.

column. A cylindrical post or support which often has three distinct parts: base, shaft and capital.

composition. The arrangement of line, form, mass, color, and so forth in a work of art.

compression. In architecture, stress that results from two forces moving toward each other.

conjunct melody. In music, melody comprising notes close together in the scale.

consonance. The feeling of a comfortable relationship between elements of a composition. Consonance may be both physical and cultural in its ramifications.

continuo (basso continuo). In music, a continuous bass line defined sharply enough to function as a clearly distinguishable part in the performance. Commonly played on a keyboard instrument.

contrapposto (counterpoise). In sculpture, the arrangement of body parts so that the weight-bearing leg is apart from the free leg, thereby shifting the hip/shoulder axis.

conventions. The customs or accepted underlying principles of an art.

Corinthian. A specific order of Greek columns employing an elaborate leaf motif in the capital.

cornice. A crowning, projecting architectural feature.

corps de ballet. The chorus of a ballet ensemble.

counterpoint. In music, two or more independent melodies played in opposition to each other at the same time.

crosscutting. In film, alternation between two independent actions that are related thematically or by plot to give the impression of simultaneous occurrence.

cruciform. Arranged or shaped like a cross.

crypt. A vaulted chamber; wholly or partly underground, that usually contains a chapel. Found in a church under the choir.

curvilinear. Formed or characterized by curved line.

cutting within the frame. Changing the viewpoint of the camera within a shot by moving from a long or medium shot to a close-up, without cutting the film.

dénouement. The section of a play's structure in which events are brought to a conclusion.

design. A comprehensive scheme, plan or conception.

disjunct melody. In music, melody characterized by skips or jumps in the scale. The opposite of *conjunct melody.*

dissonance. The occurrences of inharmonious elements in music or the other arts. The opposite of *consonance.*

dome. An architectural form based on the principles of the arch in which space is defined by a hemisphere used as a ceiling.

Doric. A Greek order of column having no base and only a simple slab as a capital.

drames bourgeois. Pseudo-serious plays utilizing middle-class themes and settings, with emphasis on pathos and morality.

dynamics. The various levels of loudness and softness of sounds; the increase and decrease of intensities.

eclecticism. In design, a combination of examples of several differing styles in a single composition.

empathy. Emotional and/or physical involvement in events to which one is a witness but not a participant.

empirical. Based on experiments, observation, and practical experience, without regard to theory.

en pointe. See *on point.*

engaged column. A column, often decorative, which is part of and projects from a wall surface.

entablature. The upper portion of a classical architectural order above the column capital.

entasis. The slight convex curving on classical columns to correct the optical illusion of concavity which would result if the sides were left straight.

entr'acte. Between acts.

ephemeral. Transitory, not lasting.

epic. A long narrative poem in heightened style about the deeds and adventures of a hero.

étude. Literally, a study, a lesson. A composition, usually instrumental, intended mainly for the practice of some technique.

façade. The front of a building or the sides if they are emphasized architecturally.

farce. A theatrical genre characterized by broad, slapstick humor and implausible plots.

ferroconcrete. Concrete reinforced with rods or webs of steel.

fluting. Vertical ridges in a column.

flying buttress. A semi-detached *buttress.*

focal point (focal area). A major or minor area of visual attraction in pictures, sculpture, dance, plays, films, landscape design or buildings.

foreground. The area of a picture, usually at the bottom, that appears to be closest to the respondent.

form. The shape, structure, configuration, or essence of something.

found object. An object taken from life that is presented as an artwork.

fresco. A method of painting in which pigment is mixed with wet plaster and applied as part of the wall surface.

frieze. The central portion of the entablature: any horizontal decorative or sculptural band.

fugue. Originated from a Latin word meaning "flight". A conventional musical composition in which a theme is developed by *counterpoint.*

full-round. See *sculpture.*

galliard. A court dance done spiritedly in triple meter.

genre. A category of artistic composition characterized by a particular style, form or content.

geometric. Based on man-made patterns such as triangles, rectangles, circles, ellipses, and so on. The opposite of *biomorphic.*

gesamtkunstwerk. A complete totally integrated artwork; associated with the music dramas of Richard Wagner in nineteenth-century Germany.

Greek cross. A cross in which all arms are the same length.

Gregorian chant. A medieval chant named for Pope Gregory I.

groin vault. The ceiling formation created by the intersection of two tunnel or barrel vaults.

harmony. The relationship of like elements such as musical notes, colors, and repetitional patterns. See *consonance* and *dissonance.*

Hellenistic. Relating to the time from Alexander the Great to the first century B.C.

heroic. Larger-than-life size.

hierarchy. Any system of persons or things that has higher and lower ranks.

hieroglyphic. A picture or symbol of an object standing for a word, idea, or sound; developed by the ancient Egyptians into a system of writing.

homophony. A musical texture characterized by chordal development supporting one melody. See *monophony* and *polyphony.*

horizon line. A real or implied line across the picture plane which, like the horizon in nature, tends to fix the viewer's vantage point.

hue. The spectrum notation of color; a specific, pure color with a measurable wavelength. There are primary hues, secondary hues, and tertiary hues.

icon. A Greek word meaning "image". Used to identify paintings which represent the image of a holy person.

iconography. The meanings of images and symbols.

idée fixe. A recurring melodic motif.

improvization. Music etc. produced on the spur of the moment; spontaneously.

intensity. The degree of purity of a hue. In

music, theatre, and dance, that quality of dynamics denoting the amount of force used to create a sound or movement.

interval. The difference in pitch between two tones.

intrinsic. Belonging to a thing by its nature.

Ionic. A Greek order of column that employs a scroll-like capital with a circular base.

jamb. The upright piece forming the side of a doorway or window frame.

key. A system of tones in music based on and named after a given tone—the tonic.

kouros. An archaic Greek statue of a standing, nude youth.

labanotation. A system of writing down dance movements.

Latin cross. A cross in which the vertical arm is longer than the horizontal arm, through whose midpoint it passes.

leitmotif. A "leading motif" used in music to identify an individual, idea, object and so on. Associated with Richard Wagner.

linear perspective. The creation of the illusion of distance in a two-dimensional artwork through the convention of line and foreshortening. That is, the illusion that parallel lines come together in the distance.

lintel. The horizontal member of a post-and-lintel structure in architecture.

loggia. A gallery open on one or more sides, sometimes with arches or with columns.

low relief. See *relief.*

madrigal. A secular two- or three-voice song with a fixed form.

masonry. In architecture, stone or brickwork.

mass. Actual or implied physical bulk, weight, and density. Also, the most solemn rite of the Catholic liturgy.

medium. The process employed by the artist. Also, the binding agent to hold pigments together.

melismatic. A single syllable of text sung on many notes.

melodrama. A theatrical genre characterized by stereotyped characters, implausible plots, and emphasis on spectacle.

melody. In music, a succession of single tones.

mobile. A constructed structure whose components have been connected by joints to move by force of wind or motor.

mode. A particular form, style, or manner.

modeling. The shaping of three-dimensional forms. Also the suggestion of three-dimensionality in two-dimensional forms.

modulation. A change of key or tonality in music.

monophony. In music, a musical texture employing a single melody line without harmonic support.

montage. The process of making a single composition by combining parts of others. A rapid sequence of film shots bringing together associated ideas or images.

monumental. Works actually or appearing larger-than-life size.

Moog synthesizer. See *synthesizer.*

motif (motive). In music, a short, recurrent melodic or rhythmic pattern. In the other arts, a recurrent element.

mullions. The vertical elements dividing windows into separate sections.

mural. A painting on a wall, usually large in size.

musique concrète. A twentieth-century

musical approach in which conventional sounds are altered electronically and recorded on tape to produce new sounds.

nave. The great central space in a church.

neoclassicism. Various artistic styles which borrow the devices or objectives of classical art.

nonobjective. Without reference to reality; may be differentiated from "abstract".

nonrepresentational. Without reference to reality; including *Abstract* and *Nonobjective*.

octave. In music, the distance between a specific pitch vibration and its double; for example, concert A equals 440 vibrations per second, one octave above that pitch equals 880, and one octave below equals 220.

on point. In ballet, a specific technique utilizing special shoes in which the dancer dances on the points of the toes. Same as *en pointe*.

opus. A single work of art.

organum. "Singing together". Earliest form of polyphony in Western music.

palette. In the visual arts, the composite use of color, including range and tonality.

pantheon. A Greek word meaning all the gods of a people.

pas. In ballet, a combination of steps forming one dance.

pas de deux. A dance for two dancers.

pathos. The "suffering" aspect of drama usually associated with the evocation of pity.

pediment. The typically triangular roof piece characteristic of classical architecture.

perspective. The representation of distance and three-dimensionality on a two-dimensional surface. See also *linear perspective* and *aerial perspective*.

plainsong (plain chant). Referring to various types of medieval liturgical music sung without accompaniment and without strict meter.

plan. An architectural drawing that reveals in two dimensions the arrangement and distribution of interior spaces and walls, as well as door and window openings, of a building as seen from above.

plasticity. The capability of being molded or altered. In film, the ability to be cut and shaped. In painting, dance, and theatre, the accentuation of dimensionality of form through *chiaroscuro*.

polyphony. See *counterpoint*.

polyrhythm. The use of contrasting rhythms at the same time in music.

post-and-lintel. An architectural structure in which horizontal pieces (lintels) are held up by vertical columns (posts).

program music. Music that refers to nonmusical ideas through a descriptive title or text. The opposite of *absolute music*.

proportion. The relation, or ratio, of one part to another and of each part to the whole with regard to size, height, width, length, or depth.

proscenium. A Greek word meaning "before the skene". The plaster arch or "picture frame" stage of traditional theatres.

prototype. The model on which something is based.

rake. To place at an angle. A raked stage is one in which the stage floor slopes slightly upward from one point, usually downstage, to another, usually upstage.

realism. A style of painting, sculpture, and theatre based on the theory that the method of presentation should be true to life.

recitative. Sung dialogue, in opera, cantata, and oratorio.

reinforced concrete. See *ferroconcrete*.

relief. See *sculpture*.

representational. Objects which are recognizable from real life.

requiem. A Mass for the dead.

rhythm. The relationship, either of time or space, between recurring elements of a composition.

rib. A slender architectural support in a vault system projecting from the surface.

sarcophagus. A stone coffin

saturation. In color, the purity of a hue in terms of whiteness; the whiter the hue, the less saturated it is.

scale. In music, a graduated series of ascending or descending musical tones. In architecture, the mass of the building in relation to the human body.

scenography. The art and study of scenery design for the theatre and film.

sculpture. A three-dimensional art object. Among the types are 1. *cast*: having been created from molten material utilizing a mold. 2. *relief*: attached to a larger background. 3. *full-round*: free-standing.

serial music. A twentieth-century musical style utilizing the tone row and serialization of rhythms, timbres, and dynamics.

shape. A two-dimensional area or plane with distinguishable boundaries.

silhouette. A form as defined by its outline.

skene. The stage building of the ancient Greek theatre.

still life. In the visual arts, an arrangement of inanimate objects used as a subject of a work of art.

strophic form. Vocal music in which all stanzas of the text are sung to the same music.

style. The identifying characteristics of a work of art which identify it with an artist, a group of artists, an era, or a nation.

stylobate. The foundation immediately below a row of columns.

summa. An encyclopedic summation of a field of learning, particularly in theology or philosophy

symbol. A form, image, or subject standing for something else.

symmetry. The balancing of elements in design by placing physically equal objects on either side of a center line.

syncopation. In a musical composition, the displacement of accent from the normally accented beat to the offbeat.

synthesis. The combination of independent factors or entities into a compound that becomes a new, more complex whole.

synthesizer (Moog synthesizer). An electronic instrument that produces and combines musical sounds.

tempo. The rate of speed at which a musical composition is performed. In theatre, film, or dance, the rate of speed of the overall performance.

texture. In visual art, the two-dimensional or three-dimensional quality of the surface of a work. In music, the melodic and harmonic characteristics of the composition.

theatricality. Exaggeration and artificiality; the opposite of *verisimilitude*.

theme. The general subject of an artwork, whether melodic or philosophical.

timbre. The characteristic of a sound that results from the particular source of the sound. The difference between the sound of a violin and the sound of the human voice is a difference in timbre, also called color.

toccata. A composition usually for organ or piano intended to display technique.

tonality. In music, the specific key in which a composition is written. In the visual arts, the characteristics of value.

tondo. A circular painting.

tonic. In music, the root tone (*do*) of a key.

tragédie bourgeois. See *drame bourgeois*.

tragedy. A serious drama or other literary work in which conflict betwen a protagonist and a superior force (often fate) concludes in disaster for the protagonist.

tragicomedy. A drama combining the qualities of tragedy and comedy.

transept. The crossing arm of a cruciform church, in contrast to the nave.

trompe-l'oeil. "Trick of the eye" or "fool the eye". A two-dimensional artwork so executed as to make the viewer believe that three-dimensional subject matter is being perceived.

tunnel vault. See *barrel vault*.

tutu. A many-layered, stiff short skirt worn by a ballerina.

twelve-tone technique. A twentieth-century atonal form of musical composition associated with Schoenberg.

tympanum. The open space above the door beam and within the arch of a medieval doorway.

value (value scale). In the visual arts, the range of tonalities from white to black.

vanishing point. In linear perspective, the point on the horizon toward which parallel lines appear to converge and at which they seem to vanish.

variation. Repetition of a theme with minor or major changes.

verisimilitude. The appearance of reality in any element of the arts.

virtuoso. Referring to the display of impressive technique or skill by an artist.

FURTHER READING

Anderson, Jack. *Dance*. New York: Newsweek Books, 1974.

Andreae, Bernard. *The Art of Rome*. New York: Harry N. Abrams, 1977.

Arnott, Peter D. *An Introduction to the Greek Theatre*. Bloomington, IN: Indiana University Press, 1963.

Artz, Frederick. *From the Renaissance to Romanticism*. Chicago: University of Chicago Press, 1962.

Bataille, Georges. *Lascaux*. Switzerland: Skira, n.d.

Bazin, Germain. *The Baroque*. Greenwich, CN: New York Graphic Society, 1968.

Bentley, Eric (Ed). *The Classic Theatre* (four vols.). Garden City, NY: Doubleday Anchor Books, 1959.

Bohn, T. W., Stromgren, R. L., and Johnson, D.H. *Light and Shadows, A History of Motion Pictures* (2nd ed.). Sherman Oaks, CA: Alfred Publishing Co, 1978.

Booth, Michael. *Victorian Spectacular Theatre 1850–1910*. Boston: Routledge and Kegan Paul, 1981.

Borroff, Edith. *Music in Europe and the United States: A History*. Englewood Cliffs, NJ: Prentice-Hall, Inc., 1971.

Brandon, S. G. F. *Religion in Ancient History*. New York: Charles Scribner's Sons, 1969.

Brindle, Reginald Smith. *The New Music: The Avant-Garde Since 1945*. London: Oxford University Press, 1975.

Brockett, Oscar G. *History of the Theatre*. Boston: Allyn and Bacon, Inc., 1968.

Campos, D. Redig de (ed). *Art Treasures of the Vatican*. Englewood Cliffs, NJ: Prentice-Hall, Inc., 1974.

Cheney, Sheldon *The Theatre: Three Thousand Years of Drama, Acting, and Stagecraft* (rev. ed.). New York: Longmans, Green, 1952.

Chujoy, Anatole. *Dance Encyclopedia*. New York: Simon and Schuster, Inc., 1966.

Clarke, Mary and Crisp, Clement. *Ballet*. New York: Universe Books, 1973.

Clough, Shepard B. et al. *A History of the Western World*. Boston: D. C. Heath and Co., 1964

Cope, David H. *New Directions in Music*. Dubuque, IA: William C. Brown and Co., 1981.

Corrigan, Robert. "The Search for New Endings: The Theatre in Search of a Fix, Part III," *Theatre Journal*, Vol. 36, No.2, May 1984, pp.153–163.

Coryell, Julie and Friedman, Laura. *Jazz-Rock Fusion*. New York: Delacorte Press, 1978.

Crocker, Richard. *A History of Musical Style*. New York: McGraw-Hill, 1966.

Diehl, Charles. *Byzantium*, New Brunswick, NJ: Rutgers University Press, 1957.

Drinkwater, John. *The Outline of Literature*. London: Transatlantic Arts, 1967

Engel, Carl. *The Music of the Most Ancient Nations*. Freeport, NY: Books for Libraries Press, 1970.

Ernst, David. *The Evolution of Electronic Music*. New York: Schirmer Books, 1977.

Fleming, William. *Arts and Ideas*. New York, Holt, Rinehart, and Winston, 1980.

Frankfort, Henri. *Kingship and the Gods*. Chicago: University of Chicago Press, 1948

Freedley, George and Reeves, John. *A History of the Theatre* (3rd ed.). New York: Crown Publishers, 1968.

Fuller, B. A. G. *A History of Philosophy*. New York: Henry Holt and Company, 1945.

Garraty, John and Gay, Peter. *A History of the World* (2 Vols.). New York: Harper and Row, 1972

Gassner, John (ed.). *A Treasury of the Theatre*. New York: Holt, Rinehart, and Winston, 1967.

Gilbert, Creighton. *History of Renaissance Art Throughout Europe: Painting, Sculpture, Architecture*. New York: Harry N. Abrams, Inc., 1973.

Glasstone, Victor. *Victorian and Edwardian Theatres*. Cambridge, MA: Harvard University Press, 1975.

Goethe, Johann Wolfgang von. *Faust: Part I*, trans. Philip Wayne. Baltimore: Penguin Books, 1962.

Graziosi, Paolo. *Palaeolithic Art*. New York: McGraw-Hill, 1960.

Griffiths, Paul. *A Concise History of Avant-Garde Music*. New York: Oxford University Press, 1978.

Grimm, Harold. *The Reformation Era*. New York: The MacMillan Co., 1954.

Groenewegen-Frankfort and Ashmole, Bernard. *Art of the Ancient World*. Englewood Cliffs, NJ and New York: Prentice-Hall, Inc. and Harry N. Abrams, Inc.

Gropius, Walter (ed). *The Theatre of the Bauhaus*. Middletown, CN: Wesleyan University Press, 1961.

Gropius, Walter *The New Architecture and the Bauhaus*. Cambridge, MA: M. I. T. Press, 1965.

Grout, Donald Jay. *A History of Western Music* (rev. ed.). New York: W. W. Norton and Co., Inc., 1973.

Hamilton, Edith. *Three Greek Plays*. New York: W. W. Norton and Co., 1965.

Hamilton, George Heard. *Nineteenth and Twentieth Century Art: Painting, Sculpture, Architecture*. New York: Harry N. Abrams, Inc. 1970.

Hartt, Frederick. *Art* (2 vols.). Englewood Cliffs, NJ and New York: Prentice-Hall, Inc. and Harry N. Abrams, Inc., 1979.

Hawkes, Jacquetta, and Wooley, Sir Leonard. *History of Mankind: Prehistory and the Beginnings of Civilization*. New York: Harper and Row, 1963.

Held, Julius and Posner, D *17th and 18th Century Art*. New York: Harry N. Abrams, n.d.

Helm, Ernest. *Music At the Court of Frederick the Great*. Norman, OK: University of Oklahoma Press, 1960.

Henig, Martin (ed.) *A Handbook of Roman Art*. Ithaca, NY: Cornell University Press, 1983.

Hewett, Bernard, *Theatre U.S.A.* New York: McGraw-Hill Book Company, 1959.

Hitchcock, Henry-Russell, *Architecture: Nineteenth and Twentieth Centuries*. Baltimore: Penguin Books, 1971

Hofstadter, Albert and Kuhns, Richard. *Philosophies of Art and Beauty*. Chicago: University of Chicago Press, 1976.

Honour, Hugh and Fleming, John. *The Visual Arts: A History* (2nd ed.) Englewood Cliffs, NJ: Prentice-Hall, Inc., 1986.

Hoppin, Richard. *Medieval Music*. New York: W. W. Norton and Co., Inc., 1978.

Hubatsch, Walther. *Frederick the Great of Prussia*. London: Thames and Hudson, 1975.

Hubert, J. Porcher, J., and Volbach, W. F. *The Carolingian Renaissance*. New York: George Braziller, 1970.

Jacobs, Lewis. *An Introduction to the Art of the Movies*. New York: Noonday Press, 1967.

Janson, H.W. *A Basic History of Art* (2nd ed.). Englewood Cliffs, NJ and New York: Prentice-Hall, Inc. and Harry N. Abrams, Inc., 1981.

Jung, Carl G. *Man and His Symbols*. New York: Doubleday and Co., Inc., 1964.

Karsavina, Tamara. *Theatre Street*. New York: E. P. Dutton, 1961.

Keutner, Hubert. *Sculpture: Renaissance to Rococo*. Greenwich, CT: New York Graphic Society, 1969.

Kjellberg, Ernst and Saflund, Gosta. *Greek and Roman Art*. New York: Thomas Y. Crowell Co. 1968.

Knight, Arthur. *The Liveliest Art: A Panoramic History of the Movies* (rev. ed.). New York: MacMillan, Inc., 1978.

Kraus, Richard. *History of the Dance*. Englewood Cliffs, NJ: Prentice-Hall, Inc., 1969.

Lange, Kurt and Hirmer, Max. *Egypt*. London: Phaidon, 1968.

Lawler, Lillian. *The Dance in Ancient Greece*. Middletown, CT: Wesleyan University Press, 1964.

Leish, Kenneth W. *Cinema*. New York: Newsweek Books, 1974.

Lippard, Lucy R. *Pop Art*. New York: Oxford University Press, 1966.

Lloyd, Seton. *The Archeology of Mesopotamia*. London: Thames and Hudson, 1978.

Lommel, Andreas. *Prehistoric and Primitive Man*. New York: McGraw-Hill, 1966.

Maas, Jeremy. *Victorian Painters*. New York: G. P. Putnam's Sons, 1969.

MacDonald, William. *Early Christian and Byzantine Architecture*. New York: George Braziller, 1967.

Machiavelli, Niccolo. *The Prince*, trans. George Bull. Baltimore: Penguin Books, 1963

Mango, Cyril. *Byzantium*. New York: Charles Scribner's Sons, 1980.

Marshack, Alexander. *The Roots of Civilization*. New York: McGraw-Hill, 1972.

Martin, John. *The Modern Dance*. Brooklyn: Dance Horizons, 1965.

McDermott, Dana Sue. "Creativity in the Theatre: Robert Edmond Jones and C. G. Jung." *Theatre Journal* (May 1984), pp.212–230.

McDonagh, Don. *The Rise and Fall of Modern Dance*. New York: E. P. Dutton, Inc., 1971.

McGiffert, Arthur. *A History of Christian Thought*. New York: Charles Scribner's Sons, 1961.

McLeish, Kenneth. *The Theatre of Aristophanes*. New York: Taplinger Publishing Co., 1980.

McNeill, William H. *The Shape of European History*. New York: Oxford University Press, 1974.

Montet, Pierre. *Lives of the Pharaohs*. Cleveland: World Publishing Co., 1968.

Moortgat, Anton. *The Art of Ancient Mesopotamia*. London: Phaidon, 1969.

Murray, Margaret. *Egyptian Sculpture*. New York: Charles Scribner's Sons, 1930.

Muthesius, Stefan. *The High Victorian Movement in Architecture* 1850 - 1870. London: Routledge and Kegan Paul, 1972.

Myers, Bernard S. *Art and Civilization*. New York: McGraw-Hill Book Company, Inc., 1957.

Nicoll, Allardyce. *The Development of the Theatre* (5th ed.). London: Harrap and Co., Ltd., 1966.

Nyman, Michael. *Experimental Music: Cage and Beyond*. New York: Schirmer Books, 1974.

Oppenheim, A. Leo. *Ancient Mesopotamia*. Chicago: University of Chicago Press, 1964.

Ostransky, Leroy. *Understanding Jazz*. Englewood Cliffs, NJ: Prentice-Hall, Inc., 1977.

Pignatti, Terisio. *The Age of Rococo*. London: Paul Hamlyn, 1969.

Raphael, Max. *Prehistoric Cave Paintings*. Washington, D.C.: Pantheon, 1946.

Read, Benedict. *Victorian Sculpture*. New Haven: Yale University Press, 1982.

Read, Herbert E. *Art and Society* (2nd ed.). New York: Pantheon Books, Inc., 1950.

Rice, David Talbot. *The Art of Byzantium*. New York: Harry N. Abrams, n.d.

Richter, Gisela. *Greek Art*. Greenwich, CN: Phaidon, 1960.

Roberts, J. M. *History of the World*. New York: Alfred A Knopf, Inc., 1976.

Robertson, Martin. *A Shorter History of Greek Art*. Cambridge, MA: Cambridge University Press, 1981.

Robinson, David. *The History of World Cinema*. New York: Stein and Day Publishers, 1973.

Roters, Eberhard. *Painters of the Bauhaus*. New York: Praeger Publishers, 1965.

Rotha, Paul. *The Film Til Now*. London: Spring Books, 1967.

Rowell, George. *The Victorian Theatre* (2nd ed.). Cambridge University Press, 1978.

Sachs, Curt. *World History of the Dance*. New York: W. W. Norton and Co., 1937.

Sachs, Curt. *The Rise of Music in the Ancient World*. New York: W. W. Norton Company, 1943.

Salzman, Eric. *Twentieth Century Music: An Introduction*. Englewood Cliffs, NJ: Prentice-Hall, Inc., 1967.

Sandars, N. K. *Prehistoric Art In Europe*. Baltimore: Penguin Books, 1968.

Schevill, Ferdinand. *A History of Europe*. New York, Harcourt Brace and Co., Inc., 1938.

Schonberger, Arno and Soehner, Halldor. *The Rococo Age*. New York: McGraw-Hill, 1960.

Sherrard, Philip. *Byzantium*. New York: Time Inc., 1966.

Sitwell, Sacheverell. *Great Houses of Europe*. London: Spring Books, 1970.

Smith, Hermann. *The World's Earliest Music*. London: W. Reeves, n.d.

Smith, W. Stevenson. *The Art and Architecture of Ancient Egypt*. Baltimore: Penguin Books, 1958.

Sorell, Walter. *Dance in its Time*. Garden City, NY: Doubleday Anchor Press, 1981.

Sorell, Walter. *The Dance Through the Ages*. New York: Grosset and Dunlap, Inc., 1967.

Southern, Richard. *The Seven Ages of the Theatre*. New York: Hill and Wang, 1961.

Sperry, Roger. *Science and Moral Priority: Merging Mind, Brain, and Human Values*. New York: Columbia University Press, 1983.

Spitz, Lewis (ed.). *The Protestant Reformation*. Englewood Cliffs, NJ: Prentice-Hall, Inc., 1966.

Sporre, Dennis J. *The Arts*. Englewood cliffs, NJ: Prentice-Hall, Inc., 1985.

Sporre, Dennis J. *Perceiving the Arts*. Englewood Cliffs, NJ: Prentice-Hall, Inc., 1981.

Stamp, Kenneth M. and Wright, Esmond (eds.). *Illustrated World History*. New York: McGraw-Hill Book Company, 1964.

Strayer, Joseph and Munro, Dana. *The Middle Ages*. Pacific Palisades: Goodyear Publishing Company, 1970.

Tierney, Brian and Painter, Sidney. *Western Europe in the Middle Ages*. New York: Alfred A. Knopf, 1974.

Tirro, Frank. *Jazz: A History*. New York: W. W. Norton and Co., In., 1977.

Ucko, Peter J. and Rosenfeld, Andree. *Paleolithic Cave Art*. London: World University Library, 1967.

Van Der Kemp, Gerald. *Versailles*. New York: The Vendome Press, 1977.

Wheeler, Robert Eric Mortimer. *Roman Art and Architecture*. New York: Praeger Publishers Inc., 1964.

Zarnecki, George. *Art of the Medieval World*. Englewood Cliffs, NJ: Prentice-Hall Inc., 1975.

300 400 500 600 700 800 900 1000 1100 1200 1250 1300 1350 1400 1450 1500

6 and 7: BYZANTIUM AND THE EARLY MIDDLE AGES

8: THE LATE MIDDLE AGES

Christianity adopted in Rome
Barbarian invasions
Council of Nicaea

Fall of Rome

Justinian
St Gregory the Great

Charles Martel

Charlemagne

Iconoclast struggle
Ottonian Empire

Henry III of Germany

First Crusade
Moslem conquest of Jerusalem
Chivalry

Magna Carta

Aquinas
Dante

100 Years' War begins

Petrarch

Black Death

Fall of Constantinople

Chaucer

Rome and Byzantium split
St Augustine

Old St Peter's

Mosaics of S Vitale
Ravenna
Hagia Sophia

Troubadors
Trouvères
Minnesänger

Palatine Chapel at Aachen

St Luke and the Virgin
Bronze doors of Hildesheim
Cluny III
Abelard

Nicola Pisano

Exeter Cathedral
Westminster Abbey

Giotto
Ars nova
Ely Cathedral
Wells Cathedral
Lincoln Cathedral

Gloucester Cathedral

Dufay
Ockegham

Lindisfarne Gospels
Gregorian chant

Song of Roland
Polyphony

Bernard of Clairvaux

Chartres
St Denis
Ars antiqua

Nibelungenlied

9: EARLY AND HIGH RENAISSANCE

Invention of printing press
Lorenzo de' Medici
Ferdinand and Isabella

Francis I of France
Emperor Charles V
Henry VIII of England
Reformation
Erasmus
Machiavelli
Rabelais

Brunelleschi

Van Eyck
Fra Angelico
Masaccio
Dürer
Donatello
Alberti

Leonardo
Raphael
Michelangelo
Bramante
Titian
Des Prez
Bruegel
Bronzino
Holbein
Tintoretto